mdeltree

```
mdeltree msdosdirectory [msdosdirectory ...]
```
The mdeltree command deletes one or more MS-DOS directories. It is similar to the DOS DELTREE command.

mkdir

```
mkdir [-p] [-m mode] [-parents] [-mode=mode] [-help]
➥ [-version] directory ...
```
The mkdir command creates one or more directories.

more

```
more [-dlfs] [-number] [+number] [file ...]
```
The more command displays one or more files, screen-by-screen, and allows for searching and jumping to an arbitrary location in the file.

mount

```
mount -a [-rvw] [-t vfstype]
mount [-rvw] [-o options [,...]] device | dir
mount [-rvw] [-t vfstype] [-o options] device dir
```
The mount command mounts a file system to a specified directory.

nslookup

```
nslookup [host | - [server]]
```
The nslookup command queries a DNS name server. It can be run in interactive mode. If no host name is provided, then the program enters interactive mode. By default, the DNS server, as specified in /etc/resolv.conf, is used unless otherwise specified. If you want to specify a server but not look up a specified host, you must provide a - in place of the host.

passwd

```
paste [-s] [-d delim-list] [-serial]
➥ [-delimiters list] [file...]
```
The passwd command changes a user's password. When run by the root user, it can be used to change a specific user's password by providing the username as an argument.

ping

```
ping [-fR] [-c number] [-i seconds]
➥ [-s packetsize] host
```
The ping command sends echo request packets to a network host to see if it is accessible on the network.

ps

```
ps [lumaxwr] [txx] [pid ...]
```
The ps command displays status reports for currently running processes. Given a specific process ID as an argument, ps displays information about that particular process. Without options or arguments, ps displays the current user's processes.

pwd

```
pwd
```
The pwd command displays the name of the current directory.

rm

```
rm [-firR] [-force] [-inter active] [-recursive]
➥ file | directory ...
```
The rm command deletes one or more files or directories.

rmdir

```
rmdir [-p] [-parents] directory ...
```
The rmdir command deletes empty directories.

rsh

```
rsh [-Knx] [-l username] host [command]
```
The rsh command opens a shell on a remote system. If a command is provided, the command is executed on the remote host, the results are returned, and the connection is terminated.

su

```
su [-flmp] [-c command] [-s shell] [-login] [-fast]
➥ [-preserve-environment] [-command=command]
➥ [-shell=shell] [-] [user]
```
The su command runs a new shell under different user and group IDs. If no user is specified, the new shell will run as the root user.

tar

```
tar [-crtuxz] [-f file] [-file file] [-create] [-delete]
➥ [-preserve] [-append] [-same-owner] [-list]
➥ [-update] [-extract] [-get] [-gzip] [-gunzip]
➥ [file | directory ...]
```
The tar command creates an archive file of one or more files or directories.

top

```
top [d delay] [q] [c] [S] [s]
```
The top command displays a regularly updated report of processes running on the system.

unzip

```
unzip [-cflptuz] file[.zip]
```
The unzip command manipulates and extracts ZIP archives.

zcat

```
zcat [-f] [file ...]
```
The zcat command uncompresses one or more compressed files and displays the results to the standard output. If no files are specified, then the standard input is uncompressed and displayed.

zip

```
zip [-efFgmrSu@] [ zipfile [ file1 file2 ...]]
```
The zip command creates a ZIP archive from one or more files and directories.

zmore

```
zmore [file ...]
```
The zmore command displays the contents of compressed text files, one screen at a time, allowing searching in much the same way as the more command. If no files are specified, the standard input will be used.

Mastering Linux

Mastering™ Linux

Arman Danesh

SYBEX®

Associate Publisher: Gary Masters
Contracts and Licensing Manager: Kristine Plachy
Acquisitions & Developmental Editor: Krista Reid-McLaughlin
Editor: Suzanne Goraj
Project Editor: Brianne Hope Agatep
Technical Editor: Cameron Reid
Book Designer: Kris Warrenburg
Graphic Illustrator: Tony Jonick
Electronic Publishing Specialist: Robin Kibby
Production Coordinators: Rebecca Rider, Julie Sakaue
Indexer: Ted Laux
Companion CD: Ginger Warner
Cover Designer: Design Site
Cover Photographer: The Image Bank

Library of Congress Card Number: 98-86867
ISBN: 0-7821-2341-4

Manufactured in the United States of America

10 9 8 7 6

Screen reproductions produced with either xv (a graphics package included with Red Hat Linux 5.1) or Collage Plus.

Collage Plus is a trademark of Inner Media Inc.

*To my parents-in-law who, through their
steadfastness in their Faith in the face of
persecution and suffering, offer a shining example
to all those who strive to stand by their beliefs.*

ACKNOWLEDGMENTS

In producing a book of this scope, there are countless people who contribute to its development, and all are deserving of recognition and acknowledgment.

Most notably, the numerous staff and contributors brought together by Sybex, including Fred Slone, Krista Reid-McLaughlin, Brianne Agatep, Suzanne Goraj, Cameron Reid, and Jim Pire, as well as all staff involved in the production and design of this book, deserve recognition for their hard work and commitment to this project.

At the same time, my colleagues and coworkers at Landegg Academy, especially Ramin Raouf and Shoba Sukumaran, deserve to be commended for their patience in the face of my sudden and mysterious periods of absence from the office while I raced to meet deadlines.

Finally, my wife, Tahirih, is owed my greatest gratitude. She tolerated the long hours and the resulting exhaustion that writing a book entail and managed to make it all bearable.

CONTENTS AT A GLANCE

TABLE OF CONTENTS

Appendixes

INTRODUCTION

Thank you for buying this book, and welcome to the world of Linux. As one of the few alternatives to Microsoft operating systems on affordable desktop-class personal computers, Linux has gained notoriety and, more recently, acclaim as an example of what can be done by a group of motivated people without any fiscal incentive.

Linux is a freely distributable, efficient, fast operating system that offers the power of Unix—once the domain of expensive servers and workstations—on hardware affordable to the budget-conscious home computer user. This has sparked a mini-revolution in the computer world leading to acceptance of free software for a wide range of tasks—from mission-critical Web sites to corporate information systems infrastructure, to education applications.

This book is designed as an introduction to the installation and use of Linux. Any operating system with the breadth of features and capabilities offered by Linux cannot be covered completely in a single book. Still, this book provides the sound knowledge of Linux needed for users to move on and learn more on their own as they use Linux in their everyday work.

Who Should Read This Book?

This book is really designed for anyone who uses a PC. Although Linux may not yet have all the ease-of-use refinements found in commercial desktop operating systems such as Windows 95/98 and the Mac OS, Linux can be used by almost anyone and mastered by anyone who can master Windows.

Having said that, learning to use any operating system is always easier if you already possess some basic computer knowledge, including an understanding of the difference between a hard disk and RAM, an understanding of the basic configuration (in Windows) of peripherals such as video cards and sound cards, and a sense of how data is organized and stored by computers (the difference between directories, subdirectories, and files, for instance).

This book aims to open the world of Linux to the average computer user. In doing so, a passing familiarity with Windows (or the Mac OS) and basic PC hardware is assumed. Without this assumption, this book would be a primer on basic computing concepts rather than a robust introduction to the Linux operating system.

If you are already comfortable using a Windows or Macintosh system and you haven't experimented with the DOS prompt, it would be helpful to do so before diving into the world of Linux, where the command line is more powerful, and therefore more heavily used, than in the Windows arena.

If you are already a power user of Windows, then you are more than ready to become a power user of Linux. Just as this book will make the everyday computer user proficient at getting their work done using Linux, it will help you become an advanced Linux user.

This book also has something to offer for the SOHO (Small Office/Home Office) user or manager of a small network. You will learn how to use Linux in many situations in your office environment, in roles that include file server, intranet Web server, and router.

What You Need to Use This Book

To use this book, you will need access to a personal computer with the following minimum specifications:

- a 486 CPU or higher (in theory, you can run Linux on a 386 system, but the performance will likely be poor enough that it isn't worthwhile for most users)

- 16MB of RAM or more (you will notice a significant performance gain if Linux has 32MB or more of memory)

- a hard disk with at least 500MB of free disk space (if you can afford 1GB or more, this will greatly enhance your freedom to experiment with Linux and Linux applications)

- a CD-ROM drive (preferably an ATAPI/IDE CD-ROM or a SCSI CD-ROM drive)

- a backup of your current system in case you need to recover existing data or applications

- a video card and VGA or better monitor

- a keyboard and mouse

Optionally, you may want to have the following:

- a printer (opt for a PCL or PostScript printer if you have a choice)

- a sound card and speakers

- a modem or ISDN modem

How This Book Is Organized

This book is divided into three sections:

- **Welcome to Linux**: This section first introduces you to Linux as an operating system and as the foundation of the GNU General Public License software model. Then we will look at the most popular distributions (versions) of Linux and make preparations to install Linux on your system.

- **Essential Linux**: This section covers the installation, configuration, and use of Linux on a stand-alone PC (which will generally be found in a home setting as opposed to an office setting). Topics covered include the installation of a stand-alone Linux system, the use of X Windows (Linux's graphical user interface), an overview of file management, system configuration, printers and peripherals, connecting to the Internet using Linux, and sending faxes from Linux.

- **Linux in the Small Office/Home Office (SOHO)**: As an inexpensive but powerful computing environment, Linux is well-suited to many small or home office tasks. In this section, we look at the installation of Linux in a networked office environment, use of Linux as a file or print server for Unix and Windows networks, awareness of basic security issues when using Linux in a networked environment, and deployment of Linux as an intranet Web server or organizational mail server. Finally, we look at DOS and Windows compatibility and integration in Linux, which allows many organizations to migrate from their current Windows environments to Linux without sacrificing their current investment in software and applications.

If you already have some experience with Linux, you probably can skip straight to the second section of the book, "Essential Linux" and begin installing a Linux system. If you have never used Linux before, start at the beginning with "Welcome to Linux" to get your feet wet and become comfortable with the world of Linux and its dynamic nature. Whatever your background, though, always remember that computers are tools that bring added power to your work, and Linux is a great way to enhance that role.

PART I

Welcome to Linux

CHAPTER
ONE

What Is Linux?

- Linux History

- Linux as an Operating System

- Linux as Free Software

If you have made it this far—buying this book, wading through the front matter, and looking at the table of contents—then you probably have some idea of what Linux and the Linux phenomenon are all about. If you don't…read on.

Linux is a truly amazing development in the computer world. It shows how quality software isn't necessarily dependent on the financial blessing of the commercial software industry.

The history of Linux illustrates how free software can evolve, grow, and become an attractive alternative to the commercial software packages with which most of us are familiar.

In addition, the technical excellence of so many aspects of Linux shows why it is a serious contender against rival operating systems from Microsoft, Novell, and IBM.

In this chapter, we will paint a quick picture of the history of Linux and then look at the key systems that make Linux a powerful alternative operating system for numerous uses. Finally, we will look at the free software model used in Linux and its implications for the whole software industry.

Linux History

The emergence of Linux onto the computing scene has grown out of the Unix culture. As an operating system (really a variety of different operating systems with similar features), Unix long predates the era of desktop computers, having been developed in the mid-1970s when minicomputers and mainframe computers were the norm in the corporate world.

Unix continues to be widely used in this corporate environment, as well as in the educational world, although it is also often found running on today's client-server intranet networks.

The problem with Unix, historically, has been its inaccessibility to programmers and developers who want to work with it outside the context of corporate or university computing centers. While versions of Unix have long been available for the PC, they never had the grace or power of those available for minicomputers, mainframes, and today's servers. In addition, the early commercial Unixes were costly, sometimes costing more than the PC hardware they were destined to run on.

This lack of accessibility ultimately gave birth to Linux as a means to make a Unix-like operating system available on a wide basis.

Linux's life began in the hands of Linus Torvalds at the University of Helsinki in Finland. While the Linux we know today has been developed with the assistance of programmers worldwide, Linus Torvalds still retains control of the evolving core of the Linux operating system: the kernel.

Torvalds originally intended to develop Linux as a hobby. Early versions didn't have the end user in mind, instead providing the barest bones of functionality to allow Unix programmers the apparent joy of programming the kernel. As the core of the operating system, the kernel keeps everything running smoothly—without a stable, powerful kernel, you don't *have* an operating system.

But as the team of programmers grew and the base software for a complete operating system emerged, it became clear to those involved that Linux was evolving to the state where it could respectably be called an operating system. In March 1992, version 1.0 of the kernel came into being, marking the first official release of Linux. At this point, Linux ran most of the common Unix tools, from compilers to networking software to X Windows.

Linux continues to evolve as the preeminent Unix-clone operating system for personal computers. Hardware support is now broad, including the most popular and common peripherals; performance is strong, giving many PCs power comparable to that of mid-range workstations such as Sun Microsystems' SPARC systems. Although technically today's Linux is not Unix because it fails to qualify for the brand name, efforts are under way to add to Linux the features needed to receive full certification as a Unix operating system.

Linux as an Operating System

The term "Linux" is actually somewhat vague. "Linux" is used in two ways: specifically to refer to the kernel itself—the heart of any version of Linux—and generally to refer to any collection of applications that run on the kernel, usually referred to as a distribution. The kernel's job is to provide the overall environment in which applications can run, including the basic interfaces with hardware and the systems for managing tasks and currently running programs.

In the specific sense, there is only one current version of Linux at any one time: the current revision of the kernel. Linus Torvalds keeps the kernel as his domain in the world of Linux development, leaving all the applications and services that sit on top of the kernel to any of the thousands of other developers in the Linux community.

In the general meaning of the term, referring to cohesive collections of applications that run on top of the Linux kernel, there are numerous versions of Linux. Each distribution has its own unique characteristics, including different installation methods, different collections of features, and different upgrade paths. But since all distributions are fundamentally Linux, in almost every case an application that works with a current version of one distribution will work with a current version of another distribution.

NOTE   A complete discussion of Linux distributions is in the next chapter, "Choosing a Distribution."

The interesting thing about this dichotomous use of the term "Linux" is that it exactly parallels the same confused usage of the term "operating system." In the commercial sense, an operating system has come to mean a large collection of applications centered around a kernel. This is what Windows 95 and Windows NT are. This is what the Mac OS is. In a purist, technical sense, an operating system is a much smaller core kernel that provides those basic system functions needed to develop any applications.

Taken in both senses, Linux is an operating system. One of the features of the Linux kernel that set it apart from many other operating systems designed to run on desktop PCs is that it is both multitasking and multiuser.

A Multitasking Operating System

You are probably familiar with the term "multitasking" even if you are not really sure what it means.

When desktop computing graduated from Windows 3.1 to Windows 95, the multitasking capabilities of the then-new Windows 95 were among its biggest claims to fame.

To say that a system can multitask is to say that it can appear to be running more than one application, or process, at a time. For instance, the system can print a document, copy a file, and dial into the Internet while the user is comfortably typing in a word processing program. Even with these background tasks happening, the foreground word processor should not freeze up or be unusable.

This is the wonder of multitasking: it allows a computer with a single processor to appear to be performing multiple tasks simultaneously. Of course, a single CPU can only execute a single instruction at a time—that is, only one action can be taking place at any one time. Multitasking creates the appearance of simultaneous activity by switching rapidly between tasks as the demands of those processes dictate.

When multitasking works well, a user running a word processor while several other things happen will not be aware of the extra work the computer is doing. All processes will seem to be running smoothly and the computer will be responsive.

Historically, Unix systems have been much better than Windows at multitasking, able to run large numbers of simultaneous applications in a way that made them ideal for large corporate servers and high-powered workstations. Today, only Windows NT can really claim to offer a similarly robust multitasking implementation. Even Windows 95, despite all of its fanfare, has trouble effectively handling large numbers of simultaneous processes.

To take things further, Linux, like Windows NT, offers support for computers with multiple processors such as dual-Pentium II systems. These systems can in fact perform two actions at exactly the same time. Combining multitasking with multiple processors greatly increases the number of simultaneous applications a computer can run smoothly.

A Multiuser Operating System

Even more important than being a multitasking operating system, Linux—like all Unixes and Unix clones—is a multiuser operating system.

All versions of Windows and the Mac OS are single-user systems. While some Windows NT services provide a semblance of multiuser capabilities, only one user can be logged in and running applications at any one time in these operating systems. It is only recently that efforts have been made to extend Windows NT into a multiuser platform under the guise of Windows NT Terminal Server.

By comparison, Linux allows multiple simultaneous users, fully leveraging the multitasking capabilities of the operating system. The great advantage of this is that Linux can be deployed as an applications server. From their desktop computers or terminals, users can log in to a Linux server across a LAN and actually run applications on the server instead of on their desktop PCs.

Linux Applications

As an operating system, Linux can be used to develop almost any type of application. Among the applications available for Linux are:

Text and word processing applications. In addition to commercial word processing software such as WordPerfect, StarOffice, and Applixware, Linux offers powerful tools for editing text files and processing text in an automated fashion.

Programming languages. There is a wide variety of programming and scripting languages and tools available for Linux and all Unix operating systems. This abundance of programming tools makes it easy to develop new applications that can run not only on Linux but also on most Unix and Unix-like operating systems.

X Windows. X Windows is Unix's answer to the graphical user interface. X Windows is a highly flexible and configurable GUI environment that runs on Linux as well as most Unix systems. Numerous applications that run in X Windows help to make Linux an easy-to-use operating system.

NOTE   Complete coverage of X Windows is provided in Chapters 6 through 9.

Internet tools. In addition to supporting well-known software such as Netscape Communicator and Mosaic, Linux provides a wide range of Internet software including character-based and graphical mail-reading applications, the full range of software needed to create Internet servers (including Web server, mail servers, and news servers), plus complete network support to connect to the Internet via local network or modem.

DOS and Windows compatibility software. As we will see in Chapter 29, "Linux and DOS/Windows," Linux can be made to run DOS software with a high degree of stability and compatibility and offers several approaches to running Windows software. In fact, the entire text of this book was written using Microsoft Word for Windows on a computer running Linux. This gives strong evidence of Linux's ability to work well in a Windows environment. In addition, emulators are available for other popular computer systems, including the Macintosh and Atari ST computer lines.

This list only touches the tip of the iceberg. Many more applications exist for Linux. A good source for finding Linux software is the Linux Software Map, which can be found on the World Wide Web at `http://www.ssc.com/lsm`.

Linux as Free Software

Given all the capabilities promised by Linux, it would be logical to think that the operating system is expensive. On the contrary; the Linux kernel and most of the applications written for Linux are freely available on the Internet, often with no restriction on the copying and redistribution of the software.

To begin with, the Linux kernel is distributed under the GNU General Public License. This special software license, developed by the Free Software Foundation, promotes the open distribution and, more importantly, open development of software. Unlike the software licenses common with most commercial software, the GNU license allows anyone to redistribute software, even for a fee, so long as in the redistribution the terms of the GNU license are still in force. In other words, anyone can take GNU software, alter it if they wish, and redistribute it, but they can't stop someone who buys their GNU-licensed software from turning around and redistributing it again.

Most of Linux is available under the GNU General Public License. This is how it is possible for so many different vendors to produce both free and commercially available Linux distributions.

This approach to free software is not the same as public domain software. With GNU products, the software authors continue to retain the rights to the software and may choose in the future to stop distributing it under the GNU license. What is special about the GNU license is that it encourages iterative development of applications by many people, each making changes they consider important or necessary and then redistributing the software.

This process is enabled by the fact that all GNU-licensed software must be distributed with its complete source code. Unlike commercial software, where the original code is unavailable and hence unalterable, GNU software not only makes it possible to alter and customize software but actually encourages interested and capable users to do so.

In fact, this model has been so successful in the development of Linux and applications for Linux that it has been adopted by Netscape for its Communicator product line. Using basic GNU principles, Netscape is making Communicator freely available and allowing anyone to license the source code for Communicator or redistribute Communicator.

Commercial versus Free

As we will see later in this book, there are commercial applications for Linux as well as commercial distributions of Linux. In these cases, most products are licensed under terms more restrictive than the GNU standards of the Linux world.

But even if a distribution of Linux includes commercial components that cannot be redistributed freely, this doesn't change the underlying GNU license that applies to the Linux kernel and those core applications found in all Linux distributions. If the original license of an application is the GNU General Public License, then the license of the redistributed copy of the software is likewise the GNU General Public License.

Where Do We Go from Here?

In this chapter, we have taken the first step into the world of Linux. We now know what the basic components and philosophy of Linux are, and have become acquainted with the features that make it an excellent choice for many applications.

In Chapter 2, we will take a look at the Linux distribution philosophy and the many distributions, or flavors, of Linux that are available.

In Chapter 3, we will begin the practical steps of preparing to install Linux on a PC.

From Chapter 4 onward, the book is divided into two sections. The first addresses the use of Linux as an end-user operating system—that is, installing Linux on a stand-alone PC and using it for common daily tasks such as word processing and Internet activities. The second section deals with the functions of Linux in a small or home office (the so-called SOHO environment), including intranet server, mail server, and gateway to the Internet for an entire network.

CHAPTER

TWO

Choosing a Distribution

- ■ What Is a Distribution?

- ■ An Overview of Major Distributions

- ■ Red Hat Linux 5

As we saw in the first chapter, the entire approach to the development of Linux breaks with traditional commercial software development. Most components that go into making a complete Linux system—including the kernel (the heart of the operating system), drivers for devices, and all the applications and utilities that make the system do useful things—are developed by small or large loosely-knit groups of developers scattered around the globe.

To top it all off, most of these components are distributed under licenses allowing free redistribution, such as the GNU Public License. (A copy of the license is shown in Appendix H.)

This all leaves the potential user of Linux at a bit of a loss as to how to put together a working Linux system and what components to include in that system.

The answer to this quandry has emerged in the form of Linux distributions. Distributions are prepackaged Linux systems that are ready to install. They come in numerous flavors from the freely available to the fully commercial, and they all offer different core sets of applications, utilities, and management tools to ease the use of Linux.

In this chapter, we are going to take a broad look at some of the major and more well-known distributions and then take a somewhat deeper look at the latest release of Red Hat Linux—the Linux distribution included on the CD-ROM with this book.

What Is a Distribution?

The concept of a distribution can be a little hard to understand in a world of commercial operating systems such as Windows 95 and NT, Mac OS, and even commercial Unix systems such as Solaris and HP-UX.

After all, in all these cases, the name of the operating system denotes a very specific product. For instance, Windows 95 defines the complete set of Windows utilities, applications, and drivers that Microsoft ships. There is no room for variation. Any application, driver, or utility that a user adds to their system is not considered part of Windows 95, and Windows 95 doesn't technically exist as a product with less than its complete set of software and tools.

In the Linux world, however, this definition becomes blurred. Linux can refer to everything from the kernel (the heart of the operating system) to any collection of Linux-based applications put together with a kernel to produce a functioning system running Linux.

This lack of a clear set of applications, utilities, drivers, and a kernel that together can clearly be identified as Linux has opened the door to different flavors of Linux that meet different needs. These are the distributions.

Distributions can be built on different versions of the kernel, can include different sets of applications, utilities, tools, and driver modules, and can offer different installation and upgrade programs to ease management of the system.

The Same but Different

It might seem that with this type of flexibility would come chaos. This is a logical deduction. After all, how is it possible to have potentially infinite varieties of Linux and yet have some level of reasonable assurance that Linux applications can be installed and run on any of these systems?

Luckily, this tends to work: in all the diversity that is Linux is an underlying thread of similarity that provides the compatibility needed to develop applications that can be used on most Linux systems.

At the heart of most Linux distributions is a common set of basic programs, utilities, and libraries that application developers can reasonably expect to find in a Linux system. In addition, most Linux distributions now adhere to such standards as the Linux File System Standard.

Therefore, large-scale commercial applications such as Netscape Communicator or Corel WordPerfect can be developed for Linux and be expected to work on the majority of Linux systems. Even if a component, such as a program or library, upon which an application is dependent is missing, it can be downloaded from large Linux software repositories on the Internet to enable the application to work.

An Overview of Major Distributions

The majority of Linux distributions are freely available. They can be downloaded from the Internet from Linux software archives such as the SunSite FTP site or the TSX-11 Linux Repository at MIT.

TIP

See Appendix E, "Sources of Linux Information," for a complete list of Linux sites offering distributions and for a list of CD-ROM vendors.

Of course, the average Linux distribution can be quite large, ranging from a few dozen to a few hundred megabytes in size, and most users will not want to spend valuable online time and bandwidth downloading a complete Linux distribution. To handle this, there are numerous sources of Linux distributions available on CD-ROM, including directly from the organizations that produce the distributions or from third-party sources, which bundle one or more distributions into CD-ROM sets that also include additional Linux software and documentation.

For instance, the Linux Developer's Resource is a set of six CD-ROMs from InfoMagic (`www.infomagic.com`). This is released quarterly and contains the latest Red Hat, Slackware, and Debian distributions, a current snapshot of the Linux archive at SunSite, and several commercial Linux applications that are available as fully-licensed copies, demonstration programs, or evaluation copies.

Generally, CD-ROM copies of free Linux distributions range in price from $10 to $50, with more popular sets such as the Linux Developer's Resource costing less than $25.

The Major Distributions

There are numerous Linux distributions. In recent years, though, three distributions have emerged as the most common: Red Hat, Slackware, and Debian. These distributions have some of the longest histories in the Linux community and together control the lion's share of the market. In addition, all three distributions are freely available, which has made them the bases for other distributions and for commercial packages that include a Linux distribution.

After these three is a second tier that includes some long-standing distributions such as Yggdrasil and newcomers to Linux such as OpenLinux from Caldera.

Red Hat

By most counts, the Red Hat Linux distribution from Red Hat Software (`www.redhat.com`) has emerged as the favorite Linux distribution for most users. This distribution is the target, or base, distribution for many commercial Linux software developers and is the benchmark against which many Linux distributions are measured.

Red Hat has gained fame particularly for its tools for installing and upgrading the operating system and for its well-designed system for installing, uninstalling, and tracking software application packages.

Red Hat Linux has also won awards, including *InfoWorld*'s Reader's Choice and Browser's Choice Awards in March 1998. Red Hat Linux came first in a survey of

InfoWorld's Web site visitors that asked readers to indicate their choice for product of the year (receiving 27 percent of the vote, well ahead of the number two package, OS/2 Warp 4, which had just over 8 percent). Red Hat Linux has also been used in projects that have proved the commercial viability of Linux, including animation work for the movie *Titanic*.

Red Hat Linux is available in a free version that can be downloaded from popular Linux archives on the Internet and in a reasonably priced $50 commercial version that includes a manual, a CD-ROM, and several commercial applications to supplement its collection of free software.

Red Hat Linux 5.1 is the current version of the distribution and is the distribution included with this book. We will take a deeper look at Red Hat 5 later in this chapter.

In addition to the Red Hat Linux 5.1 distribution included on the CD-ROM, you can always download the latest version from the Red Hat FTP server at `ftp.redhat.com` or from the SunSite Linux Archive at `sunsite.unc.edu/pub/Linux`.

Slackware

Before Red Hat Linux came to fame, Slackware was the distribution to beat. Slackware is still a popular distribution and is found on CD-ROMs from many vendors including InfoMagic and Walnut Creek, the official home of Slackware, which offers a CD-ROM set of Slackware that includes support.

The version of Slackware available from Walnut Creek at the time of this writing was Slackware 3.4. The distribution offers the full range of expected utilities, tools, and applications, including X Windows, development tools such as the GNU C Compiler, PPP support, full Java support, and the Java SDK (Developer's Kit) for Linux. Like most Linux distributions, Slackware offers the Apache Web server for using Linux to set up an intranet or Internet Web site, as well as several freely available Web browsers.

Slackware can be downloaded from Walnut Creek's FTP site at `ftp.cdrom.com` or from the SunSite Linux archive at `sunsite.unc.edu/pub/Linux`.

Debian/GNU

As one of the three major Linux players, Debian/GNU (`www.debian.org`) is the odd man out because it has no commercial organization backing it. Where Red Hat is developed by Red Hat Software and Slackware has a home at Walnut

Creek, Debian/GNU Linux is produced by a team of volunteers in much the same way as Linux development itself takes place.

Debian offers more than 1,000 software packages using its own package management system, which is designed to offer similar functionality to that offered by the Red Hat distribution.

The Debian distribution is unique in some ways. Their Web site highlights a commitment to giving back any code they generate to the free software world; they publicize their bugs, making bug reports easy to find; and they won't include applications in their distribution that don't match Debian's definition of free software (which includes free redistribution rights, available source code, and allowances for modifications and derived work).

Other Distributions

Other English-language distributions of Linux that are worth being aware of include Caldera's OpenLinux and S.u.S.E. Linux, among others. In addition, there are several non-English distributions, particularly in French and German, which are covered in Appendix C, "Linux Around the World."

Caldera OpenLinux Caldera has caused a stir in both the Linux and the broader computer markets by trumpeting the call of supportable commercial Linux. The idea here is to offer tested, stable, and supported versions of Linux that will appeal to the corporate market and to application developers who want a secure target distribution of Linux to develop for.

To some extent, this strategy has worked. WordPerfect 6 for Linux was targeted for (and only distributed with) Caldera's Network Desktop distribution. Currently, StarOffice for Linux is aimed at the latest Caldera distribution, OpenLinux, and the Linux version of Netscape's FastTrack Web server package has been ported by Caldera and is available as part of the OpenLinux package.

OpenLinux comes in three versions: a free Lite version, a Base version, and a Standard version. The Lite version consists strictly of software that can be distributed freely, and is distributed freely by Caldera. The Base version offers a non-commercial license of the StarOffice Suite, including a word processor and spreadsheet as well as NetWare client support. OpenLinux Standard takes things a step further, adding the Netscape FastTrack Web server, a commercial SQL database server, and Novell NetWare administration software.

OpenLinux's management system is based on the Red Hat package management scheme, and the distribution offers a simple installation and configuration tool.

Caldera's OpenLinux won the *Byte* Magazine Editor's Choice Award of Distinction in December 1997. In awarding OpenLinux this honor, *Byte*'s editors noted the combination of value for price, compared with other commercial server operating systems, as a strong point in favor of Caldera OpenLinux.

OpenLinux Lite can be downloaded at no cost from Caldera's Web site at `www.caldera.com`.

S.u.S.E. Linux S.u.S.E. Linux is a popular Linux distribution available primarily in Europe and offered in both English and German versions.

The version of S.u.S.E. available at the time of this writing is unique in several ways when compared against the major distributions. S.u.S.E. offers the KDE desktop (which we will learn about in Chapter 6, "An Overview of X Windows"), the latest version of the XFree86 X Windows server where some distributions are one version behind, and a system administration tool called YaST, which is useful for configuring everything from dial-up Internet connections to scanners and network cards.

S.u.S.E.'s menu-driven installation program has been lauded by some magazines as the simplest around. The distribution also includes a 400-page manual and a wide range of emulators to emulate the Amiga, Atari ST, Gameboy, and Nintendo entertainment systems.

Red Hat Linux 5

The distribution of Linux used in this book is Red Hat Linux 5.1. As mentioned earlier, Red Hat Linux is currently one of the most well-known and widely used Linux distributions.

The feature that launched Red Hat Linux into popularity was its package management system. This system allows software applications to be tested, configured, and provided in a ready-to-run state for Red Hat Linux. Using simple package management tools, new packages can be downloaded, installed, and run without the sometimes tortuous configuration required with other packages—such as software that is distributed with its own special installation program or that doesn't use the Red Hat (or the similar Debian) package management system.

Of course, package management alone is not enough to explain the success of Red Hat Linux. After all, the key software needed to implement the Red Hat package management system is made freely available by Red Hat, and other distributions also use the system.

One benefit provided by package management is upgradeability: it is possible to upgrade versions of Red Hat without having to reinstall Linux from scratch. This problem plagued earlier Slackware distributions when it was the leading distribution, and still plagues some distributions today.

Another major feature of the Red Hat distribution is that it is available not only on the Intel PC platform but also on two other platforms: Digital Alpha-based computers and Sun SPARC-based computers. These two platforms offer higher performance hardware than the typical Intel PC but generally require expensive commercial versions of Unix. Red Hat makes it possible to use Linux on all three systems and, because the distributions are fundamentally the same, management and configuration of systems running Red Hat Linux for any of the three platforms is simplified, as is the porting of software.

What's New about Red Hat 5

Version 5 of Red Hat Linux offers a lot of new features not found in earlier versions and still not found in all distributions of Linux. These features include improved installation, new and improved system administration tools, and adoption of Glibc.

Improved Installation

The Red Hat 5 installation software now does many things that earlier versions of Red Hat failed to do. This includes improved ability to recognize PCI devices, adoption of new disk-partitioning software (which eases initial configuration and offers features such as growable disk partitions that can increase in size as disk space is available), and the ability to choose which services load automatically at boot time once the system is installed.

New and Improved Administration Tools

Linux has always had a strong set of both command-line and graphical tools for configuring and administering a Red Hat Linux–based system. With Version 5 these are expanded to include a user information tool to set user information such as name and phone number, a user password tool that makes it easy to change users' passwords, and a file system tool that allows the mounting and unmounting of file systems from a graphical interface.

In addition, Version 5 includes an improved network configuration tool, which adds support for mobile systems that connect to different networks, and a new backup utility that simplifies system backups.

Red Hat Linux also offers a tool for configuring the free version of X Windows, XFree86, called Xconfigurator. Xconfigurator has always been superior to the configuration program included with XFree86, and in Red Hat Linux 5, Xconfigurator offers additional improvements such as automatic detection of video cards and their features.

All together, these improvements make Red Hat Linux easy to manage for most users and help bring to the Linux world the types of graphical management tools found in rival systems such as Windows NT.

Adoption of Glibc

This is actually a very technical subject and we won't go into it much, but Red Hat 5 is the first major release of Linux to make the switch to a newer version of the core Glibc library, which most Linux applications depend on. This switch from libc to Glibc promises to improve the performance of those applications as well as the stability of the already stable Linux operating system.

Of course, any change at a core level such as a library can wreak havoc, and this switch has meant a necessary transition period during which some applications need to be updated in order to use the new libraries. But the Linux world is increasingly moving towards Glibc-based Linux, and this issue is receding into the background.

Where Do We Go from Here?

Now that we have a firm sense of what Linux is all about and what the options are in terms of the various distributions, we are ready to focus on actually working with Red Hat Linux 5.1 (which is on the enclosed CD-ROM).

The next chapter will cover the preparation that is needed to insure that installing Red Hat Linux will go smoothly. This includes understanding some of the hardware issues involved in getting a Linux system up and running with minimum fuss, and also making sure you have all the necessary information on hand to provide the installation program the data it needs to do its job.

Following that, in Chapter 4, we will walk through the actual steps involved in installing a Red Hat Linux 5.1 system.

CHAPTER

THREE

Getting Ready to Install Linux

- What You Need

- Checking Your Hardware for Compatibility

- Recording Your Hardware Information

- Choosing an Installation Method

- Arranging Your Hard Disk

In this chapter, we finally get down to the business of installing Linux. Most of this chapter will be concerned with decisions that affect the installation process, rather than with the actual installation process itself, but this decision-making is an essential step if you want to ensure that your Linux installation goes smoothly and that you end up with a well-configured system.

We will start with a brief discussion of the minimum Linux system. What hardware is necessary to run a useful Linux system? It is possible to boot Linux from a single floppy disk, but the resulting system will be so limited as to be useless for most purposes. We will look at what equipment you need in order to make Linux a useful tool in your computing arsenal.

From there, we will look at a crucial issue: hardware compatibility. Even in the Windows world where vendors provide drivers quickly for almost every conceivable piece of hardware, things go wrong and hardware incompatibility can be the cause of long, sleepless nights trying to get Windows to work. In Linux, there is equal potential for problems, especially if you try to use hardware for which there is currently limited or no support.

What You Need

Before you can install Linux, it is important to step back and consider exactly what type of computer you need.

Linux can be installed on a wide range of hardware, including

- the ARM processor
- the Motorola 680×0 processor
- the 8086 CPU
- the DEC Alpha chip
- MIPS systems
- PowerPC-based systems
- the Acorn computer
- the Power Mac
- Intel-based PCs

By far, though, Intel-based PC hardware is the most common Linux platform. It generally provides the lowest cost-performance ratio for Linux and is the primary development platform for most Linux tools. Intel Linux offers the best selection of device drivers for peripheral hardware, the largest body of available applications (both commercial and free), and the strongest community on the Internet that can be turned to for support and assistance.

For these reasons, this book focuses on Linux for Intel x86-based computers; the enclosed CD-ROM contains Red Hat Linux for the Intel platform.

The Minimum PC for Linux

As an operating system, Linux has amazingly modest requirements for computer resources. Actually, it is possible to get Linux up and running on a 386-based computer with only 4MB of RAM. Such a machine will, of course, be limited:

- It can't run X Windows (so, no GUI interface).

- The number of simultaneous programs it can run is limited by the amount of physical RAM.

- Its performance will be slow enough to prevent its use in most mission-critical applications (for instance, as a mail server or Web server).

Given these limitations, a system like this can still play a role in an organization, such as:

- a terminal to another Linux or Unix server where applications are running

- a low-end server for services such as DNS (Domain Name Service, which helps computers translate host names such as www.yahoo.com into actual numerical [IP] addresses) or an authentication server for a small network

In fact, Linux can provide a better way to leverage this type of old hardware than DOS can. DOS has limited networking capabilities and cannot handle the server duties described above.

If you want to try to run this type of minimalist Linux system, you should turn to the Small Memory Mini HOWTO at http://sunsite.unc.edu/mdw/HOWTO/mini/Small-Memory.html for some basic tips to help you get Linux up and running in a system with limited memory.

A Good PC for Linux

This book's main focus is on running Linux on a personal workstation or as a small intranet server. Needless to say, just as you wouldn't want to run Windows on the type of machine described in the previous section, you need a somewhat more robust PC to fully enjoy the features and benefits of Linux.

Linux actually requires far fewer resources to do far more than the average Windows 98 or Windows NT system. For instance, a functional workstation can be put together with a 486-100MHz processor and 16MB of RAM. This system will be able to run X Windows (for a graphical interface), access the Internet and run Netscape Communicator, and, all the while, perform as a low-end server on a network.

Still, the average user will want a somewhat more powerful Linux system. A respectable Linux workstation needs the following specifications:

- A Pentium-class CPU. Even a Pentium 133 will do just fine for most users. It is wise to avoid certain clone chips, such as the Cyrix 686 line, because of some reported difficulties people have had running these chips. Generally, though, most Pentium-class systems work just fine.

- 32MB of RAM. Linux is exceptionally good at taking advantage of any extra memory you throw at it. 32MB is enough for the average workstation, but you will notice the difference if you can afford 64MB of RAM.

- A 2GB hard disk. You can get away with a 500MB (or even smaller) hard disk, but a roomier disk is preferable. Larger disks tend to perform better than the older, smaller ones.

- A supported video card. (See the section on hardware compatibility later in this chapter.)

With a system like this, you will have more than sufficient resources to run Linux as a desktop operating system. You don't need to go out and buy the latest 400MHz Pentium II system with all the bells and whistles to get Linux up and running at a respectable speed.

Added Bonuses

Of course, in today's computing environment, you will probably want to extend your PC's capabilities into areas such as multimedia and the Internet. There are a few add-ons that greatly enhance any Linux system, and you should consider them as a way to round out your workstation:

- A CD-ROM drive. If you are going to install one, consider an IDE/ATAPI CD-ROM drive or, if you can afford it, a SCSI CD-ROM drive. Generally, it is best to avoid proprietary CD-ROM drives that work with their own interface cards or connect directly to special interfaces on sound cards. These CD-ROM drives are usually poor performers and difficult to configure in Linux.

- A sound card. Most Sound Blaster®–compatible cards are supported in Linux; check the hardware compatibility section of this chapter.

- A modem. In terms of speed, the same rules apply here as with Windows: it is generally best to get the fastest modem you can that will be able to connect at its top speed to your Internet provider. If your Internet provider can't offer 56Kbps connections, then you may not want a 56Kbps modem at this time. One caveat, though. It is generally wise to opt for external modems in Linux. This is especially true for ISDN modems, because there is limited support for internal ISDN modems. The advantage of external modems (ISDN or analog) is that they are easier to configure and they offer external indicators so you can more easily debug configuration problems.

If you plan to use Linux as a small server on your intranet, you should consider the following add-ons:

- A SCSI card. SCSI offers much better performance for hard drives than the IDE interface and has better support for multiple devices. If you plan to run any type of multiuser system (for instance, file server, Web server, or applications server) you really need to use SCSI. Make sure you consult the hardware compatibility section before selecting a SCSI card and, if possible, choose a card with Ultra-Wide SCSI support.

- SCSI hard drive(s). The whole point of the SCSI card is to be able to use SCSI hard drives. If possible, use Ultra-Wide SCSI drives for the best performance. You may want to consider multiple disk drives. For instance, if you estimate you need 8GB of space for your users' data as well as the operating system and all installed applications, you may want to consider two 4GB drives (one for the user data and the other for the system and software). By splitting software and data, you will probably find that performance improves because the same disk is not being accessed for both.

- A tape drive. If you plan to run a server, you will want to do backups to ensure that your data is safe from system failure and other disasters. While it is possible to use some tape drives that connect through the floppy disk bus, you will find that life is a lot easier if you opt for a SCSI tape drive, if you can afford one. They are faster and better supported by Linux.

Checking Your Hardware for Compatibility

As with a Windows (especially Windows NT) system, it is important to check that your hardware will work with your Linux operating system and with the rest of the hardware in your computer before committing the dollars to purchase.

Hardware incompatibility with the operating system and other hardware can be the source of endless difficulty and time spent trying to debug and reconfigure a computer.

This issue is especially important in the Linux community. Because Linux doesn't yet enjoy widespread support among hardware vendors, vendors generally do not provide Linux drivers for their hardware, and their support staff are unable or unwilling to work with users to debug hardware conflicts and problems in a Linux environment. This means that the hardware needs to be supported by drivers included in the user's Linux distribution or by add-on software that provides drivers for the hardware in question. In addition, users must rely on the Linux community for help when problems arise.

What to Do When in Doubt

Because of the current Linux support situation, it is wise to do some research before purchasing new hardware. Here's what you can do:

- Consult the Linux Hardware Compatibility HOWTO. This document, authored by Patrick Reijnen, contains extensive lists of hardware known to work with Linux, hardware known to not work with Linux, and issues related to both types of hardware. If you purchase hardware that has the stamp of approval from the HOWTO guide, your life will be easier. Linux Hardware Compatibility HOWTO is reproduced in Appendix F.

- Consult the `comp.os.linux.hardware` newsgroup. This is a good source of information about hardware issues as they relate to Linux. If you are unsure of whether your intended hardware purchase is wise, post a question to the group asking if anyone has had any experience with the item in question. You will usually find that others have tried what you are considering, and their collective wisdom is an invaluable resource in making informed purchase decisions.

- If you are running the Red Hat Linux version that ships with this book, try consulting the archives of the Red Hat mailing list. The mailing list can be found in the support section of the Red Hat home page at `http://www.redhat.com/`.

- Try to evaluate the hardware before purchasing it. If you are considering making a corporate purchase of hardware from a vendor you use regularly, it may be possible to borrow hardware to test it with Linux before actually purchasing it. This, of course, is the only way to be certain the hardware will work the way you want it to.

Recording Your Hardware Information

Once you have put together your target Linux PC, you need to collect the hardware-related information necessary to get your hardware working. In this section, we will quickly look at the information you should note in order to get your hardware working quickly with Linux.

Video Cards

If you install Linux without X Windows (the graphical user interface for Unix systems), you will probably have no difficulties with any video card. However, with X Windows you need care and attention to detail to get your card working. You should record the following information about your video card before installing Linux:

- vendor and model of the card
- video chipset used on the card (sometimes X Windows may not provide explicit support for a particular card but will offer general support for the chipset used in the card)
- amount of video memory on the card
- type of clock chip on the card (if there is one; many common cards do not have clock chips)
- type of RAMDAC on the card (if there is one; many common cards do not have RAMDACs)

All of this information should be available in the documentation that came with your card.

Sound Cards

Sound cards require that you supply very specific information in order to get them working. The following information is critical to configuring most sound cards:

- vendor and model of the card
- IRQ(s) of the card
- I/O address(es) of the card
- DMA address(es) of the card

You may have to set the IRQ, I/O address, and DMA address manually, using jumpers or DIP switches. Refer to the card's documentation for instructions.

Monitors

As with your video card, it is important to record the technical specifications of your monitor in order to get it working optimally with X Windows. If you don't have this information, or use the wrong information, there is a risk that your monitor could be damaged. Record the following specifications after consulting your monitor's documentation:

- vendor and model of the monitor

- top resolution of the monitor

- top refresh rate of the monitor when running at its top resolution

- horizontal sync range of your monitor

- vertical sync range of your monitor

Consult Chapter 7, "Installing and Configuring X Windows," for a discussion of horizontal and vertical sync ranges as they apply to the configuration of X Windows.

Mice

In order to get your mouse working, both in Linux's character-based console mode and in X Windows, you need to note the following information:

- vendor and model of the mouse

- number of mouse buttons

- protocol of the mouse (consult the mouse's documentation for this; common protocols include the Microsoft protocol, the Mouse Systems protocol, and the PS/2 protocol)

- port where your mouse is connected to your computer (in DOS terms, this is generally COM1:, COM2:, or the PS/2 mouse port)

Hard Drives

If you plan to use Linux to repartition your hard drive during installation (see the section later in this chapter about arranging your hard disk's partitions), you may need the following information:

- total storage capacity of the hard disk

- number of cylinders

- number of heads

- number of sectors per track

Generally, you will not need to provide this information because Linux will successfully auto-detect it during boot-up.

Modems

If you have a modem, you should record the following information:

- vendor and model of the modem

- speed of the modem

- port that your external modem is connected to or that you have configured your internal modem to use (in DOS terms, this is generally COM1: or COM2:)

Other Peripherals

Many other peripherals have specific requirements for configuration. As the number and type of possible peripherals are too varied to list here, the details needed to configure these peripherals are left to the sections of this book where the hardware types are discussed. Generally, additional hardware such as specialized serial cards, specialized network hardware, and tape drives are not configured and installed at the time Linux is installed but rather after you have a running Linux system.

If you are planning to install your Linux system on a Local Area Network, consult Chapter 23, "Installing Linux for the SOHO," for information pertaining to network cards and Linux installation.

Choosing an Installation Method

Generally, Linux is distributed on CD-ROMs because of its sheer size. While Linux can be downloaded from the Internet, it is too large for most people to download unless they have access to high-speed, dedicated Internet connections.

A CD-ROM, then, is usually at the core of installing Linux, as it is in the case of the Red Hat Linux 5 distribution included with this book. While it is theoretically possible to install Linux directly off the Internet, this is too time-consuming or too expensive to be practical for most Linux users.

In this section, we will consider different approaches to installing Linux from the enclosed CD-ROM. Procedures will be similar with most other Linux distributions that are available on CD-ROM; the documentation for those distributions should be consulted to determine the differences.

From CD-ROM

If you have an IDE/ATAPI CD-ROM drive and a computer with a recent enough BIOS, it is possible to boot your computer from the Linux CD-ROM to start the installation process.

To check this, consult your computer's or main board's manual, or enter the BIOS setup of your computer while it is booting and see if you can switch the default boot device to your CD-ROM drive. If you can boot from the CD-ROM drive, insert the Red Hat 5 CD-ROM and attempt to boot your system. You should see a Red Hat 5 boot message and a boot prompt that says Lilo:.

NOTE   Even though a CD-ROM may be designed to be bootable, it still may not boot in all PCs that support bootable CD-ROMs. If you experience difficulty booting the copy of Linux that comes with this book or your own copy of Linux, then try installing from a floppy disk and CD-ROM as described in the "From Floppy Disk and CD-ROM" section in this chapter.

From Floppy Disk and CD-ROM

If you have a CD-ROM drive but can't boot from it, the next best thing is to install Linux from a combination of floppy disk and CD-ROM. In this scenario, you will boot from one or more floppy disks to start the installation process and then will proceed to install the actual Linux software from the CD-ROM.

Some preparation is necessary to do this. For most distributions of Linux, you will need to prepare a boot floppy disk and, possibly, one or more supplementary disks. Everything you need in order to do this should be included on the CD-ROM containing your Linux distribution.

In the case of Red Hat Linux 5, you will need a boot disk and a supplementary disk. From DOS or the Windows DOS prompt, you can build these two disks off the Red Hat 5 CD-ROM.

On the Red Hat 5 CD-ROM, the Images subdirectory contains two files, boot .img and supp.img, that are disk images of the floppy disks used for installing Red Hat Linux. To produce the necessary floppy disks, you will need two blank, formatted, high-density 1.44MB floppies and will use the rawrite.exe command.

For instance, assuming your CD-ROM drive is drive D, you would use rawrite.exe as follows to create the Red Hat boot install disk:

```
C:\>d:\dosutils\rawrite.exe
Enter disk image source file name: d:\images\boot.img
Enter target diskette drive: a
Please insert a formatted diskette into drive A: and press -ENTER- :
```

Similarly, you would provide **d:\images\supp.img** as the source filename to create the supplementary installation disk.

Once this is done, you can boot from the boot install disk to start the installation process.

From Hard Disk

If you have plenty of disk space, you may want to copy the entire contents of the CD-ROM to your hard disk and install from the hard disk. In order to do this, use the Windows Explorer (or the Windows 3.1 File Manager) to copy the contents of the CD-ROM to a location on your hard disk with sufficient free space to hold about 650MB of data. In addition, you will need to create the Red Hat Linux boot installation floppy disks as explained above.

Of course, if you have access to a CD-ROM drive to copy the necessary data to your hard drive, then you don't need to install from a hard disk. The only time this should really become necessary is if the Red Hat Linux installation software won't recognize your CD-ROM drive.

Arranging Your Hard Disk

When it comes time to install Linux, you are going to have to make some fundamental decisions regarding where to place the operating system on your hard disk(s).

If you are extremely lucky, then one of the following two situations applies to you:

- You have a blank hard disk, or one you can reformat, available on your system in which to install Linux.

- You have a blank partition, or one you can reformat, available in which to install Linux.

Unfortunately, most users who are looking at installing Linux for the first time will want it to coexist with their current Windows and DOS installations and will not want to reformat an existing partition or hard disk to do this.

Partitioning Concepts

In order to install Linux into an existing system with no free partitions or hard disks, you will need to find sufficient disk space and then carefully adjust your system's partitioning to free up a partition to work with during the Linux installation. Generally, if you want to install a fairly complete Linux system, you will want to free up at least 500MB of disk space. The space you free up should be on a single partition. (In Windows, each partition appears as a separate drive letter such as C, D, or E, so you need to find a drive with 500MB or more of free space.)

A Sample Partition Scheme for a Windows 98 System

Let's take a look at a simple example. You have a computer with a single 4GB hard disk divided into two 2GB partitions as drives C and D under DOS. You are able to free up 1GB of disk space on drive D and want to use this to install Linux.

There are two steps to be done before you are ready to install Linux:

1. Defragment the drive to ensure you have a large, continuous area of free space at the end of the partition.

2. Repartition the drive to make the space available for Linux installation.

Defragmenting a Drive

Defragmenting a drive under Windows 98 is fairly simple:

- In My Computer or the Windows Explorer, right-click the Drives icon.
- Select Properties from the drop-down menu.
- Click the Tools tab at the top of the Properties window.
- Click the Defragment Now... button. Wait until defragmentation is complete and then proceed to the next section.

Partitioning Your Disk with Windows 98

Once you have defragmented a drive with sufficient space to install Linux, you need to create a new partition out of the free space. Most Linux distributions, including Red Hat Linux 5, come with a free DOS tool called `fips.exe`, which is in the `dosutils` subdirectory or a subdirectory of this directory. The Red Hat version included with book, you can find the program in the `\dosutils\fips15c\ fips15c` subdirectory.

This tool allows you to adjust the size of an existing partition, making it smaller by removing empty space at the end of the partition. This empty space is then converted into another partition.

To use `fips.exe`, you first need to be in MS-DOS mode. To do this, select Shut Down from the Start menu and choose Restart in MS-DOS Mode. Windows 98 should shut down and switch to a full-screen DOS environment.

WARNING   This is a critical step. You shouldn't use a program like `fips.exe` inside a DOS window or full-screen DOS environment while Windows 98 is running. Unlike DOS, Windows 98 allows multiple programs to run simultaneously, so it is possible for other programs to try to access the partition being worked with by `fips.exe`. If this happens, your data may be corrupted and irretrievable.

Once in DOS mode, run `fips.exe` from your CD-ROM. If your CD-ROM drive is drive E, use the command:

```
c:\>e:\dosutils\fips15c\fips15c\fips.exe
```

The program will first present your partition table. In our example above of a two-partition drive, this will look something like:

```
Partition table:

      |        |    Start    |      |    End      | Start  |Number of|
Part.|bootable|Head Cyl. Sector|System|Head Cyl. Sector| Sector |Sectors  |  MB
-----+--------+----------------+------+----------------+--------+---------+----
1    |   yes  |  1   0      1|  06h| 254  222     63|      63| 3582432|1749
2    |   no   |  0  223     1|  05h| 254  286     63| 3582495| 1028160|  502
```

On most systems, identifying your partitions is easy since drive C is partition 1, drive D is partition 2, and so on. If you have trouble, use the size of the partition in megabytes in the last column to help.

You will be prompted to choose a partition. In our case, we will choose 2, since we want drive D to be adjusted. Once we choose, the partition will be scanned and summary information about the partition, similar to the following, will be presented:

```
Bytes per sector: 512
Sectors per cluster: 8
Reserved sectors: 1
Number of FATs: 2
Number of rootdirectory entries: 512
Number of sectors (short): 0
Media descriptor byte: f8h
Sectors per FAT: 145
Sectors per track: 63
Drive heads: 16
Hidden sectors: 63
Number of sectors (long): 141057
Physical drive number: 80h
Signature: 29h
```

Assuming you have free space at the end of the partition you have chosen, you will be asked which disk cylinder to use as the line where the partition is cut and split. You can use the left and right arrow keys to change the selected cylinder. As you do this, the size of the partitions in megabytes will be shown so you can make sure the new partition is large enough. The fips.exe program handles the job of ensuring that you can't choose a cylinder to split that would leave some of the data of your current partition on the new partition.

Finally, you will be presented with a revised partition table and asked to confirm that everything looks OK. In our example, you should now have three partitions, with the third being your new partition and the second being smaller in size than it was originally.

TIP   To protect against mistakes, copy `fips.exe`, `restorrb.exe`, and `errors.txt` from the `dosutils` subdirectory of the Red Hat CD-ROM to a bootable floppy disk. When asked if you want to write backup copies of your boot and root sectors to a floppy disk, answer Yes. Then, if you need to recover from a mistake, you can boot from the floppy and run `restorrb.exe` to restore your original boot and root sectors.

Where Do We Go from Here?

In this chapter, we have conducted the basic preparation needed to install Linux. Now we are ready for the actual installation.

In Chapter 4, we will run through a basic installation of Linux, discussing each screen of the installation program and how to decide what choices to make.

In Chapter 5, we will look at special cases, such as how to install Linux on multiple hard drives and how to install Linux onto an existing DOS partition.

PART II

Essential Linux

CHAPTER

FOUR

Installing Linux

- Starting the Installation

- The Installation Process

We're finally here: we are going to install Linux. By now you should be able to boot the Red Hat Linux 5 installation CD-ROM or should have produced a set of Linux boot floppy disks. You should also have determined where you will be installing Linux and made the space available.

Now we can begin. While the installation program may ask questions unfamiliar to you if you have not used a Linux-like operating system before, in reality the whole process is quite simple and many of the tough decisions are made for you by the installation software.

In fact, for the average user—who is installing Linux as a second operating system in a Windows 95 or Windows 98 system—the process is generally straightforward, with a few odd turns required.

Starting the Installation

In this chapter, we will look at a straightforward installation: installing Linux from the CD-ROM onto a non-networked, stand-alone PC.

In order to do this, you need to have selected which media to boot from to start the installation. As outlined in the last chapter, your two options are:

- Booting directly from the Red Hat CD-ROM. This requires that your computer's BIOS supports booting from your CD-ROM drive.

- Booting from a set of boot floppy disks and then installing from the CD-ROM.

In either case, insert your boot disk (floppy or CD-ROM) and boot your computer. When the computer starts booting from the floppy disk or CD-ROM, you will be presented with an initial welcome screen as shown in Figure 4.1.

Here you have three main options:

- Hit Return to start the normal installation process.

- Provide boot parameters that will allow the installation software to detect some types of obscure hardware, and then hit Return to start the normal installation process. (Most hardware is detected automatically during installation.)

- Type **expert** and hit Return to boot in expert mode. (In this mode, hardware detection is not performed and you will need to provide configuration parameters for all your hardware during the installation. You should only revert to this option if your hardware is not being detected properly and you are fairly confident of the parameters to enter.)

Generally, most users will find that all of their hardware will be successfully detected if they choose the first option, so simply hit Return to start the boot process.

FIGURE 4.1:

The Red Hat 5.1 installation boot screen

```
                     Welcome to Red Hat Linux!

    o  To install or upgrade a system running Red Hat Linux 2.0
       or later, press the <ENTER> key.

    o  To enable expert mode, type: expert <ENTER>.  Press <F3> for
       more information about expert mode.

    o  This disk can no longer be used as a rescue disk.  Press <F4> for
       information on the new rescue disks.

    o  Use the function keys listed below for more information.




[F1-Main] [F2-General] [F3-Expert] [F4-Rescue] [F5-Kickstart] [F6-Kernel]
boot:
```

NOTE   If you fail to hit any key within 60 seconds, the installation will automatically start as if you had hit Return without providing any options. To disable this timer, hit one of the help keys (F1–F6). Then you will have all the time you need to decide how to start the installation program.

The Installation Process

The installation process has several steps, which we will consider in turn. However, before doing that, we need to take a look at how to use the keyboard to work in the installation program.

Keyboard Controls

As shown in Figure 4.2, there are several elements to the average installation screen you will see. These elements include text input fields, check boxes, and buttons.

This screen contains the following elements:

- text input fields (FTP site name and Red Hat directory)
- a check box (Use non-anonymous ftp or a proxy server)
- buttons (OK and Cancel)

You can move between these elements using the Tab key (or the Alt+Tab combination to move backwards). The arrow keys can also be used to move between fields.

To toggle the state of a check box, move to the check box and press the space bar. To press a button, move the cursor to the button using the Tab or arrow keys and then press the space bar or the Enter key. With an OK button, the F12 key generally works the same as Enter or the space bar.

Choosing a Language

After starting the installation program at the boot screen as described earlier in this chapter, you will be presented with a welcome screen. Pressing the OK button will bring you to the first screen of the installation process: language selection.

As you can see in Figure 4.3, this screen has a selection list field and an OK button. When the cursor is in the selection list field, you can use the arrow keys or the Page Up and Page Down keys to move through the available languages until the desired one is selected. This selection determines the language that will be used during the installation process. (This is distinct from the language of the actual operating system, which is English, and the keyboard layout, which is chosen later.)

FIGURE 4.3:

Choosing a language

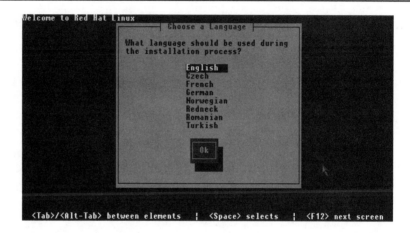

Choosing a Keyboard Type

The next screen presents a selection list field for choosing a keyboard type. In the United States and Canada, the correct choice will almost always be "us." Other common codes include those listed below.

Code	Description
uk	British English keyboard
sg	Swiss German keyboard
sf	Swiss French keyboard
fr	French keyboard (France)
de	German keyboard

PCMCIA Support

Once you have chosen a keyboard type, you will be prompted regarding your need for PCMCIA support during the installation process.

Generally, this is necessary only if you are installing Red Hat 5 on a notebook computer and will need to access a PCMCIA device during the installation. For example, you may have an external CD-ROM drive connected to your PC through a PCMCIA SCSI card.

If you need to use PCMCIA support, select this. You will be prompted to insert your supplementary boot disk at this time.

Once Red Hat 5 is installed, PCMCIA support will be available. Only choose PCMCIA support here if you need it for the installation process.

Choosing an Installation Method

Once you have made your decision about PCMCIA support and, if necessary, provided the supplementary boot disk, you will be presented with another selection list field asking you to choose the media you want to install from. Possible options include:

- CD-ROM

- NFS (from a Unix network file server)

- Hard Drive (from a hard drive partition; we will discuss this in the next chapter)

- FTP (from an FTP server)

- SMB Image (from a Windows-based file server)

In our case, we are installing from the enclosed Red Hat 5 CD-ROM, so select CD-ROM and press the OK button.

When you choose to install from a CD-ROM, the installation program will attempt to find an IDE/ATAPI CD-ROM drive, since this is the type available on most PCs today. If it fails to find your CD-ROM drive, you will be prompted to tell the installation program what type of CD-ROM drive you have. The options are SCSI or Other.

You should select SCSI if you have a SCSI CD-ROM drive. You will be prompted to select a drive for your SCSI card. Choose the drive that most closely matches your card and, if necessary, specify any options for your card.

If you have neither a SCSI nor IDE CD-ROM drive, then you need to select Other. This allows you to choose from a list of proprietary CD-ROM drives such as those directly connected to certain sound cards or proprietary interfaces. You may be prompted to provide configuration information such as I/O addresses and IRQs once you select your drive.

Installing or Upgrading

Once you have selected your installation media (a CD-ROM drive in our case), you will be asked if you are upgrading an existing installation or installing a new copy of Red Hat Linux. One of the benefits of Red Hat Linux, as opposed to some other distributions, is that it can be upgraded over old versions of Red Hat. This is a great benefit; some other distributions still require a complete reinstallation to upgrade to a new version of the distribution.

Because we are installing from scratch, press the Install button.

Checking for SCSI Adapters

If you are installing a fresh copy of Red Hat Linux, you may be asked if you have any SCSI adapters. If you do, you should indicate this so that all attached devices can be detected by the installation software.

If you indicate that you have SCSI adapters, you will be presented with a list of available drivers for SCSI cards from which you should choose the card that most closely matches your card. You may be prompted to give configuration information for the card once you choose the driver.

If you have no SCSI adapters in your system, it is important to choose No.

Setting Up Your Disk Partitions

After you provide the necessary information about your SCSI adapters, if any, you will face a decision about how to allocate disk space for your Linux installation. This is a crucial step in the process because a mistake can erase existing data on your system that you want to keep. Care needs to be taken.

We will assume that you have a single hard drive in your system; that, as directed in Chapter 3 ("Getting Ready"), you created an area of free space (preferably larger than 500MB) using the techniques described there; and that the space is now ready to be used.

The first question you will be asked is which tool you want to use to set up your partitions. The two choices are Disk Druid or fdisk.

Fdisk is the standard Linux tool for configuring disk partitions and is available for every Linux distribution. However, it is difficult to use and can be especially daunting for first-time Linux or Unix users.

To help ease this process, Red Hat 5 provides its own tool for disk partition management called Disk Druid. In this section, we will focus on using Disk Druid because it eases the initial installation process for users new to the Linux environment.

If you select the Disk Druid button, you will be presented with the main Disk Druid screen shown in Figure 4.4.

FIGURE 4.4:

The main Disk Druid screen

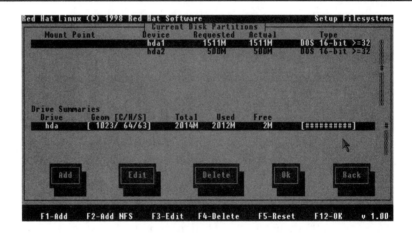

This screen has three main sections: the Current Disk Partitions section, the Drive Summaries section, and the button row.

In the Current Disk Partitions section, a single row will be displayed for each existing disk partition on your system. The following information is presented about each partition:

- Mount Point: This indicates where the partition will appear in your Linux directory structure. Linux directories all appear as subdirectories of the root directory. The root directory is / and all subdirectories start with a /, such as /home, /opt, and /usr/X11R6. At a minimum, you need to have a partition mounted as /. If you choose to mount additional partitions as subdirectories, this will spread your Linux distribution across two directories. For instance, if you mount a partition as /usr, then any content stored under this subdirectory is stored on the /usr partition while all other data is on the root-mounted (/) partition. The following indicates the primary role of the standard top-level Red Hat Linux directories:

- /bin: Standard system utilities are stored here.

- /dev: Device files are stored here.

- /home: Users' home directories are stored here.

- /opt: Optionally installed software is stored here.

- /sbin: Standard system administration files are stored here.

- /usr: Additional system software and administration tools are stored here.

- Device: This indicates the Linux device name for each partition. For IDE disks, the drives are labeled hdx, where x is a letter designating a drive (a for the primary master drive, b for the primary slave, c for the secondary master, and d for the secondary slave). Thus, if you have a single IDE hard disk, it is disk hda. SCSI Disks are labeled sdx with x again designating a drive. Partitions on the disk are then numbered consecutively starting with hda1 and moving up. Generally, partitions 1 through 4 are primary partitions and 5 and above represent the extended and logical partitions common on many DOS systems. In Figure 4.4, we see a single preexisting DOS partition, hda1.

- Requested: This indicates the minimum size of the partition in megabytes.

- Actual: This indicates the actual space allocated for a partition. Disk Druid allows the creation of growable Linux partitions, which increase in size as free space is available on the hard disk and space runs out in the partition. DOS partitions should have matching actual and requested values.

- Type: This field indicates the type of partition. Possible values include Linux native, Linux swap, and DOS 16-bit.

The next main section of the screen is the Drive Summaries section. This presents one line for each hard disk on your system and includes the following information about the drives:

- Drive: This is the device name for the hard drive, discussed above.

- Geometry: This indicates the number of cylinders, heads, and sectors (in that order) for the drive.

- Total: This indicates the total available space on the drive, in megabytes.

- Used: This indicates the total used space on the drive, in megabytes. This number actually reflects how much is used in the sense of how much has been allocated to partitions. These partitions may not be full, but the space is no longer available to be allocated to other partitions.

- Free: This indicates how much free, allocated space is available on the drive, both numerically and as a bar graph. This number must be more than zero and should be more than 500MB before proceeding, because we will need to use this space to create partitions to install Linux in. If you don't have any free space, consult the discussion in Chapter 3 where we describe how to allocate space for your Linux installation.

Finally, we have the button bar across the bottom of the screen with three task buttons, an OK button, and the typical Back button that you have already seen on some screens. We will use the Add task button to create the necessary Linux partitions for our installation and the Edit button to make sure our existing DOS and Windows data is accessible in Linux. Then we will discuss the use of the Delete button.

Adding New Partitions

To add a new partition, you simply press the Add button on the main Disk Druid screen. This will display a screen asking for the following main information:

- Mount point

- Size in megabytes

- Partition type (from a selection list field)

- Whether the drive can grow to use unallocated disk space as needed (through the Growable check box)

- Which drives the partition can be created on. If more than one drive is indicated as allowed and all allowed drives have sufficient space to create the partition, then Disk Druid will decide which disk to use. If you want to create the partition on a specific disk, make sure only that disk is checked.

We will need to use the Add button twice to create the following partitions:

- A swap partition: Linux needs a separate partition to use for swapping. This is necessary when you use up all your physical RAM and the operating system must draw on virtual memory (disk space masquerading as RAM) to keep functioning. At a minimum, you will want to match the amount of physical RAM you have on your system; if you have plenty of free disk space, make the size of the swap partition as much as double your physical RAM. So, on a 32MB system, create a swap partition of between 32 and 64 MB. The partition type should be set to `Linux swap`, no mount point should be indicated, and the Growable check box should be unselected.

- A root partition: In this chapter, we are going to install Linux in a single partition. (We will discuss the use of multiple partitions or drives for the installation of Linux in the next chapter.) To do this, we need to add another partition. You will probably want the partition to be at least 500MB to give you room to work once Linux is installed. This partition should be type `Linux native`, should have a mount point of /, and can be marked as growable if there is unallocated free space on your drive that you want to use if the partition grows larger than its initial size.

NOTE   When determining your swap partition size, keep in mind that Linux currently limits the size of a swap partition to 128MB, so you won't want to create partitions larger than that.

Editing a Partition

You can edit existing partitions by selecting them on the list of current partitions and then clicking on the Edit button. This brings up a window like the one we used when adding a new partition, except that here all the fields are filled in to match the settings of the partition we are editing.

If you have preexisting DOS partitions, you can make them available by specifying a mount point for them. To do this, select the partition you wish to make accessible in Linux, press the Edit button, and then fill in a mount point for the partition.

If you have a single DOS partition, you could mount it as /dos, for instance. If you have two DOS partitions, which are drives C and D in DOS and Windows, you could choose /dosc and /dosd (or /c and /d) respectively, as the mount points.

TIP

If you have Windows 95 or 98 FAT32 partitions, you are out of luck at the moment, since Linux currently doesn't support reading to or writing from this type of partition. In this case, don't indicate a mount point for the partition.

Deleting a Partition

If in the process of creating your Linux swap and root partitions you make a mistake (maybe the swap partition is too large or your root partition too small), you can delete the partitions and then re-add them. To do this, select the partition in the list of current partitions and then press the Delete button.

WARNING

Take care when doing this. Don't accidentally delete any partitions that already existed before you started installing Linux and that contain important data or software you want to keep.

Moving On

Once you have finished creating and configuring your partitions, you are ready to move on. You can do this by pressing the OK button.

Preparing Your Swap Space

The next step in the installation process is to prepare your swap space. You will be presented with a screen like the one in Figure 4.5.

FIGURE 4.5:

Preparing your swap space

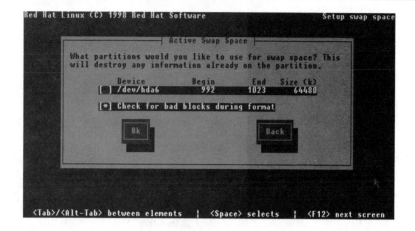

This screen lists all available partitions of type swap with a check box next to them. Any partitions that you actually want to use as swap space should be checked.

An additional check box is used to indicate that the partitions should be checked for bad blocks while being formatted for use as swap space. If the drive you are using is new, you definitely should check this option. Formatting will take longer but any problems with your hard disk will be caught early. If you are using a disk that has been in use on your computer for some time, you can consider not checking for bad blocks. Note, however, that bad blocks on your swap partition can cause your Linux system to crash. You could lose your current work when this happens, and it is even possible for data saved on your root partition to become corrupted if there are bad blocks in your swap partition.

Formatting Your Linux Partitions

The next step is to format your Linux partitions in preparation for installing Linux. You will be presented with a list of partitions of type Linux native with indications of the mount points they have. Any newly created partitions should be marked for formatting by selecting the check box next to the drive.

If you have additional partitions of type `Linux native`, they should be formatted if they are new partitions. If they already existed (this is unlikely for new Red Hat users) and you want to retain the data they hold, don't mark them for formatting.

As with the swap partition, you can indicate that a bad block check should be performed during formatting. This is a good idea, especially for new hard drives.

Selecting Packages

Now that our hard disks are configured and our Linux partitions are formatted, we are ready to begin installing the actual software. The default installation will include all necessary core software, but several optional components are also available, as shown in Figure 4.6.

FIGURE 4.6:

Selecting additional components

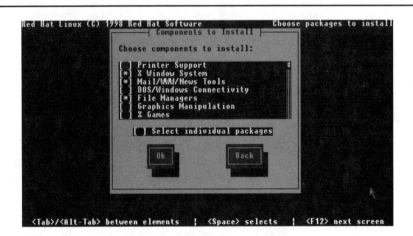

Each component is a collection of related packages for specific tasks such as dial-up connections, Web surfing, and others. You can choose the packages individually by marking their respective check boxes or you can choose the Everything option, which is the last entry in the list.

The Select Individual Packages option that appears below the list field indicates that you want to select individual packages within each component. However, if you are a first-time Linux user, it will be hard to choose the packages. Leaving this option unselected means that each component will be installed in its entirety.

If you have plenty of disk space (more than 700MB; 1GB is preferable), then select everything so that you have a complete Red Hat Linux 5 installation. If your space is in more limited supply, consider installing the following components at a minimum:

- Printer Support (If you don't have a printer, then this is unnecessary)
- X Window System
- Mail/WWW/News Tools
- DOS/Windows Connectivity
- X Multimedia Support
- Console Multimedia
- Dialup Workstation
- Extra Documentation

Once you select the components you want to install, you will be informed that a log of your installation process will be saved on your new Linux system as the file `/tmp/install.log`, and then installation will begin.

During the installation of the software, a screen will display the current status of the installation, indicating which package is currently being installed, how many packages and how many megabytes remain, and the overall progress of the installation.

Configuring Your Mouse

Once the Linux software has been successfully installed, installation will proceed to the configuration process.

The first item to be configured is your mouse. You will be presented with a list of possible mouse types from which to select. The two most common types are Microsoft-compatible serial mice and PS/2 mice. Consult your mouse's documentation to determine the type of mouse you have.

If your mouse is a two-button mouse, make sure that you check the box for three-button mouse emulation. Linux expects a three-button mouse, as do all Unix operating systems. This emulation allows you to click the left and right mouse buttons together to simulate clicking on the middle mouse button.

Configuring X Windows

X Windows is Linux's graphical user interface. We will discuss configuration of X Windows in detail in Chapter 7, "Installing and Configuring X Windows." For now, we will quickly run through the configuration process. Configuration can be quite complex and we have devoted a whole chapter to it, so any problems will be left to that chapter for resolution.

First, an attempt is made to determine what type of video card you have. If this fails, you will be presented with a list of available video cards. Select the one that most closely matches your card (if none match, leave configuration of X Windows until Chapter 7).

Next, you will be presented with a list of monitor types. If you find an exact match for your monitor, choose it; otherwise, hold off until Chapter 7. An incorrectly configured monitor can cause damage to the monitor. The match should be exact.

Next, you will be asked for the amount of video memory available on your video card. You will need to consult your video card's documentation for this information.

Once you specify the video memory, you will be presented with a list of clock chips. If your card doesn't have a clock chip or you don't know whether it does, choose No Clockchip. Do not guess on this question. If you indicate No Clockchip, you will be given a chance to probe your card for clock settings. Give this a try. If it fails, leave things until Chapter 7.

Finally, you will be presented with a list of video modes. Select the one you wish to use for X Windows.

Network Configuration

The next item to be configured is your network. Because we are installing a stand-alone system in this chapter, choose not to configure your network. We will discuss networked configuration in more detail in Chapter 23, "Installing Linux for the SOHO."

Time Zone Configuration

The next step is to configure your computer's clock and time zone. You need to make two decisions.

First, you need to indicate whether you want your system's clock set to your local time or to Greenwich Mean Time. If you run only Linux on your computer, choose to set the clock to GMT. Red Hat Linux will then convert GMT to the current time for your time zone. But if you also run other operating systems on your PC, don't select this option—leave the system's clock set to your local time.

Second, you need to choose the actual time zone from the list of available time zones.

Selecting Services

In Linux, you can easily control which services start when you boot your system. Services do everything from controlling the movement of e-mail to scheduling automated batch tasks.

Because you can change the scheduling of tasks at any point, leave the default settings on this screen for now. Later, once you have learned about many of these services, you can make changes to the start-up configuration.

Configuring a Printer

The next step is configuring a printer. Printer configuration is covered in some depth in Chapter 15, "Using Peripherals," but we will review it briefly here. If you have no printer, you can skip this step.

In this section, we will only discuss configuring a local printer—that is, a printer physically connected to your computer (as opposed to a network printer). To start this procedure, choose Local from the options presented on the first printer configuration screen.

The next screen asks for standard printer options: the name of the queue and the directory where the data should be stored while being printed. It is best to accept the defaults until our later discussions of Linux printing.

After you choose these standard options, the installation program will detect and display available parallel ports that a printer could be attached to. Linux parallel ports are named /dev/1p0, /dev/1p1, and so on, with 1p0 mapping to LPT1: in DOS and 1p1 mapping to LPT2:. Make sure the correct device is indicated in the Printer Device field.

Next, you will see the Configure Printer screen. Here you can choose the type of printer that most closely matches your printer. If the exact model is not on the list, choose the closest available type of printer. This will lead to a screen where you can specify settings for the printer that include paper size and default resolution.

The Fix Stair-Stepping of Text? option is needed if your printer doesn't automatically put a carriage return at the end of each line of text. If you aren't sure, leave this option unselected for now.

Finally, you will be presented with the configuration information for your printer and asked to confirm that everything is correct.

Setting a Root Password

As a multiuser operating system, Linux needs at least one user to exist in order for it to be used. On all systems, you have to have a root user, so you are prompted to provide a root password (twice, for confirmation). The root user is the all-powerful system administrator. When logged in as the root user, you can view all users' files, perform all system administration tasks, and, if you wanted to, delete all files on your system. This is a powerful account, and you need to keep this password secure if other people are going to have access to your system.

Creating a Boot Disk

The next step gives you a chance to create a boot disk for your system. This is a wise decision, because it allows you to boot your system in case of emergencies and then attempt to resurrect a sick system.

By choosing to create a boot disk, you will need to provide a blank floppy disk to be used for the boot disk.

Setting Up LILO

LILO is the Linux boot loader. In order for your system to boot properly, you need to configure and install LILO. LILO also provides the dual-boot features that can allow you to choose what operating system to launch at boot time, providing you with access to your existing Windows or DOS system as well as Linux.

The screen will ask you to indicate where to install LILO. You can do this in the Master Boot Record (which is recommended) or on the first sector of your root partition. If you are running an operating system, such as OS/2 or Windows NT, that has its own boot loader, you may want to choose the latter option, but then you will need to know how to make that boot loader launch your Linux system in order to get Linux working.

WARNING If you choose to skip installing LILO at this point, you will need the boot disk from the last step in order to boot your Linux system. It is highly recommended that you install LILO during this initial installation.

The next screen will prompt you to provide default options to be given to Linux at boot time. You probably don't need to use these options, but if your hard drive is configured to use logical block addressing (LBA) mode (check your BIOS), then choose the Use Linear Mode option.

Finally, you will see a screen in which all partitions are displayed and a boot label is assigned to all bootable partitions—in this case, one for your Linux system and one for your DOS/Windows system. The boot label is the name you will use to select which operating system will boot when you start your computer.

The Default column indicates which operating system will boot by default if the user makes no selection at boot time. To change this, select the operating system you wish to be your default and press F2.

Rebooting Your System

Finally, you will be prompted to remove any floppy disks from the computer and reboot. If you left Linux as the default operating system, the system will boot into Linux, giving you five seconds at the boot: prompt during start-up to select an alternate operating system.

If you chose another operating system as your default, then at the boot: prompt you will need to type the boot label of your Linux partition in order to boot into Linux.

If all goes well, you will see a Red Hat login screen similar to the one in Figure 4.7.

FIGURE 4.7:

The Red Hat 5.1 login screen

You can log in here as the root user using the username root and the password you provided earlier. You will be presented with a command prompt, as shown in Figure 4.8.

FIGURE 4.8:

A Red Hat 5.1 command prompt

We will learn about commands later, but the premise is simple: type the command and hit the Enter or Return key to execute it. Type **exit** and hit Return to log out.

Linux allows you to log in more than once, even in the initial character-based mode. Using the combinations of Alt+F1 through Alt+F6, you can switch between up to six virtual consoles. You will need to log in separately in each virtual console. You can log in as different users and perform different tasks, or log in to different virtual consoles as the same user—this is one of the features of UNIX and Linux that make them such flexible environments to work in.

Where Do We Go from Here?

By now you should have a working Linux system. If you are one of the few readers who have special circumstances that made it impossible to get your Linux system running by following the steps in this chapter, then take a look at the next chapter, where we discuss some special-case installations:

- Installing from a hard drive partition. (This is important if, for some reason, you cannot get Linux to install from your CD-ROM drive.)

- Installing to multiple partitions or hard disks. (This is useful if you have lots of disk space spread over multiple disks or need the performance gain from splitting Linux in this way.)

- Using fdisk instead of Disk Druid to configure your partitions. (Disk Druid is useful, but not standard for Linux; using fdisk allows you to learn the workings of this standard tool and provides access to the more powerful tools desired by the expert user.)

If any of these special installations are useful, turn to the next chapter. If your system booted correctly, though, you are ready to move on and learn about X Windows. Skip to Chapter 6, "An Overview of X Windows," and continue from there.

CHAPTER
FIVE

Special Installations

■ Installing from a Hard Disk Partition

■ Installing Linux on Multiple Partitions

■ Using *Fdisk* instead of Disk Druid

In the last chapter, we learned how to take the straightforward approach to installing Linux: from a local CD-ROM to a single hard disk partition.

In this chapter, we look at a few variations that are not uncommon. First among these is installing from a hard disk partition. There are cases where installing from the local CD-ROM drive is not practical. For instance, you may have one of the handful of CD-ROM drives that the Red Hat installation software can't recognize, or you may have only temporary access to a CD-ROM drive. In these cases, one option is to copy the contents of the Red Hat CD-ROM to blank space on a hard drive and then install from the hard drive.

In addition, with the low cost of hard drives today, you may have available multiple partitions or hard drives that you can use for your Linux installation. In these cases, you can maximize the performance of your system by spreading your Linux system across multiple partitions and disks.

Finally, we look at how to use the fdisk program, instead of Disk Druid, for configuring your hard disk partitions. Fdisk is standard with all distributions of Linux; Disk Druid is available only with Red Hat Linux.

Installing from a Hard Disk Partition

For some users, there are compelling reasons to install Linux from a different hard disk partition than the one they plan to run Linux from. Possible reasons include:

- A CD-ROM drive that the Red Hat installation program fails to recognize

- Lack of a permanent CD-ROM drive, but access to a CD-ROM drive to copy the CD-ROM to hard disk

- A notebook with a switchable floppy drive and CD-ROM drive that cannot be booted from the CD-ROM drive

In all these cases, the process of installing from a hard disk partition is basically the same:

1. Copy the contents of the Red Hat CD-ROM to a dedicated hard disk partition.

2. Make sure you have the correct installation floppy disks ready.

3. Start the installation process by booting from the boot installation floppy disk.

Copying the CD-ROM to a Hard Disk Partition

In order to install from a hard disk partition, you need a dedicated partition available to store the contents of the Red Hat CD-ROM. This partition should contain at least 650MB of free space in order to be able to accommodate the complete contents of the Red Hat CD-ROM.

You can copy the contents of the CD-ROM to a partition from your current Windows environment using the xcopy command from a DOS prompt window. If you have your CD-ROM drive at drive F: and the free disk partition where you want to copy the contents of the CD-ROM drive is drive E:, then you could use the command:

```
xcopy /e /h f: e:
```

The /e flag indicates that all directories on the CD-ROM should be created in the copy, even if the directory is empty, and the /h flag indicates that all files, including hidden files, should be copied.

Preparing the Installation Floppies

In Chapter 3, "Getting Ready," we discussed how to create the necessary installation floppy disks. Refer to the section "From Floppy Disk and CD-ROM" in that chapter for all the details.

In order to install from a hard disk partition, you will need both the primary boot installation floppy disk and the supplementary floppy disk, so it is best to have them both prepared before starting the installation process.

The Actual Installation Process

To begin the installation, boot from the boot floppy. Follow the steps used for a normal installation from CD-ROM (set out in Chapter 4, "Installing Linux") with the following exceptions:

1. When selecting an installation method, select Hard Drive instead of Local CD-ROM. When you do this, you will be prompted to insert the supplementary installation floppy disk.

2. After selecting and configuring your disk partitions with Disk Druid (or `fdisk`, as discussed later in this chapter), you will be prompted to indicate which partition contains your Red Hat source image. Refer back to Chapter 4 for a discussion of Linux device names for disk partitions. If you aren't sure which partition contains the Red Hat software, refer to the list of available partitions provided on the screen to try to determine which one contains your copy of the Red Hat CD-ROM. If that is not sufficient, then choose Cancel to return to the Disk Druid list of partitions, which provides more detailed information about your partitions.

Other than these two differences, the rest of your installation should proceed in much the same way as is outlined in Chapter 4.

Installing Linux on Multiple Partitions

The title of this section is something of a misnomer. After all, for any Linux installation, you are using at least two partitions: one for storing Linux and one for your swap space. However, there can be compelling reasons to use more than one partition for storing Linux.

One obvious reason for this would be if you have a disk that has two available partitions that are not physically contiguous. There is no way to delete these partitions and create one larger partition on which to store Linux. In this case, you can divide your Linux installation across the two partitions.

Even more compelling, though, is to install Linux on more than one disk. There are several ways to take advantage of having more than one disk for your Linux installation.

Putting Swap on a Separate Disk

If you have a large partition on one disk and a smaller partition (of anywhere from 32 to 200 MB) on a second disk, you may want to consider putting your swap partition on a second disk. This can noticeably improve performance if you find yourself swapping a lot.

Consider this scenario: Your Linux installation and swap partition are on the same physical disk. You are running many applications and your system has already been swapping a lot. You attempt to launch a new application, but in order for it to be launched, it needs to be loaded from disk into memory—and at the same time, existing data in memory needs to be swapped out to disk. Since only one operation can be performed by the disk at once, your disk suddenly becomes a bottleneck as the operating system tries to perform both actions nearly at the same time.

But if your swap partition is on a separate disk, there is less of a bottleneck: one disk can be reading data from the disk into memory while the other is still finishing the process of moving data from memory onto the disk. Even though the computer can't perform two instructions at the same time, the fact that the slow disk operations are spread over two disks helps minimize the time the CPU is left waiting for the disks to finish their work.

Splitting Linux across Multiple Partitions

Another way to use two or more partitions for your Linux software is to split the storage of your Linux software across the partitions in a logical manner. This can provide two benefits:

- Expanding the disk space available in critical Linux directory trees such as the /home directory tree

- Improving performance by splitting disk accesses across multiple hard disks if the available partitions are on more than one disk

Let's consider how we might want to split our Linux distribution across two partitions. As mentioned in Chapter 4 when we discussed how to specify the mount point for an existing DOS partition, we use our additional disks by specifying their mount points.

For example, if we want to store all users' home directories on a separate partition, then we make the mount point for that partition /home while leaving the mount point for our main Linux partition as /. Then, when we write to or read from any subdirectory under /home, we are actually accessing a different partition than when we access other directory trees outside /home.

There are several popular ways to split your Linux installation across two partitions:

- If you plan to install a lot of your own software (including commercial software such as word processors, Web browsers, and Windows emulation software), you will find that much of it is installed in the /opt directory tree. If your main Linux partition has plenty of room for the operating system plus user data, then consider mounting your additional partition as /opt. This will give you a separate area for all of your applications, and when you launch applications, the main system disk is still free for accessing data or running the system utilities and background tasks that Linux is always performing.

- If you expect to have a lot of users or plan to store a lot of data in users' home directories, then consider mounting your additional partition as /home. This way, you can separately monitor user disk usage, and you will get a performance gain when many users are accessing their data while other users are trying to launch applications, because these two actions will require access to separate disk partitions.

- If you find that neither partition on its own can contain your complete Linux installation, you may want to choose a fairly large directory tree such as /usr/X11R6 (the X Windows directory tree) and install that to a separate partition so that you can install your complete Linux system.

- While many new packages are installed in /opt, if you do lots of software installation you will find that /usr may also fill up quickly, making it a good candidate for a separate partition.

- If you are using Linux as a busy mail server or a heavily used, multiuser server, consider giving /var its own partition, since mail spool queues and system logs sit in this directory and can grow quickly in these types of servers.

Using *Fdisk* instead of Disk Druid

In the last chapter, we used Disk Druid to configure our disk partitions when installing Red Hat Linux 5. Disk Druid, however, is a program that is only available in the Red Hat installation process. Normally, Linux users use fdisk to configure their disk partitions, both during the installation process and later when they need to adjust their disk geographies.

In fact, fdisk is so familiar to power Linux users that Red Hat acknowledges its predominance as a tool for configuring disk partitions by offering it as an alternative to Disk Druid.

While fdisk is an extremely complex and powerful tool (and a potentially dangerous and destructive one if misused), the job of performing basic tasks such as displaying a partition table, creating a new partition from free space, and assigning types to partitions is fairly simple.

When you select fdisk instead of Disk Druid during the installation process, you are first presented with a screen that asks you which disk to work with. Unlike Disk Druid, fdisk works with only one physical disk at a time. Once you select a disk to work with, you will temporarily leave the now-familiar Red Hat installation program and will be presented with the initial fdisk screen shown in Figure 5.1.

FIGURE 5.1:

The fdisk welcome screen

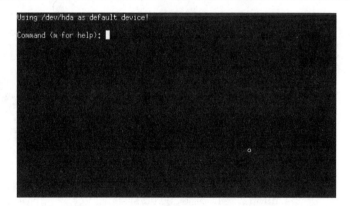

Fdisk operates using simple commands, each a single character long. To issue a command, simply type the command and hit the Return or Enter key. If the command needs additional information to perform its task, it will prompt you for the information.

The simplest command is m or ?. Either of these characters causes fdisk to display the help screen shown in Figure 5.2. This screen lists all the common fdisk commands, including all the commands we will look at in this section.

FIGURE 5.2:

The fdisk help screen

```
Using /dev/hda as default device!

Command (m for help): m
Command action
   a   toggle a bootable flag
   b   edit bsd disklabel
   c   toggle the dos compatibility flag
   d   delete a partition
   l   list known partition types
   m   print this menu
   n   add a new partition
   p   print the partition table
   q   quit without saving changes
   t   change a partition's system id
   u   change display/entry units
   v   verify the partition table
   w   write table to disk and exit
   x   extra functionality (experts only)

Command (m for help):
```

Displaying the Partition Table

One of the most useful tasks performed by fdisk is to display the current partition table for the active disk being worked with. This looks like the table in Figure 5.3.

FIGURE 5.3:

The partition table

```
Command (m for help): p

Disk /dev/hda: 255 heads, 63 sectors, 525 cylinders
Units = cylinders of 16065 * 512 bytes

   Device Boot   Begin   Start    End    Blocks   Id  System
/dev/hda1    *       1       1    223   1791216    6  DOS 16-bit >=32M
/dev/hda2          224     224    287    514080    5  Extended
/dev/hda3          288     288    515   1831410   83  Linux native
/dev/hda4          516     516    525     80325   82  Linux swap
/dev/hda5          224     224    287    514048+   6  DOS 16-bit >=32M

Command (m for help):
```

For each partition on the current disk, the device name, start and end blocks, partition size in blocks, and system type are displayed.

Adding a Partition Using Free Space

To add a new partition using existing free space on your hard disk, use the n command. As shown in Figure 5.4, you will be prompted for a partition type. Generally, you will want to choose primary as the type. With Linux fdisk, you can create four primary partitions as compared to DOS's single primary partition.

Once the partition type is selected, you assign the partition number and finally the start and end blocks. To use all remaining space (assuming all available space is at the end of the drive), take the default first and last block for your partition.

FIGURE 5.4:

Adding a new partition

```
Command (m for help): n
Command action
   e    extended
   p    primary partition (1-4)
p
Partition number (1-4): 2
First cylinder (224-525): █
```

Changing Partition Type

By default, all new partitions created with fdisk are assigned the type Linux native (type number 83). To change the type of a partition, use the t command.

You will be prompted for a partition to work with, which you can select numerically as shown in Figure 5.5, and then will be prompted for the type ID. To view a list of type IDs, use the L command at this point to see the list shown in Figure 5.5.

FIGURE 5.5:

The list of partition type IDs in fdisk

```
Command (m for help): t
Partition number (1-4): 1
Hex code (type L to list codes): 82
Changed system type of partition 1 to 82 (Linux swap)
```

The commonly used partition types are shown in the following table:

ID	Type
5	Extended
6	DOS 16-bit (larger than 32MB)
7	OS/2 HPFS
b	Windows 95 FAT32
82	Linux Swap
83	Linux Native

Deleting a Partition

Sometimes you will want to delete an existing partition to create one or more new partitions for your Linux installation. To do this, simply use the d command and, when prompted, enter the partition number you wish to delete.

Committing Your Changes

While you are working with fdisk, none of the changes you make are actually made to the physical disk. This is a safety precaution so that if you accidentally delete a partition with important data, you will be able to revert to your previous configuration before permanently deleting the partition containing the data.

For that reason, the changes you make are not actually processed until you explicitly ask fdisk to do so at the time of quitting. Therefore, before you quit from fdisk, take care to view the partition table to be sure you have done exactly what you want. If you exit and commit the changes, they are permanent, and going back is not really an option. (In theory, you can save the partition table of your disk to a floppy disk before working with fdisk and then recover from a serious mistake by replacing the new partition table with the saved one; however, this is a complicated procedure and not foolproof. You are better off taking care and making sure that the changes you make to your partition table are exactly the way you want them before committing the changes.)

The two alternative commands for quitting from fdisk are:

Command	Effect
q	Quits from fdisk without processing or saving any of your changes.
w	Processes and saves all your changes and then exits from fdisk. This is a permanent action, so take care.

Where Do We Go from Here?

Finally, we are ready to get into the business of actually using Linux. As our first step on that path, we will look at the X Windows environment. X Windows gives all Unix operating systems, including Linux, a highly flexible, mouse-driven graphical user interface.

Many Linux books start with the command line because this is really the heart of Linux. But X Windows enables new users to quickly start using Linux before they have a thorough grasp of the Linux command line.

We start the next chapter with an overview of X Windows and learn what it offers and how it compares with the Microsoft Windows environment. Then we will move on to configuration and use of X Windows and take a look at some common X Windows applications.

CHAPTER

SIX

An Overview of X Windows

- What Is X Windows?

- Microsoft Windows versus X Windows

- X Servers and Window Managers

- What Is Motif?

Now that we have succeeded in installing Linux, we are going to start our learning process by diving straight into the X Windows environment. Many Linux diehards will shudder at our considering X Windows before learning all the intricate details of the Linux command line and Linux configuration. But it is X Windows that makes Linux an acceptable alternative to Windows and the Mac OS as a productive operative system for everyday tasks such as word processing, desktop publishing, and browsing the World Wide Web.

In this chapter, we will start by learning exactly what X Windows is. X Windows offers a graphical user interface, or GUI, to the Unix world. X Windows provides a way to deliver all the now commonplace user interface paradigms such as windows, dialog boxes, buttons, and menus. It is X Windows that enables creation of the sophisticated graphics that make Unix-based workstations the systems of choice for many engineering and design applications, and it is X Windows that has made it possible for Linux to emerge a strong contender in the PC operating system market.

To fully understand what X Windows is all about, we will make a detailed comparison of Microsoft Windows and X Windows. Having done that, we will wrap up the chapter by looking at some key components of X Windows such as X servers, window managers, and Motif.

What Is X Windows?

Put in its simplest terms, X Windows is a complete graphics interface for Unix, and by extension for Linux. But that doesn't say it all. X Windows is a highly configurable environment that provides a broad range of flexible options to both the user and the application developers producing software to run under X Windows.

Basic Concepts

The core X Windows concept is the client-server framework. What this means in practical terms is that X Windows provides an environment that is not bound to a single system. Applications can run on different servers and machines on a network and display to X Windows terminals and workstations elsewhere on the net.

This separation between where an application runs and where it is displayed is a concept missing in Windows and Macintosh environments, which tie the application to the display. The benefit of this separation is that in a networking environment it is possible to have sophisticated graphical desktops displaying applications that are running on well-maintained, powerful, easy-to-manage central application servers.

In fact, this very ability is what gives Unix and X Windows such a high reputation among professional system administrators of large networks.

Another concept introduced in the X Windows environment is the separation of windowing from the interface. On an X Windows system, two applications must run to provide a complete graphical user interface. The first is the X server, which sets up the graphical display (i.e., resolution, refresh rate, and color depth), displays windows, and tracks mouse movements, keystrokes, and multiple windows. But an X server does not provide menus, window borders, or mechanisms for moving, switching, minimizing, or maximizing windows. If you look at Figure 6.1, you will see how an X server screen looks without a window manager.

FIGURE 6.1:

An X server display with no window manager

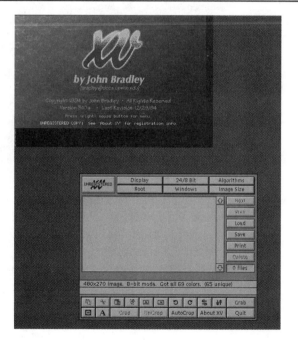

Notice the bare simplicity of things. There is no fancy color background, no sophisticated window borders or menu controls, and no other features that make a complete GUI. All these features are provided by a second application called a window manager. Figure 6.2 shows a complete X Windows desktop running the default window manager that comes with Red Hat Linux 5, the fvwm95 Window Manager. Notice the features of the window frames, including control buttons and control menus as well as a task bar and a virtual desktop system. All of these are provided by the window manager.

FIGURE 6.2:

An X Windows display running a window manager

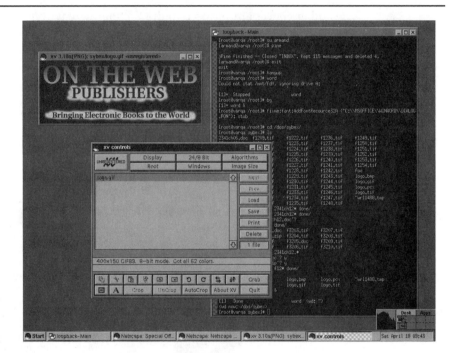

The window manager talks to the X server in a standard, predefined way, as does the X server to the X applications. This means that different window managers with different interface features can all talk in this standard way to the X server. Likewise, the variety of X servers that are available, which offer support for different graphics cards, monitors, and other performance features, also can talk in a standardized way to applications.

Microsoft Windows versus X Windows

Given some of the descriptions of X Windows we've seen, it would be natural to assume that Microsoft Windows and X Windows are pretty much the same thing. The reality, though, is that they are fundamentally different beasts.

For example, Microsoft Windows is a complete operating system, with everything from a kernel to a shell to a windowing environment and more. X Windows is just one piece of that operating system puzzle: the windowing environment. Another contrast is in the interface: Microsoft Windows' is fairly rigid while X Windows' has an amazingly flexible and customizable design.

Similarities

So, what is similar about X Windows and Microsoft's de facto standard operating system? The main similarities are that they provide graphical interfaces and make it possible to work with multiple windows. On top of this, they allow the user to interact with information using more than a keyboard and plain characters. Users can utilize a mouse as well as a keyboard and can create interfaces that combine menus, forms, windows, and dialog boxes.

Differences

There are numerous differences between the two windowing systems. The main differences are in the following areas:

- flexibility of the interface
- fine-tuned control over the interface configuration
- client-server technology

Flexible Interface

The flexibility of the X Windows interface is one of the joys of the environment for many users. As discussed already, the separation of the user interface layer from the basic windowing layer makes it possible to create multiple interfaces for X Windows through the creation of different window managers.

Multiple interfaces don't simply provide subtle differences in appearance, as some customization tools for the Microsoft Windows interface offer; rather, they allow complete redesigns of the user interface from window manager to window manager.

By way of example, Figure 6.3 shows a sample window interface running a window manager that resembles the user interface of the NeXT operating system, while Figure 6.4—running on the same system and displaying the same applications—shows a user interface resembling none of the popular PC or Macintosh operating systems.

FIGURE 6.3:

The Afterstep window manager

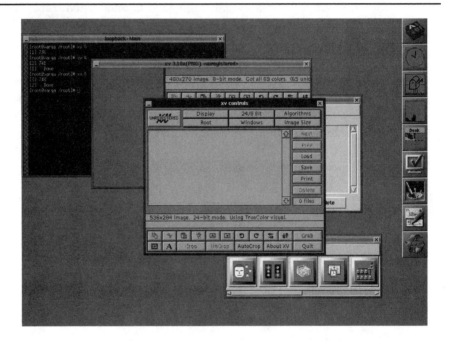

These represent just two of the many look-and-feel designs offered by X Windows window managers. We will briefly discuss the better known window managers later in this chapter.

FIGURE 6.4:

The Lesstif window manager

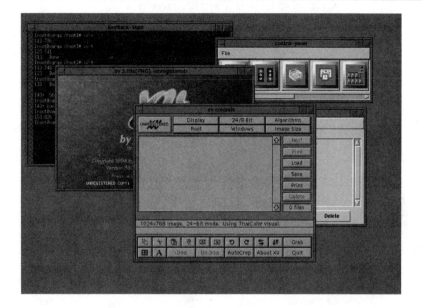

Fine-Tuned Control

Another advantage of the X Windows environment is that it offers fine-tuned control over all aspects of the windowing environment and the interface. By setting any of dozens of settings it is possible to control all aspects of the environment, from the background and foreground window colors to cursor colors, default font, and default window size. Users can also define modes of interaction. For instance, it is possible to use the mouse pointer to make a window automatically jump to the foreground or to change cursor focus to a background window.

In addition, these and other features can be defined on a per application basis, creating different settings for each application so that each launches in the most convenient way possible.

It is also possible to define which windows and applications open each time the X environment starts, as well as to have the system make logical choices about which window manager to use when starting X Windows.

We will discuss basic X Windows configuration options in Chapter 7, "Installing and Configuring X Windows."

Client-Server Environment

As mentioned above, the X Windows world works on a client-server model in which applications are clients to an X server that handles the display end of things. This has made X Windows well-adapted to network environments, allowing applications to run on one machine on the network while displaying their output on another.

The Microsoft Windows world has lacked this ability until very recently, and now has it only in a limited fashion on high-end multiuser Windows NT systems. In the Linux, Unix, and X worlds, even the lowliest of systems is capable of playing either the client or the server role in this X Windows client-server model.

X Servers and Window Managers

Now that you have a sense of where X Windows fits into things, we need to look at the fundamental components of X Windows: X servers and window managers. It is these components and the modularity they represent that provide the power and flexibility of the X Windows model.

X Servers

As we have already seen, the core of the X Windows system is the X server. The X server handles several jobs:

- support for a variety of video cards and monitor types
- resolution, refresh rate, and color depth of the X Windows display
- basic window management: displaying and closing windows, tracking mouse movements and keystrokes

Multiple X servers with this basic set of capabilities have sprung up. In the Linux world, there are three main choices: XFree86, Metro-X and Accelerated-X.

XFree86

XFree86 is the default X server with almost every noncommercial Linux distribution because it is available for free under the same sort of terms as Linux. Full source code is available, users are free to change the code to meet their own needs, and anyone can redistribute it. Red Hat Linux 5.1 ships with XFree86 3.3.2., the current version at the time of this writing.

The XFree86 Web server is designed to provide broad support for common hardware in the Intel x86 PC environment and, in more recent versions, for other platforms. While its performance is not always stellar, XFree86 is the norm for X servers in Linux and other Intel-based Unix variants and therefore is the X server that most people are familiar with.

Among the popular graphics card chipsets supported by XFree86 are Tseng's ET3000, 4000, and 6000, the full range of Trident chips, most of the Cirrus Logic line, Chips & Technologies graphics chips, and many others. You can find a full list in the XFree86 HOWTO, which was installed if you opted to install the complete documentation when you installed Linux. Use the command

```
$ zless /usr/doc/HOWTO/XFree86-HOWTO.gz
```

to read this documentation.

While the XFree86 X server goes a long way toward making Linux a complete, free Unix-like operating system, it does suffer from some drawbacks that make it less than attractive for corporate or mission-critical environments. XFree86 requires sometimes painstakingly difficult configuration and installation, has less than stable or perfect support for some graphics cards and monitors, and often will not take advantage of the accelerated features of a graphics card.

Luckily, Red Hat 5 ships with an excellent utility called Xconfigurator, which greatly eases the job of configuring XFree86, even to the point of auto-detecting some hardware and suggesting the best options for that hardware. This works great unless you present the tool with problematic hardware combinations, in which case you will be right back to configuring XFree86 manually.

Commercial X Servers

In addition to the XFree86 project, which is a vital part of making Linux a complete, free solution, there are two leading commercial X servers for the Linux world: Metro-X and Accelerated-X.

These products offer the advantage of broader support for different graphics chips and cards, and generally take full advantage of the accelerated features of those chips and cards. In addition, Metro-X and Accelerated-X offer more intelligent configuration and can usually be installed and working in a matter of minutes.

Metro-X Metro-X from MetroLink ships along with XFree86 in the commercial version of Red Hat Linux 5 as one of the added-value features of the commercial package. This gives you the option to choose the server that meets your needs.

Among the many benefits of Metro-X are a well-designed graphical configuration interface like the one in Figure 6.5, support for multi-headed displays (more than one graphics card with attached monitor on a system), support for some brands of touch screens, and more.

FIGURE 6.5:

Metro-X's configuration window

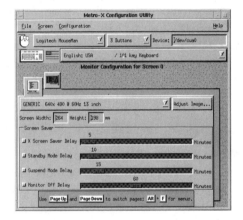

Complete information about the Metro-X server is available on the MetroLink home page at http://www.metrolink.com/. Metro-X costs U.S.$99 for Linux.

Accelerated-X X-Inside actually offers a range of X servers for Linux. These include the Accelerated-X server for Linux, a 3D Accelerated-X server, Multi-head Accelerated-X server, and a specialized Laptop Accelerated-X server. The latter is significant because the chipsets found on laptops are different than those in desktop graphics cards and because LCD screens have their own set of requirements ignored by desktop drivers.

In fact, support for laptop displays is quite limited in XFree86, and a small mistake can mean that your LCD will be damaged. If you plan to use a notebook full-time as a Linux system, look at the list of systems supported by the Laptop server and see if yours is there.

Accelerated-X offers support for more than 500 graphics cards using more than 130 chipsets and promises the best performance by 20 percent of any X server for Linux.

The multi-headed server supports up to eight screens (Metro-X supports four screens) and offers all the features of Accelerated-X on each screen.

Overall, X-Inside's servers are competitively priced. Accelerated-X costs U.S.$99.95, the Laptop server is $199.95, and the Multi-head server is $299.95. Complete information is available on the X-Inside Web site at `http://www.xinside.com/`.

Window Managers

Window managers fill out the niceties of the graphical user interface not provided by X servers. Among other features, window managers include window decorations (which provide the means to resize, move, close, and minimize windows) and mechanisms for launching applications (such as desktop menus, control panels, and button bars).

In the rest of this section, we are going to take a brief look at some of the main window managers that are available for Linux, including FVWM, fvwm95, twm, olvwm, and others. The default window manager with Red Hat Linux 5 is fvwm95, but any reasonably complete installation will include FVWM and other alternative window managers.

An overview of window managers for X Windows is available on-line at `http://www.plig.org/xwinman/`.

FVWM and fvwm95

By far the most common window manager for Linux is FVWM or some variation on this package. The name FVWM is a strange one because no one is sure what the "F" stands for in the name. Some say it stands for "Feeble" Virtual Window Manager; others argue that it is "Fine" Virtual Window Manager; still others argue that the meaning of the "F" has long been forgotten and isn't important anyway. (I tend to agree with the latter.)

FVWM is a lightweight window manager that provides a flexible, customizable windowing environment designed to look a bit like the Motif Window Manager (a commercial product). FVWM provides multiple virtual desktops and a module system for extending the window manager, and, in the more recent version 2, allows on-the-fly configuration changes and window-specific feature customization. The FVWM home page is at `http://www.hpc.uh.edu/fvwm/`. A sample FVWM desktop is shown in Figure 6.6.

FIGURE 6.6:

A sample FVWM desktop

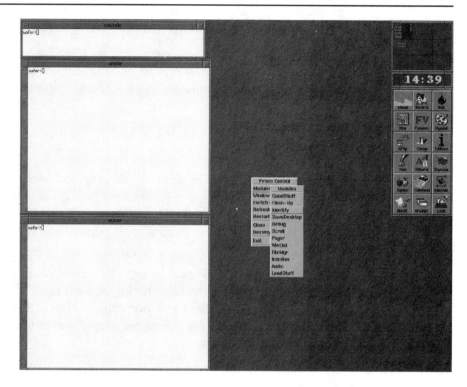

FVWM ships with almost every Linux distribution and is known for its usefulness as the basis for newer window managers with their own look and feel,
including

- fvwm95: designed to look like Windows 95

- Afterstep: designed to look like the NeXT environment

- SCWM (Scheme Configurable Window Manager): configurable using the
  Scheme language

The default window manager in Red Hat Linux 5 is the fvwm95 Window Manager, which provides a Windows 95–like look and feel. While many Linux gurus
frown on this attempt to emulate the look and feel of what they consider an inferior

operating system, Red Hat has seen that using this window manager can ease the transition to Linux for Windows users. Figure 6.7 is a screen shot of fvwm95 in action.

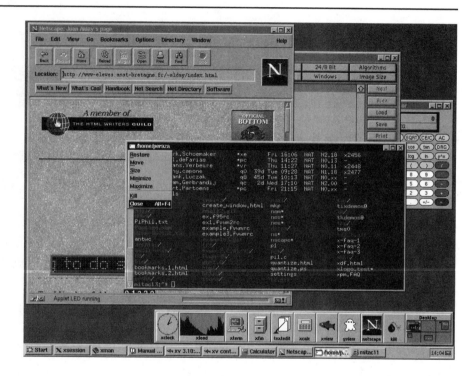

Fvwm95 is based on version 2 of FVWM and retains the flexible, easy configuration of that release. It continues to support FVWM modules but adds the modules needed to implement Windows 95 features such as the taskbar. The fvwm95 home page is at http://www.terraware.net/ftp/pub/Mirrors/FVWM95/fvwm95.html.

twm

The Tab Window Manager (twm), often called Tom's Window Manager after the name of its primary developer, is a basic, functional environment that is included with Red Hat Linux 5 as an alternate window manager. Figure 6.8 shows a typical twm desktop.

FIGURE 6.8:

The twm desktop

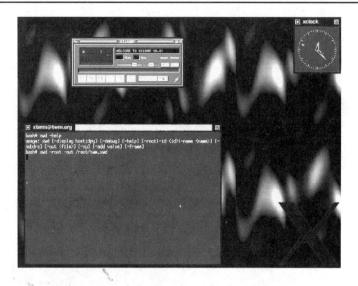

The twm window manager offers many key features that users expect in an X Windows window manager, including click-to-type or pointer-driven keyboard focus and user-defined key and button bindings. However, the interface is visually simple and some would see it as limited. Vtwm, a version of twm that includes a virtual desktop, is also available and can be downloaded from `ftp.x.org/R5contrib/vtwm-5.3.tar.gz`.

Olvwm

Olvwm, the OpenLook Virtual Window Manager, is an extension of the Open-Look Window Manager (olwm), which was the standard window manager on Sun systems for many years. While Sun systems now sport Motif and the Common Desktop Environment (discussed later in this chapter), the unique Open-Look interface is still popular among many users. Olvwm adds support for virtual desktops to the OpenLook package. Figure 6.9 shows a sample olvwm desktop.

The interface used in olvwm, especially in terms of the way in which menus and windows respond to mouse buttons, will feel awkward to many users, and this is one reason why OpenLook didn't gain huge popularity outside the Sun world. Olvwm can be downloaded from `ftp.x.org/R5contrib/olvwm4.tar.Z`.

FIGURE 6.9:

The olvwm interface

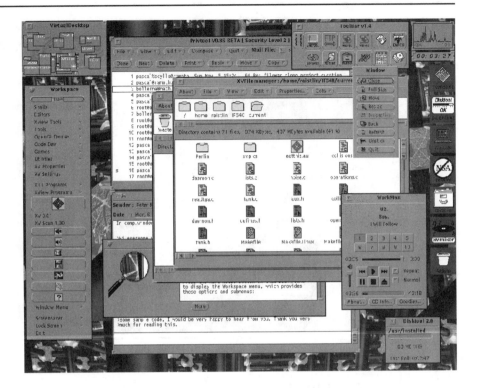

Afterstep

Afterstep, another variant on the original FVWM code, also ships as an alterna-tive window manager in Red Hat Linux 5. This product is based on an earlier window manager called Bowman and is designed to provide the look and feel of the NeXTSTEP window manager from the NeXT platform. Figure 6.10 shows a sample Afterstep desktop.

Major features drawn from NeXTSTEP are the look of title bars, buttons, and borders, the look of the style menu, and the NeXTSTEP-like icons and button bar. Since it is based on FVWM version 1 code, any modules from that version of FVWM should continue to work with Afterstep.

The Afterstep home page is at http://www.afterstep.org/.

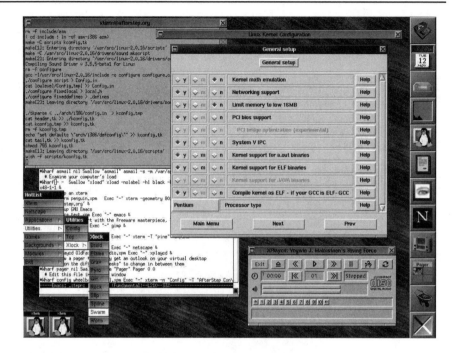

AmiWm

If you are a former user of the Amiga computer and fell in love with its interface, then AmiWm may be the window manager for you. AmiWm emulates the Amiga workbench, as shown in Figure 6.11. With support for multiple screens such as that found on the Amiga, AmiWm can ease the move to X Windows for former Amiga users.

You can learn about AmiWm and download the software from the AmiWm home page at http://www.lysator.liu.se/~marcus/amiwm.html.

Enlightenment

Enlightenment is a grand project, attempting to develop a window manager that goes beyond the conventional. It provides a useful but also visually attractive environment, and allows the user to define everything from functionality to the appearance of the window manager. Figures 6.12 and 6.13 show just two possible configurations of the Enlightenment environment. Among the many features that help Enlightenment stand out are the abilities it gives users to hand-craft the look-and-feel and to embed new features easily.

FIGURE 6.11:

The AmiWm window manager

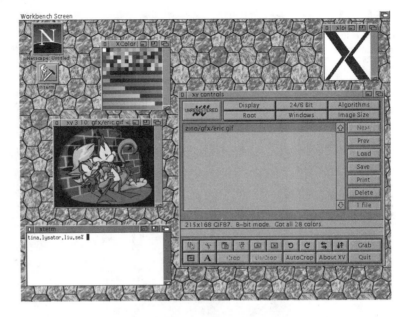

FIGURE 6.12:

The Enlightenment window manager

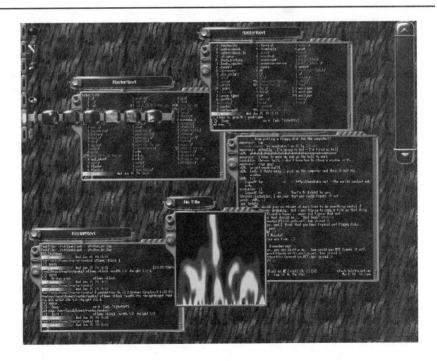

FIGURE 6.13:

Users can fully customize the Enlightenment environment

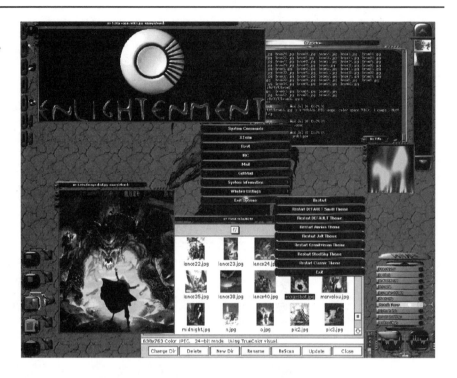

While Enlightenment is an ambitious project and offers visually stunning interfaces, installation can be a bit of a challenge for the novice user, often requiring the user to compile and install new libraries. The Enlightenment home page is at `http://www.rasterman.com/`. Note also that the authors consider Enlightenment in an early pre-release stage and therefore warn of bugs and the potential for crashes. Still, this is an interesting project and a unique concept among window managers.

The K Desktop Environment

The K Desktop Environment, or KDE, is more than just a window manager, although a window manager is at its core. KDE is an attempt to provide a free alternative to the Common Desktop Environment (discussed later in this section). In this effort, KDE combines a set of applications such as a file manager, terminal emulator, and display configuration system together with a window manager to create a consistent look and feel for X applications. Figure 6.14 shows a typical KDE desktop.

FIGURE 6.14:

A KDE desktop

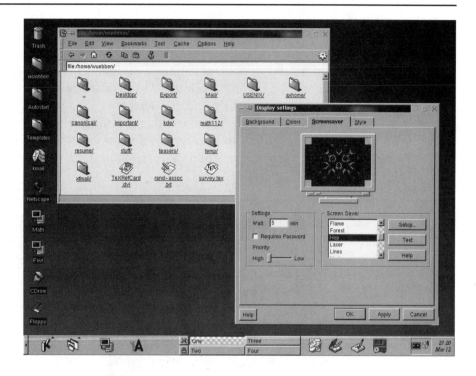

Part of the planning behind KDE is that standards be specified and the development environment be such that developers can create applications that are consistent in features as well as appearance. KDE provides an attractive, professional-looking environment in which to work, and if the necessary applications are developed for KDE, it will become a likely proposition for the business desktop. The KDE Web site is at http://www.kde.org/.

Mwm

Mwm, the Motif Window Manager, is a commercial window manager that is part of the Motif distribution. Motif as a complete environment is discussed in more detail in the next section of this chapter.

The Common Desktop Environment

CDE, or the Common Desktop Environment, is an ambitious project to standardize the graphical environment and development arena on various Unix platforms including AIX, Digital Unix, HP/UX, and Solaris. Now CDE is also available for

Linux from Red Hat (`http://www.redhat.com/`) and from X-Inside (`http://www`
`.xinside.com/`). A good FAQ about CDE is available at `http://nb.cc.utah.edu/`
`Dictionary/cde_cose_faq`.

In addition to a consistent graphical environment based on Motif, CDE offers a
set of cohesive tools and applications to standardize administrative procedures
and ease the configuration and management of a user's graphical work environment. Among the enhancements brought to the X environment by CDE are drag-
and-drop capabilities and the types of folders and icons found in other GUI
operating systems. Figure 6.15 shows a sample CDE desktop running Red Hat's
TriTeal CDE for Linux.

FIGURE 6.15:

A CDE desktop

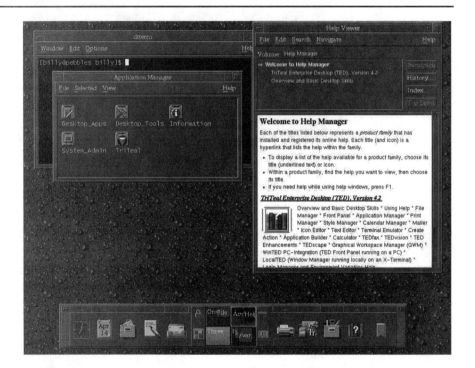

What Is Motif?

If you begin to look around the Web for X Windows applications to install on
your Linux system, you will inevitably come across applications that refer to the
fact that they use the Motif library or the Motif toolkit.

Motif is a development environment for X Windows that was introduced by the Open Software Foundation in the late 1980s to provide a consistent policy for X Windows applications. Motif provides a toolkit of widgets that developers can use in developing their applications. By using these widget libraries, Motif developers produce applications that adhere to Motif policies for consistent look and feel.

Motif, however, is commercial. Developers who want to build and distribute applications based on the Motif libraries must pay for the privilege, and users who want to have copies of the Motif libraries on their systems to improve the performance of Motif-based applications must pay for a client set of libraries.

In addition to the toolkit and libraries, the Motif distribution includes its own window manager, mwm, after which the original FVWM look-and-feel was patterned. Figure 6.16 shows a sample mwm desktop.

FIGURE 6.16:

An mwm desktop

Do I Need Motif?

For most Linux users, there is probably no need to buy Motif. Users who should consider purchasing Motif include:

- Developers who want to develop applications using the Motif toolkit

- Users who want to run applications that require the presence of the Motif libraries. Most commercial applications that use the Motif libraries either embed the necessary Motif code in the application (so it is not necessary for the user to own the license) or include a complete version of the runtime Motif libraries.

Vendors selling Motif for Linux include Red Hat (`http://www.redhat.com/`), InfoMagic (`http://www.infomagic.com/`), and X-Inside (`http://www.xinside.com/`).

An Alternative to Motif

Like so many things in the Linux world, efforts are under way to produce a freely available alternative to Motif so that developers and users won't have to pay to purchase Motif. The Lesstif Project has developed a product that is compatible with Motif version 1.2 and available under the GNU Public License. Simply put, this means the product is completely free.

Lesstif hasn't reached full maturity yet (the version at the time of this writing was 0.83), but Lesstif can already be used to develop some applications and run some software. The Lesstif FAQ on the Lesstif home page (`http://www.lesstif.org/`) is quick to point out that Lesstif is still not complete. Even so, some of the applications that use Motif can work with Lesstif 0.83, including Mosaic 2.7 and the acclaimed GIMP graphics package for Linux.

Where Do We Go from Here?

This discussion of X Windows is our first step toward hands-on use of the Linux operating system.

In the next two chapters, we will master the basics of the X Windows interface using the default window manager for Red Hat Linux 5: fvwm95. We will learn to install X Windows and begin to experiment with using some of the most common X Windows applications.

In Chapter 7, we will start with a step-by-step guide to installing and configuring X Windows.

CHAPTER

SEVEN

Installing and Configuring X Windows

- Obtaining X Windows

- Preparing to Configure X Windows

- Configuring XFree86 with Xconfigurator

- Configuring XFree86 with xf86config

Now that we have a sense of what X Windows is all about, it is time to install and configure the software so that you have a system up and running X Windows as quickly as possible.

In this chapter, we will discuss where to obtain X Windows for your system if you didn't or can't install the version of X Windows that shipped with your distribution of Linux. Following that, we will discuss how to configure XFree86 so that it works optimally on your computer.

Obtaining X Windows

If you are using the copy of Red Hat Linux 5 that came with this book and you chose to install all the key X Windows components suggested in Chapter 4 ("Installing Linux"), then you don't need to read this section because you already have obtained and installed the X Windows files. You can skip ahead to the section entitled "Preparing to Configure X Windows."

Installing from the Red Hat 5 CD-ROM

If you are using Red Hat Linux 5 but didn't install X Windows when you installed Linux, then installing X Windows is a fairly easy process. The procedure outlined here relies on techniques learned in Chapter 11 ("Working with Files") for accessing your CD-ROM drive.

Using rpm

In this section, we will be using **rpm,** a tool that is shipped with Red Hat Linux for managing Red Hat packages.

Rpm allows you to install new packages, uninstall installed packages, and look at information about packages such as what files they include.

Rather than go into a lengthy discussion of how to use **rpm** (we discuss a graphical alternative to **rpm** in Chapter 12, "Configuring Your System with the Control Panel"), we will just take a quick look at some of the main uses for **rpm**.

To install a package, use the following command:

```
$ rpm -i <package-file-name>
```

Continued on next page

To view a list of all installed packages, use the command

```
$ rpm -qa | more
```

This command presents the list of installed packages one screen at a time; you can scroll down to the next screen by pressing the space bar. The package names shown on the list are not the file names originally used when installing the packages. They are used, however, in uninstalling a package with the following command:

```
$ rpm -e <package-file-name>
```

In order to install X Windows from your Red Hat 5 CD-ROM, the first step is to mount your CD so that Linux can access it. This process is not as straightforward as it seems, because it will vary depending on the type of CD-ROM drive you have (IDE/ATAPI, SCSI, or proprietary) and on how the drive is installed. An extensive discussion of CD-ROM options is found in Chapter 21, "Linux Multimedia."

For the purposes of this chapter, we will assume that you have an IDE CD-ROM drive, since these are extremely common in today's multimedia PCs, and we will assume that it is installed as the secondary IDE slave device, since most off-the-shelf computers sold today contain only one hard drive.

Given these assumptions, your CD-ROM drive will be device /dev/hdb. For other drive types and configurations, refer to the discussion in Chapter 21 to figure out what device your drive is.

Insert the Red Hat 5 CD-ROM into your drive and type the command

```
$ mount /dev/hdb /mnt/cdrom
```

to mount the disk and make it accessible to Linux. You can use the following command to look at the contents of the CD-ROM and make sure it is accessible. The results should look like those shown here:

```
$ ls /mnt/cdrom
COPYING      RPM-PGP-KEY  TRANS.TBL   dosutils    live
rr_moved
README       Red Hat      doc         images      misc
```

The next step is to change into the directory on the CD-ROM that contains all the packages that make up Red Hat 5. This directory is the RedHat/RPMS subdirectory. Use the command

```
$ cd /mnt/cdrom/RedHat/RPMS
```

If you type the command

```
$ ls
```

you should see a long list of files scroll by and all of them should end in the extension .rpm, indicating they are Red Hat package files.

Now we are ready to install the X Windows packages. In order to do this we need to determine which packages to install. To start with, we need the general XFree86 files that are in the file XFree86-3.3.1-15.i386.rpm. Next, we need all the X Windows fonts, which are in the following files:

```
XFree86-100dpi-fonts-3.3.1-15.i386.rpm
XFree86-75dpi-fonts-3.3.1-15.i386.rpm
```

We also need the XFree86 configuration utility provided by Red Hat, which is in the file Xconfigurator-3.26-1.i386.rpm, and we want the collection of X Windows programs that can be found in X11R6-contrib-3.3.1-1.i386.rpm.

The final piece of the puzzle is to choose which XFree86 server package to install. This is dependent on your monitor and your video card. Check your video card documentation to find out what type of card you have and what chipset it uses. Compare this information to the following descriptions of the different servers designed for specific cards and video chips (the descriptions are those provided in the package files):

- XFree86-I128-3.3.1-15.i386.rpm: X server for the #9 Imagine 128 board

- XFree86-S3-3.3.1-15.i386.rpm: X server for cards built around chips from S3, including most #9 cards, many Diamond Stealth cards, Orchid Fahrenheits, Micro Crystal 8S, most STB cards, and some motherboards with built-in graphics accelerators (such as the IBM ValuePoint line)

- XFree86-Mach32-3.3.1-15.i386.rpm: X server for cards built around ATI's Mach32 chip, including the ATI Graphics Ultra Pro and Ultra Plus

- XFree86-S3V-3.3.1-15.i386.rpm: X server for cards built around the S3 VIRGE chipset

- XFree86-W32-3.3.1-15.i386.rpm: X server for cards built around the ET4000/W32 chips, including the Genoa 8900 Phantom 32i, Hercules Dynamite cards, LeadTek WinFast S200, Sigma Concorde, STB LightSpeed, TechWorks Thunderbolt, and ViewTop PCI

- XFree86-8514-3.3.1-15.i386.rpm: X server for older IBM 8514 cards and compatibles from companies such as ATI

- `XFree86-Mach64-3.3.1-15.i386.rpm`: X server for ATI Mach64-based cards such as the Graphics Xpression, GUP Turbo, and WinTurbo cards

- `XFree86-P9000-3.3.1-15.i386.rpm`: X server for cards built around the Weitek P9000 chips such as most Diamond Viper cards and the Orchid P9000 card

- `XFree86-Mach8-3.3.1-15.i386.rpm`: X server for cards built around ATI's Mach8 chip, including the ATI 8514 Ultra and Graphics Ultra

- `XFree86-AGX-3.3.1-15.i386.rpm`: X server for AGX-based cards such as the Boca Vortex, Orchid Celsius, Spider Black Widow, and Hercules Graphite

In addition to these servers that are specific to certain cards or video chips, there are three generic servers that should work with most cards and video chipsets (although they won't take advantage of any accelerated features of your video card):

- `XFree86-VGA16-3.3.1-15.i386.rpm`: Generic 16-color server for VGA boards. This works on nearly all VGA-style graphics boards, but only in low resolution with few colors.

- `XFree86-SVGA-3.3.1-15.i386.rpm`: X server for most simple framebuffer SVGA devices, including cards built from ET4000 chips, Cirrus Logic chips, Chips and Technologies laptop chips, and Trident 8900 and 9000 chips. It works for Diamond Speedstar, Orchid Kelvins, STB Nitros and Horizons, Genoa 8500VL, most Actix boards, and the Spider VLB Plus. It also works for many other chips and cards, so try this server if you are having problems.

- `XFree86-Mono-3.3.1-15.i386.rpm`: Generic monochrome (two-color) server for VGA cards, which works on nearly all VGA-style boards with limited resolutions

If you can match your video card precisely to one of the accelerated servers, you will only need to install that server. If you think you have a close match but can't be 100 percent certain, install that accelerated server as well as one of the three generic servers. If you definitely can't match one of the accelerated servers, you should only install a generic server.

Choosing which generic server to install is fairly straightforward:

- If you have a monochrome monitor and not a color monitor, you should choose the `XFree86-Mono-3.3.1-15.i386.rpm` server.

- If you have an older monitor that only supports 640×480 resolution (and nothing higher) and your video card has fewer than 512KB of video RAM, you probably want to choose the `XFree86-VGA16-3.3.1-15.i386.rpm` server.

- If you have a newer multisync monitor that supports resolutions higher than 640×480 and your video card has more than 512KB of RAM, choose the `XFree86-SVGA-3.3.1-15.i386.rpm` server.

Now that we have built a list of the files we need to install, we can use `rpm -i` to install those files. Everyone needs to install the following files:

```
$ rpm -i XFree86-3.3.1-15.i386.rpm
$ rpm -i XFree86-100dpi-fonts-3.3.1-15.i386.rpm
$ rpm -i XFree86-75dpi-fonts-3.3.1-15.i386.rpm
$ rpm -i Xconfigurator-3.26-1.i386.rpm
$ rpm -i X11R6-contrib-3.3.1-1.i386.rpm
```

Next, you need to install your selected servers. For instance, to install the generic SVGA server, use the command

```
$ rpm -i XFree86-SVGA-3.3.1-15.i386.rpm
```

or to install the server for S3 VIRGE chips, use the command

```
$ rpm -i XFree86-S3V-3.3.1-15.i386.rpm
```

Once all of this is done, all the necessary X Windows files should be installed on your system.

Installing from the Internet

If you aren't using Red Hat Linux 5 or want to install a newer version of XFree86 than is available with Red Hat 5, you can download the necessary files from the Internet and then install them.

NOTE   We discuss connecting to the Internet in Chapter 17, "Connecting Linux to the Internet," and using Netscape Communicator in Chapter 18, "Using the World Wide Web." If you aren't ready to take on these tasks in Linux and you kept your old Windows or DOS installation on your system, you can use your Windows or DOS Internet connection to download the files and then access your Windows or DOS partition from Linux to install the files.

XFree86 is developed by the XFree86 Project, which is on the Web at `http://www.xfree86.org`. Figure 7.1 shows the XFree86 Web page.

FIGURE 7.1:

The XFree86 Web page

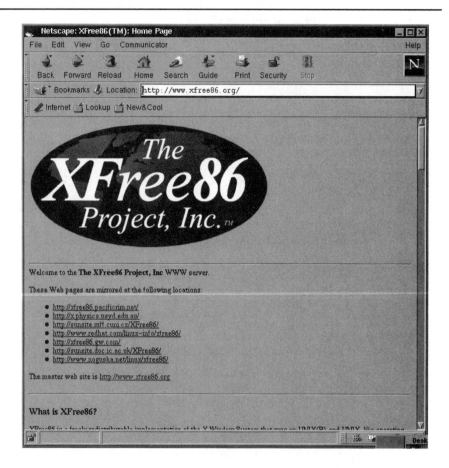

From the Web site, you can access the directory containing the files for the latest version of XFree86 at `ftp://ftp.xfree86.org/pub/XFree86/3.3.2/binaries/`. Here you will find libraries available for many versions of Linux:

- `Linux-axp`: Linux for Digital's Alpha processor

- `Linux-m68k`: Linux for Macintosh computers running the 68000-series processor

- `Linux-ix86`: Linux for Intel x86 processors, including the Pentium and Pentium II

- `Linux-ix86-glibc`: Linux versions for Intel x86 processors that use the newer Glibc libraries. As of this writing, very few Linux distributions used Glibc—with the notable exception of Red Hat 5, which is widely publicized for its adoption of Glibc.

Once you have chosen the library for your version of Linux, download the following files:

`preinst.sh`	`postinst.sh`	`extract`
`X332bin.tgz`	`X332doc.tgz`	`X332fnts.tgz`
`X332lib.tgz`	`X332man.tgz`	`X332set.tgz`
`X3322upd.tgz`	`X332cfg.tgz`	`X332f100.tgz`

In addition, you need to download the file `X332VG16.tgz` from the Servers directory, as well as any other relevant servers based on the following descriptions provided in the release notes for XFree86 3.3.2:

- `X3328514.tgz`: 8514/A server
- `X332AGX.tgz`: AGX server
- `X332I128.tgz`: I128 server
- `X332Ma32.tgz`: Mach 32 server
- `X332Ma64.tgz`: Mach 64 server
- `X332Ma8.tgz`: Mach 8 server
- `X332Mono.tgz`: Mono server
- `X332P9K.tgz`: P9000 server
- `X332S3.tgz`: S3 server
- `X332S3V.tgz`: old S3 VIRGE server (please use SVGA server)
- `X332SVGA.tgz`: SVGA server
- `X332W32.tgz`: ET4000/W32, ET6000 server

Refer to the discussion of selecting a server in the previous section, "Installing from the Red Hat 5 CD-ROM."

The next step is to create the necessary directory for the installation. We do this with the `mkdir` command, which is discussed in detail in Chapter 11, "Working with Files":

```
$ mkdir /usr/X11R6
```

Next, you need to run the installation programs provided in the files you have downloaded. Let's assume that you downloaded them to the `temp` directory of your Windows partition and that in the installation process in Chapter 4 you chose to mount this partition as `/dos`. If this is the case, you can issue the following commands to run the preinstallation script (some of these commands are discussed later in the book; just use them for now to get X Windows running and you will learn what they all mean later):

```
$ cd /usr/X11R6
$ sh /dos/temp/preinst.sh
```

The next step is to prepare and extract the files from the archives you downloaded. You do this with the following commands:

```
$ chmod 755 /dos/temp/extract
$ /dos/temp/extract /dos/temp/X332[8-z]*.tgz
$ /dos/temp/extract /dos/temp/X3322upd.tgz
```

The final step is to run the postinstallation script:

```
$ sh /dos/temp/postinst.sh
```

As cryptic as it all may seem at this point, the end result of all this typing is that the necessary files for X Windows will be installed on your Linux system.

Preparing to Configure X Windows

Before you can actually configure X Windows, you need to gather some critical information about your hardware to ensure that you do not damage your monitor in the process of trying to optimize X Windows.

The information you need is:

- the make and model of your video card
- the make and model of your monitor

- the video memory on your video card
- the type of mouse you are using
- the horizontal sync range for your monitor
- the vertical sync range for your monitor

Without this information, it is possible to make mistakes in configuring XFree86 that could potentially damage your monitor. Let's take this information one piece at a time.

Make and Model of Your Video Card

These specifications shouldn't be too difficult to obtain. Generally, if you check your card's manual you can glean this information.

If you have purchased a non–name brand video card, then the make isn't relevant. In this case, check the documentation for the video card to see what chipset is being used on the card. Common chipsets include those from Cirrus Logic, S3, and Chips and Technologies, among others. In all cases, be sure to record the model number of the chipset as well as the maker of the chips.

If you have a computer with video support built into the motherboard, check the documentation for your computer or motherboard to determine the chipset maker and model number.

Make and Model of Your Monitor

Check the manual of your monitor for the make and model of the monitor. This information may be useful in configuring XFree86 if your monitor is one of those that the configuration software knows about.

Video Memory on Your Video Card

Check the manual for your video card for the amount of memory on the card. In modern computers this is generally no less than 2MB, and on some PCs may be 4MB or as much as 8MB. On older computers or video cards, you may find as little as 256KB of video memory.

If you can't determine the amount of memory on your card from the manual, try powering on your PC and restarting it. The first screen to appear, usually very quickly, after you power on your computer is often generated by your video card and will display the make, model number, and possibly the amount of video memory on the card.

Type of Mouse You Are Using

This information is necessary in order to get your mouse working under X Windows. If you configured your mouse when installing Linux in Chapter 4, then you need the same information on hand to configure X Windows.

If you didn't configure your mouse then, you need to check the type of mouse you have. Possible types include:

- Microsoft-compatible serial mouse (usually with two buttons)
- Mouse Systems–compatible serial mouse (usually with three buttons)
- Bus Mouse
- PS/2 Mouse
- Logitech serial mouse
- Logitech MouseMan (Microsoft-compatible)
- Microsoft IntelliMouse

Most mice should be compatible with one of these types.

Horizontal Sync Range for Your Monitor

This information is crucial, especially should it turn out that your monitor is not explicitly supported by the configuration software. Without this number (and the vertical sync range numbers discussed in the next section), you risk damaging your monitor by asking your video card to provide a signal to your monitor that is outside its capability to display.

You will find the information for horizontal sync range (sometimes referred to as horizontal scanning range) in your manual, either under the monitor specifications or in the section discussing video modes. This information will be presented as a range of values in kilohertz, such as 30–70kHz. Generally, this range will start somewhere around 30kHz. You should also make note of the maximum possible value.

Vertical Sync Range for Your Monitor

Like the horizontal sync range, this range (sometimes called the vertical scanning range) is essential to preventing damage to your monitor. You should find the information in the same location as the horizontal sync range. It should appear as a range of values in hertz (not kilohertz like the horizontal value), such as 50–160Hz. (Generally, the larger number should exceed 75Hz unless you have an extremely low-end or old monitor. Monitors that cannot produce vertical scanning speeds higher than 72Hz suffer from flicker problems that can lead to eyestrain and headaches during even short-duration use.) Be sure to also note the maximum possible value for the vertical sync range.

Configuring XFree86 with Xconfigurator

Red Hat Linux comes with Xconfigurator, a configuration program for XFree86 that is much easier to use than the one that comes with XFree86. We will look first at using Xconfigurator to configure X Windows and then at configuring XFree86 on systems that do not have Xconfigurator available.

Xconfigurator is a simple, menu-driven tool that greatly simplifies the process of configuring XFree86. To run the program, use the command

```
$ Xconfigurator
```

which should run the program and display a welcome screen like the one in Figure 7.2.

FIGURE 7.2:

The Xconfigurator welcome screen

TIP   You need to be the root user to successfully complete all the steps involved in configuring X Windows.

To start using the program, hit the Return key to move past the welcome screen to the first menu, shown in Figure 7.3.

Here you choose the type of video card or chipset your system is running. Use the up and down arrows (or the page up and page down keys) to scroll through the long list of video cards and chipsets, which are presented alphabetically.

It is important to be sure you have an exact match for your card or chipset. If you don't, it is unwise to guess and choose something that seems similar—a "similar" card can in fact be distinctly different from yours. In this case, select Unlisted Card at the bottom of the list. Once you have made your selection, hit the Return key to move to the next screen.

FIGURE 7.3:

The video card menu

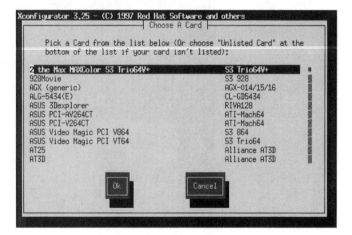

If you select Unlisted Card, you will be presented with a second menu where you can choose the appropriate server for your card, as shown in Figure 7.4. If you are uncertain, you should use the generic server you selected earlier in the section on installing X Windows. For most modern multimedia computers, this will be the SVGA server.

Once you have selected your card and possibly specified a server, the next step is to indicate your monitor on the monitor selection menu, shown in Figure 7.5.

FIGURE 7.4:

The X server menu

FIGURE 7.5:

The monitor selection menu

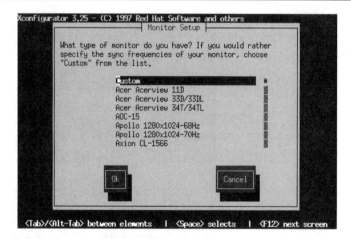

If you can't find your specific monitor on the list, then you have three choices:

- Select Custom and then specify the horizontal and vertical sync ranges for your system (as explained above).

- If you don't have the sync ranges available for your monitor and you know your monitor is a multisync monitor, select Generic Multisync.

- If you don't have the sync ranges available for your monitor and you don't know whether your monitor is a multisync monitor, then select Generic Monitor (this is the lowest common denominator and should be your selection of last resort).

If you select Custom, you will be presented with a warning screen reminding you that entering the correct ranges is critical to avoiding damage to your monitor. Hit the Return key to proceed to the horizontal sync range menu shown in Figure 7.6.

Scan through the list and see if you find an entry that matches your monitor precisely. If you do, hit Return on that entry. In Xconfigurator, the choices are not by range, but by maximum possible value. This information is provided in the same place as the sync ranges in your monitor manual. Try to match the entry with the highest resolution and sync rate possible. Never choose an entry that offers a value beyond that listed in your monitor's manual.

FIGURE 7.6:

The horizontal sync
range menu

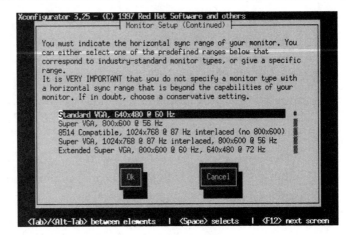

NOTE   Xconfigurator doesn't allow you to manually specify the horizontal and vertical sync ranges of your monitor. If you want to do this to take advantage of a high-end monitor, you should try using the alternate configuration method described below in the section on xf86config.

Once you make that selection, you will be presented with a menu of vertical sync ranges like the one in Figure 7.7.

FIGURE 7.7:

The vertical sync range menu

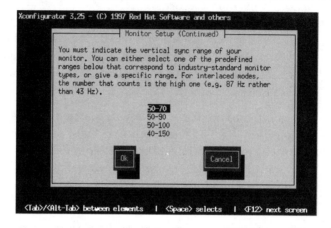

Choose a value from this menu where the larger number doesn't exceed the larger number in the vertical sync range for your monitor and the smaller number is not smaller than the smaller number in the vertical sync range for your monitor.

The next screen offered by Xconfigurator is the choice of whether or not to probe your video card for possible video modes. Generally, most new cards can be probed successfully, although attempting this with old cards and certain recent cards can cause problems.

The best bet here is to try probing. If there is an error, you will be informed and will have to proceed with manual configuration as outlined here. If probing succeeds, then you save yourself several steps.

If you choose not to probe or if probing fails, the next screen you will see will be the video memory menu shown in Figure 7.8. Choose the value that matches your video card, as discussed earlier in the section on preparing for configuration.

FIGURE 7.8:

The video memory menu

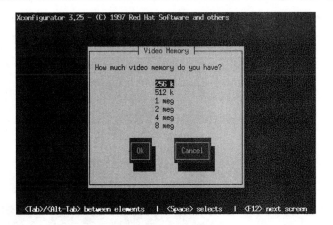

The next screen offers a selection of clock chip settings. Unless you are certain that your card has a clock chip and know the exact type of clock chip, you are better off selecting the default No Clockchip setting, as shown in Figure 7.9.

After choosing a clock chip, you will be presented with a screen like the one in Figure 7.10 where you can choose your preferred video modes.

FIGURE 7.9:

The clock chip menu

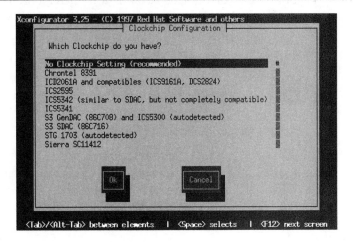

FIGURE 7.10:

The video modes screen

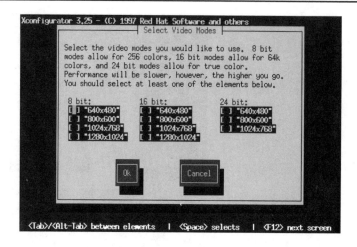

The higher bit depth you choose, the more colors will be displayed, but the slower your video performance will be. Similarly, the higher your resolution, the more desktop real estate you will have, but at the price of the size of letters and icons on the screen. You will probably want to experiment with these settings to find the best one for your system, but generally the best resolutions are 640×480 for a 14-inch monitor, 800×600 for a 15-inch monitor, and 1024×768 for a 17-inch monitor. If you have the resources for it, 16-bit or 24-bit color is worthwhile, especially for color-intensive applications such as Netscape Communicator.

To make your selection, use the Tab key to move between bit depths and the arrow keys to move between resolutions. Use the space bar to select a mode. When you have selected a mode (you can select multiple modes—there is a way to switch between modes when you are running X Windows), use the Tab key to select the OK button and hit the Return key.

This will complete the configuration process. You will be informed that a configuration file has been created, and then you can hit Return to exit Xconfigurator. In Red Hat Linux 5.1, the file that is created will be called XF86Config and will be placed in the directory /etc/X11.

Configuring XFree86 with xf86config

Xconfigurator provides only one way to configure XFree86, and this method is only available with Red Hat Linux.

XFree86 itself comes with a configuration program that is available in any distribution of Linux that includes XFree86: xf86config.

Xf86config is also menu-driven, but does less of the work for you and is somewhat more cumbersome to use than Xconfigurator. But xf86config is more flexible, allowing you to manually specify some settings where Xconfigurator does the job for you and prevents you from controlling those values precisely.

To run xf86config, use the following command:

```
$ xf86config
```

This will present a welcome screen like the one in Figure 7.11.

TIP   You need to be the root user to successfully complete all the steps involved in configuring X Windows with xf86config.

NOTE   Xf86config presents a lot of dense text on the screen during the configuration process. The welcome screen is just the first example of this. It is a good idea to read everything thoroughly if you are not familiar with xf86config so that you are fully aware of the significance of the choices you make.

FIGURE 7.11:

The xf86config welcome screen

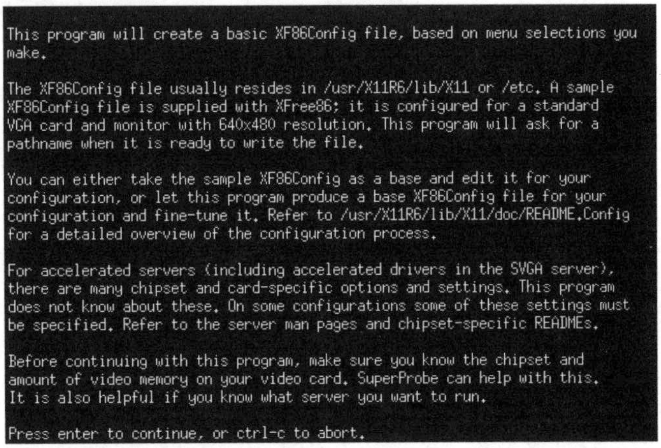

The first menu presented is the mouse menu shown in Figure 7.12. Select the correct option by typing the associated number and hitting Return. You will then be presented with a series of mouse-related questions, which may include the following:

- Do You Want to Enable ChordMiddle? If you have a three-button Microsoft-compatible mouse made by Logitech, you can select ChordMiddle to make the middle button work. Otherwise, only the left and right mouse buttons will work.

- Do You Want to Enable Emulate3Buttons? This option should be enabled when you are using a two-button mouse and a two-button mouse protocol such as the Microsoft-compatible protocol. This allows you to emulate a middle button, which is necessary in some X Windows applications, by clicking the left and right mouse buttons together.

FIGURE 7.12:

The mouse menu

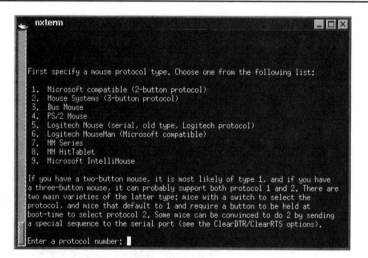

The final question related to your mouse will be a request to enter the mouse device. If you are using the same mouse you used when you installed Red Hat Linux and you configured the mouse during installation in Chapter 4, then you should enter **/dev/mouse**. Because this is the default, you can just hit Return here.

The next major section involves configuring your keyboard. The first question is Do You Want to Use XKB? XKB is a new addition to X Windows that simplifies defining the keyboard layout for particular languages and keyboard types. It is recommended that you enable this option.

If you choose to enable XKB, the next screen will be a menu of possible keyboard types, as shown in Figure 7.13.

```
List of preconfigured keymaps:

     1   Standard 101-key, US encoding
     2   Microsoft Natural, US encoding
     3   KeyTronic FlexPro, US encoding
     4   Standard 101-key, US encoding with ISO9995-3 extensions
     5   Standard 101-key, German encoding
     6   Standard 101-key, French encoding
     7   Standard 101-key, Thai encoding
     8   Standard 101-key, Swiss/German encoding
     9   Standard 101-key, Swiss/French encoding
    10   None of the above

Enter a number to choose the keymap.
```

Choose the keyboard that most closely matches yours. The Standard 101-key keyboard is the likeliest candidate for most North American computers. If none of the options fits, choose None of the Above. This choice leads to a submenu where you can choose from another series of standard keyboard models. Once you select a keyboard from this list, you will be presented with a screen from which to choose the country where the keyboard was purchased. The list of countries extends beyond one screen and you can use the Enter key to cycle to the next screen of countries.

If you opt not to choose the XKB option, then things should work fine for a standard North American English keyboard. Non-English keyboards and non-standard keyboards, however, will require manual configuration, which is discussed later in Chapter 9, "Advanced X Windows Configuration."

If you don't enable XKB, you will be presented with another option: Do You Want to Enable Special Bindings for the Alt Keys to Allow Non-ASCII Characters to Be Entered? For now you might want to answer No to this option. You will not need this enabled for most standard software, and if in the future you obtain software that is dependent on this option, you can quickly run xf86config to enable it.

After configuring your keyboard, the next step is to specify the horizontal and vertical sync ranges for your monitor. The first menu presented is the horizontal sync range menu shown in Figure 7.14.

```
You must indicate the horizontal sync range of your monitor. You can either
select one of the predefined ranges below that correspond to industry-
standard monitor types, or give a specific range.

It is VERY IMPORTANT that you do not specify a monitor type with a horizontal
sync range that is beyond the capabilities of your monitor. If in doubt,
choose a conservative setting.

     hsync in kHz; monitor type with characteristic modes
 1   31.5; Standard VGA, 640x480 @ 60 Hz
 2   31.5 - 35.1; Super VGA, 800x600 @ 56 Hz
 3   31.5, 35.5; 8514 Compatible, 1024x768 @ 87 Hz interlaced (no 800x600)
 4   31.5, 35.15, 35.5; Super VGA, 1024x768 @ 87 Hz interlaced, 800x600 @ 56 Hz
 5   31.5 - 37.9; Extended Super VGA, 800x600 @ 60 Hz, 640x480 @ 72 Hz
 6   31.5 - 48.5; Non-Interlaced SVGA, 1024x768 @ 60 Hz, 800x600 @ 72 Hz
 7   31.5 - 57.0; High Frequency SVGA, 1024x768 @ 70 Hz
 8   31.5 - 64.3; Monitor that can do 1280x1024 @ 60 Hz
 9   31.5 - 79.0; Monitor that can do 1280x1024 @ 74 Hz
10   31.5 - 82.0; Monitor that can do 1280x1024 @ 76 Hz
11   Enter your own horizontal sync range

Enter your choice (1-11):
```

If you don't find an exact match for your sync range and you have the range for your monitor on hand, select Enter Your Own Horizontal Sync Range and provide the correct range. If you don't have access to this information, choose a conservative value. For an average 15-inch multisync monitor, try the Super VGA or Extended Super VGA setting. For a low-end 14-inch monitor, it is probably safest to select Standard VGA.

Next, you will have to specify the vertical sync range for your monitor. Xf86config presents a small number of options, but you can select Enter Your Own Vertical Sync Range to specify the range for your monitor. If you don't know the range for your monitor, it is probably safest to choose the lowest and smallest range, generally 50–70 in most versions of XFree86.

Once you have specified this monitor data, xf86config will ask you to specify an identifier for your monitor, the monitor's maker, and the model name or number. These do not actually affect the configuration or performance of XFree86, but provide an easy way to identify the monitor definition in your XFree86 configuration file if you need to refer to it in the future.

Once you have all your monitor information entered, you need to specify your video card or chipset. The first screen asks if you want to look at a database of known cards and chips to make your selection. If you choose to do this, you will be presented with a menu of known cards, similar to Figure 7.15.

You can use the Return key to page forward through the menus and at any time can type the number of a specific card and hit Return to select it. If you find that there isn't a match for your card, simply hit **q** to skip this phase.

FIGURE 7.15:

The video card menu

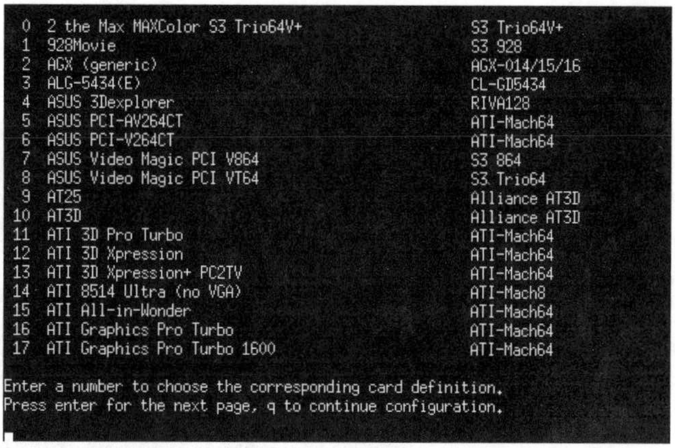

```
0  2 the Max MAXColor S3 Trio64V+        S3 Trio64V+
1  928Movie                             S3 928
2  AGX (generic)                        AGX-014/15/16
3  ALG-5434(E)                          CL-GD5434
4  ASUS 3Dexplorer                      RIVA128
5  ASUS PCI-AV264CT                     ATI-Mach64
6  ASUS PCI-V264CT                      ATI-Mach64
7  ASUS Video Magic PCI V864            S3 864
8  ASUS Video Magic PCI VT64            S3 Trio64
9  AT25                                 Alliance AT3D
10 AT3D                                 Alliance AT3D
11 ATI 3D Pro Turbo                     ATI-Mach64
12 ATI 3D Xpression                     ATI-Mach64
13 ATI 3D Xpression+ PC2TV              ATI-Mach64
14 ATI 8514 Ultra (no VGA)              ATI-Mach8
15 ATI All-in-Wonder                    ATI-Mach64
16 ATI Graphics Pro Turbo               ATI-Mach64
17 ATI Graphics Pro Turbo 1600          ATI-Mach64

Enter a number to choose the corresponding card definition.
Press enter for the next page, q to continue configuration.
```

The next screen allows you to choose which server to use. By default, you are offered four choices:

- Mono

- VGA16

- SVGA

- Accelerated (All other servers)

If you selected a card from the card database, a fifth option will be offered based on that selection. The fifth option is actually a repeat of one of the four other options, as appropriate to your card selection. If you selected a card in the early step, then select the fifth option to make sure you use the appropriate server.

WARNING   Whatever server you select, it needs to be one of the servers you installed in the installation section above. If it isn't, you need to go back and install the appropriate server before proceeding. Otherwise, your X Windows system will be configured to use a server that doesn't exist on your computer.

Once you have selected a server, you will be asked if you want xf86config to create a symbolic link to the server. It is important to answer Yes to this question. What this does is link the filename /usr/bin/X11/X to the server you selected so that, regardless of which server you are running, this filename can be used to access it.

After you set the symbolic link, you will be presented with a menu screen like the one in Figure 7.16. Here you have to select the amount of video memory on your video card.

FIGURE 7.16:

The video memory menu

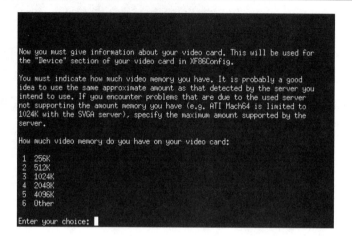

```
Now you must give information about your video card. This will be used for
the "Device" section of your video card in XF86Config.

You must indicate how much video memory you have. It is probably a good
idea to use the same approximate amount as that detected by the server you
intend to use. If you encounter problems that are due to the used server
not supporting the amount memory you have (e.g. ATI Mach64 is limited to
1024K with the SVGA server), specify the maximum amount supported by the
server.

How much video memory do you have on your video card:

    1   256K
    2   512K
    3   1024K
    4   2048K
    5   4096K
    6   Other

Enter your choice:
```

Once you have selected an amount of video memory, you will be asked to provide an identifier, maker, and model for your video card. As with your monitor, these entries have nothing to do with the proper functioning of your X Windows system, so you should enter something that you will recognize later if you ever need to manually edit your XFree86 configuration file.

The next menu, shown in Figure 7.17, allows you to select a clock chip for your card. It is generally a good idea to choose No Clockchip by hitting the Return key, since most cards lack a clock chip. You should only select a clock chip if you know for certain that your card has one and you know the type of chip.

FIGURE 7.17:

The clock chip menu

```
A Clockchip line in the Device section forces the detection of a
programmable clock device. With a clockchip enabled, any required
clock can be programmed without requiring probing of clocks or a
Clocks line. Most cards don't have a programmable clock chip.
Choose from the following list:

    1   Chrontel 8391                                                    ch8391
    2   ICD2061A and compatibles (ICS9161A, DCS2824)                     icd2061a
    3   ICS2595                                                          ics2595
    4   ICS5342 (similar to SDAC, but not completely compatible)         ics5342
    5   ICS5341                                                          ics5341
    6   S3 GenDAC (86C708) and ICS5300 (autodetected)                    s3gendac
    7   S3 SDAC (86C716)                                                 s3_sdac
    8   STG 1703 (autodetected)                                          stg1703
    9   Sierra SC11412                                                   sc11412
   10   TI 3025 (autodetected)                                          ti3025
   11   TI 3026 (autodetected)                                          ti3026
   12   IBM RGB 51x/52x (autodetected)                                  ibm_rgb5xx

Just press enter if you don't want a Clockchip setting.
What Clockchip setting do you want (1-12)?
```

If you don't choose a clock chip, the next screen will ask, "Do You Want Me to Run `X -probeonly` Now?" This program will try to detect the clock information from your card that is needed when a clock chip is unavailable.

It is important to note, however, that not all cards can be probed successfully. If, earlier in the configuration, you selected a card that does not support probing from the card database, then xf86config will warn you (on the line immediately preceding the question) not to probe. Heed the warning.

If you didn't choose a card from the card database, you won't know if your card supports probing unless you try it. If the probing fails, two possibilities can occur: either you will be given an error message like the one here:

```
X -probeonly call failed.
No Clocks line inserted.
```

or xf86config will crash completely and you will be returned to the command prompt. If the latter happens, you need to run xf86config again, and when you get to the question "Do You Want Me To Run 'X -probeonly' Now?" you need to answer No.

The next screen will prompt you for your preferred video modes. X Windows allows you to specify multiple video modes and cycle through them without restarting the X Windows environment.

You should make sure not to accept default modes that exceed the capabilities of your card and monitor. For instance, a 14-inch monitor is unlikely to support 1280×1024 resolution and a card with 512KB of video memory probably can't produce 24-bit color at any resolution.

To change video modes, first select the color bit depth you want to adjust the settings for. Once you do this, you will be presented with a menu that allows you to specify one or more resolutions for that bit depth. At the prompt, type the identification numbers of the resolutions you want, separating each number with a space, and hit Return when you are done.

This will return you to the main mode selection screen above. Repeat this process for each bit depth you need to adjust and then select The Modes Are OK, Continue.

The final question asks you if you should write the XF86Config file in its default location. You are asked this so you can make sure you don't overwrite an old, working copy of your configuration file with a new one that might not work. If you have been using X Windows successfully and are trying to reconfigure it to slightly different settings, you may want to keep a copy of your old configuration file before you allow xf86config to write the new one.

If you answer No to the question, xf86config will provide a series of alternate locations to write the file:

First you will be asked if you want to write it to the default location (usually `/usr/X11R6/lib/X11/XF86Config`). If you want to specify your own location for the file, answer No.

Next you will be asked if you want the file to be written in the current directory. If the current directory is a logical location (such as the root user's home directory or `/tmp`), then you can answer Yes. If you answer No, then you will finally be prompted to supply the complete path and filename where you want the new configuration to be saved.

In order to use this configuration (once it is working to your satisfaction), you will need to copy the file you have just saved to the correct location for the XFree86 configuration file, which for most versions of Linux is either `/etc/XF86Config` or `/etc/X11/XF86Config`. For Red Hat 5, the file should be `/etc/XF86Config`.

Another approach is to copy your current configuration file to a backup location before running xf86config; then, when you are asked if you want to overwrite the current configuration, you can simply answer Yes. We will learn how to copy files in Chapter 11 ("Working with Files"), but a simple way to make a backup copy of the Red Hat 5 XFree86 configuration file is with the following command:

```
$ cp /etc/XF86Config /etc/XF86Config.keep
```

This will create a copy of your existing configuration named `/etc/XF86 Config.keep`.

Testing Your Configuration

Now that you have finished configuring X Windows, it is time to see if the configuration you have created actually works. To do this, you need to try running X Windows. Almost every distribution of Linux comes with X Windows set up to run a default window manager and some default initial applications, so you should be ready to run once XFree86 is configured.

To start X Windows, use the following command:

```
$ startx
```

This will start X Windows running. If all goes well, you will see a number of lines of information flash by on the screen, and then the screen will switch to graphical mode and you will see your default X Windows environment. In the case of Red Hat 5, this will probably look like the one in Figure 7.18.

FIGURE 7.18:

The default fvwm95 desktop in Red Hat Linux 5

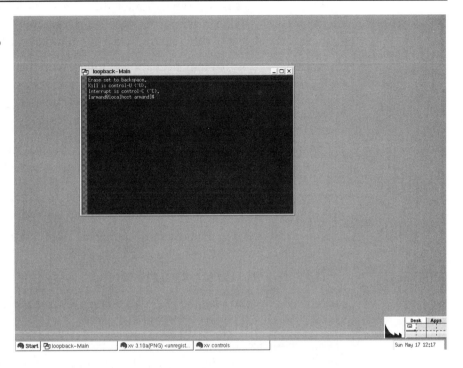

NOTE You can run X Windows as a regular user or as the root user for the purpose of verifying that it is working properly. But it is generally wise to run X Windows as a non-root user so that you minimize the chance of using X Windows applications to accidentally damage, erase, or change key system files that only the root user has permission to modify.

The real problems begin if things don't work. Failure is usually indicated in one of three ways:

- You get an error message and are returned to the command prompt without your computer ever switching to graphical mode.

- You are switched to graphical mode but are left with a blank-gray desktop, no window manager, and no functioning windows.

- You are switched to graphical mode but this is quickly exited and you are returned to the command prompt.

In the first case, this is likely an indication that XFree86 is not configured correctly. Unfortunately, the number of possible reasons for configuration failure is probably as large as the number of different hardware combinations that exist.

Here are a few tips that may help you get things working:

- Double-check your video card and monitor data.

- Try using smaller horizontal and vertical sync ranges.

- Try using a simpler server (such as the VGA16 rather than the SVGA server, or the SVGA server instead of a card-specific accelerated server).

If these attempts all fail, then you need to do some research into your specific problem. The best place to start is the XFree86 HOWTO file. You may already have this on your system if you have a fairly complete distribution. You can read this file in Red Hat Linux 5 by using the command

```
$ zless /usr/doc/HOWTO/ XFree86-HOWTO.gz
```

Alternately, you can read the HOWTO on the Web at `http://sunsite.unc` `.edu/mdw/HOWTO/XFree86-HOWTO.html`.

If you experience one of the other two problems (where your system switches to graphical mode but things don't quite work out), then the first step is to check the X Windows start-up configuration and your window manager configuration. We discuss these configurations in detail in Chapter 9, "Advanced X Windows Configuration."

Where Do We Go from Here?

Now that you should have X Windows working, it is time to actually try our hand at using the X Windows environment for practical tasks.

In the next chapter, we will take a look at the basics of using X Windows with the fvwm95 window manager, which is the default window manager in Red Hat Linux 5. Following that, we will move on to look at basic X Windows applications, including the well-known xterm program, the xfm file manager, some graphics applications, and more. By the end of the next chapter, you should have enough experience and confidence to experiment with other available X Windows applications.

CHAPTER

EIGHT

Using X Windows Applications

- X Windows Basics

- X Windows Applications

Now that we have X Windows set up and running on our systems, we are going to take a look at how to make use of the X Windows environment as it is designed in Red Hat Linux.

We will start with an overview of how to use the fvwm95 Window Manager, the default windowing environment in Red Hat Linux 5, and then we will look at some of the X Windows applications that are commonly used by Linux users.

These applications include xterm (similar to the DOS prompt of Windows), xfm (an X Windows-based File Manager that compares with the File Manager of Windows 3.1), xcalc (a scientific calculator application), several graphics programs (including The Gimp, xv and Ghostview), and others. All these applications are part of a complete Red Hat 5 installation and are ready to run once you have installed Linux and configured X Windows.

X Windows Basics

Unlike the Windows and Macintosh worlds, it is impossible to say that there is one X Windows. As we saw earlier in Chapter 6, "An Overview of X Windows," the choice of a window manager defines the graphical interface of the X Windows environment. Because there is a wide range of window managers, there are numerous look-and-feels for X Windows.

Throughout this chapter, we will discuss using X Windows with the fvwm95 window manager, since that is the default window manager in the version of Red Hat Linux accompanying this book. As mentioned in our overview of window managers in Chapter 6, fvwm95 is designed to look and feel like Windows 95.

Although Windows 95's graphical interface is often derided by die-hard Unix users, the fact that fvwm95 looks so familiar to the average Windows user makes it easy to grasp for many newcomers to Linux.

Starting X Windows and Fvwm95

Because Red Hat comes preconfigured for fvwm95, starting the window manager is as simple as starting the X Windows environment. As we learned in the last chapter ("Installing and Configuring X Windows"), begin by logging in as a user and then issue the command:

```
$ startx
```

This will start X Windows and launch the fvwm95 window manager. Initially, this produces a screen similar to the one in Figure 8.1.

FIGURE 8.1:

The default fvwm95 desktop in Red Hat Linux 5

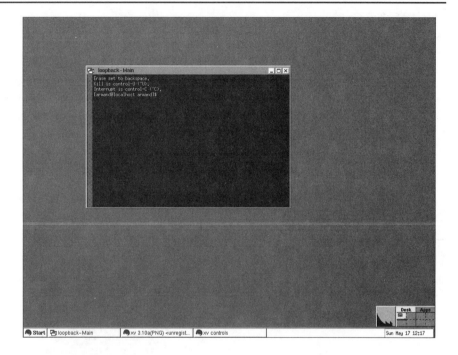

Three main components load by default when fvwm95 loads: the task bar, a virtual desktop control panel, and an `xterm` window.

NOTE   If you launch X Windows as the root user, your fvwm95 desktop will look slightly different. The text color in the `xterm` window will not be white on black but more of a tan on black, and an additional component, the Control Panel, will load at start-up. The Control Panel is covered in Chapter 12, "Configuring Your System with the Control Panel."

The Task Bar

The task bar, shown in Figure 8.2, is displayed across the bottom of the screen like Windows 95's taskbar. It includes a Start menu button at the left, a small panel displaying the time and date at the far right, and space to display buttons for each open window.

In this example task bar, you can see that there are three open Windows: loopback-Main, xv, and xv controls. Clicking once on any of these buttons opens the window if it had been temporarily minimized to the task bar and brings the window to the front of all open windows.

Using the Start Menu

The Start menu works in the same way as the Start menu in Windows 95 and Windows NT 4. Clicking the Start menu pops up a menu like the one in Figure 8.3.

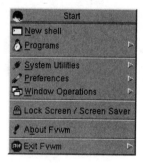

The Start menu has several items on it:

- **New shell** This option opens a new `xterm` window like the one that opens when the window manager starts. We will look at the xterm program a little later in this chapter. The full use of the command-line shell environment is covered in Chapter 13, "Understanding the Shell."

- **Programs**   This option displays a drop-down submenu of program categories that can be launched from the Start menu. The small triangle to the right of the word "Programs" indicates that clicking or highlighting this option will drop down a submenu.

- **System Utilities**   This option displays a drop-down submenu of utilities that can be used to manage your system and window environment.

- **Preferences**   This option displays a drop-down submenu that allows you to configure various aspects of your fvwm95 environment.

- **Window Operations**   This option displays a drop-down submenu that allows you to perform operations such as moving, resizing, and minimizing windows.

- **Lock Screen/Screen Saver**   This option lets you activate the screen saver with or without a password.

- **About Fvwn**   This option displays a dialog box containing information about your current fvwm95 session.

- **Exit Fvwm**   This option displays a submenu that allows you to exit the window manager and the X Windows environment.

Programs   The Programs submenu looks like the one in Figure 8.4. The menu offers further submenus, which contain different categories of programs that can be launched in the X Windows environment. These categories include administrative tools, general utilities, graphics programs, and networking applications. Some of these applications will be covered in more detail later in this chapter.

FIGURE 8.4:

The Programs submenu

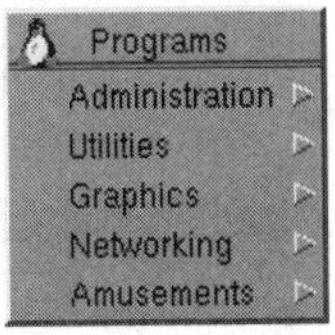

SystemUtilities   The SystemUtilities submenu looks like the one in Figure 8.5.

The options on this menu include the following:

Root shell   This option opens an `xterm` window with command prompt running as the root user. This can be used for system management tasks such as creating new users, restarting the system, or installing new software. If you are logged in as any user other than the root user, you will be prompted for the root password before being given access to the command prompt shell.

Top This option opens an `xterm` window running the program Top. This program is a useful system administration tool, as we will see in Chapter 14, "General System Administration." Top allows you to monitor memory usage, system load, and currently active processes. This window looks like the one in Figure 8.6.

FIGURE 8.5:

The SystemUtilities submenu

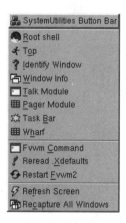

FIGURE 8.6:

The Top window

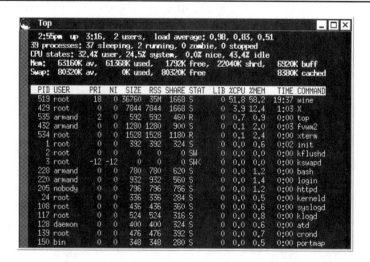

Identify Window　This option runs a program that allows you to display information about any open window. By selecting this option and then clicking an open window, an information panel like the one in Figure 8.7 will be displayed. Clicking once in the information panel will close it. The information presented includes the size and location of the current window, the title of the window, and other data that is primarily of use to developers trying to debug their applications and system administrators checking configuration of a user's X Windows environment.

FIGURE 8.7:

The Identify Window information panel

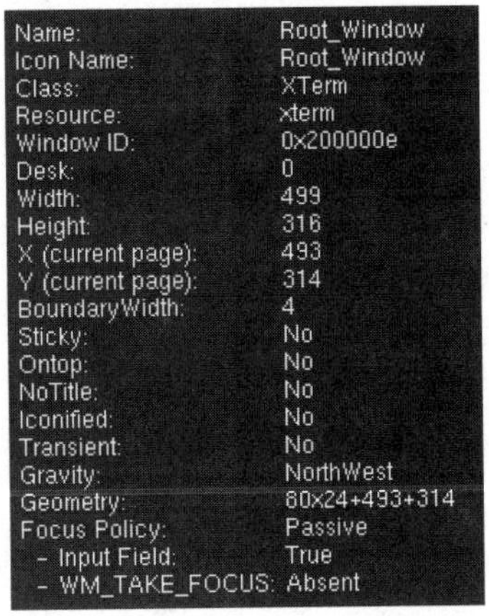

```
Name:               Root_Window
Icon Name:          Root_Window
Class:              XTerm
Resource:           xterm
Window ID:          0x200000e
Desk:               0
Width:              499
Height:             316
X (current page):   493
Y (current page):   314
Boundary Width:     4
Sticky:             No
Ontop:              No
NoTitle:            No
Iconified:          No
Transient:          No
Gravity:            NorthWest
Geometry:           80x24+493+314
Focus Policy:       Passive
 - Input Field:     True
 - WM_TAKE_FOCUS:   Absent
```

Pager Module　This option opens a pager window that gives access to fvwm95's virtual desktop feature. This small window looks like the one that opens by default when you launch fvwm95, with the exception that it lacks the graphical display of system load. The ability to launch the pager from the menu is useful when the original virtual desktop control has been closed and you need to access the virtual desktop feature.

Wharf　The Wharf option launches an alternative to the default virtual desktop window and closes the virtual desktop window. Wharf provides a NeXT-like button bar like the one in Figure 8.8. Features of the Wharf button bar include a clock, a graphical load meter, access to the virtual desktop feature of fvwm95, and quick-launch buttons to launch popular applications.

FIGURE 8.8:

The Wharf button bar

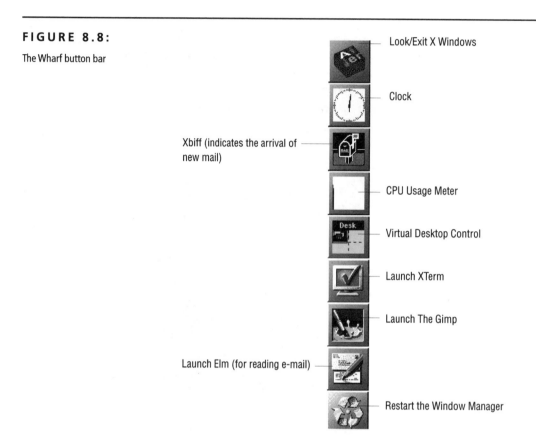

Look/Exit X Windows

Clock

Xbiff (indicates the arrival of new mail)

CPU Usage Meter

Virtual Desktop Control

Launch XTerm

Launch The Gimp

Launch Elm (for reading e-mail)

Restart the Window Manager

The SystemUtilities menu also offers other, less frequently used features, but they are generally too complicated to describe in a brief overview like this one. You can find out more about particular features by consulting man pages, documentation included with your Linux distribution, and Linux sources on the Internet.

Preferences   The Preferences menu allows you to control many aspects of the look-and-feel of the fvwm95 interface. This includes altering the background color or image, changing the default look of the mouse pointer, and changing window managers on the fly. The Preferences menu looks like the one in Figure 8.9, and we will take a look at a few of the more useful features here.

FIGURE 8.9:

The Preferences menu

Background   This option opens a window like the one in Figure 8.10. Using this window, you can choose either a solid background color for your desktop or an image for your desktop. Choosing Uniform Color allows you to specify a color by dragging the sliders for red, green, and blue in the top half of the window (the colors of each bar aren't specified, but they alter red, green, and blue, in that order).

FIGURE 8.10:

The Background Settings window

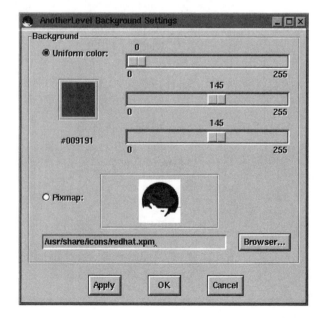

To choose a bitmap image, select Pixmap and then click the Browse button. This will bring up the File Browser dialog box, where you can choose a suitable background image file from a window like the one shown in Figure 8.11. The file you choose for a background image should be an X Windows Pixmap (XPM) file. The image will be tiled on the background of the desktop (that is, it will be repeated enough times to fill the entire display). If you want a good selection of Pixmap icons, you can try Joerg Martin's three-dimensional Pixmap collection. The most recent version is in the X11 icons directory of the SunSite Linux archive at `ftp://sunsite .unc.edu/pub/Linux/X11/icons`.

FIGURE 8.11:

The File Browser dialog box

Root Cursor   This menu item produces a submenu like the one in Figure 8.12. From this submenu you can choose from a variety of alternative cursors that will be displayed whenever the mouse pointer is over the desktop (as opposed to in a window). By default, the root cursor is a simple X symbol. But you can choose from a wide variety of alternative icons, including arrows, crosses, spray cans, and umbrellas.

FIGURE 8.12:

The Root Cursor submenu

Mouse   The Mouse submenu allows you to control the speed of the mouse tracking. This affects the distance the mouse pointer moves on screen relative to the distance you move the mouse on your desk or mousepad. This is a personal setting that you can adjust to meet your style of computing. This menu also lets you change the handedness of the mouse. By making the mouse right-handed, actions normally performed with the left button are performed by the right button and vice versa.

AutoRaise   This menu allows you to turn on and off auto-raising of windows. When enabled, AutoRaise causes windows to automatically raise to the top of other windows after having mouse focus for a specified period of time (specified in milliseconds).

Scroll Setup   This menu allows you to turn on and off scrolling functions, including limiting scrolling to only the vertical or horizontal axis.

WM Style   The WM Style submenu shown in Figure 8.13 allows you to switch to an alternate window manager without closing your existing windows and exiting the X Windows environment. By default, a complete installation of Red Hat provides the Lesstif Window Manager (designed to look like the Motif Window Manager) and Afterstep (designed to look like the NeXT computer's graphical interface). As you can see in Figure 8.14, after switching window managers, all existing windows remain open but now have the default appearance of the new window manager.

FIGURE 8.13:

The WM Style submenu

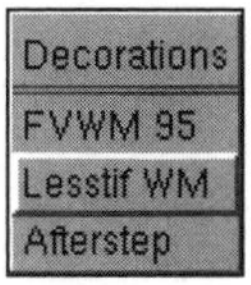

Save Desktop to new .xinitrc   After making the changes you want to your desktop, you need to save them to your personal .xinitrc file if you want them to take effect when you launch fvwm95 in the future. The .xinitrc file contains instructions and information that are used to personally customize your X Windows environment, as we will see in the next chapter ("Advanced X Windows Configuration"). Make sure you select this option before exiting fvwm95 if you have made any preference changes that you want to make permanent.

FIGURE 8.14:

Switching to the Lesstif
Window Manager

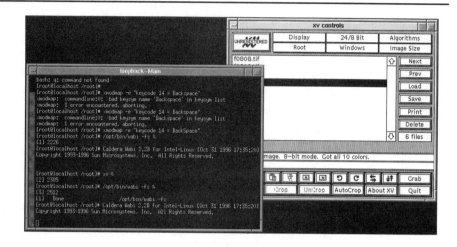

Window Operations   The Window Operations menu provides a single point of access to a wide variety of window operations, including moving, closing, resizing, and switching between windows. The menu looks like Figure 8.15.

FIGURE 8.15:

The Window
Operations menu

While many of these operations can be performed through other features of the fvwm95 interface (as we will see in the next section, "The Fvwm95 Interface"), sometimes it is necessary to use the Window Operations menu to access these functions.

The main window operations offered on the menu are outlined below:

Move   This option allows you to move any visible window. After selecting this option, click and drag anywhere in a window and that window will move with the drag. It isn't necessary to click the window's title bar to move.

WARNING   In Red Hat 5, selecting the Move option from the task bar's Start menu can cause X Windows to crash and exit. Selecting it from the Start Menu on the desktop (which we will learn about later in this chapter) works fine.

Resize   After selecting this option, simply click and drag anywhere in a window to resize it. By clicking and dragging past the right edge of the window you can make it wider, and by dragging past the bottom edge you can make it taller. When you release the mouse button, the window will redraw at the new size.

Raise   Click anywhere in a window after selecting this option to bring the window in front of all other windows.

Lower   Click anywhere in a window after selecting this option to send a window behind all other windows.

Stick   This option works in conjunction with fvwm95's virtual desktops. To use it, simply select the Stick/Unstick option and then click an open window. This sticks the window to the desktop so that when you switch between virtual desktops, the window moves with you instead of remaining in a single desktop. This allows you to have useful utilities such as a clock, a load meter, or a Top window visible at all times as you move between virtual desktops. When you stick a window, the title bar of the window changes style and displays three horizontal lines to the right of the title, as in Figure 8.16.

Unstick   Selecting the Stick/Unstick option and then clicking a window that is stuck to the desktop will release the window. The title bar of the window will return to standard style and the window will behave normally when you switch between virtual desktops.

Maximize/Reset   This selection toggles between maximizing the window and returning it to its original size.

FIGURE 8.16:

The title bar of a stuck window has three additional horizontal lines

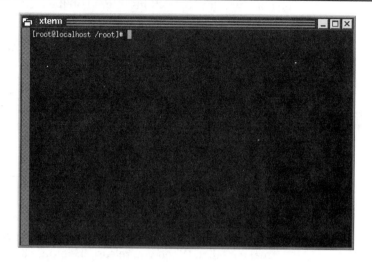

Maximize Tall/Reset   Like the previous option, this one toggles between a maximized window and its original size, except that maximization affects only the height, not the width, of the window.

Maximize Wide/Reset   As a counterpart to Maximize Tall, this option maximizes only the width, not the height, of a window.

Close   Selecting this option and then clicking anywhere in an open window causes the window to close. This is similar to but less drastic than the Kill menu option. Close simply causes the selected window to close. If a program has a single window open, closing the window in this way generally causes the application to exit.

Kill   Kill takes things a step further than Close, directly killing the process that created the window. This is a subtle but important distinction. In applications such as Netscape Communicator where it is possible to open multiple windows while running one instance of the program, choosing to Close a window closes the window selected but leaves all other Communicator windows open; choosing Kill will cause the program to exit, closing all of its windows.

ScrollBar   Choosing ScrollBar and then clicking a window adds scrollbars to a window, like those shown on the bottom and right side of the window in Figure 8.17. This is useful if the entire display area of an application can't fit in the largest possible window size and you need to be able to scroll to see hidden parts of a window. In the bottom-right corner where the scrollbars meet, you will see a raised, square button. Clicking this button removes the scrollbars and returns the window to its normal state.

FIGURE 8.17:

Scrollbars allow an application to extend beyond the bounds of its window

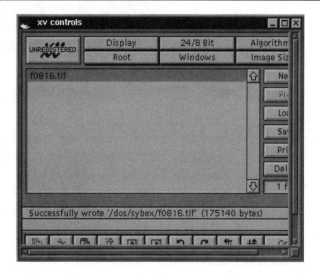

Window List Module   This option causes a special module of fvwm95 to be executed. This module displays a small list of all open windows (similar in concept to the buttons for each window on the task bar) that allows you to switch between open windows. Figure 8.18 is an example of the Window List module. You can close this window using the Close window operation.

FIGURE 8.18:

The Window List module

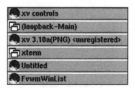

Switch to...   The Switch to… option causes a drop-down menu of all open windows to be displayed so that you can choose a window to bring to the front. A sample menu is shown in Figure 8.19.

FIGURE 8.19:

The Switch to... menu

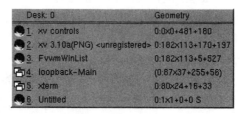

Refresh Screen   This option redraws the screen and is useful if screen redraws get distorted. Otherwise, you will rarely need to use this option.

Alternative Ways of Accessing the Start Menu   In addition to using the Start Menu button on the task bar, you can access the Start menu from the desktop by clicking with the left mouse button anywhere on the desktop except in an open window. The Start menu will pop up where you click. This is useful if, for instance, you prefer the Window List module for switching windows and want to eliminate the task bar to gain screen real estate.

The Pager

The Pager is a small window, like the one in Figure 8.20, that provides virtual desktops.

FIGURE 8.20:

The Pager

The concept of virtual desktops is simple. Let's start with a basic example. If you had two virtual desktops, this would be like having two monitors but only one power cable for those monitors. You could have two different sets of applications open, running, and displayed on the monitors and switch between these environments by switching the power cable between the monitors.

Virtual desktops provide similar functionality but without the delay, difficulty, and frustration of switching your power cable between two monitors. Each desktop in a virtual desktop system is like a brand-new work environment in which you can open windows and run applications. At the same time, these applications, regardless of which desktop they appear in, are running in the same X Windows session, which means you can cut and paste between them as if they were visually displayed on the same desktop.

By default, the Pager is configured with eight virtual desktops, four labeled Desk and four labeled Apps (although these are perfectly arbitrary names and bear no relationship to how you can use the desktops).

You can switch desktops by clicking with the left mouse button on any of the eight squares on the Pager. This will immediately switch the displayed desktop to the one selected.

Right-clicking anywhere in the Pager window brings up another screen, best explained using a different analogy. Imagine a huge 50-inch television screen that can be viewed only through a 14-inch window, which can be placed anywhere in front of the larger screen to see one 14-inch piece at a time. Virtual desktops can similarly be thought of as one large desktop that is bigger than the size of your physical monitor.

In the case of the default Pager, this larger virtual screen is eight times larger than your physical screen. This analogy is important because it illustrates how it is possible to view not only the eight marked areas of the Pager but any area at all. For instance, you can click with the right button anywhere in the Pager and the top-left corner of your physical display will be moved to the point you click. This means that it is possible to display an area that overlaps between the different desktop areas.

Also, right-clicking and dragging causes the visible area to move with the mouse as you drag, so you can watch to make sure that exactly the area you want to see is displayed.

Finally, the default Pager window also includes a load monitor to the left of the virtual desktop control. This monitor displays the current and historical demands being placed on your CPU (the processor, or heart, of your computer). This can be useful in determining whether you are trying to run too many applications (particularly background applications) or if you need to upgrade to a more powerful computer.

The Fvwm95 Interface

Fvwm95 has many key user interface elements. We will start with an overview of these elements and then focus on several specific tasks, including launching applications, manipulating windows, using desktop menus, and exiting the window manager.

Launching Applications

The Programs submenu of the Start menu is the easiest place to launch applications. If you have a complete installation of Red Hat 5 on your computer, the Programs menu and its submenus provide access to a comprehensive collection of common X applications.

For instance, file management is a common activity. You can launch an X Window file manager, like the one in Figure 8.21, by selecting xfm (which stands for X File Manager) from the File Management submenu of the Utilities submenu.

FIGURE 8.21:

An xfm window

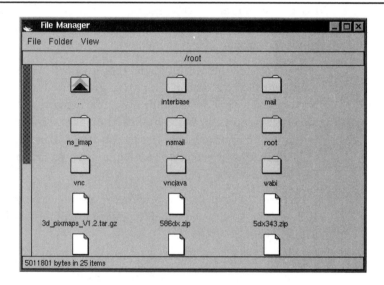

We will be looking at several of the applications on the standard Red Hat 5 Programs menu when we look at specific X Windows applications later in this chapter.

In addition to the easily accessible applications on the menu, you can launch any X Windows application from the command line if you know the name and location of the application on your computer. You can do this from an xterm window. By default, an xterm window is opened for you when you start fvwm95. If it isn't open anymore, you can open a new one by selecting New Shell at the top of the Start menu. This opens an xterm window like the one in Figure 8.22.

FIGURE 8.22:

An xterm window

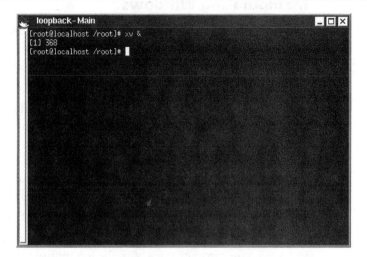

```
loopback-Main
[root@localhost /root]# xv &
[1] 368
[root@localhost /root]#
```

From the command line you can launch any X Windows application and can also pass special arguments to the application, which it is not always possible to do from the Programs menu.

For example, Netscape Communicator is not a default entry on the Programs menu. If you have installed Netscape Communicator following the instructions outlined in Chapter 18 ("Using the World Wide Web"), then you can launch Netscape Communicator by typing

$ **/opt/netscape/netscape**

at the command prompt. This launches Communicator, but there is a problem: as you will notice, you don't get back a new command prompt until you exit Communicator. This would seem to mean that you need to launch a new xterm window for each application you want to launch.

Luckily, there's a way around this. As we will learn in Chapter 13, "Understanding the Shell," it is possible to issue commands in the background. While the technical details can wait until Chapter 13, at this point it is enough to know that as soon as you issue a command to launch an X Windows application, you will get back a new command prompt allowing you to issue a new command. To start a program in the background, simply put an ampersand at the end of the command:

$ **/opt/netscape/netscape &**

Manipulating Windows

The windows in fvwm95 look a lot like their counterparts in Windows 95 and behave in much the same way. This is advantageous for Windows users, since it makes moving from Windows 95 or NT 4 to X Windows a simple process in terms of interacting with windows.

Let's take a look at the main window components: title bar, window action icons, window operations menu, and window border.

Title Bar The title bar is displayed across the top of the window. It contains the name of the window, which in most cases is the name of the application that is displaying the window. In the case of an xterm window, the title is xterm by default (although it is possible to change it, as we will see later).

The title bar area serves several functional purposes in fvwm95. As would be expected, you can click once with the left mouse button in the title bar to bring a window to the front of other open windows. (You can usually click anywhere in an open window to bring it to the front, though in some rare cases you will find it necessary to click in the title bar to do so.)

Another use of the title bar is to send a window to the back of all open windows. Right-clicking in the title bar of any open window other than the rearmost window sends that window to the back of the open windows.

Clicking and dragging with the left mouse button allows you to move the window. When you release the left mouse button, the window remains in the new location.

Finally, if you click the title bar with the middle mouse button (or, on a two-button mouse and some three-button mice, with the middle-button equivalent of right and left mouse buttons together), the Window Operations menu from the Start menu is displayed, allowing you to perform any of the window operations available.

Window Action Icons The window action icons appear as a group of three icons in the top right corner of most windows.

From left to right, these icons perform the following actions when single-clicked:

- **Minimize the window**   This action hides the window, leaving a button for it on the task bar, a button for it in the Window List module, and an entry for it on the Switch To... menu.

- **Maximize/Reset the window**   This icon acts as a toggle, switching the window between full screen (Maximize) and its original size before being maximized (Reset).

- **Close the window**   This action closes the window. In the case of multi-window applications, this does not act as a Kill operation.

Window Operations Menu   To the left of the title, in the top left corner of the window, you will see an icon representing the application that is displaying the window. In the case of common applications such as xterm windows, fvwm95 is preconfigured with special icons. In the case of other applications, a default icon is used. As we will learn in the next chapter, you can configure fvwm95 to display your own choice of icon for any application.

Regardless of the icon being used to represent the application, clicking with any of the mouse buttons on the icon displays the Window Operations menu from the Start menu.

Window Border   Most windows have a border that is five pixels wide (a default value that can be changed, as we will see in the next chapter). This border is used to visually indicate the edge of the window as well as to allow users to resize a window.

It is possible to resize a window horizontally, vertically, or both. Simply click and drag anywhere on the border. As you drag outside the existing window border, the window will resize based on the location of the mouse pointer.

This works a little differently than in Windows 95, where the resizing action varies depending whether you click and drag on an edge or on a corner of a window. Clicking the left or right edge and dragging allows only horizontal resizing in Windows 95, just as the top and bottom edges provide for only vertical resizing; the corners allow simultaneous horizontal and vertical resizing. In fvwm95, clicking and dragging anywhere on the border works in the same way as the Resize action from the Window Operations menu, allowing you to resize in both the horizontal and vertical directions regardless of which edge or corner you start dragging from.

Using Desktop Menus

As we saw earlier in the section discussing the Start menu, clicking with the left mouse button outside of any window on the desktop displays the Start menu. Clicking with the right and middle mouse buttons on the desktop also produce special menus.

Clicking with the right mouse button on the desktop produces the Programs submenu from the Start menu for quick access to its collection of applications. Clicking with the middle mouse button (or the right and left buttons together) brings up the Switch to... menu to quickly bring any open window to the front.

Exiting Fvwm95

The last entry in the Start menu is the Exit Fvwm menu. This menu offers two options: Restart and Yes, Really Quit. The third option, No, Don't Quit is actually a fake option in that it doesn't cause any action to take place.

Restart is used to exit and restart fvwm95 without exiting X Windows or closing any open windows. The benefit of this is most apparent in reconfiguring fvwm95. As we will see in the next chapter, when editing the configuration files of fvwm95, you will usually want to test changes incrementally. Instead of fully quitting X Windows and restarting to monitor changes, using the Restart option allows you to quickly activate and see changes made in the fvwm95 configuration files.

Yes, Really Quit causes fvwm95 to exit, X Windows to end, and all open windows to close. While the closing of all open windows generally also causes the applications to exit, this is not always the case. Some applications don't correctly notice the closing of the window and continue running in the background even after X Windows has exited. On a busy or heavily used system, these applications, known as dangling processes, can place an unnecessary load on the server, denying needed system resources to other applications.

For this reason, it is a good policy to close all open windows before quitting fvwm95 and X Windows.

X Windows Applications

In this section, we are going to take a look at some X Windows applications and how they can be run and used. These applications include xterm, the standard

X Windows file manager, a graphics program called The Gimp, and several X Windows utilities.

These applications have been selected on one of two criteria: they are useful in everyday Linux operations, or they are representative of the power or range of many Linux applications.

This section should give you the confidence to begin experimenting with other X Windows applications offered in any standard Linux distribution.

Using Xterm

While X Windows puts a nice-looking and user-friendly face on Linux and allows the creation of fully graphical applications, the fact remains that as a Unix clone, Linux is a command-line oriented operating system.

Although it is possible to use Linux for everyday work without ever using the command prompt, to take advantage of the real power and flexibility of a Unix-like operating system, you will need to make at least occasional forays into the world of the command line.

Fortunately, this doesn't mean abandoning the ease of X Windows. The xterm program provides a command prompt window that is fully integrated into the X Windows environment, with a scrollbar, a resizable window, and the ability to copy and paste with other X Windows applications—all features that a standard Linux console lacks.

The simplest way to launch an xterm window in Red Hat 5 is to select New Shell from the Start menu. In addition, the default Red Hat 5 configuration will launch an xterm when you start X Windows and fvwm95.

If you want to launch additional xterm windows, you can also do so from the command line of another xterm window using the command

```
$ xterm &
```

or, if you find that for some reason xterm isn't on your path,

```
$ /usr/bin/X11/xterm &
```

By default, this opens a window that is 80 characters wide and 25 lines deep (the standard size of a Linux console) with a scrollbar down the left side. The window can be resized to provide more space for viewing information and working. You will notice that in Red Hat 5, the default color scheme for new xterm windows is white characters on a black background and the default title of the window is xterm.

Customizing Xterm

The xterm program is highly customizable. Among other things, you can change the window's font, the color scheme, the default window size, the placement of new windows on the screen, and the title of the window. In this section, we will look at these options and how to use them when launching new xterm windows.

At first it might seem that this flexibility has no real value, but in reality it does. On different monitors, different color combinations produce the most readable text, so being able to change the color scheme is a valuable feature. Also, if you regularly use several xterm windows for different tasks (such as running Top, reading your e-mail, and managing your files), being able to quickly identify which window is currently being used for which task makes switching between open windows much easier.

Flags and Arguments: A Quick Unix Primer

Before going forward, we need a quick tutorial about how Unix commands work. A complete introduction to Unix and Unix commands as used in Linux comes in Chapter 10, "Introducing Linux Commands."

To execute a program (or command), you simply need to type the name of the program (and possibly the complete location of the program) and hit the Enter key.

For instance, to launch xterm, you can use

```
$ xterm
```

or, if xterm is not on your path,

```
$ /usr/bin/X11/xterm
```

But most programs either require or can accept information that alters the way they will behave or provides information to be processed. Two types of information can be provided to a command: flags and arguments.

Arguments are information provided to the program to be processed; they can be anything from file names to text to search for.

Continued on next page

Flags are options that alter the behavior of a program. They appear after the command, separated by one or more spaces and preceded by a dash. For instance, the flag -help causes xterm to print out a help message:

```
$ xterm -help
usage:
        xterm [-options ...] [-e command args]

where options include:
    -help                       print out this message
    -display display name       X server to contact
    -geometry geom              size (in characters) and position
    -/+rv                       turn on/off reverse video
    -bg color                   background color
    -fg color                   foreground color
    -bd color                   border color
    -bw number                  border width in pixels
    -fn fontname                normal text font
    -iconic                     start iconic
    -name string                client instance, icon, and title
                                strings
    -title string               title string
    -xrm resourcestring         additional resource
                                specifications
    -/+132                      turn on/off column switch
                                inhibiting
    -/+ah                       turn on/off always highlight
    -/+ai                       turn on/off active icon
etc.
```

Complex flags can also be created to provide information that the flag needs to function correctly. For instance, to set the xterm title, you use the -T flag, but you also need to provide the text that you want to appear in the title bar. The command

```
$ xterm -T Email
```

would create an xterm window with the word Email as the title.

Arguments, on the other hand, are not configuration options but information provided to a program to be processed. Arguments are not preceded by a dash as are flags. Arguments are often names of files to be opened, processed, or edited—as in the following example, which indicates that the file testfile should be opened for editing with the editor emacs:

```
$ emacs testfile
```

Setting the color scheme   Using a variety of flags, it is possible to set almost all aspects of an xterm window's color scheme from border color to the color of the cursor. In this section, we will look at the main elements of the color scheme: foreground color, background color, and cursor color.

Understanding X Windows colors   Before looking at the specific flags used to set colors of an xterm window, we need to look at how colors are referred to in X Windows.

Colors in X Windows are specified in RGB (red-green-blue) format. RGB format consists of ordered triplets of numbers with each number having a value from 0 to 255. The numbers represent the value of the red, green, and blue channels respectively, with 255 representing no color and 0 representing the highest possible value of the color.

Luckily, you don't need to figure out the color channel combinations to get your desired color. The work has already been done and is stored in a file that X Windows uses to map color names to their numerical triplets. This file, normally called rgb.txt, is usually found in the directory /usr/X11R6/lib/X11/.

The complete list of values in the Red Hat 5 rgb.txt file is in Appendix A. Users of other distributions will find a similar list on their systems. A selected list appears here to make it easy to experiment with colors as we work through this section:

snow	GhostWhite	PapayaWhip	LemonChiffon
AliceBlue	LavenderBlush	MistyRose	white
DarkSlateGray	DimGray	gray	MidnightBlue
NavyBlue	SlateBlue	blue	SteelBlue
turquoise	cyan	DarkGreen	SeaGreen
LawnGreen	green	GreenYellow	DarkKhaki
LightYellow	yellow	gold	RosyBrown
IndianRed	sienna	beige	wheat
tan	chocolate	DarkSalmon	orange
tomato	red	DeepPink	pink
maroon	magenta	violet	orchid
purple	DarkCyan	DarkRed	LightGreen

Depending on the color depth of your video display and the applications you are running, you may find that the colors you use don't appear quite the way you expect. This is due to video card limitations and differences between systems.

Background and foreground colors Setting background and foreground colors allows you to control the appearance of the text on your screen. Text will appear in the foreground color while the background color, logically, will be assigned to the background of the window.

The usual default xterm window is white text on a black background. Use the -fg and -bg flags to set the foreground and background colors:

```
$ xterm -fg black -bg white &
```

This command provides exactly the reverse color scheme of the default xterm window, causing the background to be set to white and the foreground to black. The result looks like Figure 8.23.

FIGURE 8.23:

Controlling the color scheme

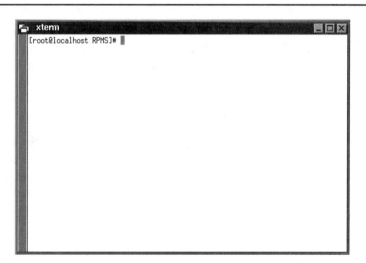

The -**bg** and -**fg** flags are not specific to xterm. In fact, they are standard X Windows flags that can be used to change the color schemes of most X Windows applications.

Cursor color If you tried the last example for setting colors, you probably noticed that the cursor stayed the same color as the default xterm color scheme (pink in most Red Hat installations). You can change this color as well, using the -cr flag. For instance, if you want a dark blue cursor, you might use the command

```
$ xterm -bg black -fg white -cr MidnightBlue &
```

Setting the window size and location When you open an xterm window (or any other application's window, for that matter), the size of the window is set to a default size and the location of the window is determined by the configuration of your window manager (we will learn how this works in fvwm95 in the next chapter).

However, you can specify the exact size and placement of windows in X Windows using the -geometry flag. This flag is a standard X Windows flag (like -bg and -fg) and works with most X Windows programs.

The basic syntax of the flag is: -geometry widthxheight+x+y, where width specifies the width of the window in pixels, height specifies the height of the window in pixels, x specifies the horizontal placement of the window as an offset in pixels from the left side of the display, and y specifies the vertical placement of the window as an offset in pixels from the top of the display.

Xterm accepts the use of the geometry flag but handles the information in a somewhat nonstandard way. When you think about it, specifying the height and width of a terminal window in pixels doesn't make a lot of sense. Instead, xterm interprets width and height as the number of columns and rows of characters to display, and sizes the window according to the font being used.

The default window size is 80 columns by 25 lines of characters. But what if we want a small 10-character by 10-character window to be placed 200 pixels from the left side of the screen and 300 pixels down from the top of the screen? We could use the command

```
$ xterm -geometry 10x10+200+300 &
```

to get a window like the one in Figure 8.24.

FIGURE 8.24:

Using the -geometry flag

By adding the -fg and -bg flags, we can also change the default color scheme at the same time we define the size of the window when it opens:

```
$ xterm -geometry 10x10+200+300 -fg DarkRed -bg cyan &
```

The result will look like Figure 8.25.

FIGURE 8.25:

Combining the -geometry flag with the color flags

Setting the window title As mentioned earlier, it is useful to be able to set the title of an xterm window to help identify what different windows are being used for. The easiest way to set the title is with the -T or -title flag (they are the same).

```
$ xterm -title Email &
```

would create an xterm window with the title Email, as would the command

```
$ xterm -T Email &
```

In order to create titles consisting of more than one word (in other words, containing spaces and other separators), you will need to quote the title so that xterm knows which part of the command to treat as the title. If you prefer to use the title My Email, you could use the command:

```
$ xterm -T "My Email" &
```

By default, the name of an xterm window in Red Hat 5.1 is nxterm unless, as we will see below, an application is specified to run inside the xterm window when it opens.

Running an application in an *xterm* window While the purpose of xterm windows is to use the command line to execute commands, you may want certain character mode programs to run by default when you launch the xterm window. For instance, if you always keep Top running inside an xterm window while working, you might want to have Top launch when you open its xterm. This is done with the -e flag:

```
$ xterm -e top &
```

This command opens a window like the one in Figure 8.26.

Launching Top when an xterm opens

When the program running inside the window quits, the xterm window will close.

It is important to note that the default window title when you use the -e flag is the name of the program launched with the -e flag.

Setting the font   The default font used by xterm is usually quite readable and suited to the average monitor. But if you have a particularly large or small monitor or use an unusually low or high resolution, you may find it wise to change the font you use in your xterm windows.

In order to do this, you use the -fn flag. But how do you refer to fonts? Fonts are referred to by names that can be as simple as 7x13 (which indicates 7 pixels wide and 12 pixels deep) or as complex as -sony-fixed-medium-r-normal-24-230-75-75-c-120-iso8859-1, which indicates the 24-point Latin character set, medium weight, Roman style font named fixed from the Sony font foundry.

X Windows offers a program, xlsfonts, that provides a list of available fonts on your X Windows system. Appendix B provides a complete list of all the fonts included in a standard Red Hat 5 installation.

To see a list of available fonts on your system, use the following command in an xterm window:

```
$ xlsfonts | more
```

The | more part of the command allows you to page through the long list of fonts (491 on my system) by hitting the space bar to move forward a page.

So, to choose the 10×20 font, you could use the command

```
$ xterm -fn 10x20 &
```

to get a window with a large font like the one in Figure 8.27.

FIGURE 8.27:

The 10×20 font

In theory, any of these fonts can be used with the -fn flag and the xterm command. In practice, though, this doesn't work. The nature of xterm is that it needs fixed-width fonts—that is, fonts in which all characters occupy the same amount of space regardless of their comparative sizes. In the world of Microsoft Windows, an example of a fixed-width font is Courier.

By contrast, many fonts are proportionally spaced. This means that a letter "i" will take up less space than a "w" because the latter is a wider letter. Xterm doesn't do a good job of handling these proportionally spaced fonts, as can be seen in Figure 8.28 where the selected font is from the Times family.

FIGURE 8.28:

Using a proportionally spaced font

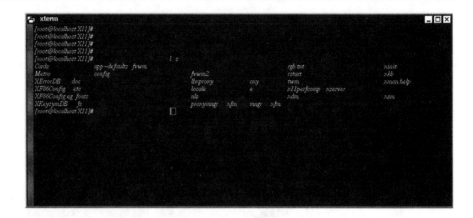

Listed below are some of the common (and easy to type) fixed-width fonts that are available in most X Windows distributions, including the one available with Red Hat 5:

5×7	6×13bold	7×14bold	9×15bold
5×8	6×9	8×13	10×20
6×10	7×13	8×13bold	12×24
6×12	7×13bold	8×16	
6×13	7×14	9×15	

If you want to experiment with other fonts, use xlsfonts to see a list of fonts, select a font, and then use the xfd command to display the font in a window. For instance, to display the Sony font -sony-fixed-medium-r-normal-24-230-75-75-c-120-iso8859-1 that we saw earlier, we could use the command:

```
$ xfd -fn -sony-fixed-medium-r-normal-24-230-75-75-c-120-iso8859-1
```

Notice the use of the -fn flag to specify the font name. The font will be displayed in a window like the one in Figure 8.29.

FIGURE 8.29:

Displaying fonts with xfd

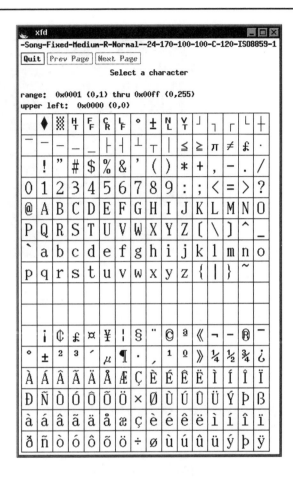

You can click the Quit button to close the window.

Other features Xterm offers many more features than the ones listed here. You can find out about them in the `xterm` man page. A man page provides information about how to use a specific program. To access the `xterm` man page, you can use the command

```
$ man xterm
```

in an `xterm` window. This will display a man page like that shown in Figure 8.30. Use the arrow keys to scroll through the man page.

FIGURE 8.30:

The xterm man page

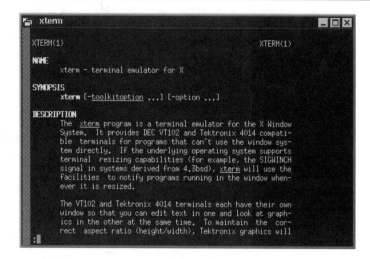

NOTE   A search program for searching popular Linux man pages is included on the CD-ROM with this book. Complete instructions for installing and using this software are provided at http://linux.juxta.com/

Managing Files in X Windows

Windows 3.1 users have the File Manager, Windows 95 users have the Explorer, and Mac OS users can make use of Finder. All of these programs provide facilities for managing files (including copying, moving, renaming, and deleting) as well as for launching applications.

In the X Windows world there is no standard tool to provide these features. Numerous applications that call themselves file managers or desktop managers attempt to provide this functionality. You can find a selected list of file managers at `http://www.xnet.com/~blatura/linapp2.html#file`.

In this section, we will look at xfm, a common X Windows file manager that you will find in most Linux distributions and on many other Unix systems.

Launching Xfm

Xfm (the X File Manager) is one of the default applications on the fvwm95 start menu in Red Hat 5. You can launch it by selecting xfm from the File Management submenu of the Utilities submenu of the Program menu.

Alternatively, you can issue the command

```
$ xfm &
```

from the command line of an xterm window or, if you need to specify the complete path,

```
$ /usr/bin/X11/xfm &
```

in a Red Hat 5 installation.

Depending on the distribution of Linux you are using, you may see one or more windows when you launch xfm. In the case of Red Hat 5, xfm is preconfigured to display two windows when it launches: a File Manager window and an Applications window.

The File Manager Window

The File Manager window looks like the one in Figure 8.31.

FIGURE 8.31:

The File Manager window

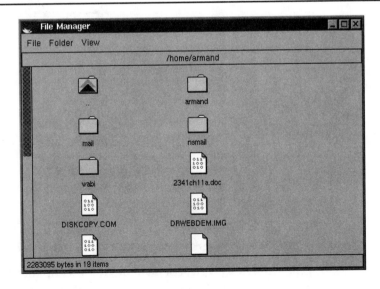

The window displays the contents of a single directory on your computer. By default, the directory displayed is the home directory of the user running the program. In Figure 8.31, user armand has run xfm so the directory displayed is his home directory: /home/armand.

In this window, there are several types of icons that represent different types of files and other elements such as directories. The most important icons to familiarize yourself with are those representing directories, text files, and binary files.

NOTE

A full discussion of file types and the directory structure of Linux is provided in Chapter 11, "Working with Files." You already have a basic understanding of the Linux directory structure from the discussion provided in Chapter 4, "Installing Linux."

The folder icon represents a directory and should be familiar to users of both Macintosh and Windows systems.

A blank piece of paper represents a text file

while a piece of paper containing a series of 1s and 0s (binary digits) represents a binary file.

Binary files are files that are not normally read or edited using a plain text editor but rather are applications, images, and other complex data.

The other elements of the File Manager window are the scrollbar and the menu.

The scrollbar is typical of many X Windows applications but will feel unfamiliar to users of both Microsoft Windows and Macintosh systems. To start with, the scrollbar is on the left side of the window and not the right. Like the one in Figure 8.32, it lacks arrows at the top and bottom.

FIGURE 8.32:

A typical X Windows scrollbar

The dark bar represents the total amount of available data being displayed and is positioned to indicate the point in that data that is currently being viewed (as you move through the document, the position of the dark bar changes). Moving through the data can be awkward at first to the new user because the procedures are a little unintuitive:

- Clicking anywhere in the scrollbar area with the left mouse button scrolls down one screen.

- Clicking anywhere in the scrollbar area with the right mouse button scrolls up one screen.

- Clicking and dragging on the dark bar with the middle mouse button drags the viewable area. (Remember: with a two-button mouse, use the left and right buttons together to simulate the middle button.)

- Clicking with the middle mouse button on the scrollbar area outside the dark bar jumps to that location.

Navigating the File System Moving through directories is fairly straight-forward. Simply double-click with the left mouse button on any folder in the File Manager window to open that directory. The contents of the window are replaced with the contents of the new directory. To move back up a folder, simply double-click with the left mouse button on the special folder icon like the one below, which represents the parent directory to the current directory.

This icon usually appears in the top left corner of the File Manager window.

Alternately, if you know exactly which directory you want to view, you can quickly get there by using the Go to... option on the Folder menu. This opens a dialog box like the one in Figure 8.33 where you can type the complete path of a directory and then click the OK button to go there. The ways in which to type the path of a directory are clearly laid out in Chapter 11, "Working with Files."

FIGURE 8.33:

The Go to... dialog box

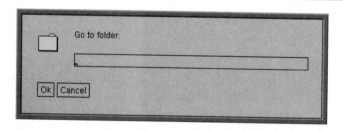

In addition to the standard Icon view of your files and directories that we have worked with so far, xfm provides two other views, which present slightly different approaches to directory navigation.

Choose Text from the View menu to get a text listing of the files and directories in the currently displayed directory. This view looks like Figure 8.34.

Notice that the names of directories appear inside square brackets like this: [*directory-name*]. Filenames have no special treatments. Several pieces of information are provided for each file, including the size, ownership, permissions, and date of creation. The complete meaning of all this information is discussed later in Chapter 11.

To open a directory, simply double-click the directory name with the left mouse button. To open the parent directory, click the special directory [..], which should appear first in the list.

A third way of viewing your directories, the Tree view, is distinctly different from the Icon or Text views. It doesn't present files but rather provides a quick way to move up and down through your directories until you get where you want to be, at which point you can switch to the Icon or Text view.

The Tree view (select Tree from the View menu) gives a view of the possible paths from the current directory, as in the sample tree in Figure 8.35.

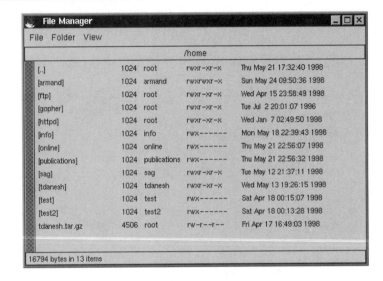

File Manager				
File	Folder	View		
/home				
[..]	1024	root	rwxr-xr-x	Thu May 21 17:32:40 1998
[armand]	1024	armand	rwxrwxr-x	Sun May 24 09:50:36 1998
[ftp]	1024	root	rwxr-xr-x	Wed Apr 15 23:58:49 1998
[gopher]	1024	root	rwxr-xr-x	Tue Jul 2 20:01:07 1996
[httpd]	1024	root	rwxr-xr-x	Wed Jan 7 02:49:50 1998
[info]	1024	info	rwx------	Mon May 18 22:39:43 1998
[online]	1024	online	rwx------	Thu May 21 22:56:07 1998
[publications]	1024	publications	rwx------	Thu May 21 22:56:32 1998
[sag]	1024	sag	rwxr-xr-x	Tue May 12 21:37:11 1998
[tdanesh]	1024	tdanesh	rwxr-xr-x	Wed May 13 19:26:15 1998
[test]	1024	test	rwx------	Sat Apr 18 00:15:07 1998
[test2]	1024	test2	rwx------	Sat Apr 18 00:13:28 1998
tdanesh.tar.gz	4506	root	rw-r--r--	Fri Apr 17 16:49:03 1998

16794 bytes in 13 items

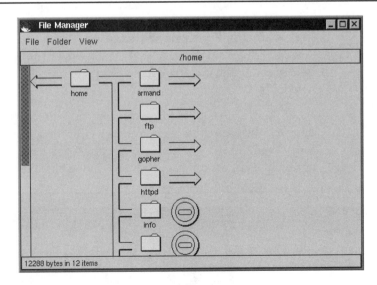

12288 bytes in 12 items

In this view, the current directory is shown as a folder at the top left. In a vertical column to its right are all its subdirectories. If the current folder has a parent, a large left-pointing arrow will appear to the left of the current directory's icon.

If you have permission to enter a subdirectory, a large right-pointing arrow appears to the right of the directory.

If you don't have permission, a No Entry sign appears to the right of the folder icon.

To move up to the parent directory, simply left-click the large left arrow. To move down into a subdirectory, left-click the large right arrow.

Manipulating Files and Directories   While xfm can perform numerous actions on files and directories, the ones you are most likely to use are copying, deleting, and moving. In addition, you will probably want to be able to create new folders.

Let's start with copying. You can copy any directory (folder) by clicking the item and then selecting Copy from the File menu, or by right-clicking the icon for the desired directory or file and selecting Copy from the pop-up menu that appears. Either action will produce a dialog box like the one in Figure 8.36.

FIGURE 8.36:

The Copy dialog box

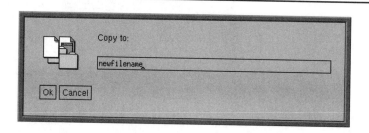

Simply enter the location you want to copy a file to (see Chapter 11, "Working with Files," to learn more about how to specify the location of files and directories) and then click the OK button. Click Cancel to cancel the operation.

Moving files and directories is a similar process. Click the icon desired to select a file or directory and choose Move from the File menu or right-click the icon and choose Move from the pop-up menu. Enter the new location of the file in the dialog box shown in Figure 8.37 and click OK.

FIGURE 8.37:

The Move dialog box

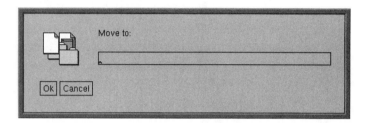

Deleting files and folders also follows a similar path: select an icon and then select Delete from the File menu or the pop-up menu to get a dialog box like the one in Figure 8.38. Clicking Continue actually deletes the file.

FIGURE 8.38:

The Delete dialog box

In the case of directories, a second confirmation dialog box appears, like the one in Figure 8.39. This is to confirm that you really want to delete the directory and all of its contents.

FIGURE 8.39:

The Directory Delete confirmation dialog box

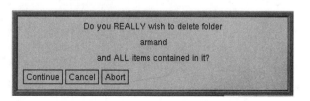

Creating new directories is also a simple process. Select New from the Folder menu to get a dialog box like the one in Figure 8.40. Enter the name of a directory (following the rules outlined in Chapter 11 regarding valid directory names) and click OK. A new folder icon will appear in the main File Manager window to represent the new directory.

FIGURE 8.40:

The New Folder dialog box

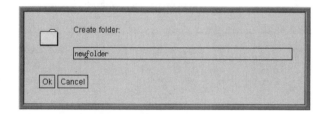

The Applications Window

The Applications window provides you with an alternate method to organize and launch the programs you regularly use. By default, the Applications window for users of Red Hat 5 will look something like the one in Figure 8.41.

FIGURE 8.41:

The Applications window

For users familiar with Windows 3.1's Program Manager, the concept of the Applications window should seem familiar. Applications are collected together into groups with each group and each application represented by an icon. For instance, in Figure 8.41 we see a Graphics Group, a Utils Group, and an Editor Group, among others. In addition, we see application icons such as Xterm, Mail and Printer.

Navigating the Applications Window   As would be expected, double-clicking with the left mouse button on an application icon launches the application. Double-clicking a group icon opens the group. For instance, Figure 8.42 shows the result of clicking the Graphics Group icon in the example above.

FIGURE 8.42:

The Graphics Group

Notice the Back button in the Graphics Group window. Because the Applications window allows for nested groups (groups that contain icons for subgroups), it is necessary to be able to move back up one level from the current open group. This is achieved with the Back button.

The Main button jumps right to the top of the main Applications window that we saw in Figure 8.41. As would be expected, the File Window button opens xfm's File Manager window.

Manipulating Groups and Applications If you right-click in the Applications window anywhere except on an icon, you will see a menu like the one in Figure 8.43.

FIGURE 8.43:

Right-clicking in the Applications window brings up this menu

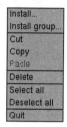

The main features of this menu are the Install and Install Group options. These allow you to create new icons for applications and groups.

Selecting Install Group brings up a dialog box like the one in Figure 8.44.

FIGURE 8.44:

The Install Group window

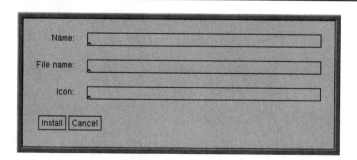

In this window are three fields that are used to define the basic information about the group. These are:

- **Name** The name of the group that appears in the Applications window

- **File Name**   The name of the file in which to store information about the group—usually it is a good idea for this name to be the same as or similar to the group name

- **Icon**   The location and filename of an icon to display for the group (we will learn more about icons and where to find them in the next chapter)

If you fill in the information and click the Install button, a new group will be created and its icon displayed.

Installing new application icons is a similar process. Simply select Install from the pop-up menu to get a dialog box like the one in Figure 8.45.

FIGURE 8.45:

The Install Application dialog box

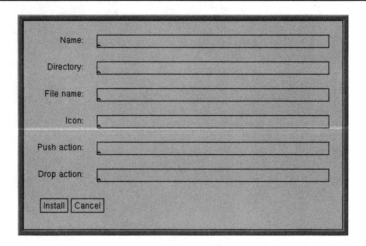

You will notice that this window contains more entries than the one for installing a new group. Still, only a few of these are crucial:

- **Name**   The name to display with the icon in the Applications window

- **Icon**   The icon to display for the application

- **Push Action**   The action to take when the icon is double-clicked

The other entries provide added functionality and are not vital to creating a functioning application icon. For complete details about how to use these fields, consult the xfm man page by typing **man xfm** in an xterm window.

Once you have created groups and applications, there will inevitably be times when you need to change the information you supplied in the original installation dialog boxes. If you right-click any icon, you will see a pop-up menu. The first entry in this pop-up menu is Edit, which brings up a dialog box like the one in Figure 8.46.

FIGURE 8.46:

The Edit dialog box

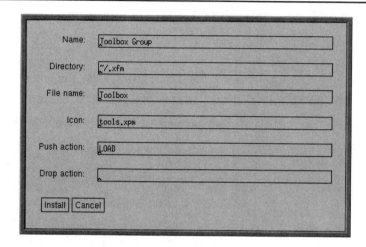

Here you can make any changes needed and click Install to update the icon's properties and behavior. Again, the xfm man page provides the complete information you need to use this window effectively.

Graphics in X Windows

So far, we have seen the most basic of X Windows applications in action: xterm and xfm. If this is all there was, it would reinforce the views of the naysayers who complain that X Windows doesn't have any applications, that Windows and the Mac OS are where the action is.

The reality, though, is that powerful, effective applications do exist for the X Windows environment. Even among the free tools out there are those that rival the features of commercial applications.

In this section, we look at two of the more popular Linux graphics applications: The Gimp and xv. Because these are both large programs with extensive feature sets, we are going to just take an overview look at the applications and what they do, and then point to where complete information on the applications is available. Mastering an application like The Gimp, after all, would require a book in itself.

The Gimp

The Gimp (General Image Manipulation Program) is an attempt to offer the Linux community a freely available, full-featured image-editing package to rival the likes of Adobe Photoshop or Corel PhotoPaint. Figure 8.47 shows The Gimp running with several of its dialog boxes and tools open.

FIGURE 8.47:

The Gimp

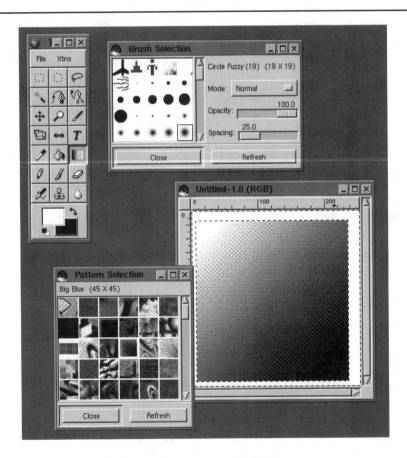

Offered under the GNU Public License, The Gimp is under constant development by Spencer Kimball and Peter Mattis at the University of California–Berkeley.

The Gimp includes all the tools expected of a full-featured image editing package, including numerous brush types, special-effects filters, intelligent scissors, bezier selection, layers, transparencies, and 24-bit image support.

The Gimp also provides a plug-in mechanism. Numerous plug-ins are freely available on the Internet to perform a variety of tasks, including despeckling, mapping to a sphere, creating mosaics, generating lens flares, and more.

In addition, the most recent version (1.0.0) includes a downloadable 590-page manual that provides the in-depth instruction and documentation often lacking in free software. This is all available from The Gimp Web site at `www.gimp.org`.

Using The Gimp   We will take just a quick look at using The Gimp. The Gimp is included on the CD-ROM as part of the standard Red Hat 5 distribution. You can run it from an `xterm` window with the command

```
$ gimp &
```

or

```
$ /usr/bin/gimp &
```

The Gimp starts up by displaying its toolbar. This window, shown in Figure 8.48, offers access to a wide range of tools plus the main File menu.

FIGURE 8.48:

The Gimp toolbar

From the file menu, you can perform basic functions such as opening and closing images, creating new images, and opening and closing dialog boxes such as the color palette, the gradient editor, and the brush selector. When working on an actual image, right-clicking anywhere in the image brings up the complete menu for The Gimp like the one shown in Figure 8.49. From this menu, you can access all the features of The Gimp—special filters, layer controls, and more.

FIGURE 8.49:

The Gimp main menu

To learn the full set of The Gimp features, refer to the manual for the software that is on The Gimp's Web site, mentioned earlier.

Xv

Xv is one of the best-known and most widely used X Windows programs. This small but powerful program is distributed as shareware that is free for personal use. While not quite as widely distributable as the rest of Linux, it still can be found in most Linux distributions, and for good reason: for basic image manipulation in the Unix world, xv is the de facto standard.

Xv supports a wide range of image file formats, both the common ones you would expect (TIF, GIF, JPG, etc.) and lesser-known formats such as PNG. It can be used to convert images, perform screen and window captures, change color depth and resolution of images, crop images, and adjust the color maps of images. In addition, xv includes a handful of its own special-effects filters, such as embossing, oil painting, and despeckling.

You can launch xv with the command

```
$ xv &
```

or

```
$ /usr/bin/X11/xv &
```

Xv also appears on the standard fvwm95 Programs menu of Red Hat 5 under the Graphics category.

Xv operations center around two windows: a controls window and a viewer window. When you launch xv, it initially opens the viewer window with its logo image displayed as in Figure 8.50.

FIGURE 8.50:

The viewer window with the xv logo

Clicking with the right mouse button in the viewer window will open and display the controls window shown in Figure 8.51.

FIGURE 8.51:

The controls window

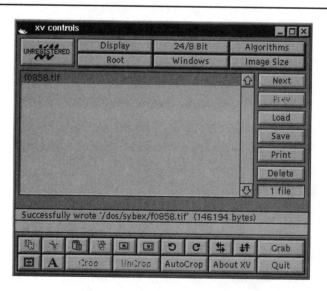

Almost everything in xv is done in the controls window. The viewer window allows you to see the results of your work.

Let's take a quick look at some of the main tasks in xv: opening and saving images, cropping an image, and capturing a window to an image file. Complete documentation exists in the form of a printable PostScript document that can be found in standard Red Hat 5 distributions at /usr/doc/xv-3.10a/xvdocs.ps. An HTML version of the documentation can be found on the Web on Shelly Johnson's Home Page at Rice University at http://is.rice.edu/~shel/. Follow the link for the xv documentation.

Opening Images   Opening images is done by clicking the Load button in the controls window. A dialog box like the one in Figure 8.52 will appear.

FIGURE 8.52:

The xv Load File window

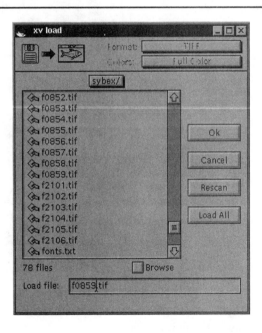

This dialog box works in a vaguely Mac-like fashion. Above the list of files, you see the name of the current directory. You can click the directory name to get a list of its parent directories and, by selecting one of these, quickly change to that directory.

To open a file, simply select the filename and click the OK button (or you can simply double-click the filename). The file will appear in the viewer window and the dialog box will close. If you check the Browse check box, then the behavior of the dialog box changes slightly: when you click a file and then click OK, the file opens in the viewer window but the dialog box remains open. This allows you to look at different files to find the file you want. Once the correct file is displayed, simply click the Cancel button to close the dialog box.

Saving Images The Save File dialog box shown in Figure 8.53 is similar to the Load File dialog box. Directory navigation works in the same fashion; you select existing filenames by clicking them in the file list, and clicking OK saves the current file to the name displayed in the Save file field.

FIGURE 8.53:

The xv Save File window

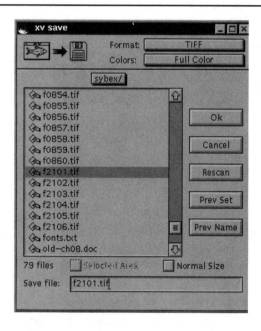

If you want to save the image to a new filename, simply type the name you want in the field.

When saving an image, you will also want to specify the type of image. In the top-right corner of the dialog box is the file format menu. By clicking this menu, you can view a list of available files. Select the file type you desire from the list. In addition, the color depth menu just below the file format menu presents any available color depth option for the file format you have selected.

Cropping an Image   Cropping an image is a simple process: select the area you want to crop to and press the Crop button in the controls window.

To select an area for cropping, you drag out a rectangle with the left mouse button in the viewer window. Figure 8.54 shows an image displayed in the viewer window with a rectangle indicating where the user has dragged the mouse.

FIGURE 8.54:

Selecting a crop area

Once you have selected an area to crop, simply click the Crop button in the controls window. The result would be something like Figure 8.55 for the above example.

FIGURE 8.55:

The result of cropping

If you don't like the results of your cropping, simply click the UnCrop button to undo the action.

Capturing a Window   One of the popular uses of xv is to create screen shots. If you want to capture an open window to an image file, you can do this using the Grab feature of xv.

Clicking the Grab button in the controls window opens the Grab dialog box like the one in Figure 8.56.

FIGURE 8.56:

The xv Grab window

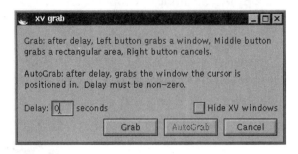

There are two easy ways to grab the contents of a window: manually or automatically.

To manually grab the contents of a window, leave the Delay value set to zero seconds. Then click the Grab button. The next window you click in will be captured. The only caveat is this: the window needs to be unobscured. Any portion of any other window overlapping the selected window will also be captured.

To give you time to bring a window to the front before capturing, enter a suitable number of seconds in the delay field (4 or 5 should work well in most situations). This means that after clicking the Grab button you have that number of seconds to work normally before xv enters the Grab mode. After the delay has expired, xv will issue a distinct beep and then the next window you click will be captured.

Automatic mode is similar to manual mode, with two differences. First, automatic grabbing requires a delay. Second, you need to click the AutoGrab button instead of the Grab button. You will have the specified number of seconds to work normally (to get the desired window to the front and unobscured), and then xv will issue the same beep and capture whichever window is underneath the mouse pointer at that time.

Once you have grabbed a window, the image of that window will appear in the viewer window and you can save it like any other image in xv.

X Windows Utilities

Before closing this chapter, we will take a look at a few handy X Windows utilities and how to use them. These utilities are:

- xedit
- xclock and oclock
- xcalc

Using Xedit

Xedit provides functionality similar to the Windows Notepad. You can use it to open and change the contents of plain text files, search and replace text, and create new files.

Admittedly, as Figure 8.57 shows, the xedit interface is a bit spartan, but for quick editing of simple text files, it does the trick.

FIGURE 8.57:

The xedit window

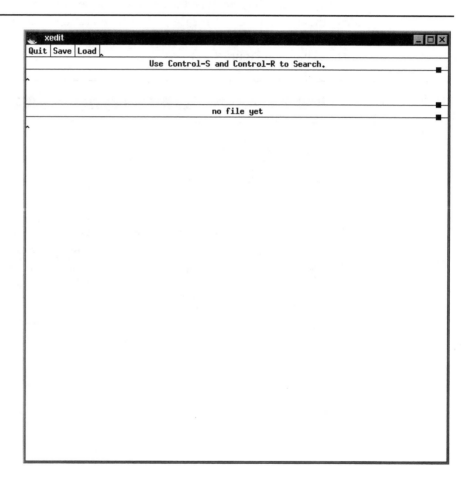

You can launch xedit with the command

```
$ xedit &
```

or, if xedit is not on your path, with

```
$ /usr/bin/X11/xedit &
```

or, if you are running fvwm95 in Red Hat 5, by selecting xedit from the Utilities submenu of the Programs menu.

The interface is simple. Across the top is the toolbar with three buttons (Quit, Save, and Load) and a filename field; below the toolbar is a small message area where the program displays the results of actions; below the message area is the main text area where the currently opened file is displayed for editing.

To load an existing file, type the name and, if needed, the complete path of the file in the filename field to the right of the Load button and then click the Load button. This will load the file and display a confirmation message in the message area, as shown in Figure 8.58.

FIGURE 8.58:

The results of loading a file

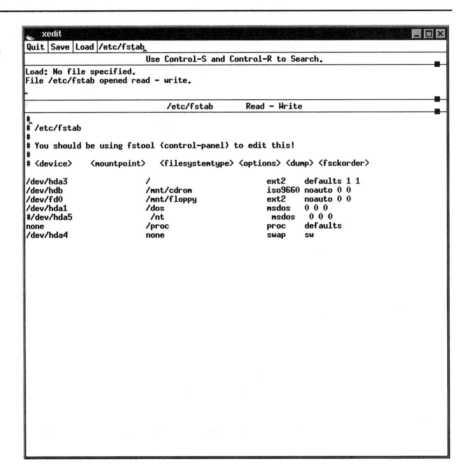

Saving a file follows a similar process: make sure the name of the file (existing or new) is in the filename field and then click the Save button.

The other two main functions of xedit are searching and replacing. As indicated below the toolbar at the top, either Control+S or Control+R can be used as the search and replace command. Pressing Control+S or Control+R brings up the search dialog box shown in Figure 8.59.

FIGURE 8.59:

The search and replace window

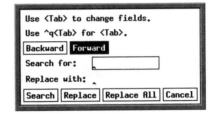

Using this dialog box is relatively simple: fill in the word to search for and click the Search button. To replace, also fill in the replacement text and click Replace to replace the next occurrence of the search term and Replace All to replace all occurrences of the search term.

The only other options in the search and replace dialog box are the Backward/Forward toggle by which you indicate whether to search the document backward or forward from the current cursor position.

X Windows Clocks

You have probably noticed the clock that appears in the toolbar of fvwm95. Some users, though, like to see a larger digital or analog clock on their desktop.

This can be achieved by using either xclock or oclock. Both of these programs ship with most Linux distributions.

Xclock is a basic clock program that allows you to create an analog or digital clock. By default, xclock displays an analog clock, so the command

```
$ xclock &
```

or

```
$ /usr/bin/X11/xclock &
```

creates a window like the one in Figure 8.60.

FIGURE 8.60:

The default xclock style

The -digital flag causes xclock to display a digital clock like Figure 8.61.

FIGURE 8.61:

A digital xclock window

Wed May 27 22:23:52 1998

The first thing you will probably notice about both the analog and digital xclock windows is the complete lack of window frames or title bars. This might suggest the window cannot be resized, moved or closed. But you can perform all of these actions by using the Windows Operations menu on the fvwm95 Start menu. Here you will find Move, Resize, and Close commands that allow you to have full control over the window size and placement.

The -digital flag is not the only flag accepted by xclock. The -hd and -hl flags help create a more interesting visual display for an analog clock. The -hd flag is used to specify a color for the hands of the clock, and the -hl flag specifies the color for the outline of the hands of the clock. (Remember our discussion of RGB colors earlier. This is one instance where you would use the RGB colors outlined in Appendix A.)

For example, the command

```
$ xclock -hd yellow -hl green &
```

would create a clock that had yellow hands with green outlines like Figure 8.62 (of course, this is hard to see in the black-and-reproduction you are looking at).

FIGURE 8.62:

Setting the color of the
clock's hands

Notice the lack of contrast between the hands and the white face of the clock. This can be rectified with a standard X Windows flag: the -bg flag that we saw earlier in our review of xterm. By specifying a background color of black with

```
$ xclock -hd yellow -hl green -bg black &
```

we end up with something like Figure 8.63.

FIGURE 8.63:

Setting the background color

While the hands are now clearly visible, a new problem has arisen: the marks that indicate the points of the clock are now not visible, since they are black and they are drawn against a black background. These marks are considered part of the foreground and their color can be changed with the standard X Windows -fg flag.

```
$ xclock -hd yellow -hl green -bg black -fg cyan &
```

gives a result like Figure 8.64.

FIGURE 8.64:

Setting the foreground color

For some users, xclock doesn't quite cut it. No matter how much you play with the colors, the appearance is quite basic, and you may be looking for something a little more visually interesting in your clock.

Many users find this in oclock, an alternative to xclock and quite common in Linux distributions. You can launch oclock with

```
$ oclock &
```

or

```
$ /usr/bin/X11/oclock &
```

to get a result like Figure 8.65.

FIGURE 8.65:

The oclock window

The most immediately noticeable aspect of the oclock window is that the clock face is not contained within a larger rectangular box. In addition, as with xclock, you need to rely on the Windows Operations menu to manipulate the window.

Oclock accepts several flags that make it more customizable than xclock:

- **-fg** sets the foreground color (that is, the color of the hands and the jewel that appears in the twelve o'clock position)

- **-bg** sets the background, or face, color

- **-jewel** sets a color for just the jewel, allowing different hand and jewel colors

- **-minute** sets a color for just the minute hand, allowing different minute- and hour-hand colors

- **-hour** sets a color for just the hour hand

- **-bd** sets the border color

- **-transparent** makes the background of the clock face transparent

For instance, let's create an oclock window with the following specifications: a dark blue face, an orange minute hand, a light yellow hour hand, a white border, and a green jewel:

```
$ oclock -bg midnightblue -minute orange -hour cornsilk -bg white -
jewel green &
```

This produces results like Figure 8.66.

FIGURE 8.66:

A colorful oclock window

The **-transparent** flag is also worth looking at. With this flag, the face of the clock becomes transparent, allowing whatever window is behind the clock to show through. In Figure 8.67, an oclock window is overlapping with an xterm window.

FIGURE 8.67:

A transparent clock

Using Xcalc

Finally, we will take a quick look at xcalc. Xcalc is the default X Windows calculator tool and should be available in every distribution of Linux that includes X Windows.

As would be expected by this point in the chapter, you can run xcalc with

```
$ xcalc &
```

or

```
& /usr/bin/X11/xcalc &
```

The xcalc window looks like Figure 8.68.

FIGURE 8.68:

The xcalc window

The calculator operates much as any standard scientific calculator does. It provides all the expected scientific functions, including trigonometric and logarithmic functions, plus a memory. The actual use of such a calculator and its functions is not really the subject of this chapter, and a full description of the meaning of these functions is best left to a mathematics text.

It is interesting to note, though, that xcalc is highly customizable. Once you are comfortable with Linux and X Windows, you can learn how to customize everything down to position and function of each key as well as the appearance of each key. But because the method of performing this customization relies on complex configuration files, the task of learning to do this is left to the determined reader. To learn more about customizing xcalc, read the xcalc man page by typing **man xcalc** at a command prompt.

One popular and comparatively simple configuration of xcalc is to use `xcalc -rpn` to get a calculator that HP calculator users will be comfortable with. Also, remember how we used `-geom`, `-fg`, and `-bg` to adjust the size and color of an `xterm` window? We can do the same for most X Windows applications, including xcalc.

Where Do We Go from Here?

By now, you should be feeling fairly comfortable navigating your chosen X Windows environment. You can control basic options of fvwm95, you can launch applications, and you can manipulate windows.

As mentioned earlier, though, the power of X Windows and its independent window manager model comes in its flexibility and configurability.

In the next chapter, we take a look at how to go about configuring X Windows and the fvwm95 Window Manager to meet your personal needs and tastes. These tasks will include configuring the XFree86 server for special situations as well as configuring the entire fvwm95 interface from menu entries to icons to color schemes.

CHAPTER

NINE

Advanced X Windows Configuration

- The XF86Config File

- The X Windows Start-Up Sequence

- X Resources

As we have already seen in this section, the X Windows environment provides a degree of flexibility and customizability not commonly found in many GUI-based operating systems. Of course, with this degree of flexibility comes some degree of complexity: to fully utilize the X Windows flexibility, you must use sometimes complex configuration methods.

In this chapter, we will look in detail at the main components of X Windows and how they can be customized. We will start with the XFree86 file, which tells the X server how to behave. It specifies everything from the type of video card and monitor in use (including the desired resolution and color depth) to the type of mouse and keyboard being used.

Once the X server is fully configured the way you like it, you will probably want to control how X Windows starts: what programs launch at start-up, what actions take place before X Windows loads, and how the Windows Manager gets launched. In addition, the X resources database provides a mechanism through which it is possible to control settings such as the colors and fonts used in windows and the behavior of windows in response to certain actions. These settings (and others) can be specified either globally or on a per-application basis.

The *XF86Config* File

The configuration of XFree86 is in the file XF86Config. This file usually can be found at /etc/XF86Config or /etc/X11/XF86Config, depending on your distribution of XFree86. Red Hat 5.1 places the file in /etc/X11. With a fresh installation of XFree86, the configuration file can be found at /usr/X11R6/lib/X11/XF86Config, but for ease of access most distributions put the file in one of the directories mentioned above instead of in this location.

If you don't know where your installation of XFree86 has placed this file, use the find command to find it:

```
# find / -name xf86config -print
```

The XF86Config file contains information pertinent to the operation of the X server, including keyboard definitions, mouse specifications, and monitor information. This file is generated by XFree86 configuration applications such as Xconfigurator and xf86config.

Sometimes, though, fine-tuning of your X Windows environment can only be achieved by directly editing the XF86Config file with your favorite text editor. Refer back to Chapter 8, "Using X Windows Applications," for an introduction to using xedit, a simple X-Windows text editor.

The XF86Config file is broken down into seven main required sections:

- Files: This section specifies where XFree86 can find its supplementary files, such as fonts and the color table.

- ServerFlags: This section is used to enable and disable X server features, such as how to handle certain key sequences.

- Keyboard: This section specifies the keyboard protocol that controls how the key map is defined and other keyboard features, such as the repeat rate.

- Pointer: This section indicates the type of mouse being used, the device port occupied by the mouse, and button behavior of the mouse.

- Monitor: This section defines the refresh rate and resolution capabilities of your monitor.

- Device: These sections define available graphic devices (display adapters).

- Screen: These sections define the behavior of available X servers (such as the generic SVGA server, the monochrome server, and so on).

Files

Files is used to specify where certain critical files are located on your system. The following is a sample Files section without the comments:

NOTE   In the XF86Config file, comments start with a hash mark (#) and continue to the end of the line. All the content contained in comments is ignored by XFree86.

```
Section "Files"

    RgbPath "/usr/X11R6/lib/X11/rgb"

    FontPath      "/usr/X11R6/lib/X11/fonts/misc/"
    FontPath      "/usr/X11R6/lib/X11/fonts/75dpi/:unscaled"
    FontPath      "/usr/X11R6/lib/X11/fonts/Type1/"
```

```
        FontPath        "/usr/X11R6/lib/X11/fonts/Speedo/"
        FontPath        "/usr/X11R6/lib/X11/fonts/75dpi/"

#       ModulePath      "/usr/X11R6/lib/modules"

EndSection
```

There are several basic rules to note here that apply to the other six sections as well:

- Each section starts with a `Section` line.

- Each section ends with an `EndSection` line.

- On the `Section` line, the name of the section is specified in double quotes (in this case, `Section "Files"`).

There are three commonly used directives in this section, as shown in Table 9.1:

TABLE 9.1: Files Directives

Directive	Effect
RgbPath	This directive specifies the name of the RGB (red-green-blue) database without the `.txt` or `.db` extension. The contents of the Red Hat 5 RGB database file are shown in Appendix A. Generally, the default value can be left untouched unless you move or change the name of your RGB database (which is not a good idea, anyway, because several applications make use of the database and expect to find it in its normal location).
FontPath	This directive is used as many times as needed to specify where X Windows can find the installed X fonts on your system. Both scaleable fonts and bitmap fonts can be indicated (the bitmap fonts, which can't be scaled, have `:unscaled` appended to the end of the directory). If you add new font directories to your system, you should add a `FontPath` directive for them here.
ModulePath	This directive is used on operating systems, like Linux, that support dynamically loaded modules. This directive indicates the path to look in for modules. With most versions of XFree86, this directive won't appear, or will be commented out as in our example. The default path for modules is `/usr/X11R6/lib/modules`, and you only need to use this directive if you need to change this value.

ServerFlags

The ServerFlags section allows you to enable and disable some features of your X server. An example section, without comments, looks like this:

```
Section "ServerFlags"

#      NoTrapSignals

#      DontZap

#      DontZoom

#      DisableVidModeExtension

#      AllowNonLocalXvidtune

#      DisableModInDev

#      AllowNonLocalModInDev

EndSection
```

Uncomment any of these directives that you want to activate; leave them commented (the usual default state) if you don't want them activated.

The directives in this example have the effects shown in Table 9.2:

TABLE 9.2: ServerFlags Directives

Directive	Effect
NoTrapSignal	This directive is used for debugging purposes. When a signal indicating an error state is received, the server performs a core dump that dumps the contents of its section of memory to a file on the disk. This can cause instability in your system but is invaluable when debugging problems, particularly with beta and test versions of different X servers. You are best advised to leave this directive commented.
DontZap	Normally, the key combination Ctrl+Alt+Backspace causes X Windows to abort and returns you to the console. With this directive enabled, Ctrl+Alt+Backspace will be ignored and the key combination will be passed on to the current application for processing. You should uncomment this line only in those rare instances when you are running an application that needs to use this key combination to function properly.

Continued on next page

TABLE 9.2 CONTINUED: ServerFlags Directives

Directive	Effect
DontZoom	Normally, the key combination Ctrl+Alt+KeypadPlus cycles through available configured screen resolutions for your X server, increasing the resolution each time, and Ctrl+Alt+KeypadMinus is similarly used to decrease the resolution. If these key combinations are needed for other purposes by an application, uncomment this line to have X Windows ignore these key combinations and pass them on to your application.
DisableVidModeExtension	This directive prevents tuning of your video display with the xvidtune client (which we don't discuss in this book; documentation for this program can be found by typing the command man xvidtune in an open xterm window). There is no need to uncomment this entry, and you can leave it commented out by default.
AllowNonLocalXvidtune	Related to the previous directive, this directive allows nonlocal (in other words, out on the network somewhere) xvidtune clients to access your X Windows system. For security reasons, it is best to leave this directive disabled.
DisableModInDev	By enabling this directive, it becomes impossible to change keyboard and mouse settings dynamically while X Windows is running.
AllowNonLocalModInDev	Uncommenting this directive allows nonlocal computers to alter your keyboard and mouse settings. It is unwise to enable this directive unless you need to.

Keyboard

As one would expect, the Keyboard section specifies information pertinent to the functioning of your keyboard, including the keyboard type and protocol. A sample section looks like this:

```
Section "Keyboard"

     Protocol      "Standard"

     AutoRepeat    500 5

#    ServerNumLock

#    Xleds         1 2 3
```

```
#    LeftAlt        Meta
#    RightAlt       ModeShift
#    RightCtl       Compose
#    ScrollLock     ModeLock

     XkbDisable

#    XkbModel       "pc102"
#    XkbModel       "microsoft"

#    XkbLayout      "de"

#    XkbOptions     "ctrl:swapcaps"

#    XkbModel       "pc101"
#    XkbLayout      "us"
#    XkbOptions     ""

     XkbKeymap      "xfree86(us)"
```

EndSection

This looks like a complicated section, but, as Table 9.3 shows, it is actually quite simple:

TABLE 9.3: Keyboard Directives

Directive	Effect
Protocol	There is only one valid value for this directive in Red Hat Linux 5: **Standard**. This directive can take other values in other versions of Linux. Make sure this directive is uncommented with the value assigned.
AutoRepeat	This directive is used to specify how long to wait while a key is pressed down before auto-repeat should start and how often the key should be repeated. All values are in milliseconds. In our example, **AutoRepeat 500 5** indicates that auto-repeat should start after a key has been held down for 500 milliseconds (half of a second) and then the key should repeat every 5 milliseconds.
ServerNumLock	Generally, this directive can remain commented out. It specifies that the server and not the application should handle processing of the NumLock key. This directive is only necessary for some older X Windows applications that require it. In a standard Linux distribution, you shouldn't need it.

Continued on next page

TABLE 9.3 CONTINUED: Keyboard Directives

Directive	Effect
Xleds	This directive specifies which keyboard LEDs can be controlled by the user using the xset command. It is probably a good idea to leave this line commented out, which is the default.
LeftAlt, RightAlt, RightCtl, and ScrollLock	X Windows originally ran on Unix workstations that had keyboards distinctly different from the standard PC keyboard. These keyboards included special keys such as Meta, ModeShift, Compose, and ModeLock. If you find that you need these keys to use your applications (which is not likely with most standard applications), then uncomment these directives.
XkbDisable	If this line is uncommented, then an extension to X Windows called XKB is disabled. When XKB is enabled (the directive is commented out), XKB determines the keyboard mapping using a series of directives, listed below. When XKB is disabled, the keyboard mapping used by the console is passed on to the X server. Generally, if you are using a non-English keyboard, you may get better recognition of some of your special keys if you use XKB. Most users using a standard US English keyboard will probably find that they can disable XKB using this directive and everything will work fine.

    • XkbModel: This directive is used when XKB is enabled to specify the keyboard model.

    • XkbLayout: This directive is used when XKB is enabled to specify which keyboard layout to use.

    • XkbOptions: This directive can be used when XKB is enabled to swap the position of your CapsLock and Ctrl keys. To do this, set the directive to the value ctrl:swapcaps.

    • XkbKeymap: This directive is used when XKB is enabled to load a keyboard mapping definition.

Pointer

The Pointer section deals with mouse-related configuration. It is here that you set such information as the type of mouse you have, the port the mouse is connected to, and the behavior associated with different mouse buttons.

```
Section "Pointer"

    Protocol    "PS/2"
    Device      "/dev/psaux"

#   BaudRate    9600
```

```
#      SampleRate 150

       Emulate3Buttons
       Emulate3Timeout     50

#      ChordMiddle

EndSection
```

Let's take these entries line-by-line in Table 9.4:

TABLE 9.4: Pointer Directives

Directive	Effect
Protocol	This directive specifies the type of mouse you are using. Possible values include BusMouse for bus mice, PS/2 for PS/2-type mice, and a series of valid serial mice: GlidePoint, IntelliMouse, Logitech, Microsoft, MMHittab, MMSeries, MouseMan, MouseSystems, and ThinkingMouse. Generally, the two most common types on today's PCs are PS/2 and Microsoft (the standard driver for serial mice).
Device	This directive is used to specify which device port your mouse is connected to. For most Linux distributions, if you configured your mouse correctly when you installed your distribution, the device /dev/mouse will point to your mouse and you can use this. If /dev/mouse isn't configured to point to your mouse, specify /dev/psaux for the PS/2 mouse port, /dev/ttyS0 for COM1 in DOS and Windows, and /dev/ttyS1 for COM2 in DOS and Windows.
BaudRate	This directive is used for only a few Logitech-brand mice. Check your mouse's documentation.
SampleRate	This directive is used for only a few Logitech-brand mice. Check your mouse's documentation.
Emulate3Buttons	This directive should be used for two-button Microsoft-compatible mice. When uncommented, clicking the left and right mouse buttons at the same time will emulate the middle mouse button on a three-button mouse. Because X Windows relies on the presence of three mouse buttons, it is a good idea to enable this for a two-button Microsoft-protocol mouse.
Emulate3Timeout	This directive is used to specify how close in time the two mouse buttons must be clicked to be considered a simultaneous click; this value is only relevant when Emulate3Buttons is enabled. By default, the time is set to 50ms. If you find it hard to get the mouse buttons to click together, lengthen the time by assigning a higher value. This directive assumes the units are in milliseconds, and you should specify only the numeric value, not the units (in other words, Emulate3Timeout 100 is valid while Emulate3Timeout 100 ms is not).
ChordMiddle	This directive is used to enable the middle button on some three-button Logitech mice. If you have a Logitech mouse and your middle button is not working, try enabling this directive.

Monitor

So far, the configuration directives we have seen have mostly been self-explanatory and not difficult to use. When it comes to configuring video hardware such as monitors, things get more complicated. Let's consider the Monitor section from our sample configuration:

```
Section "Monitor"

Identifier  "monitor"
VendorName  "LG"
ModelName   "StudioWorks"

HorizSync   30-70
VertRefresh 50-160

# 640x400 @ 70 Hz, 31.5 kHz hsync
Modeline "640x400"    25.175 640  664  760  800   400  409  411  450
# 640x480 @ 60 Hz, 31.5 kHz hsync
Modeline "640x480"    25.175 640  664  760  800   480  491  493  525
# 800x600 @ 56 Hz, 35.15 kHz hsync
ModeLine "800x600"    36     800  824  896 1024   600  601  603  625
# 1024x768 @ 87 Hz interlaced, 35.5 kHz hsync
Modeline "1024x768"   44.9  1024 1048 1208 1264   768  776  784  817
Interlace

# 640x400 @ 85 Hz, 37.86 kHz hsync
Modeline "640x400"    31.5   640  672 736   832   400  401  404  445
-HSync +VSync
# 640x480 @ 72 Hz, 36.5 kHz hsync
Modeline "640x480"    31.5   640  680  720  864   480  488  491  521
# 640x480 @ 75 Hz, 37.50 kHz hsync
ModeLine  "640x480"   31.5   640  656  720  840   480  481  484  500
-HSync -VSync
# 800x600 @ 60 Hz, 37.8 kHz hsync
Modeline "800x600"    40     800  840  968 1056   600  601  605  628
+hsync +vsync

# 640x480 @ 85 Hz, 43.27 kHz hsync
Modeline "640x400"    36     640  696  752  832   480  481  484  509
-HSync -VSync
# 1152x864 @ 89 Hz interlaced, 44 kHz hsync
```

```
ModeLine "1152x864"     65     1152 1168 1384 1480    864  865  875  985
Interlace

# 800x600 @ 72 Hz, 48.0 kHz hsync
Modeline "800x600"      50      800  856  976 1040    600  637  643  666
+hsync +vsync
# 1024x768 @ 60 Hz, 48.4 kHz hsync
Modeline "1024x768"     65     1024 1032 1176 1344    768  771  777  806
-hsync -vsync

# 640x480 @ 100 Hz, 53.01 kHz hsync
Modeline "640x480"      45.8    640  672  768  864    480  488  494  530
-HSync -VSync
# 1152x864 @ 60 Hz, 53.5 kHz hsync
Modeline  "1152x864"    89.9   1152 1216 1472 1680    864  868  876  892
-HSync -VSync
# 800x600 @ 85 Hz, 55.84 kHz hsync
Modeline  "800x600"     60.75   800  864  928 1088    600  616  621  657
-HSync -VSync

# 1024x768 @ 70 Hz, 56.5 kHz hsync
Modeline "1024x768"     75     1024 1048 1184 1328    768  771  777  806
-hsync -vsync
# 1280x1024 @ 87 Hz interlaced, 51 kHz hsync
Modeline "1280x1024"    80     1280 1296 1512 1568   1024 1025 1037 1165
Interlace

EndSection
```

Table 9.5 discusses the various directives:

TABLE 9.5: Monitor Directives

Directive	Explanation
Identifier	This directive identifies with a user-assigned name the specifications for the monitor; this is used in other parts of **XF86Config** to refer to the monitor.
VendorName	This directive identifies the vendor of the monitor being defined. This value has no effect on the operation of XFree86, so it is best to assign a meaningful value that will help you identify the definition at a later date.
ModelName	This directive identifies the model of the monitor being defined. This value has no effect on the operation of XFree86, so it is best to assign a meaningful value that will help you identify the definition at a later date.

Continued on next page

TABLE 9.5 CONTINUED: Monitor Directives

Directive	Explanation
HorizSync	This directive specifies the horizontal sync range in kHz for your monitor. You may either specify a range as shown in the example or provide discrete values in a list with values separated by commas. It is essential that you consult your monitor's documentation and provide the correct values for your monitor. If you enter the incorrect values here, you have the potential to destroy or damage your monitor.
VertRefresh	This directive specifies the vertical refresh rates in Hz supported by your monitor. You may either specify a range as shown in the example or provide discrete values in a list with values separated by commas. It is essential that you consult your monitor's documentation and provide the correct values for your monitor. If you enter the incorrect values here, you have the potential to destroy or damage your monitor.
ModeLine	This directive specifies possible modes for your monitor. Modes combine a resolution with a refresh, a dot clock, and timings to determine how to display to the monitor. Any incompatible modes found in the XF86Config file are deleted by the X server when it tries to load them. However, getting the information correct for these lines is difficult at best. Generally, it is best to let your XFree86 configuration software create these lines for you and to not alter them.

Device

The XF86Config generally can contain multiple Device sections. Device sections describe video cards that can be used by the X server. Usually the server can fill in most of this information, but it is wise to provide it manually so that mistakes aren't made. Because this information includes some highly technical specifications about your video hardware, you should let your XFree86 configuration software handle this section unless you really need to make these changes yourself.

Let's look at an example Device section:

```
Section "Device"
     Identifier   "Generic VGA"
     VendorName   "Unknown"
     BoardName    "Unknown"
     Chipset      "generic"

#    VideoRam     256

#    Clocks       25.2 28.3

EndSection
```

In Table 9.6, we see the basic entries used in the Device section:

TABLE 9.6: Device Directives

Directive	Effect
Identifier	As in the Monitor section, this directive provides a name that can be used elsewhere in the XF86Config file to identify the video card.
VendorName	This directive doesn't affect the operation of the X server but helps you identify the hardware later.
BoardName	This directive also doesn't affect operation but is an aid in identifying the device definition.
Chipset	This directive identifies your video chipset. If XFree86 doesn't support your hardware, then the generic chipset will be used.
VideoRam	This directive specifies the amount of video memory available, in kilobytes. If you don't provide this information, the server will attempt to ascertain it directly from the video card.
Clocks	This directive specifies the clock settings for your video hardware. Don't edit this line by hand, but rather let your configuration software set it.
ClockChip	This directive specifies the clock chip being used by your video hardware, if it has one. If it does, there is no need to specify a Clocks line, since the clock chip will provide all the information.

Screen

The Screen section is used to bring together the information contained in your Monitor and Device sections. You can have multiple Screen sections.

The following is an example Screen section:

```
Section "Screen"
    Driver  "ACCEL"
    Device  "VideoCard"
    Monitor "monitor"
    Subsection "Display"
            Depth           24
            Modes           "1024x768"
            ViewPort        0 0
    EndSubsection
```

```
      Subsection "Display"
              Depth           32
              Modes           "800x600"
              ViewPort        0 0
      EndSubsection
   EndSection
```

The Screen section connects a chosen X server with a device and a monitor and then defines the accessible display modes (combinations of resolution and color depth). Table 9.7 shows the four main directives used in the Screen section:

TABLE 9.7: Screen Directives

Directive	Effect
Driver	This directive specifies one of four available drivers: SVGA, VGA2 (for generic VGA), MONO (for the monochrome X server), or ACCEL (for all the card-specific accelerated X servers).
Device	This directive specifies the name of a Device identifier.
Monitor	This directive specifies the name of a Monitor identifier.
DefaultColorDepth	This directive specifies the color depth used when a Depth in the Display section is not specified.

Display

In addition to these directives, a subsection called Display is also used in the Screen section. You can use multiple Display subsections to specify available video modes.

Let's analyze the first subsection from our example above:

```
   Subsection "Display"
        Depth           24
        Modes           "1024x768"
        ViewPort        0 0
   EndSubsection
```

We are specifying three directives, as shown in Table 9.8:

TABLE 9.8: Display Subsection Directives

Directive	Effect
Depth	This directive specifies the color depth of the display in the number of bits per pixel. For instance, 8-bit allows 256 colors, 16-bit allows 65,536, and 24-bit allows 16.7 million colors.
Modes	This directive specifies the resolution of the display. Common resolutions are 1024x768, 800x600, and 640x480.
ViewPort	This directive specifies the size of a possible virtual desktop. For instance, your 640×480 screen may be a window into a larger 1024×768 virtual display. As your mouse reaches the edge of the screen, the display will scroll until the edge of the virtual display. The ViewPort entry specifies the horizontal and vertical dimensions of the vertical desktop in pixels, but the values are separated by a space rather than an x. The entry here, ViewPort 0 0, indicates that there is no virtual desktop.

The X Windows Start-Up Sequence

In addition to configuring your XFree86 server to provide the optimal display quality, you may want to configure the way in which your X Windows environment starts up. The two main files that allow each user to control their X Windows start-up sequence are .xinitrc and .Xclients. Both of these files sit in the user's home directory. They override system default files, which in Red Hat Linux 5 are /etc/X11/xinit/xinitrc and /etc/X11/xinit/Xclients.

The *.xinitrc* File

Xinit is a special program that is used to start the X server and an initial client program, usually a window manager. By default, startx first checks for the existence of the .xinitrc file in the user's home directory and runs xinit based on this file. If the user's .xinitrc file is notfound, the systemwide xinitrc file (/etc/X11/xinit/xinitrc in Red Hat 5) is used by xinit. If neither of these is found, xinit will open a single xterm window after launching the X server.

The xinitrc or .xinitrc file is an executable shell script. We will learn about shells in Chapter 13, "Understanding the Shell." Accordingly, we won't go into the details of the shell or shell scripts here; rather, we will quickly look at the default xinitrc file from Red Hat Linux 5 to see what it does. (The lines are numbered to help make our discussion easier. The line numbers are not part of the actual file.)

```
1:  #!/bin/sh
2:  # $XConsortium: xinitrc.cpp,v 1.4 91/08/22 11:41:34 rws Exp $
3:
4:  /usr/bin/X11/xhost +
5:
6:  userresources=$HOME/.Xresources
7:  usermodmap=$HOME/.Xmodmap
8:  sysresources=/usr/X11R6/lib/X11/xinit/.Xresources
9:  sysmodmap=/usr/X11R6/lib/X11/xinit/.Xmodmap
10:
11: # merge in defaults and keymaps
12:
13: if [ -f $sysresources ]; then
14:     xrdb -merge $sysresources
15: fi
16:
17: if [ -f $sysmodmap ]; then
18:     xmodmap $sysmodmap
19: fi
20:
21: if [ -f $userresources ]; then
22:     xrdb -merge $userresources
23  fi
24:
25: if [ -f $usermodmap ]; then
26:     xmodmap $usermodmap
27: fi
28:
29: if [ -z "$BROWSER" ] ; then
30:         # we need to find a browser on this system
31:         BROWSER=`which netscape`
32:         if [ -z "$BROWSER" ] || [ ! -e "$BROWSER" ] ; then
```

```
33:          # not found yet
34:                  BROWSER=
35:          fi
36: fi
37: if [ -z "$BROWSER" ] ; then
38:          # we need to find a browser on this system
39:          BROWSER=`which lynx`
40:          if [ -z "$BROWSER" ] || [ ! -e "$BROWSER" ] ; then
41:          # not found yet
42:                  BROWSER=
43:          else
44:                  BROWSER="xterm -font 9x15 -e lynx"
45:          fi
46: fi
47: if [ -z "$BROWSER" ] ; then
48:          # we need to find a browser on this system
49:          BROWSER=`which arena`
50:          if [ -z "$BROWSER" ] || [ ! -e "$BROWSER" ] ; then
51:          # not found yet
52:                  BROWSER=
53:          fi
54: fi
55: export BROWSER
56:
57: # start some nice programs
58:
59: if [ -f $HOME/.Xclients ]; then
60:     exec $HOME/.Xclients
61: elif [ -f /etc/X11/xinit/Xclients ]; then
62:     exec /etc/X11/xinit/Xclients
63: else
64:          xclock -geometry 50x50-1+1 &
65:          xterm -geometry 80x50+494+51 &
66:          xterm -geometry 80x20+494-0 &
67:          if [ -f /usr/X11R6/bin/arena -a -f
/usr/doc/HTML/index.html ]; then
68:                  arena /usr/doc/HTML/index.html &
69:          fi
70:          if [ -f /usr/X11R6/bin/fvwm ]; then
71:                  exec fvwm
72:          else
```

```
73:              exec twm
74:          fi
75: fi
```

The following steps take place:

1. Line 4: Running xhost + allows clients owned by any user from any system on the network to launch windows to the X server.

2. Lines 6 to 9: The locations of files needed throughout the script are set.

3. Lines 13 to 15: If a global Xresources file exists, apply it (see the next section for a discussion of Xresources).

4. Lines 17 to 19: If a global key map file exists, apply the rules in the file.

5. Lines 21 to 23: If the user has an .Xresources file, apply it.

6. Lines 25 to 27: If the user has a keyboard map file, apply it.

7. Lines 29 to 36: These lines determine whether a Web browser exists on the system for later use in the script by checking for the existence of Netscape's browser.

8. Lines 37 to 46: If Netscape is not found, then check whether Lynx exists (this is another Unix Web browser discussed in Chapter 18, "Using the World Wide Web") and make it the default Web browser.

9. Lines 47 to 54: If Lynx also doesn't exist, check for the existence of the Arena Web browser and, if it exists, make that the default browser.

10. Lines 59 to 75: This is where we actually start running the first clients after the X server starts. First, the script checks whether the user has a .Xclients file. If this file exists, this is run to launch any clients specified in the file. If this file doesn't exist, then the script checks for the existence of the global Xclients file and, if it exists, runs it. Finally, if neither file exists, some default programs are launched, including xclock, two xterm windows, a Web browser, and, if available, either the fvwm or twm window manager.

Xclients

As you will have noticed in the discussion of the xinitrc file, the user can override the global Xclients file with a .Xclients file in their home directory. In either case, in the Red Hat environment xinit ends up calling one of these files to launch the initial clients after the X server has started.

Like xinitrc, this file is a shell script and follows all the pertinent rules for shell scripts. To understand the types of functions that Xclients can be used for, we will look at the default Xclients file that ships with Red Hat Linux 5 (line numbers have again been added):

```
1:  #!/bin/bash
2:
3:
####################################################################
######
4:  # -*- sh -*-
5:  #
6:  #
7:  #
8:  # ~/.Xclients: used by startx (xinit) to start up a window
manager and #
9:  # any other clients you always want to start an X session
with.         #
10:  #
11:  #
12:  # feel free to edit this file to suit your needs.
13:  #
14:
####################################################################
######
15:
16:  # these files are left sitting around by TheNextLevel.
17:  rm -f $HOME/Xrootenv.0
18:  rm -f /tmp/fvwmrc*
19:
20:  # first, find an M4-enabled config file (such as
21:  # the one from AnotherLevel) for fvwm2 or fvwm95.
22:  RCFILE=""
23:  for tryfile in "$HOME/.fvwm2rc.m4"
"/etc/X11/AnotherLevel/fvwm2rc.m4"; do
24:      if [ -f "$tryfile" ]; then
25:          RCFILE="$tryfile"
26:          break
27:      fi
28:  done

29:  # if it really exists, use it; if not, fvwm2 or fvwm95 will
30:  # automagically look for a config file in the regular
places.
```

```
31:  if [ -n "$RCFILE" ]; then
32:      FVWMOPTIONS="-cmd 'FvwmM4 -debug $RCFILE'"
33:  else
34:      FVWMOPTIONS=""
35:  fi
36:
37:  # TheNextLevel is supposed to work
38:  # with both fvwm95 and fvwm2
39:  # (try fvwm95 first, then fvwm2).
40:  for FVWMVER in 95 95-2 2; do
41:      if [ -n "$(type -path fvwm${FVWMVER})" ]; then
42:          env > "$HOME"/Xrootenv.0
43:          # if this works, we stop here
44:          eval "exec fvwm${FVWMVER} ${FVWMOPTIONS}" >
"$HOME"/.FVWM${FVWMVER}-errors 2>&1
45:      fi
46:  done
47:
48:  # gosh, neither fvwm95 nor fvwm2 is available;
49:  # let's try regular fvwm (AnotherLevel doesn't work with
fvwm1).
50:  if [ -n "$(type -path fvwm)" ]; then
51:      # if this works, we stop here
52:      exec fvwm
53:  fi
54:
55:  # wow, fvwm isn't here either ...
56:  # use twm as a last resort.
57:  xterm &
58:  exec twm
```

Let's break down the steps of this file as we did for xinitrc:

1. Lines 17 to 18: Perform some cleanup by removing temporary files that may have been left behind the last time X Windows was run.

2. Lines 22 to 35: Check to see if a configuration file for fvwm95 or fvwm2 exists. If it exists, arrange to use it; otherwise, leave the options for fvwm95 alone so that it searches for its own configuration file.

3. Lines 40 to 46: Launch fvwm95, fvwm95-2, or fvwm2 if any of them exist.

4. Lines 50 to 53: If none of these exist, try launching plain old fvwm.

5. Lines 57 to 58: If fvwm doesn't exist, then launch an xterm window and run the twm window manager.

If you want to add your own clients to be run every time X Windows is started, you can copy the global Xclients file to your own .Xclients file in your home directory (we deal with file copying in Chapter 11, "Working with Files") and then edit it. The key to this process is to add the commands for the programs you want to run before the sections where the different window managers might be launched. The reason for this is that the exec keyword used to launch the different window managers causes the script to stop running as soon as the window manager is launched.

For example, if we want xclock to launch whenever X Windows is launched, add the line:

```
xclock &
```

somewhere before line 40.

X Resources

The X resources database provides applications with preferences information that controls such attributes as colors and fonts, among others. X resources can be used by most X Windows applications to control almost every aspect of behavior that is controlled by command-line flags. With the X resources database, you can specify more suitable defaults than those that are standard for the application.

How X Resources Work

In order for this all to work, application-related information needs to be categorized so that only the appropriate applications are affected by X resource entries. This is done by grouping applications into classes. Most applications have their own classes; the documentation for the application specifies the class name. For example, xload belongs to the XLoad class and xterm belongs to the XTerm class. Where a number of similar applications exist, they often are part of the same class (oclock and xclock belong to the Clock class).

For each class, a standard set of resources allows you to specify such features as foreground and background colors (foreground and background), window size and placement (geometry), and default font (font). In addition, there are resource classes that group related resources. For instance, the Foreground class includes the foreground resource plus any additional foreground-related resources the application may have. Generally, though, you will not need to pay attention to individual resources and will only work with resource classes.

Setting X Resources with *.Xdefaults*

Setting X resources involves loading entries into the X resources database. These entries take the form:

```
<ApplicationClass>|<applicationName>*<ResourceClass>|<resourceName> :
<value>
```

In Linux man pages and other documentation, the vertical bar (or pipe character: |) is often used to represent "or." Therefore, in the example above, you can use either <ApplicationClass> or <applicationName> for the first entry, and <ResourceClass> or <resourceName> for the second entry.

These values are generally placed into the .Xdefaults file for user-specific resources. Let's look at a sample .Xdefaults file:

```
XTerm*background: Black
XTerm*foreground: Wheat
XTerm*cursorColor: Orchid
XTerm*reverseVideo: false
XTerm*scrollBar: true
XTerm*reverseWrap: true
XTerm*font: fixed
XTerm*fullCursor: true
XTerm*scrollTtyOutput: off
XTerm*scrollKey: on
XTerm*titleBar: false

xclock*Geometry: 100x100+100+100
xclock*Foreground: purple
xclock*Background: mauve
```

This .Xdefaults file sets X resources for both the XTerm class of applications and for the xclock application. For the XTerm class, we find resources setting the colors, the window properties (such as the presence of a scroll bar), and more. For xclock, we see color and geometry being set. The values being taken by these resources match the values that would have been provided to command-line flags such as -fg and -geometry where applicable.

Using *xrdb* to Load X Resources

Normally the .Xdefaults file is loaded when X Windows starts in the .xinitrc file. However, new values can be loaded into the database while X Windows is running by using the xrdb command. This is particularly useful for experimenting with values until you find just the combination you want.

In order to load the contents of .Xdefaults into the database, use the command

```
$ xrdb .Xdefaults
```

Where Do We Go from Here?

With this chapter, we wrapped up our focus on X Windows. We will now move on to an area that is essential to gaining complete mastery of Linux: the command-line environment.

In the next chapter, we will learn the basics of Linux commands. We will discuss how to work with files and directories on our disk drives. We will learn about the shell, which provides a powerful command-line environment in which to work, and we will learn how to use the Red Hat Control Panel to ease some of the more obscure aspects of Linux system configuration.

CHAPTER
TEN

Introducing Linux Commands

10

- What Is a Linux Command?

- Common Linux Commands

In this chapter, we start our exploration of the Unix command-line environment.

The command-line environment is where the heart, and power, of Linux lies. We have seen that X Windows provides quick and easy access to graphical applications that can make most users productive immediately. What is missing, though, is the ability to fully manipulate and work with your Linux system. This emerges when you begin to experiment with commands.

In this chapter, we will learn to use some of the more common commands such as `ls`, `find`, and `grep`. Since these commands are found in most distributions, Unix users should immediately know what these and similar commands can do and what power they can provide in the hands of a knowledgeable user.

NOTE   For this chapter, you need to be using a Linux command line. You can get a command line in two ways: when your system boots, log in to one of the Linux virtual consoles, or, from X Windows, launch an **xterm** window.

What Is a Linux Command?

Before looking at specific commands, we need to understand exactly what we mean when we use the term "command."

Users coming from the DOS environment are probably familiar with the concept of commands that encompass core features of the operating system, such as `DIR`, `COPY`, and `ATTRIB`. These commands provided the base on which more complicated actions could be built and from which sophisticated batch files could be written.

But in the DOS world, as in the world of many operating systems, the number of available commands is limited and generally static: users don't add new commands.

In the Unix world, and by extension in Linux, the concept is different. A command is any executable file. That is, a command consists of any file that is designed to be run (as opposed to files containing data or configuration information). This means that any executable file added to a system becomes a new command on the system.

Executing a Linux Command

From our discussions of launching X Windows applications, you probably already have a sense of how to execute a command. From the command prompt, simply type the name of a command:

$ *<command>*

or, if the command is not on your path, you type the complete path and name of the command, such as:

$ */usr/bin/<command>*

NOTE   The concept of paths needs a little bit of explanation. Every user, when they log in, has a default path. The default path is a list of directories separated by colons. If a command is typed without its path indicated, then all the directories in the default path are checked, in order, for the file associated with the command. Complete details of how to set your path can be found in Chapter 13, "Understanding the Shell," and a full discussion of directories and paths is offered in Chapter 11, "Working with Files."

TIP   To find out what your current path is, type the command **echo $PATH** at a command prompt and hit the Return key.

More complex ways of executing commands, including linking multiple commands together (called piping), are discussed in Chapter 13.

Common Linux Commands

The number of Linux commands that are available in a common Linux distribution like Red Hat 5 is quite large. But on a day-to-day basis, even an advanced user will take advantage of only a small selection of these commands.

This section presents some of the most frequently used Linux commands. These commands cover a range of tasks, from moving around your directories to finding out what is running on your system to finding that file you thought was lost. The commands we will look at are:

- su

- pwd, cd, and ls

- more and less

- find and grep

- tar and gzip

- man

Su

This command is one of the most basic, and is useful in many different tasks.

The su command is generally used to switch between different users. Consider an example: You are logged in as user1 and you need to switch to user2 to perform some work and then switch back to working as user1.

You could log out, log in as user2, do the work, log out again and then log back in as user1, but that seems a little bit time-consuming. Alternately, you could log in as user1 in one virtual console and as user2 in another and switch back and forth. The problem with this is that you need to work with, and switch between, different screens.

A third option is to use the su command. If we are logged in as user1 and want to become user2, we simply use

```
$ su user2
```

We will be prompted for user2's password:

```
$ su user2
password:
```

When we are finished working, we can use the Exit command to return to user1:

```
$ exit
```

Put together, a complete session should look like this:

```
[user1@localhost user1]$ su user2
Password:
```

```
[user2@localhost user1]$ exit
[user2@localhost user1]$ <some commands>
exit
[user1@localhost user1]$
```

A common use of the su command is to become the root user, or superuser.

If you issue the su command with no username, you will be prompted for the root password and, once this is provided, will be switched to working as the root user:

```
[user1@localhost user1]$ su
Password:
[root@localhost user1]#
```

If you are logged in as the root user, you can use su to become any user on the system without a password (hence the importance of keeping your root password safe from prying eyes). This is particularly useful for the system administrator who may need to become different users to debug problems but won't necessarily know other users' passwords. For example, note how using su to become user1 doesn't cause a prompt to display when the root user issues the command

```
[root@localhost /root]# su user1
[user1@localhost /root]$
```

The su command offers many other powerful features often used in advanced system administration tasks. You can learn about these from the su man page. See the section on the man command later in this chapter to learn how to read the su man page.

Pwd, Cd, and Ls

In the next chapter, "Working with Files," we will be taking a deeper look at the pwd, cd, and ls commands. Put together, these commands provide the basic tools you need to work with your directories and files.

The pwd command (which stands for present working directory) is the most basic of the three commands. By typing the command and hitting Return, you will be informed of which directory you are currently in:

```
$ pwd
/home/armand
```

In this case, the pwd command returns /home/armand as its answer. This tells us we are in the home directory of the user armand (that's me).

The cd command does more than simply look at the current state of things: it actually changes the state. The cd command allows you to change your current directory to any accessible directory on the system.

For instance, consider the example above where the current directory is /home/armand. Using the cd command, we could change to a subdirectory of my home directory called wordfiles:

```
$ cd wordfiles
$ pwd
/home/armand/wordfiles
```

Typing the pwd command after we change directories confirms that we ended up where we wanted to be.

Similarly, we could change to the system's temporary directory, /tmp, with the command

```
$ cd /tmp
$ pwd
/tmp
```

Finally, the ls command can be used to view the contents of the current directory. For instance, if I use the ls command to view the contents of my home directory, the result looks like this:

```
$ ls
2341ch11a.doc                   dead.letter
scmp-jpc.bak
DISKCOPY.COM                    foo
svgalib-1.2.11-4.i386.rpm
DRWEBDEM.IMG                    foo.html
test.txt
Xconfigurator-3.26-1.i386.rpm   mail
wabi
Xrootenv.0                      nsmail
xserver-wrapper-1.1-1.i386.rpm
armand                          scmp-jpc
```

Notice how the files or directory names are displayed in multiple columns and the width of the columns is determined by the width of the longest name.

In addition to listing the contents of the current directory, it is possible to list the contents of any accessible directory on the system. For instance, to list the contents of the directory /usr, you would use the command ls /usr:

```
$ ls /usr
```

```
X11            doc              i486-linuxaout   lib
sbin
X11R6          dt               ibase            libexec
share
X386           etc              include          local
spool
bin            games            info             man
src
dict           i486-linux-libc5 interbase        openwin
tmp
```

As mentioned above, notice how the number and width of columns in the listing is dependent on the length of the largest name being displayed.

Of course, you probably are wondering what use a list like this really is. There is no information to tell you which names indicate files and which indicate subdirectories, or what size the files are.

This information can be determined by using an extension of the ls command: ls -l. (To understand the command's structure, refer to the complete discussion of the ls command in the next chapter.) Used in my home directory, ls -l produces these results:

```
$ ls -l
total 1807
-rw-r--r--    1 armand    armand       52224 Apr 24 23:00 2341ch11a.doc
-rw-r--r--    1 armand    armand       24325 May  9 16:06 DISKCOPY.COM
-rw-r--r--    1 armand    armand     1474979 May  9 16:06 DRWEBDEM.IMG
-rw-r--r--    1 armand    armand       52313 Jan 21 18:04 Xconfigurator-
➥ 3.26-1.i386.rpm
-rw-r--r--    1 armand    armand         396 May 19 23:09 Xrootenv.0
drwx------    2 armand    armand        1024 May 17 09:55 armand
-rw-------    1 armand    armand       10572 May 18 22:29 dead.letter
-rw-------    1 armand    root          1455 Apr 24 21:38 foo
-rw-r--r--    1 armand    armand        2646 May  7 07:32 foo.html
drwx------    2 armand    armand        1024 Jun  4 07:12 mail
drwx------    2 armand    armand        1024 May 17 09:56 nsmail
-rw-r--r--    1 armand    armand        4288 May 14 22:17 scmp-jpc
-rw-r--r--    1 armand    armand        4289 May 14 22:12 scmp-jpc.bak
-rw-r--r--    1 armand    armand      195341 Mar 25 17:32 svgalib-1.2.11-
➥ 4.i386.rpm
-rw-rw-r--    1 armand    armand          94 May 17 11:44 test.txt
drwxr-xr-x    5 armand    armand        1024 May 19 23:07 wabi
-rw-r--r--    1 armand    armand        4493 Feb  4 15:31 xserver-wrapper-
➥ 1.1-1.i386.rpm
```

Note that each file contains reference information. The most important pieces of information are to the immediate left of each name: the date of last modification of the file or directory and, in the case of files, the size of the file in bytes to the left of the date (so, for instance, a 1024 byte file is a 1KB file).

At the far left of each line, you will also notice that directories are indicated by the letter d while files are generally indicated with a simple dash (-). For instance, scmp-jpc is a file:

```
-rw-r-r-    1 armand    armand        4288 May 14 22:17 scmp-jpc
```

while mail is a directory:

```
drwx----    2 armand    armand        1024 Jun  4 07:12 mail
```

More and *Less*

The more and less commands are closely related and provide similar functionality, and the great irony is that less provides more capabilities than more.

The basic purpose of both commands is to display long files or lists of text one screen or window at a time, allowing users to page down through the text and, in some cases, move back up through the text. Both also provide capabilities to search the text being displayed.

This is useful in many instances, including to quickly look at a long text file without having to open it in an editor like xedit (see Chapter 8, "Using X Windows Applications") and to view particularly long directory listings.

More

Let's start with the more command. The more command is fairly basic, allowing users to move forward a line or a screen at a time through a large body of text as well as search that text.

For instance, if you have a large text file called textfile, you could view it a page at a time with the command

```
$ more textfile
```

After hitting Return, you will see the first screen of the file with the text –More– displayed on the last line of the screen. Hitting the space bar will jump forward a full screen length, while hitting the Return key will move forward one line at a time. When you reach the end of the body of text, you will be returned to the command prompt.

To search forward through the file, hit the slash (/) key followed by the word or phrase you want to search for and then hit Return. The display will jump forward to the first occurrence of the word or phrase being searched for and will display the occurrence near the top of the screen. You can repeat the same search by hitting the n key after the first search, avoiding the need to type the same word or phrase repeatedly.

In addition to using more to view the contents of a file, you can pass along the results of another command to more using piping (a technique discussed in detail in Chapter 13, "Understanding the Shell").

For instance, on my system, using ls -l to view the contents of the /tmp directory produces results 237 lines long—many more lines than my largest xterm window can display. In order to be able to view the results of my ls -l command a window at a time, I need to pass the results to more:

```
$ ls -l /tmp | more
```

Here we connect the ls -l command to the more command with a vertical pipe (usually Shift+\ on most English-language keyboards). The use of the pipe is the source of the term "piping." The result of this piping is that more is used to display the results of the ls -l command, which means we can move down a screen or line at a time or search the results, just as we did earlier with the contents of a file.

NOTE   Complete directions for using more are found in the more man page. We discuss how to use a man page later in this chapter in the section on the **man** command.

Less

For all intents and purposes, the less command is a vastly improved version of the more command. In addition to the basic functions described above (moving forward a screen or line at a time and searching), the following are some of the other actions that can be performed on a body of text:

- jumping directly to a line

- jumping directly to the beginning or end of the file

- moving backwards through a file

- searching backwards through a file

To jump directly to a line in a file, type the line number followed by the letter **g**. If you don't specify a line number and simply hit the g key, you will be jumped to the first line in the file. Using the uppercase G works in much the same way except that without a line number specified, G jumps you to the last line of the body of text.

It is easy to move backwards through a file using less. The up arrow moves up one line of text at a time and the down arrow moves down one line at a time. You can use Control+B to jump backwards one screen at a time.

Finally, a slash (/) followed by a word or phrase and the Return key will search forward through the text being displayed, and a question mark (?) followed by a word or phrase and the Return key will search backwards through the text.

As with the more command, you can look at the less man page for details on all the features of the command. We learn to use man pages later in this chapter in the section on the man command.

Find and Grep

The find and grep commands are powerful tools for searching for files. We will look only at their most basic uses in this section because it would be easy to devote a full chapter to using these commands. If you want a full discussion of the commands, check their man pages once we learn to use the man command later in this chapter.

While both commands are used for searching, their purposes differ: find is used to search for files by any number of criteria, including name or date of creation. Grep is used to search the contents of files.

Find

If you used computers prior to buying this book, then you have probably faced the situation where you know you have created a file but can't remember where you put it. The find command is the Unix answer to this dilemma.

The command can be used to search for files by name, date of creation or modification, owner (usually the user who created the file), size of the file, and even type of the file. Here we will look at the most frequent use: searching for files by name.

The basic structure of the find command is

```
$ find <starting-directory> <parameters> <actions>
```

The starting directory specifies where to begin searching. For instance, specifying /home means only subdirectories of /home will be searched (in other words, only the user's home directories will be searched), while specifying / means everything will be searched.

The parameters are where you specify the criteria by which to search. In our case, we use `-name filename` to specify the file we are searching for.

The actions section indicates what action to take on found files. Generally, you will want to use the `-print` action, which indicates that the full name and path of the file should be displayed. Without this, the `find` command will perform the search indicated but will not display the results, which defeats the purpose.

Putting this together, if you want to search for all files named `foo` on your system, you could use the command

```
$ find / -name foo -print
```

In my case, the results look like this:

```
$ find / -name foo -print
/tmp/foo
/home/armand/foo
/home/tdanesh/foo
```

TIP

You will notice that we attempted to search the entire system in the previous command. To do this effectively, you will need to log in as the root user so that you can access all the directories on the system. If you don't, you will get `permission denied` errors every time `find` tries to search a directory for which you don't have permission.

It is also possible to search for partial filenames. For instance, if you know that the file you are looking for begins with `fo` , then you can use the expression `fo*` to indicate all files beginning with `fo` and ending with any combination:

```
$ find / -name 'fo*' -print
/tmp/foo
/var/lib/texmf/fonts
/usr/bin/font2c
/usr/bin/mh/folders
/usr/bin/mh/folder
/usr/bin/mh/forw
/usr/bin/formail
```

```
/usr/bin/fontexport
/usr/bin/fontimport
/usr/bin/fold
etc.
```

Notice the use of the single quotation marks around fo*. When you use the * character, it is important to place the single quote marks around the entire expression. Otherwise, find will give you an error:

```
$ find / -name fo* -print -mount
find: paths must precede expression
Usage: find [path...] [expression]
```

If the results being produced by the find command are too numerous to fit in one screen, you can use piping and the more command just like we did earlier with the ls -l command:

```
$ find / -name 'fo*' -print | more
```

Grep

Where find searched for a file by its name, type, or date, grep is used to look inside the contents of one or more files in an attempt to find the occurrence of a specific pattern of text inside the files.

Consider an example: You know that you created a text file that contains the word "radio" and stored it in your home directory. However, you have forgotten the name of the file and want to quickly check which files contain "radio." This is where grep comes in handy.

Assuming you are in your home directory, the following command will search for "radio" and produce results like the ones shown:

```
$ grep radio *
ab.txt:This is a test of searching for the word radio.
pop.txt:On another radio station, he found that
```

Notice how the grep command returns one line for each occurrence of the word "radio" in a file. The name of the file is shown followed by a colon, which is followed by the complete text of the line where the word has appeared.

In general, the pattern for the grep command is

```
$ grep <text-pattern> <file-list>
```

The text pattern can be a simple word or phrase or a more complicated regular expression. (The use of regular expressions—a powerful method for searching for text patterns—with grep can be found in the grep man page.) The file list can take any form allowed by the shell. Consult Chapter 13, "Understanding the Shell," for a complete discussion of the types of expressions that constitute a file list.

Generally, though, you will either want to check the contents of a single file, which takes the form

```
$ grep <text-pattern> <file-name>
```

or the contents of all files in a directory:

```
$ grep <text-pattern> *
```

where the * is an expression indicating that all files in the current directory should be searched.

In its simplest form, the text pattern is a single word or part of a word containing no spaces. If you want to search for a phrase, such as "is a test," you need to enclose the text pattern in quotation marks:

```
$ grep "is a test" *
ab.txt:This is a test of searching for the word radio.
```

Just as it is sometimes useful to pipe the results of a command through the more or less commands, the same is true for grep. Consider the situation where you want a listing of all files in the current directory with the modification date of May 12. You could find this information by piping ls -l through a grep command:

```
$ ls -l | grep "May 12"
-rw-r-r-  1 root     root        19197 May 12 21:17 rfbprotoheader.pdf
-rw-r-r-  1 root     root       110778 May 12 21:20 rfprotoA.zip
-rw-r-r-  1 root     root        17692 May 12 23:03 svnc-0.1.tar.gz
-rw-r-r-  1 root     root        25222 May 12 19:58 vnc-
➡ 3.3.1_javasrc.tgz
drwxr-xr-x 2 root    root         1024 May 12 21:49 vncjava
```

Tar and *Gzip*

Most users of other operating systems, including Windows 95 and the Mac OS, are familiar with the concept of compressed archives. A compressed archive is a single file that contains one or more files in a compressed form.

Compressed archives are often used to distribute software on the Internet, as is the case with the ZIP files common on the Internet. While Linux provides the unzip command to access the contents of ZIP archives, in the Unix world tar archives are generally used to distribute software. These archives are then compressed using the gzip compression program, which compresses individual files.

Tar

The `tar` program was originally used to create system backups on tapes (or tape archives, hence "tar"). In its current form, it is widely used for creating archives of files for distribution.

Creation of a `tar` archive is easy:

```
$ tar cvf tar-<file-name> <file-list>
```

This command will create a new archive specified by the filename `tar-file-name` (generally, `tar` files have a `.tar` extension) and then store all the files from the file list in this archive. The file list can follow any valid expression as outlined in Chapter 13, "Understanding the Shell." It is important to remember that this process copies the files into the archive so there is no danger that the original files will be deleted in the process.

You will notice that the `tar` command is immediately followed by a series of options, in this case `cvf`. Each of these options is used to control different aspects of the behavior of the `tar` command. C indicates that we are creating an archive (as opposed to viewing an existing archive or extracting files from the archive), v indicates that the command should be run in verbose mode (which means that each filename will be displayed as it is copied into the archive), and f means we are archiving to a file (as opposed to a tape drive).

For instance, if we wanted to archive all the `.txt` files in the current directory into an archive called `text.tar`, we would use the following command:

```
$ tar cvf text.tar *.txt
ab.txt
pop.txt
```

Notice how the filenames are listed as they are copied to the archive.

Sometimes you will want to copy the entire contents of a directory into an archive. Luckily, `tar` will copy all files and subdirectories in a directory into an archive if the directory is part of the file list. So, if we have a directory called vnc and we want the entire contents of that directory to be copied to a new archive called `vnc.tar`, we could use

```
$ tar cvf vnc.tar vnc
```

and get the following results:

```
$ tar cvf vnc.tar vnc
vnc/
```

```
vnc/LICENCE.TXT
vnc/README
vnc/README.vncserver
vnc/Xvnc
vnc/classes/
vnc/classes/DesCipher.class
vnc/classes/animatedMemoryImageSource.class
vnc/classes/authenticationPanel.class
vnc/classes/clipboardFrame.class
vnc/classes/optionsFrame.class
vnc/classes/rfbProto.class
vnc/classes/vncCanvas.class
vnc/classes/vncviewer.class
vnc/classes/vncviewer.jar
vnc/vncpasswd
vnc/vncserver
vnc/vncviewer
```

You will notice that the first line indicates the creation of the vnc directory in the archive and then the copying of the files in that directory into the archive.

If we have an existing archive, we will generally want to either view a listing of the contents of a file or extract the contents of a file.

To view the contents of an archive, we replace the c option with a t. So, to view the list of files in the vnc.tar archive we just created, we could use

```
$ tar tvf vnc.tar
drwxr-xr-x root/root           0 1998-05-16 23:55 vnc/
-rw-r--r-- root/root       18000 1998-01-23 16:52 vnc/LICENCE.TXT
-rw-r--r-- root/root        6142 1998-01-23 16:53 vnc/README
-r--r--r-- root/root         601 1998-01-23 16:28 vnc/README.vncserver
-r-xr-xr-x root/root     1286834 1998-01-23 13:00 vnc/Xvnc
drwxr-sr-x root/root           0 1998-01-23 16:24 vnc/classes/
-r--r--r-- root/root        7143 1998-01-23 16:24
vnc/classes/DesCipher.class
-r--r--r-- root/root        1329 1998-01-23 16:24 vnc/classes/animated-
MemoryImageSource.class
-r--r--r-- root/root        2068 1998-01-23 16:24 vnc/classes/authentica-
tionPanel.class
-r--r--r-- root/root        1761 1998-01-23 16:24 vnc/classes/clipboard-
Frame.class
-r--r--r-- root/root        3210 1998-01-23 16:24 vnc/classes/options-
Frame.class
-r--r--r-- root/root        8309 1998-01-23 16:24
vnc/classes/rfbProto.class
```

```
-r--r--r-- root/root        7092 1998-01-23 16:24
vnc/classes/vncCanvas.class
-r--r--r-- root/root        7100 1998-01-23 16:24
vnc/classes/vncviewer.class
-r--r--r-- root/root       20564 1998-01-23 16:24
vnc/classes/vncviewer.jar
-r-xr-xr-x root/root       11433 1998-01-23 13:00 vnc/vncpasswd
-r-xr-xr-x root/root       10795 1998-05-17 00:17 vnc/vncserver
-r-xr-xr-x root/root       49685 1998-01-23 13:00 vnc/vncviewer
```

Notice how the listing of files is in a complete form, similar to the way in which
ls -l lists the contents of a directory.

To extract the contents of an archive into the current directory, we replace the c
or t with an x:

```
$ tar xvf vnc.tar
vnc/
vnc/LICENCE.TXT
vnc/README
vnc/README.vncserver
vnc/Xvnc
vnc/classes/
vnc/classes/DesCipher.class
vnc/classes/animatedMemoryImageSource.class
vnc/classes/authenticationPanel.class
vnc/classes/clipboardFrame.class
vnc/classes/optionsFrame.class
vnc/classes/rfbProto.class
vnc/classes/vncCanvas.class
vnc/classes/vncviewer.class
vnc/classes/vncviewer.jar
vnc/vncpasswd
vnc/vncserver
vnc/vncviewer
```

Gzip

While tar is useful for archiving files, it doesn't perform any compression in
the examples above. Compression in Linux is generally achieved with the gzip
command.

Unlike Windows ZIP archives, which compress many files into a single compressed archive, gzip simply compresses individual files without compressing them into an archive.

For instance, if we have a particularly large file called test.pdf that we won't use for some time and we want to compress it to save disk space, we use the gzip command:

```
$ gzip test.pdf
```

This will compress the file and add a .gz extension to the end of the filename, changing the name to test.pdf.gz.

Before compression, ls -l shows us the file size is 110,778 bytes:

```
-rw-r--r--   1 root      root          110778 Jun  5 16:54 test.pdf
```

After compression, the size has dropped to 83,729 bytes:

```
-rw-r--r--   1 root      root           83729 Jun  5 16:54 test.pdf.gz
```

As with most commands we have seen in this chapter, you can use any valid shell file expression to list more than one file. For instance,

```
$ gzip *
```

compresses all files in the current directory (but not those in subdirectories).

Uncompressing *gzip* Files To uncompress a gzip file, you can use the gzip command with the -d option:

```
$ gzip -d test.pdf.gz
```

This will uncompress the file and remove the .gz extension, returning the file to its original uncompressed state with the name test.pdf.

An alternative command, gunzip, eliminates the need to use the -d option:

```
$ gunzip test.pdf.gz
```

Combining *gzip* and *tar* Because early versions of the tar command did not compress archives, this was typically done using gzip. For instance,

```
$ tar cvf text.tar *.txt
ab.txt
pop.txt
$ gzip text.tar
```

produces a compressed archive called text.tar.gz.

To access the contents of this archive, uncompress the archive and then use `tar`:

```
$ gunzip text.tar.gz
$ tar tvf text.tar
-rw-r-r- root/root          48 1998-06-05 16:13 ab.txt
-rw-r-r- root/root           6 1998-06-05 16:13 pop.txt
```

Recent versions of `tar`, including those shipped with all current distributions, provide a method for directly accessing and creating `gzip`-compressed `tar` archives.

By simply adding a z option to any of the `tar` commands discussed earlier, we can create a compressed archive without the need for a second command.

For instance,

```
$ tar czvf vnc.tar.gz vnc
vnc/
vnc/LICENCE.TXT
vnc/README
vnc/README.vncserver
vnc/Xvnc
vnc/classes/
vnc/classes/DesCipher.class
vnc/classes/animatedMemoryImageSource.class
vnc/classes/authenticationPanel.class
vnc/classes/clipboardFrame.class
vnc/classes/optionsFrame.class
vnc/classes/rfbProto.class
vnc/classes/vncCanvas.class
vnc/classes/vncviewer.class
vnc/classes/vncviewer.jar
vnc/vncpasswd
vnc/vncserver
vnc/vncviewer
```

creates a compressed version of the `vnc.tar` archive,

```
$ tar tzvf text.tar.gz
-rw-r-r- root/root          48 1998-06-05 16:13 ab.txt
-rw-r-r- root/root           6 1998-06-05 16:13 pop.txt
```

displays the contents of our compressed `text.tar.gz` archive, and

```
$ tar xzvf text.tar.gz
ab.txt
pop.txt
```

extracts the contents of the archive.

NOTE Full details of the `tar` and `gzip` commands and their options can be found in the man pages for the commands.

Man

Throughout this chapter, you have seen references to man pages. These are manual pages that are provided in a standard format with most Linux software. Almost all the commands that ship with the Red Hat Linux 5 distribution include man pages.

Using the man command in its most basic form, you can read any existing man page:

```
$ man <command-name>
```

This will display the man page for the specified command and allow you to scroll through it and search it the same way as when you are using the less command to display text.

If the specified man page cannot be found, you will get an error:

```
$ man <non-existent-man-page>
No manual entry for non-existent-man-page
```

Xman

Since we already are familiar with X Windows, you have an alternative to using the man command to view man pages: the xman program.

To launch xman, use

```
$ xman &
```

or

```
$ /usr/bin/X11/xman &
```

This will display the initial xman window like the one in Figure 10.1.

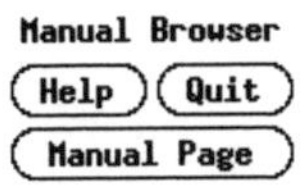

FIGURE 10.1.

The initial xman window

From here you can press the Manual Page button to display the main xman window, shown in Figure 10.2.

The main area of the window is used to display the text of the currently selected man page. Initially xman's help file is displayed. The window has two menus: Options and Sections.

The Options menu, shown in Figure 10.3, allows you to switch between listings of man pages (Display Directory) and the contents of the current man page (Display Manual Page) in addition to searching the contents of the current man page. The Help option displays the complete help file for xman, which provides detailed instructions on using xman.

FIGURE 10.2.

The main xman window

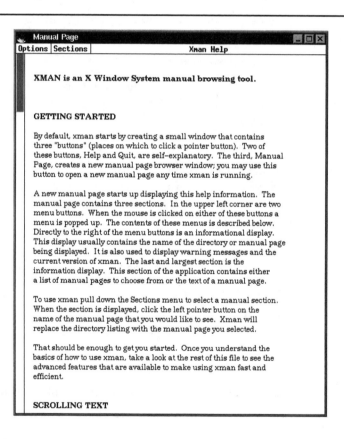

FIGURE 10.3:

The Options menu

Xman Options

Display Directory
Display Manual Page
Help
Search
Show Both Screens
Remove This Manpage
Open New Manpage
Show Version
Quit

We are more interested in the Sections menu, shown in Figure 10.4, since this is where you begin the process of finding the man page you want to read.

FIGURE 10.4:

The Sections menu

Xman Sections

(1) User Commands
(2) System Calls
(3) Subroutines
(4) Devices
(5) File Formats
(6) Games
(7) Miscellaneous
(8) Sys. Administration
(l) Local
(n) New

As you can see, the manual pages are divided into eight main categories, including user commands, system calls, and so on. Choosing one of these sections brings up a directory listing for the section like the one shown in Figure 10.5.

By double-clicking any of the command names, you can read the man page for that command.

FIGURE 10.5:

A directory listing

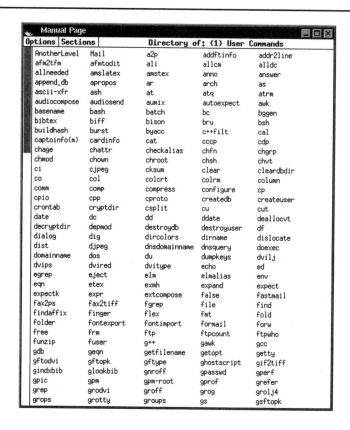

Where Do We Go from Here?

In this chapter, we've taken our first big step toward becoming real Linux users by delving into the world of the command line.

Until now we have focused on X Windows and its capabilities, but the real heart of any Unix-like operating system lies in the command line.

In the next chapter, we will learn about the powerful commands provided by Linux for working with files and directories. We will build on the commands (such as ls) discussed in this chapter and explore creating directories and other advanced tasks.

Later, in Chapter 12, we will take a close look at the Control Panel, a powerful tool for configuring your Red Hat Linux 5 system.

CHAPTER

ELEVEN

11

Working with Files

- Copying and Deleting Files

- Moving and Renaming Files

- Creating Files and Symbolic Links

- A Quick Introduction to Filename Expansion

In the last chapter, we got a glimpse of what's involved in using Linux. We saw how all commands are actually separate programs stored in separate files. We even began to learn how to manipulate files by seeing the various ways that the ls command can be used to display lists of files.

In this chapter, we are going to take a detailed look at the commands used to further manipulate files and directories, including copying, deleting, moving, renaming, and creating. We will wrap up with a quick look at filename expansion—that is, wildcards like the commonly used asterisks in DOS and Windows.

Copying and Deleting Files

Probably the two most common file manipulation tasks are copying and moving files. We regularly find ourselves replicating files all over our disk drives or copying files to floppy disks, the latter for backup purposes or to "transmit" files using the cheapest of all networking methods: our feet. Similarly, the average PC user at some point or another will run short of disk space and will strike out in search of files to delete to free up precious disk space and avoid investing in a new hard drive.

Copying Files

Anyone with even brief experience using DOS or the DOS prompt in Windows and Windows 95 is probably aware that clicking, dragging, and dropping is not the only way to copy files. In fact, DOS's copy command offers additional features, such as wildcards, that can make it quicker, easier, and more powerful to use than File Manager or the Windows 95 Explorer.

Similarly, in the Linux world, the cp command (normally found at /bin/cp) is used for copying and provides a powerful tool for copy operations.

Basic Copying

Obviously, the most basic uses of the cp command are to copy a file from one place to another or to make a duplicate file in the same directory. For instance, if I want to copy a file (ThisFile)in the current directory to a second file (to be called ThisFile-Acopy) in the same directory, I would use

```
$ cp ThisFile ThisFile-Acopy
```

Using `ls -l` to look at a directory listing of the files, I would find two files with identical sizes but different date stamps. The new file has a date stamp indicating when the copy operation took place: it is a new, separate file. Changes to `ThisFile-Acopy` will not affect the original `ThisFile` file.

Similarly, to make a copy of `ThisFile` in the `/tmp` directory (perhaps to share the file with another user), we can use

```
$ cp ThisFile /tmp
```

and if we want to copy `ThisFile` to `/tmp` but give the new file a different name, we can use

```
$ cp ThisFile /tmp/NewFileName
```

Don't Overwrite That File

The scary thing about most Linux distributions is that it is easy to accidentally overwrite a file by copying over an existing file. Consider the situation where `ThisFile` and `NewFile` both exist and we issue the command

```
$ cp ThisFile NewFile
```

In this case, the contents of NewFile would be overwritten by a copy of ThisFile and be lost forever (unless you are disciplined about backing up your system).

To avoid this difficulty, you can use the `-i` flag of the cp command, which forces the system to confirm any file it will overwrite when copying. Then, we would get a prompt like this when attempting to copy:

```
$ cp -i ThisFile NewFile
cp: overwrite `ThisFile'?
```

If you want to protect yourself, you can create an alias for the cp command. By issuing the command

```
$ alias cp=`cp -i'
```

we are defining an alias so that any time we issue the cp command, we are in fact issuing the command cp -i. In this way we will always be prompted before overwriting a file while copying. As we will learn later in Chapter 13, we can configure our Bash shell using the .bashrc file to ensure that every time we log in this alias is set. (The shell controls the command-line environment in which we work, but more about that later.)

Continued on next page

Luckily, with most Linux distributions this alias is set by default when you log in as the superuser, or root. This is especially important because making a small mistake as the root user can have drastic consequences for the whole system. Using this default can help prevent major disasters.

Copying Multiple Files in One Command

One of the drawbacks of the DOS `copy` command is that it could only copy one file or file expression at a time. For instance, we could use `copy file \temp` to copy a single file to `\temp`, or `copy *.txt \temp` to copy all text files in the current directory to `\temp`. But if there were three separate files we wanted to copy, we would need to use three commands; if we wanted to copy all text files and all executable files in the current directory, we would similarly need to use two commands.

The Linux `cp` command, however, makes this process a bit easier. The command can take more than the two arguments in the DOS version of the command. Instead, we can pass multiple arguments to the command and the last argument will be treated as the destination and all preceding files will be copied to the destination.

Let's look at an example. Suppose we want to copy the files `FileOne`, `FileTwo`, and `FileThree` in the current directory to `/tmp`. Obviously, we could issue three commands:

```
$ cp FileOne /tmp
$ cp FileTwo /tmp
$ cp FileThree /tmp
```

However, we can bundle this all together into one command, making the process easier:

```
$ cp FileOne FileTwo FileThree /tmp
```

Similarly, we can add wildcards to the mix and copy large numbers of files in one command. For instance,

```
$ cp *.txt *.doc *.bak /tmp
```

will copy all files with any one of three extensions in one command.

NOTE   When copying multiple files in this way, it is important to remember that the last argument must be a directory, since it is impossible to copy two or more files into a single file. If you forget to make the last argument a directory, then you will get an error message like this one:

```
cp: when copying multiple files, last argument must be a direc-
tory. Try `cp –help' for more information.
```

If we want to copy an entire directory and all its subdirectories, we can use the -R flag of the cp command. This command indicates that we want to recursively copy a directory. If a subdirectory called SomeDir exists in the current directory and we want to copy SomeDir in its entirety to a subdirectory in /tmp, then we could use the command

```
$ cp -R SomeDir /tmp
```

to create a directory /tmp/SomeDir as a copy of the SomeDir subdirectory in the current directory.

Advanced Copying

The cp command offers several advanced features that extend it beyond simple copying of files and directories. These capabilities include preserving the state of original files in their copies and alternate methods to protect existing files while copying.

Making Copies as Close to the Originals as Possible   If you take a close look at the copies you make, you will notice that certain aspects of the copied files bear little resemblance to the original files. These aspects include the file ownerships, permissions, date stamps, and symbolic links. Let's consider these one by one.

When you copy a file, the resulting file normally is owned by the copier as opposed to the creator of the original file. Let's say that user1 has created a file called TheFile and put it in /tmp for user2 to copy to their home directory. If we look at the file listing, the file would look something like this:

```
-rw-r-r-   1 user1    users      16992 Apr  5 12:10 TheFile
```

After user2 copies the file with

```
$ cp /tmp/TheFile ~/NewFile
```

the resulting file will have a new ownership, that of the copier (user2):

```
-rw-rw-r-   1 user2    users        16992 Apr  5 13:10 NewFile
```

Similarly, when a file is created in a directory, it has a set of default permissions assigned to it. When copying a file, the copy will have the permissions set to the default for the destination directory rather than retaining the permissions of the original file. Notice in the example above the change in permission between the original file and the new copy. The original file was only group readable but the copy is also group writable. A change has also occurred to the date of the copy, reflecting the date and time when the copy was made instead of the date stamp of the original file.

There are times, however, when you will want to retain the original owner, date, and permissions of files when they are copied. Let's say, for example, that the root account is being used to copy a set of files to a removable hard disk for storage in a vault. Unlike a regular tape backup, which would require other tools, this type of backup could be done with the cp command. However, it is important that a backup like this matches the original as closely as possible. Luckily, the cp command provides the -p flag, which preserves these attributes. Using the above example, if the command used was

```
$ cp -p /tmp/TheFile ~
```

then the resulting file would match the original quite closely:

```
-rw-r-r-   1 user1    users        16992 Apr  5 12:10 TheFile
```

Another sticky problem in copying files is how to handle symbolic links. As we learned in the last chapter, a symbolic link provides a pointer to a file from another location. In this way, you can pretend that a file is in more than one place at once. If you try to access the link, Linux actually accesses the file that the link points to.

Normally, when you copy a symbolic link the resulting file is a copy of the file pointed to by the link instead of a new link to the same file. For instance, if TheFile had been a symbolic link as in this example

```
lrwxrwxrwx   1 user1    users        16992 Apr  5 12:10 TheFile ->
➡ OtherFile
-rw-r-r-   1 user1    users            1 Apr  5 11:10 OtherFile
```

then issuing the copy command

```
$ cp /tmp/TheFile ~/NewFile
```

will result in a file that is a copy of `OtherFile`:

```
-rw-rw-r-   1 user2    users         16992 Apr  5 13:10 NewFile
```

But what if we want to copy the link instead of the file itself? What if we want the result to look like this:

```
lrwxrwxrwx   1 user2    users             2 Apr  5 13:10 NewFile ->
➥ /tmp/OtherFile
```

Well, once again the `cp` command has a flag to address the situation: the -d flag, which indicates not to dereference the symbolic link. We could simply use the command

```
$ cp -d /tmp/TheFile ~/NewFile
```

to get the desired result.

Having said all this, it is time to put it all together. What if we want to use the `cp` command to create a useful backup copy of an existing directory and all its subdirectories? Using the combination of these two flags and a recursive copy, we can do this. For instance,

```
$ cp -pdR TheDirectory /backups
```

would create an exact copy of `TheDirectory` in the directory /backups/The Directory. But the `cp` command provides a simplified way to achieve this: the -a flag, which indicates that we want an archive of a directory. It is a quick way to indicate the three flags -pdR:

```
$ cp -a TheDirectory /backups
```

Preventing Mistakes   As we saw earlier, one way to prevent mistakes is to use the -i flag, which forces interactive prompting before overwriting occurs in the course of copying files or directories. Other methods are available to provide different degrees of protection.

One method is to use the -b flag to cause the `cp` command to create a backup copy of any file about to be overwritten. By default the backup will be the original filename with a tilde after it. So, if we copy `FileOne` to `FileTwo` using the command

```
$ cp -b FileOne FileTwo
```

and `FileTwo` already exists, then a backup will be made of the original `FileTwo` called `FileTwo~`.

It is possible to alter the way in which the `cp` command names the backup files by using two different flags: `-S` and `-V`. The `-S` flag allows you to change the character used in backup names from the default tilde to something else. For instance,

```
$ cp -b -S _ FileOne FileTwo
```

would result in a backup filename `FileTwo_`.

The `-V` flag provides even more flexibility, allowing the user to specify one of three types of backup naming schemes:

- `t` or `numbered`: Create sequentially numbered backups. If an existing numbered backup file exists, then the new backup file created will be numbered sequentially after the existing backup file; the resulting filenames look like `FileName.~Number~` (`FileName.~2~` or `FileName.~11~`, for example).

- `nil` or `existing`: If a numbered backup file already exists, then create a numbered backup; otherwise, create a regular simple backup file.

- `never` or `simple`: Create a simple backup file using the default tilde or alternative character indicated by the `-S` flag.

For instance, to create a numbered backup in the example above, we would use the command

```
$ cp -b -V t FileOne FileTwo
```

or

```
$ cp -b -V numbered FileOne FileTwo
```

Similarly, both these commands create simple backup files:

```
$ cp -b -V never FileOne FileTwo
```

and

```
$ cp -b -V simple FileOne FileTwo
```

Alternative Flags

You may have noticed that we have covered a lot of flags for the `cp` command. Sometimes it is difficult to remember the flags. Fortunately, there are long forms for most of these flags that may make them easier to remember:

Short Form	Alternate Long Form
-i	—interactive
-R	—recursive
-p	—preserve
-d	—no-dereference
-a	—archive
-b	—backup
-S	—suffix
-V	—version-control

While the long forms may seem more intuitive at first, ultimately any regular Linux user will use the short forms. The long forms involve too much typing for frequent use. For instance, consider a complex copy command:

```
$ cp -i -b -V simple -S _ -R ThisDir /tmp
```

What would happen if we used the long form of these flags? We would end up with the following command:

```
$ cp —interactive —backup —version-control simple —suffix _ —recursive
➥ ThisDir /tmp
```

Sure, this command is more readable at first glance, but do we really want to type this simply to copy a directory?

Deleting Files

As it does for copying files, Linux provides a powerful command for deleting files: rm, found at /bin/rm.

In its simplest form, rm allows us to delete one or more files in the current directory:

```
$ rm ThisFile
```

will delete the file ThisFile in the current directory, and

```
$ rm *.txt
```

will remove all files with the txt extension in the current directory.

As with copying, it is possible to provide multiple arguments to the `rm` command and all referenced files will be deleted. For instance,

```
$ rm ThisFile *.txt
```

will perform the same action as the previous two commands combined.

Like the `cp` command, this can be extremely useful and potentially dangerous. After all, what would happen if, wanting to delete a backup of a document, someone accidentally issued the command:

```
$ rm thesis.doc
```

instead of

```
$ rm thesis.bak
```

This is a potential nightmare, and as unlikely as it sounds, it happens all the time, resulting in unnecessary work and headaches.

For this reason, it is wise to use the same `-i` flag for the `rm` command because it will provide the prompts to avoid disastrous mistakes:

```
$ rm -i thesis.doc
rm: remove `thesis.doc'?
```

You can also create an alias for `rm`, making this the default behavior:

```
$ alias rm=`rm-i'
```

Deleting Whole Directories

Users frequently want to delete entire directories. Consider, for instance, a directory created after unzipping a software archive downloaded from the Internet. After you have finished installing and testing the software, you will probably want to delete the whole directory. This is done using the `-r` flag. For instance, to remove a directory called `TempInstall`, you would use:

```
$ rm -r TempInstall
```

Of course, if you have been following along in this chapter, you probably have an alias for the `rm` command, forcing it to prompt you for every deletion. This can become very tedious for big directories:

```
$ rm -r TempInstall
rm: descend directory `tempInstall'? y
```

```
rm: remove `TempInstall/File1'? y
rm: remove `TempInstall/File2? y
...
rm: remove directory `TempInstall'? y
```

Just imagine if there were hundreds of files. Responding to prompts for each one would be impractical. In these instances, when you are absolutely certain that you want to delete a whole directory, you will want to use the -f flag of the rm command. This flag forces deletions, even when you have already indicated interactive operation with the -i flag in your alias:

```
$ rm -rf TempInstall
```

A Reminder...

Care needs to be taken when using the –f flag. While powerful, it is extremely dangerous.

In most versions of Linux, the superuser's account is configured so that the default alias for the rm command is rm -i. This is critically important, because even a seemingly small mistake can be disastrous. If the alias weren't being used, just consider what would happen if, in attempting to delete the /tmp directory, a space made its way in between the / and tmp:

```
$ rm -r / tmp
```

This would actually delete all the files and directories on the disk. This is why the alias for rm -i is so essential.

Similarly, using the -f flag requires great care when working as the superuser and underscores the need to limit your use of the superuser account to only essential tasks. After all,

```
$ rm -rf / tmp
```

would be just as dangerous if you did have the right alias in place.

Moving and Renaming Files

Moving files and renaming files are closely linked, and therefore they are treated together in this section. Unlike the DOS and Macintosh worlds, where renaming and moving are distinct actions, in the Linux environment renaming a file is just a special case of moving a file.

Let's start by considering the basic move operation:

```
$ mv FileOne /tmp
```

This moves the file called FileOne from the current directory to the /tmp directory.

Similarly, it is possible to move the file to the /tmp directory and change the name of the file:

```
$ mv FileOne /tmp/NewFileName
```

By using this concept, you can rename a file. Simply move a file from its existing name to a new name in the same directory:

```
$ mv FileOne NewFileName
```

See how moving and renaming are one and the same?

Moving More Than Just One File

As when copying files, it is possible to move multiple files in one go because the mv command can accept more than two arguments and the last argument will serve as the destination directory of the move (as with copying, you can't move multiple files to a file: the last argument must be a directory). Consider the situation where we want to move all files in the current directory with the extension bak, tmp, or old to /tmp. Use the command:

```
$ mv *.bak *.tmp *.old /tmp
```

This simple command moves all the specified files to the destination (/tmp) in one operation.

It is also possible to move entire directories with the mv command without using any special flags. If there was a subdirectory named TheDir in the current directory and we wanted to move it so it would become a subdirectory under /tmp, we would use the mv command just as we did earlier for files:

```
$ mv TheDir/ /tmp
```

Similarly, if we wanted TheDir to become a directory in the root directory called NewDir, we could use

```
$ mv TheDir/ /NewDir
```

NOTE   As with `cp` and `rm`, it is wise to set an alias for `mv` to `mv -i` to ensure that you don't accidentally overwrite files when moving. You can do this with `$ alias mv='mv -i'`. This is set by default for the superuser account in most Linux distributions.

Creating Files and Symbolic Links

We have already learned several ways to create files. After all, we create files when we copy files. We create files when we move files. Other obvious ways of creating files include creating a word processing document, saving an e-mail attachment, or making a screen capture.

However, there are cases where it is necessary to create a new file, even if the file is empty and has a length of zero. The most obvious instance of this would be in cases where a script needs to create a file to indicate a special state. The best example of this is a programming technique called file locking. If a script opens a file to make changes, it also creates a special file called a lock file that indicates to other programs and scripts that the current file is opened for editing and is therefore unavailable to be changed. Once the script closes the file, it deletes the lock file to make the file once again available.

In order to be able to create these lock files quickly and efficiently without exacting excessive disk space requirements, we need a shortcut method of signifying an empty file of a specified name. This is achieved with the `touch` command. This command creates a file. For instance,

```
$ touch NewFile
```

creates a new file of zero length with the name `NewFile`:

```
-rw-rw-r-  1 armand   armand        0 Apr  6 21:06 NewFile
```

Another main use of the `touch` command is to change the modification date stamp of an existing file. Many programs depend on the date stamp of files they are working with to determine what action to take. The `touch` command can let you change the modification date of a file without opening and editing the file.

Creating Symbolic Links

In addition to creating files, there are times when it is necessary to create symbolic links. Symbolic links (which are simply pointers to a real file in another location) are usually used by system administrators and application developers. Consider a programmer who has several versions of a program that is under development. The current version for testing may be prog5, prog8, or prog10, depending how far along the development is. In order to ensure that the latest version is always being executed during testing, the programmer can create a symbolic link from prog to the latest version. By doing this, executing prog always executes the desired revision of the application.

There are two possible approaches to creating a symbolic link. The first is to use the ln command with the -s flag to indicate a symbolic link. The command takes two arguments: a file to be linked to and the location and name of the symbolic link to that file.

For instance, to create a link to /bin/cp in the current directory, MyCopy, we could use the command

```
$ ln -s /bin/cp MyCopy
```

Using ls -l to see the listing of MyCopy shows us a symbolic link:

```
lrwxrwxrwx   1 armand   armand          7 Apr  6 22:50 MyCopy ->
/bin/cp
```

Another, far less common, way to create a symbolic link is to use the cp command with the -s flag:

```
$ cp -s /bin/cp MyCopy
```

A Quick Introduction to Filename Expansion

Before closing out this chapter, we need to take a quick look at an important subject: filename expansion. We take a closer look at this in Chapter 13 when we discuss the Unix shell, but since we have already seen examples of filename expansion in this chapter, we need to put it in context.

Filename expansion refers to a special syntax that can be used to expand a compact expression into a list of one or more file or directory names. The simple examples we have seen in this chapter involve the use of the asterisk (*) to represent zero or more characters. For instance, the expression `*.txt` could match any of the following filenames:

- `.txt`

- `a.txt`

- `file.txt`

- `txt.txt`

The default Bash shell provides a rich syntax for filename expansion. We will explore this later, but a few of the more useful symbols are outlined below:

- `?`: Matches any single character, so `file.?` would match `file.c` but not `file.txt`.

- `[CharacterList]`: Matches any single character in the character list, so `file.[abc]` would match `file.a`, `file.b`, and `file.c` but not `file.d` or `file.txt`.

Where Do We Go from Here?

We've come a long way. We now know how to use X Windows and have begun to delve into the real depths of Linux: the command line and the shell. We have reviewed some of the major programs available in the command prompt environment and are able to manipulate files in sophisticated ways using concise and powerful commands.

The next step, which we will take in the next chapter, is to learn to perform some important system configuration tasks using Red Hat Linux's Control Panel utility. These functions include setting up printers for use in Linux, managing users, and more. After that, in Chapter 13, we will take a close look at the shell since the shell is where the real power of the command line environment lies.

CHAPTER

TWELVE

12

Configuring Your System with the Control Panel

- Launching the Control Panel

- Managing Users and Groups

- Configuring Printers

- Setting the Time and Date

- Configuring a Modem

- Managing Packages

- Other Control Panel Features

While avid Linux power users and system administrators will want to roll up their sleeves and get down to the business of hand-editing the files that control the behavior of their systems, the everyday computer user who wants to use Linux as a productivity tool finds this a daunting and overwhelming proposition.

In fact, the thought of having to hand-edit configuration files is so daunting that it may be one of the leading reasons why Linux is seen as user-unfriendly and Windows is perceived as user-friendly.

However, Red Hat has long striven to integrate tools into their distribution of Linux that will help shield the user from dealing with the underlying configuration of a basic Linux workstation.

At the center of these tools is the Control Panel. Like its namesake in the Windows world, the Red Hat Control Panel provides facilities to perform the most common system management tasks through easy-to-use graphical dialog boxes and windows.

Among the tasks that can be performed with the Control Panel are adding users and groups, managing printers, configuring networks, and handling installation and removal of software packages.

In this chapter, we will take a close look at the most frequently used features of the Control Panel.

Launching the Control Panel

If you have a relatively complete installation of Red Hat Linux 5, then you will already have all the files on your system required to run the Control Panel. The best way to find out if everything necessary is installed is to use the *Red Hat* package management system.

First check to see if the Control Panel is installed at all by using the command:

```
$ rpm -qa | grep control
```

This should produce a result like

```
control-panel-3.5-1
```

if Control Panel is installed.

If you find the package is not installed (rpm will tell you this quite clearly: control-panel is not installed), use rpm to install the package:

```
$ rpm -i control-panel-3.5-1.i386.rpm
```

assuming you are in the RedHat/RPMS subdirectory on the Red Hat CD-ROM.

If you are missing any required packages, rpm will inform you, and you can install them using the same command as above in order to make sure that Control Panel will work. Some of the packages which are commonly missing are: fstool, modemtool, printtool, netcfg, and usercfg. These provide the actual individual modules which allow the Control Panel to do its magic.

Once you are sure the Control Panel is installed, you can try to run it. There are two things to keep in mind about the Control Panel: it requires X Windows to run, and it must be run by the root user because it will attempt to edit system configuration files that only the root user should have permission to alter.

By default, the root account is configured to launch the Control Panel when you start the X Windows environment as the root user. So, assuming you haven't changed the global default window manager or root's own Window Manager, simply log in as root and issue the command

```
$ startx
```

If all is well, you will see X Windows start and the Control Panel will appear on the screen, as shown in Figure 12.1.

FIGURE 12.1:

The Red Hat Control Panel

If the Control Panel doesn't appear, from an `xterm` issue the command

```
$ control-panel
```

and the Control Panel should launch. The full path of the Control Panel is normally `/usr/bin/control-panel`.

Control Panel Features

Once you have the Control Panel running, there are a few features to look at. First, you will notice that the application runs in a vertical mode. If you prefer a horizontal Control Panel, you can choose Change Orientation from the File menu, as shown in Figure 12.2.

FIGURE 12.2:

The Orientation option in the File menu

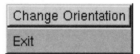

This will change the Control Panel window to look like the one in Figure 12.3.

FIGURE 12.3:

A horizontal Control Panel window

The Control Panel window consists of numerous icons representing functions. For instance, the icon pictured in Figure 12.4 represents User and Group Configuration. Holding the mouse over each icon for a few seconds will display small help balloons indicating the meaning of each icon.

FIGURE 12.4:

The User and Group Configuration icon

To launch the Control Panel applet associated with a given icon, simply click the icon once. For instance, clicking the icon once in Figure 12.4 launches the User Configurator applet pictured in Figure 12.5.

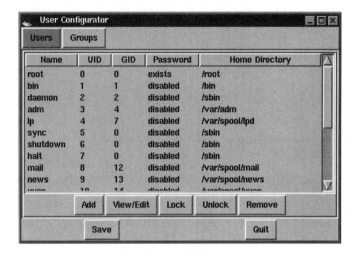

Managing Users and Groups

The first Control Panel applet we will look at is the User Configurator, which we saw at the end of the last section.

The User Configurator is launched by clicking the icon shown in Figure 12.4. The User Configurator window (see Figure 12.5) consists of three main sections: section buttons across the top, a user or group list in the center, and function buttons across the bottom. We will consider these in turn.

Users or Groups

The top part of the User Configurator window consists of two buttons, as pictured in Figure 12.6, that allow you to work with either users or groups. Although these two tasks are handled separately, making changes in one section can affect the contents of the other (as we will see later).

FIGURE 12.6:

Use these buttons to work
with users or groups.

Managing Users

When working with users you use the middle pane of the window, which has
details of existing users as well as a row of function buttons immediately below
it. These are shown in Figure 12.7.

FIGURE 12.7:

Use the list of users and the
row of function buttons to
manage users.

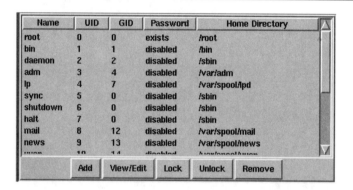

Using the User Configurator, it is possible to add new users, edit properties of
existing users or view their current properties, lock and unlock users, and permanently remove users from the system.

Adding a New User

To add a new user, click the Add button. This brings up a dialog box titled Edit
User Definition, like the one shown in Figure 12.8. Most of the information fields
in the dialog box are empty, waiting for you to enter information about the new user.

Username   The first field in the box is the Username field. In this field you
should enter the username of the user. That is, enter the name they will type to
log in to the system rather than their complete name. These usernames should
not contain spaces and should start with a letter or number.

FIGURE 12.8:

Adding a new user

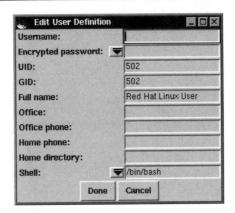

For instance, for a user named Arman Danesh you might choose any of the following usernames:

- armand
- adanesh
- arman
- danesh
- arman_danesh
- ArmanDanesh

because they all relate in some way to the name of the user.

Encrypted Password   The Encrypted Password field is supposed to contain the encrypted password of the user. When adding a new user, you have several options:

- Give no password to the user and allow them to specify their own password.
- Assign an arbitrary password to the user.
- Assign no password to the user with the intention of later assigning them a password.

You choose what you want to do with this field by using the drop-down menu next to the field. The drop-down menu is indicated with the symbol shown in Figure 12.9.

FIGURE 12.9:

FIGURE 12.9:

This symbol indicates a
drop-down menu

Clicking this symbol produces a drop-down menu like the one in Figure 12.10.

FIGURE 12.10:

The Encrypted Password
drop-down menu

The Original option means to assign no password to the new user—the same meaning as the No Password option. With this option, the user will be able to log in without a password until a password is assigned, either by the user or by the system administrator. The advantage of this is that new user accounts can be created without a password and the user can create their own, completely secret password. The disadvantage is that until a password is created, the new account is a security hole in the system, allowing anyone logging in with that username access to the system without a password.

The Change option will allow you to change the password from the default original to one that you assign. By selecting this option, you will be presented with a dialog box like the one in Figure 12.11. You will be prompted to enter the password twice, after which the encrypted form of the password will be displayed (as in Figure 12.12) and you can choose to click Done to apply the password, to reenter a different password, or to click Cancel to create no password for the user.

FIGURE 12.11:

Enter a password to create
one for the user.

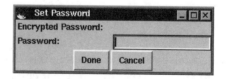

FIGURE 12.12:

After the password is
entered, the encrypted
password is displayed.

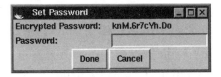

Finally, the Lock option can be used to lock the user account so that the account has no password but cannot be accessed the way it can be with the No Password option. This allows you to assign a password at a later time after the account has been created.

UID and GID   The UID and GID fields represent the user and group ID numbers for the user. Each user on a Linux system needs a UID and GID that can be shared with other users.

By default, Red Hat Linux is set up to give each user a unique UID and a GID that matches, meaning that by default each user is a member of their own group to which no other user belongs. This makes the user's account as secure as possible.

The User Configurator will, by default, select the next available user and group number for the new user. Unless you have your own scheme for the naming and numbering of users, you are probably best off keeping the preselected numbers that User Configurator assigned.

Full Name   The Full Name field is where you can type the full name of the user. The full name is used, for example, in constructing the From line of the user's e-mails, including both the e-mail address of the user, which is derived from the username, and the full name of the user.

Office, Office Phone, and Home Phone   These fields are optional and are left blank on many systems. If you wish to use these fields, fill in the necessary information as indicated.

Home Directory   The Home Directory field indicates the full path of the user's home directory. By default on a Red Hat Linux system, this is a subdirectory of the /home directory and the directory name is the same as the username. In fact, once you enter the username in the User Name field, User Configurator automatically displays this default home directory in the Home Directory field.

For example, the home directory for a user with the username armand would be /home/armand. Unless you have a large multi-user server or are implementing a custom scheme for placing home directories on your system, it is best to leave the default entry as is.

Shell The Shell field is used to indicate the user's default shell, which governs the way in which their command line environment will function. (To learn about different shells and their features, see Chapter 13, "Understanding the Shell.")

The default shell for all new users in Red Hat Linux is the Bash shell and will show up in the field as /bin/bash. Clicking the drop-down menu next to the field will produce a menu like the one in Figure 12.13. From this list you can choose alternate shells such as /bin/false (which prevents the user from logging in even if their username and password are entered correctly), variations on Bash such as the Ash shell, or the C-Shell and the Enhanced C-Shell (/bin/tcsh).

FIGURE 12.13:

The Shell drop-down menu

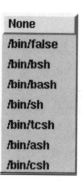

Editing or Viewing a User

To view the details or change the information for a user, simply select their name from the list of users and click the View/Edit button. This will bring up a dialog box like the one in Figure 12.14. This dialog box looks the same as the one we saw when we tried to add a new user, with one major difference: all the fields contain information relating to the user selected from the list. In addition, the Username field is not editable.

You can use this form to change any information about the user except the username. To change the username, you must create a new user and then remove the existing user.

There is one important point to note about the options on the Encrypted Password drop-down menu. When you add a new user, choosing the Original option assigns a new password to the user. When you view and edit a user, choosing Original leaves the user's password unchanged.

Viewing and editing a user

If you make changes to a user and want to commit those changes to the user list, simply click the Done button. Otherwise, you can click the Cancel button to exit the dialog box without saving changes.

Locking and Unlocking Users

Locking and unlocking users is a useful concept. The idea behind locking a user is to temporarily deactivate the user's account without permanently removing it from the system. This allows the user to be reinstated later. Examples of when this type of functionality is used would include an Internet Service Provider who temporarily suspends access privileges when a user is in arrears with their access charges.

To lock a user's account, simply select the user from the user list and click Lock. This will bring up a dialog box like the one in Figure 12.15.

The Lock User dialog box

When locking a user, several things take place. The most important is that the user's password will be locked. That is, an asterisk (*) will be appended to the start of the user's password, thus making it impossible for the user to log in.

In addition to this, several other options are available in the dialog box, including ways to handle the user's home directory, incoming mail queue, and other files.

The User's Home Directory When locking a user's account, you have three options regarding how to handle the user's home directory, as displayed in Figure 12.16.

FIGURE 12.16:

Home Directory options

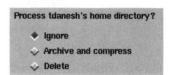

The Ignore option leaves the user's home directory untouched. The Archive and Compress option will compress all the files in the user's directory into a single compressed archive using the gzip compression utility. This operation is completely reversible and is reversed when the user's account is unlocked. Choose this option to save disk space while the user's account is inactive.

The third option, Delete, should be used with great care. Because the deletion of files is irreversible (unless you have a good, recent backup), this should only be used when you are sure you won't want the files available upon unlocking a user's account.

The User's Mail Queue Another option presented in the Lock User dialog box is whether to delete the user's incoming mail queue, also known as the mail spool. If selected, this action is irreversible and the incoming mail queue will be irretrievably lost. Use with care.

The User's Other Files The last set of options, as shown in Figure 12.17, concerns how to deal with any files owned by the user that exist outside the user's home directory.

FIGURE 12.17:

Dealing with a user's
other files

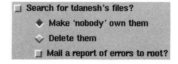

The Search for *Username*'s Files? option is used to indicate whether the files should be ignored or not. If you select this option, then the next three options are looked at to choose what action to take on the files.

If you decide to search the user's files, then you need to choose one of two possible actions: changing the ownership of the files to the user nobody or deleting them completely. Neither action is reversible, so be careful using this feature. After all, if you change the ownership of all the user's other files to nobody, there will be a problem when you unlock the user: the User Configurator will have no way of distinguishing between these files and any other files owned by the user nobody.

Finally, since you will be searching the whole file system and trying to manipulate files you find, there is a chance that errors will occur. Choosing the third option lets you bypass error message boxes for each file and instead have an error report e-mailed to the root user to be read at another time.

Completing the Lock Once you have chosen all the relevant options and want to lock the user, simply click the Lock button. This will present a confirmation dialog box like the one in Figure 12.18, giving you one more chance to review the options you selected before committing to the decision.

FIGURE 12.18:

Confirming before locking a user's account

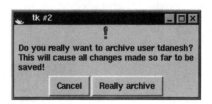

Simply select Really Archive to cause the actions to take place, or click Cancel to cancel.

Unlocking a User To unlock a locked user, simply select the user's name from the user list and click Unlock. This will cause a confirmation dialog box like the one in Figure 12.19 to be displayed.

FIGURE 12.19:

The Unlock confirmation
dialog

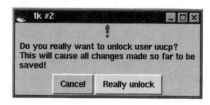

If you click Really Unlock, all reversible actions taken during the locking process will be undone. If you want to leave the user locked, click Cancel.

Deleting a User

The final option in managing users is to delete a user from the system. Once done, you can only bring a user back by recreating the user's account. To delete a user, select the user from the user list and click Remove. This will bring up a dialog box like the one in Figure 12.20. The box looks just like the one used for locking users, and the options have the same meaning.

The difference between locking a user and deleting a user is that instead of simply changing the password to make it impossible to use the account to log in, deleting a user removes the account's entry from the user list, meaning the user no longer exists in any way on the system. To completely remove all traces of a user, you choose to delete the user's home directory, mail spool, and other files.

FIGURE 12.20:

The Delete User dialog box

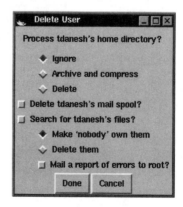

Once you click Done, you will be presented with a confirmation dialog box like the one in Figure 12.21. Clicking Really Delete will delete the user.

Managing Groups

The second aspect of managing users and groups is to work with groups. To switch to group management in the User Configurator, click the Groups button at the top of the User Configurator window. When managing groups, you work with a groups list and a row of function buttons like those in Figure 12.22. Groups are discussed in detail in Chapter 15, "General System Administration."

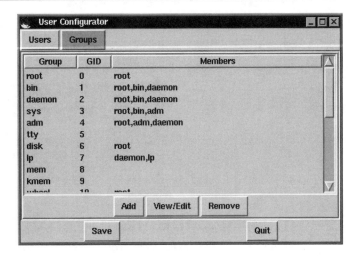

Adding Groups

To add a new group to the groups list, simply click the Add button. This will bring up a dialog box like the one in Figure 12.23.

FIGURE 12.23:

Adding a group

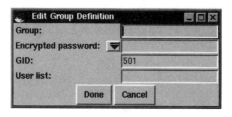

This looks like a scaled-down version of the dialog box used for adding users to the system. Here you can assign a group name, select a GID for the group if you don't like the default one provided by the system, and assign a password to the group in the same way you did for a new user.

In addition, you can specify which users belong to a given group by entering a comma-separated list of users in the User List field.

Editing and Viewing Groups

To edit or view a group's details, simply select the group from the groups list and click View/Edit to get a dialog box like the one in Figure 12.24.

FIGURE 12.24:

Editing and viewing a group

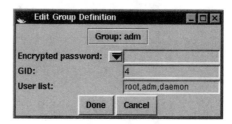

Notice that the dialog box looks like it did when you added a group, except that here all the data is filled in. You can change the password, GID, or user list for a group but not the name, as this amounts to creating a new group.

Deleting Groups

Deleting groups couldn't be simpler. Just select a group from the groups list and click Remove. A word of warning, though: Unlike deleting a user, where you are prompted for confirmation, the Red Hat 5 User Configurator doesn't prompt for confirmation when deleting a group—it just proceeds to delete the group as soon as you click the button.

Saving and Quitting

At the very bottom of the User Configurator window are the Save and Quit buttons. These warrant some discussion.

When you make changes in the User Configurator, the changes are reflected in the data shown in the User Configurator but are not automatically saved in the system configuration files. In order to save the changes to the system (making them permanent), you need to click the Save button.

If you click the Quit button, you will be given one last chance to save your changes. You will be presented with a confirmation dialog box like the one in Figure 12.25.

FIGURE 12.25:

The Quit confirmation dialog box

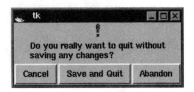

If you select Abandon, User Configurator will quit without saving any changes you made in the current session since Save was last clicked. This provides a final opportunity to reverse major changes, such as deleting users and groups, before they are permanently saved to the system.

Clicking Save and Quit will first save all changes since Save was last clicked and then close the User Configurator. Cancel will return you to the User Configurator.

Configuring Printers

Probably one of the more intimidating configuration tasks in Unix is trying to get a printer working—especially a PCL printer—by manually editing the necessary system configuration files.

Red Hat has done an admirable job of making this task manageable (if not exactly easy) using the Print System Manager applet of the Red Hat Linux Control Panel. To launch the Print System Manager, click the icon shown in Figure 12.26. This will bring up the Print System Manager, as shown in Figure 12.27.

FIGURE 12.26:

Click this icon to launch the
Print System Manager.

The Print System Manager consists of four menus (PrintTool, lpd, Tests, and Help), a list of existing printers, and three function buttons (Edit, Add, and Delete).

FIGURE 12.27:

The Print System Manager

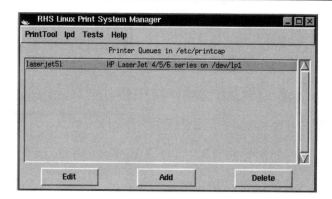

The PrintTool Menu

The PrintTool menu provides three entries: Reload, About, and Quit.

Reload is used to reload the system's `printcap` file, found at `/etc/printcap`. This is the configuration file where the system stores all configuration information for all installed printers and remote printers on the system. This allows you to refresh the display of available printers should the `printcap` file be changed manually or by another program while the Print System Manager is running.

About does exactly what is expected, presenting a dialog box with some detailed information about the Print System Manager. This dialog box looks like the one in Figure 12.28.

Finally, Quit quits without any confirmation. Unlike the User Configurator, when you make changes in the Print System Manager, they are immediately written to the relevant system configuration files.

FIGURE 12.28:

The About dialog box

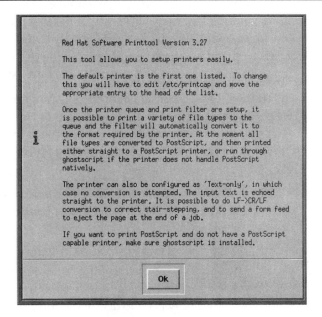

Red Hat Software Printtool Version 3.27

This tool allows you to setup printers easily.

The default printer is the first one listed. To change this you will have to edit /etc/printcap and move the appropriate entry to the head of the list.

Once the printer queue and print filter are setup, it is possible to print a variety of file types to the queue and the filter will automatically convert it to the format required by the printer. At the moment all file types are converted to PostScript, and then printed either straight to a PostScript printer, or run through ghostscript if the printer does not handle PostScript natively.

The printer can also be configured as 'Text-only', in which case no conversion is attempted. The input text is echoed straight to the printer. It is possible to do LF->CR/LF conversion to correct stair-stepping, and to send a form feed to eject the page at the end of a job.

If you want to print PostScript and do not have a PostScript capable printer, make sure ghostscript is installed.

Ok

The Lpd Menu

The lpd menu contains a single entry: Restart lpd.

When you make changes to the printer setup on your system—whether those changes involve adding new printer queues, deleting existing printers, or changing the configuration of printers—they don't take effect until the line printer daemon, known as lpd, is restarted.

Lpd is a system program that runs in the background and handles the spooling of print jobs for all printers configured on a Linux system. To get lpd to look at its configuration files for new information requires that the program be restarted.

The Tests Menu

The Tests menu allows you to test a configured printer by sending sample print jobs to the printer. The first two tests print an ASCII or PostScript test file to the printer selected in the list of available printers. This tests the configuration of the printer.

If a job fails to print, you will want to test that you have the printer configured and connected to the correct serial or parallel port on your system. You can use the third option, Print a Test File Directly to the Port, to bypass the lpd-managed printer queue and send data directly to the printer's configured port to see if the physical connection is correct and on the port expected by lpd.

The usefulness of this quickly becomes apparent. For instance, if you print a test PostScript file to a printer and it fails to print, two possible things could be wrong: the configuration of the printer queue in question is incorrect (a software problem) or there is a physical connection problem.

For instance, if you have configured your printer to be connected to /dev/lp0 (LPT1: in DOS and Windows) but have connected it to /dev/lp1 (LPT2:), then printing test pages will fail. Or you may have a bad printer cable, which can cause a print job to fail.

Using the Direct to Port test tells you whether the problem is hardware or software. If you print directly to the port and the text prints, then you know the printer is connected correctly to the port indicated in the printer queue configuration. This means you only need to debug the configuration of the queue to solve any printing problems.

The Help Menu

The Help menu provides access to two help screens: General Help, which offers general guidance about using the Print System Manager, and Troubleshooting, which offers useful pointers about solving printing difficulties.

The Edit Button

If you select an existing printer and click the Edit button, you will be shown a dialog box like the one in Figure 12.29.

FIGURE 12.29:

The Edit printer dialog box

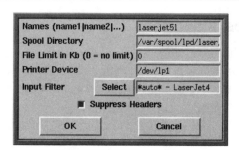

This dialog box displays the relevant properties of the specified printer queue, including the name(s) of the printer, the spool directory, any limit on the size of print jobs, the port where the printer is connected, and the Input Filter. In addition, indication is given about whether headers should be suppressed when printing to this printer. For a remote printer, the dialog box will look a little different, showing the host name and queue name of the printer on the remote host instead of the port where the printer is connected. This looks like Figure 12.30.

FIGURE 12.30:

Editing a remote printer

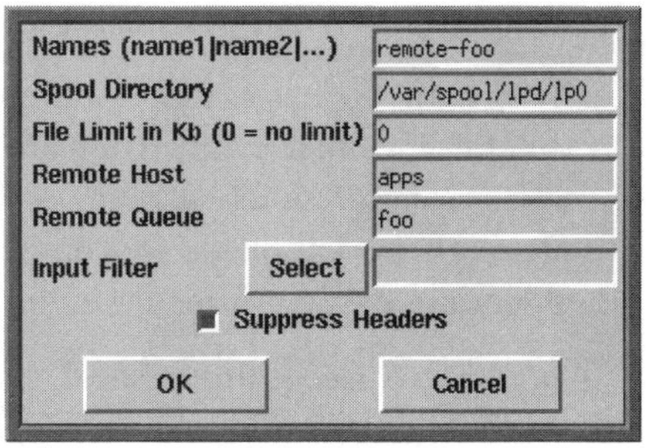

Printer Names

You can give any name to a printer queue that doesn't include spaces—letters and numbers are best. If you want to give a printer more than one name, separate the names with the pipe symbol (|).

You might want to create more than one name for the default printer on your system, for instance. By default, the commands used to print and query a printer look for a printer named lp when none is specified. This is considered the default printer of the system.

But most users would prefer to name their printers with names that reflect some useful information about the printer, such as the type or location. For the default printer, then, you might want to use two names such as laserjet51|lp.

Spool Directory

The spool directory is the location on your system where print jobs are stored while in the queue waiting to be sent to the printer. Normally this location is a subdirectory under the directory /var/spool/lpd with the same name as the first name given the printer.

By default, the Print System Manager will copy the first name of a printer to the Spool Directory field so that a printer named `laserjet5l` will have a spool directory of `/var/spool/lpd/laserjet5l`. Normally you should leave the default unless there is a compelling reason to change the location, such as disk space limitations.

File Limit

The File Limit field specifies any limit on the size of print jobs in kilobytes. This can be especially useful in two instances:

1. Where a printer has extremely small memory and sending large jobs to the printer can leave it in an error state and inaccessible. This is especially critical in a situation where a printer is being shared on a network and this error state might go unnoticed for some time while people assume the jobs they are sending to the printer are being printed.

2. Where disk space is limited and a large print job can cause the partition or disk containing the spool directories to quickly fill up.

In these cases, specify any limits in kilobytes in this field. If you want to place no limit on the size of print jobs, enter zero in this field.

Printer Device

This field is used to indicate which device to send print jobs to. The following table indicates which Linux devices map to which DOS devices and what type of port they are.

Linux Device	DOS Device	Type
/dev/lp0	LPT1:	Parallel
/dev/lp1	LPT2:	Parallel
/dev/lp2	LPT3:	Parallel
/dev/ttyS0	COM1:	Serial
/dev/ttyS1	COM2:	Serial
/dev/ttyS2	COM3:	Serial
/dev/ttyS3	COM4:	Serial

Note that the numbering of devices differs from DOS and Windows. Linux numbering starts at 0 where DOS and Windows start at 1.

Remote Host and Queue

The Print System Manager handles remote network printers as well as local printers. In the Unix and Linux world, a remote printer is handled in essentially the same way as a local printer. A queue exists on the local machine with its own spool directory. But instead of indicating a device for the printer, the Print System Manager specifies a remote host and remote queue name, and files sit in the local queue until they can be sent to the print queue on the remote host.

Given this, it is easy to configure remote printers. When editing a remote printer, you will see Remote Host and Remote Queue fields instead of the Printer Device field.

Let's consider an example. What if there was a printer in the Finance department connected to a Linux system called Finance. On this system, the printer queue for the local printer might be called `lj4p`, indicating that the printer is a LaserJet 4P.

If you wanted to create a print queue on your own Linux system pointing to that remote printer, you might want to call the print queue `finance-printer`, since you also have a LaserJet 4P and using a similar name would be confusing.

In this example, the printer name on your system would be `finance-printer`, the remote host would be `finance`, and the remote queue would be `lj4p`.

Input Filter

Generally speaking, Linux programs that offer printing capabilities send one of two types of data to a printer queue: ASCII or PostScript. Depending on your printer, however, one or the other or both of these types of data might be inappropriate. For instance, a PostScript printer won't print a plain ASCII file and a PCL printer won't print a PostScript file.

In order to address this problem, you need to use input filters. Input filters are generally programs or scripts that can translate a variety of file formats including ASCII, PostScript, pictures, and more into the right format for a printer. When you edit a printer queue entry, the Input Filter field will display the filter in a special format such as `*auto*` - `LaserJet4` for a LaserJet 4–compatible printer.

Luckily, the Print System Manager provides a graphical interface for selecting the correct input filter for your printer. Simply click the Select button next to the Input Filter field, and a dialog box like the one in Figure 12.31 will be displayed.

FIGURE 12.31:

The Configure Filter dialog box

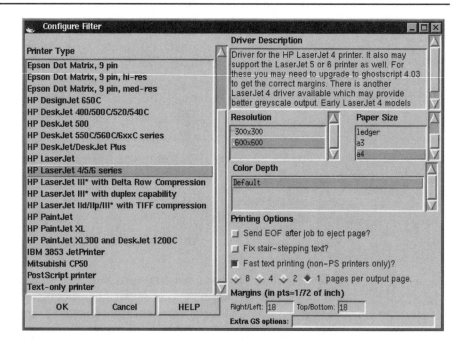

The Configure Filter dialog box offers a selection of printer types including popular dot matrix, ink jet, and laser printers. If you select the closest printer to the one you are using, it often works. For instance, owners of HP LaserJet 6 series printers can select HP LaserJet 4/5/6 Series, which is actually a LaserJet 4 series filter that usually works with newer models.

Once you select the appropriate filter, you can configure details such as default resolution, paper size, and more. Generally, aside from the Resolution, Paper Size, and Color Depth entries, the default entries selected when you choose an input filter will be the best ones for your printer.

Suppress Headers

Selecting the Suppress Headers option turns off the printing of header pages. Header pages are used in a networked environment to indicate who printed a given document and are helpful in sorting print jobs. However, some printers will have trouble with the header pages. If you experience difficulty because of header pages, deselect this option.

The Add Button

As would be expected, adding a new printer is closely related to editing an existing printer. When you click the Add button, you will be presented with a dialog box like the one in Figure 12.32 asking you what type of printer queue you wish to create.

Select the correct type (local or remote) and then click OK to get a dialog box like the one in Figure 12.33 or 12.34.

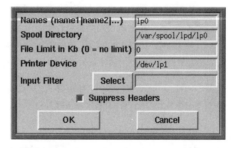

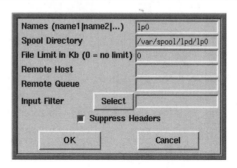

These dialog boxes look like the ones used to edit local and remote printers and work in the same way. You need to fill in the correct information for your printer and click OK to add the printer.

The Delete Button

Deleting a printer is a fairly simple process. Select the appropriate printer from the list of available printers and click the Delete button. A confirmation dialog box like the one in Figure 12.35 will come up.

FIGURE 12.35:

The Delete Printer confirmation dialog

If you want to delete the printer, click Continue; otherwise, click Cancel. If you choose to delete a printer, you will be reminded to delete the spool directory manually. There is no requirement to do so, but doing this will keep your system well-organized and uncluttered by unneeded directories.

Remember, as soon as you click Continue to delete a printer, it will be removed from the necessary configuration file. There is no second chance after that.

Working with Windows Printers

You may have noticed the reference to LAN Manager Printers in the Add dialog box. These are printers shared by a Windows 95 or NT system using standard Windows networking and the Server Message Block Protocol(SMB). When adding this type of printer, you will see a dialog box like the one in Figure 12.36.

The key differences here are the need to know the host name of the server, the IP address of the server, and the username and password of the shared printer. If you want to integrate a Linux system into an existing Windows network with shared printers, you can get this information from your Windows network system administrator.

FIGURE 12.36:

Adding a Windows printer

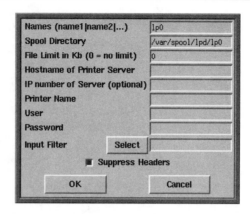

Setting the Time and Date

The Control Panel lets you set the system time and date using the Time Machine. You can launch the Time Machine by clicking the icon shown in Figure 12.37. The Time Machine window looks like Figure 12.38.

FIGURE 12.37:

The Time Machine icon

The time and date are displayed at the top of the window. You can click any part of the time or date (the hour, the minutes, the seconds, the month, the day etc.) and adjust it using the arrows. When you make these changes, the system clock doesn't update; you can reset the time to the system clock's time by clicking the Reset Time button. If you prefer to view the time in 24-hour format in the Time Machine, select the 24 Hour Time option. This option has no impact on the time stored in the system clock, since the system clock doesn't make the distinction between 12- and 24-hour clocks.

FIGURE 12.38:

The Time Machine window

After changing the time here, you can change the time of the system clock by clicking Set System Clock. This will bring up a warning screen like the one in Figure 12.39.

FIGURE 12:39

System time change warning

The warning suggests that you reboot your system immediately after changing the system time or else risk system instability. This is not an idle threat. There are system processes that rely on the system clock and can get confused by changes in the clock. If you aren't in a position to reboot your system when you are changing the time, it is best to put off changing the time until you plan to shut down your system.

If you still want to change the system time once the warning is displayed, click Continue and the system clock will be updated.

Configuring a Modem

The Control Panel provides a simple modem configuration applet that is accessed by clicking the icon shown in Figure 12.40. This brings up the Configure Modem window, as shown in Figure 12.41.

This window offers very little to choose from: you can simply select the port your modem is connected to or, in the case of an internal modem, configured to use. This will create the necessary link so that programs that expect the modem to be on the device /dev/modem will find your modem.

This setting is independent of the configuration of programs that will use the modem for accessing the Internet or faxing. These programs will be discussed in later chapters such as Chapter 17, "Connecting Linux to the Internet."

Managing Packages

As we saw in the section on installing RedHat, Red Hat has implemented a package management system to make it easy to install and uninstall software packages and keep track of what is installed on your system.

At the core of this system is a command-line program called rpm. While very powerful, this tool is complex to use and requires care. For this reason, Red Hat offers a package management applet in the Control Panel so that you can install, uninstall, and query packages without resorting to the rpm command.

To launch the package management applet, simply click the icon shown in Figure 12.42 to display the package management window shown in Figure 12.43.

FIGURE 12.42:

The package management icon

FIGURE 12.43:

The package management window

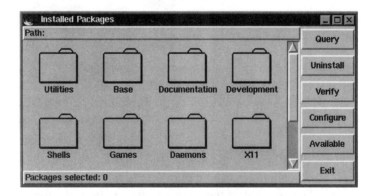

This graphical package management system is known as Glint, which stands for Graphical Linux INstallation Tool. Initially, Glint presents a view of currently installed packages using a series of hierarchical folders reminiscent of the Windows 95 My Computer metaphor. You can select a package by double-clicking down through the folders to the package you want to work with, and then select an action from the buttons on the right side of the window.

Selecting Packages

You can select one or more packages in the window by single-clicking with the left mouse button on each package. As you click each package, it will be highlighted by a red box, and the number of selected packages displayed at the bottom of the window will increase. For instance, in Figure 12.44, two packages are selected and highlighted and the number of selected packages is indicated as two.

FIGURE 12.44:

Selecting multiple packages

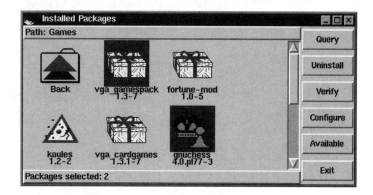

To deselect a package, simply click it again with the left button.

Another way to select and deselect packages is to right-click a package's icon. This brings up a context-sensitive menu that displays all appropriate actions available for the object. In the case of installed packages, this menu will look like the one in Figure 12.45.

FIGURE 12.45:

A context-sensitive menu

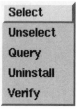

Once you have selected all the packages you want to work with, you can select an action from the buttons on the right side of the window.

Querying Packages

Querying packages brings up a window like the one in Figure 12.46 that displays information about the selected packages. This information includes the full name of the package, a description of the package, and a complete list of all the files in the package.

FIGURE 12.46:

Querying packages

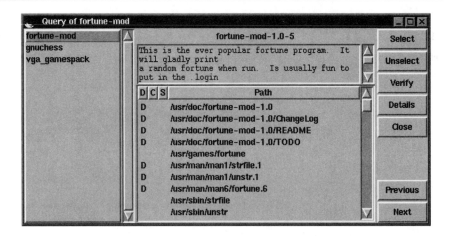

You can use the Next and Previous buttons to cycle through the selected packages that are displayed at the left side of the window. The Details button on the right side of the window brings up a window like the one in Figure 12.47 for the currently selected package. This window displays version information, the source of the package, the size of the package, and when the package was created. Such data is useful in keeping track of versions and ensuring you have the latest package installed.

FIGURE 12.47:

The package details window

Verifying Packages

You can verify selected packages by clicking the Verify button on the right side of the main window. The verification process checks all files in a package to be sure they are installed, have the correct size and permissions, and are uncorrupted. This is done by confirming all the information against a database maintained for all installed packages. If you feel that a program is misbehaving because of problems in any of the areas mentioned above, you can try verifying the package to see if it needs to be reinstalled.

For instance, in Figure 12.48, we can see that the file /usr/games/vga_spider is missing from the indicated package.

FIGURE 12.48:

Verifying a package's files

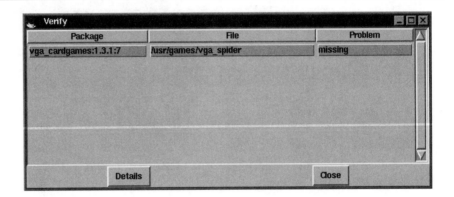

Uninstalling Packages

When you click the Uninstall button to uninstall your selected packages, you will be presented with a window like the one in Figure 12.49 listing the packages you have chosen to install and confirming that you wish to proceed.

If you click Yes, the packages will be removed from your system. Clicking No cancels the uninstall.

FIGURE 12.49:

Confirming an uninstall
request

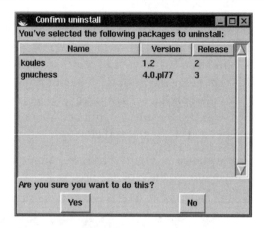

Installing New Packages

Installing new packages requires a few preparatory steps:

1. Mount your Linux CD-ROM in its normal location. For most users, this will be /mnt/cdrom.

2. Configure Glint to look in the CD's RedHat/RPMS subdirectory for new RPM files.

3. Display a list of available packages.

Configuring Glint

Glint offers only one configuration option, accessed by clicking the Configuration button in the main window. This brings up a dialog box like the one in Figure 12.50 that allows you to set the path where Glint should look for new packages. For most systems, this will be /mnt/cdrom/RedHat/RPMS.

FIGURE 12.50:

Configuring Glint

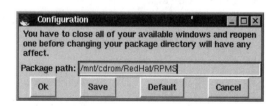

Listing Available Packages

Once you have made sure Glint is configured correctly, click the Available button to list all packages available for installation. A new window will open, similar to the one in Figure 12.51. This window resembles the one that displays installed packages, except that it displays uninstalled packages available for installation.

FIGURE 12.51:

The Available Packages window

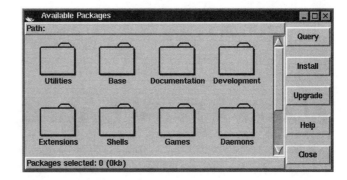

Because Glint must scan all packages in the specified directory and compare them against the list of installed packages to create a list of available packages, this window can take anywhere from a few seconds to a few minutes to appear.

The procedures for using this window are the same as with installed packages. You select packages with the left mouse button and use the right mouse button to get a context-sensitive menu.

Installing New Packages

Once you have selected the packages you want to install, click the Install button on the right side of the window. This will install all selected packages. During the installation, a window charting the progress of the installation, like the one in Figure 12.52, will be displayed.

FIGURE 12.52:

The installation progress meter

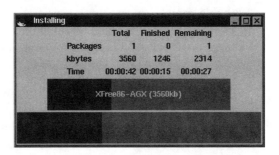

Upgrading Packages

When a new version of a package is released, you will want to install it on your system without first uninstalling the existing version. This is done by upgrading. In fact, it is preferable to upgrade a package rather than uninstall it and reinstall a new version, because any custom configurations you made are preserved during an upgrade.

To upgrade, select the packages you wish to upgrade and click the Upgrade button. A progress meter like the one used during package installation will be displayed.

Other Control Panel Features

You probably have noticed that many of the Control Panel icons were not discussed in this chapter. These icons bring up tools for performing advanced system configuration that requires deeper knowledge of system administration. Some of these will be discussed in the appropriate sections of this book:

- The File Manager will be discussed in Chapter 8, "Using X Windows Applications."

- The Network Configurator will be discussed in Chapter 16, "Understanding Linux Networking."

Where Do We Go from Here?

This chapter has given you a grounding in how to confirm some of the most basic components of your system—components that you will use every day, such as printers, modems, and packages.

With this knowledge and your basic grasp of Unix and managing Linux files, you are ready to delve into the world of the shell. The shell is the program that provides you with the powerful command-line environment that is loved by the Unix guru but feared by the Linux novice.

In the next chapter, we will take a look at the role played by the shell compare many of the available shells (including the ever-popular Bash and C shells), and then take a deeper look at Bash, the default shell of almost every Linux distribution.

CHAPTER

THIRTEEN

13

Understanding the Shell

- Comparing Shells

- Overview of the Bash Shell

Now that we have learned some basic Unix commands, it is important that we understand the command-line environment we are using to enter them. This command-line environment is known as the shell—a command interpreter, similar to the DOS prompt in Windows 3.1 and Windows 95, that allows you to type commands, launch programs, and manipulate files.

Unlike the Windows world where the DOS prompt is a fixed environment with limited flexibility, Unix shells are small application programs that run as processes when you log in and provide a variety of command-line interface features and capabilities to suit different users and applications.

In the Unix world, and by extension in Linux, there are numerous shells to choose from. Each shell offers you a different set of features and capabilities and most offer their own scripting languages, which, as we will see in the chapter on scripting later in the book, allow us to create sophisticated, self-executing programs similar to—but more powerful than—DOS batch files (with the familiar .BAT extension).

First, we will take a quick look at some of the major shells, including the Bourne Shell, the C Shell, and the Korn Shell, and then we will take an in-depth look at the Bourne Again Shell, known as Bash, which is the default shell installed with most Linux distributions.

Comparing Shells

The earliest Unix shell was very limited, with no history list, no command-line editing, and no job control. It was with the emergence of the Bourne Shell and the C Shell in the 1970s that shells began to garner serious attention in the Unix world. Today there is a plethora of shells available to Unix users, with a wide variety of unique features distinguishing them from each other.

There are two main classes of shell—those that derive their essential syntax and design from the Bourne Shell and those that base their model on the C Shell. Before taking a close look at the Bourne Again Shell—the default shell that ships with most Linux distributions—let's take a quick look at some of the major Unix shells.

TIP
If you want to keep track of the latest developments in the world of Unix shells, consider subscribing to the `comp.unix.shell` newsgroup.

Bourne Shell (*sh*)

The Bourne Shell is seen by many as the original Unix shell. In many ways it is rather limited, lacking features such as a history list and command-line editing. But as the original Unix shell, many features of the Bourne Shell, including its core command set, are found in many modern shells. It is rare, however, to find modern systems that use the Bourne Shell as their default shell. Instead, the Bourne Again Shell or the Enhanced C Shell are commonly found in most Linux distributions.

The Bourne Shell is well-known for introducing many key shell concepts, such as the ability to test programs for success or failure status when they exited, which allowed for sophisticated scripting. This concept is now standard in all Unix shells.

C Shell (*csh*)

The C Shell was an early Unix shell that was developed to provide a command set and scripting environment derived from the syntax of the popular C programming language. Like the early Bourne Shell, the C Shell lacked some important features, such as command-line editing. Still, the C Shell introduced many key ideas, including command aliases and command histories. An Enhanced C Shell (tcsh), which adds command-line editing and other features found in Bash, is usually shipped with most Linux distributions as an alternate shell.

The C Shell is generally hailed for introducing several key concepts that today are found even in shells based on the Bourne Shell. These include the idea that certain shell functions, such as arithmetic calculations and comparison testing, could be performed by the shell itself. In the case of the Bourne Shell, these tasks required calling external programs.

TIP   If your Linux distribution didn't come with the Enhanced C Shell and you want to try it out, you can download the original source code from `ftp://ftp.gw.com/pub/unix/tcsh/`. However, if you have any mainstream distribution, including Red Hat, Slackware, or Debian Linux, you should find that a precompiled version of this shell is included.

Bourne Again Shell (*bash*)

The Bourne Again Shell is the most common shell installed with Linux distributions. Known as Bash, this shell is based on the Bourne Shell (as the name implies) but provides a broad additional feature set including command-line editing, a history list, and filename completion. With Bash, it is possible to write sophisticated shell scripts using a Bourne Shell-like syntax. As the most common Linux shell, Bash will be the focus of most of this chapter and is the default shell being used in all examples in this book.

Korn Shell (*ksh*)

The Korn Shell is another of the family of shells that is derived from the original Bourne Shell. By some counts, the Korn Shell is the most popular Unix shell in use; however, it is generally not the default shell on most Linux systems. The Korn Shell was probably the first to introduce many of the popular features we now see in Bash, including command-line editing. The Korn Shell was also one of the first shells to bring many features introduced in the C Shell into the Bourne Shell world.

Other Shells

There are numerous other shells available, all of which provide their own unique command-line interfaces. None of these, however, is sufficiently popular or well known to be shipped with most Linux distributions. These shells include The Adventure Shell (ash), a subset of the Bourne Shell; Extensible Shell (es), which provides a completely reprogrammable shell environment; ERGO Shell (esh), a shell that aims to provide a more ergonomic, structured approach to a shell; and Z Shell (zsh), which, like Bash, brings together features from several shells and is similar to the Korn Shell.

TIP   An excellent source of alternate shells for your Linux system is at the SunSite Linux archive. In their Shells directory at `ftp://sunsite.unc.edu/pub/Linux/system/shells/`, you will find all the shells listed here as well as a collection of less common shells such as `lsh`, `pash`, and `pdksh`.

Experimenting with Different Shells

At this point, you are probably wondering how you can try out these different shells without making them your default shell. You can do this by simply executing the shell as a program from within your default shell. For instance, most Linux distributions come with the Enhanced C Shell preinstalled even though Bash is set up to be the default shell for all users. If you want to try out `tcsh` you just need to enter the command

```
$ tcsh
```

(This command assumes `tcsh` is on your path; if not, you will need to include the appropriate path to the shell, such as `/bin/tcsh`.) Once you do this, the Enhanced C Shell will run and you will be switched to that shell. Simply typing `exit` will return you to your default shell.

On most Linux systems, you will find a symbolic link from `/bin/sh` to `/bin/tcsh`, so using the command

```
$ csh
```

will also launch the Enhanced C Shell.

If you plan to experiment with different shells, you can use this technique to try them all out before switching your default shell. In order to change the default shell that runs when you log in to your system, you will need to change your entry in the Unix password file. You can do this using the `chsh` command.

Consider a user `someuser` whose default shell is currently `/bin/bash` (the Bourne Again Shell). Their current entry in the Unix password file might look like:

```
someuser::790:103:Some User:/home/someuser:/bin/bash
```

In this password entry, the last section specifies the shell as `/bin/bash`. Running the command

```
$ chsh -s /bin/tcsh someuser
```

changes the shell for `someuser` to `/bin/tcsh`. The resulting entry for `someuser` in the Unix password file would be

```
someuser::790:103:Some User:/home/someuser:/bin/tcsh
```

and the next time they log in, Enhanced C Shell would be their shell instead of the Bourne Again Shell.

Overview of the Bash Shell

Now that we've reviewed many of the other shells, let's take a closer look at Linux's most common shell, the Bash shell. As the first step to learning where the Bash shell fits into the Linux universe, it is important to understand the whole login process. When you log in at the Login: prompt, several things take place. The first of these is the launching of your shell (in this case Bash), followed by the execution of any configuration file you may have created for your personal Bash environment.

In order to provide a personalized configuration to Bash, you need to create a file called .bashrc in your home directory. This is a simple text file that is executed by Bash whenever you launch the shell—generally, when you log in.

The .bashrc file can contain any legitimate combination of commands and Bash functions that you would type at the normal Bash prompt, as well as sophisticated scripting command.

It is in the .bashrc file that you can configure the behavior of Bash, set environment variables such as your path, and launch any programs that you may want to launch every time you run the Bash shell. The following is the content of a simple .bashrc file that creates a customized prompt, sets a command alias called which, and assigns some environment variables:

```
PS1="[\u@\h \W]\\$ "
alias which="type -path"
export PATH=$PATH:.:~/bin
export EDITOR=emacs
```

There are several major features of the Bash shell at play in this seemingly small example, including:

- Setting of environment variables

- Command aliases

- Pattern expansion

All of these will be discussed in the rest of this chapter, along with the following major features of the Bash shell:

- Input and output redirection

- Filename completion

- Full command-line editing

- Command history list

- Job control

Setting Environment Variables in Bash

Each shell has its own syntax for the setting of environment variables. In Bash this is generally done in two steps:

1. Set the value of a variable.

2. Export the variable to the environment.

For instance, if we want to assign emacs as our default text editor, we might set the `EDITOR` environment variable with

```
$ EDITOR=emacs
```

and export it with

```
$ export EDITOR
```

The two steps can also be combined into a single step where we assign a value to `EDITOR` and export `EDITOR` in one command:

```
$ export EDITOR=emacs
```

As we will learn in greater detail when we discuss pattern expansion, the value of environment variables can be accessed by adding a $ at the beginning of the name of the variable in a Bash command. In this way, we can add information to the current value of an environment variable. For instance, if the PATH variable currently contains

```
/bin:/usr/bin:/usr/X11R6/bin
```

we could add `/usr/local/bin` to the path by using the command

```
$ export PATH=$PATH:/usr/local/bin
```

Notice how we use $PATH to include the current value of the PATH variable in our new value of the PATH variable. The resulting value of the variable would be

```
/bin:/usr/bin:/usr/X11R6/bin:/usr/local/bin
```

Input and Output Redirection

One of the most useful concepts in the Unix world is that of standard input and standard output. Often, non-interactive programs receive their input data through the standard input—usually the keyboard. Similarly, they display their results to the standard output—usually the screen.

However, most shells provide the ability to redirect standard input and output, which allows you to build complex command combinations out of multiple commands and data files. As we saw in the last chapter, the use of the pipe (|) allows the redirection of both standard input and standard output. For instance, in the command

```
$ ls -l | more
```

the output of the ls -l command is not displayed to standard output but is instead redirected to the standard input of the more command. The more command processes this redirected input and then displays the results to the standard output.

There is another way to redirect standard input and output in Bash: using the < and > redirection symbols. For instance, consider a situation where we want to save a directory listing to a file for later processing. We can use the > symbol to redirect the standard output:

```
$ ls -l > filelist
```

This command saves the output of the ls -l command in a file called filelist. Similarly, if we want to use the contents of a file as the standard input for a command, we would use the < symbol:

```
$ mail user@juxta.com < filelist
```

This would cause the contents of the file filelist to be used as the input data for the mail command, effectively causing the contents of the file to be used as the body of the resulting e-mail message.

Filename Completion

Sometimes called word completion, filename completion is a simple but very useful concept. It works like this: if you type enough characters to uniquely identify a file, command, or directory name, Bash can complete the rest of the name. Consider if you typed

```
$ /usr/lo
```

On most systems, `/usr/lo` will uniquely identify the directory `/usr/local/`. By simply hitting the Tab key, Bash will attempt to complete the name. If only one file, command, or directory begins with `/usr/lo`, then Bash will complete the name for you, in this case filling in the text to read `/usr/local/`.

Of course, there are going to be times when you don't provide enough information for Bash to know how to complete a name. In this situation, the shell is able to provide you with all possible alternatives to match the name you are trying to complete. For instance, if you type

```
$ /usr/l
```

`/usr/local/` and `/usr/lib/` would usually be matched. If you hit Tab, then Bash is confused—it doesn't know which name to complete with, and so cannot complete the name. If you hit Tab a second time, Bash will display all the possible alternatives, like this:

```
lib          local
```

You are free to type enough characters to uniquely identify the name you want and then hit Tab again. In the example above, if you type an additional o and then hit Tab, Bash would complete the name as `/usr/local/`.

By now you are probably asking: What happens if I want to type a filename in the local directory or somewhere else on my path without providing the complete path to the file? Can Bash complete filenames for me then? Luckily, the answer is "yes." If you attempt to complete a file or directory name without providing a complete path, as in the case of

```
$ gr
```

Bash will search the path for names that match the entered characters. For most systems, the example above will match only a few commands, including `grep` and `groff`, and Bash will present you with a list of possible alternatives:

```
grep      groff     grotty
```

If you want the command `grep`, all you would need to do is type e and then hit Tab again, and Bash will complete the command name for you.

Command Alias

Command aliasing is a powerful feature of the Bash shell that allows you to define your own custom commands. For instance, if you regularly check all running processes on your system, you might use a command like

```
$ ps -aux | more
```

Rather than needing to type **ps -aux | more** whenever you want to check all the processes running on your system, you can save yourself unnecessary keystrokes by defining an alias using Bash's built-in `alias` command.

In this example, let's say you want to create an alias called `psa` to use whenever you want to check all the running processes. You could define this using

```
$ alias psa="ps -aux | more"
```

Once you do this, typing **psa** at the Bash prompt will run `ps -aux | more`. The alias will remain in place until the end of your current Bash session. When you log out and Bash exits, the aliases you have defined will be lost.

If you want to create more permanent command aliases, you should set the aliases in your `.bashrc` file using the same method we used earlier to make emacs the default text editor.

In addition to providing a way to create shortcuts to commonly used commands, command aliasing can be used to protect yourself from major mistakes. For instance, if you are logged in as the root user, normal use of the `cp`, `mv`, and `rm` commands can be quite dangerous. One mistake can overwrite or erase files, directories, or whole file systems without your realizing it. For this reason, many distributions of Linux configure the Bash shells of the root account to have the following set of default aliases:

```
alias cp='cp -i'
alias mv='mv -i'
alias rm='rm -i'
```

In all these cases, the `-i` flag forces the command to interactively prompt the user for all actions it takes to overwrite or erase files. In order to cause the commands to run without prompting for each action, the user would have to explicitly ask for this with the appropriate flags (for instance, `rm -f`).

Command-Line Editing

One feature of Bash that was missing in some earlier shells such as the Bourne Shell and the C Shell is the ability to edit a command line. Without this feature, once you type a sequence of characters on the command line, you are not free to go back to that sequence—your only choice would be to delete all the characters back to the one you want to edit, fix the character, and then retype the rest of the line. For instance, if you had typed:

```
$ /usr/kocal/bin/mycommand
```

and subsequently realized that koca1 had to be 1oca1, you would have had to delete all the way back to the k, replace the k with an 1, and then retype the rest of the line. Needless to say, this would be a rather inefficient way to work.

For this reason, most modern shells, including Bash, provide full command-line editing. This allows you to use the arrow keys to move through the current line, delete and insert characters as needed, and hit Return to execute the command without moving the cursor to the end of the line. By default, Bash has inserting turned on, so if you type new characters, they are inserted at the cursor rather than overwriting existing characters.

Bash provides several useful key shortcuts to speed up editing, especially with long command lines. Table 13.1 highlights these shortcuts:

TABLE 13.1: Useful Editing Key Shortcuts

Keystroke	Action
Ctrl+A	Jump to the start of the line
Ctrl+E	Jump to the end of the line
Ctrl+B	Move back one character
Ctrl+F	Move forward one character
Esc, B	Move back one word
Esc, F	Move forward one word
Ctrl+L	Clear the screen and display the current command as the first line of the screen
Ctrl+D	Delete the character at the current cursor position
Backspace	Delete the character to the left of the cursor
Ctrl+T	Transpose the character to the left of the cursor with the character at the current cursor position
Esc, T	Transpose the word to the left of the cursor with the word at the current cursor position
Esc, U	Uppercase the current word
Esc, L	Lowercase the current word
Esc, C	Capitalize the current word
Ctrl+K	Delete from the current cursor position to the end of the line

If you are familiar with the emacs editor, you will probably notice that many of the above keystrokes are the same as the ones you use in emacs. This is because the default editing mode of Bash is designed to use emacs-like commands. Alternatives include a vi-like mode, but since familiarity with vi and its more obscure style of editing is generally limited to programmers and advanced system administrators, we won't look at how to use the vi editing mode in this book.

The list of commands outlined in Table 1 represents only a small portion of all the editing commands available in Bash. It covers the core set of editing functions needed by most users to become efficient with Bash. If you want to delve more deeply into the editing functions of Bash, you should read the READLINE section of the bash man page, which you can find by typing **man bash** at the shell prompt.

Command History List

The idea behind the command history list is really rather simple. Every command you execute (by hitting Return instead of Ctrl+C) is added to a history list buffer, which you can access in reverse order starting with the most recent command executed and ending with the least.

To access the history list, the simplest method is to press the up arrow key to cycle through the history list until you find the command you are looking for.

The history list is most often used for two purposes:

• Fixing mistakenly entered commands

• Repeating commands many times during a session

Let's address the first application of the history list. Let's say you have just tried to view the contents of the file testfile by typing

```
$ moer testfile
```

When you hit the Return key, an error message will be generated along the lines of

```
bash: moer: command not found.
```

To quickly correct and execute the command, you could simply hit the up arrow key to recall the last command, change moer to more using the editing functions discussed above, and hit Return to view the file.

Similarly, let's consider the situation where you are experimenting with the configuration for a program you are installing. You might want to repeat the process of editing the configuration file and executing the program several times. You can do this by using the history list to repeatedly perform each step of this two-step process.

A quick method to access commands on the history list is to use the ! symbol. By typing ! followed by the first few letters of a command in the history list, the most recent command starting with the specified letters will be executed.

For instance, if we had previously used the command

```
$ ps -aux | grep httpd | more
```

and we wanted to execute the same command again, typing the command

```
$ !ps
```

would execute the previous command as long as no other ps command had been used after ps -aux | grep httpd | more was used. Using !ps would execute the most recent command starting with ps in the history list.

As with command-line editing, there are some advanced key shortcuts to perform more advanced functions with the command history list. Table 13.2 outlines these keystrokes:

TABLE 13.2: Command History Key Shortcuts

Keystroke	Action
Ctrl+P	Move to the previous command in the history list
Ctrl+N	Move to the next command in the history list
Esc, <	Jump to the top of the history list (the least recent command)
Esc, >	Jump to the end of the history list (the most recent command)
Ctrl+R	Reverse-search through the history list
Ctrl+O	Execute the current line and fetch the next line in the history list for editing and executing

The most interesting of these is Ctrl+R, which allows you to search backwards through the history list in a dynamic, interactive fashion: as you start to type a command, Bash will show the most recent command that matches what you have typed so far. The more you type, the more you narrow down your search to the command you are looking for.

Let's say you want to execute a complicated `find` command you have already executed once. You could use `Ctrl+R` to start a reverse search. When you do this, Bash presents an interactive search prompt:

```
(reverse-i-search)`':
```

As you type the letters in the `find` command, Bash finds the most recent command that has a match for the currently entered string. For instance, just typing `f` might bring up

```
(reverse-i-search)`f': pico info/.signature
```

and continuing on to `fi` might produce

```
(reverse-i-search)`fi': rm -rf StarOffice-3.1
```

until finally `fin` displays

```
(reverse-i-search)`fi': find / -name 'foo' -print
```

which is the command you are looking for. You can now hit Return to execute the command.

Job Control

The concept of job control is particularly useful in Linux given the multitasking nature of the operating system. Using job control, it is possible to use a single shell to execute and control multiple programs running simultaneously.

Normally, when you execute a command, it runs in the foreground. That is, the shell executes the command and the prompt doesn't return until the command is finished. In the case of interactive programs such emacs, this means the program takes over the screen or window where the shell is running and only when you quit the program does the command prompt become available again. In the case of non-interactive programs such as `find`, the program will run and, even if it displays nothing on the screen, the command prompt is not returned until the program finishes.

Consider the command

```
$ find / -name '*.tmp' -print > templist
```

This command searches the entire directory structure of a Linux system for files with the `.tmp` extension and prints all of those filenames to the standard output.

With the above command, the output is redirected to a file called `templist` that can be used for later processing. This means that nothing will be printed to the display—but you still won't be able to run other commands while `find` is running.

Such a limitation runs against the very notion of multitasking. There should be a way to start the `find` command and then continue with other work while `find` finishes running.

This is where the idea of running a program in the background comes into play. Rather than running it in the foreground, thus preventing the simultaneous execution of other commands, placing a job in the background allows the command to run while the user issues new commands at the command prompt.

The easiest way to place a job in the background is to add an ampersand (&) to the end of the command when you run it. This tells Bash to run the command in the background and immediately gives you a new command prompt. To put the `find` command in the background, we would use

```
$ find / -name '*.tmp' -print > templist &
```

Once we hit the Return key to execute this command, we would immediately be presented with a new command prompt; at the same time, `find` would begin executing.

Using Bash's `jobs` command, it is possible to track the jobs that are running in the background. Using `jobs` might produce results like:

```
$ jobs
[1]+  Running                 find / -name '*.tmp' -print >templist &
```

Here the `jobs` command returns results telling us that there is one background (note the &) job running, and that the first job running is `find / -name '*.tmp' -print >templist &`.

If we have several jobs running in the background, we might get results such as

```
[1]-  Running                 find / -name '*.tmp' -print >templist &
[2]+  Running                 ls -lR / >dirlist &
```

from the `jobs` command.

If you have already started a program in the foreground and want to put it in the background, you can do so. The key shortcut Ctrl+Z is interpreted by Bash as a request to temporarily suspend the current process. For instance, if our `find` command is running in the foreground and we type Ctrl+Z, the process is temporarily stopped. Typing the `jobs` command at this point produces a result like this:

```
[1]+  Stopped                 find / -name '*.tmp' -print >templist
```

Notice how the status of the job is `Stopped` instead of `Running`. We can then place the job in the background with the `bg` command:

```
$ bg 1
```

where 1 specifies the number of the job. If there is only one stopped job, it is not necessary to specify the job number, and

```
$ bg
```

will place the single stopped job in the background. Once a stopped job is placed in the background, typing `jobs` will produce a result showing the job as `Running`.

Sometimes it is useful to temporarily suspend a job without placing it in the background. This is particularly true when you are using an interactive application such as emacs or another text editor and want to run one or more commands and then return to your editing. Instead of completely quitting from the editor, it is easier to use Ctrl+Z to stop the editor job, execute your desired commands, and then return the stopped job to the foreground. By their nature, though, interactive applications are not well-suited to being run in the background, and they are best left stopped while they are not in use.

To send a stopped job (or a background job) to the foreground, you can use the `fg` command. For instance, if you were running emacs but stopped it with Ctrl+Z, executed some commands, and then wanted to return to emacs, you could use

```
$ fg
```

If you have one or more stopped or background jobs, it is best to specify the job number with the `fg` command. If your `emacs` command was job number two, then

```
$ fg 2
```

would return it to the foreground, and you could continue editing.

Finally, there may be times when you will want to terminate or kill a stopped or background job. The `kill` command can be used to kill a command on the basis of a process ID (PID). Use the `ps` command to find out the process ID (check the `ps` man page for details) or to directly kill stopped and background jobs in Bash.

For instance, if we have two background jobs and the jobs command produces

```
[1]-  Running        find / -name '*.tmp' -print >templist &
[2]+  Running        ls -lR / >dirlist &
[3]+  Stopped        emacs somefile
```

then we could kill the ls command using the kill command, like this:

```
$ kill %2
```

Notice that, unlike killing a PID, killing a job requires that a percent sign (%) appear before the job number. Without the percent sign, kill would attempt to kill the process with the PID of 2 rather than job number two in the current shell. This is an important distinction because the job number and the PID of a job are extremely unlikely ever to be the same.

Consider the following example: You already have a background process running in your shell and you start a new one as job number 2. When you launch this new job, the system automatically assigns the job a PID from a list of PIDs. This number might be 100, 999, or 25,678. Generally, small process IDs (especially those below 100) are used up by all types of system processes that start when Linux boots and stay running until you shut the computer off. Therefore, it is unlikely that the PID of your job will match the job number.

Pattern Expansion

One of the strengths of many modern shells, including Bash, is the ability to use powerful patterns to specify one or more commands or files.

Let's consider a simple example to illustrate the concept. Normally, if we use the command

```
$ ls -l
```

we get a full listing of all files in the current directory. Suppose we want to find a specific file and all we know is that the filename starts with the letter z. Then the command

```
$ ls -l z*
```

could be used. Here, we pass z* as an argument. The pattern z* says to list any file whose filename starts with z followed by zero or more characters. This is the same function of the * that any DOS or Windows user is probably familiar with. What really happens here is that Bash builds a list of all filenames starting with z and then replaces z* with this list, effectively passing all filenames as arguments to the ls -l command.

Unlike DOS and the Windows DOS prompt, however, Bash offers a greater pattern of possibilities for the simple * symbol.

Pathname Expansion

One form of pattern expansion is pathname expansion. In addition to the *, we can use up to two other major special symbols to expand pathnames, as shown in Table 13.3:

TABLE 13.3: Pathname Expansion in Bash

Symbol	Description
?	Match any single character
[...]	Match one of the characters enclosed in the brackets
[A-F]	Match any single character that falls between the first character and the second
[^...] or [!...]	Match any single character other than those specified in the brackets
[^A-F] or [!A-F]	Match any single character other than those that fall between the first character and the second

Let's look at some examples.

Suppose we want to list all files whose names are three letters long and start with a and end with z. We could use

```
$ ls -l a?z
```

Similarly, if we want to match any files whose names simply start with a and end with z, we could use

```
$ ls -l a*z
```

The difference is that the ? matches exactly one character in the first example, forcing the filename to be three characters long. In the second example, the * matches zero or more characters, meaning the filename could be two or more characters in length.

Next, let's consider the situation where we want to see a listing of all files starting with the letters a, b, c, or d. We could use the command

```
$ ls -l a* b* c* d*
```

but this is rather inefficient and becomes cumbersome when we want to see files starting with more letters. To make the process easier, we could use

```
$ ls -1 [abcd]*
```

which tells us to list any file starting with one of a, b, c, or d followed by zero or more characters.

However, because a, b, c, and d are a continuous sequence of letters, we could use

```
$ ls -1 [a-d]*
```

making the pattern even more concise.

Finally, we need to consider the case where we want to exclude a particular character or pattern and include all others. Consider cases where we are producing a compressed archive of all the home directories on a system for backup purposes. Let's say that, for whatever reason, we want to produce an archive of all home directories except those starting with the letter m. We could use

```
$ tar czvf home.tar.gz /home/[a-l]* /home/[n-z]*
```

However, we can make things easier with

```
$ tar czvf home.tar.gz /home/[!m]*
```

which indicates that all home directories starting with any letter except m should be processed by the command.

Taking things one step further, we could exclude all directories starting with the letters m, n and o by using

```
$ tar czvf home.tar.gz /home/[^mno]*
```

or

```
$ tar czvf home.tar.gz /home/[!m-o]*
```

Brace Expansion

Closely related to the pathname expansion is brace expansion. Brace expansion provides a method by which it is possible to expand an expression regardless of whether the names being generated actually exist as files or directories at all.

An example of a brace expression is:

```
$ mkdir testdir{1,2,3,4}
```

which causes the directories `testdir1`, `testdir2`, `testdir3`, and `testdir4` to be created.

Here each element in the braces is separated by a comma, and one by one these are used to produce the resulting names. Unlike the [. . .] expressions we saw earlier, the use of a comma means that the elements between the braces can be more than one character in length:

```
$ mkdir testdir{01,02,03,04}
```

It is important to keep in mind that a brace expression must contain at least one comma.

An interesting feature of both pathname expansion and brace expansion is that they can be used within another brace expression. This is possible because the first expansion to take place is brace expansion.

Consider the example:

```
$ mkdir newdir/{firstdir,firstdir/dir{01,02}}
```

This command would create the following directories:

```
firstdir
firstdir/dir01
firstdir/dir02
```

Here we used the brace expression {01,02} inside the outer brace expression.

Similarly, we can use any of the pathname expansion symbols inside a brace. The command

```
$ chmod 644 testfile.{tx?,bak,0[0-9]}
```

would change the permissions on a series of files including any file matching the expression testfile.tx?, testfile.bak and testfile.00 through testfile.09.

Command Substitution

Finally, we will take a look at command substitution, another form of pattern expansion. In some ways this is similar to piping commands together, but the difference is that in piping, the standard output of a command is passed to the standard input of another command. With command substitution, though, the standard output of one command becomes an argument or parameter to another command.

For instance, consider an example where we want to compress all files that have a .bak extension. We can get a list of all these files by using

```
$ find / -name '*.bak' -print
```

Using the exec flag of the find command we could compress all the files in question:

```
$ find / -name '*.bak' -exec gzip {} \;
```

The other option is to use command substitution:

```
$ gzip `find / -name '*.bak' -print`
```

Here the find command is contained in backwards single quotes. These quotes indicate that the results of the command should be used as part of the command line, in this case as arguments to the gzip command.

An alternative to the backwards single quotes is the following form, which has the same meaning and gets the same result:

```
$ gzip $(find / -name '*.bak' -print)
```

The main difference between these two forms is the meaning of the special character \. In the latter form no characters have special meanings, while in the former the backslash retains special meaning except when followed by $, ` or \.

NOTE   In addition to the types of expansion we have reviewed here, there are other types of expansion available in Bash. These are outlined in detail in the **bash** man page. However, the pattern expansion forms in this chapter provide a lot of power. If you find yourself needing more powerful pattern and expansion abilities, check out the man page by using the command **man bash**.

Where Do We Go from Here?

Now that we are shell power users and can perform lots of nifty magic in the world of Bash, it is time to move on to working with real, productive applications in Linux.

In the next chapter, we are going to look at essential tasks of system administration. These include managing users and groups of users as well as scheduling tasks for automated execution and controlling the way in which a Linux system boots.

CHAPTER
FOURTEEN

14

General System Administration

- Managing Users

- Managing Groups

- System Start-Up

- Scheduling Jobs

- Managing Logs

In this chapter, we are going to look at some of the basic administrative tasks that are necessary for maintaining a working Linux system.

Fundamental to any Linux system, from a network server to a home computer shared by family members, is user management. This runs the gamut from creating new user accounts to changing user passwords to ensuring that a user's home directory is just the way you, as the system administrator, want it when their accounts are created.

On even a moderately sophisticated system, user access to system resources will be governed on both a per-user basis and a per-group basis, where a group consists of a number of users associated in a common organizational entity with a single name. Linux provides facilities to associate users in groups and to use these groups to manage access to system resources.

Another administrative essential—one that is crucial to taking full advantage of Linux—is the automation of tasks, both at start-up and on a scheduled basis. Linux's notion of run levels provides a powerful mechanism to specify what will occur at what point in the start-up process (and in the shutdown process as well). And the Unix Cron facility offers a mechanism to schedule one-time jobs as well as operations that are repeated daily, weekly, monthly, or yearly.

Finally, Linux provides sophisticated logging capabilities that make it possible to know exactly what is happening on your system. Of course, for logs to be of use, they need regular management. After all, if your log contains one year's worth of entries, it becomes too large to be useful for analysis or for quickly tracking down problems or potential problems.

Managing Users

You were introduced to user management in Chapter 12 ("Configuring Your System with the Control Panel") when we looked at Red Hat Linux 5's Control Panel. However, the Control Panel is not universally available in all distributions of Linux, and to fully master the administration of Linux you must learn to manage users without this tool.

Creating Users

Creation of users in Linux is done through `useradd` (generally found in `/usr/sbin/`; it may be called `adduser` on some systems). The versions of this program that come with various distributions of Linux can differ, so you should refer to the man page for yours (`man adduser` or `man useradd`) to learn the details of using the version you have.

The version of `useradd` shipped with Red Hat 5 is a highly complex tool that can make the creation of new user accounts exceptionally easy. Let's start with the simplest example and work up to more complicated cases. The simplest case is to create a user with all the default settings. For instance, to create a new user called `testuser1`, we simply type:

```
# useradd testuser1
```

This command creates the user by performing the following actions:

- Creating an entry for the user in the `/etc/passwd` file without a password. In some Linux distributions, the account would be created so that anyone can log in to the account without first being assigned a password. In Red Hat Linux 5, a password needs to be assigned before the user is able to log in.

- Assigning a user ID to the user. Generally, this is the next available user ID in numerical order. In Red Hat Linux 5, the default is to use the smallest number greater than 99 that is greater than all other users' IDs.

- Adding the user to the appropriate group. In Red Hat Linux 5, this means creating a group for the user to which only that user belongs. On other distributions of Linux, all users may belong to the same group by default.

- Creating a home directory for the user (at `/home/testuser1` on most Linux systems) and copying the contents of `/etc/skel` to the home directory. Skeleton directories are discussed in more detail in the section "Setting Up Default Home Directories" later in this chapter.

NOTE   On Red Hat Linux 5 systems, the default behavior to create users' home directories is automatically specified in the file `/etc/login.defs` and is generally true by default. To force `useradd` to create the home directory regardless of the entry in `/etc/login.defs`, add the -m flag: `# useradd -m testuser`.

Using the command above to add users leaves the system administrator free to assign a password for the user, utilizing the techniques described in the next section, "Changing Passwords."

What happens, though, if you want to override the system defaults for assignment of the user ID? Consider an organization where Red Hat Linux user IDs are based on the individual's corporate identification number. In this case, you will want to force the assignment of a particular ID. This is done with the -u flag:

```
# useradd -u 10001 testuser1
```

This creates the account for testuser1 with the assigned user ID of 10001.

Similarly, what if you want to force the assignment of a particular group to the user as their default group. For instance, if testuser1 should be assigned to the collective group named users rather than to an individual group as is the default in Red Hat Linux, you could use the -g flag:

```
# useradd -g users testuser1
```

Let's go a step further and assume that testuser1 should belong to the groups group1 and group2 in addition to the default group of users. You could create the user as indicated above and then manually add them to the groups, as shown below in the section on managing groups. But useradd offers the -G flag, which allows the specification of additional groups to add the new user to when the account is created:

```
# useradd -g users -G group1,group2 testuser1
```

Finally, to specify an alternate home directory for a user, use the -d flag:

```
# useradd -d /other/home/directory testuser1
```

Changing *Useradd* Defaults

There are some defaults used by useradd that you may want to override every time you create a user. For example, you may want all home directories to be created in /users instead of /home. Similarly, you may want all new users to belong to the default group users instead of their own private groups.

These defaults can be reset using the -D flag of the useradd command and several supplementary flags. The -D flag indicates that the command should not create a new user but should assign new defaults.

The -D flag is used in conjunction with supplementary flags. Here we will look at the -b and -g flags for resetting the default home directory path and default group, respectively.

To set the default home directory path to /users, use the command

```
# useradd -D -b /users
```

Similarly, to set the default group for all new users to users, use the command

```
# useradd -D -g users
```

These commands can be combined into one:

```
# useradd -D -b /users -g users
```

Changing Passwords

Changing passwords is accomplished with the passwd command. Any user can change their password by simply typing the command at the prompt; they will be asked to enter their current password followed by their new password twice for confirmation:

```
$ passwd

Changing password for test
(current) UNIX password:
New UNIX password:
Retype new UNIX password:
passwd: all authentication tokens updated successfully
```

In many versions of Linux, the passwd command checks to see if a password is too short, too simple, too similar to the username, or too similar to the previous password. An invalid password produces errors like these:

```
$ passwd
Changing password for test
(current) UNIX password:
New UNIX password:
BAD PASSWORD: it does not contain enough DIFFERENT characters
New UNIX password:
BAD PASSWORD: it is too short
New UNIX password:
BAD PASSWORD: is too simple
passwd: Authentication token manipulation error
```

WARNING With some versions of the `passwd` command, the type of protection against invalid passwords described above can be circumvented if the user is stubborn enough and keeps supplying the same password. Eventually the `passwd` program gives up and accepts the password.

The root user has the power to change any user's password by supplying the username as an argument to the `passwd` program. In this case, the only prompts are to enter the new password twice:

```
# passwd test
New UNIX password:
Retype new UNIX password:
passwd: all authentication tokens updated successfully
```

Setting Up Default Home Directories

You will have noticed a reference to skeleton directories earlier in the section on adding users. By default, every user is given a home directory, usually in the /home directory. When the user's account is created, their home directory is created and populated with a default set of files. This default set of files is copied from the /etc/skel directory, which contains the skeleton directory for new home directories.

In order to include a file in every new home directory, simply create the file and place it in /etc/skel with the same name you would want it to have in users' home directories. All users added after you place the file there will find the file in their home directories when their accounts are created.

Removing Users

Deleting users is a parallel process to adding users: you use the `userdel` command. Fortunately, though, this command is far simpler to use than the `useradd` command. To delete a user's account and remove their entry from relevant system files such as /etc/passwd, simply provide the username as an argument:

```
# userdel <username>
```

The problem here is that the user's files are not deleted. To delete the user's home directory at the same time, provide the -r flag:

```
# userdel -r <username>
```

This leaves one other issue: What if the user owned files elsewhere on the system that need to be deleted? This can be achieved by using the `find` command after deleting the user. In order to do this, make a note of the user's user ID from the password file before deleting the user, and then use the `find` command:

```
# find / -type f -uid 503 -print -exec rm {} \;
```

Let's break this down. The forward slash (/) indicates that we search the entire directory structure from the top level; `-type f` indicates that we should only find files; `-uid 503` indicates that only files owned by the user with ID 503 should be returned (this number should be substituted with the user ID of the user you are deleting); `-print` indicates that the filenames should be printed as they are found so that you can track the progress of the command; finally, `-exec rm {} \;` indicates that the command `rm` should be performed on every file found, effectively removing the files.

WARNING Great care needs to be taken when using the `find` command described above. Because it runs as the root user, a mistake in typing the command or in the ownership of files on your system could cause critical data to be lost. Use `find` only if the user is likely to own files outside their home directory.

Managing Groups

Managing groups—collections of associated users—is as simple as managing users and parallels the user management process. As with user management, Linux provides commands to automate the creation and modification of groups. On some systems, these commands may behave differently than described below, so you should check the documentation for your Linux distribution if you are not using the enclosed copy of Red Hat 5.1.

Creating Groups

You can add new groups to your system using the `groupadd` command (this command is called `addgroup` on some distributions). To create a group, simply provide the group name as an argument:

```
# groupadd <groupname>
```

The group will be created and assigned a new user number based on the following rule from the man page for groupadd: "The default is to use the smallest ID value greater than 500 and greater than every other group."

If you want to specify the group number, simply use the -g flag to indicate the number:

```
# groupadd -g 503 <groupname>
```

This should produce an entry similar to the following in /etc/group:

```
<groupname>::503:
```

This entry shows an empty group with the specified name and group ID.

Adding Users to Groups

Unfortunately, there is no standard program available to easily add users to a group. In order to do this, the easiest thing is to directly edit the file /etc/group. Each line in this file represents the definition for a group and takes the form

```
<groupname>:<password>:<groupid>:<userlist>
```

The groupname entry is the name of the group. The password entry represents an encrypted password for the group; passwords generally are not applied to groups, so this is usually blank. The groupid is the numeric ID for the group and should be unique for the group. Finally, the userlist entry is a comma-separated list of users who belong to the group. For instance, if user1, user2, and user3 all belong to the group named group1 whose group ID is 505, the entry for the group would look like:

```
group1::505:user1,user2,user3
```

If you want to add users to an existing group, simply edit the file /etc/group with your favorite text editor and add the user's names to the end of the user list, separating each user with a comma.

Deleting Groups

Deleting groups is achieved with the groupdel command. This command is truly simple; no flags or options are available. Simply provide the group name to delete as an argument, and the group will be deleted:

```
# groupdel <groupname>
```

For all its simplicity, though, there are some caveats:

1. Files belonging to the group won't be deleted or have their group changed.

2. If the group serves as the primary group for a user (in other words, is indicated as the user's group in the password file), the group won't be deleted.

The first issue can be handled much as we dealt with deleting a user's files once the user had been deleted. First, we need to note the group ID of the group we are deleting (this can be found in the /etc/group file). Once the group is deleted with groupdel, we can use the find command to change the group ownership of all files that belonged to the deleted group:

```
# find / -type f -gid 503 -print -exec chgrp newgroupname {} \;
```

This find command will find all files belonging to the group whose ID is 503 and then use the chgrp command to change the group ownership of the file to the group named newgroupname.

System Start-Up

One area that is a mystery to many Unix users (as opposed to system administrators) is the boot sequence, when all those arcane messages flash by on the screen.

NOTE   Start-up messages are saved in the system log file /var/log/messages. Log files are discussed later in this chapter.

What Happens during Booting?

The boot cycle is really simpler than the boot-time messages suggest. Basically, there are two stages to the boot process:

1. Booting the kernel. During this phase, the kernel loads into memory and prints messages as it initializes each device driver.

2. Executing the program init. After the kernel finishes loading and initializing devices, the program init runs. Init handles the launching of all programs, including essential system daemons and other software that is specified to load at boot time.

The *Init* Program

We are going to take a closer look at the init program because it is here that you are able to easily customize which programs load during the boot cycle. Init has the job of launching new processes and restarting other processes when they exit. A perfect example of this is the set of processes that provide the virtual login consoles in Linux. On most Linux systems, six of these are initially loaded at boot time. When you log out of a console window, that process dies and init starts a new one so that six console windows are always available.

The rules that govern the operation of the init program are stored in the file /etc/inittab. Red Hat Linux 5's /etc/inittab file looks like this:

```
#
# inittab       This file describes how the INIT process should set up
#               the system in a certain run-level.
#
# Author:       Miquel van Smoorenburg, <miquels@drinkel.nl.mugnet.org>
#               Modified for RHS Linux by Marc Ewing and Donnie Barnes
#

# Default runlevel. The runlevels used by RHS are:
#   0 - halt (Do NOT set initdefault to this)
#   1 - Single user mode
#   2 - Multiuser, without NFS (The same as 3, if you do not have
➥ networking)
#   3 - Full multiuser mode
#   4 - unused
#   5 - X11
#   6 - reboot (Do NOT set initdefault to this)
#
id:3:initdefault:

# System initialization.
si::sysinit:/etc/rc.d/rc.sysinit

l0:0:wait:/etc/rc.d/rc 0
l1:1:wait:/etc/rc.d/rc 1
l2:2:wait:/etc/rc.d/rc 2
l3:3:wait:/etc/rc.d/rc 3
l4:4:wait:/etc/rc.d/rc 4
```

```
l5:5:wait:/etc/rc.d/rc 5
l6:6:wait:/etc/rc.d/rc 6

# Things to run in every runlevel.
ud::once:/sbin/update

# Trap CTRL-ALT-DELETE
ca::ctrlaltdel:/sbin/shutdown -t3 -r now

# When our UPS tells us power has failed, assume we have a few minutes
# of power left.  Schedule a shutdown for 2 minutes from now.
# This does, of course, assume you have powerd installed and your
# UPS connected and working correctly.
pf::powerfail:/sbin/shutdown -f -h +2 "Power Failure; System Shutting
Down"

# If power was restored before the shutdown kicked in, cancel it.
➡ pr:12345:powerokwait:/sbin/shutdown -c "Power Restored; Shutdown
➡ Cancelled"


# Run gettys in standard runlevels
1:12345:respawn:/sbin/mingetty tty1
2:2345:respawn:/sbin/mingetty tty2
3:2345:respawn:/sbin/mingetty tty3
4:2345:respawn:/sbin/mingetty tty4
5:2345:respawn:/sbin/mingetty tty5
6:2345:respawn:/sbin/mingetty tty6

# Run xdm in runlevel 5
x:5:respawn:/usr/bin/X11/xdm -nodaemon
```

While it is not important to learn how to write your own inittab file, it is useful to understand what this file is telling us.

Linux has a system of run levels. A run level is a number that identifies the current state of the system and which processes init should run and keep running in that system state. In the inittab file, the first entry specifies the default run level that loads at boot time. In the above example, it is a multiuser console mode, run level 3. Then, each entry in the inittab file specifies which run level it applies to in the second field of the entry (each field is separated by a colon). So, for run level 3, the following lines are relevant:

```
l3:3:wait:/etc/rc.d/rc 3
1:12345:respawn:/sbin/mingetty tty1
2:2345:respawn:/sbin/mingetty tty2
3:2345:respawn:/sbin/mingetty tty3
4:2345:respawn:/sbin/mingetty tty4
5:2345:respawn:/sbin/mingetty tty5
6:2345:respawn:/sbin/mingetty tty6
```

The last six lines set up the six virtual consoles provided in Linux. The first line runs the start-up script /etc/rc.d/rc 3. This will run all the scripts contained in the directory /etc/rc.d/rc3.d. These scripts represent programs that need to start at system initialization, such as sendmail, PCMCIA services, the printer daemon, and crond. Generally, you will not want to edit these scripts or change them; they are the system defaults.

What is important to note is that the last script in rc3.d to be executed will be the S99local script. This script is actually a link to the file /etc/rc.d/rc.local; it is here that you can put any custom start-up programs that you want to launch at boot time.

On other Linux systems, the structure of /etc/inittab may differ, as will the organization of the /etc/rc.d directory. In all systems, however, the file /etc/rc.d/rc.local represents the file in which you can add your own start-up commands.

Using the *Rc.local* File

The default Red Hat Linux 5 rc.local file sets up the login prompt and does nothing else:

```
#!/bin/sh

# This script will be executed *after* all the other init scripts.
# You can put your own initialization stuff in here if you don't
# want to do the full Sys V style init stuff.

if [ -f /etc/redhat-release ]; then
        R=$(cat /etc/redhat-release)
else
```

```
        R="release 3.0.3"
fi

arch=$(uname -m)
a="a"
case "_$arch" in
        _a*) a="an";;
        _i*) a="an";;
esac

# This will overwrite /etc/issue at every boot.  So, make any
➥ changes you
# want to make to /etc/issue here or you will lose them when you
reboot.
echo "" > /etc/issue
echo "Red Hat Linux $R" >> /etc/issue
echo "Kernel $(uname -r) on $a $(uname -m)" >> /etc/issue

cp -f /etc/issue /etc/issue.net
echo >> /etc/issue
```

This may look complicated, but it is actually quite simple. The steps here are:

1. Determine the Red Hat release being used.

2. Determine the hardware architecture (such as i386 for Intel or axp for Alpha).

3. Store the contents of the login prompt in /etc/issue; this file is displayed at each console prompt.

Because the rc.local file is a standard shell script, you can do anything here that is legitimate in a shell script, including assigning environment variables and launching programs. For instance, on one system I manage, we launch a database daemon in our rc.local file with the command:

```
/usr/local/Minerva/bin/msqld &
```

Feel free to use the rc.local file to add any start-up programs that you would like to run. For instance, if you want to receive an e-mail every time a particular machine on the network finishes booting, you can use the rc.local file on the machine in question to run the command

```
/bin/mail -s "I have booted - machinename" username@some.domain
```

to send a quick mail message to username@some.domain with the subject line I have booted - machinename.

Shutting Down

Closely related to system start-up is system shutdown. In Linux, as in all other multitasking operating systems, it is essential to shut down your system cleanly in order to prevent corruption of data stored on attached hard disk drives. Generally, this is done by the root user with the `shutdown` command:

```
# shutdown -h now
```

The use of the `now` argument tells the program to shut down the system immediately. The `-h` flag tells the system to halt after shutting down. When you see the message `System Halted`, it is safe to power off your computer.

Closely related to the shutdown command is the `reboot` command, which cleanly shuts down the system and then reboots it. Hitting the key combination Control+Alt+Delete invokes the `reboot` command.

Scheduling Jobs

One of the great powers of a multiuser server-class operating system like Linux is that much can happen in an unattended manner. If you use Linux as a mail server, Web server, or FTP server, unattended activity occurs every time one of these applications answers incoming connections and requests for service. Similarly, individual users and the system administrator can configure Linux to perform prescheduled tasks in an unattended manner.

This activity is achieved through the facility of a daemon called `crond`. This daemon is standard in almost every distribution of Linux and is generally installed to start every time the system boots.

How *Crond* Works

The way in which `crond` works is amazingly simple. Once `crond` starts (generally at boot time), it wakes up every minute and checks whether any jobs have been scheduled to run during that minute. If so, the job is executed and the resulting output is sent by e-mail to the user who scheduled the job.

Because `crond` checks the date stamps on its configuration files every minute, any changes to schedules are noted without the necessity of restarting the `crond` process.

Scheduling Jobs

Scheduling jobs is an easy matter. All scheduled jobs are stored in an individual configuration file (known as a `crontab` file) for the user, with each line representing a job that has been scheduled.

We will start by looking at the format of `crontab` file entries before moving on to how we actually edit the `crontab` file to create scheduled jobs.

Each entry takes the form

```
<time-date> <command>
```

The `time-date` entry consists of five numeric fields, each separated by spaces, which indicate when a job should be run. The five fields (in order) are:

- Minute: Possible values are 0-59

- Hour: Possible values are 0-23

- Day of month: Possible values are 0-31

- Month: Possible values are 0-12 (or the first three letters of the month's name)

- Day of week: Possible values are 0-7 where both 0 and 7 represent Sunday (or the first three letters of the day's name)

For all these fields, several rules provide flexibility:

- Ranges of numbers can be used. For instance, 1-3 in the hour field says to schedule the command for 1:00 A.M., 2:00 A.M., and 3:00 A.M. Similarly, 2-4 in the day of the week field schedules the job for Tuesday, Wednesday, and Thursday.

- Ranges can be stepped through in increments greater than one. For instance, to indicate every other hour from midnight to midnight, use the range 0-23 and combine it with the step of 2, separating them with slashes: 0-23/2.

- An asterisk (*) indicates the entire range for a field from smallest value to largest value. Thus, * in the day of the month field is the same as 0-31 and in the day of the week field is the same as 0-7.

Sample Times and Dates

Let's take a look at some example time-date fields:

`0 1 * * *`	This field indicates a job that should run every day at 1:00 a.m.
`30 14 * * 0`	This field indicates a job that should run every Monday at 2:30 p.m.
`0 12 1 * *`	This field indicates a job that should run at noon on the first day of every month.
`0 12 * 1 mon`	This field indicates a job that should run at noon on every Monday in January every year.
`0 12 2 feb *`	This field indicates a job that should run at noon on February 2nd every year.

The Command Field

The time-date field is separated from the command field by one or more spaces and runs until the end of the line. The commands are processed by the `/bin/sh` shell.

For instance, the `crontab` entry

```
0 1 * * *     /usr/local/bin/backup
```

will run the program `/usr/local/bin/backup` daily at 1:00 a.m.

Sometimes commands (such as the `mail` command) require information to be entered through the standard input. This is achieved using percent signs (%). The first percent sign marks the start of standard input, and each subsequent percent sign serves as a new line character in the standard input.

So, the `crontab` entry

```
30 14 * * fri     /bin/mail -s "TGIF" armand@landegg.edu%Thank God It's
Friday%%Me.
```

will send the following e-mail message:

```
Thank God It's Friday

Me.
```

to `armand@landegg.edu` each Friday afternoon at 2:30 p.m.

Editing the *Crontab* File

A user can edit their crontab file with the crontab command. Two approaches are available: create a file containing all the entries desired in their crontab file and then load it with the crontab command or edit the crontab file directly with the crontab command.

Loading Entries from a File In order to load entries from a file, it is first necessary to create a file (using your favorite text editor) containing all the entries you wish to have appear in your crontab file. A sample file might contain two entries:

```
0 1 * * *      /usr/local/bin/backup
30 14 * * fri      /bin/mail -s "TGIF" armand@landegg.edu%Thank God
It's Friday%%Me.
```

This file needs to be saved, under a suitable name such as cronjobs.

Once the file is created and saved, it can be loaded into a user's crontab file by issuing the command:

```
$ crontab cronjobs
```

The contents of cronjobs will overwrite any current entries in the crontab file for the user. Using this method, any user can manipulate their own crontab file.

The root user has special privileges that allow them to edit the crontab entries for any user. Using the -u flag, the root user can specify that another user's crontab file, rather than the root user's crontab file, should be altered. For instance, the command

```
# crontab -u username cronjobs
```

will load the file cronjobs as the crontab file for the user username.

Editing *Crontab* Files Directly Instead of creating a separate file and loading it into the crontab file, the crontab command provides the -e flag, which allows the user to edit the crontab file directly.

By default, crontab -e will attempt to edit the crontab file using the vi editor. The vi editor is a powerful but hard-to-master editor popular among longtime Unix users. If you prefer to use another editor, such as xedit, you need to set the value of the EDITOR environment variable to this program:

```
$ export EDITOR=xedit
```

Then, the command

```
$ crontab -e
```

will open the `crontab` file for editing using the specified editor, as shown in Figure 14.1.

FIGURE 14.1:

Editing the crontab file
with xedit

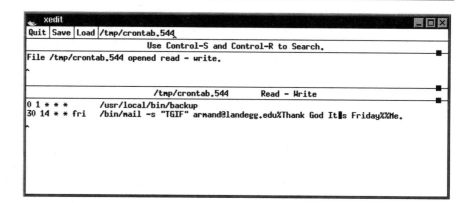

As when we loaded a file into the `crontab` file using the `-u` flag, the root user can directly edit another user's `crontab` file:

```
$ crontab -u <username> -e
```

Viewing the Contents of the *Crontab* File   In order to view the contents of the `crontab` file, simply use the `-1` flag:

```
$ crontab -1
# DO NOT EDIT THIS FILE - edit the master and reinstall.
# (/tmp/crontab.555 installed on Mon Jul 13 00:07:05 1998)
# (Cron version - $Id: crontab.c,v 2.13 1994/01/17 03:20:37
➥ vixie Exp $)
0 1 * * *        /usr/local/bin/backup
30 14 * * fri    /bin/mail -s "TGIF" armand@landegg.edu%Thank God
➥ It's Friday%%Me
```

Notice that the `crontab` file has several comment lines at the beginning that start with the hash mark (#).

As with editing the `crontab` file, the root user can view the contents of any user's `crontab` file with the `-u` flag:

```
# crontab -u <username> -1
```

Removing the *Crontab* File In order to erase the contents of a user's `crontab` file, the user can use the `-r` flag:

```
$ crontab -r
```

Similarly, the root user can clear any user's `crontab` file with the `-u` flag:

```
# crontab -u <username> -r
```

Managing Logs

One of the benefits of Linux and all forms of Unix is that they provide standardized mechanisms for the logging of activity from the numerous daemons and programs running on the system. These logs can be used to debug system problems as well as track usage of the system, covering everything from possible security breaches to advanced warning of possible hardware failure.

For example, the following extract of the main Red Hat 5 system log file (`/var/log/messages`) provides numerous pieces of information from a two-minute period:

```
Apr 16 03:55:29 localhost login: ROOT LOGIN ON tty1
Apr 16 03:55:58 localhost syslog: Warning - secret file /etc/paus
➥ has world and/
or group access
Apr 16 03:55:58 localhost kernel: CSLIP: code copyright 1989 Regents
➥ of the Univ
ersity of California
Apr 16 03:55:58 localhost kernel: PPP: version 2.2.0 (dynamic
➥ channel allocation
)
Apr 16 03:55:58 localhost kernel: PPP Dynamic channel allocation
➥ code copyright
1995 Caldera, Inc.
Apr 16 03:55:58 localhost kernel: PPP line discipline registered.
Apr 16 03:55:58 localhost kernel: registered device ppp0
Apr 16 03:55:58 localhost pppd[207]: pppd 2.2.0 started by root, uid 0
Apr 16 03:55:59 localhost chat[208]: send (ATDT8447077^M)
Apr 16 03:56:00 localhost chat[208]: expect (CONNECT)
Apr 16 03:56:32 localhost chat[208]: ATDT8447077^M^M
Apr 16 03:56:32 localhost pppd[207]: Serial connection established.
Apr 16 03:56:32 localhost chat[208]: CONNECT - got it
```

```
Apr 16 03:56:32 localhost chat[208]: send (^M)
Apr 16 03:56:33 localhost pppd[207]: Using interface ppp0
Apr 16 03:56:33 localhost pppd[207]: Connect: ppp0 <-> /dev/cua1
Apr 16 03:56:36 localhost pppd[207]: Remote message:
Apr 16 03:56:36 localhost pppd[207]: local  IP address 194.209.60.112
Apr 16 03:56:36 localhost pppd[207]: remote IP address 194.209.60.97
```

What exactly do we learn here? We see the login program informing us that the root user has logged in, we have a warning about the security of information in a file that should be secure, we see the kernel loading its PPP module successfully, and we see the pppd process establish a connection to the Internet.

What Gets Logged?

It is important to make a distinction between different types of logs in a Linux system. Basically, there are two types of logs: system logs and application logs. We will be looking at system logs because all systems have them. Application-specific logs are dependent on the applications being run and how these applications are configured to generate their logs.

In the system logs, you are likely to find messages and warnings from the kernel that include information about modules that have loaded, data from the sendmail daemon that provides a trail of the messages that have been processed in the system, and messages about the success or failure of authentication (login) attempts.

System logs are generated by the syslogd daemon, which loads at boot time. The daemon accesses messages at eight levels of severity from various system processes such as the kernel, the mail system, user programs configured to use syslogd, and authentication programs such as the login program.

These levels of messages are, in order of increasing severity:

- debug
- info
- notice
- warning
- err
- crit

- alert

- emerg

These levels are used in the /etc/syslog.conf file to tell syslogd where to create logs for different types of information. The /etc/syslog.conf file contains multiple entries, one on each line, each containing two fields separated by one or more spaces: a facility-level list and a log file location.

The facility-level list is a semicolon-separated list of facility-level pairs. Facilities are indicated by facility names such as mail, kern (for the kernel), user (for user programs), and auth (for authentication programs). Sample facility-level pairs include:

- mail.err: errors generated by the mail daemon

- *.info: all information messages

- kern.emerg: emergency messages from the kernel

Let's look at the default /etc/syslog.conf file that is included with Red Hat Linux 5 to get a sense of how this works:

```
# Log all kernel messages to the console.
# Logging much else clutters up the screen.
#kern.*                                   /dev/console

# Log anything (except mail) of level info or higher.
# Don't log private authentication messages!
*.info;mail.none;authpriv.none            /var/log/messages

# The authpriv file has restricted access.
authpriv.*                                /var/log/secure

# Log all the mail messages in one place.
mail.*                                    /var/log/maillog

# Everybody gets emergency messages, plus log them on another
# machine.
*.emerg                                            *

# Save mail and news errors of level err and higher in a
# special file.
```

```
uucp,news.crit                                /var/log/spooler
```

The first important line is

```
*.info;mail.none;authpriv.none               /var/log/messages
```

This line logs information messages from all facilities except mail and authentication (hence, `mail.none;authpriv.none`) to the file `/var/log/message`. This is followed by

```
authpriv.*                                    /var/log/secure
```

which places all authentication messages in `/var/log/secure`.

Next we find the following line, which specifies that all mail log messages should be placed in `/var/log/maillog`:

```
mail.*                                        /var/log/maillog
```

followed by

```
uucp,news.crit                                /var/log/spooler
```

which logs certain mail- and news-related messages to `/var/log/spooler`.

The first thing you will probably notice is that log messages are separated into different files. The goals behind this practice are to keep the size of each log manageable and to keep the information in each log related so that tracking down log messages will be easy. If every message of every level from every facility ended up in a single log file, the information would be practically useless because the volume of information in the file would be unmanageable.

Other Linux distributions may break the messages down differently than shown in our example, but it is unlikely that all system log messages would end up in a single log file. You can check `/etc/syslog.conf` on your system to find out where your messages are being logged.

If you want to change your logging strategy by editing `/etc/syslog.conf`, you can do this by editing the `syslog.conf` file and then telling `syslogd` to reload the configuration with the command

```
# kill -HUP 'cat /var/run/syslogd.pid'
```

Notice the use of the back quotes. These indicate that the command they contain should be run and the resulting standard output should be provided as an argument to the `kill -HUP` command. The `-HUP` flag of the `kill` command indicates that the process should reread its configuration but keep running.

Rotating Logs

In order for logs to remain useful, they need to be rotated on a regular basis. This allows the size of the logs to be manageable and clears them of old information that is no longer of particular value. Also, because the size of logs will continue to grow, rotating them frees up the disk space they are using.

The simplest strategy for rotating logs is to remove them and restart syslogd. When syslogd restarts, it will create a new, empty log file to replace any that have been removed. For instance, the following commands:

```
# rm /var/log/messages
# kill -HUP 'cat /var/run/syslogd.pid'
```

remove the /var/log/messages file and restart syslogd to create a new, empty /var/log/messages file.

This strategy of removing files works well on a single-user or home system where historical logs may not serve a valuable purpose. On multiuser servers, however, historical information is of particular value, especially for tracking possible security breaches. In this case, the strategy may be slightly different. For instance, to keep one generation of historical logs, you can move the current logs to a new filename and then restart syslogd to create a new current log file:

```
# mv /var/log/messages /var/log/messages.1
# kill -HUP 'cat /var/run/syslogd.pid'
```

Similarly, if you want to create two generations of historical log files, you need to move the first generation files to the second generation filename and then move the current logs to the first generation filename:

```
# mv /var/log/messages.1 /var/log/messages.2
# mv /var/log/messages /var/log/messages.1
# kill -HUP 'cat /var/run/syslogd.pid'
```

On most systems, you may want to automate this procedure, running it every week at a set time. To do this, you first want to create a script that performs the necessary actions to rotate your log files. For instance, on a Red Hat Linux 5 server where you keep one generation of logs, the script would look something like this:

```
#!/bin/sh

mv /var/log/messages /var/log/messages.1
mv /var/log/secure /var/log/secure.1
mv /var/log/maillog /var/log/maillog.1
```

```
mv /var/log/spooler /var/log/spooler.1
kill -HUP 'cat /var/run/syslogd.pid'
```

This script file needs to be created with a text editor in a logical location (such as /usr/local/bin/newlogs) and then made into an executable file:

```
# chmod 755 /usr/local/bin/newlogs
```

Next, you need to edit the root user's crontab file, using the methods described earlier in this chapter, and add an appropriate entry. For instance, to run the script every Sunday morning at 12:01 a.m., we would use the entry:

```
1 12 * * sun /usr/local/bin/newlogs
```

Where Do We Go from Here?

In this chapter, we have learned a handful of useful general system administration tasks relating to users, scheduling, and logs.

In the next chapter, we consider how to configure and use two of the most popular PC peripherals: printers and modems.

We will learn how to configure both PostScript and PCL printers and will discuss the mechanics of the Unix print spool systems. Then we will look at modem configuration and experiment with the minicom program to test and use our modems.

CHAPTER
FIFTEEN

Using Peripherals

- Printers

- Modems

In this chapter, we learn how to configure the two most common types of peripherals: printers and modems. We will get an understanding of how Linux ports work, take a look at the files that control the Linux printing system, and become acquainted with minicom, a standard Linux terminal emulator that you can use to access your modem.

Printers

In Chapter 12, "Configuring Your System with the Control Panel," we learned how to easily configure printers in Red Hat Linux 5 using the Control Panel. In this chapter, we will discuss the basics of configuring printers manually. A good reference for this process is the Printing HOWTO at `http://sunsite.unc.edu/mdw/` `HOWTO/Printing-HOWTO.html`.

What Printer to Use

Before discussing configuration of printers in Linux, let's take a quick look at which printers work with Linux and how to go about using them.

First, though, a word of warning: printers that use the Windows Printing System (also called GDI printers) generally cannot be used with Linux. These printers are essentially "dumb" printers that require the computer to do the job of preparing a document for printing and rely on specialized Windows software provided by the printer manufacturer. You are best off avoiding a GDI printer for use in Linux.

Having said that, most other printers are supported as follows:

- PostScript printers: Most Unix software generates PostScript output for printing, so you are best off with a PostScript printer. Of course, low-end laser printers and inkjet printers don't support PostScript.

- Non-PostScript printers supported by GhostScript: If your printer doesn't support Printer Control Language (PCL), it is probably supported by the GhostScript application, a software-based PostScript interpreter that is standard in most Linux distributions. To see if your printer is supported, check the GhostScript home page at `http://www.cs.wisc.edu/~ghost/`. The following is a partial list of printers supported by GhostScript:

Canon BubbleJet BJ10e	HP DeskJet 682C
Canon BubbleJet BJ200	HP DeskJet 683C
Canon BubbleJet BJC-210 (4.01)	HP DeskJet 693C
Canon BubbleJet BJC-240 (3.33, 4.03)	HP DeskJet 694C
Canon BubbleJet BJC-250 (5.10)	HP DeskJet 850
Canon BubbleJet BJC-70 (5.10)	HP DeskJet 855
Canon BubbleJet BJC-600	HP DeskJet 870Cse
Canon BubbleJet BJC-4000	HP DeskJet 870Cxi
Canon BubbleJet BJC-4100	HP DeskJet 890C
Canon BubbleJet BJC-4200	HP DeskJet 672C
Canon BubbleJet BJC-4300	HP DeskJet 680
Canon BubbleJet BJC-4550	HP DeskJet 1100C
Canon BJC-210	HP DeskJet 500C
Canon MultiPASS C2500 color printer/fax/copier	HP DeskJet 510
Canon BJC-240	HP DeskJet 520
Canon BJC-70	HP LaserJet 5
Canon BubbleJet BJC-800	HP LaserJet 5L
Canon BubbleJet BJC-7000	HP LaserJet 6L
HP DeskJet	Oki OL410ex LED printer
HP DeskJet Plus	NEC SuperScript 860
HP DeskJet 500	HP PaintJet XL300
HP DeskJet Portable	HP DeskJet 1200C
HP DeskJet 400	HP DeskJet 1600C
HP DeskJet 500C	Ricoh 4081 laser printer
HP DeskJet 540C	Ricoh 6000 laser printer

HP DeskJet 690C	Epson Stylus Color
HP DeskJet 693C	Epson Stylus Color II
HP DeskJet 550C	Epson Stylus 500
HP DeskJet 560C	Epson Stylus 600
HP DeskJet 600	Epson Stylus 800
HP DeskJet 660C	

The *Printcap* File

The printcap file is found in the /etc directory and is the core of Linux printer configuration. This file contains entries for each printer that is available to your Linux system. When the Linux printer daemon, lpd, is loaded (generally at boot time), it looks at this file to learn about the printers it will be managing.

A basic entry in the printcap file looks like this:

```
# LOCAL
djet500lp|dj|deskjet:\
    :sd=/var/spool/lpd/dj:\
    :mx#0:
    :lp=/dev/lp0:\
    :sh:
```

The entry contains numerous fields separated by colons. If the entry needs to span more than one line, the backslash indicates that the entry continues on the next line.

Here we have a printer with three possible names: djet500lp, dj, and deskjet. This printer has a spool directory at /var/spool/lpd/dj where lpd can store temporary files while they are waiting to be printed. The printer is connected to the first parallel port (/dev/lp0) and no header pages should be printed (sh). This all might seem very cryptic, and to a certain extent it is. The printcap file can take literally dozens of different fields. These are outlined in the printcap man page:

```
$ man printcap
```

If this information was all that was needed to get a printer to work, configuring your printers wouldn't be so bad. But lpd is essentially stupid. With an entry like the one above, whatever data is provided to lpd is sent directly to the printer. If the data provided is not understood by the printer, we will get gibberish or nothing in return. Consider the following possible problems:

- An ASCII text file sent to a PostScript printer will not print.

- An ASCII text file sent to a PCL printer will not print with the correct formatting unless the control codes in the file are adjusted.

- A PostScript file sent to a PCL printer will print out as a long list of PostScript commands instead of the actual page image defined by the commands.

These are just some of the problems encountered when printing using a barebones `printcap` entry like the one outlined above. They can be resolved by the use of print filters.

Print Filters

Print filters are special programs or scripts that process data before it is sent to the printer. For instance, if we have a PCL printer we could write one script to process ASCII text before sending it to the printer so it will appear in correct format, and another to send PostScript data through GhostScript to generate correct PCL output. But if we do this manually, we will need to have multiple printer entries in our `printcap` file, one for each type of filter we plan to make available:

```
# PCL Printer with ASCII filter
ascii-pcl:\
    :sd=/var/spool/lpd/ascii-pcl:\
    :mx#0:
    :lp=/dev/lp0:\
    :sh:\
    :if=/var/spool/lpd/ascii-pcl/filter

# PCL Printer with PostScript filter
ps-pcl:\
    :sd=/var/spool/lpd/ps-pcl:\
    :mx#0:
    :lp=/dev/lp0:\
    :sh:\
    :if=/var/spool/lpd/ps-pcl/filter
```

```
# PCL Printer with no filter
pcl:\
      :sd=/var/spool/lpd/pcl:\
      :mx#0:
      :lp=/dev/lp0:\
      :sh:\
```

These filters would generate correct output but they would add complications to the printing process. Users would need to know what type of output is being generated by their application (plain text, PostScript, or PCL) and then select the correct printer accordingly. There might also be confusion because the filters suggest that there are three physical printers available when there is really only one.

These difficulties are addressed by magic filters. Magic filters, which are available for downloading from the Internet, handle all the printcap configuration for most supported printers and provide filters that can determine the type of data being sent to the printer and perform the correct filtering on that basis.

The APS Print Filter System

The leading magic filter package is the APS Filter system, which we will look at here. You can download the latest version of the APS Filters from ftp://sunsite .unc.edu/pub/Linux/system/printing/. At the time of this writing, the version available was 4.91 and the file to download was **aps-491.tgz**.

To install the software, use the tar command to uncompress and extract the archive in a logical location, such as /usr/local. You will need to create a directory in which to store the uncompressed files. The following commands assume you have downloaded the original archive in /tmp.

NOTE   You need to perform these steps as the root user.

```
# cd /usr/local
# mkdir apsfilter
# cd apsfilter
# tar /tmp/tzvf aps-491.tgz
```

To configure APS to work with your printer, the next step is to run the setup script that comes with the package:

```
# ./SETUP
```

This will bring up a welcome screen. Hit Return and the setup script will present its first question:

```
For which printer type do you want to setup apsfilter...

        1 - for a Postscript printer
        2 - for HP Deskjets
        3 - for another printer who doesn't support the
            Postscript language

?
```

At this prompt, select the type of printer you are installing; we will take each type in turn.

A PostScript Printer If you choose to install a PostScript printer, the process is relatively easy. The next question is about the resolution of your printer:

```
Very fine, you have a real PS printer...Please select a printer
driver that fits your PS-printers resolution:

 [ PS_300dpi PS_400dpi PS_600dpi PS_800dpi ]

?
```

Here you need to select the appropriate option by typing the complete name presented. For instance, if you have a 600 dpi laser printer, type **PS_600dpi** and hit Return.

The next question is about the color capabilities of your printer:

```
Is your printer a  (c)olor printer
           or a  (m)ono printer ?

?
```

Type **c** or **m** as appropriate. For most PostScript laser printers, monochrome is the right choice.

Once you have selected the color status of your printer, you need to indicate the default paper you are using:

```
What paper form do you use (i.e.: a3, a4, letter,...)
See /usr/local/apsfilter/doc/paper for valid sizes...
Note: enter the paper form in lowercase letters:

?
```

In the U.S., this will usually be letter (or on occasion legal); outside the U.S. the most likely size is a4.

The next question asks about the port you are using to connect the printer to your computer:

```
Do you have a (s)erial or a (p)arallel printer interface ?

?
```

Any respectable printer sold today will use the parallel interface, so unless you are using an extremely old printer or are trying to get some Macintosh printers to work with your PC, you should type **p** and hit Return.

Now you need to specify the Linux device that is associated with your printer:

```
What's the device name for your parallel printer interface ?
For Linux Systems with kernel <= 1.1.X :)
Device Name Major Minor  I/O address!
/dev/lp0    6     0       0x3bc  (1. parallel device)
/dev/lp1    6     1       0x378  (2. parallel device)
/dev/lp2    6     2       0x278  (3. parallel device)

type in the full path name, i.e.: /dev/lp0

?
```

As discussed earlier, LPT1: on DOS maps to /dev/lp0, and LPT2: in DOS is the same as /dev/lp1.

Following this, the setup program will create several files and then prompt you to hit Return after being presented with different pieces of information about your configuration. As it continues the job of configuring your print system, the setup program will periodically present screens of information that you should read so you'll understand what's happening.

Finally, you will be greeted with the message We made it ! and returned to the command prompt.

A DeskJet Printer   Configuring a DeskJet printer is subtly different than configuring a PostScript printer. After selecting this type of printer, you will be presented with a list of DeskJet printers.

You can use the up and down arrow keys to scroll through the list. Once you have finished reading the list and identified a likely printer, hit **Q** to exit the list and return to the main part of the setup script. You will be presented with a prompt like this:

```
which printer driver do you want to use ?

------------------------
cdjmono        *1   300, 300,   1, 4, 0, 1
cdeskjet       *1   300, 300,   3, 4, 2, 1
cdjcolor       *1   300, 300,  24, 4, 2, 1
cdj500         *1   300, 300, bpp, 4, 2, 1
cdj550         *1   300, 300, bpp, 0, 2, 1
deskjet        +    300, 300,   1, -  -  -
djet500        +    300, 300,   1, -  -  -
djet500c       *2   300, 300,   3, -, 1, 1
------------------------


Perhaps good choices are:
For a HP Deskjet  (b&w):   deskjet
For a Deskjet 500 (b&w):   djet500
For a color Deskjet:       cdeskjet

What driver do you want for your deskjet ?
```

Select the appropriate driver and hit Return. From there, the setup script will continue on to ask you about the color capabilities of your printer, your default paper size, the type of connection being used, and the Linux device associated with your printer, just as it did for a PostScript printer.

Other Non-PostScript Printers If you choose the third type of printer, configuration is subtly different again. Here you will be presented with a list of printer drivers to choose from:

```
Select one of the following gs(1) printer driver ...

[ appledmp bj10e bj200 declj250 eps9high epson epsonc escp2
  ibmpro jetp3852 la50 la75 laserjet lbp8 lj250 ljet2p ljet3
  ljet4 ljet4l ljetplus ln03 m8510 necp6 nwp533 oki182 paintjet
  pj pjxl pjxl300 r4081 sparc t4693d2 t4693d4 t4693d8 tek4696
  gs V3.X: st800 ]

Do you need a more verbose description of the printer
drivers ? y/n ?
```

If you see one that clearly matches your printer, type **n** and hit Return to move on to the selection prompt. Otherwise, hit **y** to view a detailed description of the drivers (use the up and down arrow keys to scroll through the list) and hit the **Q** key when you are done to move on to the prompt:

```
[ appledmp bj10e bj200 declj250 eps9high epson epsonc escp2
    ibmpro jetp3852 la50 la75 laserjet lbp8 lj250 ljet2p ljet3
    ljet4 ljet4l ljetplus ln03 m8510 necp6 nwp533 oki182 paintjet
    pj pjxl pjxl300 r4081 sparc t4693d2 t4693d4 t4693d8 tek4696
    gs V3.X: st800 ]
```

```
Which printer driver do you want ?
```

Enter the driver name and hit Return to make your selection.

From there, the *setup* script will continue on to ask you about the color capabilities of your printer, your default paper size, the type of connection being used, and the Linux device associated with your printer, just as it did for a PostScript printer.

After Configuration   After configuration, you should have a `printcap` file that looks something like this:

```
# LABEL apsfilter
# apsfilter setup Mon Jul 27 17:17:05 CEST 1998
#
# APS_BASEDIR:/usr/local/apsfilter
#
#
ascii|lp1|escp2-a4-ascii-mono|escp2 ascii mono:\
        :lp=/dev/lp1:\
        :sd=/usr/spool/escp2-a4-ascii-mono:\
        :lf=/usr/spool/escp2-a4-ascii-mono/log:\
        :af=/usr/spool/escp2-a4-ascii-mono/acct:\
        :if=/usr/local/apsfilter/filter/aps-escp2-a4-ascii-mono:\
        :mx#0:\
        :sh:
#
lp|lp2|escp2-a4-auto-mono|escp2 auto mono:\
        :lp=/dev/lp1:\
        :sd=/usr/spool/escp2-a4-auto-mono:\
        :lf=/usr/spool/escp2-a4-auto-mono/log:\
```

```
            :af=/usr/spool/escp2-a4-auto-mono/acct:\
            :if=/usr/local/apsfilter/filter/aps-escp2-a4-auto-mono:\
            :mx#0:\
            :sh:
#
lp3|escp2-a4-ascii-color|escp2 ascii color:\
            :lp=/dev/lp1:\
            :sd=/usr/spool/escp2-a4-ascii-color:\
            :lf=/usr/spool/escp2-a4-ascii-color/log:\
            :af=/usr/spool/escp2-a4-ascii-color/acct:\
            :if=/usr/local/apsfilter/filter/aps-escp2-a4-ascii-color:\
            :mx#0:\
            :sh:
#
lp4|escp2-a4-auto-color|escp2 auto color:\
            :lp=/dev/lp1:\
            :sd=/usr/spool/escp2-a4-auto-color:\
            :lf=/usr/spool/escp2-a4-auto-color/log:\
            :af=/usr/spool/escp2-a4-auto-color/acct:\
            :if=/usr/local/apsfilter/filter/aps-escp2-a4-auto-color:\
            :mx#0:\
            :sh:
#
raw|lp5|escp2-a4-raw|escp2 auto raw:\
            :lp=/dev/lp1:\
            :sd=/usr/spool/escp2-raw:\
            :lf=/usr/spool/escp2-raw/log:\
            :af=/usr/spool/escp2-raw/acct:\
            :if=/usr/local/apsfilter/filter/aps-escp2-a4-raw:\
            :mx#0:\
            :sh:
```

Regardless of the printer you configure for use with Linux, the APS filter system will always make the following three print queues available:

- ascii: a queue that is exclusively for printing plain text files

- lp: an automatic filter that will detect the file type and process it accordingly

- raw: an unfiltered print queue that can be used if the software you are using generates output in the native format required by your printer

Printing   Now you are ready to print. You can do this with the `lpr` command. The `-P` flag specifies which printer queue to use. For instance, the command

```
$ lpr -Pascii /etc/printcap
```

would print the `printcap` file out through the plain text print queue, while

```
$ lpr -Plp /etc/printcap
```

would print the same file through the automatic filter.

Modems

Modems are among the simplest types of peripherals to get working in Linux. Generally, external modems can be plugged into an available serial port and be expected to work, while standard internal modems should be equally easy to get up and running under Linux.

NOTE   Not all internal modems are supported under Linux. If you have one, try it. If you are buying a new modem, it is probably worth the extra cost to buy an external one.

In this section, we will look at how Linux handles ports, since this is essential to the understanding of Linux modem management, and then will look at simple ways to use your modem.

Understanding Linux Ports

In the Linux environment, every physical peripheral or connection port is associated with one or more files in the special directory `/dev`. This includes hard disk drives, CD-ROM drives, parallel ports, and serial ports.

The concept behind this is easy to understand. Let's look at hard drives as an example.

Each IDE hard drive is named hd*x* where *x* is a letter starting with a for the first drive on the primary IDE bus, b for the second drive on the primary IDE bus, c for the first drive on the secondary IDE bus, and so on. Thus, the secondary master drive is associated with `/dev/hdc`.

In addition, each partition on the drive is associated with a `/dev` entry. The second partition on the primary slave drive, for instance, is `/dev/hdb2`, while the first partition of the secondary master drive is `/dev/hdc1`.

Parallel Ports and Linux

So far, this is a simple concept.

Let's consider parallel ports. In the DOS and Windows world, parallel ports are referred to as LPT1:, LPT2:, LPT3:, and so on. On most PCs, there is generally only one parallel port, so we usually only have to deal with LPT1:.

In the Linux world, the parallel ports correspond to the device files `lpx`, where x is the number of the port. Here is where the crucial difference lies: Linux starts counting the ports at 0 instead of 1, so LPT1: is actually `/dev/lp0` and LPT2: is `/dev/lp1`.

Now, on to serial ports. We need to fully understand all of this to understand how to get our modems working.

Serial Ports and Linux

In Linux, serial ports are generally each associated with two device files: one for outgoing connections and one for incoming connections. Let's start with outgoing connections: these are `ttySx`, where x is a number starting from 0. So, DOS's COM1: maps to `/dev/ttyS0` in Linux and COM2: to `/dev/ttyS1`.

But Linux serial ports also are associated with another device file for incoming connections: `cuax`, where x is a number starting from 0. Therefore, COM1: is both `/dev/ttyS0` and `/dev/cua0`, while COM4: is both `/dev/ttyS3` and `/dev/cua3`.

Simple, right?

NOTE   It isn't uncommon for Linux distributions to maintain a link from `/dev/modem` to the serial port device for the modem. In this way, the modem can be referred to through the device `/dev/modem`.

Getting Your Modem Ready

In order for a modem to work properly, it must meet several criteria:

- It must be properly connected to the PC.

- It must be using a dedicated serial port.

- It must not have an IRQ or I/O address conflict with another device.

Connecting a Modem to Your PC

Connecting a modem is fairly simple. If you have an external modem, you need to connect it to one of your existing serial ports. If you have no free ports, you need to consider purchasing a serial card and should consult your PC or modem vendor about this. Generally, though, most PC users only need two external serial ports: one for their mouse and one for their modem. The usual practice is to connect your mouse to the first serial port (COM1:, /dev/ttyS0, /dev/cua0) and your modem to the second serial port (COM2:, /dev/ttyS1, /dev/cua1).

Internal modems usually need to be placed into a free slot inside your PC. If you are wary about opening your PC, then you may want to consider getting a technician from the store where you bought your PC or your modem to install the modem.

Choosing a Serial Port

When installing an external modem, you select a serial port by simply choosing which physical port to connect the modem to. In doing this, it is important to make sure that you have not installed an internal device that is using the same serial port. If you haven't installed any hardware inside your PC, consult your PC's documentation to see if there are any preinstalled internal devices that are using the same serial port as one of your external connections. Generally, though, unless you already have an internal modem installed, you aren't likely to have an internal device conflicting with one of your available external serial ports.

Installing an internal modem requires a bit more work. Most standard internal modems need to be configured to use a specific serial port in order to function. For instance, DIP switches or jumpers on the modem card are commonly used to specify a particular serial port. You need to consult your modem's documentation for instructions on how to do this.

As with external modems, you must make sure you don't choose a port that matches one already in use by an external device. For instance, you definitely wouldn't make your modem use the first serial port if you have a mouse connected to the external connector for this port. The third or fourth serial port is usually the best choice for an internal modem.

IRQs and I/O Addresses

Associated with each serial port is an interrupt request (IRQ) and an input/output (I/O) address. This is numerically-specified information that ensures that your PC and operating system always know which physical device is providing data or information or is asking for the attention of the system.

The following table outlines the four common serial ports and their associated IRQs and I/O addresses:

TABLE 15.1: Serial Port IRQs and I/O Addresses

DOS Name	Linux device files	IRQ	I/O Address
COM1:	/dev/ttyS0,/dev/cua0	4	0x3f8
COM2:	/dev/ttyS1,/dev/cua1	3	0x2f8
COM3:	/dev/ttyS2,/dev/cua2	4	0x3e8
COM4:	/dev/ttyS3,/dev/cua3	3	0x2e8

You will probably notice that the first and third ports share the same IRQ and the second and fourth ports also share the same IRQ. This poses certain issues that have to be considered. The fact that port 1 and port 3 share the same IRQ but have different I/O addresses basically means that they cannot be used simultaneously. That is, you can't have devices on these two ports (or on ports 2 and 4) that will need to be in use at the same time.

This means, for example, that you can't have a mouse on the first port and put a modem on the third port unless you will never be using the mouse while the modem is in use. If you use X Windows, this is a highly improbable scenario. Therefore, when installing an internal modem, you also need to take care not to create an IRQ conflict. If you use a mouse on the first serial port, then you will probably want to put your internal modem on the fourth port to eliminate all possible conflicts with your mouse.

Finally, there is one more consideration: Internal modems often allow you to configure special IRQ and I/O addresses for the card that differ from the norms for the four serial ports. This should only be done if you have so many serial devices already on your system that you simply cannot make the modem work in any other way. In this situation, you will need to consult the serial devices HOWTO at `ftp://sunsite.unc.edu/pub/Linux/docs/HOWTO/unmaintained/Serial-HOWTO` to get a stronger sense of how to do this safely and correctly in Linux.

Plug-and-Play Modems

The introduction of Plug-and-Play motherboards and internal cards with Windows 95 has caused some problems with other operating systems. Many Plug-and-Play devices (modems included) are often designed to work expressly with Windows and are configured using special Windows 95 or 98 software that is not available in Linux. If you have a card like this, you usually have one of two options:

1. If you are lucky, after you configure the modem in Windows 95 or 98, you can reboot to Linux and the modem will retain its configuration.

2. If you are unlucky, the modem will need to be configured every time the computer is power-cycled and Windows will have to do this during the boot process. If this is the case, you need to start Linux from within Windows using `loadln` (see Chapter 5, "Special Installations," for more information about this) to start Linux without rebooting the system.

Generally, though, you are best off without a Plug-and-Play modem, and should really consider spending the small amount of extra money required to get an external modem.

Software for Working with Your Modem

There are numerous types of software in Linux that you will be using with your modem. These include:

- minicom: a basic, text-based terminal emulation package
- seyon: an X Windows–based terminal emulation package

- pppd: a daemon used for establishing PPP connections to the Internet (see Chapter 17, "Connecting Linux to the Internet")

- efax: a collection of programs used for sending and receiving faxes (see Chapter 20, "Faxing from Linux")

In the next section, we will take a quick look at using minicom to make sure your modem is working properly.

Using Minicom to Test Your Modem

The first step to using minicom is to create a global configuration file. This is done by running minicom as the root user with the -s flag:

```
# minicom -s
```

This will launch the minicom configuration environment as shown in Figure 15.1.

FIGURE 15.1:

Configuring minicom

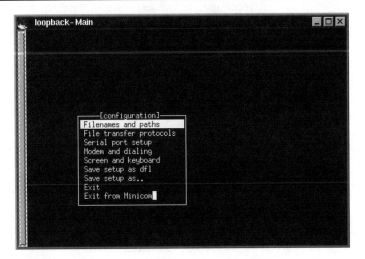

You can use the up and down arrow keys to move through the menu and the Return key to select menu items.

The critical settings for testing your modem are under Serial Port Setup. Selecting this option displays the Serial Port Setup screen shown in Figure 15.2.

FIGURE 15.2:

Configuring your serial port

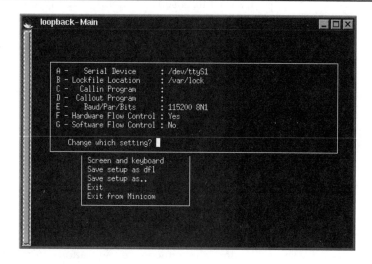

In order to change the values, you simply select them by letter.

First, you need to set your serial device. This is done with choice A. You should change this location to the appropriate device file. For instance, if your modem is on the second serial port, you could set this to /dev/ttyS1 since you are using minicom for an outgoing connection.

You also need to configure option E to match your modem's settings and the settings required by the system you will be connecting to (usually an Internet provider's system). Option E displays the communication parameters screen shown in Figure 15.3.

At the top of the screen, the current settings are shown. You can change the settings by selecting the appropriate letters.

For speed, you should choose your modem's top compressed connection speed. This is generally four times the speed of your modem. For instance, for a 14.4Kbps modem, this would be 57600bps; for a 28.8Kbps modem, this should be set to 115200bps. If you have a faster modem, choose 115200bps.

FIGURE 15.3:

Configuring communication
parameters

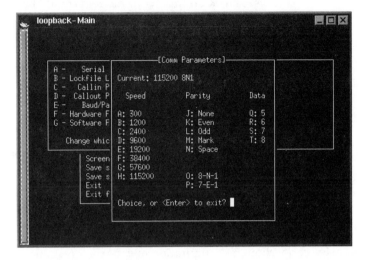

For parity and data bit, the norm for most connections today is no parity
(option J), and 8 stop bits (option T). Confer with the administrator of the system
you will be connecting to in order to determine the correct settings.

When you are done, hit the Enter key to return to the Serial Port Setup screen.
Hitting the Enter key here will return you to the main menu.

This information should be sufficient to allow you to test your modem. Select
Save Setup as dfl to save the configuration as the default setting, and then select
Exit to exit the setup screen and use minicom with the settings you have selected.
This will bring up the minicom terminal emulator, as shown in Figure 15.4.

FIGURE 15.4:

The main minicom screen

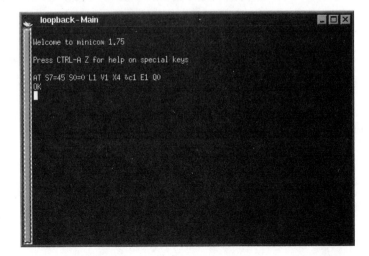

If you see an OK prompt, your modem should be configured correctly and working. You can test this further by typing **AT** and hitting Return. You should get back an OK message:

```
AT
OK
```

If this works, you can try dialing into a system to see if you can connect:

```
ATDT1234567
```

If this works, you may hear the sound of a connection and then should see a connection message and possibly some messages or prompts from the remote system:

```
ATDT1234567
CONNECT 115200
```

If you have problems with any of these stages, then your modem's physical connection or configuration may be incorrect. In this case, you should refer to the serial devices HOWTO at `ftp://sunsite.unc.edu/pub/Linux/docs/HOWTO/unmaintained/Serial-HOWTO` for a detailed discussion of getting a modem to work with Linux.

Issues with ISDN Adapters

ISDN adapters can be a little problematic with Linux. The difficulties stem from the fact that internal and external adapters function in fundamentally different ways, and among internal adapters there are distinctly different technological approaches.

External ISDN adapters are your best choice for a Linux system because external adapters mimic the behavior of external modems, making the use of them generally transparent to Linux.

Internal modems pose issues, though. Some emulate standard serial modems and others emulate standard network cards, and both can be made to work with Linux. There are those known not to work, however.

Consult the Linux ISDN page at `http://www.caliban.org/linux_isdn.html` for a detailed discussion of Linux and ISDN.

Where Do We Go from Here?

Now that we know how to get our modems to work in Linux, we will move on to the basics of Linux networking.

In the next chapter, we will learn the basic networking concepts in Linux and TCP/IP. Following that, in Chapters 17 and 18 we will explore how to connect Linux to the Internet using our modems and PPP, the standard method of connecting to Internet providers today. Chapter 19 will look at common Internet software such as Netscape Communicator and e-mail clients such as pine.

Finally, Chapter 20 will discuss another use for your modem: faxing in Linux.

CHAPTER

SIXTEEN

16

Understanding Linux Networking

- TCP/IP Fundamentals

- TCP and UDP Services and Ports

- Routing Concepts

In this section, we will dive into a topic that is of interest to most computer users these days: networking.

We start in this chapter by considering the basic Linux networking concepts, including the basics of TCP/IP networks and routing. We will learn about the basic idea behind TCP/IP and the basic components of a TCP/IP configuration, such as IP addresses, netmasks, ports, and gateways. Then we will look at the types of services that typically run on the TCP/IP connection of a standard Linux system.

TCP/IP Fundamentals

We are considering TCP/IP networks in this chapter for a simple reason: in the world of Unix, TCP/IP networks are undoubtedly the standard.

When we refer to a type of network (such as TCP/IP, IPX/SPX, or Novell), we are referring to the protocols, or languages, used to communicate between machines connected to the network. This is independent of the type of physical connection on which the network is built.

At a physical level, today's networks are built using a variety of Ethernet technologies, including 10-Base-2, 10-Base-T, and 100-Base-TX Ethernet, as well as fiber optic and other technologies. In fact, a TCP/IP network can be built up of components running on different types of network infrastructures: Ethernet components, components connected via telephone serial connections, and connections running on infrared transmitters and receivers. At the level of the network protocol, it doesn't matter what type of hardware and cabling is actually used to move the data around the network.

This abstraction, or separation, of the logical (the protocols) from the physical (the hardware and cabling) makes it possible to talk about networking without concern for the types of connections being made.

What Is TCP/IP?

Possibly because the genesis of the Internet occurred on a series of interconnected Unix systems, the networking standard for most Unix networks and for the Internet is the same: TCP/IP.

TCP/IP is a two-part name. TCP stands for Transmission Control Protocol and IP stands for Internet Protocol. Together they make up one of the most pervasive networking protocols in use today.

This powerful combo allows the Internet to act as a global TCP/IP network. In fact, connecting a TCP/IP-based LAN to the Internet can be a simple job because the same technology is being used on the internal network (the LAN) and the external network (the Internet).

Taken separately, the job of IP is to act as the mechanism for routing and transmitting TCP packets (packages of information) as well as packets that use the User Datagram Protocol (UDP), a relative of TCP. TCP and UDP are the protocols utilized by programs such as FTP and Telnet to build meaningful packets to be shared across the network. TCP and UDP know nothing about the mechanics of delivering these packets across the network; they leave that work to IP.

The metaphor that is often used to explain the relationship is that of addressed envelopes and their contents. TCP and UDP packets are letters placed in envelopes with the destination address on the outside. IP then acts as the postal system, delivering the packet to the destination where the package is opened and handed back to TCP or UDP.

TCP/IP Configuration Essentials

In order to understand how TCP/IP is configured and networks are designed, it is important to understand some fundamental concepts:

- IP addresses
- subnetworking and netmasks
- broadcast addresses
- gateway addresses
- name servers

IP Addresses

In the world of TCP/IP, each machine (or host) connected to the network is assigned a unique address known as an IP address. An IP address is a four-part number that uniquely identifies the host. Each machine that has direct access to the Internet has a unique IP address. If you dial into the Internet through an Internet provider, for the duration of your connection you will possess and use a unique IP address assigned to you by your Internet provider.

IP addresses are made up of four one-byte integer numbers separated by dots. A one-byte integer is any integer that can be represented by eight binary digits (eight binary digits, or bits, is one byte). This means each of the four parts of an IP address can take a value between 0 and 255. For instance, possible IP addresses include 194.148.43.194, 134.65.98.0, 23.98.45.23, and 65.87.99.254. Invalid IP addresses would include 194.148.43.294, 341.65.98.0, 222.98.145.256, and 230.980.450.230.

The total number of IP addresses available, then, is 256 to the power of 4, or 4,294,967,296. This may seem like a lot of addresses, but with the rate at which the Internet has grown in recent years and continues to grow, IP addresses are increasingly becoming rare commodities. Efforts are under way to upgrade the structure of IP addresses to consist of four 32-bit integers for a total of 340,282,366,920,938,463,463,374,607,431,768,211,456 addresses, which is the total number of existing IP addresses to the power of 4.

Today's over four billion addresses are not simply randomly used around the globe. Rather, they are assigned in chunks, known as networks, for use by organizations, Internet providers, and other groups needing IP addresses for use on the Internet.

There are three types of TCP/IP networks available: Class A, Class B, and Class C networks.

- In a Class A network, the network is identified by the first byte of the IP addresses while the remaining three bytes identify specific machines on the network, for a total of 16,777,216 available addresses.

- In a Class B network, the network is identified by the first two bytes of the IP address while the remaining two bytes identify specific machines on the network, for a total of 65,536 machines.

- In a Class C network, the network is identified by the first three bytes of the IP address while the remaining byte identifies specific machines on the network, for a total of 256 machines.

As an example, in a Class C network, the machine identified by the IP address 194.148.43.194 is machine 194 on the network 194.148.43. Similarly, on a Class B network, the machine 194.148.43.194 would be the machine 43.194 on the network 194.148.

It is not uncommon for organizations with large IP address needs to obtain a Class B network and then subdivide (subnetwork) it into 256 Class C networks. A perfect example of this would be a large Internet provider that needs to provide Class C networks to its corporate clients and does this by dividing up a Class B network.

Subnetworking and Netmasks

There is a potential for confusion in this situation. How can a machine know what type of network it is on? If a machine has an IP address of 194.148.43.194, there is no immediately apparent way for it to know if it is on the Class A network 194, the Class B network 194.148, or the Class C network 194.148.43.

This situation is resolved by the use of a network mask (or subnetwork mask), also known as a netmask (or subnetmask). A netmask is another set of dot-separated one-byte integers that serves to define which portion of the IP address identifies the network. This is done by combining the IP address and the netmask with a logical AND. Let's consider how this works with a simple eight-bit number.

If we have an eight-bit number of 194, its binary representation is:

11000010

If we want to split this number in two, with the first four bits representing the network and the last four the host, then our netmask, when combined with this number using logical AND, needs to leave zeros in the last four bits and should ensure that the first four bits are left unchanged.

Logical AND follows this set of rules:

- 1 and 1 is 1

- 1 and 0 is 0

- 0 and 1 is 0

- 0 and 0 is 0

and each bit is matched with the corresponding bit in the same position.

Therefore, if we want to create a netmask that keeps the first four bits of an eight-bit number intact, our netmask, in binary form, would be:

```
11110000
```

Consider our value of 194 from above:

```
11000010 and
11110000 is
11000000
```

Now, let's apply this to a bigger example of an actual IP address and network mask combination. Consider an IP address of 194.148.43.194. If we want a network mask to indicate a Class B network and its network address, we need to make all the bits in the first two bytes 1 (each byte will have a value of 255) and all the bits in the last two bytes 0 (each byte will have a value of 0). The end result is a netmask of 255.255.0.0.

Similarly, for a Class C address, the netmask would have the first three bytes set to 255 and the last to zero: 255.255.255.0.

The value returned by combining the netmask and the IP address is your network address. In our Class B example above, using logical AND to combine 194.148.43.194 and 255.255.0.0 produces a Class B network address of 194.148.0.0. Similarly, using the netmask of 255.255.255.0 produces a Class C network address of 194.148.43.0.

Because the network address of a Class C network uses up the first IP address (the one with 0 in the last byte), this IP address can't be used for an actual host on the network.

Broadcast Addresses

The broadcast address is a special address that can be used when sending information to all hosts on the network. Instead of sending a separate packet to each host, a single packet can be sent out and all machines listening can receive it (like radio or television signals).

The broadcast address is based on the network address with the host portions replaced by 255. So, for our Class B network 194.148.0.0, the broadcast address is 194.148.255.255, and for the Class C network 194.148.43.0, the broadcast address is 194.148.43.255.

As with the network address, the broadcast address is also reserved and can't be used for an actual host.

Therefore, counting out the network and broadcast addresses leaves an actual 254 available host addresses on a Class C network and 65,534 on a Class B network.

Gateway Addresses

As we will see later in the section on routing, a computer configured for the local network or subnetwork has no knowledge of how to communicate with machines on external networks (for instance, on the Internet).

A gateway is a machine that provides a route to the outside world. It generally has at least two network interfaces: one connected to the local network and one to the outside world. The gateway reroutes packets on and off the local network as appropriate.

For a host to connect to external networks, it will need to know the IP address of at least one gateway off the local network.

Name Servers

While it is great to be able to communicate on the local and external networks, it is impractical for users to remember IP addresses for every machine they want to connect to.

This is resolved by the Domain Name System (DNS). DNS provides a mechanism to map domain names (such as `landegg.edu`) and host names (`www.landegg.edu`) into IP addresses for actual use. For each registered domain, there are at least two DNS servers responsible for answering lookup queries for hosts in the domain.

In addition, every host that wants to be able to resolve host names into IP addresses needs the services of at least one DNS server that can handle the task of contacting other DNS servers to get name lookup answers.

For this reason, when configuring TCP/IP, it is usually necessary to provide the IP address of at least one name server.

TCP and UDP Services and Ports

When two machines wish to use TCP/IP to communicate with each other, they generally specify the destination by using a combination of the IP address and a port. Ports are 16-bit integers that identify the service that is being used and that should receive the data. Think of ports as the mailboxes in an apartment block.

Let's look at an example: the Web. A Linux Web server will run a process known as a daemon whose job it is to listen to a specific port for incoming Web connections. Widely used services such as TCP/IP, the Web, FTP, and e-mail all have well-known ports that daemons listen to for incoming connections. Table 16.1 is a list of common TCP and UDP ports.

TABLE 16.1: Common TCP and UDP Ports

Service Name	Port	Type	Description
FTP	21	TCP	File Transfer Protocol
Telnet	23	TCP	Telnet connections
SMTP	25	TCP	Simple Mail Transfer Protocol
Name	42	TCP	Domain Name System services
HTTP	80	TCP	Hypertext Transfer Protocol (World Wide Web)
POP3	110	TCP	Post Office Protocol 3 mail readers
IMAP	143	TCP	Internet Message Access Protocol mail readers

A more complete list of TCP and UDP services and ports can be found on the Internet at `http://www.con.wesleyan.edu/~triemer/network/docservs.html`.

Back to our Web example. Since port 80 is the default port for the Web, our Web daemon will listen on port 80 for an incoming connection. A Web client will initiate a connection requesting a document on port 80.

When the daemon notices an incoming connection, it answers, and the daemon and client are able to communicate. However, if the daemon returns the document being requested on port 80, it will tie up port 80, preventing new incoming requests.

This is resolved by the fact that the Web client is dynamically assigned its own port and sends this port along to the Web daemon, allowing the Web daemon to return the document requested on the client's own port, thus leaving port 80 free for further incoming requests. This is how it is possible for a Web daemon to handle a large number of incoming requests while listening on a single port.

Routing Concepts

In our discussion of gateways earlier in this chapter, we alluded to the notion of routing. Routing is the mechanism by which it is possible for the apparently chaotic Internet to work.

After all, when you use Netscape Communicator to connect to Yahoo!'s Web site, your machine knows nothing about the actual physical location of the Yahoo! Web server. Still, your request somehow makes it to Yahoo! and Yahoo!'s response finds its way back to you.

Let's start with a simple example of routing: You are connected to a small corporate LAN that has an Internet connection. The Internet connection is made through a router connected to the corporate LAN and your company's leased line connection to its Internet provider. This network layout is shown in Figure 16.1.

Because your LAN has only a single connection to the outside world through the router, routing is a simple matter. Each machine on the Internet is configured with a default gateway that points to the router. Whenever a host on the LAN is trying to connect with a machine off the local network, it sends the packets to the router and the router is responsible for redirecting the information.

In this way, the entire outside world is a black box: all outward-bound information is simply sent to the router as if the router encapsulated the entire network beyond the LAN. The router has a simple decision to make. Whenever it receives a packet, the router looks at the destination address. If the address is for the local LAN, the router sends it to the local LAN Ethernet; if the packet is addressed to any external address, the router simply sends it across the leased line to the Internet provider.

FIGURE 16.1:

A LAN connected to the
Internet

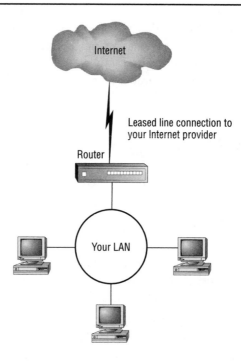

Let's take things a step further and enlarge our black box to include the Internet provider's network and its connection to the Internet, as shown in Figure 16.2.

Now things get a bit more interesting. Let's consider the Internet provider's LAN. Here we see two routers: Router A, which connects their LAN to the leased line to your local LAN and Router B, which connects their LAN to the leased line to the Internet through their provider.

Since each network needs a default gateway, Router B becomes the default gateway: when a host on the Internet provider's LAN is trying to connect to a host not on the local LAN and for which no known route exists, it sends the information to Router B.

But if the Internet provider only specifies Router B as the default gateway for machines on its LAN, then information destined for your local LAN will actually be sent to Router B and from there out to the Internet. We solve this with the addition of a static route.

FIGURE 16.2:

The LAN and its Internet provider

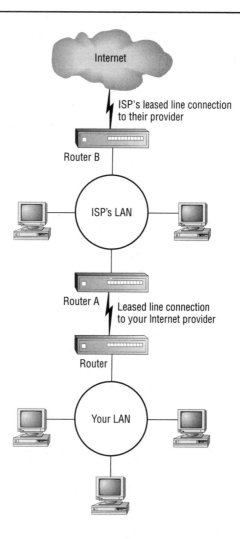

A static route specifies that information for a specific network or host should be sent to a different gateway than the default gateway. In this way, a static route can be defined for sending all traffic from the Internet provider for your local LAN to Router A. For hosts on the Internet provider's LAN, then, there is a series of three routing rules to follow:

1. If a packet is destined for a host on the local LAN, send it directly to the host.

2. If a packet is destined for the LAN connected via Router A, send the packet to Router A.

3. Send all packets not destined for the Router A LAN to Router B.

The process should be clear now. When incoming packets destined for your network arrive, they come from the Internet to Router B. Router B looks at the destination of the packet, sees it is for your LAN, and follows the static route, sending the packet to Router A. Router A looks at the destination of the packet, determines it is for your local LAN, and sends the packet directly to the destination host on your local LAN.

Routing can become extremely complex in large organizations with multiple sites, multiple LANs, and multiple connections to the Internet. In these cases, routing has to be carefully designed to ensure the most efficient routing of information in the most secure manner possible. For instance, two remote locations may have a leased-line connection between them plus their own connections to the Internet. It wouldn't make sense to route packets between these sites through the public Internet. This is both inefficient and an unnecessary security hole.

Complex routing of large networks is beyond the scope of this book and belongs in tomes dedicated to networking. The discussion here should provide sufficient background to understand the typical network routing environment in which most Linux users will find themselves.

Where Do We Go from Here?

In this chapter, we have learned the basic concepts of TCP/IP networking and routing.

Taking this theoretical knowledge into the realm of the practical, in the next chapter we will learn how to connect a Linux PC to the Internet through a dial-up PPP connection like those commonly offered by Internet providers.

In the chapters that follow, you will learn how to use specific Internet services such as the World Wide Web and e-mail from Linux.

CHAPTER
SEVENTEEN

17

Connecting Linux to the Internet

- What Is PPP?

- Necessary Hardware and Software

- Your First PPP Connection

- Automating Your Internet Connection

The subject of connecting a Linux system (or any computer system, for that matter) to the Internet is a complex one and one that can require deep knowledge of that system's network environment.

Still, for many users, this process is simple enough that both Windows and Linux work on the first attempt.

In this chapter, we will start with a quick look at PPP and its role in the Internet world. We will continue by reviewing the hardware and software requirements for connecting to the Internet. Then we will work through the mechanics of manually making a PPP connection, and finally we will wrap up by learning how to automate these connections.

What Is PPP?

Most Internet users are probably familiar with the acronym PPP, simply because the type of account they have with their Internet provider is a PPP account. Many users, though, really don't understand what PPP is all about.

PPP stands for Point-to-Point Protocol and is designed to provide a method by which TCP/IP is extended across an analog modem connection. In this way, when you are connected to the Internet using PPP, you become part of your Internet provider's network, are an actual host on the Internet, and have an IP address.

Traditionally, dial-up Internet connections were done using terminal software and Unix shell accounts on central servers. In this environment, the terminal software on the client system merely acted as a display for the server, and only the server really existed as a node on the Internet. This contrasts sharply with today's PPP connections, which bring the Internet right up to your modem.

The great flexibility of Internet connection technologies allows a great variety of PPP connection types. You can have PPP connections with fixed IP addresses or dynamic IP address assignments. Connections can use special authentication protocols such as PAP (Password Authentication Protocol), or can use standard text-based prompt-and-response mechanisms. Connections can be made manually or can be made automatically as needed.

In this chapter, we will discuss the most common Internet connection scenario: connecting by modem to an Internet provider that offers PPP connections with dynamically-assigned IP addresses.

Necessary Hardware and Software

In order to make PPP work properly, some preparation is needed. Hardware and software needs to be in place and configured before you can get PPP to work properly. Three key components need to be considered:

- A modem needs to be installed, configured, and working.

- PPP support needs to be compiled into the Linux kernel.

- PPP software needs to be installed.

The Modem

Because PPP is designed for dial-up connections, a modem is an essential piece of the PPP puzzle.

In Chapter 15, "Using Peripherals," we discussed modems and how to install them, test them, and get them working. Refer to that chapter to get your modem up and running and to make a test connection to be sure everything is in order.

To configure PPP, you will need to know the speed of your modem connection and which device it uses in Linux (probably /dev/modem or one of /dev/cua0 through /dev/cua3).

PPP in the Kernel

The Linux kernel is designed to be highly flexible. It can be compiled to include (or exclude) support for numerous technologies ranging from serial mice right up to networking facilities such as PPP.

In order to make a PPP connection with Linux, it is necessary for the kernel to include PPP support. In most Linux distributions, including many releases of Red Hat Linux, the default kernel that is installed by the distribution has PPP support built right in.

You can check to see if support is there by watching the messages that scroll by while the operating system is booting. If you see a series of lines like these:

```
PPP: version 2.2.0 (dynamic channel allocation)
PPP Dynamic channel allocation code copyright 1995 Caldera, Inc.
PPP line discipline registered.
registered device ppp0
PPP: ppp line discipline successfully unregistered
```

then PPP is compiled into your kernel. If you find the messages scroll by too quickly, you can use the dmesg command to see the part of the start-up messages that should include the PPP messages:

```
$ dmesg | more
```

NOTE   If you find you need to recompile your kernel, you should visit the Web site for this book at http://linux.juxta.com/. Recompiling the kernel is an advanced topic and one that many users won't face. In order to fully understand it and to succeed in recompilation attempts, you need to understand its complexities. For this reason, it is beyond the scope of this book. On the Web site you will find links to references that discuss recompiling the kernel, which can help guide you through the process.

Installing PPP Software

Most Linux distributions install PPP software with a complete or default installation. Red Hat Linux 5 is no exception.

Two programs are used to establish a PPP connection: /usr/sbin/pppd and /usr/sbin/chat. In Red Hat 5, these are part of the ppp -2.3.3-2 package and you can see if these are installed by using rpm:

```
$ rpm -q ppp
ppp -2.3.3-2
```

If you find you are lacking either pppd or chat, you need to install a new set of PPP software before continuing.

If you are running Red Hat 5, mount the Red Hat CD-ROM at a suitable location (such as /mnt/cdrom) and then install the package ppp-2.3.3-2.i386.rpm:

```
$ rpm -i ppp-2.3.3-2.i386.rpm
```

Alternately, you can download the latest sources for PPP from Sunsite's Linux archive in the directory ftp://sunsite.unc.edu/pub/Linux/system/network/serial/ppp. The current version of PPP is 2.3.4 and the filename is ppp-2.3.4.tar.gz.

You need to expand the archive in a suitable location with

```
$ tar xzvf ppp-2.3.4.tar.gz
```

and then read through the README.linux file carefully. Installation of a new PPP package involves not only compiling the software but also upgrading your Linux kernel source files and recompiling the Linux kernel to match the version of the PPP software being installed.

Detailing this process would take up a whole chapter, so it is best left to the documentation. If you are unfortunate enough to be running a Linux distribution that doesn't include PPP and you don't feel confident enough (or adventurous enough) to install PPP on your own, then you are probably best advised to install a new Linux distribution such as the one included with this book.

Your First PPP Connection

Now that we have the necessary software and hardware in place, we are ready to work out the details of our first connection. First, it is necessary to understand how things work.

In Linux, the PPP connection is made and maintained by pppd. But pppd assumes that a modem connection has already been made between your modem and your Internet provider's modem, that all the necessary logging in has taken place, and that the Internet provider's system is also trying to establish a PPP connection on top of the same modem connection.

This sounds like a lot of conditions, but it really isn't that bad. On almost every Internet provider's system, the connection process goes like this:

1. The modem connection is made.

2. The login process occurs.

3. Once the user is authenticated, the Internet provider begins to try to make a PPP connection by sending the IP address of the client to the client system.

The pppd program requires steps 1 and 2 to have occurred before number 3 gets under way.

Given this process, it is necessary to make a modem connection to the Internet provider before attempting to run pppd. Once the connection is made, the PPP connection can be established with pppd.

Making a PPP Connection

Fortunately, the pppd software is designed to bring things together and work with the chat program to handle the entire connection process.

Before attempting to connect, we need to gather some information:

- Are you assigned an IP address each time you connect, or do you have a permanently assigned IP address? Because most Internet providers work on the basis of assigning a dynamic IP address with each connection, we will also work on this basis.

- How do you log in to your Internet provider? One option uses plain text prompt-and-response logins; the other uses a special authentication protocol called PAP. If you attempt to dial into your Internet provider with minicom or other terminal software and are presented with a login prompt of some sort, then you are logging in with plain text prompts. If you see random characters after connecting, or no characters at all, then you are probably using PAP authentication.

> **NOTE** All the examples in this section assume that you are working as the root user on your machine. Because the process of connecting via PPP requires manipulation of interfaces and creation and deletion of network routes, the programs involved need to be run by the root user.

Connecting with Plain Text Prompts

We will start with plain text prompts because they are a little easier to work with.

Because pppd by itself can take control of your modem device but cannot perform the actual dialing or logging in, we need a way to issue commands to the modem and provide the necessary login information. This is achieved with the chat program. The chat program allows you to create a conversational exchange.

For instance, the normal dialing process on a modem is to run a terminal editor and in an empty terminal window type a dial command such as **ATDT12345678**. The response to this is usually a connect string such as CONNECT 9600, to which the user doesn't respond.

This exchange can be turned into a simple chat script:

```
"" ATDT1234567 CONNECT ""
```

This script is made up of two expect-send pairs: `""` `ATDT1234567` and `CONNECT` `""`. An expect-send pair contains two pieces of information separated by spaces. In our first pair, chat is told to expect nothing and in response send back the string `ATDT1234567`. In other words, as soon as the script starts processing, the first action is to send the dial string. Next, the second pair is processed and chat is told to expect the string `CONNECT` and in response to do nothing. If this were the complete script, chat would finish at this point and exit.

Of course, our chat script will need to be a bit longer. In order to complete our chat script, we need to find out exactly what our login session looks like. We can do this by logging in with regular terminal software such as minicom.

Login prompts at most Internet providers generally take the form of

```
Username:
Password:
```

or

```
Login:
Password:
```

We will take the first case as our example in this chapter. If you find your login prompts are different, substitute accordingly as we work through the section.

NOTE   It may be necessary for you to leave off the first letter of the prompts. This is because different operating systems handle the case of the first letter differently, and with some Internet providers you can't be sure which operating system will be providing the prompt to you when you log in. By waiting for the `ogin:` or `assword:` your scripts will work regardless of the case of the first letter.

So, what is our next expect-send pair? After connecting, we are presented with a `Username:` prompt, in response to which we provide a username (let's say our username is "testuser"). The expect-send pair for this interaction would be `Username:` **`testuser`**.

Once a username is provided, we get a `Password:` prompt, to which we provide a password (let's assume this is "testpassword"). This produces the pair `Password:` **`testpassword`**.

For many Internet providers this is sufficient, and PPP starts on the provider's system after the correct password is entered. On a smaller number of systems, the provider's computers will present you with a command prompt at which you have to type a command to start PPP. In this case, you will need to create an additional pair.

For our example, the complete chat script looks like this:

```
"" ATDT1234567 CONNECT "" Username: testuser Password: testpassword
```

To use this with the chat program (which is normally in /usr/sbin), we simply provide the script as an argument to chat:

```
/usr/sbin/chat "" ATDT1234567 CONNECT "" Username: testuser Password:
➥ testpassword
```

Note, however, that you don't want to type this at the command line and hit Enter. Without being integrated with pppd and provided access to the modem through that program, chat will attempt to chat in the console. You can use this to test your script, though. Simply type the command at the command prompt. When you see ATDT1234567, type **CONNECT** and then type **Username:**; you should see testuser in response. Follow this by typing **Password:**, and you should see testpassword in response.

NOTE   If you need to work out problems with your chat script, try adding the -v flag to your chat command. This causes the output of the script to appear in the system log, where you can analyze the results to find problems.

Once you have a working script, you need to integrate it with pppd. We are going to use a handful of pppd options to do this. (The pppd application takes many additional options, which can be found in the pppd man page.) The options we will use are the following:

- connect   This option is employed to specify a program or command used to establish a connection on the serial line being utilized. In this case, we use this option to specify the chat program and its script.

- noipdefault   The default behavior of pppd is to determine the IP address of the local machine on the basis of its host name. But if the Internet provider assigns a dynamic IP address, then the noipdefault is used to tell pppd to get the IP address from the remote machine to which it is connecting.

- defaultroute   This option tells pppd to add a default route to the system's routing table, using the remote system as the default gateway. The entry is removed when the connection is broken.

The structure of the pppd command is:

```
pppd device-name device-speed options
```

If we are connecting with the device /dev/modem and the modem has a top compressed speed of 57600bps (in other words, a 14.4Kbps modem), then we would use the following command to connect with our chat script:

```
$ pppd /dev/modem 57600 connect '/usr/sbin/chat "" ATDT1234567 CONNECT
➡ "" Username: testuser Password: testpassword' noipdefault
➡ defaultroute
```

When this command is issued, the modem should dial and, after connecting, authenticate and establish a PPP connection. If this process is successful, two things should happen.

First, issuing the command ifconfig with no flags or arguments should return a list of interfaces including a PPP interface similar to this one:

```
ppp0      Link encap:Point-to-Point Protocol
          inet addr:194.209.60.101  P-t-P:194.209.60.97
➡ Mask:255.255.255.0
          UP POINTOPOINT RUNNING  MTU:1500  Metric:1
          RX packets:10 errors:0 dropped:0 overruns:0
          TX packets:11 errors:0 dropped:0 overruns:0
```

Second, entries should be added to the routing table to create a default route through the remote machine (check for this using the route command with no flags or arguments):

```
Kernel IP routing table
Destination    Gateway        Genmask          Flags Metric Ref     Use
➡ Iface
du1.paus.ch    *              255.255.255.255 UH    0      0         0
➡ ppp0
default        du1.paus.ch    0.0.0.0          UG    0      0         0
➡ ppp0
```

In this example, the du1.paus.ch is the remote machine in the PPP connection and is serving as the default gateway.

Connecting with PAP Authentication

Connecting with PAP authentication follows the same basic principles as the text prompt example we just worked through, except that the method of providing the username and password differs.

The first major difference is that we don't provide the username and password on the command line as part of a PAP script. Instead, we create entries in a special secrets file that is used during the PAP authentication process. In Red Hat Linux 5, this file is /etc/ppp/pap-secrets. By default, the permissions on this file make it readable and writable only by the root user. Other users do not have read access for this file.

The format of entries in this file are:

```
username device/interface password
```

For instance, if we use our test username and password from the section above, our entry might be:

```
testuser * testpassword
```

The * indicates that this password can be used for connections on any interface. If we have a single PPP interface (ppp0), we can limit use of this password to that device by changing the entry:

```
testuser ppp0 testpassword
```

Comments in the pap-secrets file start with a hash mark (#).

Once your username and password are in the file, you need to write a new chat script. For most Internet providers, as soon as the modem connection is established, PAP authentication can begin. Therefore, our chat script gets simpler:

```
"" ATDT12345678 CONNECT ""
```

This script dials the Internet provider and makes sure that a connect message is received before ending the chat program and proceeding on to authentication.

Finally, we need to introduce one more option for pppd: user. This option indicates which PAP user from the pap-secrets file is to be authenticated. The end result is the following pppd command:

```
$ pppd /dev/modem 57600 connect '/usr/sbin/chat "" ATDT1234567 CONNECT'
➡ noipdefault defaultroute user testuser
```

As with our earlier text login example, you can check that everything is in order using `ifconfig` and `route`.

Once You Have a Connection

Once you have an Internet connection, you need to make sure you can fully connect to the Internet. In order to do this, you will need to verify that your DNS services are properly configured to point to your Internet provider's name server.

This is done by editing two files: `/etc/host.conf` and `/etc/resolv.conf`. Both of these files are discussed more fully in Chapter 27, "Setting Up Linux for an Ethernet Network." Here we will just cover the necessary basics of the files so that you can quickly get online.

The file `/etc/host.conf` should contain the following two lines:

```
order hosts,bind
multi on
```

For most Linux distributions, including Red Hat 5, this should be the default.

Next, `/etc/resolv.conf` should contain at least two lines:

```
search
nameserver 100.100.100.100
```

In your case, replace the IP address 100.100.100.100 with the IP address of your Internet provider's name server. Your Internet provider can provide this information. If your Internet provider provides you with a list of more than one name server, create a separate line for each name server, following the form of the `nameserver` line above:

```
search
nameserver 100.100.100.100
nameserver 200.200.200.200
```

Once this is done, you should be able to resolve names and thus access the Internet. You should also be able to run Internet software such as Netscape and FTP. These programs are discussed in later chapters, such as Chapter 20, "Using the World Wide Web."

Hanging Up

When you are finished using the Internet, you will want to hang up to reduce phone costs and online charges. To do this, you need to kill the pppd process.

You can find out the process ID of the pppd program using the `ps` command as the root user:

```
$ ps x | more
```

The entry for pppd should look something like

```
1316  a1 S    0:00 /usr/sbin/pppd /dev/cua1 115200 connect
➤ /usr/sbin/chat "" AT
```

and the first number is the process ID. You can kill this process with the `kill` command:

```
$ kill 1316
```

When pppd is killed, the modem should hang up.

Automating Your Internet Connection

While it is great to be able to establish PPP connections to the Internet, if you have to type the long `pppd` and `chat` commands each time you connect, the practicality of using Linux to connect to the Internet will be limited.

To improve the situation, we can create two scripts: one for dialing and one for hanging up.

Your Scripts

The two scripts we are going to create are called `dial` and `hangup` (logical choices, yes?). You will want to place these files in a directory on your path such as `/usr/local/bin`.

Because we haven't reviewed scripting yet, these two scripts will be presented here with a brief discussion so that you can get right down to using them. These scripts can be created in any text editor. It is important to make sure that lines that appear as one line here stay as one line in your files.

For the `dial` script, we will assume that our PAP example earlier in the chapter is the way we want to connect to the Internet.

Once you have created the scripts, you will want to make them executable with the chmod command:

```
$ chmod 700 dial hangup
```

The permission 700 makes the script readable, writable, and executable by the root user and no one else. This will work fine since you need to be running as root in order to make a PPP connection.

The *Dial* Script

The `dial` script should look like this:

```
#!/bin/sh
/usr/sbin/pppd /dev/modem 57600 connect \
'/usr/sbin/chat "" ATDT1234567 CONNECT' \
noipdefault defaultroute user testuser
```

The first line tells Linux to process the script through the Bourne Shell, which is at /bin/sh. You will notice that our pppd command is split across three lines. We do this in order to make the script more readable and the individual lines shorter. The backslashes at the ends of the first and second lines indicate that the line breaks shouldn't be treated as line breaks and that the command continues on the next line of the file.

The *Hangup* Script

The hangup script should look like this:

```
#!/bin/sh
kill `cat /var/run/ppp0.pid`
```

As with the `dial` script, we start by specifying that the script should be processed with the Bourne Shell. Next we kill the process in a slightly different way than we learned to before.

We rely on the fact that the pppd process writes its process ID to a file that usually sits in /var/run on most modern Linux systems. The filename consists of the device name followed by a .pid extension. If you have only one modem and one PPP connection active at a time, you can assume the device is ppp0 and write **/var/run/ppp0.pid** directly into your script.

The cat command simply displays the contents of the ppp0.pid file on the standard output. We put the cat command in back quotes to pass the result of the cat command (which is the process ID of the pppd process) to the kill command.

But what happens if you have multiple PPP interfaces and want to be able to specify which one to hang up? A quick modification of the hangup script makes this possible:

```
#!/bin/sh
kill `cat /var/run/$1.pid`
```

Here we have replaced ppp0 with $1. The $1 indicates that the value of the first argument to the script should be placed in this location. Now we can pass the interface name to the script as an argument. $ **hangup ppp1** will hang up the modem that is being used for the ppp1 interface.

Where Do We Go from Here?

In this chapter, we took a big step. We brought our Linux systems from the isolation of a lone computer on a desktop and connected them to the world with a PPP connection.

In the upcoming chapter, we will take advantage of this new ability and look at using Netscape Communicator, the premier Web browser and Internet client for the Linux platform.

Following that, in Chapter 19, we will look at the rich variety of e-mail software available for Linux so that you can choose the one that best supports your style of using e-mail.

CHAPTER
EIGHTEEN

Using the World Wide Web

- An Overview of Linux Browsers

- Installing and Using Netscape Communicator

- Installing and Using Xmosaic

- Installing and Using Lynx

Now that we have our Linux systems connected properly to the Internet, the first thing most of us will want to do is get out there and browse the World Wide Web.

In this chapter, we will take a brief tour through the numerous Web browsers that are available for Linux, and then take a closer look at three browsers: Netscape Communicator, Xmosaic, and Lynx.

Netscape Communicator is the latest version of the free Web browser and Internet client from Netscape. This full-featured package is available for Windows, Macintosh, and almost every conceivable Unix variant including Linux.

After Netscape Communicator, Xmosaic warrants a look because it is the grandparent of today's graphical browsers. Before anyone had heard of Netscape (and probably even before Marc Andreesen had conceived of it), Mosaic was quietly revolutionizing the World Wide Web by taking a text-based hypertext system and making it graphical. Mosaic started life in the Unix and X Windows worlds and later made its way to the Windows world, so looking at Mosaic in the X environment is truly looking at where the Web as we know it today began.

Finally, we will look at Lynx, the de facto standard in Unix text-based browsers. Lynx has a longer history than either Netscape or Mosaic, going back to when Web technology was used to deliver small amounts of scientific information in a simple text-based hypertext system. Lynx has continued to evolve and ships with almost every distribution of Linux. While it lacks the fancy graphics and icon-driven interface of Netscape Communicator, for a quick way to go online, check some information, and go offline, nothing beats Lynx.

An Overview of Linux Browsers

There are several browsers available for the X Windows environment that work with Linux. These browsers range from the test platform Amaya, developed at the World Wide Web Consortium (W3C), to mainstream browsers such as Netscape. We will take a quick look at some of these browsers so that you have a sense of the breadth of available Web software for Linux.

Amaya

Amaya is a Web browser developed by the W3C as a testbed for new Web protocols and data formats. Since this is the organization that maintains such standards as HTML and cascading style sheets (CSS)—both key Web technologies—it makes sense that the Consortium should develop its own software as part of developing new standards for the World Wide Web.

Amaya is a combination Web browser and authoring tool that is supposed to support cascading style sheets and HTML along with new graphics formats such as PNG. Amaya also includes a powerful mathematical expression editor.

Although Amaya offers leading-edge features, it does not support all the features of the Web that are currently supported by commercial browsers such as Netscape.

The Amaya home page is on the Web at `http://www.w3.org/Amaya/`.

Arena

Arena is a free Web browser currently sponsored by Yggdrasil, which produces its own Linux distribution. A copy is included with Red Hat 5 and is normally installed at `/usr/X11R6/bin/arena`. To test Arena, simply issue the command

```
$ /usr/X11R6/bin/arena
```

from an `xterm` window.

Arena was designed as a free browser in the days before Netscape Navigator and Microsoft Internet Explorer, and it claims many of the innovations that now appear in these two browsers. Arena was the original W3C testbed for HTML 3.0 and cascading style sheets, but it currently does not have a complete implementation of HTML 3.2 or CSS1. The W3C is now focusing its efforts on Amaya. A sample Arena window is shown in Figure 18.1.

Unfortunately, Arena is now falling out of date, and while Yggdrasil promises to continue developing the product, the current version is missing support for critical features of the Web and contains bugs that cause the software to crash unexpectedly. Still, Yggdrasil has done well developing their distribution of Linux, and there is every reason to expect that Arena will eventually be a full-featured and competitive browser for the Linux environment. The Arena home page is at `http://www.yggdrasil.com/Products/Arena/`.

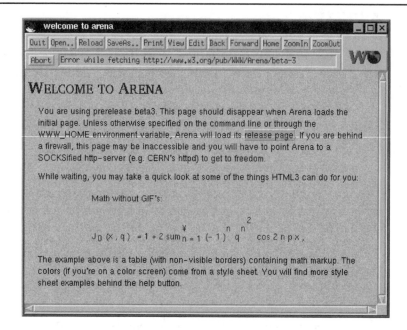

Lynx

Lynx is the de facto standard for text browsers for the World Wide Web and is available for all versions of Unix, Windows 95 and NT, and DOS. Work is underway for a Macintosh version. The Lynx home page is available at `http://lynx .browser.org/`.

You may be wondering what possible use a text browser could be. In the Unix world, it has many uses:

- Browsing HTML documentation or the Web on a system without X Windows running, such as a server console or a character terminal connected to a Unix network

- Quickly accessing the Web to download information without inflicting the system load that launching Netscape or a similar graphical browser would have

- Accessing the Web from low-end hardware such as a 386 PC

Whatever the reason, Lynx has evolved into an ideal offline browser with the means to cope with most of the advanced features of the Web today, including a way to view a site using frames. Figure 18.2 shows Lynx running in an `xterm` window. Detailed coverage of Lynx is provided later in this chapter.

FIGURE 18.2:

Lynx

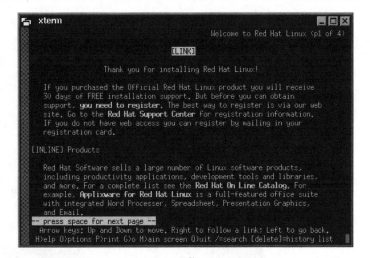

Xmosaic

The emergence of Mosaic from the labs of the National Center for Supercomputer Applications was the first indication that Web technology could mean more than a simple alternative to the omnipresent Gopher, which was the hypertext system of choice until the early 1990s.

Early versions of Mosaic ran in the X Windows environment of popular Unix systems such as Sun's. Users of the then-fledgling World Wide Web were dazzled by Mosaic's pages of combined graphics and text and the new, easy-to-navigate, mouse-driven interface.

While Mosaic is no longer under active development, the last release version (2.6 in the case of X Windows) is still available at the Mosaic Web page at the University of Illinois at Urbana-Champaine, http://www.ncsa.uiuc.edu/SDG/Software/Mosaic/. Figure 18.3 provides a sense of what the early pioneers of the Web used as their browser of choice.

We will discuss Xmosaic in more detail later in this chapter.

FIGURE 18.3:

The last version of Mosaic for X Windows

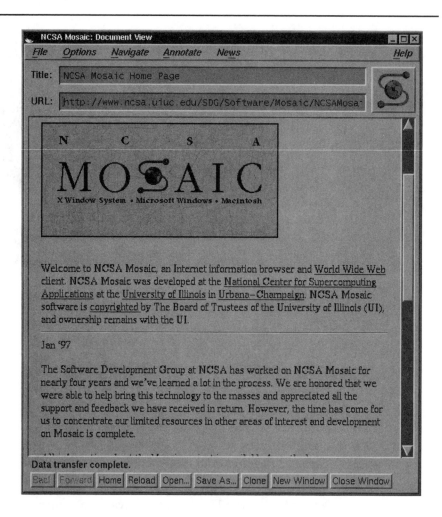

Netscape Communicator

Netscape Communicator, which includes the Navigator Web browser, can really be considered the flagship browser of the World Wide Web, and has been the source of many browser features that we now consider standard. While Microsoft can now be regarded as an equal competitor to Netscape in the Web browser market, Netscape still retains a large majority share by some counts, helped in part by the decision to release Communicator and its source code for free redistribution and alteration in early 1998.

In fact, at the time of this pricing policy change, Netscape highlighted Linux as an example of the open source model that Netscape was adopting for Communicator.

As would be expected, Netscape Communicator looks pretty much the same and behaves pretty much consistently on all the platforms it is available for, including Linux. Figure 18.4 shows Netscape Communicator for Linux. At first glance, it looks much the same as its Windows counterpart.

FIGURE 18.4:

Netscape Communicator for Linux

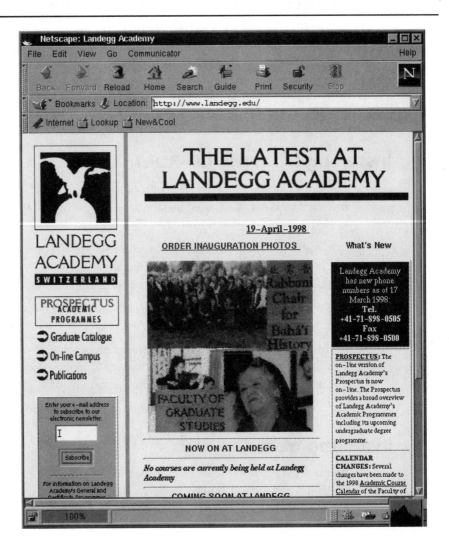

We discuss Netscape Communicator for Linux in detail later in this chapter.

Installing and Using Netscape Communicator

Netscape Communicator version 4.05 is included on the CD-ROM that accompanies this book. You can also download new copies of Communicator from Netscape's Web site at `http://home.netscape.com/`.

We will take a quick look at installing Communicator in Linux, and then take a brief introductory tour of the software. This tour is not intended to provide a comprehensive guide to Communicator, but rather to provide enough information so that you can use it to get online. Netscape Communicator includes complete online help that has all the information needed to take full advantage of Communicator's features.

Installing from the CD-ROM

Netscape Communicator 4.05 is part of Red Hat 5.1 and is likely to have been installed by default for most installations. If you find that Netscape is not on your system, you can install it from the CD-ROM that accompanies this book.

In order to install Communicator, you first must mount your CD-ROM to a logical location, such as /mnt/cdrom. Next, you want to use the rpm command to install the Netscape Communicator packages as follows:

```
$ rpm -i/mnt/cdrom/RedHat/RPMS/netscape-common-4.05-4.i386.rpm
$ rpm -i/mnt/cdrom/RedHat/RPMS/netscape-communicator-4.05-4.i386.rpm
```

This will install the complete version of Netscape Communicator on your system. If you prefer to install only the Navigator component of Communicator and not the whole package, replace the second rpm command with

```
$ rpm -i/mnt/cdrom/RedHat/RPMS/netscape-navigator-4.05-4.i386.rpm
```

Installing from the Web

If you decide to download a newer version of Communicator from the Netscape Web site, installation will be somewhat different. At the time of this writing, the most recent version of Netscape Communicator was version 4.05 and was available as a compressed `tar` archive called `communicator-v405-export` `.x86-unknown-linux2.0.tar.gz`.

You need to download this archive to a temporary location, such as `/tmp/`. Next, create a temporary directory to hold the installation files, such as `/tmp` `/netscape/`, and then change directories (using the `cd` command) into this directory. Next, uncompress the archive with the command:

```
$ tar xzvf /tmp/communicator-v405-export.x86-unknown-linux2.0.tar.gz
```

This will create several files in your temporary directory, including a README file and the `ns-install` script. You can proceed to install by running the installation script:

```
$ ./ns-install
```

From there, the procedure will be the same as if you were installing from the CD-ROM.

NOTE   If you download a newer version of Communicator than 4.05, there is the chance that the installation procedure is different than outlined here. In this case, check the installation files for a `README` file or an `INSTALL` file and take a look at the instructions in the file using the `more` command. When in doubt, accept the default options for all questions asked during installation, as this will help ensure that installation goes smoothly.

Accessing the World Wide Web

Accessing the Web with Communicator requires no additional preparation. Simply connect to the Internet (as outlined in the previous chapter) and then issue the command

```
$ /opt/netscape/netscape
```

or w1hatever is appropriate for your installation to launch Communicator.

This will bring up a window similar to the one in Figure 18.5.

From here, Netscape works pretty much in the same way as it does on Windows or Macintosh computers.

FIGURE 18.5:

The initial Netscape Communicator window

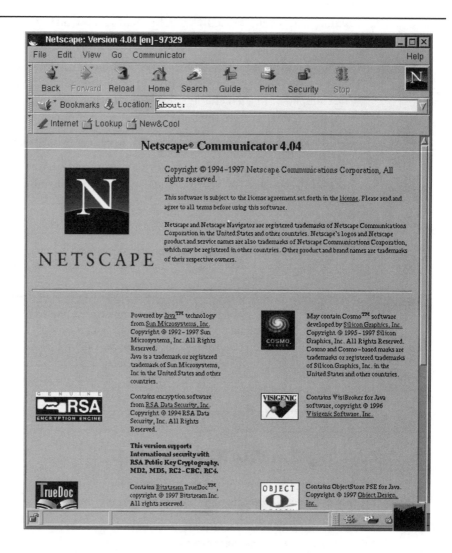

Opening a Web Page

You can open a Web page in several ways. The first is to type the URL of the desired page directly into the location field of the main window, as shown in Figure 18.6. As you can see in the figure, when you start typing a new URL in the location field, the name of the field changes to Go To, indicating that the URL being displayed is not the URL of the currently loaded document. When you hit Return, Communicator will attempt to load the URL you have typed.

FIGURE 18.6:

The Location/Go To field

Another method of opening a new page is to select Open Page from the File menu, as shown in Figure 18.7. This will bring up the Open Page dialog box like the one in Figure 18.8. Simply type the URL you want to open and click the Open in Navigator button to open the Web page.

FIGURE 18.7:

The File menu

FIGURE 18.8:

The Open Page dialog box

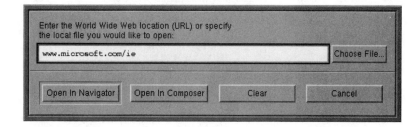

Returning to Previous Pages

Returning to the previously viewed page is as simple as clicking the Back button in the Communicator toolbar. The toolbar is shown in Figure 18.9; the Back button is the first button at the left.

FIGURE 18.9:

The Communicator toolbar

You can also return to the previous page by choosing Back from the Go menu shown in Figure 18.10. The Go menu shows the history of documents you have viewed, and you can return to any displayed document by selecting it from the Go menu.

FIGURE 18.10:

The Go menu

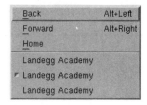

Printing Pages

You can print Web pages from Communicator as long as you have already installed and configured a printer as discussed in Chapter 12, "Configuring Your System with the Control Panel," and Chapter 15, "Using Peripherals."

To print a displayed page, simply click the Print button in the toolbar or select Print from the File menu. This will bring up a dialog box like the one in Figure 18.11.

FIGURE 18.11:

The Print dialog box

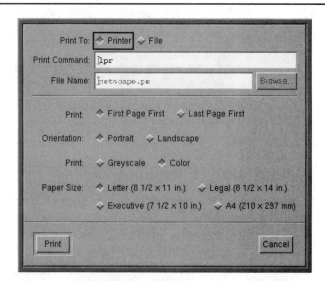

You can use this dialog box to print to a file or print to a configured printer queue.

Printing to a File   Printing to a file causes Netscape to generate a PostScript image of the page being printed. The resulting file can be viewed with a Post-Script viewer such as Ghostscript, or can be used with software that can handle PostScript files (including word processors, graphics, and other applications) and sent directly to a printer at a later date.

To print to a file, select Print To: File at the top of the dialog box and then fill in the complete path and file name where you want Netscape to create the resulting file. All the other options are the same as printing to a printer (see below) and should be selected as appropriate depending on the intended use of the resulting file.

Printing to a Print Queue   To print to a printer queue, select Print To: Printer at the top of the dialog box. Next, you need to enter the complete print command for your printer. For instance, if you want to print to a printer with a print queue called `laserjet51`, you would use the print command `lpr -Plaserjet51`. You may need to specify the full path of the `lpr` command, in which case your print command would be `/usr/bin/lpr -Plaserjet51`. The `lpr` command was covered in detail in Chapter 15, "Using Peripherals."

The choice of printing First Page First or Last Page First will be dependent on the way in which pages come out of your printer. Generally, if they come out face down, choose First Page First; if they come out face up, select Last Page First.

Choose your orientation based on the nature of the document you are printing. If the document is a tall document with lots of text, Portrait will probably look best. If the document has some wide images, try Landscape to see how things look.

Selecting the correct option of Greyscale or Color is important. If you have a black-and-white printer, you should select Greyscale; some black-and-white printers will produce unusable results if Color is selected, printing all colors as black and rendering documents unreadable. If you have a color printer, you can choose either option depending on whether you want your final printout to be black-and-white or color.

Finally, choose the correct paper size to match the paper in your printer and click the Print button.

Using Help

Netscape Communicator includes complete online help for the software. The online help system is accessible by selecting the Help Contents entry in the Help menu, shown in Figure 18.12.

FIGURE 18.12:

The Help menu

The Communicator help window looks like the one shown in Figure 18.13.

FIGURE 18.13:

The Netscape NetHelp window

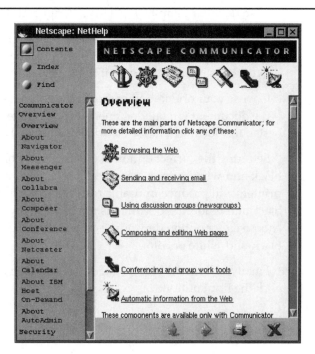

The help system includes a table of contents down the left side. The text contains underlined hypertext links that allow you to quickly jump to content of interest. In addition, you can click the Index button to view and search an index of the help contents.

Accessing Your E-Mails with Communicator

In addition to a Web browser, Netscape Communicator includes an integrated mail package, Messenger Mailbox, that you can use to read mail stored on POP or IMAP servers. In order to use the Mailbox, you first need to configure Communicator to know where to find your mail and how to send your mail.

Configuring Communicator for E-Mail

Communicator can be configured with the Preferences dialog box, accessed by selected Preferences from the Edit menu. Figure 18.14 shows the Preferences dialog box when it is first opened.

FIGURE 18.14:

The Preferences dialog box

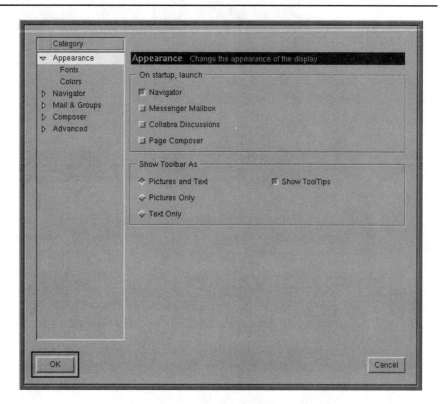

The dialog box contains numerous sections and subsections that are used to configure Communicator. To set up Communicator to read your mail, you need to open Mail & Groups by clicking the right-facing triangle next to its name. This will open the first configuration panel, as shown in Figure 18.15, and will show a submenu of configuration panels for the Mail & Groups section.

FIGURE 18.15:

The Mail & Groups section

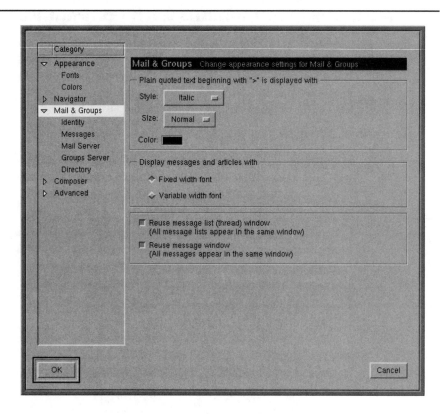

In order to get your mail working, you will need to use the Identity and Mail Server panels, at a minimum. The other panels provide configuration options that you may want to consider, but these are not essential to basic e-mail operation.

The Identity Panel   You use the Identity panel to configure the information (such as your e-mail address, name, and organization) that will appear on all e-mails you send. This panel is shown in Figure 18.16.

The fields that you really need to fill in are Your Name, which should contain your full name as you would wish mail recipients to see it, and Email Address, which should contain your complete e-mail address as it needs to appear on the From line of your e-mails.

FIGURE 18.16:

The Identity panel

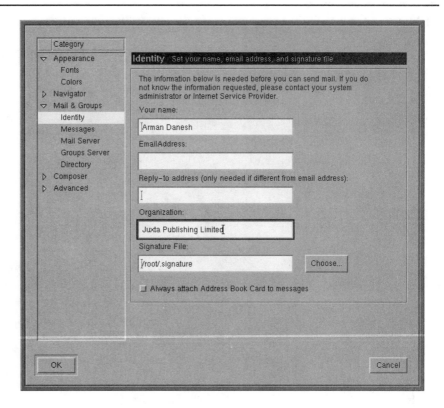

Fill in the Reply-to Address field if the address that people should use to reply to your messages is different than the From line of your outgoing e-mails. You can also fill in the Organization field. This information will be included in the header of all e-mails you send and will be displayed in some mail readers, including Communicator.

The Signature File field specifies a file containing a signature to be appended at the end of all the e-mails you send. This field can be left blank if you want no signature on outgoing e-mails.

The Mail Server Panel   The Mail Server panel is used to tell Communicator how to find your inbox and how to send mail you compose. It looks like Figure 18.17.

The information required by the Mail Server panel will generally be given to you by your Internet provider, or by your system administrator if you are on a corporate LAN.

FIGURE 18.17:

The Mail Server panel

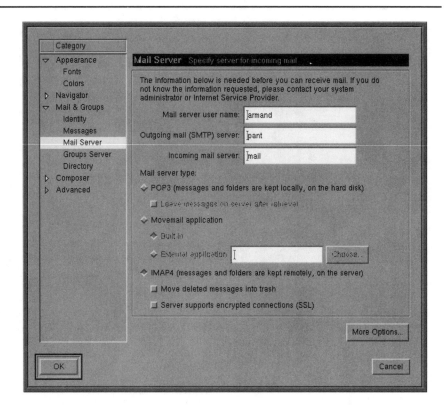

The Mail Server User Name you need to specify is the name that identifies you to the mail server that has your inbox on it. This may not be the same as your e-mail address. The Outgoing Mail Server (the SMTP server) specifies the server that will route your outgoing Internet mail. In the case of many Internet providers, this may be the same as the incoming mail server.

The choice of Mail Server Type is dependent on the type of mail server you are connecting to:

- If you are using an Internet provider, it will likely be a POP3 server. When first configuring Communicator to use a POP3 server, you will want to select "Leave messages on server after retrieval" to make sure you don't lose any e-mails by misconfiguration or other problems with your Communicator setup.

- On a corporate LAN, you may find that you are accessing an IMAP4 server. The information for this type of server will be provided by your system administrator.

Finally, Communicator for Linux includes one mail server option that is not available on the Windows version of Communicator: the Movemail application. The Movemail application can be used if Sendmail or another mail transport agent is running on your system and delivering your mail to a local mailbox (which is normally found in `/var/spool/mail/`). In this case, you can use Communicator's built-in Movemail application to move mail from this type of Linux inbox into Communicator's Mailbox.

Reading Mail

Once you have configured Communicator for your mail account, you can read mail by clicking on the Mailbox icon, which appears either in a component button bar docked in the bottom right corner of the main Communicator window (as in Figure 18.18) or in a floating component window (as in Figure 18.19). Alternately, you can select Messenger Mailbox from the Communicator menu shown in Figure 18.20.

FIGURE 18.18:

The docked Communicator component bar

FIGURE 18.19:

The floating Communicator component bar

Any of these selections will open the Mail & Discussions window as shown in Figure 18.21.

FIGURE 18.20:

The Communicator menu

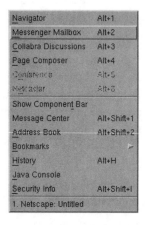

FIGURE 18.21:

The Mail & Discussions window

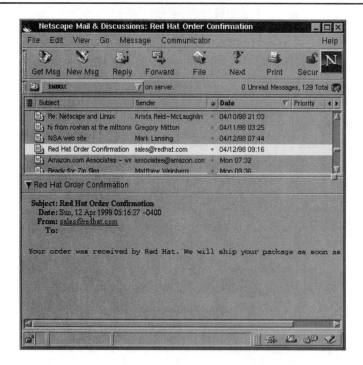

The Mail & Discussions window consists of a menu and toolbar at the top, a message list pane showing the headers of messages in the mailbox currently being viewed, and a message pane showing the contents of the message currently selected in the message list.

If, after opening the Mail & Discussions window, you want to check your mail again, simply click the Get Msg button in the Mail & Discussions toolbar shown in Figure 18.22.

FIGURE 18.22:

The Mail & Discussions toolbar

Composing a New Message

You can compose a new message by selecting the New Msg button on the toolbar, as shown in Figure 18.22. This will bring up a message composition window like the one in Figure 18.23. In this window you can fill in one or more recipients by hitting Return after each recipient's name. Clicking the To at the left of each e-mail address allows you to select alternate modes of addressing a recipient, such as Cc and Bcc.

FIGURE 18.23:

The Message Composition window

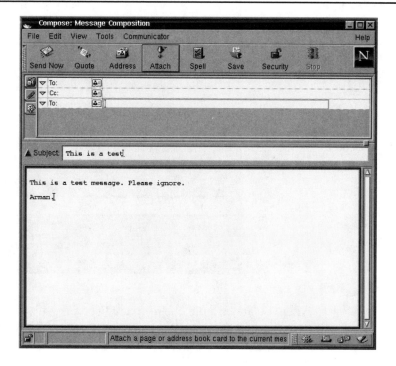

After filling in the recipients, subject, and message text, you have several options: you can add an attachment, you can spell-check the document, you can send the document immediately, or you can queue the document to send later.

Attaching a File In order to attach a file, simply click the Attach button on the Message Composition toolbar shown in Figure 18.24.

FIGURE 18.24:

The Message Composition toolbar

This will produce a drop-down menu that will let you attach a file or Web page. If you choose File, you will be presented with a dialog box, like the one in Figure 18.25, from which you can select the file to attach.

FIGURE 18.25:

Selecting a file to attach

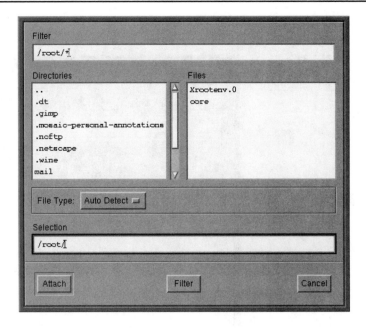

After you attach a file, the recipient list pane will switch to an attachment list pane. Figure 18.26 shows this changed view, with a file named core as the attachment. If you attach more files, more than one icon will appear.

FIGURE 18.26:

The attachment list

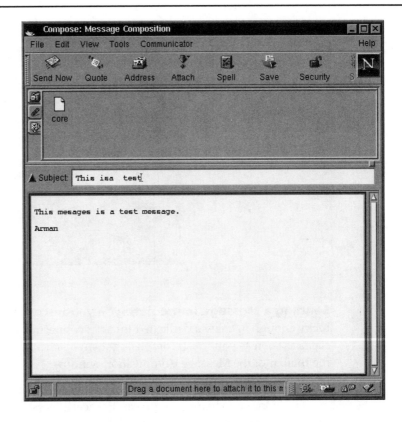

If you want to switch back to the recipient list to add or remove recipients, simply select Address Pane from the View menu.

Spell Checking To spell-check your message before sending it, simply click the Spell button on the toolbar of the Message Composition window. This will bring up the spell check dialog box shown in Figure 18.27. Each word that is not found in the system's dictionary will be presented to you with a list of suggestions. Click Replace to correct a misspelled word, Ignore to skip a word, or Learn to add a word to the dictionary.

At any time during the process of spell checking a message you can click the Stop button to cancel the operation.

FIGURE 18.27:

The Spell Check dialog box

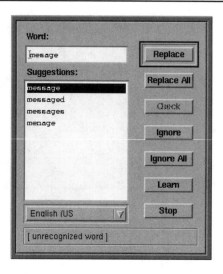

Sending a Message Immediately If you are connected to the Internet (or are lucky enough to enjoy a dedicated Internet connection), you can send your messages as soon as you finish composing them by clicking the Send Now button on the toolbar of the Message Composition window.

This will immediately connect to your outgoing mail server and deliver the message. Once this happens, you can't cancel a message. The message is en route to the recipients and can't be stopped.

Queuing a Message for Later Delivery Most users who connect to the Internet through an Internet provider will want to compose messages offline and then quickly connect to their provider to send all messages that they have written. You can do this with Netscape Communicator by selecting Send Later from the File menu when you are done composing the message.

Then, when you finally connect to the Internet, simply select Send Unsent Messages from the File menu of the main Mail & Discussions window to send all messages that are queued for delivery.

Replying to a Message

Replying to a message is closely related to composing a new message. Simply select the message you want to reply to in the Mail & Discussions window and then click the Reply button in the toolbar.

This will bring up a pre-addressed Mail Composition window with the subject line preset, and the text of the original message displayed if you selected the Automatically Quote Original Message when Replying option when configuring Communicator. By default, reply messages are addressed only to the sender of the original message. If you want to send a reply to the sender and all other recipients of the message, simply click and hold the Reply button. A drop-down menu like the one in Figure 18.28 will appear, and you can select To Sender and All Recipients.

FIGURE 18.28:

The Rer'.y drop-down menu

When you finish composing your reply, you can send it in the same way as described above for a new message.

Installing and Using Xmosaic

Xmosaic is the X Windows version of the browser that has become famous for bringing graphics to the World Wide Web and launching the Internet as we know it today.

While development on Mosaic no longer continues, you can still download the binary installation of Mosaic for Linux if you want to run the program to see what all the fuss was about. Some people even end up using Mosaic as their browser of choice, although they are becoming increasingly rare.

Installing Xmosaic

You can download the compressed Mosaic binary file for Linux from the Mosaic home page at `http://www.ncsa.uiuc.edu/SDG/Software/Mosaic/`. The current version of Xmosaic for Linux (version 2.6) is the file `Mosaic-linux-2.6.Z`.

This file is not an archive of multiple files, but is a single file compressed using the `compress` program. To install the software, move the compressed file to the directory where you want to install Mosaic (consider `/usr/local/bin/` or `/opt/bin/`, depending on your preference) and then uncompress the file with the command

```
$ uncompress Mosaic-linux-2.6.Z
```

This will uncompress the file and remove the `.Z` extension. Next, you need to make the file executable with the command

```
$ chmod w+x Mosaic-linux-2.6
```

Finally, since `Mosaic-linux-2.6` is a lot to type to launch the application, consider making a symbolic link to the file called `mosaic` or `xmosaic`:

```
$ ln -s Mosaic-linux-2.6 xmosaic
```

Now it is possible to launch Mosaic with the command

```
$ xmosaic
```

to get a window like the one in Figure 18.29.

FIGURE 18.29:

The Mosaic window

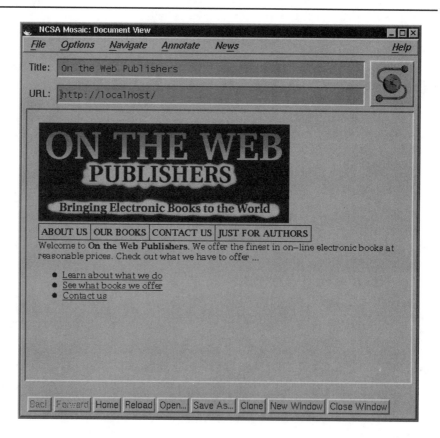

Using Mosaic

Because development stopped on Mosaic some time ago, Mosaic offers far fewer features than Netscape Communicator. This makes Mosaic much simpler to use—but also makes it less intuitive, since less effort has been poured into its interface.

Opening a Page

Xmosaic offers several ways to open a URL. The simplest is to type the URL into the URL field at the top of the window (as shown in Figure 18.30).

FIGURE 18.30:

The URL field

Alternately, you can click the Open... button on the toolbar at the bottom of the window (shown in Figure 18.31) or choose Open URL from the File menu (shown in Figure 18.32). These two options bring up a dialog box like the one in Figure 18.33, where you enter the URL you want to access and then click the Open button.

FIGURE 18.31:

The Mosaic toolbar

| Back | Forward | Home | Reload | Open... | Save As... | Clone | New Window | Close Window |

FIGURE 18.32:

The File menu

FIGURE 18.33:

The Open URL dialog box

Accessing Previous Pages

The toolbar at the bottom of the window offers a Back button that allows you to cycle back through your history of pages one page at a time. In addition, selecting Window History from the Navigate menu shown in Figure 18.34 brings up the window history list in a dialog box like Figure 18.35.

FIGURE 18.34:

The Navigate Menu

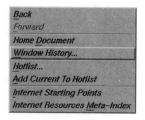

FIGURE 18.35:

The Where You've Been dialog box

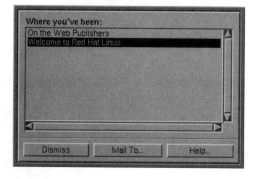

From this window you can double-click any entry to open that page, or click the Mail To button to mail the selected page to another person.

Using Mosaic's Help

Mosaic offers complete online help in HTML format in the form of documentation stored on the Mosaic Web site. You can access this help by selecting the appropriate subject from the Help menu shown in Figure 18.36.

FIGURE 18.36:

The Mosaic Help menu

Options on the Help menu include an FAQ and a Manual, as shown in Figure 18.37.

FIGURE 18.37:

The online manual

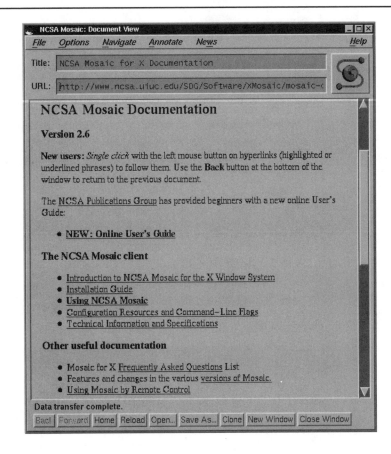

Installing and Using Lynx

The final browser we will take a look at is Lynx, by far the most common text browser in use in the Unix and Linux worlds. Lynx is included in most Linux distributions, among them the RedHat distribution bundled with this book.

You can check whether Lynx is installed with the command

```
$ rpm -qa | grep lynx
```

If you find that Lynx is not installed, use rpm to install lynx-2.7.2-1.i386.rpm from the RedHat/RPMS subdirectory of the CD-ROM:

```
$ rpm -i lynx-2.7.2-1.i386.rpm
```

Once it is installed, you can find Lynx at /usr/bin/lynx.

Downloading a Newer Version

The version of Lynx included with this book is version 2.8. If you are interested in a newer version, you can check the Lynx home page at http://lynx.browser.org/. At the time of this writing, the most current version of Lynx was version 2.8.

Lynx comes as source code that you will need to compile, but don't let this stop you from installing a newer version if you intend to make regular use of Lynx. The archive of version 2.8 is called lynx2-8.zip. Simply download it to a temporary location (such as /tmp/) and then follow the steps below to compile and install this version of Lynx.

Compiling Lynx from Source Code

Once you have downloaded the archive, use cd to change to the /tmp/ directory and then unzip the archive with the command:

```
$ unzip /tmp/lynx2-8.zip
```

This will create a subdirectory called lynx2-8. Change to this directory.

To start compiling Lynx, simply issue the command

```
$ make linux-ncurses
```

while in this directory. The linux-ncurses argument ensures that the correct options for Linux are set while compiling and that the ncurses library is used.

The ncurses library, which provides a collection of functions for manipulating character-mode screens, is included with the distribution of Red Hat on the CD-ROM.

Once this is done, you should see a message informing you that Lynx has been successfully compiled. Next, issue the command

> $ **make install**

to install the new Lynx binary file in /usr/local/bin/.

Starting Lynx

To use Lynx, you will want to launch it in an xterm window or in a character console. If you launch Lynx without any arguments, Lynx will attempt to load its default page. In the case of the binary version distributed with Red Hat Linux, this default page is an HTML documentation page that is installed with the operating system. If you compiled Lynx yourself, then this page is probably http://lynx.browser.org/.

Starting Lynx produces a screen like the one in Figure 18.38.

FIGURE 18.38:

Lynx

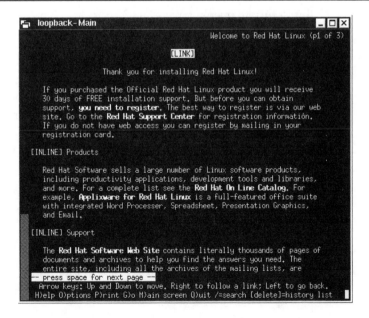

If you want to directly access a specific page or file when you launch Lynx, simply provide the page URL or the filename as an argument to Lynx:

```
$ lynx http://www.yahoo.com/
```

or

```
$ lynx /tmp/filename
```

Lynx also takes numerous flags that can alter its behavior. You can view the complete list with the –? argument:

```
$ lynx -?
```

Generally, however, you won't need to use any of these command-line arguments when browsing the Web with Lynx.

Opening a New Page

As you will notice, the bottom line of the Lynx screen displays the main key commands that you can use to browse the Web. To open a new page once Lynx is running, you can use the Go command by hitting the G key.

Lynx will prompt you with the prompt URL to Open:. Simply enter a URL and hit Return to open the page.

Following Links

Links in a document show up in bold text when running in an `xterm` window and as blue text when running in color mode in a console window. You can select a link to follow by using the Tab key to move forward through the links or the up and down arrows to move backwards and forwards through the links. The currently selected link will appear in reverse text in an `xterm` window or in red text in a console window.

Once you have selected a link to follow, hit Return or the right arrow key to follow the link. You can return to the previously visited page by using the left arrow key.

Viewing Images

If you are running Lynx in an `xterm` window, you can configure things so that you can view images embedded in pages in a separate window using the `xv` program.

In order to do this, you need to configure Lynx so that it knows to use xv to display images. You do this by editing the file /etc/lynx.cfg using your favorite text editor.

In this file, you will find two lines that start with #XLOADIMAGE_COMMAND. One will appear under the header VMS and the other under the header Unix. We will work with the one under the header Unix. Change this line to read

```
XLOADIMAGE_COMMAND:/usr/bin/X11/xv %s &
```

Notice that the pound sign (#) at the start of the line has been removed. This uncomments the line so that Lynx will pay attention to it when Lynx loads.

Once you have done this, save the changed file and launch Lynx. Next you need to turn on the images-as-links mode. This is done with the asterisk (*). If you press this, all pages will now display images as links. Following one of these links will cause xv to load and the image to be displayed in xv.

Online Help

You can access Lynx's online help with the key H. This connects to a Web site on the Internet containing the complete documentation for Lynx, so it is necessary to be connected to the Internet to access the online help system.

Where Do We Go from Here?

Now that we managed to get online and browse the Web using Linux, we are ready to look at the full range of options for the other major Internet function: e-mail.

We have already reviewed one of the popular mail-reading applications, Netscape Communicator. But Communicator is only one of many alternatives.

Linux offers a broad range of mail clients, both commercial and free. These range from powerful (but complicated) prompt-oriented systems to comprehensive and lightweight character-mode mail readers (such as the well-known Pine and Elm packages) to graphical mail readers (such as Xmail).

In the next chapter, we will take a broad look at the mail readers available for Linux and then take a closer look at some of the more common mail readers available.

CHAPTER

NINETEEN

Reading E-Mail

■ Local versus Remote Mailboxes

■ Offline Mail Readers

■ Online Mail Program

In this chapter, we are going to discuss the different approaches and programs available in Red Hat Linux for reading, composing, and sending e-mail.

The discussion will start with a look at mailboxes. Most home users of the Internet have remote mailboxes maintained on their Internet provider's servers. But when they read the mail using a mail reader such as Eudora or Netscape Communicator's built-in mail reader, they permanently copy their messages into a mailbox created locally by their mail software.

Another approach is to read mail online. In this way, the mailbox remains on the server and is simply manipulated by the mail software without permanently creating a local mailbox as new mail is read.

This chapter will cover all approaches available in Linux for online and offline mail reading. It will move on to various types of mail software for offline reading and online access to a remote mailbox.

Local versus Remote Mailboxes

The distinction between local and remote mailboxes may seem subtle and not a major issue, but this distinction is fundamental to understanding the various types of mail software in the Unix world.

In most Unix networks, users' mail is stored in local mailboxes in a format known as Berkeley Mail Folders (after the University of California at Berkeley where this type of folder originated). Unix mail systems such as Sendmail, which is responsible for routing incoming and outgoing mail, automatically store new messages in users' personal mailboxes in this standard format. Users can then use any of numerous standard Unix-based mail applications to read their mail, compose new messages, and organize their mailboxes.

All of this is available in the Linux world. All the common Unix mail tools are available for Linux, and, as we will see later in the book when we discuss small business networks, the Berkeley Mail Folder with Sendmail and a Unix mail client is a common solution for providing users with e-mail capabilities.

But for a home user, mail generally sits in a mailbox on a remote server managed by their Internet provider. There is no way for software to access these remote folders as if they were local Berkeley Mail Folders. Instead, it is necessary to use mail software that speaks either the POP3 or IMAP4 protocol. These protocols provide different ways for accessing remote mailboxes.

POP3 Mail Servers

Most users of Windows- or Mac-based mail software whose mail sits on an Internet provider's mail server probably use the POP3 protocol.

In the POP3 model, users connect to the Internet, download new mail from their mailboxes, and then optionally delete the original copy from the mailboxes on the remote server. This effectively creates a local mailbox that can be read offline. The local mailbox contains a complete copy of the contents of the original mailbox on the server. Users can read their messages, compose replies and new messages, and organize their mail while offline, and then reconnect to send messages they have composed and check for new mail.

This is a simple protocol and is a familiar one to most users. It is ideal where the cost of online time is expensive or bandwidth is limited. Because it is designed for working offline, it is well-suited to users with limited network access. But the simplicity of the protocol creates some fundamental limitations.

For instance, consider the user who needs to access a remote mailbox from two or more locations. It is possible to leave copies of all downloaded messages on the remote server using POP3. This would allow all messages to be downloaded using mail software on two different PCs in two different locations. But there is no way to know whether a message has been answered from the other location, and if a message is deleted off the remote server for any reason before it is downloaded to both locations, then one location will have an incomplete mailbox.

Consider this scenario of a user who uses two PCs, one at home and one on the road. Both PCs are used to read mail from the same mailbox using POP3 mail software. First thing in the morning, the home PC is used to download the day's mail. There are 50 messages including 33 junk messages. The user immediately deletes the junk messages, responds to 7 messages, and files 10 messages for later processing.

Later in the afternoon, this same user proceeds to access their mailbox using their portable system. They proceed to download their mail. The number of messages now numbers 58. This includes the 33 junk messages that were deleted on the home machine, the 7 messages that have been replied to, and the 10 messages kept for later processing, in addition to 8 new messages to be handled.

This situation, which is not uncommon, can lead to a lot of unnecessary repetition in trying to work with the same mail in two or more locations.

IMAP4 Mail Servers

One solution to this problem is an IMAP4 mail server.

In the IMAP model, mailboxes exist on remote servers and remain there. Users then open and access these mailboxes using their client applications, but instead of copying the messages to a local mailbox, they are simply manipulating the remote mailbox without ever creating a local copy.

IMAP offers several benefits to address the problems found in POP3 systems. This includes the ability to work with, and maintain, a single mailbox from multiple locations and computers. This is achieved by the fact that the mail remains in a single remote mailbox instead of replicating into multiple local mailboxes. If a user deletes a message from the mailbox from one location and then accesses the mailbox from another, the message won't be there.

However, the very nature of IMAP4—manipulating a remote mailbox—makes it necessary to work online to read, reply to, and process mail. Thus, IMAP4 is best suited to situations where a network connection is either permanent or essentially free. For instance, in a location with flat-rate Internet costs and flat-rate local phone costs, POP3 and IMAP4 mail connections would cost the same. But if a user

is paying per-minute Internet and phone call costs, then IMAP4 will prove much more expensive than POP3.

In addition, not many Internet providers give users access to their mailboxes through IMAP4 servers. IMAP4 systems are far more common in corporations and allow users to access their mailboxes at work and from home without the difficulties introduced by POP3 systems.

Offline Mail Readers

For most users, accessing a remote mailbox with POP3 is the right solution. This can be done using any of numerous available mail applications for Linux—including Netscape Communicator, which is available on the enclosed CD-ROM.

We will take a look at Netscape Communicator in this section because it is becoming one of the most popular graphical mail clients today and because users coming to Linux from the Windows and Macintosh platforms should already be familiar with Netscape's product. There are many other POP and IMAP mail readers available for Linux. You can check the Linux Applications and Utilities Page at `http://www.xnet.com/~blatura/linapps.html` for a list of alternative packages.

Netscape Communicator

It is fairly simple to configure Netscape Communicator to read your remote POP3 mailbox and to use it to compose messages offline and queue them. To launch Netscape Communicator, you can issue the command

```
$ /opt/netscape/netscape
```

from an `xterm` window, assuming you installed Communicator in the default location (see the section about installing Netscape Communicator in Chapter 18, "Using the World Wide Web").

Configuring Netscape Communicator for E-Mail

Once Communicator is launched, you can configure its mail reader from the Preferences dialog box by following the steps in the section "Configuring Netscape Communicator for E-Mail" in Chapter 18.

Here you have the option of setting up a POP3 or IMAP4 mail server. In this section, we will discuss using Netscape Communicator in a POP3 configuration. Configure your POP3 server in the Mail Server panel of the Preferences dialog box. Figure 19.1 shows a sample POP3 configuration.

Mail Server User Name The mail server user name is the name of your POP3 mail account. Generally, this will be the same as the part of your e-mail address before the @ symbol, although sometimes it can bear no relationship to the e-mail address. This value is generally specified by your e-mail provider.

Outgoing Mail Server The outgoing mail server, also known as an SMTP server, indicates where to send outgoing messages (messages you are sending) for delivery. The name or address of the server will be provided by your Internet provider. In the example above, the Internet provider is different than the mailbox provider, and all outgoing mail is sent out via a server from the Internet provider (`paus.ch`).

FIGURE 19.1:

Configuring Netscape Communicator to read mail from a POP3 server

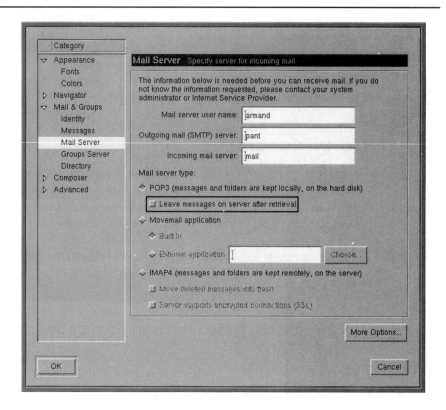

Incoming Mail Server   In the case of a POP3 configuration, this should indicate the name of the POP3 mail server where your mailbox sits. In our example, this is with an e-mail provider (landegg.edu) that is different from the Internet provider. For most users with a normal Internet account, the Internet provider and e-mail provider are one and the same. The name of the server will be specified by the provider.

Mail Server Type   There are three choices of mail server type in Netscape Communicator:

- POP3   Used when your mail sits on a POP3 server

- Movemail   Used when your mail sits in a local Berkeley Mail Folder

- IMAP4   Used when your mail sits on an IMAP4 server

Each of these server types offers a selection of options for working with mail folders. In the case of POP3 mail, there is one option: `Leave messages on server after retrieval`. This is useful especially when you access your mail from more than one location and don't want to miss mail at any location. If you only access your mailbox from one location, you will probably want to unselect this option once you have tested that everything is working. Many Internet providers impose disk space limitations on the size of inboxes, and if you don't delete messages after downloading them, your inbox on the server will grow without restriction.

More Options Clicking the More Options button brings up a dialog box like the one in Figure 19.2.

FIGURE 19.2:

More Mail Server options

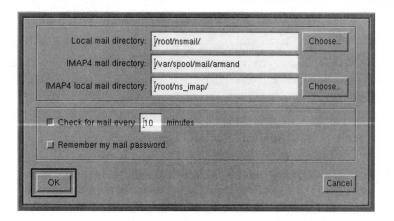

The local mail directory field indicates where Netscape should create its local mailboxes and folders. This is usually a subdirectory of a user's home directory called `nsmail`. For instance, for a user named `joeb`, Netscape will default to `/home/joeb/nsmail/` as the local mail directory. You can, of course, change this value, but there is little reason to do so unless you have very specific and unique needs.

The IMAP4 options are not relevant to a POP3 configuration and can be left with their default settings. The last two options, however, are of interest to a POP3 user.

You can specify how often Communicator should automatically check for new mail. If you rarely connect to the Internet and are usually online for very short periods of time, you will probably want to unselect this option so that you can check your mail manually.

Checking `Remember my mail password` means that you will only be prompted for your password the very first time you access your mailbox; from then on, Communicator will remember the password and you won't have to provide it again. This, of course, is a security risk if there is any chance of an unauthorized person using your computer. They will be able to access your inbox without providing a password.

As an alternative, you can leave this option unselected. Then you will be prompted for your mail password the first time you access your inbox after launching Communicator. Communicator will remember the password until you quit the program, and the next time you launch it to access your inbox it will prompt you for your password again.

Reading Mail with Netscape Communicator

Once you have configured Netscape Communicator to access your mailbox, you are ready to try reading messages. But before you are able to access your mailbox, you need to do two things:

1   Connect to the Internet (follow the method discussed in Chapter 17).

2   Launch Netscape Communicator.

By default, Communicator launches with a Web browser window open. You can open the mailbox window in two ways:

1.   Click the mailbox icon, which will appear either in a floating toolbar

or in a smaller, fixed toolbar in the bottom right corner of the Communicator windows.

Both toolbars show a mailbox icon.

2. Select Messenger Mailbox from the Communicator menu (or press Alt+2), as shown in Figure 19.3.

FIGURE 19.3:

The Communicator menu

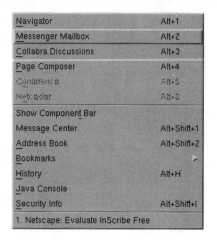

The mailbox window looks like the one in Figure 19.4.

The mailbox window is divided into three distinct regions, two on the top and one on the bottom. The top-left pane is used to display a list of mail folders, including your inbox and any local folders you create to organize your e-mail. The top-right pane displays the list of messages in the current folder. The information displayed includes the date, subject, sender, and size of the message. Finally, the bottom pane displays the contents of the current mail message.

FIGURE 19.4:

The Messenger Mailbox window

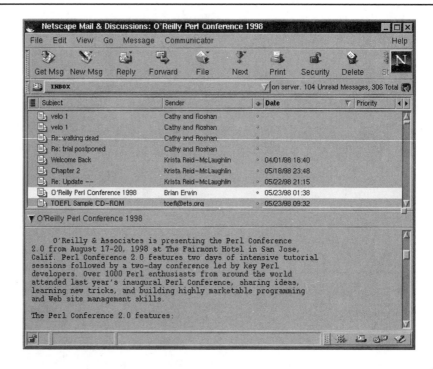

Because Communicator supports HTML mail, a mail message formatted using HTML will be displayed in the mailbox window just as if it were a Web page. Links are highlighted, as expected, and are clickable. Clicking a link will open the requested document in a browser window instead of in the mailbox window.

Composing Messages in Communicator

The flip side of reading messages is being able to compose new messages. Composing new messages is actually quite simple. Simply click the New Message icon.

This will bring up a message composition window like the one in Figure 19.5.

FIGURE 19.5:

The message composition
window

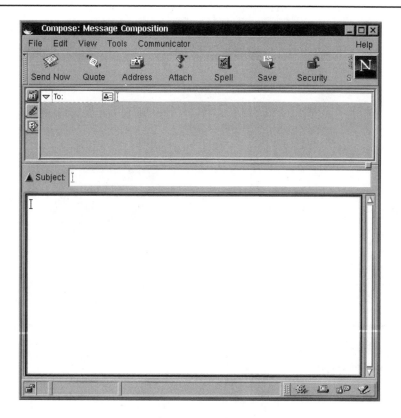

To address a message, simply fill in the address in the field next to the To:. Hitting the Return key after the address will create a new, blank To: field on the next line so you can address your message to multiple recipients. If you want some of the recipients to receive the message as a carbon copy (Cc:) or blind carbon copy (Bcc:), click the down arrow key next to the To: for the addressee you wish to change. This will bring up an address field menu where you can specify the correct option.

To add an attachment to your message, click the Attach button on the toolbar.

Attach

This will drop down the attachment menu, where you can choose to attach a file or a Web page.

If you choose to attach a file, this will open the file selection dialog box shown in Figure 19.6, where you can choose a file and click the Attach button.

FIGURE 19.6:

The file selection dialog box

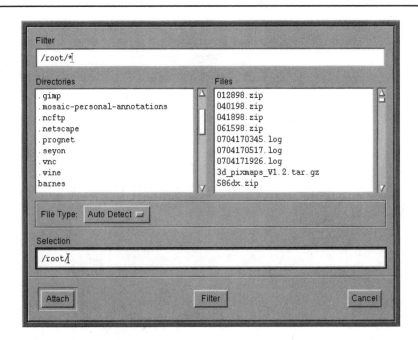

As shown in Figure 19.7, once you attach a file, the Attachments tab will be displayed with an icon for your attachment.

An attached file in the
Attachments tab

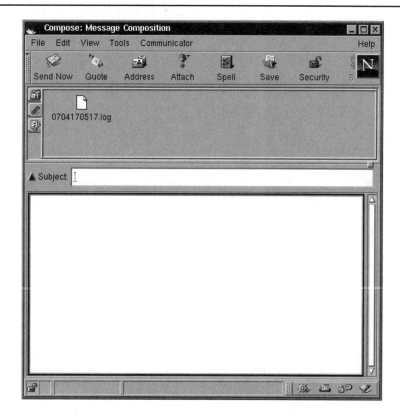

Type the subject of the message in the subject field and the body of the message in the large text editing area, as shown in the completed message in Figure 19.8.

Finally, hit the Send Now button to send the message (assuming you are connected to the Internet when you finish composing the message).

FIGURE 19.8:

A completed message

Queuing Messages   Usually, users with a POP mail connection to an Internet provider will want to compose their messages while offline, queuing them for later delivery when they connect to their Internet provider. This is achieved quite easily. Once a message is composed, instead of clicking the Send Now button on the composition window's toolbar, simply select Send Later from the File menu shown in Figure 19.9. This will queue the message for later delivery.

FIGURE 19.9:

The message composition file menu

Once you have finished composing your messages, connect to the Internet, and from the main Messenger Mailbox window, select Send Unsent Messages from the File menu shown in Figure 19.10.

FIGURE 19.10:

The Messenger Mailbox's file menu

New	▶
New Folder...	
Open Message	Alt+O
Save As...	Alt+S
Edit Message	
Empty Trash Folder	
Compress This Folder	Alt+K
Compress All Folders	
Get Messages	▶
Send Unsent Messages	
Clean Up Disk	
Join Discussion Groups...	
Print...	Alt+P
Close	Alt+W
Exit	Alt+Q

Any unsent, queued messages will be sent.

Replying to Messages and Forwarding Messages   Closely related to composing new messages are replying to messages and forwarding messages to other people.

Let's start with replying, since it is the more common activity for most people. To reply to a message, select the message in your mailbox and then click the Reply button on the toolbar.

This will bring up a pre-addressed message composition window like the one in Figure 19.11. If you have configured Netscape Communicator to do so, the window will include the contents of the original message in the message body pane.

FIGURE 19.11:

Replying to a message

Similarly, to forward a message, select the message and click the Forward button.

This will bring up an unaddressed mail-composition window with the selected message attached to your message and a subject line indicating a forwarded message, as shown in Figure 19.12.

FIGURE 19.12:

Forwarding a message

Online Mail Programs

In this section, we take a look at mail programs whose primary purpose is to read local Unix mailboxes; some mail programs can access IMAP4 servers as well. What distinguishes these from the offline software like Netscape Communicator is that they are designed to send messages at the time they are composed, rather than queuing them for later delivery. This is not uncommon on Unix systems: even on a system that is not connected to the Internet, you can run a mail server that handles the job of queuing messages for all users and sending them when a connection is periodically established. As far as the mail client software is concerned, you are always connected to the Internet, so the mail client can send a message immediately by passing it over to a mail server.

Pine and Elm

In the Unix world, and by extension in the Linux world, the two most common mail programs are pine and elm. These programs are both designed to work in a character-based environment, so they can be used at the console or in an `xterm` window. They are both designed to read local Berkeley Mail inboxes, and both are highly flexible with a large number of configurable options.

NOTE   An interesting bit of history: elm predates pine. Pine was written to make some aspects of elm easier to handle for the average user. Pine is known to stand for "Pine Is Not Elm."

Both elm and pine are commonly found in universities, where many students still have shell accounts to access e-mail. Because of space limitations, we will take a close look at only one of these programs: pine. The choice of pine versus elm is a highly subjective one and many die-hard Linux and Unix users may argue that elm should be presented instead of pine.

The logic behind my choice is this: both elm and pine are powerful packages, neither superior to the other. Most users are now likely to use graphical packages such as Netscape Communicator to manage their mail, since today's average PC is more than capable of running processing-intensive graphical applications of that type. To give users a sense of these traditional (and still popular) Unix mail programs, I chose pine because it is somewhat more user-friendly for a newcomer to Linux. And at the university where I work as a system administrator, all users use pine as their mail application, and this has proven to be quite a successful choice.

Using Pine

At first glance, pine may seem very complicated, but in reality it isn't. For the average user who wants to send and receive e-mail, pine is quite easy to use.

Most Linux systems will include pine already installed if the complete suite of networking applications was selected during the installation process. If yours doesn't, you can find pine at `http://www.washington.edu/pine/`. The version of pine included with Red Hat 5 is version 3.96. Version 4.00 is now available from this Web site.

Simply type the command

$ **pine**

to launch the program. The default configuration on most Linux systems should work without any tweaking.

When it first launches, pine will present its default main menu, as shown in Figure 19.13.

FIGURE 19.13:

The pine main menu

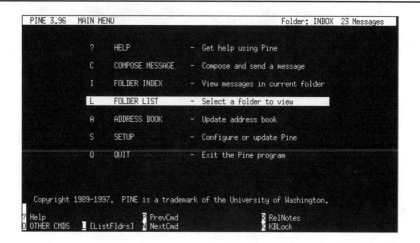

The pine screen contains four main areas:

- The top line presents the version number of pine that you are running, the name of the currently open folder (INBOX when pine first starts), and, if applicable, the current message being read along with the total number of messages in the folder.

- The bottom two lines present the more common commands accessible from the current screen. These commands change as the context dictates.

- The line above the menus is where pine displays prompts asking the user for input (Figure 19.14 provides an example of how this line is used) as well as information messages for the user.

- The rest of the screen represents the main work area.

FIGURE 19.14:

A user prompt

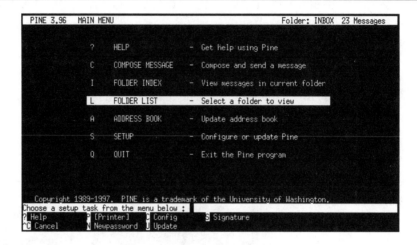

From the main menu, there are four main options:

- C (Compose Message): This command is used to compose and send a new message; this command can also be accessed when viewing the contents of a mail folder.

- I (Folder Index): This command is used to view the contents of the current folder (as displayed on the top line of the screen).

- L (Folder List): This command is used to view a list of available folders.

- A (Address Book): This command is used to access the address book.

We will look at the first two. All the commands are documented fully in pine's online help, which is available from the main menu with the HELP command (the ? key).

Opening and Working in a Folder Index To open a folder index, use the up or down arrow keys to select the FOLDER INDEX command and hit the Return key. Alternately, use the I key. This will open an index of the current folder (initially the inbox), as shown in Figure 19.15.

FIGURE 19.15:

A folder index

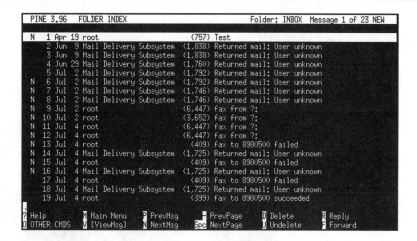

In the folder index, the top line of the display will show the currently selected message, the number of messages in the folder, and the status of the message (such as NEW for a new, unread message or ANS for an answered message).

Each message in the inbox is presented on a single line showing, from left to right, the status of the message (N for new, A for answered, D for deleted), the number of the message, the date the message was received, the sender of the message, the size of the message in bytes, and, finally, the subject line of the message.

To select a message, use the up and down arrow keys until the desired message is highlighted. Alternately, use the P key to move to the previous message or the N key to move to the next message.

To delete the currently selected message, hit the D key. This will mark the message for deletion and will change the status indication for that message to show it has been marked for deletion. The message won't be deleted, however, until you quit from pine. Until then, you can undelete the message by selecting it and hitting the U key.

If you have a folder index that is longer than one screen, you can move through it quickly using the space bar to jump down a page and the hyphen key to jump up a page. In addition, you can jump directly to a specific message by its message number. Hit the J key, and, when prompted, enter the message number and hit Return.

To read a message in a folder, simply select the message and hit the Return key or the V key to view the message. The message will be displayed as shown in Figure 19.16.

FIGURE 19.16:

Viewing a message

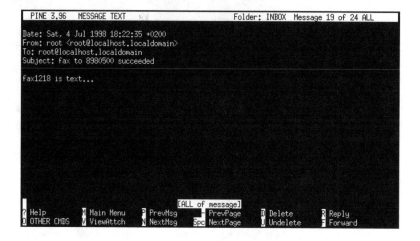

```
  PINE 3.96   MESSAGE TEXT                    Folder: INBOX  Message 19 of 24 ALL

Date: Sat, 4 Jul 1998 18:22:35 +0200
From: root <root@localhost.localdomain>
To: root@localhost.localdomain
Subject: fax to 8980500 succeeded

fax1218 is text...




                                    [ALL of message]
? Help        M Main Menu    P PrevMsg    - PrevPage   D Delete      R Reply
O OTHER CMDS  V ViewAttch    N NextMsg  Spc NextPage   U Undelete    F Forward
```

While viewing a message, you can continue to use the P and N keys to move through messages in the folder, and can use D and U to delete and undelete messages.

If the message is more than one screen long, you can use the space bar to move down a screen and the hyphen key to move up a screen.

To return to the main menu from the folder index or while viewing a message, simply type the M key.

Composing a Message You can start composing a message from the main menu or while viewing a folder index or a message. To do this, simply type the C key (from the main menu, you can also select the COMPOSE MESSAGE command and hit Return). This will bring up a blank message form like the one in Figure 19.17.

This screen is divided into two parts, one above the Message Text dividing line and one below. Above the dividing line you can specify the recipients, the subject, and other details; below the line, you write the message. You can move between sections and fields using the up and down arrow keys.

FIGURE 19.17:

The message composition
screen

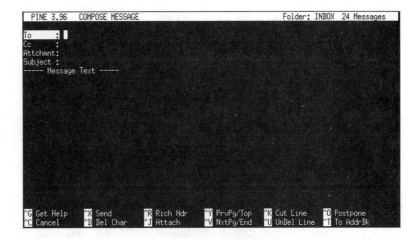

The To: and Cc: fields can take any number of e-mail addresses separated by
commas. When the cursor leaves the field, the display will refresh to show each
address on a separate line, as in Figure 19.18.

FIGURE 19.18:

Multiple message recipients

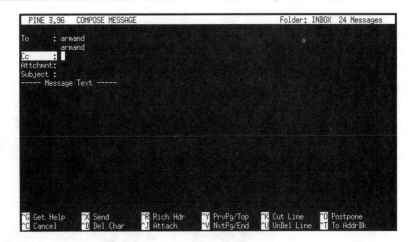

If you want to send a blind carbon copy, you can expand the available message
header fields by pressing Ctrl+R while the cursor is in the header (not in the body
of the message text). This calls up the rich headers feature, as shown in Figure 19.19.

Rich headers

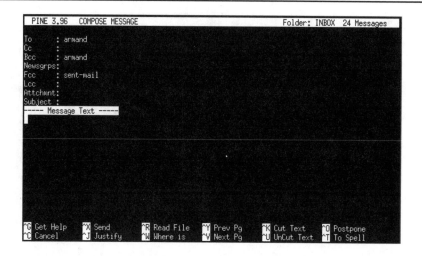

Here you will find a Bcc: field for sending blind carbon copies of e-mail messages. The other fields provide more obscure functions such as specifying an alternate location for storing a copy of the outgoing message or copying the message to a newsgroup as a posting.

Below the Message Text divider, you can type the body of your message. Figure 19.20 shows a completed message.

FIGURE 19.20:

A completed message

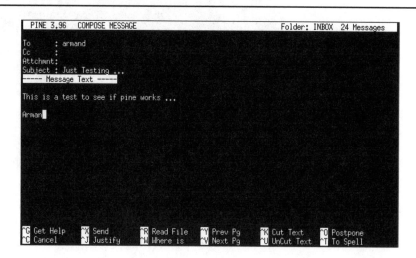

Once you are finished, you have two choices: you can send the message or you can cancel it. To send the message, use Ctrl+X; you will be prompted to confirm that you want to send the message, to which you can answer y for yes or n for no. To cancel the message, use Ctrl+C; again, you will be prompted to confirm that you want to cancel the message. Once the message is canceled you won't be able to recover its contents.

The *Pico* Editor

When you are editing messages in pine, you are using its integrated text editor called pico. The following commands should help you use pico effectively:

- Ctrl+V: page down
- Ctrl+Y: page up
- Ctrl+K: cut a line of text
- Ctrl+U: uncut (paste) cut text
- Ctrl+A: jump to the start of a line
- Ctrl+E: jump to the end of a line
- Ctrl+J: justify (adjust the layout of) the current paragraph

Cutting and pasting of text requires some explanation. When you press Ctrl+K, a single line of text is cut and placed in a buffer in memory. If you use Ctrl+K to cut multiple lines in succession (these have to be continuous lines in the document), then all the lines are copied into the buffer. Ctrl+U, to uncut text, copies the entire contents of the buffer to the current cursor location but does not clear the contents of the buffer. In other words, you can paste multiple copies of cut text back into your messages.

Replying to and Forwarding Messages   Replying to messages and forwarding them to other recipients is much the same as composing a new message. To reply to a message, select the message and hit the R key (from the folder index or while viewing the message). You will be prompted with one or two questions:

- Include original message in Reply?   If you answer affirmatively to this question, the entire contents of the message you are replaying to will appear in your reply.

- Reply to all recipients?   You will be presented with this question if there are multiple recipients of the original message (either on the To: line or the Cc: line). If you answer Yes, then everyone who received the message will receive your response. If you answer No, then only the person who sent the message will get your response.

Next, a message composition screen will be displayed with the appropriate recipients, subject line, and any necessary body text already in place. An example of this is shown in Figure 19.21.

FIGURE 19.21:

Replying to a message

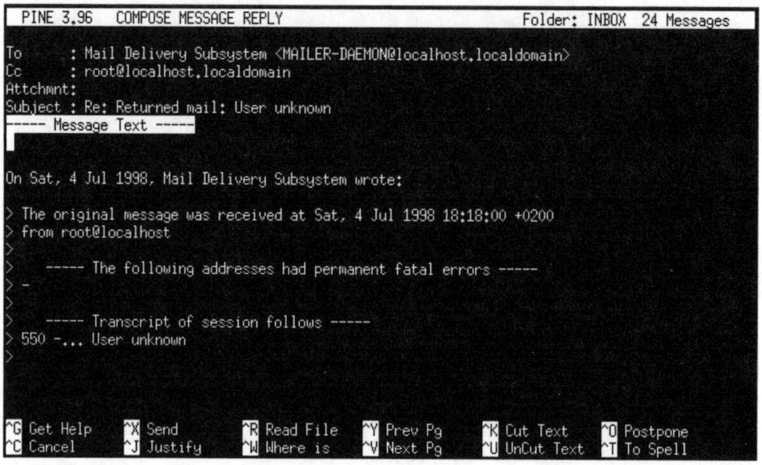

```
    PINE 3.96   COMPOSE MESSAGE REPLY                    Folder: INBOX  24 Messages

To      : Mail Delivery Subsystem <MAILER-DAEMON@localhost.localdomain>
Cc      : root@localhost.localdomain
Attchmnt:
Subject : Re: Returned mail: User unknown
----- Message Text -----


On Sat, 4 Jul 1998, Mail Delivery Subsystem wrote:

> The original message was received at Sat, 4 Jul 1998 18:18:00 +0200
> from root@localhost
>
>       ----- The following addresses had permanent fatal errors -----
> -
>
>       ----- Transcript of session follows -----
> 550 -... User unknown
>

^G Get Help    ^X Send      ^R Read File   ^Y Prev Pg    ^K Cut Text    ^O Postpone
^C Cancel      ^J Justify   ^W Where is    ^V Next Pg    ^U UnCut Text  ^T To Spell
```

Just as you did when composing a new message, use Ctrl+X to send your reply and Ctrl+C to cancel it.

Forwarding a message is similar to sending one: select the message and hit the F key. This will bring up a message composition window like the one in Figure 19.22, with the text of the message in place and an appropriate subject line.

FIGURE 19.22:

Forwarding a message

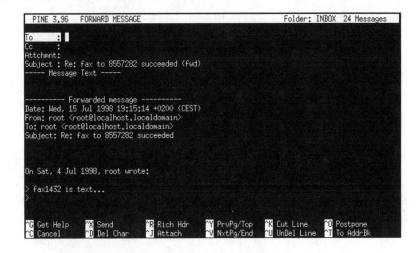

Where Do We Go from Here?

We now know how to perform the two most common Internet operations: browsing the Web and sending and receiving e-mails.

However, there is one more very popular use of modems to be discussed: faxing.

In the next chapter, we will look at the software that allows us to send, receive, and print faxes on a Linux system. Among other tasks, we will learn how to send faxes in the same way that we print from our applications and how to set up an automated fax reception system.

CHAPTER
TWENTY

Faxing from Linux

- Linux Fax Software

- Efax for Linux

We have already addressed the use of modems to establish network connections, mostly with the goal of accessing the Internet and its myriad services. In this chapter, we look at the other popular use of modems: sending and receiving faxes.

There are plenty of fax software packages available for Linux. As would be expected in the Linux and Unix world, at their heart these fax packages are powerful, fast command-line tools that make it possible to send a large variety of documents by fax and to build fax services into automated processes.

On top of this, it is possible with many fax packages for Linux to extend these command-line tools to allow faxing through the print features of some applications, or to allow users to send faxes in the same way that they send e-mails.

In this chapter, we will take a broad look at Linux faxing and consider the major fax packages. Then we will take a detailed look at efax, a common fax package that is found in many Linux distributions, including the Red Hat 5 distribution accompanying this book.

Linux Fax Software

In the Linux world, and in the Unix world in general, there are only a few main software packages for sending and receiving faxes: efax, NetFax, mgetty+sendfax, and HylaFax.

Of all these, efax is generally considered the easiest to configure and install because it is ideally suited to a single-user system. For many home users of Linux, this will suffice.

As a basic package, of course, efax doesn't have many of the sophisticated features that make HylaFax and NetFax well-suited to multiuser network environments. Nonetheless, efax offers sufficient capabilities to meet the needs of all but the most demanding single and small office users.

Efax for Linux

Efax is almost the de facto standard fax software for Linux, because it ships with many Linux distributions (including the version of Red Hat Linux 5 on the enclosed CD-ROM). We will therefore focus this chapter on using efax for Linux.

TIP

If you are interested in other fax packages for Linux, see the listing at the Linux Applications and Utilities page at `http://www.xnet.com/~blatura/linapp4 .html#comm`.

NOTE

The discussion in this chapter assumes that you have a functioning fax modem installed in your system. Chapter 15, "Using Peripherals," discusses how to configure a modem for use with Linux, and you should follow the guidelines there to make sure your modem is properly configured.

Installing Efax in Linux

The first step to getting fax capabilities up and running on your system is to make sure you have the efax software installed on your system. If you have installed the version of Linux included with this book, you may already have the software installed. You can check this with the `rpm` command:

```
$ rpm -qv efax
```

If efax is installed, then `rpm` will inform you by displaying the name of the efax package, such as `efax-0.8a-5`. If the package is not installed, then `rpm` will inform you with a message similar to this: `package efax is not installed`.

If efax is not installed, then you have two choices:

- Install it from the Red Hat 5 CD-ROM.
- Download and install it from the Internet.

Installing Efax from the Red Hat CD-ROM

If you have installed Red Hat Linux from the CD-ROM accompanying this book and want to install the version of efax that comes with the distribution, you need to mount your CD-ROM at your standard location—typically at /mnt/cdrom—using the mount command (here we assume the CD-ROM is the device /dev/hdc):

```
$ mount /dev/hdc /mnt/cdrom
```

Once the CD-ROM is mounted, you need to use rpm to install the package efax-0.8a-5.i386.rpm:

```
$ rpm -i /mnt/cdrom/RedHat/RPMS/efax-0.8a-5.i386.rpm
```

Downloading and Installing Efax from the Internet

If you want to install the latest version of efax, you can obtain it by FTP from ftp://sunsite.unc.edu/pub/Linux/apps/serialcomm/fax/. At the time of this writing, the most recent version of the software is version 0.8a and the name of the file to be downloaded is efax08a.tar.gz.

Once you have downloaded the file, use tar to unarchive the files into a temporary location:

```
$ tar xzvf efax08a.tar.gz
```

Next, change your working directory to the temporary one where you unarchived the files and, as the root user, issue the following command:

```
$ make
```

This will cause the efax software to be compiled.

Assuming there are no errors during compilation (a safe assumption, since efax is a fairly simple program), you can install efax to its default location using the command

```
$ make install
```

For full instructions regarding the compilation and installation of the efax software, read the README file included with the distribution.

Configuring Efax for Linux

Before sending your first fax, you need to specify a few parameters that will allow efax to function properly. In order to do this, you need to edit the file /usr/bin/fax and set certain information:

- Find the line that starts with FROM and set the value to your phone number (e.g., FROM="+1 212 555 1212").

- Find the line starting with CLASS and set the class of the fax modem to match the specifications of your modem (either CLASS=1 or CLASS=2).

- Find the line starting with PAGE and set the default page size for your country (probably PAGE=letter, PAGE=legal, or PAGE=a4).

When editing the file, note that lines starting with a hash mark (#) are comments and do not affect the configuration. You can comment out an existing line with a hash mark and add in your own variation on the line so that you can easily switch back to the default configuration.

This is the minimum configuration needed to run efax for Linux.

Sending Your First Fax

The efax package has three main components: efax, efix, and fax.

Efax is the core of the system. It sends and receives faxes to and from files in the standard fax file format: Group 3 compressed TIFF files. You can't use efax to send a text file or a PostScript file or any other type of file without first converting it to the necessary Group 3 compressed TIFF file format needed for faxing.

The efix program is used for conversion purposes, providing the ability to convert files to and from text, bitmap, and the fax TIFF format. By combining efax and efix, it is possible to send many images and text files as faxes.

Finally, the fax program provides an integrated layer from which it is possible to create, send, receive, view, and print faxes. This program integrates efax, efix, and other Linux components to provide fairly complete Linux faxing functionality.

In order to learn how to send and receive faxes with efax, we will focus on the fax program, since it brings together all the functionality we need.

Sending Faxes

The fax program makes it easy to send a fax from a text file or a PostScript file. For the purposes of sending, the syntax of the fax command is `fax send <options> <number> <file>`.

There are three available options that can be used when sending a fax:

- `-l`: Use low resolution (96 dots per inch).

- `-v`: Provide verbose messages and program status.

- `-m`: Assume the phone number has already been dialed (in which case the phone number should not be provided).

The phone number should be provided in the same form that you would use to dial it. For instance, if you want to dial the local phone number 555-1212, you could use 5551212 or 555-1212 as the phone number entry. If you need to dial 9 for an outside line, then use 95551212 or 9-5551212 or 9-555-1212.

Let's take an example. We have a text file called `textfile` in the directory `/tmp` and we want to send it as a low-resolution fax to the number 123-4567, using 9 to access an outside line. To do this, we would use the command:

```
$ fax send -l 9-123-4567 /tmp/textfile
```

Given a text file containing the following text:

```
FAX TRANSMISSION:

TO: Arman Danesh

FROM: Arman Danesh

NOTE:

This is a test of the efax package. Using the fax command, we can send
text files as faxes.
```

this will produce a fax that looks like the one in Figure 20.1.

FIGURE 20.1:

A sample efax fax

```
FAX TRANSMISSION:

TO: Arman Danesh

FROM: Arman Danesh

NOTE:

This is a test of the efax package. Using the fax command, we can send
text files as faxes.
```

Sending Multiple Files as One Fax

In addition to sending a single file as a fax, you can use fax to send multiple files as a single fax. For instance, if we want to send the contents of /tmp/textfile followed by the contents of another text file called /tmp/textfile2, we could use the command

```
$ fax send 9-123-4567 /tmp/textfile /tmp/textfiles
```

to send the files in the specified order.

> **NOTE**
> You can only combine multiple text files in this way. If you try to combine a Post-Script file with text files or with another PostScript file, the process will not work.

But what if we want to send the pages out of order or only send some of the pages in a file? To do this, we need to first convert the file into a fax-formatted TIFF file. Each page of the fax will then be placed in a separate file, and we can choose which pages to send by faxing only those files.

Here we utilize the fax program's ability to create fax-formatted files. For instance, if we have a PostScript file called /tmp/psfile that is three pages long, we can convert it into three fax-formatted TIFF files using the command:

```
$ fax make /tmp/psfile
```

The resulting pages will be contained in three separate files named /tmp/psfile .001, /tmp/psfile.002, and /tmp/psfile.003.

When you convert a file into fax format, the resulting pages will retain the same name as the original file with three-digit, numerically-ordered extensions. For instance, the file `test.txt` would create fax pages named `test.txt.001`, `test.txt.002`, and so on.

The only option available to us when using `fax make` is to choose low-resolution mode using the `-1` option:

```
$ fax make -1 /tmp/psfile
```

Back to the three-page document we converted earlier. If you wanted to send the third page followed by the first and not send the second page, you could use the command

```
$ fax send /tmp/psfile.003 /tmp/psfile.001
```

Sending a Fax by Printing

While it is great to be able to send faxes using the `fax` command, this isn't very useful when it comes to printing from applications such as Netscape, WordPerfect, or Applix Words.

NOTE　　Of course, if you have only one modem and are using this to browse the Internet with Netscape, you won't be able to send a fax from Netscape as long as the modem is being used to connect to the Internet.

For instance, consider the Netscape example. It is possible to print from Netscape to a file, generating a PostScript file as a result. But sending the page as a fax adds a second step to the process, requiring that the user switch to the command line to send the file as a fax.

Unfortunately, this isn't quite as simple as faxing from Windows or Macintosh applications, where faxing is generally as simple as printing.

Fortunately, it is possible to create a special printer device in Linux that uses efax to send the file being printed as a fax.

The process is fairly simple. The `lpd` printing system allows for input filters to be specified. If an input filter is specified for a printer queue, then the file being sent to the queue is sent to an input filter before being placed in the queue. If the filter doesn't return any data, but instead faxes the file, the job will never be sent to a printer.

There are three steps to setting up the necessary printer queue for printing to the fax modem:

1. Configuring the printer queue

2. Setting up the faxlpr script

3. Preparing the spool directory

All of this preparation needs to be done as the root user on your system.

Configuring the Printer Queue

You can set up the printer queue for faxing using the printer configuration Control Panel applet. This applet is discussed in Chapter 15, "Using Peripherals."

When you create the queue, make sure it is configured as a local printer queue, set the spool directory to /var/spool/fax, set the printer device to /dev/null, set the input filter to /usr/bin/faxlpr, and make sure that headers are not being suppressed. Figure 20.2 shows how the printer configuration dialog should look for a fax queue named fax.

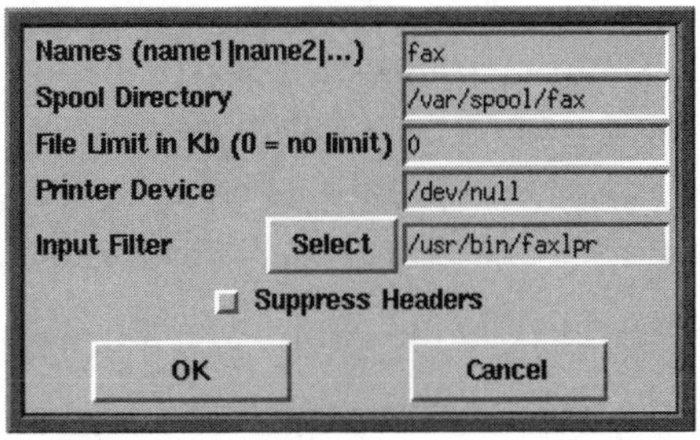

FIGURE 20.2:

Configuration of a fax printer queue

If you prefer to edit your printer configuration file manually, you can edit /etc/printcap and add the following entry:

```
fax:\
        :sd=/var/spool/fax:\
        :lp=/dev/null:\
        :if=/usr/bin/faxlpr:
```

This entry specifies the name of the queue as `fax`, sets the spool directory to `/var/spool/fax`, sets the print device to `/dev/null`, and sets the input filter to `/usr/bin/faxlpr`.

Finally, restart the `lpd` daemon using the printer configuration Control Panel applet or by killing and restarting `/usr/sbin/lpd`.

Setting Up the *faxlpr* Script

The `fax` program is actually a highly flexible shell script. When the script is called by its regular name (`fax`), it assumes that the command is coming from the command line and behaves accordingly. If the script is called by an alternate name (`faxlpr`), the script assumes it is being asked to send a fax via an `lpd` printer queue.

In order to prepare for this, you need to create a link to `/usr/bin/fax` called `faxlpr`:

```
$ ln /usr/bin/fax /usr/bin/faxlpr
```

Next, we need to make some simple alterations in the `faxlpr` file. We have to do this because of problems inherent in the version of efax that ships with Red Hat 5 (the version included with this book).

Use your favorite editor to edit the file `/usr/bin/faxlpr` and find the following pair of lines, which should appear around line 597 in the file:

```
0) echo "$1" | mail -s "fax to $num succeeded" $user@$host - ;;
*) echo "$1" | mail -s "fax to $num failed   " $user@$host - ;;
```

You need to edit these lines to remove the dash near the end of the line:

```
0) echo "$1" | mail -s "fax to $num succeeded" $user@$host ;;
*) echo "$1" | mail -s "fax to $num failed   " $user@$host ;;
```

Preparing the Spool Directory

The final step in preparing to use a printer queue to send faxes is to prepare the spool directory, `/var/spool/fax`.

First, check that the directory exists by using `ls /var/spool` and see if the `fax` subdirectory is there. The installation of efax should create this directory, so it should be there.

Next, set the permissions on the directory to world read and write so that any user can send a fax:

```
$ chmod 777 /var/spool/fax
```

Finally, you need to create a lock file and give it the appropriate permissions:

```
$ touch /var/spool/fax/lock ; chmod 644 /var/spool/fax/lock
```

Sending Faxes through the Print Queue

Once this is all done, you are ready to send your first fax using the lpd system. Just as you could print a file using the lpr command, now you can fax a text or PostScript file in the same way. The only new notion is that you use the -J argument of the lpr command to specify the phone number to send the fax to.

For instance, if we have a file called /tmp/testfile that we want to fax to 555-1212 using the print queue called fax, we could use the command

```
$ lpr -Pfax -J 5551212 /tmp/testfile
```

The lpd daemon will pass the file over to the input filter (faxlpr), which will attempt to fax the file. Following the attempt, faxlpr will send the user transmitting the fax an e-mail indicating the success or failure of the process.

You can print in this way from any program that allows you to specify options to the lpr command and that generates PostScript output (including, but not limited to, Netscape Communicator, WordPerfect for Linux, and StarOffice for OpenLinux).

Receiving Faxes

Receiving faxes is a fairly straightforward process. There are three ways in which you can arrange to receive a fax: manually, automatically for a specific incoming call, or automatically for all incoming calls.

Manually Receiving a Fax

To manually receive a fax, you need to tell the modem to answer the telephone and receive the fax once the phone is ringing. This is done with the receive option of the fax command.

If the line is ringing and you know the call is an incoming fax, you simply need to issue the command

```
$ fax receive
```

to receive the fax.

With the `fax receive` command, you can specify a filename for the incoming fax. Each page of the fax will be saved in separate files with sequentially numbered extensions (001, 002, 003, etc.). For instance, if you receive a three-page fax with the command

```
$ fax receive testfax
```

the resulting fax will be stored in three files named `testfax.001`, `testfax.002`, and `testfax.003`. To view the fax, use the `fax view` command as shown later in this section.

If you don't specify a filename for the incoming fax, then the `fax` command will build a 10-digit filename derived from the date and time the fax is received. For instance, a fax received on December 24 at 9:52:35 p.m. will be saved in a series of files names `1224095235.001`, `1224095235.002`, `1224095235.003`, etc.

Faxes are stored in the default `/var/spool/fax` directory. You can view the contents of the fax spool directory with the fax queue command:

```
$ fax queue

Fax files in /var/spool/fax :

-rw-r--r--    1 root      root            247 Jul  2 17:49 0702174857.001
-rw-r--r--    1 root      root            247 Jul  2 17:59 0702175842.001
-rw-r--r--    1 root      root            247 Jul  4 17:14 0704171330.001
```

To view these faxes, use the `fax view` command while running X Windows:

```
$ fax view 0704171330.001
```

This will cause the fax to be filtered and displayed by the xv program as shown in Figure 20.3.

A fax displayed in xv

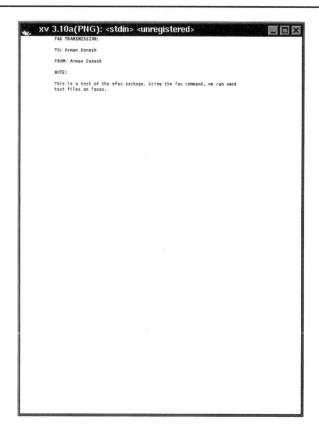

Printing is equally simple using the fax print command:

```
$ fax print 0704171330.001
```

This would print the same fax to the default printer queue, usually called lp.

Automatically Receiving a Fax for a Specific Call

If you are expecting that the next phone call you receive will be an incoming fax, you can set things up so that the fax program will wait for the call, answer the phone, receive the fax, hang up, and then exit. To do this, you use the answer option of the fax command:

```
$ fax answer
```

The `fax` program will start, sit and wait patiently for the phone to ring, and then answer after the second ring. As with `fax receive`, the incoming fax will be stored using the date to generate a filename and can be viewed and printed using the `fax view` and `fax print` commands.

Automatically Receiving All Incoming Faxes

If your fax modem is connected to a dedicated phone line that you wish to use for incoming faxes, you can make the `fax` program continually monitor the line for incoming faxes while still allowing outgoing calls.

Using the `wait` option of the `fax` command causes the program to run as a daemon waiting for incoming calls to the fax modem:

```
$ fax wait
```

This works by having `fax wait` run as a daemon. The daemon runs `fax answer` to wait for a call. When `fax answer` exits (usually because an incoming fax has been received or a call has been answered), the daemon starts `fax answer` again to continue waiting for the next call.

This process can be monitored using the `status` option:

```
$ fax status
USER       PID %CPU %MEM  SIZE   RSS TTY STAT START   TIME COMMAND
root       721  0.0  0.7   936   456 p0 S <  17:28   0:00
/usr/bin/efax -d/dev/

from: /var/spool/fax/modem.721

efax: 28:14 opened /dev/modem
efax: 28:16 waiting for activity
```

You can also specify a number of seconds after the `fax status` command, which causes the status display to be updated continually at the interval that has been specified. To cause the status to be displayed every five seconds, use `fax status 5`:

```
$ fax status 5
USER       PID %CPU %MEM  SIZE   RSS TTY STAT START   TIME COMMAND
root       721  0.0  0.7   936   456 p0 S <  17:28   0:00
➥ /usr/bin/efax -d/dev/

from: /var/spool/fax/modem.721

efax: 28:14 opened /dev/modem
```

```
efax: 28:16 waiting for activity
--------
USER       PID %CPU %MEM  SIZE   RSS TTY STAT START   TIME COMMAND
root       721  0.0  0.7   936   456 p0  S <  17:28   0:00
➥ /usr/bin/efax -d/dev/

from: /var/spool/fax/modem.721

efax: 28:14 opened /dev/modem
efax: 28:16 waiting for activity
efax: 31:00 activity detected
--------
etc.
```

Luckily, the `fax wait` daemon doesn't lock the modem, so you can continue sending faxes (for instance, using `fax send`) while the daemon is running.

If you want your system to answer faxes all the time, you can consider putting the command `fax wait` in your `/etc/rc.d/rc.local` start-up file so that the daemon runs every time you launch Linux.

If you need to stop the answering daemon, you can use the command

`$ fax stop`

to kill the daemon. When the last `fax answer` process dies (or is killed by you), then all automatic answering ceases.

Where Do We Go from Here?

By now you should feel comfortable sending and receiving faxes using your Linux system.

In the next chapter, we move on to an area that most users find important: multi-media. We will look at how to install and configure common multimedia peripherals such as sound cards, and will take a quick tour through common Linux multimedia software.

# CHAPTER TWENTY-ONE

Linux Multimedia

■ Configuring Sound Blaster Cards

■ Using XPlaycd

■ Other Multimedia Applications

This chapter looks at an area of Linux that, unfortunately, is not as well-developed as it is on competitive platforms such as Windows and the Mac OS: multimedia.

We will look at Red Hat 5.1's built-in support for Sound Blaster Cards and discuss how to configure the cards. Next, we will look at a representative multimedia application, XPlaycd, and then review other available multimedia applications.

Unfortunately, fully mastering multimedia for Linux can be somewhat complicated. You should consult the Linux Sound HOWTO at `http://www.linux-howto` `.com/ptHOWTO/Sound-HOWTO` for a detailed discussion of how to work with sound in Linux. Also, consult the Linux Hardware Compatibility List in Appendix F to see what sound cards are best supported under Linux.

Configuring Sound Blaster Cards

Generally, Linux's support for sound cards is sketchy. Strong support is provided for Sound Blaster cards and those cards that are compatible on a hardware register-level with genuine Sound Blaster cards. Other cards that are labeled compatible don't work with the standard Sound Blaster drivers.

A collection of other drivers for sound cards can be found, but they all have their own quirks and unique ways of being configured, so we will only address the Sound Blaster line of cards in this chapter. The Linux Sound HOWTO mentioned above is a good reference if you find yourself facing another card on your Linux system.

With most versions of Linux, adding sound support may mean recompiling your kernel from source code. This is a task best reserved for expert Linux users. Making the right decisions in compiling the kernel is tricky, and taking a wrong step can render your system non-bootable and difficult to return to a working state.

For this reason, Red Hat has developed the Sound Blaster driver into a loadable module so it is possible to add Sound Blaster support to your Red Hat 5.1 system without reconfiguring your kernel. If you are using another version of Linux that requires kernel reconfiguration to enable Sound Blaster support, consult the Linux Sound HOWTO.

> **NOTE**
>
> In order to configure your card, you will need to know all the relevant hardware settings of the card such as I/O port, IRQ, and DMA addresses. Consult your card's documentation for instructions on how to determine the settings of your card.

Using *Sndconfig*

Red Hat includes the `sndconfig` program for configuring the Sound Blaster module. To run the program, type the command

```
# sndconfig
```

at a command prompt in the console or an `xterm` window.

After an initial screen, you will be presented with a screen like the one in Figure 21.1. This screen asks you to identify your sound card type. You can select from a list of standard Sound Blaster types. If you think you have a proper hardware-compatible card, select the type of card it is supposed to be compatible with.

FIGURE 21.1:

Selecting a Sound Blaster card

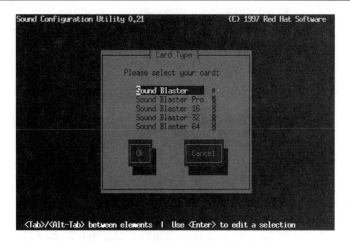

The next screen you see will depend on the type of card you select. The screen will ask you to provide relevant hardware settings such as I/O port, IRQ, and DMA addresses for your card. Figure 21.2 shows this screen for a regular Sound Blaster card.

FIGURE 21.2:

Specifying hardware settings for a Sound Blaster card

Once you specify these settings, sndconfig will add the entries to the /etc/conf.modules file (and back up your original conf.modules file) and then will attempt to play a test sound.

In Case of Silence

If sndconfig fails to play a sound, then several things may be wrong.

First, check that your sound card is properly inserted in your PC and that your speakers are correctly plugged into the card and are turned on and have power.

If all these physical things are OK, then there are two likely sources of difficulty:

1. You have chosen the wrong card type or have provided the wrong hardware settings. Check all these details and try running sndconfig again.

2. Your card is not supported by the Red Hat Sound Blaster module. You will need to consult the Linux Sound HOWTO for more details about Linux sound and building a new kernel with the correct driver for your card.

Using XPlaycd

One popular use of sound cards is to play audio CD-ROMs through the speakers of the sound card. You can do this with the XPlaycd program. This is an X Windows application that ships with Red Hat Linux 5 and provides a simple, graphical interface to your CD-ROM drive.

As Figure 21.3 shows, XPlaycd should be familiar to anyone with an audio CD player as part of their stereo.

FIGURE 21.3:

The XPlaycd window

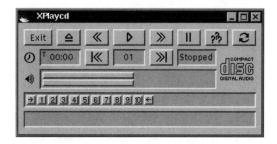

From right to left, the control buttons in the top row perform the following functions:

- Exit: quits XPlaycd
- Open/Close: alternately ejects and closes the CD tray for drives that support software-controlled eject
- Rewind: scans backwards through the current track in two-second intervals
- Play/Stop: alternately plays and stops the current track
- Fast Forward: scans forward through the current track in two-second intervals
- Pause/Continue: alternately pauses and resumes playing
- Shuffle/Resort: alternately plays tracks in a random order or returns tracks to their physical order
- Repeat: continuously repeats the playlist

Immediately below the rewind button is the back track button. Pressing the button once jumps to the start of the current track and pressing it again moves back one track at a time. Immediately below the fast forward button is the forward track button, which jumps to the start of the next track.

The third row of controls is the volume control. You can control each channel separately or change both channels' values together. To change the setting of either volume bar, click to the left or the right of the current setting to move the bar one notch in the desired direction.

To move both bars in either direction, you need to click the desired side, but exactly between the two bars.

Finally, below the volume controls is the playlist. The playlist shows a small icon for each track, initially in numerical order. The start icon is represented by a right arrow and the end icon is marked with a left arrow.

The playlist is played from the start icon to the end icon, playing each track between the two icons as they appear on the playlist in order from left to right. You can click and drag any icon to the right or left to change its place on the playlist. Figure 21.4 shows an altered playlist in which all tracks are played, but not in their original order.

FIGURE 21.4:

A reordered playlist

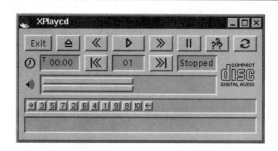

By moving the start and end icons, it is possible to create a playlist that excludes some of the tracks, as shown in Figure 21.5.

FIGURE 21.5:

Adjusting the start and end
of the playlist

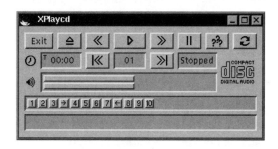

Other Multimedia Applications

While the availability of slick, fancy multimedia applications and games falls
short of what is available on some other platforms, that hasn't prevented a
healthy number of applications from being developed for Linux.

On the Linux Applications and Utilities page at `http://www.hongik.com/
linux//linapp5.html#mm`, you can find a list of many available multimedia
applications for Linux. We will take a brief look at a small selection of these in
this section.

MpegTV Player 1.0

This application, a U.S.$10 shareware application, is a real-time MPEG video/audio
player for Linux and many other Unix platforms. It provides a simple, intuitive
control panel that allows the user to control the playing of files, jump to any location in an open file, and adjust the volume. The software can be downloaded from
`http://www.mpegtv.com/`.

Festival Speech Synthesis System

Currently in a state of development, the Festival system is designed to offer a
powerful, multilingual (currently English, Spanish, and Welsh) speech synthe-
sis system that can be used to convert text to speech and provides the necessary

tools for application developers to add speech to their own software. The current release of the package is available at `http://www.cstr.ed.ac.uk/projects/festival/festival.html`.

MiXViews

MiXViews is an X Windows–based digital sound editor that is freely distributable. Multiple files can be displayed and edited, allowing for cutting and pasting between files and for applying sound modifications to the data. The MiXViews home page is at `http://www.ccmrc.ucsb.edu/~doug/htmls/MiXViews.html`.

MMaudio

MMaudio is an X Windows–based audio player that supports many popular formats including AU, WAV, and MPEG 1 files. The program can record and encode MPEG files and is capable of playing MPEG files directly off a Web server, thanks to its built-in MIME support. The software can be found at `http://www.powerweb.de/mpeg/unix.html`.

RealPlayer

The RealPlayer from RealNetworks is the popular player software for playing RealAudio and RealVideo files in real-time, streamed across the Internet. Many of the popular Web-based, radio, television and music sites use RealAudio and RealVideo technology, and the RealPlayer is needed to view or listen to this content. Free and enhanced commercial versions of the player are available for download from `http://www.real.com/products/player/50player/index.html?src=404`.

FreePhone

FreePhone is an Internet audio-conferencing tool similar in concept to the Internet phone software that can be found for Windows and Macintosh systems. It is more than a one-to-one phone system; users can create unicast or multicast audio conferences. FreePhone supports a variety of popular audio compression systems and uses the Internet's multimedia Mbone backbone. The software is online at `http://www.inria.fr/rodeo/fphone/`.

Where Do We Go from Here?

In this chapter, we have looked at just the tip of the multimedia iceberg. Multimedia in the Linux environment can be very technically demanding (as it can be in Windows as well), and a general book like this one can only offer a cursory look at the subject.

If you are using a genuine Sound Blaster card or a truly compatible one, you should now have it working with your Red Hat Linux system. You should have been able to download and test some multimedia applications and should feel at least comfortable with using multimedia applications in Linux.

If you really want to delve into multimedia and all its related specialties, such as sound and video editing, IP Audio, and streaming media, you should start by consulting *The Linux Multimedia Guide* by Jeff Tranter and Andy Oram (O'Reilly & Associates, 1996).

In the next section of the book, we move into a whole new area: Linux in the small office/home office (SOHO) environment. We will start by considering how to install Linux in a network environment, look at basic network configuration, and then move on to the types of services Linux can be used for in a SOHO environment, including mail server, intranet Web server, and file server for UNIX, Windows, and Novell networks.

PART III

Linux in the Small Office/Home Office

CHAPTER

TWENTY-TWO

22

Where to Use Linux in the SOHO

- Linux as a File Server

- Linux as a Print Server

- Linux as an Intranet Server

- Linux as an Applications Server

- Linux as a Router

- Linux as a Workstation

At this point in the book, we are going to shift our focus. By now you have a firm grasp of using Linux on a stand-alone workstation, and perhaps even use Linux as your preferred operating system at home to access the Internet, surf the Web, compose e-mails and letters, and more.

Still, Linux's real home is in a networked world. Perhaps you run a small office at home with two PCs that you want to see networked. Linux makes a great file and print server in most networks. Perhaps in your business you are thinking about setting up an intranet. Linux provides an inexpensive way to move your business into an intranet environment by offering powerful Web and database servers.

If you want to connect a network of PCs to the Internet, Linux can be an excellent router. In many cases, it is far less costly to use a Linux computer as a router than to purchase a hardware router to connect your network to the world.

Finally, if you find that your current Windows-based desktops lack the performance or stability you would like to see on your home or office network, Linux as a workstation operating system may be the answer to your problems. It is possible to access both Windows and Unix applications from within Linux, network with other Unix, Windows, and Novell network systems, and easily share files and data with the rest of the world without worrying about bothersome crashes.

In this chapter, we take a quick look at these uses of the Linux operating system for small offices and home offices (commonly known as SOHO) where the cost of deploying expensive commercial solutions may be prohibitive.

Linux as a File Server

Perhaps the most fundamental need on a small network is a file server. File servers supply common places to store data, thus allowing shared files to be accessed by all users who need them and providing centralized locations for backing up files (thereby eliminating the need for daily data backups on each workstation on a network).

On a Windows or Novell network, this is generally done in two ways:

- Using dedicated file servers
- Using peer-to-peer networks

Dedicated File Servers

A dedicated file server is a system that is not used as a workstation but is set up as a central file server for the network. Users at different workstations or computers on the network can access directories on the file server as if these were directories or disk drives on their own computers.

Dedicated file servers offer the advantage of centralizing the management of shared data and the backup process, but they cost more than peer-to-peer networks. They also offer the benefit of being able to set up network access control policies for confidential, core, or shared data to ensure that unauthorized users don't have easy access to the information.

Linux is ideally suited to run as a low-cost file server for a small network. Linux can act as a file server to Unix, Windows, and Novell networks, making it an easily deployed universal file server for a network containing different types of computers and workstations. In addition, the stability and true multitasking capabilities of Linux make it a better choice than some other well-known options (such as Windows 95) when a robust file server solution is needed.

In Chapter 25, "Integrating Linux in Windows and Novell Networks," we discuss how to set up Linux as a file server.

Peer-to-Peer File Sharing

In a peer-to-peer network, there is no central file server. Instead, each user decides which directories and drives on their PC should be shared on the network and what level of access control to impose. In this way, each workstation or computer on the network becomes a small file server.

While there is a flexibility to this approach, allowing users to decide what data to share and with whom, there are also drawbacks. These include no centralized management of file sharing and access control policies, no centralized location for the backing up of critical data, and a performance impact on a user's desktop when several other individuals on the network are accessing shared files on that user's PC.

Linux can act as a reasonable peer-to-peer file server because of its ability to share with multiple types of networks. In addition, the true multitasking abilities of Linux mitigate much of the impact on performance when multiple users access files on a PC being used for other work.

Ultimately, though, the low cost of setting up a Linux-based dedicated file server for a small network makes the dedicated file server approach more attractive because of the management and centralized backup benefits it provides.

Linux as a Print Server

In addition to file servers, print servers are another component of the network. Generally, a dedicated file server will also play the role of offering print services to the network, serving double duty.

It is not uncommon to find print services provided in both a centralized, dedicated fashion and the peer-to-peer method on the same network. Some users who use a printer heavily may warrant their own printers at their desks, while others who use the printers less frequently may share a printer located in a common area. Often, a user with a dedicated printer will share it on the network so that other users can print documents for his or her attention directly to the dedicated printer rather than the common shared printer.

Linux, of course, can work in both environments. Linux supports a healthy range of printers including most PostScript and HP-compatible PCL printers. In addition, its printer sharing options include the ability to share printers to Unix, Windows, and Novell networks.

In Chapter 25, "Integrating Linux in Windows and Novell Networks," we discuss how to set up Linux as a print server.

Linux as an Intranet Server

If you follow the computing trends today, you have probably heard a lot about intranets: internal corporate networks that use Internet technology such as TCP/IP, Web browsers, and Internet-standard e-mail to share information and applications within an organization.

Many articles discussing intranets and the hardware and software used to deploy them depict intranets as expensive endeavors only suited to large corporations and organizations. This couldn't be further from the truth.

Even in small offices, an intranet can provide a convenient way to publish information to be read by all employees through a Web browser, and with a little forethought some of the paperwork in your office can be eliminated by introducing electronic, online, Web-based forms for everything from leave requests to expense report submissions.

In addition, if you have small databases scattered across your organization, each used on a daily basis by different users, an intranet can provide a common means by which occasional users of the data can access the information contained in a database without needing full access to the database tools used to create, maintain, and update the data. By integrating the database with an intranet Web server, simple Web-based forms can be used to query the database.

Linux, which offers a wealth of powerful, flexible Web servers as well as fully functional relational database systems, can allow the creation of an intranet server without the cost involved in deploying Windows NT, a commercial database such as Oracle, and an expensive Web-database integration tool. There are even some free tools for Linux that make it relatively easy to produce intranet programs and applications that make use of your corporate databases.

In Chapter 27, "Building Your Own Web Server," we discuss the basics of getting a Linux-based intranet server up and running.

Linux as an Applications Server

Unlike Windows NT as a server platform, Linux is by nature designed to act as both a file/print/intranet server and a full-fledged applications server.

With an applications server, applications actually run on the server and are only displayed on a terminal or workstation, using the X Windows protocol or a terminal connection such as Telnet. In the typical Windows network, the applications run on the desktop and the data is stored on the server and accessed there.

For some types of applications and in some situations, centralizing the running of applications can bring both performance and management benefits.

If you are running a Windows or Novell network, a Linux system can act as an applications server for several purposes:

- Running character-based programs such as powerful Unix mail software

- Running a custom-developed, character-based database interface to a centralized Linux database

- Accessing custom in-house applications, such as a corporate telephone book, designed to run in a Unix shell

If you install an X server on a Windows-based desktop, you can even deliver centrally managed X Windows applications to the desktop while running the applications on a Linux applications server.

Where budgets are low, Linux can create full-fledged GUI networks without the hardware or software expense of running Windows 95 or NT. For instance, I have deployed a 10-desktop network running Linux exclusively. The desktops are all 486-class machines with 8MB of RAM. It would be exceptionally difficult to run Windows 95 plus Microsoft Office on them, and the cost for the necessary software licenses would run over U.S.$300 per desktop.

But, with Linux on their older hardware, these systems can act as simple X terminals, displaying applications that run on a single applications server. In this case, the applications server is a Pentium 200MHz system with just 96MB of RAM. The only software license fee needed here is the cost of the desired Unix office suite for the number of concurrent users who will use the software.

A network like this can provide performance to the user that feels like a low-end Pentium system with 16MB of RAM running Windows 95. All of the management of software, user accounts, backups, and system maintenance can be done centrally on one or two servers.

Of course, this type of solution takes a fundamental strategic decision: not to use popular Windows-based productivity applications. But where cost is of the essence or the availability of modern hardware is limited, Linux makes a strong candidate for an organization-wide computing platform.

Linux as a Router

The concept of a router is simple: where two or more networks need to be connected, a router is the device that makes it possible to communicate between the networks.

Routers come in all shapes and sizes, from software-based routers running on Windows NT servers to hardware routers from famous names such as Cisco. Routers can connect to networks in different ways, using technology ranging from regular modems to Ethernet cards to ISDN connections.

Let's consider an example: an office with a small network that is connected to the Internet by an ISDN connection. That is, a small company has a single dial-up ISDN connection to the Internet but has a network of two or more computers that would like to share the connection.

A router for this situation would offer a single Ethernet connection connected to the local network and a single ISDN modem connection connected to the phone line. All computers on the network will send all packets to the router. The router will decide if the packet is destined for another location on the local network or for an outside address (in other words, somewhere on the Internet). A diagram of this network looks like Figure 22.1.

FIGURE 22.1:

A typical Ethernet-to-ISDN routing diagram

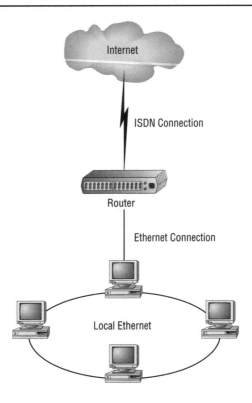

All local packets will be sent by the router back out on the Ethernet connection to the local network. If a packet is destined for the outside world, an ISDN connection is established, the information is sent, and, after a specified period of non-use, the connection will be dropped.

Similar routing situations include connecting two separate Ethernet networks through a router that has two or more Ethernet connections (see Figure 22.2) or connecting a local Ethernet network to the Internet through a leased-line connection such as a T1 connection.

FIGURE 22.2:

Connecting two Ethernet networks with routers

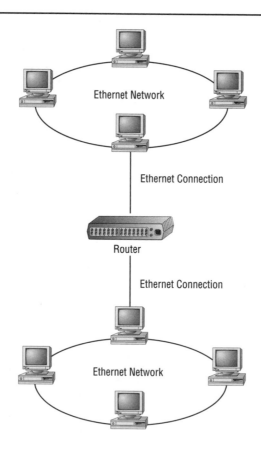

Linux has all the features needed to act as a router:

- Support for multiple Ethernet cards

- Support for ISDN and regular modems

- Support for IP forwarding (the means by which packets can be received, analyzed, and re-routed by the Linux-based router)

In fact, for small Ethernet-to-Ethernet interconnectivity or Ethernet-to-ISDN Internet routing, a Linux-based solution can be far less expensive than dedicated hardware routers, and once it is properly configured can be very reliable.

We look at using Linux as a router in Chapter 26, "Security and Linux as an Inexpensive Router."

Linux as a Workstation

A final use of Linux in a small office environment is as the actual desktop operating system. If the application base available in Linux is suitable to the work of the office, then Linux-based desktops provide these advantages:

- Stability and performance

- Full remote management by the network administrator

- Full network backup capabilities

- Lower cost of ownership in comparison with Windows-based desktops

Where money is available, high-powered Linux workstations can offer speed rivaling more expensive Windows-based systems, including peer-to-peer networking that is more robust and offers better performance than is seen on many systems, especially those running Windows 95.

Also, as mentioned in the previous section, Linux can enable low-end or old hardware that can't run the latest Windows software to become full-fledged X terminals, providing performance on obsolete desktop hardware that feels like that of a low-end Pentium system.

Where Do We Go from Here?

In this chapter, we have used broad brushstrokes to paint a picture of the ways in which Linux can be used in a small home or office network environment.

The next chapters of this book will cover this topic in more detail. We will start by learning how to install Linux in an Ethernet network environment, move in to Linux in different capacities such as file server, print server, router, and intranet server, and then consider the advanced system administration techniques you can use to get the most out of your office Linux systems.

The next chapter looks at specific points of installing Linux in a networked environment.

CHAPTER

TWENTY-THREE

Installing Linux for the SOHO

- Choosing Packages for a LAN Installation

- Configuring Network Support during Installation

- Installing from an NFS Source

- Installing from an SMB Source

- Installing from an FTP Source

In this chapter, we move from considering principles that apply to Linux in the often-isolated context of a home workstation to examining another common role for Linux: as a desktop or server operating system in a local area network.

In fact, Linux has an increasingly important role to play in the small-office, home-office market, where Linux can deliver enterprise-class networking capabilities at a fraction of the cost of commercial Unix solutions.

Linux can easily be configured to work with most LANs and brings with it a wide range of tools, including Web servers, mail servers, and news servers, all essential components of successful intranet solutions.

Choosing Packages for a LAN Installation

An important piece of a network puzzle is consideration of what packages to install on a networked Linux system.

If, as discussed in Chapter 4 ("Installing Linux"), you find yourself unable to install all Red Hat 5.1 components on your system, consider the guidelines shown in Table 23.1 when selecting packages to install on your network-enabled system.

T A B L E 2 3 . 1 : Suggested Packages for Different Network Installations

Type of System	Packages to Install
Networked Workstation	• Mail/WWW/News Tools • Networked Workstation • NFS Server • SMB (Samba) Connectivity
Network Management Workstation	Everything for a Networked Workstation plus: • IPX/Netware Connectivity (if needed) • Network Management Workstation
Network Server	Everything for a Network Management Workstation plus: • Anonymous FTP/Gopher Server • Print Server • News Server • Web Server • DNS Name Server

Configuring Network Support during Installation

During the Linux installation process, you will get a chance to configure Local Area Network (LAN) support for your Linux system. While Chapter 24 ("Configuring Linux for an Ethernet Network") discusses how to configure an existing Linux system to communicate on a LAN, this is generally easier to do during the installation process.

In order for LAN configuration to work, you need to have a network card already installed in your computer before you install Linux. This is important because the installation program will attempt to communicate with the card when networking is being configured.

Regardless of what media you choose to install from (CD-ROM, hard disk partition, or network mount), you will have a chance to configure your network environment. Normally, you will be given the option to configure your network following installation of the Linux files. In Chapter 4, we intentionally chose not to configure LAN support when prompted. In the case of a networked system, however, we need to answer "Yes" at this prompt. Once we do, we will need to provide information in a minimum of four screens to fully configure our network.

NOTE
Much of the information requested during the network configuration process is covered in Chapter 16, "Understanding Linux Networking," and Chapter 24, "Configuring Linux for an Ethernet Network." These discussions include definitions of such terms as IP address, network mask, and nameserver.

Choosing a Network Interface Card

The first step to configuring your network is to select a network interface from the provided list of network cards, which is the first screen you should see during the configuration process. Most popular cards are supported, so you should find a reasonable match on the list.

Once you have selected a card, you may be asked to indicate how the card's settings should be determined. The two options are Specify Options and Autoprobe. Autoprobe causes Linux to attempt to determine the settings of the card automatically. With many cards this will succeed. With some cards, though, this can fail or even cause your system to freeze, making it necessary to start the Linux installation process again. If you find that autoprobing doesn't work for your card, you will need to specify the card's settings manually. When you select Specify Options, you will be presented with a screen asking for information specific to the card you have selected.

Selecting a Boot Protocol

Once the card's settings are determined, you need to indicate how the system will obtain its network identity, including IP address, nameserver and other crucial settings. This is done using the Boot Protocols screen. The three options on this screen are:

- Static IP Address
- BOOTP
- DHCP

With the Static IP Address option, all network configuration information is stored locally. BOOTP or DHCP allows your system to acquire its network configuration information from a server at boot time instead of storing information locally (and having to change the information locally when configuration changes are required).

Unless you know that you should be using DHCP or BOOTP to configure your network, it is necessary to choose Static IP Address. With this option, you can manually specify all the information necessary to make your system talk successfully with the rest of your LAN.

Configuring Your Network

Having chosen to configure your network settings manually, you will be presented with the next two screens.

In the first screen, you are asked for the following information: IP address, network mask, default gateway, and primary nameserver. If you don't know the correct values for these entries, consult your network administrator. For any LAN connected to the Internet, a default gateway and a primary nameserver are essential. For isolated networks, you may not need a gateway or a nameserver, so these fields can be left blank if your network administrator indicates they are not needed.

In the second screen, you have the opportunity to provide the following supplementary network configuration information:

- Domain Name: This is the domain name of your network. This is essential for Internet-connected networks but may not be needed for isolated LANs that do not use the Domain Name System for resolving host names.

- Host Name: This is the fully qualified host name for your machine. In the case of systems on LANs where a domain name was specified, this value will include the host name of the machine as well as the domain name.

- Secondary and Tertiary Nameservers: Many networks and systems connected to the Internet use more than one nameserver to ensure reliability of their domain name system. If you use two or three nameservers, enter the second and third servers IP addresses in these two fields.

Once these screens are completed, your network is installed and configured. When your system reboots after the installation, you should find that it is configured correctly to work with your LAN.

Installing from an NFS Source

If your system is connected to a LAN during the installation process, then it is possible to install Red Hat 5 from a source image located on a server on the network.

In a Unix network, it is most common for the image to exist on a Network File System (NFS) server, which is the norm for sharing resources in Unix and Linux operating systems.

If your Red Hat 5 CD-ROM is being made available from an NFS server on your network, you can use the boot install disk to install from this source.

When prompted for the source for your installation, instead of choosing Local CD-ROM, simply select NFS Image. You will immediately be prompted to configure your network as outlined above, and then the NFS Setup screen will be displayed.

In this screen you need to provide two pieces of information: the IP address (or host name) of the NFS server you want to use and the path on the server where the Red Hat 5 source image is located.

For instance, if your Red Hat 5 CD-ROM is mounted on the NFS server at /mnt/cdrom and the NFS server has the IP address 10.10.10.1, you would enter **10.10.10.1** as the NFS server name and **/mnt/cdrom** as the RedHat Directory.

The rest of the installation procedure should proceed in the same way as when you install from a local CD-ROM drive.

Installing from an SMB Source

If you are installing a Linux system onto a largely Windows network, then it is unlikely that an NFS server is available. Instead, you can choose to install Linux from a shared Windows resource, otherwise known as an SMB (Server Message Block) share.

> **NOTE**
>
> Installing from an SMB source requires the supplemental installation disk. After selecting SMB Image, you will be prompted to insert the disk, so be sure it is ready before you start your installation. See Chapter 3, "Getting Ready," for information on producing Red Hat 5 boot and supplementary installation disks.

Consider this example: You have a Windows NT file server with a CD-ROM drive at IP address 10.10.10.1. The Red Hat 5 CD-ROM is in the drive and the drive has been shared with the resource name CDROM.

In this case, when selecting the source for the installation you could choose SMB Image instead of Local CD-ROM or NFS Image. If you do this, the installation will proceed normally and, after you finish configuring your partitions using Disk Druid or fdisk and select and format your swap partition, you will then be prompted to configure your network, as outlined earlier in this chapter.

Once the network has been configured, the SMB Setup screen will be displayed, prompting you for the following information:

- SMB Server Name: The name of the server sharing the Red Hat files (in our example, this would be 10.10.10.1)

- Share Volume: The resource name of the share (in our example, this would be CDROM)

- Account Name and Password: If required by the resource you are accessing, your username and password

Once this information is provided, the rest of your installation should proceed normally.

Installing from an FTP Source

If neither NFS nor SMB sources are an option and you need to install from a network server, you can install Linux from an FTP server. Using this option, you have two choices:

- Install from an FTP server on your LAN.

- Install from the Red Hat FTP server on the Internet. (Keep in mind that this could prove painfully slow unless you have a fast, dedicated Internet connection.)

If you want to use the FTP option, you will need to select FTP at the point where we selected SMB Image and NFS Image in the previous two sections. As with the SMB option, using FTP to install Linux requires the supplementary installation disk.

You will be prompted to configure your network once you have finished configuring disk partitions and selecting your swap partition. After the network is configured, you will be presented with the FTP Setup screen. In this screen, you can provide three pieces of information:

- FTP Site name: This is the name of the FTP server you plan to use. If you want to install from the Red Hat FTP server, use `ftp.redhat.com`.

- Red Hat Directory: This is the directory on the FTP server where the Red Hat source files are located. To install Red Hat 5.1 from the Red Hat FTP server, use `/pub/redhat/redhat-5.1/i386/`.

- Use Non-anonymous FTP or Proxy: Select this option if you are required to log in to the FTP server you plan to use or if your site is connected to the Internet through a proxy server and you plan to install Linux from the Red Hat FTP site.

If you select the last option, then another screen will be displayed after you select OK on the FTP Setup screen. This supplementary screen, the Further FTP Setup screen, allows you to provide the account name and password you need to use for non-anonymous FTP, as well as the host name or IP address of your proxy server if those are required to access the Internet.

Where Do We Go from Here?

Now that you have installed a networked Linux system, we are going to look at the details of Linux Ethernet configuration. This information will allow you to install existing non-networked Linux systems onto an Ethernet LAN or reconfigure existing network configurations as needed.

Once we have learned these details, we will spend much of the rest of the book looking at some of the roles that Linux can play in a small intranet, including:

- serving as an inexpensive router or firewall
- acting as an intranet Web server
- handling e-mail services for your network

CHAPTER
TWENTY-FOUR

24

Configuring Linux for an Ethernet Network

- Preparing and Configuring the Network

- Manual Network Configuration

- Sharing Files on a Unix Network

- Basic Network Security

In the last chapter, "Installing Linux for the SOHO," we looked at how to install Linux on a computer and connect it to a TCP/IP Ethernet network in the process.

In this chapter, we learn how to configure an already-installed Linux system to connect to a Linux network. These steps including preparing your PC for a network, configuring the network, and testing the network. We will cover the entire process.

Preparing and Configuring the Network

As you saw in the last chapter, there are two main steps that need to be taken to get your network working:

- Installing and setting up a network card

- Setting up your TCP/IP parameters

We will look at how to configure these essentials after Linux has been installed. This process can be used to install new PCs onto the network or to change the configuration of current PCs.

Installing and Setting Up a Network Card

Installing and setting up a network card is highly dependent on the type of network card you plan to use. You should consult the discussion of network cards in Chapter 23, "Installing Linux for the SOHO," to decide what type of card to use and what information is needed to configure it properly with Linux.

Having selected a card (in this chapter, we will assume you select an Etherworks 3c59x class card, such as the 3Com Etherlink III card), you need to first install the hardware according to the instructions that come with the card and then restart your computer and let Linux load.

Having done this, log in as the root user and start X Windows. If you haven't changed your configuration, the Control Panel should launch automatically when X Windows starts. If it doesn't, start the Control Panel as outlined in Chapter 12, "Configuring your System with the Control Panel."

In the Control Panel, single-click the kernel daemon configuration icon

to launch the kernel daemon configuration applet shown in Figure 24.1.

FIGURE 24.1:

The kernel daemon
configuration window

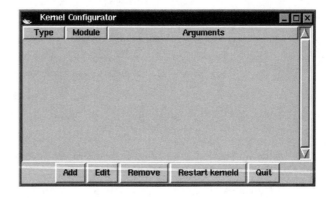

This window will display any installed kernel modules. These kernel modules represent support for devices that, instead of being compiled into the kernel, are loaded at boot time or later. In addition to Ethernet cards, these devices can include SCSI cards, CD-ROM drives, and other hardware.

If you are adding a new Ethernet card to your system, click the Add button to get the Choose Module Type dialog box shown in Figure 24.2. Here you can click the Module Types to produce a drop-down list of device types. For Ethernet cards, choose the eth device type, which is the Linux abbreviation for Ethernet.

FIGURE 24.2:

The Choose Module Type
dialog box

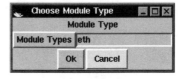

Having done this, you will be presented with the Define Module dialog box shown in Figure 24.3. In this box, you need to specify the exact device name and type of hardware being used. Click the Which Module Type? button to drop down a list of Ethernet device names such as eth0, eth1, and eth2. Generally, the first Ethernet card in a system is eth0, the second is eth1, and so on. If you are installing a new card in a system that previously had no Ethernet card, choose eth0.

FIGURE 24.3:

The Define Module dialog box

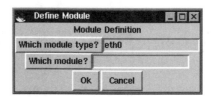

Next, click the Which Module? button to select the type of Ethernet card you are installing from a list of available cards. In our case, we want to select 3c59x.

This will result in a dialog box asking you to provide any configuration information necessary for your card. In some cases, this will include the IRQ and base I/O address of the card. You will need to consult your card's manual for information about how to determine and set your card's hardware configuration. In the case of our chosen card, we are offered a chance to provide additional arguments; these are not necessary for a standard installation, so we just click the Done button and our new card will appear in the kernel daemon configuration window as shown in Figure 24.4.

FIGURE 24.4:

Adding a new Ethernet card

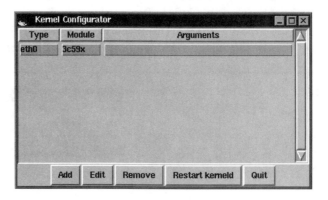

The final step to installing a new Ethernet card is to restart the `kerneld` process, which will force `kerneld` to load any configuration information related to the card. In order to do this, simply click the Restart Kerneld button.

Checking whether the Module Loaded

Verifying the configuration is not the easiest task. Until you try to make the network work in the next section, there is no quick way to see if your Ethernet card is configured correctly. But you can check whether the module will load by manually using the `insmod` command to install a loadable kernel module.

In order to do this, either go to a console command line or open an `xterm` window as `root`. First, you need to change your current directory to the following:

```
$ cd /lib/modules/2.0.32/net/
```

Here we are assuming you have installed the Red Hat 5 distribution that shipped with this book and have not upgraded the kernel. In this case, the kernel version is `2.0.32`, which is reflected in the path of the directory.

Once you are in the correct directory, load your desired module (in this case, for the 3c59x series of cards) with the `insmod` command:

```
$ insmod 3c59x.o
```

Notice that the filenames for the modules have a `.o` extension.

If successfully configured, your card will load and a series of messages will be generated by the driver. In the case of our chosen card, the messages will look something like this:

```
3c59x.c:v0.46C 10/14/97 Donald Becker
http://cesdis.gsfc.nasa.gov/linux/drivers/vortex.html
loading device 'eth0'…
etho: 3Com 3c905 Boomerang 100baseTx at 0x1440, 00:60:08:71:ad:8c,
➥ IRQ 11
  8k word-wide RAM 3:5 Rx:Tx split, autoselect/MII interface.
eth0: MII transceiver found at address 24.
eth0: Overriding PCI latency timer (CFLT) setting of 64, new value
➥ is 248.
```

If no errors appear, then the module has loaded successfully and your card should be configured just fine. If you continue to experience trouble configuring your network card, refer to the Ethernet HOWTO at `http://sunsite.unc.edu/mdw/ HOWTO/Ethernet-HOWTO.html`.

Setting Up Your TCP/IP Parameters

The next step is to set up your TCP/IP parameters using the network configuration applet, which is accessed using the network configuration icon in the Control Panel.

The network configuration window looks like the one shown in Figure 24.5.

FIGURE 24.5:

The Network Configurator dialog box

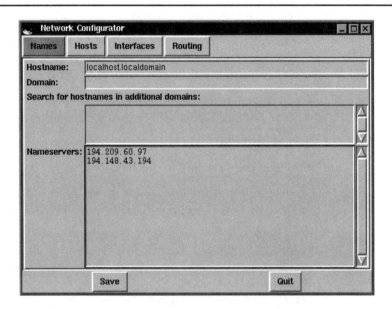

It is in this dialog box that you specify critical information about your machine in relation to the network it is connected to. This information includes the name and address of your machine, the names and addresses of other machines on your network, how each available network interface should be used, and how to correctly route traffic so that it reaches its destination.

NOTE

If you are connecting to an existing network, much of the information needed for this section will come from your network's administrator. If you plan to deploy your own network from scratch, it is a good idea to read up on the fundamentals of TCP/IP networking and network design.

The first step is to configure your computer's name and nameserver. This is done in the Names panel, which is displayed by default when you open the network configuration dialog box. Figure 24.5 shows this default panel.

Three main pieces of information need to be provided in the Names panel:

- Your complete host name: This includes the name of your machine plus the complete domain name in which the machine exists. For instance, the machine foobar in the domain foo.com would have the host name foobar.foo.com.

- The domain in which your machine exists: This is the latter part of the host; in the example above, this would be foo.com.

- Your nameservers: This is a list, one per line, of machines that provide domain name services to your network. Domain name services allow you to look up the names of systems on internal and external networks (such as the Internet) but are not used on all networks. If you need to provide a list of nameservers, list them as IP addresses—the job of the nameserver is to convert names into IP addresses, and if you provide the list of nameservers as names and not addresses, your system won't be able to look up the name of the nameserver in order to connect to it.

The next step involves the host table for your machine. The host table, which actually is kept in the file /etc/hosts, is the simplest form of name lookup. The host table file contains lists of names and their associated IP addresses. In small networks that don't run their own domain name servers, it is common for the host table to contain the names and addresses of all machines on the network. At a minimum, though, a machine connected to a local area network needs two entries:

- A local host entry

- An entry with the machine's name and IP address

To add an entry to the list, click the Add button. This will display a dialog box like the one in Figure 24.6.

FIGURE 24.6:

Adding a host

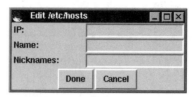

In this dialog box, you will find three fields that you can fill in. At the very least, fill in the IP address and the complete name of the machine that you are configuring (such as `foobar.foo.com`). In the Nicknames field, you can enter alternative names for the machine separated by spaces. Frequently, system administrators will place the unqualified host name (in the case of `foobar.foo.com` the unqualified name is `foobar`) in this field. When you are finished, click the Done button.

Editing entries in the host table is similar to adding new entries. Select an existing entry and then click the Edit button to get a dialog box like the one in Figure 24.7.

FIGURE 24.7:

Editing the host table

Here you find the same three fields as when you were adding a new entry to the host table. Once you finish editing the contents of the entry, you can click the Done button to commit the changes to the host table.

The next panel is where you configure the network interfaces on your system. Interfaces can include modem-based PPP connections, Ethernet connections through an Ethernet card, and even Token Ring connections. By default, this table should include at least one entry, called `lo` (this is the local loopback entry and is needed for Linux to work without a network present). Each interface is associated with an IP address.

The first step to adding a new interface (assuming yours isn't there) is to click the Add button. This will initially bring up a dialog box like the one in Figure 24.8, where you can select the type of interface you are adding.

FIGURE 24.8:

The Choose Interface Type
dialog box

In the case of a LAN, you will want to select the same type of device as you did earlier when setting up the module for your network card. This will probably be an Ethernet interface.

After clicking OK, you will be presented with a dialog box where you can configure the properties of the interface. In the case of an Ethernet interface, this will look like the one in Figure 24.9.

FIGURE 24.9:

Configuring an Ethernet
interface

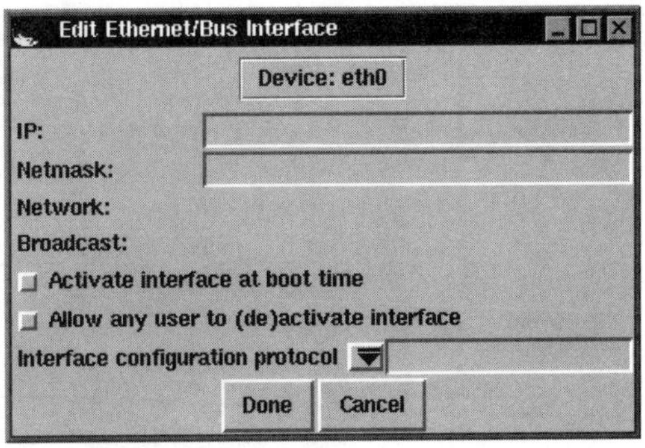

At the very least, you need to provide the IP address of the interface and a netmask for the network. If you have only one network interface, then the IP address should be the same one you entered for the machine in the Names and Hosts panels. The other available options are:

- Activate Interface at Boot Time: Select this if you want the network to be enabled every time you boot your computer; if you don't select this, you will need to manually enable your network. It is usually preferable to select this option for an Ethernet LAN connection.

- Allow Any User to (De)activate Interface: Normally, only the root user can activate or deactivate a network interface. Allowing any user to do so is particularly useful for dial-up interfaces, such as PPP, where any user may want or need to dial out to establish a network connection. If you are dealing strictly with an Ethernet LAN connection and are activating the interface at boot time, then you probably won't need to enable this feature.

- Interface Configuration Protocol: On some networks, special servers provide network workstations with the information they need to operate on the network. This makes it easier to configure your workstation because instead of performing the complete network configuration, you can allow the computer to obtain its configuration from the server every time the network interface is activated. If your network uses BOOTP or DHCP for this purpose, select the option here. If your network doesn't use a boot protocol such as BOOTP or DHCP, select None.

The final piece of the network configuration puzzle is the setting of routes. Click the Routing button at the top of the window to display the routing table panel shown in Figure 24.10.

FIGURE 24.10:

The routing table panel

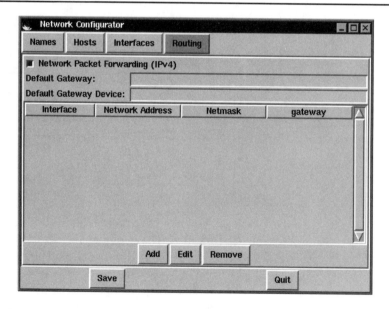

The routing table is used to tell the computer how to direct data that is destined for different locations on the network. In the case of a small LAN that is not connected to another LAN or to an external network such as the Internet, configuration of routes can be an easy job.

If your network uses a default gateway, you may be able to simply indicate the IP address of the default gateway and the network device on your system that is used to send information to the gateway (if you have a single Ethernet card, this should be the device eth0). If you have multiple interfaces (such as more than one Ethernet card), you can specify when to use these devices by creating static routes.

For example, let's say your computer has two Ethernet cards, one attached to your main corporate network (eth0) and another connected to a small network you are using to test some software (eth1). Your routing configuration would indicate that your default gateway device should be eth0 and a static route for your test network should use eth1, as shown in Figure 24.11.

FIGURE 24.11:

Using static routes

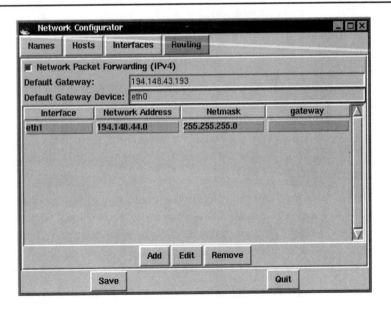

It is not uncommon to include a static route for the local Ethernet network you are connected to.

Testing Your Network

The next step is to test your network connection to make sure everything is healthy.

First, you need to test basic network connectivity. You can do this with the `ping` command, which allows you to send a query to a specific IP address to see if any machine is currently on and alive at the address.

Let's use a fictional network with IP addresses in the range of 194.148.43.0 to 194.148.43.255. You are configuring your workstation to act as 194.148.43.100. On your network is a file server with the IP address 194.148.43.10. If your network is correctly configured, at the very least you should be able to talk to this server. Test this with the command:

```
$ ping 194.148.43.10
```

If you get back the following errors:

```
ping: sendto: Network is unreachable
ping: wrote 194.148.43.10 64 chars, ret=-1
ping: sendto: Network is unreachable
ping: wrote 194.148.43.10 64 chars, ret=-1
etc.
```

then you immediately know that you have a problem with the configuration of your Ethernet card's driver module or a basic configuration error such as the wrong IP address or netmask for the device. You should go back and review these settings to make sure they are correct. First check that the module for the Ethernet card is loading successfully; once it is, double-check your IP address and netmask entries.

Once you can ping on the local network, you need to see if your default gateway and access to networks outside your local network are functional. You can do this by using `ping` for an external IP address. If you don't know the IP address of any external system, you can skip this step or ask your system administrator for an appropriate IP address to test.

Just as we did before, use the `ping` command:

```
$ ping 194.148.8.10
```

If this succeeds, then your routing is correctly set up and you can access external networks through your default gateway.

The final step is to see if name lookups are working. To test this, you can use the `nslookup` command to try to look up a host name using your default DNS server. For instance, you can try looking up www.yahoo.com:

```
$ nslookup www.yahoo.com
```

If successful, the `nslookup` command should produce results that look like this:

```
Server:   du1.paus.ch
Address:   194.209.60.97

Name:     www5.yahoo.com
Address:   204.71.177.70
Aliases:   www.yahoo.com
```

Notice that the name and address of the name server being used are displayed (you can use this to confirm you have configured your DNS services correctly), and then the results of the name lookup are provided.

Assuming all three of these steps work, then you probably have a fully functional network connection. If not, you may want to refer to the networking HOWTO document at `/usr/doc/HOWTO/NET-3-HOWTO.gz`:

```
$ zless /usr/doc/HOWTO/NET-3-HOWTO.gz
```

Manual Network Configuration

If you are using a Linux distribution other than Red Hat, you may not have access to the Red Hat Control Panel for the purposes of network configuration.

If this is the case, you have a number of choices.

First, you can check the documentation of your distribution to see if it provides a utility for configuring network connections as Red Hat Linux does. If it does, try using this utility. It should ask for information similar to that needed by the Control Panel network configuration applet.

Failing that, you will need to edit some configuration files by hand to get your network working. Depending on the version of Linux that is running, these files can sit in different places. Because of this, we will look at a series of steps that can be taken to configure your network regardless of the Linux distribution you are using. These steps assume you have your Ethernet card's module loaded.

Setting Up the Interface

The first step is to activate the network interface you wish to use. If you are trying to activate eth0 as IP address 100.100.100.10, then you can use the ifconfig command to activate the interface:

```
$ ifconfig eth0 100.100.100.10 netmask 255.255.255.0 up
```

This command tells the system to assign the IP address 100.100.100.10 and the netmask 255.255.255.0 to the eth0 interface, and then activates the interface with the up argument.

To test whether the interface has been successfully activated, you can use the ifconfig command without any parameters or arguments to see a list of enabled interfaces like the one below:

```
lo        Link encap:Local Loopback
          inet addr:127.0.0.1  Bcast:127.255.255.255  Mask:255.0.0.0
          UP BROADCAST LOOPBACK RUNNING  MTU:3584  Metric:1
          RX packets:2142848 errors:0 dropped:0 overruns:0
          TX packets:2142848 errors:0 dropped:0 overruns:0

eth0      Link encap:10Mbps Ethernet  HWaddr 00:C0:F0:0D:76:5A
          inet addr:100.100.100.10  Bcast:100.100.100.255
➥ Mask:255.255.255.0
          UP BROADCAST RUNNING MULTICAST  MTU:1500  Metric:1
          RX packets:11239889 errors:0 dropped:0 overruns:0
          TX packets:16384520 errors:3 dropped:0 overruns:0
          Interrupt:3 Base address:0x300
```

This list will generally contain at least a loopback device (device lo) plus any network devices you have enabled. In our case, we are looking for the eth0 interface. Most Linux distributions will set things up to configure a loopback device at boot time. To keep your system running happily, you should make sure you have a local loopback device configured. If lo is not set up on your system, you can configure it with the following ifconfig command:

```
$ ifconfig lo 127.0.0.1 up
```

Setting Up a Name Server

The next step is to set up your name server. In order to do this, you need to edit the file /etc/resolv.conf using your favorite text editor. This file tells the system everything it needs to know to go out and find the address for host names.

Generally, you will want at least two lines in your `resolv.conf` file such as:

```
domain landegg.edu
nameserver 194.148.43.194
```

The `domain` line specifies the domain name of the local system. If your machine is being placed on a network whose domain is `foo.bar`, then this line should read `domain foo.bar`. The second line specifies the IP address of the primary name server that you will be using. This may be a machine on your local network, a server running at your Internet provider, or a public name server on the Internet. Your network administrator can provide you with this information.

Many sites use multiple name servers for redundancy. If one is down or not available for some reason, users should still be able to look up names using the alternate servers. You can specify multiple servers by including multiple `name-server` lines in `resolv.conf`:

```
domain landegg.edu
nameserver 194.148.43.194
nameserver 194.148.43.196
nameserver 194.148.8.10
nameserver 194.148.1.10
```

In a situation like this, the first listed server will be the first tried when looking up a name. If this attempt fails, Linux will move on to the second machine on the list and so on. If all listed name servers fail to respond to the query, then Linux will give up and the attempted name lookup will fail.

Setting Up a Local Hosts File

While it is theoretically possible to use a DNS name server to look up every name, including those of hosts on the local network, this is hugely inefficient. As an alternative to using a name server to look up the names of machines on moderately sized networks, you can use a local hosts file to perform these lookups.

A local hosts file sits on your system and contains a list matching IP addresses with host names. To enable a local hosts file, you first need to edit the file `/etc/host.conf` with your favorite text editor. This file tells Linux how to go about looking up names, and needs to contain the following two lines to enable a local hosts file:

```
order hosts,bind
multi on
```

The first line says that when a name is being looked up, first check the local hosts file (hosts) and then check the Domain Name System (bind stands for Berkeley Internet Name Daemon) by following the instructions in /etc/resolv.conf.

Next, you need to create the local hosts file, which is called /etc/hosts. Edit this file with your favorite text editor and create a one-line entry for each host being listed. The entry should take the form

<IP Address> <hostname> <alias> <alias> <alias> ...

Each section of the line (IP address, hostname, alias) can be separated by one or more spaces. Comment lines begin with a hash mark (#) and can be used to structure and explain the entries in larger hosts files.

Let's consider an example. The following four entries are from a hosts file:

```
194.148.43.194      serv1.landegg.edu
194.148.43.195      apps.landegg.edu         apps
194.148.43.196      serv3.landegg.edu        serv3      www.landegg.edu
194.148.43.215      office15.landegg.edu     office15
```

Notice that all lines start with the IP address and then provide a host name and any aliases for the host. Aliases are not required. You will notice that for many machines, the aliases include a short form of the host name without the complete domain name. This is done so that you can access machines on the local network without having to type the complete host name with domain name. In our example, apps.landegg.edu can be accessed locally as apps, and office15.landegg.edu as office15.

Setting Up Routes

The final step is to set up the necessary routes that allow you to talk to the network and the rest of the world. Basically, for each interface you need a routing entry that tells Linux what network is connected on that interface. In addition, you need an entry specifying a default gateway if your network is connected through a gateway to other non-local networks.

Let's start with the loopback device. We can use the route command to specify that the local machine is accessed through the loopback device:

```
$ route add -host 127.0.0.1 lo
```

This command says that the host 127.0.0.1 (the local host) should be accessed through the device lo.

Next, let's consider our `eth0` device from earlier in this section. This device connects the PC to a network with the network address 100.100.100.0 and a netmask of 255.255.255.0. We use the `route` command again to tell Linux to send all information for the local network out on the `eth0` interface:

```
$ route add -net 100.100.100.0 netmask 255.255.255.0 eth0
```

Finally, we can use the `route` command once more to specify the default gateway that can be used to access remote networks. If our default gateway is at the IP address 100.100.100.1, we could use the command:

```
$ route add default gw 100.100.100.1 eth0
```

This indicates that the default gateway (gw) is at the address 100.100.100.1 and can be accessed by sending information destined for the gateway out through the `eth0` interface.

Finally, we can check all our routing entries by using the `route` command with no parameters or arguments. This should return a routing table like this:

```
Kernel IP routing table
Destination     Gateway        Genmask         Flags Metric Ref  Use Iface
100.100.100.0   *              255.255.255.0   U     0      0    317 eth0
127.0.0.0       *              255.0.0.0       U     0      0      6 lo
default         100.100.100.1  0.0.0.0         UG    0      0   2605 eth0
```

Automating Network Configuration at Boot Time

By now, you should have a fully functional network connection. However, it would be laborious to have to type all of those commands each time you started your Linux system.

Luckily, you can place all the needed `ifconfig` and `route` commands into one of the system's start-up scripts, such as `/etc/rc.d/rc.local`. In the case of the examples used here, you could add the following lines to your `rc.local` file using a text editor:

```
/sbin/ifconfig eth0 100.100.100.10 netmask 255.255.255.0 up
/sbin/ifconfig lo 127.0.0.1 up
/sbin/route add -host 127.0.0.1 lo
/sbin/route add -net 100.100.100.0 netmask 255.255.255.0 eth0
/sbin/route add default gw 100.100.100.1 eth0
```

Sharing Files on a Unix Network

Now that we have our Linux system talking with other machines on a local TCP/IP network, we should look at one of the most basic networking tasks: sharing files. In the Unix and Linux world, this is generally done using NFS, the Network File System.

Sharing takes place in two directions:

- Accessing directories and files on other hosts on the network that have been shared

- Sharing files and directories on your PC for other users on the network to access

Accessing Remote File Systems

Accessing remote files and directories is done using the `mount` command. The command takes the form

```
mount <remote-directory-name> <local-directory>
```

where the remote directory is specified with the form *<hostname:/directory-name>*, and the local directory is an existing directory, preferably empty, that will become the location through which the remote directory is accessed.

Let's consider an example. You want to access the directory `/test/dir` on the machine `foo.bar` on your local network; the directory has been made available for remote mounting via NFS. You have an empty directory called `/foo` on your machine, which will be the mount point for the remote directory.

To assign this directory, you use the `mount` command:

```
$ mount foo.bar:/test/dir /foo
```

This command says to mount the directory `/test/dir` on machine `foo.bar` to the local directory `/foo`. Once this is done, you will have access to the files and subdirectories in the remote directory on the basis of the file permissions assigned to the files. Listing the contents of `/foo` will actually list the contents of `/test/dir` on `foo.bar`.

WARNING There is one caveat to the NFS system. On your local system, the root user has godlike power to open, read, or erase a file anywhere on the system regardless of who created or owns the file. But in a remotely mounted directory, `root` has severe restrictions under the NFS model: it can only access files and directories for which explicit permission has been granted.

Mounting Remote Directories at Boot Time

If there are remote directories that you frequently use, you will probably want them to mount automatically at boot time. To do this, you can use the File System configuration applet in the Red Hat Control Panel, which is accessed through the File System configuration icon.

To add a new NFS mount, select Add Mount from the NFS menu on the menu bar at the top of the window. This will open a dialog box like the one in Figure 24.12.

FIGURE 24.12:

The Add NFS Mount
dialog box

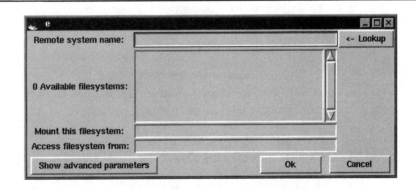

To enter the remote mount example used above, enter **foo.bar** for Remote System Name, **/test/dir** for Mount This Filesystem, and **/foo** for Access Filesystem From. If you want the mount to occur automatically at boot time, click the Show Advanced Parameters button. The dialog box will expand to show additional options like the ones in Figure 24.13.

FIGURE 24.13:

Additional NFS mount options

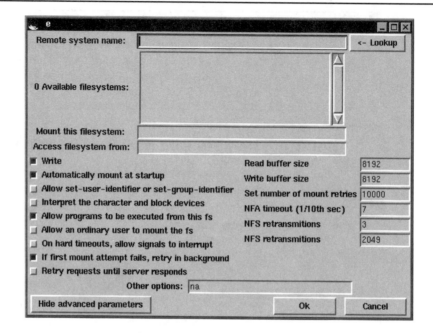

Make sure Automatically Mount at Startup is selected and then click the OK button.

This whole procedure will add an entry to the /etc/fstab file similar to the following:

```
foo.bar:/test/dir /foo nfs defaults 0 0
```

If you want to manually create an automatic mount that will mount at boot time, or if you aren't using Red Hat Linux, you can add a similar entry to /etc/fstab on your system using a text editor.

Sharing Directories on the Network

The flip side of the whole equation is sharing your files and directories to users on the network. After all, before we mounted the remote file system on the machine foo.bar in the last section, foo.bar had to make the directory available to the network.

Exporting directories with NFS requires the used of two daemons, /usr/sbin/rpc.nfsd and /usr/sbin/rpc.mountd plus one configuration file, /etc/exports. (On some Linux distributions, the rpc. prefix is dropped from the nfsd and mountd daemons' names.) The files rpc.mountd and rpc.nfsd should be installed on most systems. If they're not on your system, you can install them from the enclosed Red Hat CD-ROM from the RPM file nfs-server-2.2beta29-2 .i386.rpm.

The first step to sharing a directory on the network is to edit /etc/exports using a text editor and add one entry for each directory being shared. The entries take the form

> /*<directory>* *<host>*<(*options*)>

The following is a sample /etc/exports file from the man page for /etc/exports:

```
# sample /etc/exports file
/                 master(rw) trusty(rw,no_root_squash)
/projects         proj*.local.domain(rw)
/usr              *.local.domain(ro)
/home/joe         pc001(rw,all_squash,anonuid=150,anongid=100)
/pub              (ro,insecure,all_squash)
/pub/private      (noaccess)
```

Let's break the file down line by line:

- Line 1: This is a comment line, as indicated by a hash mark (#); and is ignored.

- Line 2: Two machines are being given different levels of access to the / directory: master with read and write permission (the rw option), and trusty with read and write permission enabled and permission for the root user to have full access to all the files and subdirectories being exported (the no_ root_squash option). In other words, a root user on trusty will have the same permissions as root on the local system.

- Line 3: Any host whose name starts with proj and is part of the domain local.domain is given read and write access to the directory /projects.

- Line 4: Any host in the domain local.domain has read-only (the ro option) access to /usr.

- Line 5: The host pc001 is being given read and write access to the directory /home/joe. All users accessing this mount from pc001 will be treated as the anonymous user (the all_squash option), and the anonymous user will be considered to have the user ID of 150 and group ID of 150 (the anonuid=150 and anongid=150 options).

- Line 6: The directory /pub is being made available to all hosts with access to the exporting system. Access is granted on a read-only basis with all users treated as anonymous users. The insecure option allows clients that don't use a reserved TCP/IP port for NFS to access the mount.

- Line 7: Access is denied (the noaccess option) to all hosts for the directory /pub/private.

Other options for the /etc/exports file can be found in the exports man page, which is accessed with the command:

```
$ man exports
```

Once you have specified your exported directories in /etc/exports, you need to restart the rpc.nfsd and rpc.mountd processes (which usually run at boot time). First, use ps to check the process IDs of the two processes:

```
$ ps aux | grep rpc.nfsd
root 1103  0.2  0.8  872  508  ?  S  22:25  0:00 /usr/sbin/rpc.nfsd
$ ps aux | grep rpc.mountd
root 1105  0.0  0.7  836  500  ?  S  22:25  0:00 /usr/sbin/rpc.mountd
```

Next, kill and restart the processes:

```
$ kill 1103 1105; /usr/sbin/rpc.nfsd; /usr/sbin/rpc.mountd
```

Your new exports will be made available on the network for remote users to access.

Basic Network Security

While it is great to be able to connect to a network and access all of its resources, this does present a security risk. Luckily, Linux provides a basic mechanism that gives some control over which machines on the network can actually attempt to connect to services on your Linux system.

The basic security mechanism consists of two files: /etc/hosts.allow and /etc/hosts.deny. Together, these files are part of a three-part basic security chain:

1. Allow access to any daemon-client combination in hosts.allow.

2. Deny access to any daemon-client combination in hosts.deny.

3. Grant access to everyone else.

By default, most Linux distributions have no entries in hosts.allow or hosts .deny, so they will default to option 3: anyone can attempt to connect to the system. Of course, this doesn't prevent individual services such as Telnet and FTP from requiring further authentication, but it also doesn't prevent those initial probing attempts to connect that can be the start of many hackers' joyrides through unknown systems.

Creating entries for hosts.allow and hosts.deny is straightforward:

```
<Daemon List>: <Client List>
```

Any entry like this specifies which network daemons (e.g., ftpd, in.telnetd, in.rshd) should allow connections from which hosts (in hosts.allow) or deny connections from which hosts (in hosts.deny). Any network daemon can be listed. For instance, the entry

```
ftp: host1
```

in the file hosts.allow would allow incoming FTP connections from the specified host, host1.

A few special keywords help make things easy, preventing the necessity of listing out all daemons and clients individually. The ALL keyword can match any client or any daemon. For instance, the entry

```
ALL: ALL
```

in hosts.allow allows any type of access from any client, while the same entry in hosts.deny would stop all access.

The EXCEPT keyword allows exceptions in a network that is otherwise thrown wide open by ALL. For instance, the entry

```
ALL EXCEPT ftpd: ALL
```

in hosts.deny would deny access to all clients accessing all services except FTP services. Similarly,

```
ALL: .local.domain EXCEPT foo.local.domain
```

in hosts.allow would allow access to all services to any machine in the domain local.domain (note the necessary "." in front of local.domain) except foo .local.domain.

Finally, the LOCAL keyword makes it easy to provide access to all machines in the local domain:

```
ALL: LOCAL
```

in `hosts.allow` would allow any type of access from machines in the local domain.

The `hosts.allow` and `hosts.deny` files can take a very rich set of entries that provide more finely grained control than most users need. This is detailed in the man page for `hosts.allow`:

```
$ man hosts.allow
```

Where Do We Go from Here?

In this chapter, we have learned the basics of connecting a Linux PC to an Ethernet network using TCP/IP. This allows Linux to communicate easily with other Unix systems on the network, including other Linux systems.

However, fully integrating your Linux system with Windows and Novell networks requires more work. In the next chapter, we will take a look at the basics of integrating your Linux system with Windows and Novell.

# CHAPTER TWENTY-FIVE

Integrating Linux in Windows and Novell Networks

- Sharing Linux Files and Printers with Windows Networks

- Accessing Windows Network Files and Printers from Linux Systems

- Connecting Linux to a Novell Network

In this chapter, we look at capabilities of Linux that make it an attractive addition to many existing intranet networks.

If your organization is running a standard Windows network, Linux is able to step in and play the role of an effective, efficient, and powerful file and print server. With a price-point far lower than Windows NT and stability that exceeds that of Windows 95 and Windows 98, Linux may be the ideal file and print server for budget-conscious offices that need to share files between Windows desktops on a network.

Working from the other direction, Linux can also access files on Windows file servers as if they were local hard disks on the Linux system. This serves any number of purposes. For instance, suppose you run a Linux-based Web server but your Web developer performs development on a Windows system. The Linux Web server could automatically connect to a pre-specified directory on the Windows development system and copy new files onto the Web server, preventing any need to manually update the Web server's content.

Finally, we will look at integration of a Linux system into a Novell network. These tools are not as well-developed and robust as those available for integration with Windows networks, but we will discuss the Novell options and point you to sources of information on the subject.

Sharing Linux Files and Printers with Windows Networks

The most common method of Linux-Windows network integration is to make a Linux system act as a file and print server to Windows clients on the network. This is achieved through the use of Samba. Samba is a collection of software that makes Linux capable of the SMB (Server Message Block) protocol that is the basis of Windows network file and print sharing. Possible clients to a Linux-based SMB server include LAN Manager, Windows NT, OS/2, and other Linux systems.

Installing Samba

If you are running the version of Red Hat Linux that comes with this book, you may already have installed Samba when you installed Linux. You can check this using the `rpm` command:

```
$ rpm -q samba
```

If you find that Samba is not installed, you can install it from the Red Hat CD-ROM by mounting the CD-ROM to a logical location (such as `/mnt/cdrom`) and then using `rpm` to install the file `samba-1.9.17p4-3.i386.rpm`:

```
# rpm -i /mnt/cdrom/ samba-1.9.17p4-3.i386.rpm
```

Installing Samba from the Internet

If you are using another Linux distribution or simply want the latest version of Samba available, you can download the latest Samba source code from `ftp://samba.anu.edu.au/pub/samba/`.

Once you download the file, you will need to extract the compressed archives and read the documentation for instructions about how to compile and install Samba from the source code. Because these procedures can change from version to version, they aren't included here.

Alternatively, if you are wary of compiling from the source code, the easiest approach is to install the binaries that come with almost every major Linux distribution.

What Gets Installed

When you install Samba, several files will be installed, including:

- `/usr/sbin/smbd`: the Samba server that handles connections from clients
- `/usr/sbin/nmbd`: the NetBIOS server that allows clients to locate servers on a Windows network
- `/usr/bin/smbclient`: a basic Samba client for accessing SMB servers
- `/etc/smb.conf`: the Samba configuration file

Configuring Samba

The entire Samba configuration is contained in the file /etc/smb.conf. This file may not exist in some distributions, but you will find a sample configuration, possibly at /etc/smb.conf.sampl, that you can copy to /etc/smb.conf with the cp command to provide a starting point for configuring Samba.

The smb.conf file consists of multiple entries that contain a header followed by multiple parameters. For instance, the following entry shares the /tmp directory on the network:

```
[temp]
    comment = Temporary file space
    path = /tmp
    read only = no
    public = yes
```

Notice that the header is contained in square brackets ([tmp]), that each parameter is on a separate line, and that the structure of parameters is parameter=value.

The *[global]* Section

Most smb.conf files start with a [global] section that defines some essential parameters that affect the overall behavior of Samba. Common parameters in the [global] section include:

- printing: Specifies the type of print system being used; on Linux systems, this should be bsd.

- printcap name: Specifies the location of the printcap file; generally, this is /etc/printcap.

- load printers: Should be set to yes if you will be sharing printers.

- guest account: Indicates which Linux user to use for attempted guest connections; most Linux administrators will make this nobody because of its extremely limited privileges.

- lock directory: Indicates where to place lock files for file locking. This is usually /var/lock/samba; this directory must exist and be world readable (use chmod 755 /var/lock/samba to make it world readable).

- share modes: Specifies whether multiple users can share the same file. This should be set to yes to ensure that the necessary locking mechanisms are used to protect the integrity of shared files.

- workgroup: Indicates the Windows workgroup or domain to which the Samba server belongs.

- security: Specifies how to authenticate users for access to system resources; when set to user, Samba will authenticate out of the local Unix password file. If this parameter is set to server, Samba will authenticate from a Windows NT domain server specified by the password server parameter.

Consider the following [global] section in the smb.conf file of the Landegg Academy server that I manage:

```
[global]
    printing = bsd
    printcap name = /etc/printcap
    load printers = yes
    guest account = nobody
    lock directory = /var/lock/samba
    share modes = yes
    workgroup = testgroup
    security = user
```

This section specifies the type of printing system used in Landegg, sets up the guest account to use the Linux user nobody, points to a lock directory, makes the server part of the testgroup Windows workgroup, and specifies that Samba should use the local Unix password file for authentication.

The *[homes]* Section

The [homes] section is used to specify how to share users' home directories to the Windows network. Without this section, users' home directories need to be shared individually, as we will see later.

The following [homes] section comes from the default Red Hat smb.conf file:

```
[homes]
    comment = Home Directories
    browseable = no
    read only = no
    preserve case = yes
    short preserve case = yes
    create mode = 0750
```

The comment parameter provides additional information about the section but doesn't affect operation. The browseable parameter is used to indicate whether other users can browse the directory; setting it to no limits access to those users with permission. The `read only` parameter is set to no so that users can both read and write files in their home directories. The `preserve case` and `short preserve case` parameters ensure that case-insensitive Windows systems do not mess up the case of letters in filenames, because Linux is case sensitive. Finally, the `create mode` parameter specifies what permission to give to files created by users connected through Samba; in this case, 0750 indicates that the files should be readable, writable, and executable by the owner, readable and executable by the file's group, and off-limits to everyone else.

In order for a user to access their home directory from a Windows system, they use their username for the share name. For instance, for the user `username` to access their home directory on `smbserv`, they would access the share `\\smbserv\username`.

The *[printers]* Section

As the [homes] section was used to share all users' home directories, the [printers] section is used to share all Linux printers to the Windows network.

The following table outlines common parameters in the [printers] section:

TABLE 25.1: [Printers] Section Parameters

Parameter	Description
comment	Provides information about the section but does not affect operation.
path	Specifies the spool path; you may want to create your own spool directory for Samba and point there (for instance, Red Hat Linux creates /var/spool/samba and points there).
browseable	As with the home directories, setting this to no ensures that only users with permission can browse the printers.
printable	This should be set to yes, otherwise printing won't work (how does one print to a non-printable printer?).
public	If set to yes, then the guest account can print; on many networks, it is wise to set this to no to prevent excessive printing by guest users.
writable	Printers are not writable, so this should be no.
create mode	This specifies the permissions on spool files created during printing; this is often set to 0700.

Put together, these can be used to produce a fairly common [printers] section like the default Red Hat Linux one shown here:

```
[printers]
    comment = All Printers
    path = /var/spool/samba
    browseable = no
    printable = yes
    public = no
    writable = no
    create mode = 0700
```

Accessing Linux printers from Windows works the same way as with directories. The share name is the Linux printer name in the printcap file. For instance, to access the printer printername on smbserv, Windows users should access \\smbserv\printername.

Sharing a Directory for Public Access

Sometimes it is necessary to create a publicly accessible directory that is accessible by all users and is read-only. The directory can be set up to share information centrally in a way that prevents users from altering the information.

Consider this entry:

```
[public]
    path = /public/directory
    public = yes
    read only = yes
    printable = no
```

This entry creates a share named public that is accessible by all users (hence, public=yes) but is read only (hence, read only=yes).

Consider another example: sharing /tmp as a publicly accessible temporary directory that can be read and written to by all users. This can be achieved with the following entry:

```
[temp]
    path = /tmp
    read only = no
    public = yes
```

Sharing a Directory for Private Access

In addition to sharing directories for public access, it is sometimes necessary to create shared directories accessible by a limited number of users.

Consider a situation where we want to share the directory /private/directory as the share named private. Suppose, as well, that this directory is only to be accessible by three users: user1, user2, and user3. This could be achieved with an entry similar to the following:

```
[private]
     path = /private/directory
     valid users = user1 user2 user3
     public = no
     writable = yes
     printable = no
     create mask = 0765
```

Here we see the use of a new parameter: valid users. This parameter takes as its value a list of users with permission to access the resource, with spaces separating the usernames.

Note, as well, that public is set to no to prevent unwanted prying eyes and writable is yes so that it is a fully writable resource.

Putting It All Together

Now, let's put this all together into a complete smb.conf file. There are two things to note here:

- Blank lines are ignored.

- Comment lines start with a semicolon and continue to the end of the line.

Our completed file looks like this:

```
; Sample smb.conf

; Global Settings
[global]
     printing = bsd
     printcap name = /etc/printcap
     load printers = yes
; The guest user is nobody
```

```
    guest account = nobody
    lock directory = /var/lock/samba
    share modes = yes
    workgroup = testgroup
    security = user

; Export All Home Directories to the Network
[homes]
    comment = Home Directories
    browseable = no
    read only = no
    preserve case = yes
    short preserve case = yes
    create mode = 0750

; Make All Printers Accessible on the Network
[printers]
    comment = All Printers
    path = /var/spool/samba
    browseable = no
    printable = yes
    public = no
    writable = no
    create mode = 0700

; Create Public read-only Directory
[public]
    path = /public/directory
    public = yes
    read only = yes
    printable = no

; Provide a Public Temporary Directory
[temp]
    path = /tmp
    read only = no
    public = yes

; Export a Private Workspace for user1, user2 and user3
[private]
    path = /private/directory
    valid users = user1 user2 user3
```

```
public = no
writable = yes
printable = no
create mask = 0765
```

Running Samba

If your network is running on TCP/IP, configuration is complete and you are ready to run Samba. However, if you have a NetBIOS network, you need to perform one more step. In the file /etc/services, look for the following lines (and if they aren't there, add them):

```
netbios-ns      137/tcp              # NETBIOS Name Service
netbios-ns      137/udp
netbios-dgm     138/tcp              # NETBIOS Datagram Service
netbios-dgm     138/udp
netbios-ssn     139/tcp              # NETBIOS session service
netbios-ssn     139/udp
```

Now that you have Samba configured, it is time to run the software. By default, the Red Hat Linux version of Samba is installed to start at boot time so that it is always available. In addition, the system script /etc/rc.d/init.d/smb can be used to manually start and stop Samba.

For example, you can start Samba with

 # /etc/rc.d/init.d/smb start

and stop it with

 # /etc/rc.d/init.d/smb stop

On other distributions, you may need to manually add the necessary entries to your start-up files to start Samba at boot time. To do this, you need to add the following two commands to an appropriate start-up file, such as rc.local:

/usr/sbin/smbd -D
/usr/sbin/nmbd -D

Similarly, these two commands can be used on the command line by the root user to manually start Samba.

Without a handy system script to stop Samba, you will probably have to use a brute-force combination of ps and kill to stop Samba:

```
# ps aux | grep smbd
root        929  0.0  1.0  1112   664  ?  S    13:47   0:00
➥/usr/sbin/smbd -D
# ps aux | grep nmbd
root        931  0.0  0.9   976   608  ?  S    13:47   0:00
/usr/sbin/nmbd -D
➥# kill 929 931
```

Accessing Windows Network Files and Printers from Linux Systems

The flip side of this procedure is for Linux to be able to access SMB shared files and printers.

There are several ways in which this can be achieved. The most basic way involves use of two client programs that come with the Samba installation: smbclient and smbprint.

While this approach works, it is somewhat limited, particularly for file access. Smbclient provides an FTP-like way in which to access a remote share. Of course, this doesn't allow use of regular Unix commands such as cp and mv to manipulate files and, thus, prevents access to shares from other applications (unlike NFS-mounted remote file systems, which appear as local file systems to Linux applications).

This problem is effectively addressed using an alternative method: the smbfs package, which allows SMB shared file systems to be mounted on Linux as are NFS file systems and local file systems.

Using *Smbclient*

The smbclient program is normally installed in /usr/bin. The program can be used to move files to and from shared resources on an SMB server using an FTP-like interface.

The first step to using `smbclient` is to establish a connection to a resource on the SMB server. In its simplest form, the command looks like this:

```
$ smbclient \\<server>\<resourcename>
```

Of course, things are rarely that simple. If you need to provide a password, for instance, to access a protected resource, your command gets moderately more complicated:

```
$ smbclient \\<server>\<resourcename> <password>
```

In addition to this, there are several flags that alter the way in which `smbclient` connects to the server. The major flags are outlined in the table below.

TABLE 25.2: Smbclient Flags

Flag	Effect
-L host	This flag displays a list of services available on a server specified by **host**; when using this flag, a resource does not need to be specified.
-I IP Address	This is useful when the address for the named server can't be looked up; it forces `smbclient` to assume the machine is at the specified IP address.
-N	This flag suppresses the password prompt. It is especially useful when a resource doesn't require a password; if this flag is not specified when a password is not required, the user is still prompted for a password and must hit Return to supply a null password.
-P	This flag indicates that the service being connected to it is a printer and should be treated as such; this affects what commands can be used to move data to the resource, as we will see later in this section.
-U <username>	Using this flag, you can specify the username to use to connect to a resource. Without this flag, the server uses the content of the **USER** or **LOGNAME** environment variables; if these are empty, no username is provided to the server. You can send a password along to the server by putting a percent sign (%) after the username and following it by the password: -U **username%password**.
-W <workgroup>	This flag specifies which workgroup is to be used when connecting to the server.
-T <tar options>	This flag allows you to move data into or out of a **tar** file on the local Linux system. For instance, -Tx **backup.tar** restores files from **backup.tar** to the remote share, while -Tc **backup.tar** creates a **tar** file called **backup.tar** that contains all files and directories in the remote share.

By way of example, let's build our own `smbclient` command based on this information:

```
$ smbclient \\server\resourcename -U username%password -W workgroup
```

This command will attempt to connect to `resourcename` on `server` in the workgroup named `workgroup`, with the user `username` using the password `password`.

Available Operations for File Resources

Once connected to a file resource, there are a number of commands available for moving data back and forth. These are outlined in the table below.

TABLE 25.3: File Operations Commands

Operation	Description
`cd <directory>`	Changes to another directory on the SMB shared resource.
`del <file>`	Deletes the specified file on the server (can also use **rm**).
`dir`	Displays the current directory listing from the server (can also use **ls**).
`get <file>`	Gets the specified file from the remote server and saves it with the same name in the current directory on the local system; optionally, you can specify a different name for the file on the local system: `get <file> <localfilename>`.
`lcd <directory>`	Change to the specified directory on the local system.
`mget <filemask>`	Gets all files on the remote server matching the specified filemask.
`mkdir <directory>`	Makes the specified directory on the remote server (can also use **md**).
`mput <filemask>`	Puts all files in the local directory matching the specified filemask into the current directory on the remote server.
`prompt`	Toggles prompting on and off for multiple file operations (**mput** and **mget**). When on, users will be prompted for each file copied.
`put <file>`	Copies the specified file in the current local directory to the current directory on the remote server and keeps the name of the file the same; the name of the file on the remote server can also be changed: `put <file> <remotefilename>`.
`quit`	Exits **smbclient** (can also use **exit**).

Continued on next page

TABLE 25.3 CONTINUED: File Operations Commands

Operation	Description
recurse	Toggles directory recursion on and off for multiple file operations (mput and mget). When on, the commands will search down all directories under the current directory when copying files.
rmdir <directory>	Removes the specified directory from the remote server (can also use rd).

Let's look at some examples:

1. To change the local directory to the subdirectory foo: use lcd foo.

2. To change the remote directory to the directory ../foo: use cd ../foo.

3. To copy the file foo in the local directory to the remote share and give the copy the name newfoo: use put foo newfoo.

4. To get all files ending in .txt from the remote share's current directory: use mget *.txt.

5. To create a new directory on the remote share called foo: use mkdir foo.

Available Operations for Printer Resources

When you use smbclient to connect to a printer resource, the following commands are available for working with the printer:

- print file: Prints the specified file using the current resource based on the mode specified by printmode.

- printmode option: Sets the printer mode based on the specified option; possible options are graphics or text, where graphics indicates any binary data.

- queue: Displays the current status of the remote print queue.

- quit (or exit): Exits smbclient.

Of course, this is a little cumbersome. If someone wants to print a text file, they can't simply print it from the application they used to create it the way they might normally do with a Unix print queue. Instead, they need to connect to the printer with smbclient and then issue the command printmode text followed by print <filename>. Printing more complicated print formats gets even more difficult.

For instance, what if the remote printer is a PCL printer and the software being used only generates PostScript output (as is often the case in the Unix world)? In that case, the user needs to print to a file, pass this file through gs to convert it to PCL, connect the printer with smbclient, set the print mode, and then print the file. This is a lot of work.

Luckily, smbprint helps to solve this problem.

Using *Smbprint*

The smbprint script is a tool that makes it possible to print using smbclient via a standard Unix print queue. Smbprint makes printing to remote SMB printer resources virtually seamless for users.

With some Samba installations, you will find the script at /usr/bin/smbprint. In Red Hat Linux 5, the script is hidden away at /usr/doc/samba-1.9.17p4/examples/printing/smbprint. If you plan to use it, copy it to a convenient location such as /usr/sbin/smbprint.

In order to use the script, it is necessary to create a printcap entry for the remote printer and create a configuration file that indicates where the printer is.

First, the printcap entry:

```
queuename:\
             :sd=/var/spool/samba:\
             :af=/var/spool/samba/accountingfile:\
             :if=/usr/bin/smbprint:\
             :mx=0:\
             :lp=/dev/null:
```

Let's look at the important entries here:

- sd=/var/spool/samba: Specifies the spool directory.

- af=/var/spool/samba/accountingfile: Specifies the accounting file (this file should be in the same directory as the configuration file, probably in your spool directory).

- if=/usr/bin/smbprint: Specifies that the input filter should be smbprint.

- lp=/dev/null: Indicates that the printer is not physically connected to the machine where the printcap file exists.

Next, we need to create a configuration file called `.config` in the same directory as our accounting file. This file contains three entries and looks like this:

```
server=<SERVERNAME>
service=<PRINTERNAME>
password=<"password">
```

Once this is done, most files should be printable using the `lpr` command:

```
$ lpr -P<queuename> <filename>
```

Because this is the way applications such as Netscape Communicator handle printing, this configuration will work for many printers and applications.

Using *Smbfs*

The `smbfs` package allows the direct mounting of SMB shares to Linux in the same way that NFS volumes are mounted by Linux. Usage of `smbfs` is fairly straightforward once it is installed.

Installing *smbfs*

If you are using Red Hat Linux 5, you can install `smbfs` from the CD-ROM. Mount the CD-ROM in a convenient location and then install the file with `rpm`:

```
# rpm -i /mnt/cdrom/RedHat/RPMS/smbfs-2.0.1-2.i386.rpm
```

Failing that, you can download the latest version of `smbfs` from the Linux LAN Web page at `http://samba.SerNet.DE/linux-lan/`. This is a source distribution that can be difficult to install because it may require recompilation of the Linux kernel in order to work. To make things easier, try to find the binary version of `smbfs` that comes with your Linux distribution or is available preconfigured for your distribution.

Using *smbmount*

At the core of the `smbfs` system is the `smbmount` program. The `smbmount` program is the tool you use to mount SMB shares to your Linux system.

At its most basic, `smbmount` takes the form:

```
# smbmount //servername/resourcename mountpoint
```

As with the mount command, the mount point must be an existing directory (which can be, and probably should be, empty) on your system. Forward slashes are used instead of back slashes in the specification of SMB shares to avoid problems using back slashes in some shells.

There is one caveat here: smbmount doesn't use NetBIOS to look up the server name. Therefore, if the SMB server name is different than the TCP/IP host name for the server, things won't work. In this situation, use the Unix host name for the server in question.

The submount command can be followed by several options, the more common of which are outlined in the table below.

TABLE 25.4: Submount Flags

Flag	Explanation
-n	Suppresses the password prompt where none is required.
-P *<password>*	Provides a password where one is required.
-s *<server name>*	If the NetBIOS is different than the Unix host name, use the Unix host name to specify the resource and then provide the NetBIOS name with the -s flag.
-c *<client name>*	If the local client's NetBIOS name and Unix host name are different, specify the NetBIOS name here.
-U <username>	Specifies the username to be used in accessing the SMB resource.
-D *<domain name>*	Specifies the SMB domain to use in accessing the resource.

For example, to mount the resource testdir on the SMB server smbserv to the local directory /smbdir as user user1 using the password testpass, you would use the command:

```
# smbmount //smbserv/testdir /smbdir -U user1 -P testpass
```

Complete documentation for the smbmount command is in the smbmount man page (man smbmount).

Connecting Linux to a Novell Network

The world of NetWare-Linux integration is far less robust than Windows-Linux integration. For that reason, we will only discuss available options without going into the details of implementation.

In the realm of freely available software, a fairly limited Novell NetWare client package called `ncpfs` is available, as is a still-beta NetWare server product called `mars_nwe`. Both of these products are limited as to the versions of NetWare they support and the types of NetWare products they can interact with.

To get a robust NetWare solution, it is necessary to turn to commercial Linux offerings such as Caldera's OpenLinux

Ncpfs and *Mars_nwe*

Together, `ncpfs` and `mars_nwe` provide the closest thing to a complete free Linux NetWare solution. Both are available for download from the Linux LAN Web page at `http://samba.SerNet.DE/linux-lan/`.

Both products are limited, however. For example:

- Both are only NetWare 3.*x* compatible.

- `Ncpfs` is not backward-compatible with NetWare 2.*x* servers.

- `Ncpfs` does not work with some NetWare-compatible servers, such as Windows NT 3.51.

A Solution That Works: Caldera OpenLinux

Caldera (`http://www.caldera.com`) is doing a lot to integrate the Linux and Novell NetWare worlds. Their OpenLinux Standard product includes basic NetWare support, including:

- An NDS-capable NetWare client (which will work with recent versions of the NetWare environment)

- NetWare administration tools with a GUI interface

- The ability to log into multiple NDS trees simultaneously

In mid-1998, they introduced Caldera NetWare, which is helping to turn Linux systems into full NetWare servers. In public beta testing at the time of writing this book, Caldera NetWare for Linux promised:

- File, print, and directory services running on Linux
- NetWare 4.10b compatible file services
- Integration of NetWare print services with the Unix print spool
- An NDS version 611 server

Initial indications are that a version of Caldera NetWare for Linux with a three-user license will be available for free download, with additional licenses being sold by Caldera.

Where Do We Go from Here?

In this chapter, we learned how to integrate Linux into Windows intranets, enabling file sharing between Linux and Windows.

In the next chapter, we will look at an interesting topic: how to use Linux as an inexpensive router. As a robust networking operating system, Linux is ideally suited to act as a router for a small network, connecting it to the Internet through a regular modem or ISDN connection or connecting to another LAN as an inter-LAN router.

Specifically, we will consider the typical example for many small offices: connecting an entire LAN to the Internet on a dial-up connection that provides only one real IP address.

CHAPTER
TWENTY-SIX

Security and Linux as an Inexpensive Router

- Basic Security Issues

- Creating a Linux-Based Router

In this chapter, we address two related topics: security and connecting networks to the Internet.

We will look at Linux security at several levels, first considering how to keep individual Linux systems secured and then discussing the broader issue of keeping a LAN secure when it is connected to the Internet.

Finally, we will take a look at the Linux Router Project, which can allow you to use a single floppy disk containing a special distribution of Linux to create a Linux-based router that can act as a gateway between your network and your existing Internet connection.

Basic Security Issues

The area of computer security is actually a huge one that cannot be addressed adequately in a single chapter of a book. In fact, whole books are devoted to only small areas of computer and network security.

Given the scope of the subject, we will take a look at computer security in general and point out the basic concepts that you can consider applying to your specific circumstances.

Securing a Stand-Alone System

If you have a stand-alone Linux system, your security needs are the most basic. Because the system is not connected to a LAN and, assuming you connect to the Internet through a modem, is not left connected permanently or for long periods of time, your security concerns will be relatively minor.

Still, there are some fundamental security issues that you should address:

- Make sure your passwords are sufficiently complex that they can't be guessed or cracked easily. This includes combining letters and numbers and other characters into non-word passwords. Passwords should also be changed frequently. It is especially important that your root password be a non-word, complex password that is changed regularly.

- Make sure your computer is kept physically secure. If it contains important data, don't leave it in an unlocked office while you go to lunch. Similarly, don't walk out of the office and leave the system logged in, especially if you have logged in as `root` at the console or in a terminal window.

- Do not create unnecessary user accounts. If only two people will be using the machine on a regular basis, create accounts only for those users and not for anyone else. This makes it easier to keep track of who is using the system and where any security violations originate.

- Most important of all, do not share passwords (user or root), even with people who are authorized to use the system on a regular basis. Especially keep the root password secure. All it takes is the wrong user obtaining the root password and you could find all the data on your system erased one day.

- Because no system can be completely secure, consider encrypting important data. Many tools exist for doing this, including PGP encryption. A step-by-step guide to PGP encryption can be found on the Internet at the Linux Focus Web site at `http://mercury.chem.pitt.edu/~angel/LinuxFocus/ English/November1997/article7.html`.

Securing a Linux System on a LAN

The instant you connect your Linux system to a LAN, new security issues appear. After all, even if you follow all the rules outlined above for a stand-alone system (which you should also follow when the system is on a LAN), it is still possible for the intent hacker to gain access to your Linux system by exploiting any number of security weaknesses via the network.

Several simple policies can help minimize this problem:

- Do not run unnecessary network services. If you do not need to allow telnetting into your system, make sure the telnet daemon (probably `/usr/sbin/ in.telnetd`) is not installed and there is no entry for the daemon in `/etc/ inetd.conf`. Similarly, if your machine does not act as a mail server, consider not running the `sendmail` daemon, which can open up several unwanted security holes. The same rules go for most network services: FTP, finger, news, DNS, and many others. Only run those network service daemons that you require to connect to the network and perform the tasks that you are using your Linux system for.

- Make effective use of `/etc/hosts.allow` and `/etc/hosts.deny`, which are discussed in Chapter 24, "Configuring Linux for an Ethernet Network." Not only should you deny access from all IP addresses to all the services you chose not to run in the previous point, but you should be sure you are only allowing incoming access to services you are running to hosts with permission to use those services. For instance, if you are running an FTP server to allow incoming FTP access by only two users, allow just those two systems access to the FTP service instead of allowing any user on your LAN to make an FTP connection.

Keeping Your Network Secure

Even if you keep your Linux system fairly secure on your LAN, if your LAN is connected to the Internet, the rest of your network is open to a wide range of possible security threats and attacks.

Keeping a network secure is a large job and requires detailed knowledge of network security. Fundamentally, though, there are two main techniques (and many variations on them) for ensuring at least minimal network security.

Remember that your network will be connected to the Internet through some type of router that has the job of moving data on and off the LAN as appropriate. Generally, a router can provide some level of security to ensure that the most malicious attacks cannot infiltrate your LAN.

Router-level protection is usually provided in one of two ways:

Using a packet-filtering firewall: Packet filtering is a process that every router is capable of performing. Whenever a packet of information from the Internet is received by the router and is destined for a system on the LAN, the originating IP address, destination IP address, and port of the connection are examined and compared to a table to determine whether the packet is allowed into the LAN. If the packet is not allowed, it essentially vanishes into the ether. In this way, connections from specific hosts, to specific hosts, or for specific ports (or any combination of these) can be allowed or denied.

Using a proxy firewall: A proxy firewall is a different approach because it prevents direct connections between the machines inside the firewall and those on the Internet. If a host on your LAN makes a connection to a host on the Internet, it actually connects to the proxy system and then the proxy system makes the actual connection to the system on the Internet, serving as the relay for all data traveling back and forth. Similarly, if you allow any incoming connections to your LAN, the proxy plays the same role of middleman. In addition to keeping the LAN and the Internet totally separate, the proxy firewall has capabilities similar to a packet-filtering firewall. It can be configured to allow only certain types of traffic through the firewall in either direction, or to deny connections on the basis of several variables, including originating IP address, destination IP address, and port being used.

To really understand the fundamentals of network security, you should read the Linux Security HOWTO at `http://sunsite.unc.edu/LDP/HOWTO/Security-HOWTO.html`.

A Linux system can easily be configured to act as a router between your LAN and the Internet, providing connections over standard analog phone modems or ISDN lines. This router can also be configured to act as a packet-filtering or proxy firewall as well. Setting up a Linux-based router generally costs less than buying complete hardware router solutions and offers more security options than do many hardware-based routers.

Creating a Linux-Based Router

In this section, we will walk through the basic steps for creating a Linux-based router using the Linux Router Project's distribution of Linux.

Designed as a minimalist Linux installation, the Linux Router Project's distribution of Linux can fit on a single 1.44MB floppy disk for most sites and provides all the components needed to route between two Ethernet LANs or between an Ethernet LAN and the Internet via PPP. With add-on modules, support is available for additional hardware for WAN connections as well as other features such as SNMP management.

The benefit of setting up a router using the Linux Router Project's Linux distribution instead of full-scale versions of Linux such as Red Hat is that all the hard work has been done for you. You won't need to make the effort to identify what needs to be installed to get routing to work. In addition, the software includes a simple, menu-driven configuration system that allows you to check that everything that needs configuration is done.

The Linux Router Project software is included with the CD-ROM accompanying this book. For complete information, updates, and add-ons for the router distribution, visit the Linux Documentation Project Web site at `http://www.linuxrouter.org/`.

What We Will Create

We will use the Linux Router Project software to create a router that serves as a firewall, protecting the private areas of your LAN from the Internet. First, we will make two assumptions:

- You have an existing Internet connection, most likely through a leased line and an existing router or through an ISDN connection and an ISDN router.

- You want to allow some incoming access to servers on your network. For instance, you may have a Web server that the public should be able to access, but you don't want any incoming access to the sensitive file, application, and database servers on the rest of your network.

Given these assumptions, your network arrangement will resemble Figure 26.1.

FIGURE 26.1:

A typical firewall-protected network

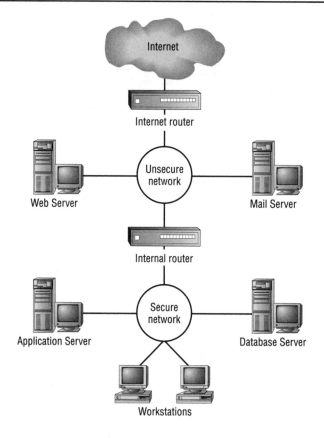

Notice that the router connecting you to the outside world provides looser protection than does the router between your unsecure and secure networks. This means that, at the worst, only the systems sitting on your unsecure network are directly open to possible attacks from outside. Because your second router, between the unsecure and secure LANs, does not allow incoming connections into the secure network, your systems are—as far as this is possible in a networked environment—safe from outside attack.

It is this second router, between the unsecure and secure LANs, that we will implement using the Linux Router Project software.

Getting Ready

There isn't room on the CD-ROM that comes with this book to include a floppy disk image for the Linux Router Project. Instead, an image designed to work as a dual-Ethernet router can be found on the Web page for this book at `http://linux.juxta.com/`.

To prepare the Linux Router Project floppy disk, you will need a blank floppy disk. (Any data on the floppy disk will be erased, so be sure there is nothing there that you want to keep). The following instructions assume you are creating the disk from within an existing Linux system.

- Step 1: Download the Linux image file and save it in a convenient location, for instance `/tmp/disk.img`.

- Step 2: Change your current directory to the directory containing the downloaded file with a command such as `cd/tmp`.

- Step 3: Copy the disk image file to your floppy disk using a `cat` command like this: `cat disk.img > /dev/fd0`.

Once this is done, you will have a boot floppy disk for the Linux Router Project distribution.

You will want to be sure you have sufficient hardware to run the router. While a 386SX with 8MB of RAM can function as a router and a 486DX2 66MHz with 12MB of RAM will be respectable, these days you really want to run a Pentium 100MHz or faster system with at least 16MB of RAM. No hard drive is needed, just a floppy drive to boot from. If you want to add many add-ons to your Linux Router Project configuration, then the software may exceed the size of your floppy disk, in which case you should consider booting from a hard disk or a bootable Zip drive and increasing your RAM to 32MB. Details of how to boot from other media can be found on the Linux Router Project home page.

The PC needs to have two Ethernet cards. One will be used to connect to the unsecure network and the other will connect to the secure network.

The Operating Environment

Before starting the Linux router software, let's define the environment in which the router will run so that all the configuration we perform later will make sense.

First, we need to determine IP addresses. Our unsecure network will use the addresses 200.200.200.0 through 200.200.200.255 with the netmask 255.255.255.0. The router connecting the network to the outside world is at 200.200.200.1 and the router we will build has the IP address 200.200.200.254 on the unsecure side of the router. These are genuine IP addresses in that the rest of the Internet knows they exist and they are unique on the Internet. If our router to the external world allows it, machines on the Internet can communicate directly with any host on the unsecure LAN.

Our secure network will use the addresses 10.10.10.0 through 10.10.10.255 with the netmask 255.255.255.0. The router connecting the secure and unsecure LANs will use the IP address 10.10.10.1 on the secure side of the router. These are fake, or non-routable, IP addresses. The rest of the world doesn't know about the existence of hosts on the internal network, and no direct communication is possible with hosts on the internal network: our router, in its firewall role, hides the existence of the secure network from the rest of the world (including our unsecure network).

In the router we are building, the device eth0 will be connected to the unsecure LAN (with IP address 200.200.200.254) and the device eth1 will be connected to the secure LAN (with the IP address 10.10.10.1).

We will allow only outgoing connections from the secure LAN—no incoming connections. What's more, we will use a feature of the Linux kernel known as IP masquerading in order to implement a security feature known as network address translation. Under network address translation, the router not only handles the work of routing data into and out of the secure LAN but, when a machine inside the secure LAN makes a connection through the router, also hides the IP address of that machine and translates it into an address on the unsecure LAN. In this way, the connection cannot be traced back to the real IP address of the host, thus helping to hide the existence of hosts on the secure network from the rest of the world.

Because the secure network uses non-routable IP addresses, the hosts on our unsecure network do not know about the existence of hosts on that network and cannot attempt to communicate with them. Similarly, the router connecting the unsecure network to the Internet doesn't know about the existence of the internal, secure network and so will never route packets directly to hosts on the internal network.

Starting the Linux Router

To boot your computer as a Linux-based router, simply insert the floppy disk and restart your computer. Your computer should boot from the floppy disk.

The Linux Router Project software will then create a RAM disk and load the contents of the boot disk into the RAM disk. Then the entire router will run from RAM. Any configuration changes you make can be saved back to the boot disk so that the next time you boot, your configuration is retained.

After you boot, you will be prompted to log in. Log in as root with no password and the Linux router software will start, presenting you with a configuration menu. We will walk through the following steps to get a minimal network running as described above:

1. Basic settings: configuration of the IP addresses, network masks, and routes of the two Ethernet cards

2. Basic security: configuration of the network security needed to implement network address translation

3. Further configuration: configuration of additional network parameters, such as nameservers and host tables

The menus are entirely numeric and are accessed by typing the number of a selection and hitting Return. For instance, typing **1** for Network Settings on the main configuration menu causes the network settings submenu to be displayed. Selecting an entry on a submenu will open the file for editing (for configuration purposes) in a simple editor. To use the editor effectively, you really only need to know how to save (type **Ctrl+W** and then hit Return to confirm the filename) and quit (type **Ctrl+C**). You can use the editor to do more than this, but we are only going to perform basic editing tasks here.

Configuring Basic Network Settings

The first thing to do is configure our basic network settings: tell our router who we are, which interface is connected to which network, and so on.

To do this, we need to edit the main network settings file, which is option 1 on the network settings submenu (accessed by selecting option 1 on the main configuration menu). The main network settings file will open in the editor.

First, we need to assign IP addresses and network masks to our Ethernet cards. Find the lines

```
#IF0=eth0
IPADDR0=192.168.1.1;          NETMASK0=255.255.255.0
BROADCAST0=192.168.1.255      NETWORK0=192.168.1.0
```

Change them to the correct settings for eth0 and activate the interface by removing the # from the first line:

```
IF0=eth0
IPADDR0=200.200.200.254;      NETMASK0=255.255.255.0
BROADCAST0=200.200.200.255    NETWORK0=200.200.200.0
```

Next, find the lines

```
#IF0=eth1
IPADDR0=192.168.2.1;          NETMASK0=255.255.255.0
BROADCAST0=192.168.2.255      NETWORK0=192.168.2.0
```

and likewise change them to the correct settings for eth1 (our internal, secure network) and remove the hash mark:

```
IF0=eth1
IPADDR0=10.10.10.1;           NETMASK0=255.255.255.0
BROADCAST0=10.10.10.255       NETWORK0=10.10.10.0
```

These steps configure the respective Ethernet cards in the router to communicate with their assigned networks. (Make sure the Ethernet cards are physically connected to the correct networks.)

Other sections of the configuration file set up default routes without requiring additional configuration.

Setting Up Basic Security

Basic security setup takes place in the same file as basic network setup, so for this reason we haven't saved the file yet.

First, an overview of the default setting: The router is configured by default to deny all traffic across the router. In addition, IP spoofing—where an external host pretends to be a host on the secure network by feigning the same IP addresses—is monitored and prevented.

What we need to do is use network address translation to explicitly allow outgoing traffic from the secure network. To do this, find the section of the file called IP Masquerade (aka NAT) and uncomment the first entry:

```
#[ "IF$" ] && ipfwadm -F -a -m -S "$NETWORK1"/24 -D 0.0.0.0/0
```

Without going into the syntax of ipfwadm (which you can find at http://kac .poliod.hu/cgi-bin/dwww?type=man&location=/usr/man/man8/ipfwadm .8.gz), we can note that this command does the following:

- Enables IP forwarding for outgoing connections from the secure network to the outside world

- Enables IP masquerading so that the source address of all outbound connections is the external IP address of the router, rather than the original host address on the secure network

- Handles all return connections to make sure data in response to an outgoing connection is returned to the correct host

Now we can save the file (**Ctrl+W**) and quit the editor (**Ctrl+C**).

Further Network Configuration

There are other network settings that you would be wise to configure. They include:

- Giving the router a host name (number 2 on the network settings submenu)

- Providing a host table (number 3 on the network settings submenu)

- Providing a correct resolv.conf file (number 6 on the network settings submenu)

Configuration of these settings should be straightforward on the basis of what you learned in Chapter 24, "Configuring Linux for an Ethernet Network."

A final note: The `hosts.allow` and `hosts.deny` files are designed to protect the router itself from unwanted attack by denying attempts to log in to the router remotely across the network. In other words, the router needs to be configured at the console rather than through a network login. It is probably wise to leave these files unchanged.

Saving Your Changes

Once you have configured the router, it is necessary to save your changes back to the boot floppy. You can do this by choosing b from the main configuration menu. You are backing up the `etc` module because you have changed files in the `/etc` directory only. You can do this by selecting 2 from the backup menu.

After writing the changes back to the boot floppy, you are ready to reboot your system to enable your new configuration. Now you should have a functioning router serving as a basic firewall.

Going Further

Using these basic principles, it is possible to work with the Linux Router Project distribution to implement (among other things) more advanced routers that support ISDN connections, dial-up PPP users, and leased-line Internet connections. These all require additional combinations of modules and system-specific configuration. More information is available on the Linux Router Project Web site at `http://www.linuxrouter.org`.

Where Do We Go from Here?

In this chapter, we saw how flexible Linux is, allowing us to turn a PC into not just a powerful workstation or network server, but also a router and a security firewall.

In the next chapter, we continue our look at Linux in a networked environment with a detailed discussion of how to use Linux as an intranet Web server. Linux is an increasingly popular platform for Internet and intranet Web servers because of the availability of high-performance, industry-standard Web server software that can be run on inexpensive hardware.

In fact, the reliability and speed of Linux Web servers makes them popular in many circumstances where high-cost, commercial Web server solutions could have been used.

If you don't have a background in Web development or design, the chapter still provides the basic knowledge you need to begin setting up your own Web server in your organization.

CHAPTER

TWENTY-SEVEN

Building Your Own Web Server

- What is a Web Server?

- Linux Web Servers

- Installing Apache

- Configuring Apache

- Managing Your Web Server

- Building a Web Site

We've come a long way in our study of Linux and are ready to look at one of the most popular applications of Linux: using the operating system as the basis for small and medium-sized Web servers.

In fact, Linux is widely used for deploying Web servers for a number of reasons: it provides the flexibility and manageability of Unix, it costs little or nothing to set up and run, and it provides a strong breadth of tools for building fairly sophisticated Web sites.

In this chapter, we will cover the basics of turning a Linux PC into a Web server for an intranet or Internet site. We will start with an overview of the job played by a Web server and then examine some of the major Web servers available for Linux.

We will then take a detailed look at installing, configuring, and managing the Apache Web server, arguably the most popular Web server on the Internet and the one that currently ships with Red Hat Linux 5.

We will close by taking a guided tour through building a simple Web site using Apache. By the end of the chapter, you should be in a position to create your own Web site using Linux and Apache and feel confident enough to experiment with other Web servers available for Linux.

What Is a Web Server?

If you have used the Web at all, you have probably heard the term "Web server" bandied about but may not have a clear picture of what a Web server does.

While it is often the case that the term serves a dual purpose—referring to physical machines as well as the software they run—"Web server" correctly refers to the software that can be run to answer requests from Web clients such as Web browsers.

Web server software is designed to serve a simple purpose: to answer requests from clients, using the Hypertext Transfer Protocol (HTTP), for documents available from the Web site being handled by the software.

What happens is this: The client requests a document using a URL; the Web server receives the request, maps the URL to a physical file on the system (which could be an HTML file or any one of numerous other file types), and then, after making sure that the client has permission to retrieve the file, returns the file to the client. In addition, the Web server will generally keep logs of who has requested what documents and how many times requests were made, which allows the production of statistics used to determine how popular Web sites are.

More Than Just Retrieving Files

The description above is overly simplistic, but that explanation serves to describe the work done by the majority of Web servers most of the time.

Of course, as you browse the Web you quickly become aware that the Web is more than simply a set of static documents that a Web server sends to Web browsers on request. Forms can be used to request information from the server or provide information to the organization running the server. Products can be ordered, credit cards can be verified, and many other types of transactions can take place.

In order for all this interactivity to occur, modern Web servers must do more than simply answer HTTP requests. Web servers generally provide two mechanisms for interactions:

- The Common Gateway Interface (CGI)
- Server Application Program Interfaces (APIs)

The Common Gateway Interface

CGI is the most widely deployed method for adding interactivity to a Web server. Under the CGI model, a very simple extension is added to the HTTP protocol for requesting static files.

CGI provides a standardized method for causing a program to be run on the server and for data from a form to be passed to the program for processing. These programs can be written in almost any programming or scripting language—C, Perl, and Java are commonly used.

When a user requests a CGI program—possibly by submitting a form or by clicking a link to the program—the Web server passes the user's data to the CGI program and waits for the program to return data. Any data returned by the program is passed straight back to the client in the same way that the contents of a static file are returned to a browser. It is the program's job to produce valid content to be returned to the browser and to handle all contingencies so that valid content is returned to the client.

Overall, the CGI concept has worked quite well. The simplicity of the way data is passed from the server to the CGI program, and the way in which the program needs to build the data it returns to the server, means that simple CGI programs can be written with little programming experience.

In addition, it is easy to change and test CGI programs, since popular scripting languages such as Perl can be used to write them.

The standard nature of the CGI interface also means that a CGI script or program written for one Linux Web server will likely function without alteration on any other Linux Web server—and possibly on any other Unix server, if it is written using a language commonly found in all operating systems.

Still, for all its advantages, CGI suffers from some serious drawbacks that make it unattractive for some Web sites. Its two main weaknesses pertain to security and speed.

Since the emergence of the Web, significant security holes in the CGI interface have been discovered that, if a script is poorly written, can allow a system running a Web server to be completely accessible to a knowledgeable hacker. This makes CGI less than desirable where the security of the data on the Web server is paramount, as it would be on most corporate Internet and intranet servers—and especially on sites offering online financial transactions and credit card sales.

In addition, the CGI interface is not very efficient. The Web server runs one or more processes that answer client requests. The browser then starts child processes for the CGI program, passing data to this new process and waiting for it to finish. On a busy site, this can lead to large numbers of new processes needing to start in short periods of time, especially where CGI scripts are being heavily used. Each request for a CGI program will lead to a separate process for each request.

This is a highly inefficient way to process large amounts of data and requests, and the reason why many leading Web servers have implemented their own APIs for writing server-side programs.

Application Program Interfaces

APIs provide a way to write programs that integrate tightly into the Web server and generally don't require new processes for each request.

API has enabled the development of Web-based applications that are capable of handling large numbers of requests as compared to similar CGI-based solutions. In addition, API-based solutions have been the subject of less criticism with regard to security.

API-based programs can generally do the same jobs as CGI programs do, such as processing information provided in forms, accessing data in databases, and verifying credit cards.

The biggest disadvantage of server APIs is that they commit an application to a particular Web server. Moving an application to a new server can require significant reprogramming, and with a large application this can be impractical.

Just remember that a server needs to be well-tested as to security, performance, and flexibility before you deploy a large application on it using the server's built-in API.

Linux Web Servers

The Unix world is where the Web emerged, so it isn't surprising that Unix platforms enjoy the broadest choice of available Web servers.

As with most things in the Unix world, this same range of Web servers is available for Linux. The majority of Linux Web servers are free. The most well-known are:

- NCSA httpd
- Apache
- AOLserver
- Boa
- WN
- W3C/Cern

In addition to these free servers, there are an increasing number of commercial alternatives available for Linux, including:

- FastTrack
- Java Web Server
- Stronghold
- Zeus

Apache

By some counts, Apache is the most widely used Web server software. Standing for "A Patchy Server," Apache grew out of efforts to patch NCSA httpd, one of the original Web servers, to fix some problems and add functionality.

Since then, Apache has emerged as the non-commercial server of choice for Unix systems. More recently, it has been ported to Windows and can be used as a Web server on Windows NT systems.

Apache offers numerous features that make it attractive for Unix system administrators. Besides using a configuration based on the original NCSA httpd configuration files, Apache is available in full source code and is collectively developed, like many other popular applications for the Linux environment.

Apache offers its own API, which can be used as an alternative to CGI (which is also supported by Apache). In addition, the API can be used to produce plug-in modules that serve numerous purposes. Among available modules are:

- Alternative authentication systems, including authentication from NIS authentication servers or from LDAP (Lightweight Directory Access Protocol) databases

- Server-side scripting environments that serve the same function as Microsoft Active Server Pages or Netscape LiveWire, including PHP/FI and HeiTML

- Modules designed to improve the performance of traditional CGI. For instance, the FastCGI module uses shortcuts to minimize the time it takes to execute a CGI program and return the results. The Perl module allows Perl scripts to run in a single process and to be compiled on first execution only, making Perl-based CGI perform almost as fast as compiled CGI programs and some API-based Web applications.

The original source code for the latest version of Apache is available from www.apache.org, along with precompiled binaries for many different systems including Linux. Apache is included as the default Web browser installed with Red Hat Linux.

NCSA Httpd

NCSA httpd is one of the two original Web servers (along with the Cern Web server) upon which the Web was first built. NCSA httpd comes out of the National Center for Supercomputer Applications at the University of Illinois at

Urbana-Champaign, which is also the home of Mosaic, the original graphical Web browser that launched the Web onto the road to widespread popularity.

NCSA httpd offers a core set of functions designed to meet the needs of all but the most demanding of Web sites. These features include built-in support for multiple hosts, Basic and Digest authentication, directory-level access controls, server-side includes, and full CGI support.

The original source code and precompiled binaries are available from hoohoo .ncsa.uiuc.edu.

AOLserver

AOLserver has an interesting history, moving from a commercial offering in 1995 to one of the most full-featured free servers currently available.

AOLserver started its life as NaviPress, one of the first commercial servers available. In late 1995, AOL acquired the company producing NaviPress and began to use the server internally. In early 1997, AOL released the server as a free product for distribution on the Internet.

At the time of this writing, the latest release (2.2) of AOLserver included the following features:

- Built-in full-text indexing for offering a search function on a Web site

- A built-in API that is accessible from C and the Tcl scripting language

- Full CGI and server-side include support

- Server-side dynamic page functionality similar to Microsoft's Active Server Pages

- Database connectivity for building database-driven dynamic applications without needing third-party Web-database integration tools

AOLserver can be downloaded from the AOLserver Web site at www.aolserver .com/server/index.html.

W3C/Cern

The Cern Web server was one of the first Web servers to be created. After all, the Web was born at Cern, and the Cern server was the platform for this fledgling Web.

Now the server is distributed as a public-domain server by the World Wide Web Consortium (W3C), the Internet standards body that defines such standards as HTML and cascading style sheets.

In terms of overall features, the Cern server doesn't have a lot in it to recommend it against today's crop of servers. Many of today's free servers are derived from the NCSA server and follow its style of configuration and management. Cern is decidedly different from these, and many Webmasters prefer the NCSA approach.

Probably the most compelling feature of the W3C server is that it can perform the role of both a Web server and a proxy server, allowing users behind a firewall to access the Internet. The server continues to be used as a proxy by many sites.

The W3C maintains a page about the server at `www.w3.org/Daemon`.

WN

Our survey of free servers is now moving down toward less commonly used servers. Still, these niche market servers help us to see the diversity possible in Web server technology and features.

WN is another freely available server with unique features that set it apart from other Web servers.

For instance, WN allows full text searching of what the developer refers to as a logical HTML document: a document that consists of more than one file. In addition, users can search files on the server and easily obtain matching documents. Users can also download a single logical document made up of multiple linked documents, making it easy for them to print files that are structured as a series of small documents.

Another unique feature of the WN server is its ability to serve up conditional documents. That is, it is possible to create a single document with definitions that cause the correct version to be sent to a client on the basis of such variables as the IP address of the client or the browser version of the client.

The security model of the WN server also sets it apart from the likes of Apache and the NCSA Web server. In the latter servers, the default action is to serve a file unless permission is specifically denied. With WN, no file is served unless permission is specifically granted for the file. This potentially makes the server more secure and provides finer-grained control over access to files.

You can get a copy of WN at `hupf.math.nwu.edu/docs/manual.html`.

Boa

The last free server in our survey is the Boa server. This is a little-known server that is still in a pre-1.0 release as of the writing of this book.

Boa is included here to show that servers can be small, simple, and basic and still serve a useful role. Boa offers very basic functionality and less fine-grained access control than Apache or WN.

But Boa is designed in a way that makes it potentially faster than almost any other available Web server for Linux. In fact, the creators of Boa claim that the server is twice as fast as Apache, although more real-world testing on large Web sites is needed to prove the claim.

Boa achieves this performance gain through a single-tasking design. Where traditional Web servers create multiple processes to listen for requests, and then create a process to handle each request, the Boa server runs as a single process and handles all the processing and juggling of multiple requests internally rather than allowing the operating system's multitasking mechanism. Boa only spawns a child process when a CGI request is made.

You can learn more about Boa at `www.boa.org`.

Stronghold

Stronghold may well be the best-known commercial Web server for Linux. Stronghold is a commercially available version of Apache that offers full support as well as a feature lacking in the free version of the server: SSL support.

SSL support, or support for the Secure Sockets Layer, is necessary for creating the secure browser-server links used in online shopping applications, or anywhere where data moving from client to server and back needs to be encrypted and hidden from prying eyes.

Stronghold provides all the tools you need to set up a secure server, including Certificate Authority tools. With a Certificate Authority you can, if necessary, issue digital certificates approved by third-party certificate authorities such as VeriSign.

In addition, since Stronghold comes with full source code, you can use it for everything you use Apache for, including compiling in Apache modules and writing your own modules.

Stronghold is distributed by C2 Software, which is on the Web at `www.int.c2.nt`.

FastTrack

FastTrack is one of Netscape's well-known family of Web servers. Unfortunately, until its recent decision to release its browser and browser source code into the public domain, Netscape never had any interest in developing Web servers for noncommercial operating systems such as Linux.

Instead, for less popular operating systems, Netscape would license their servers to other companies, which would port the server. In the case of Linux, the FastTrack server has been ported by Caldera, which sells the server and bundles it with some versions of their OpenLinux product.

FastTrack is an easy-to-manage Web server. All configuration and administration is done through Web-based forms. These forms allow a Webmaster to do everything from creating users to controlling access to files at the directory level.

FastTrack provides support for server-side includes, CGI, and Netscape's own API for developing applications. In addition, FastTrack can support Netscape's server-side JavaScript development environment, LiveWire.

The server is also capable of being used as a secure server using SSL technology.

If you want to learn more about the Linux version of FastTrack or want to place an order, contact Caldera at www.caldera.com (see Figure 27.1).

FIGURE 27.1:

Information about the FastTrack server for Linux is available from the Caldera Web site

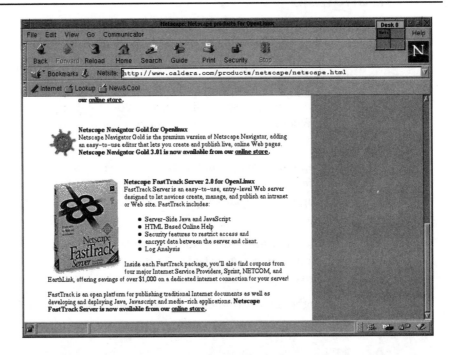

Java Web Server

The Java Web Server from Sun's JavaSoft division is a unique Web server on this list. Instead being developed specifically for Linux, the Java Web Server is developed fully in Java and can theoretically run on any platform with a Java Virtual Machine.

The Java Web Server offers numerous features that make it a competitive commercial offering, including a server applet framework for writing applications without falling back on CGI and full support for SSL so that the server can be used in secure applications such as online storefronts.

To help improve performance, it is possible to produce compiled pages that contain both HTML and program code. For statistical purposes, user sessions can be tracked in programs using a built-in server tracking mechanism.

You can read the complete specifications of the Java Web Server at the JavaSoft home page at `www.javasoft.com`.

Zeus

The final Web server we are covering in this survey is the Zeus Web server.

Zeus is a Web server for Unix and Windows NT. It offers built-in clustering support, which clearly positions it as a potential choice for high-volume sites. With clustering, it is possible to serve a single Web address from multiple Web servers. This allows the load of requests to be distributed over a group of servers and means that more simultaneous hits can be handled.

In addition, Zeus offers support for ISAPI, the API from Microsoft's Internet Information Server, and offers this support on Unix as well as Windows NT. Zeus also supports Java servlets like those used in the Java Web Server, and offers integrated database connectivity using the JDBC standard for accessing databases.

Perhaps most interesting is that Zeus offers SSL with full 128-bit encryption worldwide. Because the U.S. government limits the export of 128-bit encryption technology, the majority of secure products being exported by U.S. companies have offered only watered-down 40-bit encryption. Most reported occurrences of people cracking the encryption of products such as Netscape have involved the 40-bit-encryption versions of products.

Zeus information is available at `www.zeus.co.uk`.

Installing Apache

In the rest of this chapter, we will take a detailed look at the Apache Web server. We do this for two reasons: the Apache server is the default Web server that ships with Red Hat Linux (including Red Hat 5 on the CD-ROM accompanying this book) and, since Apache is the most popular Web server currently on the Internet, it is most likely to be the Web server you will want to use.

If you performed a reasonably complete installation when you set up your Linux system, in all likelihood you already have Apache installed. There are several ways you can check this. You can use `rpm`:

```
$ rpm -qa | grep apache
```

If you have Apache installed, you should get back a result like:

```
apache-1.2.4-4.i386.rpm
```

If you get back an indication that Apache is installed, you can skip forward to the section titled "Configuring Apache."

Installing Apache from the Red Hat CD-ROM

The simplest way to install Apache is from the Red Hat CD-ROM that came with this book. In order to do this, simply mount the CD-ROM (normally at `/mnt/cdrom`) and then `cd` to the directory `/mnt/cdrom/RedHat/RPMS`. (If you mounted your CD-ROM somewhere other than `/mnt/cdrom`, you will need to change to the appropriate directory based on your mount point.) This directory contains all the rpm files for the complete Red Hat Linux distribution. Here you simply use `rpm` to install the package:

```
$ rpm -i apache-1.2.5-1.i386.rpm
```

Alternately, you can use the Package Management module of the Control Panel, as discussed in Chapter 12, "Configuring Your System with the Control Panel" (see Figure 27.2). You will find the Apache package under the `Networking/Daemons` section.

FIGURE 27.2:

FIGURE 27.2:

You can install Apache from the Package Management Control Panel module

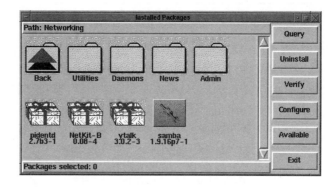

Downloading the Latest Version of Apache

If you plan to run a mission-critical or high-volume Web server, you may want to download the latest version of Apache from www.apache.org (see Figure 27.3). By using the latest version, you can be sure that small bugs that wouldn't affect the average site won't come to plague your more complex or heavily used site.

FIGURE 27.3:

The Apache Web site

All discussion of configuration and management of Apache assumes you are using the version of Apache on the Red Hat CD-ROM included with this book. Generally, new versions of Apache are backward-compatible. That is, the configuration files we look at in this chapter should work with newer versions of Apache.

When downloading Apache from the Apache Web site, you will have the option of downloading the original source code or precompiled binary files for Linux. While there are compelling reasons to use the source code version, especially if you plan to develop programs using the Apache API or you want to build extra modules into your server, you should download the precompiled binaries to set up a Web site with the basic Apache feature set. In this book, we won't discuss compiling your own copy of Apache, since this requires a much deeper discussion of Web servers than can be provided in a single chapter.

If you want to obtain the latest binary distribution from Apache, point your browser at the Apache Web site (`www.apache.org`) and select the "Download" link there. This will lead to a directory of files and a link called "binaries." After following the binaries link, select your operating system (in our case, linux_2.x). Here you will find a list of available files. At the time of writing, this list was:

```
apache-1.2.4-i486-whatever.README
apache-1.2.4-i486-whatever.tar.Z
apache-1.2.4-i486-whatever.tar.gz
apache-1.2.4-i586-whatever.README
apache-1.2.4-i586-whatever.tar.Z
apache-1.2.4-i586-whatever.tar.gz
```

From these filenames, you will notice that the current version is Apache 1.2.4. The i486 and i586 designations indicate that the package has been compiled with optimizations for either 486 processors or Pentium-class processors.

The README files are text files; it is a good idea to read them before downloading. The files with the .Z extension are compressed files using the Unix `compress` utility. The .gz files are compressed using the `gzip` utility. Since Red Hat Linux (and almost all current distributions of Linux) supports the `gzip` format, it is best to download the .gz file for your system since these files are smaller than .Z files.

Once you have your chosen package downloaded, you will want to expand the file in a temporary location. You can use the command

```
$ tar xzvf apache-file-name
```

to expand the archive into a subdirectory of the current directory. In this case, the subdirectory is called `apache-1.2.4`, but this may be different depending on the version of Apache that is available when you download the binaries. Inside this directory is the complete source code for the version you have downloaded, along with sample configuration files and full documentation in HTML format.

In order to install the binaries you have downloaded, you will need to change directories to the `src` subdirectory. There you will find the compiled binary file for the server. The name of the file will look something like `httpd-i586-whatever-linux2`, which is the file in the Pentium version of Apache 1.2.4. You will want to copy this file to a useful location on your system such as `/usr/sbin/httpd`, which is the common place for the `httpd` binary on most systems.

Once you have the binary file in place, you will want to copy the `conf` subdirectory to a logical location on your system. You may want to follow the Red Hat default of using `/etc/httpd/conf` for the Apache configuration subdirectory.

Finally, you may want the tools in the `support` subdirectory. Here you will find tools that can be used in Apache's access control system to create users. These tools are not provided in binary format and you will need to compile them by changing your current directory to the `support` subdirectory and issuing the command `make`. This will create a variety of tools in the directory, including `htpasswd`, `dbmanage`, and `htdigest`. You will want to copy these utilities to your preferred directory for these types of binaries, such as `/usr/sbin/` or `/usr/local/bin/`. We will see how to use some of these tools later in this chapter when we discuss managing your Apache server.

The binary Apache distributions include complete instructions for compiling the application from the included source code, so if you find that the binaries you have downloaded are not working as expected (perhaps because of problems such as incompatible libraries in your version of Linux), you may want to follow those instructions and try building your own Apache binaries.

Configuring Apache

Apache is configured using three main configuration files: `httpd.conf`, `srm.conf`, and `access.conf`. In the standard Red Hat installation of Apache, these files are found at `/etc/httpd/conf/`, although this location can easily be changed (as we will see later when we discuss starting the Apache Web server).

The roles of these three configuration files are not very clearly defined and there is some overlap, but essentially they are used as follows:

- httpd.conf: This file is used to set general settings such as the port number used by the server. This file also indicates where to find the srm.conf and access.conf files.

- srm.conf: This file sets other general settings such as the root document tree of the server and the rules related to CGI programs.

- access.conf: This file can be used to set access control restrictions for the server or for specific directories.

We will now discuss the handful of major settings that any Webmaster should consider before running Apache on an open Web server.

Httpd.conf

The structure of the httpd.conf file is fairly straightforward. Below is a listing from a sample Web site:

```
# This is the main server configuration file. See URL http://www.apache.org/
# for instructions.

# Do NOT simply read the instructions in here without understanding
# what they do, if you are unsure consult the online docs. You have been
# warned.

# Originally by Rob McCool
# Revised by Arman Danesh for linux.juxta.com

# ServerType is either inetd, or standalone.
ServerType standalone

# If you are running from inetd, go to "ServerAdmin".
# Port: The port the standalone listens to. For ports < 1023, you will
# need httpd to be run as root initially.
Port 80

# HostnameLookups: Log the names of clients or just their IP numbers
#    e.g.   www.apache.org (on) or 204.62.129.132 (off)
HostnameLookups on
```

```
# If you wish httpd to run as a different user or group, you must run
# httpd as root initially and it will switch.

# User/Group: The name (or #number) of the user/group to run httpd as.
#  On SCO (ODT 3) use User nouser and Group nogroup
User nobody
Group nobody

# ServerAdmin: Your address, where problems with the server should be
# e-mailed.
ServerAdmin user1@juxta.com

# ServerRoot: The directory the server's config, error, and log files
# are kept in
ServerRoot /etc/httpd

# BindAddress: You can support virtual hosts with this option. This option
# is used to tell the server which IP address to listen to. It can either
# contain "*", an IP address, or a fully qualified Internet domain name.
# See also the VirtualHost directive.
#BindAddress *

# ErrorLog: The location of the error log file. If this does not start
# with /, ServerRoot is prepended to it.
ErrorLog /var/log/httpd/error.log

# TransferLog: The location of the transfer log file. If this does not
# start with /, ServerRoot is prepended to it.
TransferLog /var/log/httpd/access.log

# PidFile: The file the server should log its pid to
PidFile /var/run/httpd.pid

# ScoreBoardFile: File used to store internal server process information
ScoreBoardFile /var/log/httpd/apache.status

# ServerName allows you to set a host name which is sent back to clients for
# your server if it's different than the one the program would get (i.e. use
# "www" instead of the host's real name).
# Note: You cannot just invent host names and hope they work. The name you
# define here must be a valid DNS name for your host. If you don't understand
```

```
# this, ask your network administrator.
#ServerName new.host.name
ServerName linux.juxta.com


# CacheNegotiatedDocs: By default, Apache sends Pragma: no-cache with each
# document that was negotiated on the basis of content. This asks proxy
# servers not to cache the document. Uncommenting the following line disables
# this behavior, and proxies will be allowed to cache the documents.
#CacheNegotiatedDocs


# Timeout: The number of seconds before receives and sends time out
#   n.b. the compiled default is 1200 (20 minutes !)
Timeout 400


# KeepAlive: The number of Keep-Alive persistent requests to accept
# per connection. Set to 0 to deactivate Keep-Alive support
KeepAlive 5


# KeepAliveTimeout: Number of seconds to wait for the next request
KeepAliveTimeout 15


# Server-pool size regulation.  Rather than making you guess how many
# server processes you need, Apache dynamically adapts to the load it
# sees -- that is, it tries to maintain enough server processes to
# handle the current load, plus a few spare servers to handle transient
# load spikes (e.g., multiple simultaneous requests from a single
# Netscape browser).
# It does this by periodically checking how many servers are waiting
# for a request.  If there are fewer than MinSpareServers, it creates
# a new spare.  If there are more than MaxSpareServers, some of the
# spares die off.  These values are probably OK for most sites --
MinSpareServers 1
MaxSpareServers 2


# Number of servers to start -- should be a reasonable ballpark figure.
StartServers 5


# Limit on total number of servers running, i.e., limit on the number
# of clients who can simultaneously connect -- if this limit is ever
# reached, clients will be LOCKED OUT, so it should NOT BE SET TOO LOW.
# It is intended mainly as a brake to keep a runaway server from taking
# Unix with it as it spirals down...
MaxClients 15
```

```
# MaxRequestsPerChild: the number of requests each child process is
#  allowed to process before the child dies.
#  The child will exit so as to avoid problems after prolonged use when
#  Apache (and maybe the libraries it uses) leak.  On most systems, this
#  isn't really needed, but a few (such as Solaris) do have notable leaks
#  in the libraries.
MaxRequestsPerChild 30


# Proxy Server directives. Uncomment the following line to
# enable the proxy server:
#ProxyRequests On


# To enable the cache as well, edit and uncomment the following lines:
#CacheRoot /home/httpd/proxy
#CacheSize 5
#CacheGcInterval 4
#CacheMaxExpire 24
#CacheLastModifiedFactor 0.1
#CacheDefaultExpire 1
#NoCache adomain.com anotherdomain.edu joes.garage.com


# Listen: Allows you to bind Apache to specific IP addresses and/or
# ports, in addition to the default. See also the VirtualHost command

#Listen 3000
#Listen 12.34.56.78:80


# VirtualHost: Allows the daemon to respond to requests for more than one
# server address, if your server machine is configured to accept IP packets
# for multiple addresses. This can be accomplished with the ifconfig
# alias flag, or through kernel patches like VIF.
# Any httpd.conf or srm.conf directive may go into a VirtualHost command.
# See alto the BindAddress entry.
#<VirtualHost host.foo.com>
#ServerAdmin webmaster@host.foo.com
#DocumentRoot /www/docs/host.foo.com
#ServerName host.foo.com
#ErrorLog logs/host.foo.com-error_log
#TransferLog logs/host.foo.com-access_log
#</VirtualHost>
```

The first thing to notice is that the file consists of comments and actual configuration entries. Comments are preceded by the hash mark (#). Configuration entries consist of an entry name followed by an entry value.

ServerType

Let's start looking at the more important entries in the file. The first entry is Server-Type. The Apache server can run in two ways: in a standalone mode with its own processes listening for connections or in inetd, which we have seen in the section on networking. In the inetd mode, inetd listens for connections and then starts an Apache process when a connection comes. If this is your first time running a Web server, you are best off running Apache in standalone mode unless you are familiar with inetd and have compelling reasons for running the server in this way.

Port

The second important entry is the Port entry. By default, a Web server is supposed to run on port 80. When a browser requests a URL without a port, it assumes that the URL is being requested from a server on port 80.

Because of the vulnerability of processes running below port 1024, if you are running a Web server that is not being made publicly available on the Internet and want to avoid the risks associated with these ports, you can try running the server on a port above 1024. Common ports for these types of Web servers are 8000 and 8080, but you can choose any free port.

User and Group

The User and Group entries are critical entries because the very security of your system is affected by them. Normally, the httpd process is fired by the root account, but this process does not listen for connections. Rather, this process launches one or more child processes as the user and group (which are specified by name or ID number) indicated with these configuration directives.

This is done because all processes fired by the Web server, including CGI programs, would otherwise be run as root. This would pose a huge security risk, especially if a poorly written CGI script left a large security hole. By running the Web server and its related children as a user with limited power, it is possible to limit these security holes.

The norm is to run the Web server as nobody with a group of nobody or #-1. I generally use user nobody and group nobody, since they are easily identifiable when reading the configuration file. This user has limited privileges on the system, and potential hackers will be able to wreak only limited havoc if a CGI script lets them into the system.

ServerRoot

ServerRoot is used to indicate the base directory where configuration files and logs for the server can be found. Red Hat sets this up in the directory /etc/httpd. Inside this directory is a conf directory containing the three configuration files plus a logs directory as a link to /var/logs/httpd.

You are free to move the directory anywhere on your system to match the style of management you are using. However, it is usually easiest to keep things where your distribution of Linux puts them.

ServerName

The ServerName configuration directive identifies the host name returned to clients with the pages they request. This will be one of the legitimate names for your Web server as identified in a DNS record or host table on your network. In an intranet environment, you can define a host name in host tables, using NIS, or in the DNS server for your site. For an Internet Web server, you should make sure that the name you indicate here is a valid name in your domain's DNS record. If you aren't sure, you should consult with whoever manages the domain name records for your domain.

In the case of our example file, ServerName is linux.juxta.com.

ServerAdmin

This directive indicates the e-mail address of the administrator of the Web site. When the server generates an automated error message, such as one indicating that a page is not found, then this e-mail address is usually added to the page indicating who to contact to report the problem.

Make sure that this is a valid address and that the address is the correct one for the server's administrator.

Srm.conf

The srm.conf file has the same basic structure as the httpd.conf file. The srm.conf file for linux.juxta.com is shown here:

```
# With this document, you define the name space that users see of your http
# server.  This file also defines server settings which affect how requests are
# serviced, and how results should be formatted.

# See the tutorials at http://www.apache.org/ for
# more information.

# Originally by Rob McCool; Adapted for Apache
# Adapted by Arman Danesh for linux.juxta.com

# DocumentRoot: The directory out of which you will serve your
# documents. By default, all requests are taken from this directory, but
# symbolic links and aliases may be used to point to other locations.

DocumentRoot /home/httpd/html

# UserDir: The name of the directory which is appended onto a user's home
# directory if a ~user request is received.

UserDir public_html

# DirectoryIndex: Name of the file or files to use as a pre-written HTML
# directory index.  Separate multiple entries with spaces.

DirectoryIndex index.html index.htm index.shtml

# FancyIndexing is whether you want fancy directory indexing or standard

FancyIndexing on

# AddIcon tells the server which icon to show for different files or filename
# extensions

AddIconByEncoding (CMP,/icons/compressed.gif) x-compress x-gzip

AddIconByType (TXT,/icons/text.gif) text/*
AddIconByType (IMG,/icons/image2.gif) image/*
```

```
AddIconByType (SND,/icons/sound2.gif) audio/*
AddIconByType (VID,/icons/movie.gif) video/*

AddIcon /icons/binary.gif .bin .exe
AddIcon /icons/binhex.gif .hqx
AddIcon /icons/tar.gif .tar
AddIcon /icons/world2.gif .wrl .wrl.gz .vrml .vrm .iv
AddIcon /icons/compressed.gif .Z .z .tgz .gz .zip
AddIcon /icons/a.gif .ps .ai .eps
AddIcon /icons/layout.gif .html .shtml .htm .pdf
AddIcon /icons/text.gif .txt
AddIcon /icons/c.gif .c
AddIcon /icons/p.gif .pl .py
AddIcon /icons/f.gif .for
AddIcon /icons/dvi.gif .dvi
AddIcon /icons/uuencoded.gif .uu
AddIcon /icons/script.gif .conf .sh .shar .csh .ksh .tcl
AddIcon /icons/tex.gif .tex
AddIcon /icons/bomb.gif core

AddIcon /icons/back.gif ..
AddIcon /icons/hand.right.gif README
AddIcon /icons/folder.gif ^^DIRECTORY^^
AddIcon /icons/blank.gif ^^BLANKICON^^

# DefaultIcon is which icon to show for files which do not have an icon
# explicitly set.
DefaultIcon /icons/unknown.gif

# AddDescription allows you to place a short description after a file in
# server-generated indexes.
# Format: AddDescription "description" filename

# ReadmeName is the name of the README file the server will look for by
# default. Format: ReadmeName name
# The server will first look for name.html, include it if found, and it will
# then look for name and include it as plaintext if found.
# HeaderName is the name of a file which should be prepended to
# directory indexes.
ReadmeName README
HeaderName HEADER
```

```
# IndexIgnore is a set of filenames which directory indexing should ignore
# Format: IndexIgnore name1 name2...
IndexIgnore */.??* *~ *# */HEADER* */README* */RCS

# AccessFileName: The name of the file to look for in each directory
# for access control information.
AccessFileName .htaccess

# DefaultType is the default MIME type for documents which the server
# cannot find the type of from filename extensions.
DefaultType text/plain

# AddEncoding allows you to have certain browsers (Mosaic/X 2.1+) uncompress
# information on the fly. Note: Not all browsers support this.
AddEncoding x-compress Z
AddEncoding x-gzip gz

# AddLanguage allows you to specify the language of a document. You can
# then use content negotiation to give a browser a file in a language
# it can understand.  Note that the suffix does not have to be the same
# as the language keyword -- those with documents in Polish (whose
# net-standard language code is pl) may wish to use "AddLanguage pl .po"
# to avoid the ambiguity with the common suffix for perl scripts.
AddLanguage en .en
AddLanguage fr .fr
AddLanguage de .de
AddLanguage da .da
AddLanguage el .el
AddLanguage it .it

# LanguagePriority allows you to give precedence to some languages
# in case of a tie during content negotiation.
# Just list the languages in decreasing order of preference.
LanguagePriority en de fr

# Redirect allows you to tell clients about documents which used to exist in
# your server's namespace, but do not anymore. This allows you to tell the
# clients where to look for the relocated document.
# Format: Redirect fakename url

# Aliases: Add here as many aliases as you need (with no limit). The format is
# Alias fakename realname
#Alias /icons/ /home/httpd/icons/
```

```
# ScriptAlias: This controls which directories contain server scripts.
# Format: ScriptAlias fakename realname
ScriptAlias /cgi-bin/ /home/httpd/cgi-bin/

# If you want to use server side includes, or CGI outside
# ScriptAliased directories, uncomment the following lines.
# AddType allows you to tweak mime.types without actually editing it, or to
# make certain files to be certain types.
# Format: AddType type/subtype ext1

# AddHandler allows you to map certain file extensions to "handlers",
# actions unrelated to filetype. These can be either built into the server
# or added with the Action command (see below)
# Format: AddHandler action-name ext1

# To use CGI scripts:
AddHandler cgi-script .cgi

# To use server-parsed HTML files
AddType text/html .shtml
AddHandler server-parsed .shtml

# Uncomment the following line to enable Apache's send-asis HTTP file
# feature
#AddHandler send-as-is asis

# If you wish to use server-parsed imagemap files, use
AddHandler imap-file map

# To enable type maps, you might want to use
#AddHandler type-map var

# Action lets you define media types that will execute a script whenever
# a matching file is called. This eliminates the need for repeated URL
# pathnames for oft-used CGI file processors.
# Format: Action media/type /cgi-script/location
# Format: Action handler-name /cgi-script/location

# For example to add a footer (footer.html in your document root) to
# files with extension .foot (e.g. foo.html.foot), you could use:
#AddHandler foot-action foot
#Action foot-action /cgi-bin/footer
```

```
# Or to do this for all HTML files, for example, use:
#Action text/html /cgi-bin/footer

# MetaDir: specifies the name of the directory in which Apache can find
# meta information files. These files contain additional HTTP headers
# to include when sending the document

#MetaDir .web

# MetaSuffix: specifies the file name suffix for the file containing the
# meta information.

#MetaSuffix .meta

# Customizable error response (Apache style)
#   these come in three flavors
#
#     1) plain text
#ErrorDocument 500 "The server made a boo boo.
#   n.b.  the (") marks it as text, it does not get output
#
#     2) local redirects
#ErrorDocument 404 /missing.html
#   to redirect to local url /missing.html
#ErrorDocument 404 /cgi-bin/missing_handler.pl
#   n.b. can redirect to a script or a document using server-side-includes.
#
#     3) external redirects
#ErrorDocument 402 http://other.server.com/subscription_info.html
```

DocumentRoot

The DocumentRoot configuration entry specifies where the root directory for html files is located. In the case of Red Hat Linux, the default is usually set to /home/httpd/html, and I have kept this setting for linux.juxta.com. Thus, the file /home/httpd/html/file.html would be accessed using the URL http://linux.juxta.com/file.html.

UserDir

UserDir is a directive that is useful when a Webmaster wants to enable each user on the system to have their own personal Web site that they manage through a directory in their home directory. This directive indicates the name of the subdirectory in their home directory that should be considered as their Web directory.

The norm is to use `public_html`. So, if user testuser had a directory /home/testuser/public_html, this directory could be accessed via the Web using the URL http://servername/~testuser.

DirectoryIndex

`DirectoryIndex` is an important directive in that it indicates which files should be considered default files. This is how it is possible for a URL such as http://www.juxta.com/ to access the correct file.

For instance, in the sample `srm.conf` file above, there are three entries given for the Directory Index: `index.html`, `index.htm`, and `index.shtml`. This means that for any URL that doesn't specify a filename and only gives a directory, the server will first try to return `index.html` from the specified directory. If that file is missing, `index.htm` is returned; if that file is missing, `index.shtml` is sent back to the client.

If no file match is found, the server either returns a directory listing or an error message based on other configuration options.

AccessFileName

`AccessFileName` is used to specify the filename that will contain access control information for a given directory. As we will see later when we discuss the `access.conf` file and when we build our sample site, it is possible to store access control information in the `access.conf` file or in files in each directory.

Here we indicate that if a file `.htaccess` exists in a directory, then that file contains access control information for the directory.

ScriptAlias

It is important to set the `ScriptAlias` directive so that you will be able to set up a directory to store CGI programs and scripts. `ScriptAlias` specifies which directory is used for CGI scripts and what the URL is for that directory. Unless other permissions are given to run CGI programs on the basis of file extensions (as we will see in the next section when we talk about the `AddHandler` directive), this is the only directory where you can place CGI programs.

For instance, in our sample file above, we used the directive

```
ScriptAlias /cgi-bin/ /home/httpd/cgi-bin
```

This line indicates that the URL `http://linux.juxta.com/cgi-bin/` points to `/home/httpd/cgi-bin/`. In this directory, files are considered CGI scripts and the server will attempt to execute the files instead of returning them directly to the requesting client.

AddHandler and AddType

The `AddHandler` and `AddType` directives really need to be considered together.

`AddHandler` allows files with a specified extension to be mapped to a particular action, which can be a built-in action in the server (such as running CGI programs) or an external action that generally invokes a special program outside the server and passes the file in question through that program.

`AddType` creates a new MIME type for a specific extension. MIME types are important in informing the client how to handle a file. For instance, if a file is passed with MIME type `text/plain` to the browser, the browser won't attempt to interpret the file for any HTML it contains, while a MIME type of `text/html` causes the browser to process the file it receives as an HTML file.

Two of the main uses of these directives are to allow the execution of CGI scripts outside the specified CGI script directory and to enable server-parsed HTML, which allows special tags embedded in an HTML file to be processed by the server before it returns the page to the client.

Enabling CGI Scripts You can use the `AddHandler` directive to enable CGI processing outside the specified CGI directory. In our sample `srm.conf` file, we use

```
AddHandler cgi-script .cgi
```

to indicate that any file with the extension `.cgi` that is found outside the specified CGI directory should be treated as a CGI program and handled in that way. Without this directive, a CGI script found outside the CGI directory will not be processed as a CGI program; instead, the contents of the file will simply be returned to the client. Generally, this means that the user will see the actual program code of a script rather than the results of running a script.

Enabling Server-Parsed HTML   Both the AddHandler and AddType directives are used to enable server-parsed HTML. The normal usage for Apache is:

```
AddType text/html .shtml
AddHandler server-parsed .shtml
```

Here AddType ensures that the results of a server-parsed HTML file (those with the extension .shtml) will be viewed as HTML by the client browser and will be displayed as such.

The AddHandler line indicates that files with the extension .shtml should be handled by the server-parsed action of the server. This effectively enables server-parsed HTML for .shtml files.

Access.conf

The role of access.conf is a little bit different than httpd.conf and srm.conf. This file defines when, where, and by whom certain types of actions are allowed. It can be used for a number of purposes, including to specify access restrictions and to limit where scripts can be executed (overriding the settings in srm.conf).

```
# access.conf: Global access configuration
# Online docs at http://www.apache.org/

# This file defines server settings which affect which types of
# services are allowed, and in what circumstances.

# Each directory to which Apache has access, can be configured with
# respect to which services and features are allowed and/or disabled in
# that directory (and its subdirectories).

# Originally by Rob McCool
# Adapted by Arman Danesh for linux.juxta.com

# This should be changed to whatever you set DocumentRoot to.

<Directory /home/httpd/html>

# This may also be "None", "All", or any combination of "Indexes",
# "Includes", "FollowSymLinks", "ExecCGI", or "MultiViews".

# Note that "MultiViews" must be named *explicitly* -- "Options All"
# doesn't give it to you (or at least, not yet).
#
# Options Indexes FollowSymLinks
```

```
Options Includes

# This controls which options the .htaccess files in directories can
# override. Can also be "All", or any combination of "Options",
# "FileInfo", "AuthConfig", and "Limit"

AllowOverride All

# Controls who can get stuff from this server.

# order allow,deny
# allow from all

order allow,deny
allow from all

</Directory>

# /usr/local/etc/httpd/cgi-bin should be changed to whatever your
# ScriptAliased CGI directory exists, if you have that configured.

<Directory /home/httpd/cgi-bin>
AllowOverride None
Options None
</Directory>

# Allow server status reports, with the URL of http://servername/status
# Change the ".nowhere.com" to match your domain to enable.

#<Location /status>
#SetHandler server-status

#order deny,allow
#deny from all
#allow from .nowhere.com
#</Location>

# You may place any other directories or locations you wish to have
# access information for after this one.
```

At a minimum, `access.conf` needs to set up the necessary permissions to enable the root HTML directory and the CGI directory. You will usually find it easier to implement access control for specific directories using `.htaccess` files located in the directories in question. As we saw in the section discussing the `srm.conf` file above, you must enable this directory-level access control file for it to work.

In the next section, we will discuss how to set up `access.conf` to enable the HTML and CGI directories.

Enabling the HTML Directory

The code below is the section of our sample `access.conf` dealing with the HTML document root directory, without any comments.

```
<Directory /home/httpd/html>
Options Includes
AllowOverride All
order allow,deny
allow from all
</Directory>
```

The structure of the entry is to enclose the necessary directives inside opening and closing `<Directory>` and `</Directory>` tags. The opening tag specifies the directory that all directives between the tags should apply to, in this case `/home/httpd/html`.

Inside the `<Directory>` and `</Directory>` tags we see four directives.

The `Options` directive is used to indicate what special actions can be taken on the files contained in the directory and its subdirectories. Possible values include `None`, `All`, `Indexes`, `Includes`, `FollowSymLinks`, `ExecCGI`, and `MultiViews`. Commonly used values for HTML directories are `None` when only normal HTML files and images will appear on a site and `Includes` when you plan to enable server-parsed HTML (some server-parsed HTML files offer an ability to include other files in the contents of a file, and this value allows this action to occur).

The next directive is the `AllowOverride` entry, which indicates how much power a local `.htaccess` file will have to override entries in the global `access.conf` file. Possible values include `None`, `All`, `Options`, `FileInfo`, `AuthConfig`, and `Limit`. For instance, the `Options` value limits the `.htaccess` file to overriding the `Options` directive. On servers where the Webmaster has good control over all content, it is usually easiest to allow full right to override. When you run a server with multiple users controlling their own directories' content, it may be wise to limit the power of these users to override global access configuration.

Finally, the `order` and `allow` directives go together to control who has access to pages in the directory. Here, `order allow,deny` indicates that first the `allow` directive should be used, and if that directive doesn't allow the user to obtain the file in question then any `deny` directive should be applied.

Normally, when you are not applying access control you will want to use `order allow,deny`. When you are attempting to implement access controls, `order deny,allow` is the best entry (as we will see later when we build our small sample site with access control).

Following the `order` directive is the `allow` directive, which indicates that all users should be allowed access. If you want to fully understand how to deny users, you should read the Apache documentation available online at `http://www.apache.org/`.

Enabling the CGI Directory

Things look a little bit different with our CGI directory entry:

```
<Directory /home/httpd/cgi-bin>
AllowOverride None
Options None
</Directory>
```

You are probably surprised by the lack of the `ExecCGI` option for the `Options` directive. Because `/home/httpd/cgi-bin` has been specified as the CGI directory with the `ScriptAlias` directive in `srm.conf`, it is not necessary to enable CGI execution here. However, if you want to allow script execution outside this directory you will need to allow it using the `ExecCGI` option.

Notice, also, that all overrides have been disallowed. This is generally a wise idea, since CGI is a security hole even on a well-configured system and it is prudent to prevent all possible security mistakes with CGI directories.

Managing Your Web Server

In addition to being able to start and stop your Web server, once you have your Web server up and running there are a few tasks that you will need to do occasionally to make sure your server continues to run without incident. These steps include creating and deleting users and groups, protecting directories by using access control, and maintaining the server logs so that they continue to be useful.

Starting and Stopping Apache

If you installed Apache when you installed Red Hat, then your start-up files have been set up to start Apache at boot time. This occurs in the file `/etc/rc.d/init.d/httpd.init`. This file is an executable script that takes two possible arguments: `start` and `stop`. If you are planning to use the version of Apache included with your Red Hat installation and don't plan to move the location of the configuration files, then you can start and stop your Web server manually, using

```
$ /etc/rc.d/init.d/httpd.init start
```

to start the server and

```
$ /etc/rc.d/init.d/httpd.init stop
```

to stop the server.

NOTE   All starting and stopping of your Web server will need to be done by **root** so that the main server process can change users to launch child processes to listen for connections.

However, if you want to install your own binaries or compile new binaries from source code, or if you wish to change the location of the configuration files, you will need to know how to invoke the `httpd` command by hand.

Usually, `httpd` is found in `/usr/sbin/`. Two flags are available:

- `-f` specifies the location of the `httpd.conf` file.
- `-d` specifies the server root, overriding the configuration file.

Usually, using -f is sufficient since ServerRoot is specified in httpd.conf. For instance, if you keep your configuration files in /home/httpd/conf, then you could issue the command

```
$ /usr/sbin/httpd -f /home/httpd/conf/httpd.conf
```

to start the server.

If you want to stop your server manually and you started it yourself without using /etc/rc.d/init.d/httpd.init, you will need to know the correct process ID (PID) for the server. You can determine the PID of the server by using the ps command:

```
$ ps -aux | grep httpd
```

This will produce a list of processes similar to the one shown here:

```
nobody   545  0.1  3.8  1104  572  ?  S  17:52  0:00 /usr/sbin/httpd
nobody   546  0.0  3.8  1104  572  ?  S  17:52  0:00 /usr/sbin/httpd
nobody   547  0.2  3.8  1104  572  ?  S  17:52  0:00 /usr/sbin/httpd
nobody   548  0.1  3.8  1104  572  ?  S  17:52  0:00 /usr/sbin/httpd
nobody   549  0.0  3.8  1104  572  ?  S  17:52  0:00 /usr/sbin/httpd
nobody   550  0.3  3.8  1104  572  ?  S  17:52  0:00 /usr/sbin/httpd
root     544  0.5  4.0  1104  592  ?  S  17:52  0:00 /usr/sbin/httpd
```

Notice that all the processes are owned by nobody, except for one owned by root. This is the parent process of all the httpd processes, and this is the one that needs to be stopped, in this case with the command

```
$ kill 544
```

Managing Users and Groups

As we will see in the next section on protecting directories, one main method of protection is by username and password, restricting access to a specified list of users who must correctly provide their username and password to gain access to a protected directory.

Creating users is straightforward and is done using the command htpasswd, which in the default installation of Apache that comes with Red Hat Linux is found at /usr/sbin/htpasswd. This program is used both to create a password file and to create individual users.

The password file serves as the repository for usernames and encrypted passwords, which can then be used by Apache for access control.

You create the password file the first time you create a user, using the command

```
$ htpasswd -c <filename> <username>
```

Here, the file specified by `filename` will be created and the first user will be added to the file. The `-c` flag indicates that the file needs to be created. You can store your password file anywhere that is accessible by the Apache Web server. A good place to store it is with your configuration files. For instance,

```
$ htpasswd -c /etc/httpd/conf/users user1
```

would create a `users` file in the same directory as the other Apache configuration files and would create the user user1.

When you issue the command above, you will be prompted to enter the password for the user twice to make sure it has been entered correctly. Then the password will be encrypted and stored in `/etc/httpd/conf/users`. The entry looks like this:

```
user1:N31mVAxFtivO
```

The format of the entries is the username followed by a colon followed by the encrypted password. Each user entry is on a separate line.

While it looks like the passwords in the system password file (`/etc/passwd`) and the Apache password file are encrypted in the same way, the encryption process used by `htpasswd` is different and you can't simply copy encrypted passwords from `/etc/passwd` to create your Apache password file.

To add additional users once the file is created, simply use the `htpasswd` command without the `-c` flag:

```
$ htpasswd /etc/httpd/conf/users user2
```

This would add the user `user2`, again evoking two prompts for the password. The resulting password file would contain two entries:

```
user1:N31mVAxFtivO.
user2:WROTrbH6.3pPk
```

In addition to creating users, you will usually want to create groups. Groups associate multiple users together under a single name, making it easier to address related users when configuring access control for directories.

To create groups, make a `groups` file by simply editing the file using a text editor such as pico or emacs. You should probably place the `groups` file in the same directory as your `users` file. (In the sample site used in this book, we use `/etc/httpd/conf/groups`.) This file contains one or more entries, each on a separate line, with the format:

```
<groupname>: <username1> <username2> <username3> ...
```

For instance, to create a group called `authors` with the two users we created before as members, we would use the entry:

```
authors: user1 user2
```

Protecting Directories with Access Control

As noted above in the section about `access.conf`, it is possible to configure access control on a directory-by-directory basis. Normally, this is done by creating a file called `.htaccess` in the directory we want to protect and then placing the necessary configuration directives in the file.

The main directives used in this file for access control purposes are:

- `AuthGroupFile`
- `AuthUserFile`
- `AuthName`
- `AuthType`
- `require`
- `order`
- `deny`
- `allow`

AuthUserFile and AuthGroupFile

These directives are used to specify the location of the `users` and `group` files we learned to create in the last section. In our example, these directives would read

```
AuthUserFile /etc/httpd/conf/users
AuthGroupFile /etc/httpd/conf/groups
```

These directives are important because without them, the server won't know where to look for the users and their passwords.

AuthName

AuthName is used to specify the domain of the authentication. Ultimately, this is a prompt that is displayed to the user so they know which username and password to provide. For instance,

```
AuthName Authors Only
```

will display an Authors Only prompt to the user when asking for username and password.

Require

The require directive is used in limiting access for users and groups. The directive can be used to restrict access to all users in the password file, to a list of specific users, or to a list of specific groups.

To restrict access to any existing user, use the directive

```
require valid-user
```

To restrict access to specific users, use the format

```
require user <username1> <username2> <username3> ...
```

Finally, to restrict by group, use the entry

```
require group <groupname1> <groupname2> <groupname3> ...
```

Order

The order directive is used in conjunction with the deny and allow entries to control access based on host rather than user. Using order, deny, and allow, it is possible to permit access only to specified hosts by IP address or host name.

The order directive specifies the order in which the deny and allow directives should be applied.

For instance,

```
order allow,deny
```

says that the allow directive should be applied first, and if the client host does not fall within those specified by the directive, then the deny directive should be applied.

Similarly,

```
order deny,allow
```

reverses the order, testing the deny directive first.

Deny

The deny directive specifies which hosts should be denied access to a directory. Possible values include all, a partial host name, or a partial or full IP address. For instance,

```
deny from all
```

means that all hosts are denied. Similarly,

```
deny from .juxta.com
```

denies access to all hosts in the juxta.com domain. With IP addresses, the format is the same:

```
deny from 194.148.43.195
```

denies access to the specified host.

Allow

The allow directive is the opposite of the deny directive, specifying which hosts should be allowed access to the directory in question. It takes the same possible values as the deny directive.

Putting It All Together

Let's consider now how this all fits together with two examples: enabling access by group and allowing access by domain name.

Enabling Access by Group The following sample .htaccess file would enable access to the specific directory only for users in the group authors:

```
AuthName Authors Only
AuthUserFile /etc/httpd/conf/users
AuthGroupFile /etc/httpd/conf/groups
require group authors
```

Notice that we specify an `AuthName` for the prompt, identify the password and group file, and then indicate that a user must be part of the group `authors` in order to access the directory.

Enabling Access by Domain Name   The following sample `.htaccess` file would enable access to the specific directory only to users accessing the Web site from hosts in the `juxta.com` domain:

```
order allow,deny
allow from .juxta.com
deny from all
```

In this example, notice the order of `allow` and `deny`. The logic works like this: When a host accesses a directory, the host's domain is first compared with the domain `juxta.com`. If the host falls within the specified domain, access is granted. If the host does not, the `deny` directive is looked at and, because it indicates that all hosts should be denied access, the host in question is denied access.

Maintaining Logs

The final management function we are going to consider is log management. Apache produces two important logs: an access log and an error log. Together, these provide information vital for several functions, including debugging buggy CGI scripts and producing statistical access reports with detailed information about usage patterns for your Web site.

However, left on their own, these log files will continue to grow, reaching extremely large sizes. As their size grows, their value decreases as it becomes more difficult to process the volumes of data they contain.

For this reason, it is wise to establish a schedule for rotating your logs. Rotating logs means saving the existing version to an archive and starting afresh with a new, empty log. Depending on how many hits you receive, the ideal frequency for rotating logs can be anything from monthly to weekly to daily.

In order to rotate logs, you use the `rotatelogs` utility that comes with the Apache distribution. By default, Red Hat Linux installs this at `/usr/sbin/rotatelogs`. In order to use the program, you need to add an entry to `httpd.conf`:

```
TransferLog "|/usr/sbin/rotatelogs /some/location/file time"
```

The entry /some/location/file provides a base filename for the rotated logs. A number indicating the system time at which the log starts will be appended to the filename. The time parameter specifies in seconds how often to rotate the logs.

Building a Web Site

Now that you have your Web site configured and running smoothly, let's create a small sample Web site that shows how to deploy content for the Web.

The site that we are going to build will be the information for a small publishing company we will call On The Web Publishers. This site will offer a list of new titles, general information about the publisher, a contact form, and a password-protected section exclusively for the use of authors with contracts with the publisher.

All together, this will let us create a site that includes HTML and images, uses CGI programming, and implements access control for the password-protected section of the site.

First, we need to identify the structure of our site, as we see in Figure 27.4.

FIGURE 27.4:

The structure of our Web site

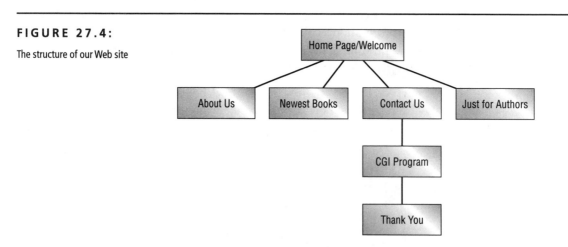

Having done this, we need to create the necessary files to implement this structure. Assuming the configuration used in the sections earlier in this chapter, the root document tree for HTML files is at /home/httpd/html and the CGI directory is at /home/httpd/cgi-bin. Therefore, our directory and file tree for the site might include the following files:

```
/home/httpd/html/index.html
/home/httpd/html/about/index.html
/home/httpd/html/books/index.html
/home/httpd/html/contact/index.html
/home/httpd/html/authors/index.html
/home/httpd/cgi-bin/formmail
```

With the exception of the last file, which we will shortly deal with, all files are HTML files. Any supporting images that are used by the HTML files could be placed in the same directory as the HTML files, but to keep things clean, many Webmasters prefer to place all their images in another directory. In our case, that directory could be:

```
/home/httpd/html/images/
```

Since we aren't learning HTML in this chapter, let's just look at two of the HTML files as examples of how they might be written. Let's start with the main home page at /home/httpd/html/index.html. In our example, the source code for the file would be:

```
<HTML>

    <HEAD>
    <TITLE>On the Web Publishers</TITLE>
    </HEAD>

    <BODY BGCOLOR=lightcyan TEXT=midnightblue>

    <DIV ALIGN=CENTER>
        <A HREF="/"><IMG SRC="/images/logo.gif" BORDER=0></A>
        <TABLE BORDER=0 CELLPADDING=5 CELLSPACING=5
            BGCOLOR=lightpink>
        <TR>
            <TD ALIGN=CENTER><A HREF="about">ABOUT
                US</A></TD>
            <TD ALIGN=CENTER><A HREF="books">OUR
                BOOKS</A></TD>
            <TD ALIGN=CENTER><A HREF="contact">CONTACT
                US</A></TD>
            <TD ALIGN=CENTER><A HREF="authors">JUST FOR
```

```
                     AUTHORS</A></TD>
          </TR>
          </TABLE>
      </DIV>

      <FONT SIZE=5>W</F>elcome to <STRONG>On the Web
      Publishers</STRONG>. We offer the finest in
      on-line electronic books at reasonable prices.
      Check out what we have to offer ...

      <UL>
      <LI><A HREF="about">Learn about what we do</A>
      <LI><A HREF="books">See what books we offer</A>
      <LI><A HREF="contact">Contact us</A>
      </UL>

      </BODY>

   </HTML>
```

This would produce results like those in Figure 27.5.

FIGURE 27.5:

The main home page

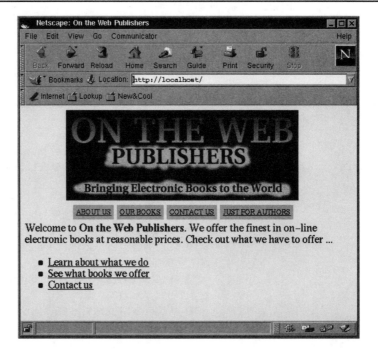

The other pages would have similar-looking source code with the exception of the contact form at /home/httpd/html/contact/index.html. This page would look like Figure 27.6, which is produced by the following source code:

```
<HTML>

    <HEAD>
    <TITLE>On the Web Publishers</TITLE>
    </HEAD>

    <BODY BGCOLOR=lightcyan TEXT=midnightblue>

    <DIV ALIGN=CENTER>
        <A HREF="/"><IMG SRC="/images/logo.gif" BORDER=0></A>
        <TABLE BORDER=0 CELLPADDING=5 CELLSPACING=5
            BGCOLOR=lightpink>
        <TR>
            <TD ALIGN=CENTER><A HREF="/about">ABOUT
                US</A></TD>
            <TD ALIGN=CENTER><A HREF="/books">OUR
                BOOKS</A></TD>
            <TD ALIGN=CENTER BGCOLOR=yellow>CONTACT
                US</TD>
            <TD ALIGN=CENTER><A HREF="/authors">JUST FOR
                AUTHORS</A></TD>
        </TR>
        </TABLE>

        <H1>Drop Us A Line ...</H1>
    </DIV>

    <TABLE ALIGN=CENTER><TR><TD>
    <FORM METHOD=POST ACTION="/cgi-bin/formmail">
    <INPUT TYPE=TEXT WIDTH=30 NAME=name> Name<BR>
    <INPUT TYPE=TEXT WIDTH=30 NAME=address> Address<BR>
    <INPUT TYPE=TEXT WIDTH=30 NAME=city> City<BR>
    <INPUT TYPE=TEXT WIDTH=30 NAME=state> State<BR>
    <INPUT TYPE=TEXT WIDTH=30 NAME=zip> Zip/Post Code<BR>
    <INPUT TYPE=TEXT WIDTH=30 NAME=country> Country<BR>
    <INPUT TYPE=TEXT WIDTH=30 NAME=email> E-mail<BR>
    Comments:<BR>
    <TEXTAREA ROWS=10 COLS=30 NAME=comments
```

```
      WRAP=HARD></TEXTAREA><BR>
<INPUT TYPE=SUBMIT VALUE="Send Comments">
</FORM>
</TD></TR></TABLE>

</BODY>

</HTML>
```

FIGURE 27.6:

The contact form

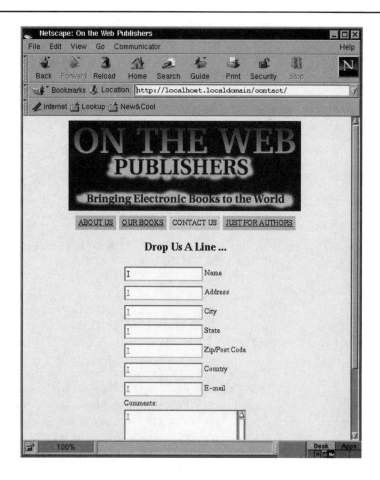

What makes this page special is that it includes a form and a reference to a CGI program that processes the data in the form. The program we are using in this case is called formmail, a freely available CGI script written in Perl, which takes the contents of a form and mails them to a predefined mail address. In this way, the contact information from the form can be e-mailed to the bookstore's main e-mail address.

Formmail is written by Matthew M. Wright and is available at `http://www .worldwidemart.com/scripts/formmail.shtml`. Even though we aren't discussing Perl or CGI programming in this chapter, the source code is presented here so you can see how simple it is to create basic CGI programs with little effort:

```perl
#!/usr/bin/perl
###############################################################################
# FormMail                     Version 1.6                                    #
# Copyright 1995-1997 Matt Wright mattw@worldwidemart.com                     #
# Created 06/09/95              Last Modified 05/02/97                         #
# Matt's Script Archive, Inc.:    http://www.worldwidemart.com/scripts/       #
###############################################################################
# COPYRIGHT NOTICE                                                            #
# Copyright 1995-1997 Matthew M. Wright  All Rights Reserved.                 #
#                                                                             #
# FormMail may be used and modified free of charge by anyone so long as this #
# copyright notice and the comments above remain intact.  By using this      #
# code you agree to indemnify Matthew M. Wright from any liability that       #
# might arise from its use.                                                   #
#                                                                             #
# Selling the code for this program without prior written consent is         #
# expressly forbidden.  In other words, please ask first before you try and #
# make money off of my program.                                              #
#                                                                             #
# Obtain permission before redistributing this software over the Internet or #
# in any other medium.  In all cases copyright and header must remain intact #
###############################################################################
# Define Variables                                                           #
#    Detailed Information Found In README File.                              #

# $mailprog defines the location of your sendmail program on your unix       #
# system.                                                                    #

$mailprog = '/usr/lib/sendmail';

# @referers allows forms to be located only on servers which are defined     #
# in this field.  This security fix from the last version which allowed      #
# anyone on any server to use your FormMail script on their web site.        #
```

```perl
@referers = ('linux.juxta.com');

# Done                                                                       #
##############################################################################

# Check Referring URL
&check_url;

# Retrieve Date
&get_date;

# Parse Form Contents
&parse_form;

# Check Required Fields
&check_required;

# Return HTML Page or Redirect User
&return_html;

# Send E-Mail
&send_mail;

sub check_url {

    # Localize the check_referer flag which determines if user is valid.    #
    local($check_referer) = 0;

    # If a referring URL was specified, for each valid referer, make sure   #
    # that a valid referring URL was passed to FormMail.                    #

    if ($ENV{'HTTP_REFERER'}) {
        foreach $referer (@referers) {
            if ($ENV{'HTTP_REFERER'} =~ m|https?://([^/]*)$referer|i) {
                $check_referer = 1;
                last;
            }
        }
    }
    else {
        $check_referer = 1;
    }
```

```
        # If the HTTP_REFERER was invalid, send back an error.           #
        if ($check_referer != 1) { &error('bad_referer') }
    }

    sub get_date {

        # Define arrays for the day of the week and month of the year.    #
        @days   = ('Sunday','Monday','Tuesday','Wednesday',
                   'Thursday','Friday','Saturday');
        @months = ('January','February','March','April','May','June','July',
                   'August','September','October','November','December');

        # Get the current time and format the hour, minutes and seconds.  Add  #
        # 1900 to the year to get the full 4 digit year.                  #
        ($sec,$min,$hour,$mday,$mon,$year,$wday) =
    (localtime(time))[0,1,2,3,4,5,6];
        $time = sprintf("%02d:%02d:%02d",$hour,$min,$sec);
        $year += 1900;

        # Format the date.                                                #
        $date = "$days[$wday], $months[$mon] $mday, $year at $time";

    }

    sub parse_form {

        # Define the configuration associative array.                    #
        %Config = ('recipient','',          'subject','',
                   'email','',              'realname','',
                   'redirect','',           'bgcolor','',
                   'background','',         'link_color','',
                   'vlink_color','',        'text_color','',
                   'alink_color','',        'title','',
                   'sort','',               'print_config','',
                   'required','',           'env_report','',
                   'return_link_title','',  'return_link_url','',
                   'print_blank_fields','', 'missing_fields_redirect','');

        # Determine the form's REQUEST_METHOD (GET or POST) and split the form  #
        # fields up into their name-value pairs.  If the REQUEST_METHOD was  #
        # not GET or POST, send an error.                                 #
        if ($ENV{'REQUEST_METHOD'} eq 'GET') {
            # Split the name-value pairs
            @pairs = split(/&/, $ENV{'QUERY_STRING'});
```

```perl
    }
elsif ($ENV{'REQUEST_METHOD'} eq 'POST') {
    # Get the input
    read(STDIN, $buffer, $ENV{'CONTENT_LENGTH'});

    # Split the name-value pairs
    @pairs = split(/&/, $buffer);
}
else {
    &error('request_method');
}

# For each name-value pair:                                            #
foreach $pair (@pairs) {

    # Split the pair up into individual variables.                     #
    local($name, $value) = split(/=/, $pair);

    # Decode the form encoding on the name and value variables.        #
    $name =~ tr/+/ /;
    $name =~ s/%([a-fA-F0-9][a-fA-F0-9])/pack("C", hex($1))/eg;

    $value =~ tr/+/ /;
    $value =~ s/%([a-fA-F0-9][a-fA-F0-9])/pack("C", hex($1))/eg;

    # If they try to include server side includes, erase them, so they
    # aren't a security risk if the html gets returned.  Another
    # security hole plugged up.
    $value =~ s/<!-(.|\n)*->//g;

    # If the field name has been specified in the %Config array, it will #
    # return a 1 for defined($Config{$name}}) and we should associate    #
    # this value with the appropriate configuration variable.  If this   #
    # is not a configuration form field, put it into the associative     #
    # array %Form, appending the value with a ', ' if there is already a #
    # value present.  We also save the order of the form fields in the   #
    # @Field_Order array so we can use this order for the generic sort.  #
    if (defined($Config{$name})) {
        $Config{$name} = $value;
    }
    else {
        if ($Form{$name} && $value) {
            $Form{$name} = "$Form{$name}, $value";
        }
```

```
                elsif ($value) {
                    push(@Field_Order,$name);
                    $Form{$name} = $value;
                }
            }
        }

        # The next six lines remove any extra spaces or new lines from the     #
        # configuration variables, which may have been caused if your editor   #
        # wraps lines after a certain length or if you used spaces between field #
        # names or environment variables.                                      #
        $Config{'required'} =~ s/(\s+|\n)?,(\s+|\n)?/,/g;
        $Config{'required'} =~ s/(\s+)?\n+(\s+)?//g;
        $Config{'env_report'} =~ s/(\s+|\n)?,(\s+|\n)?/,/g;
        $Config{'env_report'} =~ s/(\s+)?\n+(\s+)?//g;
        $Config{'print_config'} =~ s/(\s+|\n)?,(\s+|\n)?/,/g;
        $Config{'print_config'} =~ s/(\s+)?\n+(\s+)?//g;

        # Split the configuration variables into individual field names.       #
        @Required = split(/,/,$Config{'required'});
        @Env_Report = split(/,/,$Config{'env_report'});
        @Print_Config = split(/,/,$Config{'print_config'});
}

sub check_required {

    # Localize the variables used in this subroutine.                          #
    local($require, @error);

    if (!$Config{'recipient'}) {
        if (!defined(%Form)) { &error('bad_referer') }
        else                 { &error('no_recipient') }
    }

    # For each require field defined in the form:                              #
    foreach $require (@Required) {

        # If the required field is the email field, the syntax of the email    #
        # address if checked to make sure it passes a valid syntax.            #
        if ($require eq 'email' && !&check_email($Config{$require})) {
            push(@error,$require);
        }

        # Otherwise, if the required field is a configuration field and it      #
```

```perl
        # has no value or has been filled in with a space, send an error.    #
        elsif (defined($Config{$require})) {
            if (!$Config{$require}) {
                push(@error,$require);
            }
        }

        # If it is a regular form field which has not been filled in or      #
        # filled in with a space, flag it as an error field.                 #
        elsif (!$Form{$require}) {
            push(@error,$require);
        }
    }

    # If any error fields have been found, send error message to the user.   #
    if (@error) { &error('missing_fields', @error) }
}

sub return_html {
    # Local variables used in this subroutine initialized.                   #
    local($key,$sort_order,$sorted_field);

    # If redirect option is used, print the redirectional location header.   #
    if ($Config{'redirect'}) {
        print "Location: $Config{'redirect'}\n\n";
    }

    # Otherwise, begin printing the response page.                           #
    else {

        # Print HTTP header and opening HTML tags.                           #
        print "Content-type: text/html\n\n";
        print "<html>\n <head>\n";

        # Print out title of page                                            #
        if ($Config{'title'}) { print "  <title>$Config{'title'}</title>\n" }
        else                   { print "  <title>Thank You</title>\n"        }

        print " </head>\n <body";

        # Get Body Tag Attributes                                            #
        &body_attributes;
```

```perl
# Close Body Tag                                                            #
print ">\n  <center>\n";

# Print custom or generic title.                                           #
if ($Config{'title'}) { print "   <h1>$Config{'title'}</h1>\n" }
else { print "   <h1>Thank You For Filling Out This Form</h1>\n" }

print "</center>\n";

print "Below is what you submitted to $Config{'recipient'} on ";
print "$date<p><hr size=1 width=75\%><p>\n";

# Sort alphabetically if specified:                                        #
if ($Config{'sort'} eq 'alphabetic') {
    foreach $field (sort keys %Form) {

        # If the field has a value or the print blank fields option  #
        # is turned on, print out the form field and value.          #
        if ($Config{'print_blank_fields'} || $Form{$field}) {
            print "<b>$field:</b> $Form{$field}<p>\n";
        }
    }
}

# If a sort order is specified, sort the form fields based on that.  #
elsif ($Config{'sort'} =~ /^order:.*,.*/) {

    # Set the temporary $sort_order variable to the sorting order,  #
    # remove extraneous line breaks and spaces, remove the order:   #
    # directive and split the sort fields into an array.            #
    $sort_order = $Config{'sort'};
    $sort_order =~ s/(\s+|\n)?,(\s+|\n)?/,/g;
    $sort_order =~ s/(\s+)?\n+(\s+)?//g;
    $sort_order =~ s/order://;
    @sorted_fields = split(/,/, $sort_order);

    # For each sorted field, if it has a value or the print blank   #
    # fields option is turned on print the form field and value.    #
    foreach $sorted_field (@sorted_fields) {
        if ($Config{'print_blank_fields'} || $Form{$sorted_field}) {
            print "<b>$sorted_field:</b> $Form{$sorted_field}<p>\n";
        }
    }
}
```

```
            # Otherwise, default to the order in which the fields were sent.    #
            else {

                # For each form field, if it has a value or the print blank    #
                # fields option is turned on print the form field and value.   #
                foreach $field (@Field_Order) {
                    if ($Config{'print_blank_fields'} || $Form{$field}) {
                        print "<b>$field:</b> $Form{$field}<p>\n";
                    }
                }
            }

            print "<p><hr size=1 width=75%><p>\n";

            # Check for a Return Link and print one if found.                   #
            if ($Config{'return_link_url'} && $Config{'return_link_title'}) {
                print "<ul>\n";
                print "<li><a
href=\"$Config{'return_link_url'}\">$Config{'return_link_title'}</a>\n";
                print "</ul>\n";
            }

            # Print the page footer.                                            #
            print <<"(END HTML FOOTER)";
            <hr size=1 width=75%><p>
            <center><font size=-1><a
href="http://www.worldwidemart.com/scripts/formmail.shtml">FormMail</a>
V1.6 &copy; 1995 -1997  Matt Wright<br>
A Free Product of <a href="http://www.worldwidemart.com/scripts/">Matt's
Script Archive, Inc.</a></font></center>
            </body>
            </html>
(END HTML FOOTER)
    }
}

sub send_mail {
    # Localize variables used in this subroutine.                               #
    local($print_config,$key,$sort_order,$sorted_field,$env_report);

    # Open The Mail Program
    open(MAIL,"|$mailprog -t");
```

```perl
print MAIL "To: $Config{'recipient'}\n";
print MAIL "From: $Config{'email'} ($Config{'realname'})\n";

# Check for Message Subject
if ($Config{'subject'}) { print MAIL "Subject: $Config{'subject'}\n\n" }
else                    { print MAIL "Subject: WWW Form Submission\n\n" }

print MAIL "Below is the result of your feedback form.  It was submitted
by\n";
print MAIL "$Config{'realname'} ($Config{'email'}) on $date\n";
print MAIL "-" x 75 . "\n\n";

if (@Print_Config) {
    foreach $print_config (@Print_Config) {
        if ($Config{$print_config}) {
            print MAIL "$print_config: $Config{$print_config}\n\n";
        }
    }
}

# Sort alphabetically if specified:                                    #
if ($Config{'sort'} eq 'alphabetic') {
    foreach $field (sort keys %Form) {

        # If the field has a value or the print blank fields option    #
        # is turned on, print out the form field and value.            #
        if ($Config{'print_blank_fields'} || $Form{$field} ||
            $Form{$field} eq '0') {
            print MAIL "$field: $Form{$field}\n\n";
        }
    }
}

# If a sort order is specified, sort the form fields based on that.    #
elsif ($Config{'sort'} =~ /^order:.*,.*/) {

    # Remove extraneous line breaks and spaces, remove the order:      #
    # directive and split the sort fields into an array.               #
    $Config{'sort'} =~ s/(\s+|\n)?,(\s+|\n)?/,/g;
    $Config{'sort'} =~ s/(\s+)?\n+(\s+)?//g;
    $Config{'sort'} =~ s/order://;
    @sorted_fields = split(/,/, $Config{'sort'});

    # For each sorted field, if it has a value or the print blank      #
```

```perl
        # fields option is turned on print the form field and value.          #
        foreach $sorted_field (@sorted_fields) {
            if ($Config{'print_blank_fields'} || $Form{$sorted_field} ||
                $Form{$sorted_field} eq '0') {
                print MAIL "$sorted_field: $Form{$sorted_field}\n\n";
            }
        }
    }

    # Otherwise, default to the order in which the fields were sent.          #
    else {

        # For each form field, if it has a value or the print blank          #
        # fields option is turned on print the form field and value.          #
        foreach $field (@Field_Order) {
            if ($Config{'print_blank_fields'} || $Form{$field} ||
                $Form{$field} eq '0') {
                print MAIL "$field: $Form{$field}\n\n";
            }
        }
    }

    print MAIL "-" x 75 . "\n\n";

    # Send any specified Environment Variables to recipient.                  #
    foreach $env_report (@Env_Report) {
        if ($ENV{$env_report}) {
            print MAIL "$env_report: $ENV{$env_report}\n";
        }
    }

    close (MAIL);
}

sub check_email {
    # Initialize local email variable with input to subroutine.              #
    $email = $_[0];

    # If the e-mail address contains:                                        #
    if ($email =~ /(@.*@)|(\.\.)|(@\.)|(\.@)|(^\.)/ ||

        # the e-mail address contains an invalid syntax.  Or, if the         #
        # syntax does not match the following regular expression pattern     #
        # it fails basic syntax verification.                                #
```

```perl
        $email !~ /^.+\@(\[?)[a-zA-Z0-9\-\.]+\.([a-zA-Z]{2,3}|[0-
9]{1,3})(\]?)$/) {

        # Basic syntax requires:  one or more characters before the @ sign,  #
        # followed by an optional '[', then any number of letters, numbers,   #
        # dashes or periods (valid domain/IP characters) ending in a period   #
        # and then 2 or 3 letters (for domain suffixes) or 1 to 3 numbers     #
        # (for IP addresses).  An ending bracket is also allowed as it is     #
        # valid syntax to have an email address like: user@[255.255.255.0]    #

        # Return a false value, since the e-mail address did not pass valid   #
        # syntax.                                                             #
        return 0;
    }

    else {

        # Return a true value, e-mail verification passed.                    #
        return 1;
    }
}


sub body_attributes {
    # Check for Background Color
    if ($Config{'bgcolor'}) { print " bgcolor=\"$Config{'bgcolor'}\"" }

    # Check for Background Image
    if ($Config{'background'}) { print "
➥ background=\"$Config{'background'}\"" }

    # Check for Link Color
    if ($Config{'link_color'}) { print " link=\"$Config{'link_color'}\"" }

    # Check for Visited Link Color
    if ($Config{'vlink_color'}) { print " vlink=\"$Config{'vlink_color'}\"" }

    # Check for Active Link Color
    if ($Config{'alink_color'}) { print " alink=\"$Config{'alink_color'}\"" }

    # Check for Body Text Color
    if ($Config{'text_color'}) { print " text=\"$Config{'text_color'}\"" }
}
```

```
sub error {
    # Localize variables and assign subroutine input.                    #
    local($error,@error_fields) = @_;
    local($host,$missing_field,$missing_field_list);

    if ($error eq 'bad_referer') {
        if ($ENV{'HTTP_REFERER'} =~ m|^https?://([\w\.]+)|i) {
            $host = $1;
            print <<"(END ERROR HTML)";
Content-type: text/html

<html>
 <head>
  <title>Bad Referrer - Access Denied</title>
 </head>
 <body bgcolor=#FFFFFF text=#000000>
  <center>
   <table border=0 width=600 bgcolor=#9C9C9C>
    <tr><th><font size=+2>Bad Referrer - Access Denied</font></th></tr>
   </table>
   <table border=0 width=600 bgcolor=#CFCFCF>
    <tr><td>The form attempting to use
     <a
href="http://www.worldwidemart.com/scripts/formmail.shtml">FormMail</a>
     resides at <tt>$ENV{'HTTP_REFERER'}</tt>, which is not allowed to access
     this cgi script.<p>

     If you are attempting to configure FormMail to run with this form, you
need
     to add the following to \@referers, explained in detail in the README
file.<p>

     Add <tt>'$host'</tt> to your <tt><b>\@referers</b></tt> array.<hr size=1>
     <center><font size=-1>
      <a href="http://www.worldwidemart.com/scripts/formmail.shtml">FormMa
➥ il</a> V1.6 &copy; 1995 - 1997  Matt Wright<br>
      A Free Product of <a href="http://www.worldwidemart.com/scripts/">Matt's
Script Archive, Inc.</a>
     </font></center>
    </td></tr>
   </table>
  </center>
```

```
 </body>
</html>
(END ERROR HTML)
        }
        else {
            print <<"(END ERROR HTML)";
Content-type: text/html

<html>
 <head>
  <title>FormMail v1.6</title>
 </head>
 <body bgcolor=#FFFFFF text=#000000>
  <center>
   <table border=0 width=600 bgcolor=#9C9C9C>
    <tr><th><font size=+2>FormMail</font></th></tr>
   </table>
   <table border=0 width=600 bgcolor=#CFCFCF>
    <tr><th><tt><font size=+1>Copyright 1995 - 1997 Matt Wright<br>
        Version 1.6 - Released May 02, 1997<br>
        A Free Product of <a
href="http://www.worldwidemart.com/scripts/">Matt's Script Archive,
        Inc.</a></font></tt></th></tr>
   </table>
  </center>
 </body>
</html>
(END ERROR HTML)
        }
    }

    elsif ($error eq 'request_method') {
            print <<"(END ERROR HTML)";
Content-type: text/html

<html>
 <head>
  <title>Error: Request Method</title>
 </head>
 <body bgcolor=#FFFFFF text=#000000>
  <center>
   <table border=0 width=600 bgcolor=#9C9C9C>
```

```
    <tr><th><font size=+2>Error: Request Method</font></th></tr>
    </table>
    <table border=0 width=600 bgcolor=#CFCFCF>
    <tr><td>The Request Method of the Form you submitted did not match
      either <tt>GET</tt> or <tt>POST</tt>.  Please check the form
➥ and make sure the
      <tt>method=</tt> statement is in upper case and matches <tt>GET</tt> or
<tt>POST</tt>.<p>

      <center><font size=-1>
      <a href="http://www.worldwidemart.com/scripts/formmail.shtml">ForMa
➥ il</a> V1.6 &copy; 1995 - 1997  Matt Wright<br>
        A Free Product of <a href="http://www.worldwidemart.com/scripts/">Matt's
Script Archive, Inc.</a>
      </font></center>
    </td></tr>
    </table>
  </center>
 </body>
</html>
(END ERROR HTML)
    }

    elsif ($error eq 'no_recipient') {
            print <<"(END ERROR HTML)";
Content-type: text/html

<html>
 <head>
  <title>Error: No Recipient</title>
 </head>
 <body bgcolor=#FFFFFF text=#000000>
  <center>
   <table border=0 width=600 bgcolor=#9C9C9C>
    <tr><th><font size=+2>Error: No Recipient</font></th></tr>
    </table>
    <table border=0 width=600 bgcolor=#CFCFCF>
    <tr><td>No Recipient was specified in the data sent to FormMail.  Please
      make sure you have filled in the 'recipient' form field with an e-mail
      address.  More information on filling in recipient form fields can be
      found in the README file.<hr size=1>
```

```
      <center><font size=-1>
        <a href="http://www.worldwidemart.com/scripts/formmail.shtml">FormMa
➡ il</a> V1.6 &copy; 1995 - 1997  Matt Wright<br>
        A Free Product of <a href="http://www.worldwidemart.com/scripts/">Matt's
Script Archive, Inc.</a>
        </font></center>
      </td></tr>
    </table>
   </center>
 </body>
</html>
(END ERROR HTML)
    }

    elsif ($error eq 'missing_fields') {
        if ($Config{'missing_fields_redirect'}) {
            print "Location: $Config{'missing_fields_redirect'}\n\n";
        }
        else {
            foreach $missing_field (@error_fields) {
                $missing_field_list .= "        <li>$missing_field\n";
            }

            print <<"(END ERROR HTML)";
Content-type: text/html

<html>
 <head>
  <title>Error: Blank Fields</title>
 </head>
  <center>
   <table border=0 width=600 bgcolor=#9C9C9C>
    <tr><th><font size=+2>Error: Blank Fields</font></th></tr>
   </table>
   <table border=0 width=600 bgcolor=#CFCFCF>
    <tr><td>The following fields were left blank in your submission form:<p>
     <ul>
$missing_field_list
     </ul><br>

    These fields must be filled in before you can successfully
➡ submit the form.<p>
```

```
        Please use your browser's back button to return to the form
➥ and try again.<hr size=1>
        <center><font size=-1>
        <a href="http://www.worldwidemart.com/scripts/formmail.shtml">FormMa
➥ il</a> V1.6 &copy; 1995 - 1997  Matt Wright<br>
        A Free Product of <a href="http://www.worldwidemart.com/scripts/">Matt's
Script Archive, Inc.</a>
        </font></center>
      </td></tr>
    </table>
  </center>
 </body>
</html>
(END ERROR HTML)
          }
      }
      exit;
}
```

What is important to note is that the program is designed to return an HTML page to the user, indicating that the contact information in the form has been processed or indicating an error, if there was one. This is an important component of all CGI programs: they should either return valid data to the browser (such as HTML or the contents of an image file) or they should redirect the browser to a valid URL.

The formmail program offers many other features, such as the ability to set the subject line of e-mails and ensure that the script is not abused by users on other Web sites. Full details are available at the Web site for the program.

The last important piece of our basic site is to create access restrictions for the directory /home/httpd/html/authors/ so that only authorized users will have access to the files in this directory. To do this requires a two-step process. First, we need to create a users file with the necessary users in it, as we did in the last section when we discussed protecting directories with access control.

We do this for all users we wish to give access to the directory. Next, we want to create a group—let's call it authors—to make the job of managing access to the directory easier. We create this group by adding an entry for the group to our Web server's group file that looks like:

```
authors: <author1> <author2> <author3>
```

In this entry we have assumed that there are three users being given access to the directory.

Finally, we need to create a .htaccess file called /home/httpd/html/authors/ ("Auth" in these directives refers to authentication, not to our authors group):

```
AuthName Just For Authors
AuthType Basic
AuthUserFile /etc/httpd/conf/users
AuthGroupFile /etc/httpd/conf/groups
require group authors
```

The contents of this file are fairly straightforward. AuthName specifies the prompt presented to the user, which you can see in Figure 27.7. AuthUserFile tells the server where to find the list of valid usernames and passwords, just as AuthGroupFile tells the server where the list of valid groups is. Finally, the require directive indicates that only members of the group authors should be given access to the directory.

FIGURE 27.7:

The user prompt box

Now, when a user tries to access the directory in question for the first time in a session, they will be presented with an authentication dialog box by their browser, like the one in Figure 27.8 produced by Netscape Communicator.

FIGURE 27.8:

An authentication dialog box in Netscape Communicator

By default, if a user fails to authenticate properly, they will receive a page like the one in Figure 27.9. In order to provide a customized page indicating failure like the one shown here, we can edit the `srm.conf` file to indicate a custom error message by adding the following entry to the file:

```
ErrorDocument 401 /error.html
```

This entry indicates that when error 401 (Authorization Required) occurs, the server should return the indicated URL instead of the default message. Now when a user fails to authenticate, they will receive the page shown in Figure 27.10.

FIGURE 27.9:

The standard error page when a user fails to authenticate

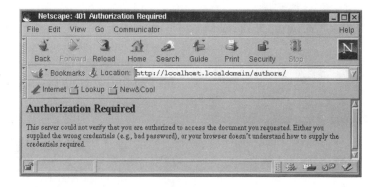

FIGURE 27.10:

A customized error page

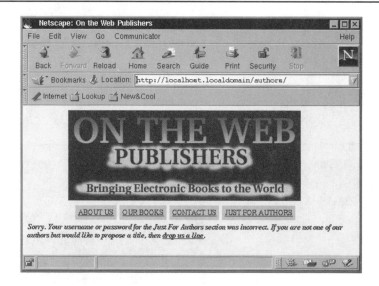

NOTE   All the files for this sample site appear on the included CD-ROM. In addition, you can see this site on the Web site for this book at `linux.juxta.com/OnTheWeb`. This Web site is running using the Apache Web server on a Red Hat Linux system.

Where Do We Go from Here?

This chapter has shown us how the Linux operating system provides a flexible tool as a network server, in this case a Web server.

In the next chapter, we look at another important role that Linux can play in an intranet: the job of a mail server. A mail server handles the processing of all incoming and outgoing mail for a network, deciding which messages are destined for internal users and directing these messages to the users' mailboxes, and directing messages bound for external networks onto the Internet for delivery.

Setting up a mail server can be a daunting task in a UNIX environment, especially using the Sendmail program, which is the dominant Linux mail server. Still, for many networks the job is manageable and, once it is done, a Linux mail server can be relied on to deliver high volumes of messages with little day-to-day administration.

CHAPTER
TWENTY-EIGHT

28

Linux as a Mail Server: The Power of Sendmail

- The Concept of a Mail Transport Agent

- Sendmail as the Foremost MTA

- Configuring Sendmail with M4

In this chapter, we are going to consider how to turn Linux into an organizational mail server using the Sendmail Mail Transport Agent.

The need for a mail server arises when you begin to connect together multiple desktops on a network and want to provide e-mail services to them. Using Sendmail, it is possible to configure a Linux system to act as the mail server for internal messages as well as for outgoing and incoming messages to and from the Internet.

We will first consider the concept of a mail transport agent (MTA), and then take a quick look at Sendmail, the foremost MTA in the Unix world, and some alternative MTAs. Finally, we will get down to the business of configuring Sendmail.

The Concept of a Mail Transport Agent

Normally, when users think of e-mail systems, they think of the software they use to read, compose, and send messages. This may be Netscape Communicator's mail module, Eudora, Pegasus Mail, or pine, but in all cases these programs are simply an interface to the back-end systems that really do the work of routing and delivering mail.

In none of these cases does the user's software actually handle delivery of outgoing mail or receipt of incoming mail. These programs are mail user agents (MUAs). There are numerous MUAs, and their job is to provide the user interface to the world of e-mail.

Behind these MUAs are the mail transport agents. MTAs handle the job of delivering, receiving, and routing mail messages. Generally, they all adhere to certain standard protocols (such as the Simple Mail Transport Protocol, or SMTP) that make up the Internet's e-mail system (and the e-mail system of almost every Unix-based network).

This distinction between an MUA and an MTA is an important one. In order to set up a mail server for an organization or any other network of computers, it is necessary to work with mail transport agents.

Sendmail as the Foremost MTA

There is little doubt that in the Unix world, the foremost MTA is the Sendmail program. This program defines the mail system we are familiar with on the Internet, providing the addressing structure we all know (`username@some.domain`) and the features we have come to expect (such as automatic mail forwarding).

In its dominance, Sendmail has grown to be the most powerful and complex Unix MTA available. In fact, configuration and management of a Sendmail system can be so complex in a large organization that an entire book is dedicated to the subject of designing a Sendmail system, configuring it, and keeping it running happily.

In this chapter, we will focus our attention on the configuration and use of Sendmail, since this is the default MTA included with Red Hat Linux and since it is so common on Unix networks.

TIP   This chapter only gives a cursory look at Sendmail and how to configure it. To gain a deeper insight into the subject, visit the Web site `www.sendmail.org`.

First, though, we will take a brief survey of some of the alternative MTAs available for Linux.

Smail

Sendmail may be the dominant Unix mail transport agent, but in the Linux world, smail is widely used as an MTA. Its configuration can be easier than Sendmail's (though not always), and it offers similar features, including SMTP support and UUCP support, that make it well-suited to an online mail server configuration.

Red Hat Linux 5 uses Sendmail as its default MTA and doesn't include the smail package. You can download the latest version of smail from `ftp://ftp.uu.net/networking/mail/smail/`.

Qmail

Qmail is a an alternative to Sendmail that hasn't garnered the same fame as smail but has several features that make it a strong contender in the MTA arena.

The author of qmail has made security a stated priority for the package. Over the years, Sendmail has had a number of security bugs exposed, though they have always been closed subsequently. The qmail philosophy is to do everything possible to avoid hidden holes because mail is a perpetually running service and therefore constantly open to hacking attempts.

Qmail also tries to make the delivery process as reliable as possible, with an inbox format that will be safer than most from corruption should a system crash occur while a message is being delivered to the inbox.

To top it off, qmail brings together features that are kept in separate applications in traditional MTAs: forwarding, aliasing, mailing lists, load management, and more.

The qmail home page is at `http://www.qmail.org/top.html`.

Configuring Sendmail with M4

As mentioned earlier, configuration of Sendmail can be a daunting task for even an experienced Unix system administrator. Mastering the intricacies of the system can take years.

Sendmail's configuration is stored in `/etc/sendmail.cf`, and just a look at the default configuration file that ships with Red Hat Linux 5 shows the complexity of the configuration. The file is so long that it is included here in a separate appendix, Appendix D.

If you look through this file, you will see that it consists of a large number of extremely cryptic rules that define the behavior of Sendmail. To expect anyone other than an expert in Sendmail to configure a basic system would be unreasonable if it were necessary to manually create and edit this type of configuration file.

Luckily, Sendmail provides a facility for creating a configuration file: a program called m4. M4 allows you to produce much simpler configuration files. M4 then processes these files and converts them into full-fledged Sendmail configuration files. All but the most knowledgeable users should create their Sendmail configurations in this manner.

NOTE You can find a discussion of m4 Sendmail configuration in the **README** file included with the configuration files at **/usr/lib/sendmail-cf/README**. For examples of how to configure Sendmail using m4, see **/usr/lib/sendmail-cf/cf**.

In this section, we will start by installing the necessary Sendmail configuration files for m4 to work and then will look at the configuration of an online mail server.

Installing the Sendmail Configuration Files

Depending on your distribution, the Sendmail configuration files may not have been installed by default when you installed Linux. In the case of Red Hat Linux 5, they are not. To determine whether you have the files, check to see if the directory /usr/lib/sendmail-cf exists.

In the case of Red Hat Linux 5, installing the files is easy. Mount the CD-ROM that comes with this book to a convenient location (such as /mnt/cdrom) and use rpm to install the file sendmail-cf-8.8.7-12.i386.rpm:

```
$ rpm -i /mnt/cdrom/RedHat/RPMS/sendmail-cf-8.8.7-12.i386.rpm
```

For other distributions of Linux, look at your documentation to find out how to install the configuration files for Sendmail.

Creating an Online Mail Server

Now we can look at the configuration file for an online mail server. We do this because online mail servers are a little bit easier to configure and understand than offline servers.

NOTE Even though the m4 system eases Sendmail configuration, the number of options is still immense. We will discuss only those options that appear in the configuration files in this chapter.

An online mail server is a mail server for a network that is fully connected to the Internet by a dedicated line. When someone outside the network directs a mail message to a user on the local network, it can be delivered directly, and when a user on the network sends a message, it will be sent immediately.

In our case, we need to configure Sendmail to direct incoming messages to users' mailboxes and to immediately attempt to deliver messages sent by users. Messages will only be queued for later delivery if there is a problem delivering a message, such as a failure in the Internet connection while attempting to deliver the message.

Our m4 configuration file will look something like this:

```
include(`../m4/cf.m4')
OSTYPE(`linux')
undefine(`UUCP_RELAY')
undefine(`BITNET_RELAY')
FEATURE(redirect)
FEATURE(always_add_domain)
MAILER(local)
MAILER(smtp)
```

Let's break this down line-by-line.

- Line 1: `include(`../m4/cf.m4')`. These are the generic configuration files needed to build a Sendmail configuration file.

- Line 2: `OSTYPE(`linux')`. Our operating system type is defined as Linux so that the appropriate defaults are set.

- Line 3: `undefine(`UUCP_RELAY')`. By not defining a UUCP relay, we are indicating that there is no host to receive UUCP-directed mail and that UUCP recipients must be directly connected. Given that UUCP mail was designed for the era when most networks were not directly connected, most sites will leave UUCP_RELAY undefined.

- Line 4: `undefine(`BITNET_RELAY')`. Because we are not connected to the Bitnet network, we leave this undefined; addresses using the Bitnet format will not work.

- Line 5: `FEATURE(redirect)`. If set, any mail addressed to `address.REDIRECT` will be rejected with a message indicating the user's new address. In this way, when a user leaves, their new address can be aliased to their old address with .REDIRECT appended.

- Line 6: FEATURE(always_add_domain). This feature ensures that the From line always contains the local domain so that messages can be replied to by the recipients.

- Line 7: MAILER(local). Local mailer support allows Sendmail to deliver mail to local Unix mailboxes.

- Line 8: MAILER(smtp). SMTP mailer support allows Sendmail to send messages directly to recipient mail servers. This works in a system where the server is connected to the Internet and DNS services are available.

To create our Sendmail configuration file from the m4 configuration file, we need to create the m4 file in the directory /usr/lib/sendmail-cf/cf. In this case, let's call the file online.mc. The extension .mc is the generally accepted one for m4 configuration files.

Next, change the directory to /usr/lib/sendmail-cf/cf and issue this command:

```
$ m4 online.mc > online.cf
```

This will process the file using m4 and generate a Sendmail configuration file called online.cf.

The next step is to make a backup of your existing sendmail.cf file and then replace it with the one we just created. This needs to be done by the root user:

```
# cp /etc/sendmail.cf /etc/sendmail.cf.keep
# cp online.cf /etc/sendmail.cf
```

The last and final step is to restart the Sendmail daemon:

```
# killall -HUP sendmail
```

The killall command sends the specified signal to all processes running the named program, in this case Sendmail.

When the Sendmail daemon starts at boot time, it will now load your new configuration file. If you want to load Sendmail manually, use the command:

```
# sendmail -bd
```

By default, the Sendmail daemon loads at boot time in most distributions of Linux unless you choose to disable it. You can use the `sendmail -bd` command in your `rc.local` file if you need to add Sendmail to your boot cycle.

TIP   If you plan to run a large Sendmail site, then the book *Sendmail* from O'Reilly & Associates (2nd ed., 1997) is the definitive reference. The book is authored by Bryan Costales and Eric Allman. Be prepared for a long read, though.

Where Do We Go from Here?

With this chapter, we have now covered all the main topics related to setting up Linux as a server in an intranet.

In the next chapter, we take a look at an important topic in today's corporate world: the ability to run DOS and Windows software in Linux.

To a surprising extent, Linux is able to support DOS applications using its `dosemu` software. On top of that, efforts are under way, albeit still at an early stage, to write a Windows emulator called Wine that is capable of running 16-bit and 32-bit Windows applications. Although not ready for deployment as a tool for day-to-day work in a corporate environment, Wine is currently able to run Microsoft Word and other popular Windows applications. We will discuss the features and uses of these two compatibility packages.

Finally, we will look at Wabi, a Windows emulation environment created by Sun Microsystems for the Solaris operating system and ported to Linux by Caldera. Wabi offers stable, reliable Windows 3.1 emulation and the certified ability to run dozens of popular Windows 3.1 applications.

CHAPTER

TWENTY-NINE

29

Linux and DOS/Windows

■ Running DOS Applications in Linux

■ Windows with Wabi

■ Why Not Wine?

One of the biggest arguments against using Linux as a day-to-day operating system for productivity tasks such as word processing is that there is a lack of applications for Linux. Add to that the inability to run Windows applications (at least OS/2 can do that, right?) and Linux is just an oddity, a curious example of great technology with poor marketing.

The problem with that whole argument is that Linux can in fact run the majority of DOS applications and many Windows applications, and there is promise of even wider-ranging Windows compatibility.

DOS support has been available for Linux for some time, to the extent that numerous popular DOS applications can be run under Linux with little effort.

Also, several efforts are currently under way to provide complete Windows compatibility within the Linux environment. Commercially, Sun Microsystems' Wabi environment has been ported to Linux by Caldera and is available at a very reasonable cost. But, in true Linux spirit, a team of Linux developers has taken up the task of delivering a freely available, better-than-commercial Windows compatibility package called Wine.

In this chapter, we are going to look at all three endeavors: DOS emulation, Wabi, and Wine.

Running DOS Applications in Linux

Support for DOS applications is the strongest compatibility offering in Linux and is included with most Linux distributions.

Most Linux distributions, including Red Hat 5.1, ship with the DOS emulation application DOSEmu. Under this environment, it is possible to install and run DOS, including recent versions such as DOS 6.2, and then run most DOS applications. There are limitations, of course, including those that affect some graphics and font operations, but overall things work well.

In addition, a DOS environment can run inside a separate window in X Windows, making it easy to run DOS applications next to Linux programs.

Among the features offered by DOSEmu are:

- the ability for multiple users to run DOS applications simultaneously
- the ability to mount Unix directories to specific drive letters in the DOS environment
- the ability to print to Unix printer spools

Running DOSEmu

There are numerous configurations that can be used to run DOSEmu in Linux. These include:

- booting DOS from a floppy disk
- booting DOS from a disk image
- booting DOS from a separate partition

For the sake of simplicity, and to get a glimpse into how the software works, we will look at booting DOS from a disk image. Advanced configuration, including booting from other media, is well covered in the documentation, which for Red Hat 5 can be found at /usr/doc/dosemu-0.66.7/.

NOTE   Detailed information and documentation for DOSEmu is available at http://www.suse.com/~dosemu/. You can also download the latest version, with complete installation instructions, from this site.

In order to get DOS running, it is necessary to have a configuration file called /etc/dosemu.conf. This is a highly complex file that has extensive documentation.

However, Red Hat 5.1 makes things easy, coming with a preconfigured disk image file and a dosemu.conf file designed to boot from that disk image. The disk image itself is located at /var/lib/dosemu/hdimage. It contains a free variant of DOS called FreeDOS and many useful commands and utilities, including fdisk, format, unix2dos, and lredir (a utility for redirecting Linux directories to DOS drive letters).

To get a sense of what is involved in configuring a typical DOSEmu environment, the following is the contents of the default Red Hat 5.1 `dosemu.conf` file (all comment lines have been removed for brevity):

```
debug { off }
dosbanner on
timint on

terminal { charset latin  updatefreq 4  color on }

X { updatefreq 8 title "DOS in a BOX" icon_name "xdos" }
mathco on
cpu 80386
xms 1024
ems 1024

ifdef h_oddhost.hell.com
  abort "this host is not allowed to use dosemu"
endif

ifdef guest
  define restricted
  define c_dexeonly
  keyboard {  layout us  keybint on  rawkeyboard off  }
  HogThreshold 1
  video { vga }
  sound_emu off
else
  keyboard {  layout us  keybint on  rawkeyboard off  }
  HogThreshold 0
  video { vga }
  ifndef restricted
  endif
  sound_emu off
endif

ifdef restricted
  define c_normal
  secure on
  dexe { secure }
  ifndef guest
    ifndef c_dexerun
```

```
        disk { image "/var/lib/dosemu/hdimage" }
      endif
    endif
    dpmi off
    speaker emulated
    ipxsupport off
    printer { options "%s"  command "lpr"  timeout 20 }
  else
    secure off
    dexe { allowdisk }
    ifndef vbootfloppy
      bootA
      ifndef c_dexerun
        # If you are following the QuickStart guide, use this line:
        # disk { image "/var/lib/dosemu/hdimage.first" }
        disk { image "/var/lib/dosemu/hdimage" }
      endif
    endif
  ifndef vbootfloppy
      floppy { device /dev/fd0 threeinch }
    else
      bootA
      floppy { heads 2  sectors 18  tracks 80 threeinch  file
/var/lib/dosemu/disk
image }
    endif
    dpmi 4086
    irqpassing off
    speaker native
    ipxsupport off
    printer { options "%s"  command "lpr"  timeout 20 }
  endif

  ifdef restricted
    undef c_all
    ifdef guest
      undef c_normal
      define c_dexe
      define c_nice
      define c_x
    endif
  endif
```

Launching DOS

The simplest way to run DOSEmu is using the dos command from the console or inside an xterm window. When you issue the command

```
$ dos
```

DOSEmu will load and boot from the specified boot device in /etc/dosemu.conf. By default, in Red Hat 5, this means booting from the provided disk image file. Figure 29.1 shows the DOS prompt in an xterm window after the dos command has been issued.

FIGURE 29.1:

Running DOS in an xterm window

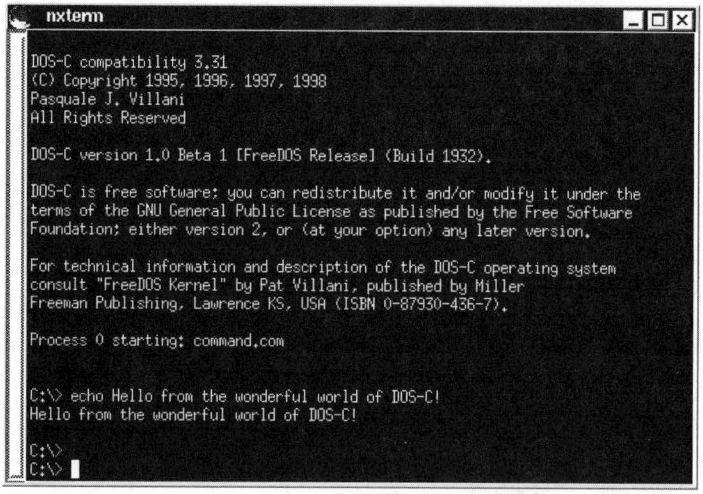

```
DOS-C compatibility 3.31
(C) Copyright 1995, 1996, 1997, 1998
Pasquale J. Villani
All Rights Reserved

DOS-C version 1.0 Beta 1 [FreeDOS Release] (Build 1932).

DOS-C is free software; you can redistribute it and/or modify it under the
terms of the GNU General Public License as published by the Free Software
Foundation; either version 2, or (at your option) any later version.

For technical information and description of the DOS-C operating system
consult "FreeDOS Kernel" by Pat Villani, published by Miller
Freeman Publishing, Lawrence KS, USA (ISBN 0-87930-436-7).

Process 0 starting: command.com

C:\> echo Hello from the wonderful world of DOS-C!
Hello from the wonderful world of DOS-C!

C:\>
C:\>
```

Once DOS is running, you can use standard DOS commands and syntax to run programs from floppy disks or, as we will see later in this chapter, to run applications contained in redirected directories.

Launching DOS in a Separate X Window

In addition to running DOS in the current window, DOS can be launched in its own window when running X Windows. You can do this by running the command

```
$ xdos
```

Xdos is actually a link to the main dos binary file. Running the program through the xdos link has the same effect as the command

```
$ dos -X
```

Running DOS in its own X window produces results like those in Figure 29.2.

FIGURE 29.2:

Running DOS in its own
X window

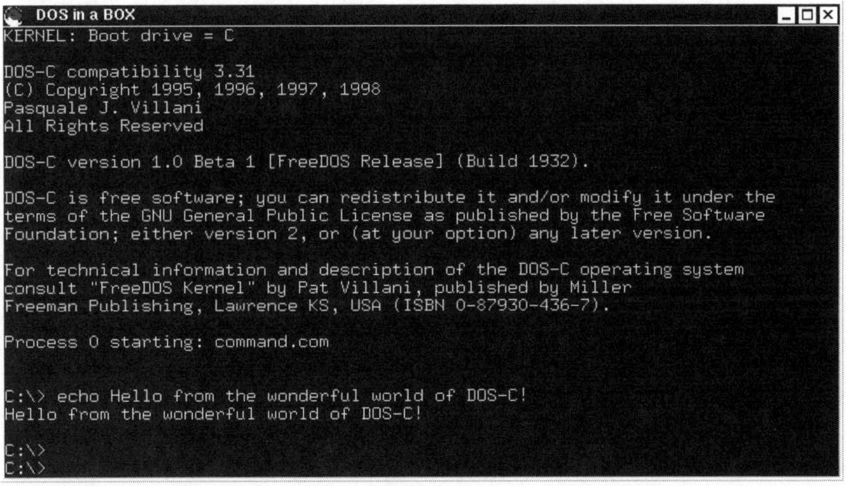

Useful DOSEmu Commands

The disk image that comes with DOSEmu, which Red Hat 5.1 boots from by default, contains several useful commands and utilities as outlined in the following table.

TABLE 29.1: DOSEmu Commands

Command	Description
eject.com	Ejects the CD-ROM drive
emumouse.com	Tunes the DOSEmu mouse driver
exitemu.com	Exits DOSEmu
lredir.com	Redirects a Unix directory to a DOS drive letter
unix.com	Executes a Linux command from within DOSEmu

Mounting Directories with *Lredir*

For DOSEmu to be useful, it needs to do more than work with disk images or floppy disks. It must be able to access parts of the Linux directory structure as if they were DOS disk drives. This ability allows your DOS environment to access data and applications that are stored on any existing DOS or Linux partitions or hard drives on your system.

The first step of the process takes place before the DOSEmu environment is launched: you need to make sure that the partitions you want to access are mounted at a logical location in your Linux directory structure. For instance, if you have an existing DOS partition, you could mount it at /dos.

Once all the directories and partitions you want to make available are accessible in Linux, you can start your DOS environment with

$ **dos**

or

$ **xdos**

Once DOS is running, you can use the lredir command to redirect Linux directories to DOS drive letters. The basic syntax is:

```
lredir <drive letter>: linux\fs/<linux directory>
```

This will cause the specified Linux directory to be made available in DOS using the specified drive letter. For instance, to make a DOS partition mounted as /dos in Linux available in your DOSEmu environment as D:, you could use the command

lredir D: linux\fs/dos

Another useful application of lredir is to make users' home directories available to them on a pre-specified DOS drive letter. To do this, use the following variation on the lredir command we just saw:

lredir E: linux\fs\${HOME}

Here, a user's home directory is being obtained from the Linux environment variable HOME, where Red Hat (and most versions of Linux) store the current user's home directory.

Finally, if you are booting initially from the provided disk image but want all booting from the loading of the `config.sys` file onward to occur from another location (such as a mounted DOS partition), you can use a simple two-step trick:

1. Edit the `config.sys` file on the initial disk image that is used to boot the DOSEmu environment. Make the following line the first line of the file (assuming the DOS partition is mounted under Linux at `/dos`):

   ```
   install=c:\lredir.exe c: linux\fs/dos
   ```

2. Make sure the `config.sys` files on the disk image and the DOS partition are identical. This means including the line from step 1 in the `config.sys` file on your DOS partition.

Now, before executing the rest of `config.sys` and then `autoexec.bat`, the disk image will be unmounted and the DOS partition will be redirected to `C:` in the DOS environment.

Windows with Wabi

While it is great to be able to run DOS applications, for most users the ability to run at least a handful of major Windows applications is more important than being able to run the majority of DOS applications.

Two main solutions are available for doing this: Wabi, which we will look at now, and Wine, which is discussed in the next section.

Wabi is a product that originated with Sun Microsystems, which developed it as a way to run Windows 3.1 and key Windows 3.1 applications on their Sun Solaris platform. The program has since been ported to Linux and is available from Caldera (`http://www.caldera.com`). You don't need to use Caldera's OpenLinux to run Wabi; it should work fine on most other modern Linux distributions. In fact, 75 percent of this book was written using Microsoft Word 6 for Windows running through Wabi on a Red Hat Linux 5 system (the other 25 percent used Wine instead of Wabi to run Word 6, but we'll get to that later).

In this section, we will look at the capabilities of Wabi. If you are interested in more information, visit the Caldera Web site mentioned above. The software comes with a manual and clear installation instructions that will work with most Linux distributions.

How Wabi Works

The concept behind Wabi is really quite simple: It translates Microsoft Windows' calls into X Windows and Linux calls, displaying windows and applications that look strikingly similar to Windows 3.1 in the X Windows environment. Figure 29.3 shows an X Windows desktop with an `xterm` window overlapping Windows' Program Manager.

FIGURE 29.3:

Wabi and X Windows can co-exist

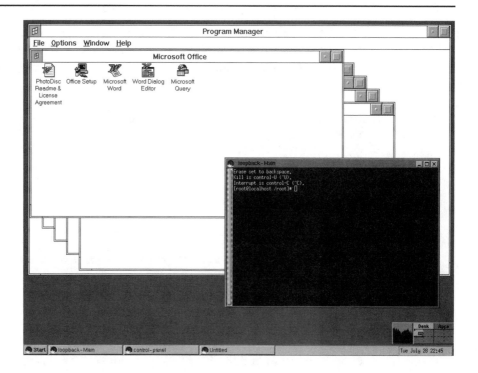

Luckily, because both Windows and Linux with Wabi run on Intel's x86 processors, the vast majority of commands in a Windows program (which are general x86 instructions, not Windows-specific) can be sent directly to the processor for processing. It is only those Windows-specific calls that Wabi has to handle in a special way, converting them to the appropriate Linux or X Windows instructions and requests.

Wabi allows copying and pasting between Windows applications and X Windows applications, supports object linking and embedding between Windows applications, supports Windows sockets networking, and can access the PC's serial and parallel ports.

In some ways, though, Wabi provides even better Windows than Windows 3.1 itself. Because Wabi is running in the true multiuser, multitasking environment of Linux, it allows the following benefits that are missing in Windows 3.1:

- true multitasking of Windows applications

- ability for multiple users to run Windows applications simultaneously on the same system

- remote display of Windows applications (using the X Windows environment)

In addition, Wabi supports a useful drive-mapping capability in which any mounted Linux directory can be mapped to any drive letter under Windows, giving Wabi users access to their important Linux files.

Limitations of Wabi

Of course, Wabi is not a perfect environment. Several limitations make Wabi unsuitable for some potential users. These limitations include:

- lack of support for MIDI audio devices

- lack of support for NetWare networks

- lack of support for applications requiring Windows VGA display drivers

- inability to format floppy disks

- lack of support for virtual device drivers

- lack of support for Adobe Type Manager

In addition, Wabi cannot run the 32-bit Windows applications popular in Windows 95, 98, and NT, which limits its usefulness to older versions of popular applications. Sun Microsystems is no longer actively developing Wabi, so it is unlikely to have support for newer Windows applications in the future.

> **NOTE**   It is also important to note that Wabi is not a Windows emulator. A licensed copy of Windows 3.1 and the original installation disks are necessary to complete the Wabi installation process. You will need to use these disks to install Windows 3.1 on your Linux system.

Wabi Application Support

Wabi is designed to provided full support for a list of certified applications. For a complete list, you can visit the Caldera Wabi Web page at `http://www.caldera.com/products/wabi`. The current list of supported applications include those shown in the following table.

TABLE 29.2: Wabi-supported Windows 3.1 Applications

Application	Versions
CorelDRAW!	3.0, 4.0
Harvard Graphics	2.0, 3.0
Lotus 1-2-3	4.0, 5.0
Lotus Ami Pro	3.1
Lotus cc:Mail client	2.03, 2.2
Lotus Approach	2.1, 3.02
Lotus Freelance Graphics	2.01, 2.1
Lotus Notes client	3.0c, 3.3
Lotus SmartSuite	3.1, 4.0
Lotus WordPro	96
Microsoft Access	2.0
Microsoft Excel	4.0, 5.0
Microsoft Mail client	3.2
Microsoft Office	4.3
Microsoft PowerPoint	3.0, 4.0
Microsoft Project	3.0, 4.0
Microsoft Schedule+	1.0
Microsoft Word	2.0, 6.0
PageMaker	4.0, 5.0

Continued on next page

TABLE 29.2 CONTINUED: Wabi-supported Windows 3.1 Applications

Application	Versions
Paradox	4.5, 5.0
Procomm Plus	1.02, 2.11
Quattro Pro	5.0, 6.0
Quicken	3.0, 4.0
Quicken Deluxe	4.0
WordPerfect	6.0a, 6.1

In addition to the list of certified applications, there are numerous other applications that are known to run in Wabi but that are not certified by Sun Microsystems or Caldera.

Why Not Wine?

Wine is a completely different product than Wabi for two reasons: It is not commercial and it aims to provide a completely free environment in which to run Windows applications on Linux systems.

The latter point is especially significant. While current development versions of Wine still rely on an existing Windows installation for some of the Windows system files, the goal of the project is to provide a complete alternative: If you install Wine on your Linux system, you won't need to install any version of Windows to run Windows applications.

As is typical of many open source Linux applications, Wine is under constant development and revision and is considered pre-release software. In fact, the release notes for Wine indicate that the software is considered alpha code, not even beta (and some people even refer to it as pre-alpha code), and should be used with caution. The Wine home page is at http://www.winehq.com/; new releases of Wine happen frequently and you can always get the latest from this Web site.

The compilation, configuration, and installation of Wine reflect this early development phase. Even so, it is possible to get some heavy-duty Windows applications, including Word 6, to run under Wine (25 per cent of this book was written that way).

The Future of Wine

The Wine team has a lot of plans for the Wine project that make it significant. These include:

- Being able to run Windows 3.1, 95, 98, and NT software on major PC Unix platforms, including Linux, FreeBSD, OpenBSD, and Solaris.

- Being able to run Windows applications without having an installed, licensed version of Windows available. Wine plans to provide a complete alternative set of system DLLs that are free of Microsoft code (you can still use your original Windows system DLLs if you have them, but they won't be required when Wine is finished). Planned support includes:

  - partial DirectX support for Windows games

  - full GDI support

  - support for native Windows 16-bit printer drivers

  - support for Winsock networking

  - support for scanners

  - limited support for Unicode

  - support for multiple languages

Wine is officially alpha developers-only code, and is not yet suitable for general use. Nevertheless, many people find it useful in running many different Windows applications in Linux, with some versions of Wine supporting a surprising range of Windows applications.

Where Do We Go from Here?

This chapter wraps up the main body of this book by noting several available paths for running your existing Windows and DOS applications. With this knowledge in hand, plus the experience you now have in using, configuring, and managing Linux systems, you should be able to perform every computing task you need to, using Linux or Windows and DOS applications running under Linux.

The rest of this book consists of several Appendixes, many of which you will find helpful in your daily use of Linux. In particular, "Linux Command Reference" (Appendix G) provides a quick guide to the syntax of major Linux commands, many of which you will find yourself using on a regular basis.

In addition, you should refer to Appendix E, "Sources of Linux Information," for useful resources for expanding your Linux knowledge and skills. Linux is a vast terrain that cannot be mastered quickly. Even the most adept Linux experts find themselves learning new tricks, secrets, and skills on an almost daily basis. Don't be afraid to do the same. More importantly, don't be afraid to ask questions in the Linux newsgroups and of the authors of popular Linux applications. Most often, the authors are more than happy to provide guidance, insight, and advice to fledgling Linux users. After all, it is in the interest of Linux developers and users to foster knowledge, awareness, and skill among the growing community of Linux users.

X Windows Colors

The following list contains the complete contents of the Red Hat 5 `rgb.txt` file. This file contains a set of predefined RGB colors that can be used in specifying colors for X Windows and Window Manager configurations and color schemes.

255 250 250	snow	248 248 255	ghost white	248 248 255	GhostWhite
245 245 245	white smoke	245 245 245	WhiteSmoke	220 220 220	gainsboro
255 250 240	floral white	255 250 240	FloralWhite	253 245 230	old lace
253 245 230	OldLace	250 240 230	linen	250 235 215	antique white
250 235 215	AntiqueWhite	255 239 213	papaya whip	255 239 213	PapayaWhip
255 235 205	blanched almond	255 235 205	BlanchedAlmond	255 228 196	bisque
255 218 185	peach puff	255 218 185	PeachPuff	255 222 173	navajo white
255 222 173	NavajoWhite	255 228 181	moccasin	255 248 220	cornsilk
255 255 240	ivory	255 250 205	lemon chiffon	255 250 205	LemonChiffon
255 245 238	seashell	240 255 240	honeydew	245 255 250	mint cream
245 255 250	MintCream	240 255 255	azure	240 248 255	alice blue
240 248 255	AliceBlue	230 230 250	lavender	255 240 245	lavender blush
255 240 245	LavenderBlush	255 228 225	misty rose	255 228 225	MistyRose
255 255 255	white	0 0 0	black	47 79 79	dark slate gray
47 79 79	DarkSlateGray	47 79 79	dark slate grey	47 79 79	DarkSlateGrey
105 105 05	dim gray	105 105 105	DimGray	105 105 105	dim grey
105 105 105	DimGrey	112 128 144	slate gray	112 128 144	SlateGray
112 128 144	slate grey	112 128 144	SlateGrey	119 136 153	light slate gray
119 136 153	LightSlateGray	119 136 153	light slate grey	119 136 153	LightSlateGrey
190 190 190	gray	190 190 190	grey	211 211 211	light grey
211 211 211	LightGrey	211 211 211	light gray	211 211 211	LightGray
25 25 112	midnight blue	25 25 112	MidnightBlue	0 0 128	navy
0 0 128	navy blue	0 0 128	NavyBlue	100 149 237	cornflower blue

100	149	237	CornflowerBlue	72	61	139	dark slate blue	72	61	139	DarkSlateBlue
106	90	205	slate blue	106	90	205	SlateBlue	123	104	238	medium slate blue
123	104	238	MediumSlateBlue	132	112	255	light slate blue	132	112	255	LightSlateBlue
0	0	205	medium blue	0	0	205	MediumBlue	65	105	225	royal blue
65	105	225	RoyalBlue	0	0	255	blue	30	144	255	dodger blue
30	144	255	DodgerBlue	0	191	255	deep sky blue	0	191	255	DeepSkyBlue
135	206	235	sky blue	135	206	235	SkyBlue	135	206	250	light sky blue
135	206	250	LightSkyBlue	70	130	180	steel blue	70	130	180	SteelBlue
176	96	222	light steel blue	176	196	222	LightSteelBlue	173	216	230	light blue
173	216	230	LightBlue	176	224	230	powder blue	176	224	230	PowderBlue
175	238	238	pale turquoise	175	238	238	PaleTurquoise	0	206	209	dark turquoise
0	206	209	DarkTurquoise	72	209	204	medium turquoise	72	209	204	MediumTurquoise
64	224	208	turquoise	0	255	255	cyan	224	255	255	light cyan
224	255	255	LightCyan	95	58	160	cadet blue	95	158	160	CadetBlue
102	205	170	medium aquamarine	102	205	170	MediumAquamarine	127	255	212	aquamarine
0	100	0	dark green	0	100	0	DarkGreen	85	107	47	dark olive green
85	107	47	DarkOliveGreen	143	188	143	dark sea green	143	188	143	DarkSeaGreen
46	139	87	sea green	46	139	87	SeaGreen	60	179	113	medium sea green
60	179	113	MediumSeaGreen	32	178	170	light sea green	32	178	170	LightSeaGreen
152	251	152	pale green	152	251	152	PaleGreen	0	255	127	spring green
0	255	127	SpringGreen	124	252	0	lawn green	124	252	0	LawnGreen
0	255	0	green	127	255	0	chartreuse	0	250	154	medium spring green
0	250	154	MediumSpringGreen	173	255	47	green yellow	173	255	47	GreenYellow
50	205	50	lime green	50	205	50	LimeGreen	154	205	50	yellow green
154	205	50	YellowGreen	34	139	34	forest green	34	139	34	ForestGreen
107	142	35	olive drab	107	142	35	OliveDrab	189	183	107	dark khaki

189 183 107	DarkKhaki	240 230 140	khaki	238 232 170	pale goldenrod
238 232 170	PaleGoldenrod	250 250 210	light goldenrod yellow	250 250 210	LightGoldenrod Yellow
255 255 224	light yellow	255 255 224	LightYellow	255 255 0	yellow
255 215 0	gold	238 221 130	light goldenrod	238 221 130	LightGoldenrod
218 165 32	goldenrod	184 134 11	dark goldenrod	184 134 11	DarkGoldenrod
188 143 143	rosy brown	188 143 143	RosyBrown	205 92 92	indian red
205 92 92	IndianRed	139 69 19	saddle brown	139 69 19	SaddleBrown
160 82 45	sienna	205 133 63	peru	222 184 135	burlywood
245 245 220	beige	245 222 179	wheat	244 164 96	sandy brown
244 164 96	SandyBrown	210 180 140	tan	210 105 30	chocolate
178 34 34	firebrick	165 42 42	brown	233 150 122	dark salmon
233 150 122	DarkSalmon	250 128 114	salmon	255 160 122	light salmon
255 160 122	LightSalmon	255 165 0	orange	255 140 0	dark orange
255 140 0	DarkOrange	255 127 80	coral	240 128 128	light coral
240 128 128	LightCoral	255 99 71	tomato	255 69 0	orange red
255 69 0	OrangeRed	255 0 0	red	255 105 180	hot pink
255 105 180	HotPink	255 20 147	deep pink	255 20 147	DeepPink
255 192 203	pink	255 182 193	light pink	255 182 193	LightPink
219 112 147	pale violet red	219 112 147	PaleVioletRed	176 48 96	maroon
199 21 133	medium violet red	199 21 133	MediumVioletRed	208 32 144	violet red
208 32 144	VioletRed	255 0 255	magenta	238 130 238	violet
221 160 221	plum	218 112 214	orchid	186 85 211	medium orchid
186 85 211	MediumOrchid	153 50 204	dark orchid	153 50 204	DarkOrchid
148 0 211	dark violet	148 0 211	DarkViolet	138 43 226	blue violet
138 43 226	BlueViolet	160 32 240	purple	147 112 219	medium purple
147 112 219	MediumPurple	216 191 216	thistle	255 250 250	snow1

238	233	233	snow2	205	201	201	snow3	139	137	137	snow4
255	245	238	seashell1	238	229	222	seashell2	205	197	191	seashell3
139	134	130	seashell4	255	239	219	AntiqueWhite1	238	223	204	AntiqueWhite2
205	192	176	AntiqueWhite3	139	131	120	AntiqueWhite4	255	228	196	bisque1
238	213	183	bisque2	205	183	158	bisque3	139	125	107	bisque4
255	218	185	PeachPuff1	238	203	173	PeachPuff2	205	175	149	PeachPuff3
139	119	101	PeachPuff4	255	222	173	NavajoWhite1	238	207	161	NavajoWhite2
205	179	139	NavajoWhite3	139	121	94	NavajoWhite4	255	250	205	LemonChiffon1
238	233	191	LemonChiffon2	205	201	165	LemonChiffon3	139	137	112	LemonChiffon4
255	248	220	cornsilk1	238	232	205	cornsilk2	205	200	177	cornsilk3
139	136	120	cornsilk4	255	255	240	ivory1	238	238	224	ivory2
205	205	193	ivory3	139	139	131	ivory4	240	255	240	honeydew1
224	238	224	honeydew2	193	205	193	honeydew3	131	139	131	honeydew4
255	240	245	LavenderBlush1	238	224	229	LavenderBlush2	205	193	197	LavenderBlush3
139	131	134	LavenderBlush4	255	228	225	MistyRose1	238	213	210	MistyRose2
205	183	181	MistyRose3	139	125	123	MistyRose4	240	255	255	azure1
224	238	238	azure2	193	205	205	azure3	131	139	139	azure4
131	111	255	SlateBlue1	122	103	238	SlateBlue2	105	89	205	SlateBlue3
71	60	139	SlateBlue4	72	118	255	RoyalBlue1	67	110	238	RoyalBlue2
58	95	205	RoyalBlue3	39	64	139	RoyalBlue4	0	0	255	blue1
0	0	238	blue2	0	0	205	blue3	0	0	139	blue4
30	144	255	DodgerBlue1	28	134	238	DodgerBlue2	24	116	205	DodgerBlue3
16	78	139	DodgerBlue4	99	184	255	SteelBlue1	92	172	238	SteelBlue2
79	148	205	SteelBlue3	54	100	139	SteelBlue4	0	191	255	DeepSkyBlue1
0	178	238	DeepSkyBlue2	0	154	205	DeepSkyBlue3	0	104	139	DeepSkyBlue4
135	206	255	SkyBlue1	126	192	238	SkyBlue2	108	166	205	SkyBlue3
74	112	139	SkyBlue4	176	226	255	LightSkyBlue1	164	211	238	LightSkyBlue2

141 182 205	LightSkyBlue3	96 123 139	LightSkyBlue4	198 226 255	SlateGray1
185 211 238	SlateGray2	159 182 205	SlateGray3	108 123 139	SlateGray4
202 225 255	LightSteelBlue1	188 210 238	LightSteelBlue2	162 181 205	LightSteelBlue3
110 123 139	LightSteelBlue4	191 239 255	LightBlue1	178 223 238	LightBlue2
154 192 205	LightBlue3	104 131 139	LightBlue4	224 255 255	LightCyan1
209 238 238	LightCyan2	180 205 205	LightCyan3	122 139 139	LightCyan4
187 255 255	PaleTurquoise1	174 238 238	PaleTurquoise2	150 205 205	PaleTurquoise3
102 139 139	PaleTurquoise4	152 245 255	CadetBlue1	142 229 238	CadetBlue2
122 197 205	CadetBlue3	83 134 139	CadetBlue4	0 245 255	turquoise1
0 229 238	turquoise2	0 197 205	turquoise3	0 134 139	turquoise4
0 255 255	cyan1	0 238 238	cyan2	0 205 205	cyan3
0 139 139	cyan4	151 255 255	DarkSlateGray1	141 238 238	DarkSlateGray2
121 205 205	DarkSlateGray3	82 139 139	DarkSlateGray4	127 255 212	aquamarine1
118 238 198	aquamarine2	102 205 170	aquamarine3	69 139 116	aquamarine4
193 255 193	DarkSeaGreen1	180 238 180	DarkSeaGreen2	155 205 155	DarkSeaGreen3
105 139 105	DarkSeaGreen4	84 255 159	SeaGreen1	78 238 148	SeaGreen2
67 205 128	SeaGreen3	46 139 87	SeaGreen4	154 255 154	PaleGreen1
144 238 144	PaleGreen2	124 205 124	PaleGreen3	84 139 84	PaleGreen4
0 255 127	SpringGreen1	0 238 118	SpringGreen2	0 205 102	SpringGreen3
0 139 69	SpringGreen4	0 255 0	green1	0 238 0	green2
0 205 0	green3	0 139 0	green4	127 255 0	chartreuse1
118 238 0	chartreuse2	102 205 0	chartreuse3	69 139 0	chartreuse4
192 255 62	OliveDrab1	179 238 58	OliveDrab2	154 205 50	OliveDrab3
105 139 34	OliveDrab4	202 255 112	DarkOliveGreen1	188 238 104	DarkOliveGreen2
162 205 90	DarkOliveGreen3	110 139 61	DarkOliveGreen4	255 246 143	khaki1
238 230 133	khaki2	205 198 115	khaki3	139 134 78	khaki4
255 236 139	LightGoldenrod1	238 220 130	LightGoldenrod2	205 190 112	LightGoldenrod3

139	129	76	LightGoldenrod4	255	255	224	LightYellow1	238	238	209	LightYellow2
205	205	180	LightYellow3	139	139	122	LightYellow4	255	255	0	yellow1
238	238	0	yellow2	205	205	0	yellow3	139	139	0	yellow4
255	215	0	gold1	238	201	0	gold2	205	173	0	gold3
139	117	0	gold4	255	193	37	goldenrod1	238	180	34	goldenrod2
205	155	29	goldenrod3	139	105	20	goldenrod4	255	185	15	DarkGoldenrod1
238	173	14	DarkGoldenrod2	205	149	12	DarkGoldenrod3	139	101	8	DarkGoldenrod4
255	193	193	RosyBrown1	238	180	180	RosyBrown2	205	155	155	RosyBrown3
139	105	105	RosyBrown4	255	106	106	IndianRed1	238	99	99	IndianRed2
205	85	85	IndianRed3	139	58	58	IndianRed4	255	130	71	sienna1
238	121	66	sienna2	205	104	57	sienna3	139	71	38	sienna4
255	211	155	burlywood1	238	197	145	burlywood2	205	170	125	burlywood3
139	115	85	burlywood4	255	231	186	wheat1	238	216	174	wheat2
205	186	150	wheat3	139	126	102	wheat4	255	165	79	tan1
238	154	73	tan2	205	133	63	tan3	139	90	43	tan4
255	127	36	chocolate1	238	118	33	chocolate2	205	102	29	chocolate3
139	69	19	chocolate4	255	48	48	firebrick1	238	44	44	firebrick2
205	38	38	firebrick3	139	26	26	firebrick4	255	64	64	brown1
238	59	59	brown2	205	51	51	brown3	139	35	35	brown4
255	140	105	salmon1	238	130	98	salmon2	205	112	84	salmon3
139	76	57	salmon4	255	160	122	LightSalmon1	238	149	114	LightSalmon2
205	129	98	LightSalmon3	139	87	66	LightSalmon4	255	165	0	orange1
238	154	0	orange2	205	133	0	orange3	139	90	0	orange4
255	127	0	DarkOrange1	238	118	0	DarkOrange2	205	102	0	DarkOrange3
139	69	0	DarkOrange4	255	114	86	coral1	238	106	80	coral2
205	91	69	coral3	139	62	47	coral4	255	99	71	tomato1
238	92	66	tomato2	205	79	57	tomato3	139	54	38	tomato4

255	69	0	OrangeRed1	238	64	0	OrangeRed2	205	55	0	OrangeRed3
139	37	0	OrangeRed4	255	0	0	red1	238	0	0	red2
205	0	0	red3	139	0	0	red4	255	20	147	DeepPink1
238	18	137	DeepPink2	205	16	118	DeepPink3	139	10	80	DeepPink4
255	110	180	HotPink1	238	106	167	HotPink2	205	96	144	HotPink3
139	58	98	HotPink4	255	181	197	pink1	238	169	184	pink2
205	145	158	pink3	139	99	108	pink4	255	174	185	LightPink1
238	162	173	LightPink2	205	140	149	LightPink3	139	95	101	LightPink4
255	130	171	PaleVioletRed1	238	121	159	PaleVioletRed2	205	104	137	PaleVioletRed3
139	71	93	PaleVioletRed4	255	52	179	maroon1	238	48	167	maroon2
205	41	144	maroon3	139	28	98	maroon4	255	62	150	VioletRed1
238	58	140	VioletRed2	205	50	120	VioletRed3	139	34	82	VioletRed4
255	0	255	magenta1	238	0	238	magenta2	205	0	205	magenta3
139	0	139	magenta4	255	131	250	orchid1	238	122	233	orchid2
205	105	201	orchid3	139	71	137	orchid4	255	187	255	plum1
238	174	238	plum2	205	150	205	plum3	139	102	139	plum4
224	102	255	MediumOrchid1	209	95	238	MediumOrchid2	180	82	205	MediumOrchid3
122	55	139	MediumOrchid4	191	62	255	DarkOrchid1	178	58	238	DarkOrchid2
154	50	205	DarkOrchid3	104	34	139	DarkOrchid4	155	48	255	purple1
145	44	238	purple2	125	38	205	purple3	85	26	139	purple4
171	130	255	MediumPurple1	159	121	238	MediumPurple2	137	104	205	MediumPurple3
93	71	139	MediumPurple4	255	225	255	thistle1	238	210	238	thistle2
205	181	205	thistle3	139	123	139	thistle4	0	0	0	gray0
0	0	0	grey0	3	3	3	gray1	3	3	3	grey1
5	5	5	gray2	5	5	5	grey2	8	8	8	gray3
8	8	8	grey3	10	10	10	gray4	10	10	10	grey4
13	13	13	gray5	13	13	13	grey5	15	15	15	gray6

15	15	15	grey6		18	18	18	gray7		18	18	18	grey7

15	15	15	grey6	18	18	18	gray7	18	18	18	grey7
20	20	20	gray8	20	20	20	grey8	23	23	23	gray9
23	23	23	grey9	26	26	26	gray10	26	26	26	grey10
28	28	28	gray11	28	28	28	grey11	31	31	31	gray12
31	31	31	grey12	33	33	33	gray13	33	33	33	grey13
36	36	36	gray14	36	36	36	grey14	38	38	38	gray15
38	38	38	grey15	41	41	41	gray16	41	41	41	grey16
43	43	43	gray17	43	43	43	grey17	46	46	46	gray18
46	46	46	grey18	48	48	48	gray19	48	48	48	grey19
51	51	51	gray20	51	51	51	grey20	54	54	54	gray21
54	54	54	grey21	56	56	56	gray22	56	56	56	grey22
59	59	59	gray23	59	59	59	grey23	61	61	61	gray24
61	61	61	grey24	64	64	64	gray25	64	64	64	grey25
66	66	66	gray26	66	66	66	grey26	69	69	69	gray27
69	69	69	grey27	71	71	71	gray28	71	71	71	grey28
74	74	74	gray29	74	74	74	grey29	77	77	77	gray30
77	77	77	grey30	79	79	79	gray31	79	79	79	grey31
82	82	82	gray32	82	82	82	grey32	84	84	84	gray33
84	84	84	grey33	87	87	87	gray34	87	87	87	grey34
89	89	89	gray35	89	89	89	grey35	92	92	92	gray36
92	92	92	grey36	94	94	94	gray37	94	94	94	grey37
97	97	97	gray38	97	97	97	grey38	99	99	99	gray39
99	99	99	grey39	102	102	102	gray40	102	102	102	grey40
105	105	105	gray41	105	105	105	grey41	107	107	107	gray42
107	107	107	grey42	110	110	110	gray43	110	110	110	grey43
112	112	112	gray44	112	112	112	grey44	115	115	115	gray45
115	115	115	grey45	117	117	117	gray46	117	117	117	grey46

120 120 120	gray47	120 120 120	grey47	122 122 122	gray48
122 122 122	grey48	125 125 125	gray49	125 125 125	grey49
127 127 127	gray50	127 127 127	grey50	130 130 130	gray51
130 130 130	grey51	133 133 133	gray52	133 133 133	grey52
135 135 135	gray53	135 135 135	grey53	138 138 138	gray54
138 138 138	grey54	140 140 140	gray55	140 140 140	grey55
143 143 143	gray56	143 143 143	grey56	145 145 145	gray57
145 145 145	grey57	148 148 148	gray58	148 148 148	grey58
150 150 150	gray59	150 150 150	grey59	153 153 153	gray60
153 153 153	grey60	156 156 156	gray61	156 156 156	grey61
158 158 158	gray62	158 158 158	grey62	161 161 161	gray63
161 161 161	grey63	163 163 163	gray64	163 163 163	grey64
166 166 166	gray65	166 166 166	grey65	168 168 168	gray66
168 168 168	grey66	171 171 171	gray67	171 171 171	grey67
173 173 173	gray68	173 173 173	grey68	176 176 176	gray69
176 176 176	grey69	179 179 179	gray70	179 179 179	grey70
181 181 181	gray71	181 181 181	grey71	184 184 184	gray72
184 184 184	grey72	186 186 186	gray73	186 186 186	grey73
189 189 189	gray74	189 189 189	grey74	191 191 191	gray75
191 191 191	grey75	194 194 194	gray76	194 194 194	grey76
196 196 196	gray77	196 196 196	grey77	199 199 199	gray78
199 199 199	grey78	201 201 201	gray79	201 201 201	grey79
204 204 204	gray80	204 204 204	grey80	207 207 207	gray81
207 207 207	grey81	209 209 209	gray82	209 209 209	grey82
212 212 212	gray83	212 212 212	grey83	214 214 214	gray84
214 214 214	grey84	217 217 217	gray85	217 217 217	grey85
219 219 219	gray86	219 219 219	grey86	222 222 222	gray87

222 222 222	grey87		
227 227 227	gray89		
229 229 229	grey90		
235 235 235	gray92		
237 237 237	grey93		
242 242 242	gray95		
245 245 245	grey96		
250 250 250	gray98		
252 252 252	grey99		
169 169 169	dark grey		
169 169 169	DarkGray		
0 139 139	dark cyan		
139 0 139	DarkMagenta		
144 238 144	light green		

RGB	Name	RGB	Name	RGB	Name
222 222 222	grey87	224 224 224	gray88	224 224 224	grey88
227 227 227	gray89	227 227 227	grey89	229 229 229	gray90
229 229 229	grey90	232 232 232	gray91	232 232 232	grey91
235 235 235	gray92	235 235 235	grey92	237 237 237	gray93
237 237 237	grey93	240 240 240	gray94	240 240 240	grey94
242 242 242	gray95	242 242 242	grey95	245 245 245	gray96
245 245 245	grey96	247 247 247	gray97	247 247 247	grey97
250 250 250	gray98	250 250 250	grey98	252 252 252	gray99
252 252 252	grey99	255 255 255	gray100	255 255 255	grey100
169 169 169	dark grey	169 169 169	DarkGrey	169 169 169	dark gray
169 169 169	DarkGray	0 0 139	dark blue	0 0 139	DarkBlue
0 139 139	dark cyan	0 139 139	DarkCyan	139 0 139	dark magenta
139 0 139	DarkMagenta	139 0 0	dark red	139 0 0	DarkRed
144 238 144	light green	144 238 144	LightGreen		

APPENDIX

B

X Windows Fonts

The following list is the result of running the `xlsfonts` program in Red Hat 5. It provides the complete font names for all X Windows fonts installed in a Red Hat 5 installation.

```
-adobe-courier-bold-i-normal--0-0-0-0-m-0-iso8859-1
-adobe-courier-bold-o-normal--0-0-75-75-m-0-iso8859-1
-adobe-courier-bold-o-normal--10-100-75-75-m-60-iso8859-1
-adobe-courier-bold-o-normal--10-100-75-75-m-60-iso8859-1
-adobe-courier-bold-o-normal--12-120-75-75-m-70-iso8859-1
-adobe-courier-bold-o-normal--12-120-75-75-m-70-iso8859-1
-adobe-courier-bold-o-normal--14-140-75-75-m-90-iso8859-1
-adobe-courier-bold-o-normal--14-140-75-75-m-90-iso8859-1
-adobe-courier-bold-o-normal--18-180-75-75-m-110-iso8859-1
-adobe-courier-bold-o-normal--18-180-75-75-m-110-iso8859-1
-adobe-courier-bold-o-normal--24-240-75-75-m-150-iso8859-1
-adobe-courier-bold-o-normal--24-240-75-75-m-150-iso8859-1
-adobe-courier-bold-o-normal--8-80-75-75-m-50-iso8859-1
-adobe-courier-bold-o-normal--8-80-75-75-m-50-iso8859-1
-adobe-courier-bold-r-normal--0-0-0-0-m-0-iso8859-1
-adobe-courier-bold-r-normal--0-0-75-75-m-0-iso8859-1
-adobe-courier-bold-r-normal--10-100-75-75-m-60-iso8859-1
-adobe-courier-bold-r-normal--10-100-75-75-m-60-iso8859-1
-adobe-courier-bold-r-normal--12-120-75-75-m-70-iso8859-1
-adobe-courier-bold-r-normal--12-120-75-75-m-70-iso8859-1
-adobe-courier-bold-r-normal--14-140-75-75-m-90-iso8859-1
-adobe-courier-bold-r-normal--14-140-75-75-m-90-iso8859-1
-adobe-courier-bold-r-normal--18-180-75-75-m-110-iso8859-1
-adobe-courier-bold-r-normal--18-180-75-75-m-110-iso8859-1
-adobe-courier-bold-r-normal--24-240-75-75-m-150-iso8859-1
-adobe-courier-bold-r-normal--24-240-75-75-m-150-iso8859-1
-adobe-courier-bold-r-normal--8-80-75-75-m-50-iso8859-1
-adobe-courier-bold-r-normal--8-80-75-75-m-50-iso8859-1
-adobe-courier-medium-i-normal--0-0-0-0-m-0-iso8859-1
-adobe-courier-medium-o-normal--0-0-75-75-m-0-iso8859-1
-adobe-courier-medium-o-normal--10-100-75-75-m-60-iso8859-1
-adobe-courier-medium-o-normal--10-100-75-75-m-60-iso8859-1
-adobe-courier-medium-o-normal--12-120-75-75-m-70-iso8859-1
-adobe-courier-medium-o-normal--12-120-75-75-m-70-iso8859-1
-adobe-courier-medium-o-normal--14-140-75-75-m-90-iso8859-1
-adobe-courier-medium-o-normal--14-140-75-75-m-90-iso8859-1
-adobe-courier-medium-o-normal--18-180-75-75-m-110-iso8859-1
-adobe-courier-medium-o-normal--18-180-75-75-m-110-iso8859-1
-adobe-courier-medium-o-normal--24-240-75-75-m-150-iso8859-1
```

```
-adobe-courier-medium-o-normal--24-240-75-75-m-150-iso8859-1
-adobe-courier-medium-o-normal--8-80-75-75-m-50-iso8859-1
-adobe-courier-medium-o-normal--8-80-75-75-m-50-iso8859-1
-adobe-courier-medium-r-normal--0-0-0-0-m-0-iso8859-1
-adobe-courier-medium-r-normal--0-0-75-75-m-0-iso8859-1
-adobe-courier-medium-r-normal--10-100-75-75-m-60-iso8859-1
-adobe-courier-medium-r-normal--10-100-75-75-m-60-iso8859-1
-adobe-courier-medium-r-normal--12-120-75-75-m-70-iso8859-1
-adobe-courier-medium-r-normal--12-120-75-75-m-70-iso8859-1
-adobe-courier-medium-r-normal--14-140-75-75-m-90-iso8859-1
-adobe-courier-medium-r-normal--14-140-75-75-m-90-iso8859-1
-adobe-courier-medium-r-normal--18-180-75-75-m-110-iso8859-1
-adobe-courier-medium-r-normal--18-180-75-75-m-110-iso8859-1
-adobe-courier-medium-r-normal--24-240-75-75-m-150-iso8859-1
-adobe-courier-medium-r-normal--24-240-75-75-m-150-iso8859-1
-adobe-courier-medium-r-normal--8-80-75-75-m-50-iso8859-1
-adobe-courier-medium-r-normal--8-80-75-75-m-50-iso8859-1
-adobe-helvetica-bold-o-normal--0-0-75-75-p-0-iso8859-1
-adobe-helvetica-bold-o-normal--10-100-75-75-p-60-iso8859-1
-adobe-helvetica-bold-o-normal--10-100-75-75-p-60-iso8859-1
-adobe-helvetica-bold-o-normal--12-120-75-75-p-69-iso8859-1
-adobe-helvetica-bold-o-normal--12-120-75-75-p-69-iso8859-1
-adobe-helvetica-bold-o-normal--14-140-75-75-p-82-iso8859-1
-adobe-helvetica-bold-o-normal--14-140-75-75-p-82-iso8859-1
-adobe-helvetica-bold-o-normal--18-180-75-75-p-104-iso8859-1
-adobe-helvetica-bold-o-normal--18-180-75-75-p-104-iso8859-1
-adobe-helvetica-bold-o-normal--24-240-75-75-p-138-iso8859-1
-adobe-helvetica-bold-o-normal--24-240-75-75-p-138-iso8859-1
-adobe-helvetica-bold-o-normal--8-80-75-75-p-50-iso8859-1
-adobe-helvetica-bold-o-normal--8-80-75-75-p-50-iso8859-1
-adobe-helvetica-bold-r-normal--0-0-75-75-p-0-iso8859-1
-adobe-helvetica-bold-r-normal--10-100-75-75-p-60-iso8859-1
-adobe-helvetica-bold-r-normal--10-100-75-75-p-60-iso8859-1
-adobe-helvetica-bold-r-normal--12-120-75-75-p-70-iso8859-1
-adobe-helvetica-bold-r-normal--12-120-75-75-p-70-iso8859-1
-adobe-helvetica-bold-r-normal--14-140-75-75-p-82-iso8859-1
-adobe-helvetica-bold-r-normal--14-140-75-75-p-82-iso8859-1
-adobe-helvetica-bold-r-normal--18-180-75-75-p-103-iso8859-1
-adobe-helvetica-bold-r-normal--18-180-75-75-p-103-iso8859-1
-adobe-helvetica-bold-r-normal--24-240-75-75-p-138-iso8859-1
-adobe-helvetica-bold-r-normal--24-240-75-75-p-138-iso8859-1
-adobe-helvetica-bold-r-normal--8-80-75-75-p-50-iso8859-1
-adobe-helvetica-bold-r-normal--8-80-75-75-p-50-iso8859-1
-adobe-helvetica-medium-o-normal--0-0-75-75-p-0-iso8859-1
```

```
-adobe-helvetica-medium-o-normal--10-100-75-75-p-57-iso8859-1
-adobe-helvetica-medium-o-normal--10-100-75-75-p-57-iso8859-1
-adobe-helvetica-medium-o-normal--12-120-75-75-p-67-iso8859-1
-adobe-helvetica-medium-o-normal--12-120-75-75-p-67-iso8859-1
-adobe-helvetica-medium-o-normal--14-140-75-75-p-78-iso8859-1
-adobe-helvetica-medium-o-normal--14-140-75-75-p-78-iso8859-1
-adobe-helvetica-medium-o-normal--18-180-75-75-p-98-iso8859-1
-adobe-helvetica-medium-o-normal--18-180-75-75-p-98-iso8859-1
-adobe-helvetica-medium-o-normal--24-240-75-75-p-130-iso8859-1
-adobe-helvetica-medium-o-normal--24-240-75-75-p-130-iso8859-1
-adobe-helvetica-medium-o-normal--8-80-75-75-p-47-iso8859-1
-adobe-helvetica-medium-o-normal--8-80-75-75-p-47-iso8859-1
-adobe-helvetica-medium-r-normal--0-0-75-75-p-0-iso8859-1
-adobe-helvetica-medium-r-normal--10-100-75-75-p-56-iso8859-1
-adobe-helvetica-medium-r-normal--10-100-75-75-p-56-iso8859-1
-adobe-helvetica-medium-r-normal--12-120-75-75-p-67-iso8859-1
-adobe-helvetica-medium-r-normal--12-120-75-75-p-67-iso8859-1
-adobe-helvetica-medium-r-normal--14-140-75-75-p-77-iso8859-1
-adobe-helvetica-medium-r-normal--14-140-75-75-p-77-iso8859-1
-adobe-helvetica-medium-r-normal--18-180-75-75-p-98-iso8859-1
-adobe-helvetica-medium-r-normal--18-180-75-75-p-98-iso8859-1
-adobe-helvetica-medium-r-normal--24-240-75-75-p-130-iso8859-1
-adobe-helvetica-medium-r-normal--24-240-75-75-p-130-iso8859-1
-adobe-helvetica-medium-r-normal--8-80-75-75-p-46-iso8859-1
-adobe-helvetica-medium-r-normal--8-80-75-75-p-46-iso8859-1
-adobe-new century schoolbook-bold-i-normal--0-0-75-75-p-0-iso8859-1
-adobe-new century schoolbook-bold-i-normal--10-100-75-75-p-66-iso8859-1
-adobe-new century schoolbook-bold-i-normal--10-100-75-75-p-66-iso8859-1
-adobe-new century schoolbook-bold-i-normal--12-120-75-75-p-76-iso8859-1
-adobe-new century schoolbook-bold-i-normal--12-120-75-75-p-76-iso8859-1
-adobe-new century schoolbook-bold-i-normal--14-140-75-75-p-88-iso8859-1
-adobe-new century schoolbook-bold-i-normal--14-140-75-75-p-88-iso8859-1
-adobe-new century schoolbook-bold-i-normal--18-180-75-75-p-111-iso8859-1
-adobe-new century schoolbook-bold-i-normal--18-180-75-75-p-111-iso8859-1
-adobe-new century schoolbook-bold-i-normal--24-240-75-75-p-148-iso8859-1
-adobe-new century schoolbook-bold-i-normal--24-240-75-75-p-148-iso8859-1
-adobe-new century schoolbook-bold-i-normal--8-80-75-75-p-56-iso8859-1
-adobe-new century schoolbook-bold-i-normal--8-80-75-75-p-56-iso8859-1
-adobe-new century schoolbook-bold-r-normal--0-0-75-75-p-0-iso8859-1
-adobe-new century schoolbook-bold-r-normal--10-100-75-75-p-66-iso8859-1
-adobe-new century schoolbook-bold-r-normal--10-100-75-75-p-66-iso8859-1
-adobe-new century schoolbook-bold-r-normal--12-120-75-75-p-77-iso8859-1
-adobe-new century schoolbook-bold-r-normal--12-120-75-75-p-77-iso8859-1
-adobe-new century schoolbook-bold-r-normal--14-140-75-75-p-87-iso8859-1
```

```
-adobe-new century schoolbook-bold-r-normal--14-140-75-75-p-87-iso8859-1
-adobe-new century schoolbook-bold-r-normal--18-180-75-75-p-113-iso8859-1
-adobe-new century schoolbook-bold-r-normal--18-180-75-75-p-113-iso8859-1
-adobe-new century schoolbook-bold-r-normal--24-240-75-75-p-149-iso8859-1
-adobe-new century schoolbook-bold-r-normal--24-240-75-75-p-149-iso8859-1
-adobe-new century schoolbook-bold-r-normal--8-80-75-75-p-56-iso8859-1
-adobe-new century schoolbook-bold-r-normal--8-80-75-75-p-56-iso8859-1
-adobe-new century schoolbook-medium-i-normal--0-0-75-75-p-0-iso8859-1
-adobe-new century schoolbook-medium-i-normal--10-100-75-75-p-60-iso8859-1
-adobe-new century schoolbook-medium-i-normal--10-100-75-75-p-60-iso8859-1
-adobe-new century schoolbook-medium-i-normal--12-120-75-75-p-70-iso8859-1
-adobe-new century schoolbook-medium-i-normal--12-120-75-75-p-70-iso8859-1
-adobe-new century schoolbook-medium-i-normal--14-140-75-75-p-81-iso8859-1
-adobe-new century schoolbook-medium-i-normal--14-140-75-75-p-81-iso8859-1
-adobe-new century schoolbook-medium-i-normal--18-180-75-75-p-104-iso8859-1
-adobe-new century schoolbook-medium-i-normal--18-180-75-75-p-104-iso8859-1
-adobe-new century schoolbook-medium-i-normal--24-240-75-75-p-136-iso8859-1
-adobe-new century schoolbook-medium-i-normal--24-240-75-75-p-136-iso8859-1
-adobe-new century schoolbook-medium-i-normal--8-80-75-75-p-50-iso8859-1
-adobe-new century schoolbook-medium-i-normal--8-80-75-75-p-50-iso8859-1
-adobe-new century schoolbook-medium-r-normal--0-0-75-75-p-0-iso8859-1
-adobe-new century schoolbook-medium-r-normal--10-100-75-75-p-60-iso8859-1
-adobe-new century schoolbook-medium-r-normal--10-100-75-75-p-60-iso8859-1
-adobe-new century schoolbook-medium-r-normal--12-120-75-75-p-70-iso8859-1
-adobe-new century schoolbook-medium-r-normal--12-120-75-75-p-70-iso8859-1
-adobe-new century schoolbook-medium-r-normal--14-140-75-75-p-82-iso8859-1
-adobe-new century schoolbook-medium-r-normal--14-140-75-75-p-82-iso8859-1
-adobe-new century schoolbook-medium-r-normal--18-180-75-75-p-103-iso8859-1
-adobe-new century schoolbook-medium-r-normal--18-180-75-75-p-103-iso8859-1
-adobe-new century schoolbook-medium-r-normal--24-240-75-75-p-137-iso8859-1
-adobe-new century schoolbook-medium-r-normal--24-240-75-75-p-137-iso8859-1
-adobe-new century schoolbook-medium-r-normal--8-80-75-75-p-50-iso8859-1
-adobe-new century schoolbook-medium-r-normal--8-80-75-75-p-50-iso8859-1
-adobe-symbol-medium-r-normal--0-0-75-75-p-0-adobe-fontspecific
-adobe-symbol-medium-r-normal--10-100-75-75-p-61-adobe-fontspecific
-adobe-symbol-medium-r-normal--10-100-75-75-p-61-adobe-fontspecific
-adobe-symbol-medium-r-normal--12-120-75-75-p-74-adobe-fontspecific
-adobe-symbol-medium-r-normal--12-120-75-75-p-74-adobe-fontspecific
-adobe-symbol-medium-r-normal--14-140-75-75-p-85-adobe-fontspecific
-adobe-symbol-medium-r-normal--14-140-75-75-p-85-adobe-fontspecific
-adobe-symbol-medium-r-normal--18-180-75-75-p-107-adobe-fontspecific
-adobe-symbol-medium-r-normal--18-180-75-75-p-107-adobe-fontspecific
-adobe-symbol-medium-r-normal--24-240-75-75-p-142-adobe-fontspecific
-adobe-symbol-medium-r-normal--24-240-75-75-p-142-adobe-fontspecific
```

```
-adobe-symbol-medium-r-normal--8-80-75-75-p-51-adobe-fontspecific
-adobe-symbol-medium-r-normal--8-80-75-75-p-51-adobe-fontspecific
-adobe-times-bold-i-normal--0-0-75-75-p-0-iso8859-1
-adobe-times-bold-i-normal--10-100-75-75-p-57-iso8859-1
-adobe-times-bold-i-normal--10-100-75-75-p-57-iso8859-1
-adobe-times-bold-i-normal--12-120-75-75-p-68-iso8859-1
-adobe-times-bold-i-normal--12-120-75-75-p-68-iso8859-1
-adobe-times-bold-i-normal--14-140-75-75-p-77-iso8859-1
-adobe-times-bold-i-normal--14-140-75-75-p-77-iso8859-1
-adobe-times-bold-i-normal--18-180-75-75-p-98-iso8859-1
-adobe-times-bold-i-normal--18-180-75-75-p-98-iso8859-1
-adobe-times-bold-i-normal--24-240-75-75-p-128-iso8859-1
-adobe-times-bold-i-normal--24-240-75-75-p-128-iso8859-1
-adobe-times-bold-i-normal--8-80-75-75-p-47-iso8859-1
-adobe-times-bold-i-normal--8-80-75-75-p-47-iso8859-1
-adobe-times-bold-r-normal--0-0-75-75-p-0-iso8859-1
-adobe-times-bold-r-normal--10-100-75-75-p-57-iso8859-1
-adobe-times-bold-r-normal--10-100-75-75-p-57-iso8859-1
-adobe-times-bold-r-normal--12-120-75-75-p-67-iso8859-1
-adobe-times-bold-r-normal--12-120-75-75-p-67-iso8859-1
-adobe-times-bold-r-normal--14-140-75-75-p-77-iso8859-1
-adobe-times-bold-r-normal--14-140-75-75-p-77-iso8859-1
-adobe-times-bold-r-normal--18-180-75-75-p-99-iso8859-1
-adobe-times-bold-r-normal--18-180-75-75-p-99-iso8859-1
-adobe-times-bold-r-normal--24-240-75-75-p-132-iso8859-1
-adobe-times-bold-r-normal--24-240-75-75-p-132-iso8859-1
-adobe-times-bold-r-normal--8-80-75-75-p-47-iso8859-1
-adobe-times-bold-r-normal--8-80-75-75-p-47-iso8859-1
-adobe-times-medium-i-normal--0-0-75-75-p-0-iso8859-1
-adobe-times-medium-i-normal--10-100-75-75-p-52-iso8859-1
-adobe-times-medium-i-normal--10-100-75-75-p-52-iso8859-1
-adobe-times-medium-i-normal--12-120-75-75-p-63-iso8859-1
-adobe-times-medium-i-normal--12-120-75-75-p-63-iso8859-1
-adobe-times-medium-i-normal--14-140-75-75-p-73-iso8859-1
-adobe-times-medium-i-normal--14-140-75-75-p-73-iso8859-1
-adobe-times-medium-i-normal--18-180-75-75-p-94-iso8859-1
-adobe-times-medium-i-normal--18-180-75-75-p-94-iso8859-1
-adobe-times-medium-i-normal--24-240-75-75-p-125-iso8859-1
-adobe-times-medium-i-normal--24-240-75-75-p-125-iso8859-1
-adobe-times-medium-i-normal--8-80-75-75-p-42-iso8859-1
-adobe-times-medium-i-normal--8-80-75-75-p-42-iso8859-1
-adobe-times-medium-r-normal--0-0-75-75-p-0-iso8859-1
-adobe-times-medium-r-normal--10-100-75-75-p-54-iso8859-1
-adobe-times-medium-r-normal--10-100-75-75-p-54-iso8859-1
```

```
-adobe-times-medium-r-normal--12-120-75-75-p-64-iso8859-1
-adobe-times-medium-r-normal--12-120-75-75-p-64-iso8859-1
-adobe-times-medium-r-normal--14-140-75-75-p-74-iso8859-1
-adobe-times-medium-r-normal--14-140-75-75-p-74-iso8859-1
-adobe-times-medium-r-normal--18-180-75-75-p-94-iso8859-1
-adobe-times-medium-r-normal--18-180-75-75-p-94-iso8859-1
-adobe-times-medium-r-normal--24-240-75-75-p-124-iso8859-1
-adobe-times-medium-r-normal--24-240-75-75-p-124-iso8859-1
-adobe-times-medium-r-normal--8-80-75-75-p-44-iso8859-1
-adobe-times-medium-r-normal--8-80-75-75-p-44-iso8859-1
-adobe-utopia-bold-i-normal--0-0-0-0-p-0-iso8859-1
-adobe-utopia-bold-r-normal--0-0-0-0-p-0-iso8859-1
-adobe-utopia-medium-i-normal--0-0-0-0-p-0-iso8859-1
-adobe-utopia-medium-r-normal--0-0-0-0-p-0-iso8859-1
-adobe-utopia-regular-i-normal--0-0-75-75-p-0-iso8859-1
-adobe-utopia-regular-i-normal--10-100-75-75-p-55-iso8859-1
-adobe-utopia-regular-i-normal--10-100-75-75-p-55-iso8859-1
-adobe-utopia-regular-i-normal--12-120-75-75-p-67-iso8859-1
-adobe-utopia-regular-i-normal--12-120-75-75-p-67-iso8859-1
-adobe-utopia-regular-i-normal--15-140-75-75-p-79-iso8859-1
-adobe-utopia-regular-i-normal--15-140-75-75-p-79-iso8859-1
-adobe-utopia-regular-i-normal--19-180-75-75-p-100-iso8859-1
-adobe-utopia-regular-i-normal--19-180-75-75-p-100-iso8859-1
-adobe-utopia-regular-i-normal--25-240-75-75-p-133-iso8859-1
-adobe-utopia-regular-i-normal--25-240-75-75-p-133-iso8859-1
-adobe-utopia-regular-r-normal--0-0-75-75-p-0-iso8859-1
-adobe-utopia-regular-r-normal--10-100-75-75-p-56-iso8859-1
-adobe-utopia-regular-r-normal--10-100-75-75-p-56-iso8859-1
-adobe-utopia-regular-r-normal--12-120-75-75-p-67-iso8859-1
-adobe-utopia-regular-r-normal--12-120-75-75-p-67-iso8859-1
-adobe-utopia-regular-r-normal--15-140-75-75-p-79-iso8859-1
-adobe-utopia-regular-r-normal--15-140-75-75-p-79-iso8859-1
-adobe-utopia-regular-r-normal--19-180-75-75-p-101-iso8859-1
-adobe-utopia-regular-r-normal--19-180-75-75-p-101-iso8859-1
-adobe-utopia-regular-r-normal--25-240-75-75-p-135-iso8859-1
-adobe-utopia-regular-r-normal--25-240-75-75-p-135-iso8859-1
-b&h-lucida-bold-i-normal-sans-0-0-75-75-p-0-iso8859-1
-b&h-lucida-bold-i-normal-sans-10-100-75-75-p-67-iso8859-1
-b&h-lucida-bold-i-normal-sans-10-100-75-75-p-67-iso8859-1
-b&h-lucida-bold-i-normal-sans-12-120-75-75-p-79-iso8859-1
-b&h-lucida-bold-i-normal-sans-12-120-75-75-p-79-iso8859-1
-b&h-lucida-bold-i-normal-sans-14-140-75-75-p-92-iso8859-1
-b&h-lucida-bold-i-normal-sans-14-140-75-75-p-92-iso8859-1
-b&h-lucida-bold-i-normal-sans-18-180-75-75-p-119-iso8859-1
```

```
-b&h-lucida-bold-i-normal-sans-18-180-75-75-p-119-iso8859-1
-b&h-lucida-bold-i-normal-sans-19-190-75-75-p-122-iso8859-1
-b&h-lucida-bold-i-normal-sans-19-190-75-75-p-122-iso8859-1
-b&h-lucida-bold-i-normal-sans-24-240-75-75-p-151-iso8859-1
-b&h-lucida-bold-i-normal-sans-24-240-75-75-p-151-iso8859-1
-b&h-lucida-bold-i-normal-sans-8-80-75-75-p-49-iso8859-1
-b&h-lucida-bold-i-normal-sans-8-80-75-75-p-49-iso8859-1
-b&h-lucida-bold-r-normal-sans-0-0-75-75-p-0-iso8859-1
-b&h-lucida-bold-r-normal-sans-10-100-75-75-p-66-iso8859-1
-b&h-lucida-bold-r-normal-sans-10-100-75-75-p-66-iso8859-1
-b&h-lucida-bold-r-normal-sans-12-120-75-75-p-79-iso8859-1
-b&h-lucida-bold-r-normal-sans-12-120-75-75-p-79-iso8859-1
-b&h-lucida-bold-r-normal-sans-14-140-75-75-p-92-iso8859-1
-b&h-lucida-bold-r-normal-sans-14-140-75-75-p-92-iso8859-1
-b&h-lucida-bold-r-normal-sans-18-180-75-75-p-120-iso8859-1
-b&h-lucida-bold-r-normal-sans-18-180-75-75-p-120-iso8859-1
-b&h-lucida-bold-r-normal-sans-19-190-75-75-p-122-iso8859-1
-b&h-lucida-bold-r-normal-sans-19-190-75-75-p-122-iso8859-1
-b&h-lucida-bold-r-normal-sans-24-240-75-75-p-152-iso8859-1
-b&h-lucida-bold-r-normal-sans-24-240-75-75-p-152-iso8859-1
-b&h-lucida-bold-r-normal-sans-8-80-75-75-p-50-iso8859-1
-b&h-lucida-bold-r-normal-sans-8-80-75-75-p-50-iso8859-1
-b&h-lucida-medium-i-normal-sans-0-0-75-75-p-0-iso8859-1
-b&h-lucida-medium-i-normal-sans-10-100-75-75-p-59-iso8859-1
-b&h-lucida-medium-i-normal-sans-10-100-75-75-p-59-iso8859-1
-b&h-lucida-medium-i-normal-sans-12-120-75-75-p-71-iso8859-1
-b&h-lucida-medium-i-normal-sans-12-120-75-75-p-71-iso8859-1
-b&h-lucida-medium-i-normal-sans-14-140-75-75-p-82-iso8859-1
-b&h-lucida-medium-i-normal-sans-14-140-75-75-p-82-iso8859-1
-b&h-lucida-medium-i-normal-sans-18-180-75-75-p-105-iso8859-1
-b&h-lucida-medium-i-normal-sans-18-180-75-75-p-105-iso8859-1
-b&h-lucida-medium-i-normal-sans-19-190-75-75-p-108-iso8859-1
-b&h-lucida-medium-i-normal-sans-19-190-75-75-p-108-iso8859-1
-b&h-lucida-medium-i-normal-sans-24-240-75-75-p-136-iso8859-1
-b&h-lucida-medium-i-normal-sans-24-240-75-75-p-136-iso8859-1
-b&h-lucida-medium-i-normal-sans-8-80-75-75-p-45-iso8859-1
-b&h-lucida-medium-i-normal-sans-8-80-75-75-p-45-iso8859-1
-b&h-lucida-medium-r-normal-sans-0-0-75-75-p-0-iso8859-1
-b&h-lucida-medium-r-normal-sans-10-100-75-75-p-58-iso8859-1
-b&h-lucida-medium-r-normal-sans-10-100-75-75-p-58-iso8859-1
-b&h-lucida-medium-r-normal-sans-12-120-75-75-p-71-iso8859-1
-b&h-lucida-medium-r-normal-sans-12-120-75-75-p-71-iso8859-1
-b&h-lucida-medium-r-normal-sans-14-140-75-75-p-81-iso8859-1
-b&h-lucida-medium-r-normal-sans-14-140-75-75-p-81-iso8859-1
```

```
-b&h-lucida-medium-r-normal-sans-18-180-75-75-p-106-iso8859-1
-b&h-lucida-medium-r-normal-sans-18-180-75-75-p-106-iso8859-1
-b&h-lucida-medium-r-normal-sans-19-190-75-75-p-108-iso8859-1
-b&h-lucida-medium-r-normal-sans-19-190-75-75-p-108-iso8859-1
-b&h-lucida-medium-r-normal-sans-24-240-75-75-p-136-iso8859-1
-b&h-lucida-medium-r-normal-sans-24-240-75-75-p-136-iso8859-1
-b&h-lucida-medium-r-normal-sans-8-80-75-75-p-45-iso8859-1
-b&h-lucida-medium-r-normal-sans-8-80-75-75-p-45-iso8859-1
-b&h-lucidabright-demibold-i-normal--0-0-75-75-p-0-iso8859-1
-b&h-lucidabright-demibold-i-normal--10-100-75-75-p-59-iso8859-1
-b&h-lucidabright-demibold-i-normal--10-100-75-75-p-59-iso8859-1
-b&h-lucidabright-demibold-i-normal--12-120-75-75-p-72-iso8859-1
-b&h-lucidabright-demibold-i-normal--12-120-75-75-p-72-iso8859-1
-b&h-lucidabright-demibold-i-normal--14-140-75-75-p-84-iso8859-1
-b&h-lucidabright-demibold-i-normal--14-140-75-75-p-84-iso8859-1
-b&h-lucidabright-demibold-i-normal--18-180-75-75-p-107-iso8859-1
-b&h-lucidabright-demibold-i-normal--18-180-75-75-p-107-iso8859-1
-b&h-lucidabright-demibold-i-normal--19-190-75-75-p-114-iso8859-1
-b&h-lucidabright-demibold-i-normal--19-190-75-75-p-114-iso8859-1
-b&h-lucidabright-demibold-i-normal--24-240-75-75-p-143-iso8859-1
-b&h-lucidabright-demibold-i-normal--24-240-75-75-p-143-iso8859-1
-b&h-lucidabright-demibold-i-normal--8-80-75-75-p-48-iso8859-1
-b&h-lucidabright-demibold-i-normal--8-80-75-75-p-48-iso8859-1
-b&h-lucidabright-demibold-r-normal--0-0-75-75-p-0-iso8859-1
-b&h-lucidabright-demibold-r-normal--10-100-75-75-p-59-iso8859-1
-b&h-lucidabright-demibold-r-normal--10-100-75-75-p-59-iso8859-1
-b&h-lucidabright-demibold-r-normal--12-120-75-75-p-71-iso8859-1
-b&h-lucidabright-demibold-r-normal--12-120-75-75-p-71-iso8859-1
-b&h-lucidabright-demibold-r-normal--14-140-75-75-p-84-iso8859-1
-b&h-lucidabright-demibold-r-normal--14-140-75-75-p-84-iso8859-1
-b&h-lucidabright-demibold-r-normal--18-180-75-75-p-107-iso8859-1
-b&h-lucidabright-demibold-r-normal--18-180-75-75-p-107-iso8859-1
-b&h-lucidabright-demibold-r-normal--19-190-75-75-p-114-iso8859-1
-b&h-lucidabright-demibold-r-normal--19-190-75-75-p-114-iso8859-1
-b&h-lucidabright-demibold-r-normal--24-240-75-75-p-143-iso8859-1
-b&h-lucidabright-demibold-r-normal--24-240-75-75-p-143-iso8859-1
-b&h-lucidabright-demibold-r-normal--8-80-75-75-p-47-iso8859-1
-b&h-lucidabright-demibold-r-normal--8-80-75-75-p-47-iso8859-1
-b&h-lucidabright-medium-i-normal--0-0-75-75-p-0-iso8859-1
-b&h-lucidabright-medium-i-normal--10-100-75-75-p-57-iso8859-1
-b&h-lucidabright-medium-i-normal--10-100-75-75-p-57-iso8859-1
-b&h-lucidabright-medium-i-normal--12-120-75-75-p-67-iso8859-1
-b&h-lucidabright-medium-i-normal--12-120-75-75-p-67-iso8859-1
-b&h-lucidabright-medium-i-normal--14-140-75-75-p-80-iso8859-1
```

```
-b&h-lucidabright-medium-i-normal--14-140-75-75-p-80-iso8859-1
-b&h-lucidabright-medium-i-normal--18-180-75-75-p-102-iso8859-1
-b&h-lucidabright-medium-i-normal--18-180-75-75-p-102-iso8859-1
-b&h-lucidabright-medium-i-normal--19-190-75-75-p-109-iso8859-1
-b&h-lucidabright-medium-i-normal--19-190-75-75-p-109-iso8859-1
-b&h-lucidabright-medium-i-normal--24-240-75-75-p-136-iso8859-1
-b&h-lucidabright-medium-i-normal--24-240-75-75-p-136-iso8859-1
-b&h-lucidabright-medium-i-normal--8-80-75-75-p-45-iso8859-1
-b&h-lucidabright-medium-i-normal--8-80-75-75-p-45-iso8859-1
-b&h-lucidabright-medium-r-normal--0-0-75-75-p-0-iso8859-1
-b&h-lucidabright-medium-r-normal--10-100-75-75-p-56-iso8859-1
-b&h-lucidabright-medium-r-normal--10-100-75-75-p-56-iso8859-1
-b&h-lucidabright-medium-r-normal--12-120-75-75-p-68-iso8859-1
-b&h-lucidabright-medium-r-normal--12-120-75-75-p-68-iso8859-1
-b&h-lucidabright-medium-r-normal--14-140-75-75-p-80-iso8859-1
-b&h-lucidabright-medium-r-normal--14-140-75-75-p-80-iso8859-1
-b&h-lucidabright-medium-r-normal--18-180-75-75-p-103-iso8859-1
-b&h-lucidabright-medium-r-normal--18-180-75-75-p-103-iso8859-1
-b&h-lucidabright-medium-r-normal--19-190-75-75-p-109-iso8859-1
-b&h-lucidabright-medium-r-normal--19-190-75-75-p-109-iso8859-1
-b&h-lucidabright-medium-r-normal--24-240-75-75-p-137-iso8859-1
-b&h-lucidabright-medium-r-normal--24-240-75-75-p-137-iso8859-1
-b&h-lucidabright-medium-r-normal--8-80-75-75-p-45-iso8859-1
-b&h-lucidabright-medium-r-normal--8-80-75-75-p-45-iso8859-1
-b&h-lucidatypewriter-bold-r-normal-sans-0-0-75-75-m-0-iso8859-1
-b&h-lucidatypewriter-bold-r-normal-sans-10-100-75-75-m-60-iso8859-1
-b&h-lucidatypewriter-bold-r-normal-sans-10-100-75-75-m-60-iso8859-1
-b&h-lucidatypewriter-bold-r-normal-sans-12-120-75-75-m-70-iso8859-1
-b&h-lucidatypewriter-bold-r-normal-sans-12-120-75-75-m-70-iso8859-1
-b&h-lucidatypewriter-bold-r-normal-sans-14-140-75-75-m-90-iso8859-1
-b&h-lucidatypewriter-bold-r-normal-sans-14-140-75-75-m-90-iso8859-1
-b&h-lucidatypewriter-bold-r-normal-sans-18-180-75-75-m-110-iso8859-1
-b&h-lucidatypewriter-bold-r-normal-sans-18-180-75-75-m-110-iso8859-1
-b&h-lucidatypewriter-bold-r-normal-sans-19-190-75-75-m-110-iso8859-1
-b&h-lucidatypewriter-bold-r-normal-sans-19-190-75-75-m-110-iso8859-1
-b&h-lucidatypewriter-bold-r-normal-sans-24-240-75-75-m-140-iso8859-1
-b&h-lucidatypewriter-bold-r-normal-sans-24-240-75-75-m-140-iso8859-1
-b&h-lucidatypewriter-bold-r-normal-sans-8-80-75-75-m-50-iso8859-1
-b&h-lucidatypewriter-bold-r-normal-sans-8-80-75-75-m-50-iso8859-1
-b&h-lucidatypewriter-medium-r-normal-sans-0-0-75-75-m-0-iso8859-1
-b&h-lucidatypewriter-medium-r-normal-sans-10-100-75-75-m-60-iso8859-1
-b&h-lucidatypewriter-medium-r-normal-sans-10-100-75-75-m-60-iso8859-1
-b&h-lucidatypewriter-medium-r-normal-sans-12-120-75-75-m-70-iso8859-1
-b&h-lucidatypewriter-medium-r-normal-sans-12-120-75-75-m-70-iso8859-1
```

```
-b&h-lucidatypewriter-medium-r-normal-sans-14-140-75-75-m-90-iso8859-1
-b&h-lucidatypewriter-medium-r-normal-sans-14-140-75-75-m-90-iso8859-1
-b&h-lucidatypewriter-medium-r-normal-sans-18-180-75-75-m-110-iso8859-1
-b&h-lucidatypewriter-medium-r-normal-sans-18-180-75-75-m-110-iso8859-1
-b&h-lucidatypewriter-medium-r-normal-sans-19-190-75-75-m-110-iso8859-1
-b&h-lucidatypewriter-medium-r-normal-sans-19-190-75-75-m-110-iso8859-1
-b&h-lucidatypewriter-medium-r-normal-sans-24-240-75-75-m-140-iso8859-1
-b&h-lucidatypewriter-medium-r-normal-sans-24-240-75-75-m-140-iso8859-1
-b&h-lucidatypewriter-medium-r-normal-sans-8-80-75-75-m-50-iso8859-1
-b&h-lucidatypewriter-medium-r-normal-sans-8-80-75-75-m-50-iso8859-1
-bitstream-charter-black-i-normal--0-0-0-0-p-0-iso8859-1
-bitstream-charter-black-r-normal--0-0-0-0-p-0-iso8859-1
-bitstream-charter-bold-i-normal--0-0-0-0-p-0-iso8859-1
-bitstream-charter-bold-r-normal--0-0-0-0-p-0-iso8859-1
-bitstream-charter-medium-i-normal--0-0-0-0-p-0-iso8859-1
-bitstream-charter-medium-i-normal--0-0-0-0-p-0-iso8859-1
-bitstream-charter-medium-i-normal--0-0-75-75-p-0-iso8859-1
-bitstream-charter-medium-i-normal--10-100-75-75-p-55-iso8859-1
-bitstream-charter-medium-i-normal--10-100-75-75-p-55-iso8859-1
-bitstream-charter-medium-i-normal--12-120-75-75-p-65-iso8859-1
-bitstream-charter-medium-i-normal--12-120-75-75-p-65-iso8859-1
-bitstream-charter-medium-i-normal--15-140-75-75-p-82-iso8859-1
-bitstream-charter-medium-i-normal--15-140-75-75-p-82-iso8859-1
-bitstream-charter-medium-i-normal--19-180-75-75-p-103-iso8859-1
-bitstream-charter-medium-i-normal--19-180-75-75-p-103-iso8859-1
-bitstream-charter-medium-i-normal--25-240-75-75-p-136-iso8859-1
-bitstream-charter-medium-i-normal--25-240-75-75-p-136-iso8859-1
-bitstream-charter-medium-i-normal--8-80-75-75-p-44-iso8859-1
-bitstream-charter-medium-i-normal--8-80-75-75-p-44-iso8859-1
-bitstream-charter-medium-r-normal--0-0-0-0-p-0-iso8859-1
-bitstream-charter-medium-r-normal--0-0-0-0-p-0-iso8859-1
-bitstream-charter-medium-r-normal--0-0-75-75-p-0-iso8859-1
-bitstream-charter-medium-r-normal--10-100-75-75-p-56-iso8859-1
-bitstream-charter-medium-r-normal--10-100-75-75-p-56-iso8859-1
-bitstream-charter-medium-r-normal--12-120-75-75-p-67-iso8859-1
-bitstream-charter-medium-r-normal--12-120-75-75-p-67-iso8859-1
-bitstream-charter-medium-r-normal--15-140-75-75-p-84-iso8859-1
-bitstream-charter-medium-r-normal--15-140-75-75-p-84-iso8859-1
-bitstream-charter-medium-r-normal--19-180-75-75-p-106-iso8859-1
-bitstream-charter-medium-r-normal--19-180-75-75-p-106-iso8859-1
-bitstream-charter-medium-r-normal--25-240-75-75-p-139-iso8859-1
-bitstream-charter-medium-r-normal--25-240-75-75-p-139-iso8859-1
-bitstream-charter-medium-r-normal--8-80-75-75-p-45-iso8859-1
-bitstream-charter-medium-r-normal--8-80-75-75-p-45-iso8859-1
```

```
-bitstream-courier-bold-i-normal--0-0-0-0-m-0-iso8859-1
-bitstream-courier-bold-i-normal--0-0-0-0-m-0-iso8859-1
-bitstream-courier-bold-r-normal--0-0-0-0-m-0-iso8859-1
-bitstream-courier-bold-r-normal--0-0-0-0-m-0-iso8859-1
-bitstream-courier-medium-i-normal--0-0-0-0-m-0-iso8859-1
-bitstream-courier-medium-i-normal--0-0-0-0-m-0-iso8859-1
-bitstream-courier-medium-r-normal--0-0-0-0-m-0-iso8859-1
-bitstream-courier-medium-r-normal--0-0-0-0-m-0-iso8859-1
-daewoo-gothic-medium-r-normal--0-0-100-100-c-0-ksc5601.1987-0
-daewoo-gothic-medium-r-normal--16-120-100-100-c-160-ksc5601.1987-0
-daewoo-mincho-medium-r-normal--0-0-100-100-c-0-ksc5601.1987-0
-daewoo-mincho-medium-r-normal--16-120-100-100-c-160-ksc5601.1987-0
-daewoo-mincho-medium-r-normal--24-170-100-100-c-240-ksc5601.1987-0
-dec-terminal-bold-r-normal--0-0-75-75-c-0-dec-dectech
-dec-terminal-bold-r-normal--0-0-75-75-c-0-iso8859-1
-dec-terminal-bold-r-normal--14-140-75-75-c-80-dec-dectech
-dec-terminal-bold-r-normal--14-140-75-75-c-80-dec-dectech
-dec-terminal-bold-r-normal--14-140-75-75-c-80-iso8859-1
-dec-terminal-bold-r-normal--14-140-75-75-c-80-iso8859-1
-dec-terminal-medium-r-normal--0-0-75-75-c-0-dec-dectech
-dec-terminal-medium-r-normal--0-0-75-75-c-0-iso8859-1
-dec-terminal-medium-r-normal--14-140-75-75-c-80-dec-dectech
-dec-terminal-medium-r-normal--14-140-75-75-c-80-dec-dectech
-dec-terminal-medium-r-normal--14-140-75-75-c-80-iso8859-1
-dec-terminal-medium-r-normal--14-140-75-75-c-80-iso8859-1
-isas-fangsong ti-medium-r-normal--0-0-72-72-c-0-gb2312.1980-0
-isas-fangsong ti-medium-r-normal--16-160-72-72-c-160-gb2312.1980-0
-isas-song ti-medium-r-normal--0-0-72-72-c-0-gb2312.1980-0
-isas-song ti-medium-r-normal--16-160-72-72-c-160-gb2312.1980-0
-isas-song ti-medium-r-normal--24-240-72-72-c-240-gb2312.1980-0
-jis-fixed-medium-r-normal--0-0-75-75-c-0-jisx0208.1983-0
-jis-fixed-medium-r-normal--16-110-100-100-c-160-jisx0208.1983-0
-jis-fixed-medium-r-normal--16-150-75-75-c-160-jisx0208.1983-0
-jis-fixed-medium-r-normal--24-170-100-100-c-240-jisx0208.1983-0
-jis-fixed-medium-r-normal--24-230-75-75-c-240-jisx0208.1983-0
-misc-fixed-bold-r-normal--0-0-75-75-c-0-iso8859-1
-misc-fixed-bold-r-normal--13-100-100-100-c-70-iso8859-1
-misc-fixed-bold-r-normal--13-100-100-100-c-80-iso8859-1
-misc-fixed-bold-r-normal--13-120-75-75-c-70-iso8859-1
-misc-fixed-bold-r-normal--13-120-75-75-c-80-iso8859-1
-misc-fixed-bold-r-normal--14-130-75-75-c-70-iso8859-1
-misc-fixed-bold-r-normal--15-120-100-100-c-90-iso8859-1
-misc-fixed-bold-r-normal--15-140-75-75-c-90-iso8859-1
-misc-fixed-bold-r-semicondensed--0-0-75-75-c-0-iso8859-1
```

```
-misc-fixed-bold-r-semicondensed--13-100-100-100-c-60-iso8859-1
-misc-fixed-bold-r-semicondensed--13-120-75-75-c-60-iso8859-1
-misc-fixed-medium-r-normal--0-0-75-75-c-0-iso646.1991-irv
-misc-fixed-medium-r-normal--0-0-75-75-c-0-iso8859-1
-misc-fixed-medium-r-normal--0-0-75-75-c-0-iso8859-8
-misc-fixed-medium-r-normal--0-0-75-75-c-0-jisx0201.1976-0
-misc-fixed-medium-r-normal--0-0-75-75-c-0-jisx0208.1983-0
-misc-fixed-medium-r-normal--10-100-75-75-c-60-iso8859-1
-misc-fixed-medium-r-normal--10-70-100-100-c-60-iso8859-1
-misc-fixed-medium-r-normal--13-100-100-100-c-70-iso8859-1
-misc-fixed-medium-r-normal--13-100-100-100-c-80-iso8859-1
-misc-fixed-medium-r-normal--13-100-100-100-c-80-iso8859-8
-misc-fixed-medium-r-normal--13-120-75-75-c-70-iso8859-1
-misc-fixed-medium-r-normal--13-120-75-75-c-80-iso8859-1
-misc-fixed-medium-r-normal--13-120-75-75-c-80-iso8859-8
-misc-fixed-medium-r-normal--14-110-100-100-c-70-iso8859-1
-misc-fixed-medium-r-normal--14-130-75-75-c-140-jisx0208.1983-0
-misc-fixed-medium-r-normal--14-130-75-75-c-70-iso8859-1
-misc-fixed-medium-r-normal--14-130-75-75-c-70-jisx0201.1976-0
-misc-fixed-medium-r-normal--15-120-100-100-c-90-iso8859-1
-misc-fixed-medium-r-normal--15-140-75-75-c-90-iso8859-1
-misc-fixed-medium-r-normal--20-140-100-100-c-100-iso8859-1
-misc-fixed-medium-r-normal--20-200-75-75-c-100-iso8859-1
-misc-fixed-medium-r-normal--7-50-100-100-c-50-iso8859-1
-misc-fixed-medium-r-normal--7-70-75-75-c-50-iso8859-1
-misc-fixed-medium-r-normal--8-60-100-100-c-50-iso8859-1
-misc-fixed-medium-r-normal--8-80-75-75-c-50-iso646.1991-irv
-misc-fixed-medium-r-normal--8-80-75-75-c-50-iso8859-1
-misc-fixed-medium-r-normal--9-80-100-100-c-60-iso8859-1
-misc-fixed-medium-r-normal--9-90-75-75-c-60-iso646.1991-irv
-misc-fixed-medium-r-normal--9-90-75-75-c-60-iso8859-1
-misc-fixed-medium-r-semicondensed--0-0-75-75-c-0-iso646.1991-irv
-misc-fixed-medium-r-semicondensed--0-0-75-75-c-0-iso8859-1
-misc-fixed-medium-r-semicondensed--0-0-75-75-c-0-iso8859-8
-misc-fixed-medium-r-semicondensed--12-110-75-75-c-60-iso646.1991-irv
-misc-fixed-medium-r-semicondensed--12-110-75-75-c-60-iso8859-1
-misc-fixed-medium-r-semicondensed--12-90-100-100-c-60-iso8859-1
-misc-fixed-medium-r-semicondensed--13-100-100-100-c-60-iso8859-1
-misc-fixed-medium-r-semicondensed--13-100-100-100-c-60-iso8859-8
-misc-fixed-medium-r-semicondensed--13-120-75-75-c-60-iso8859-1
-misc-fixed-medium-r-semicondensed--13-120-75-75-c-60-iso8859-8
-misc-nil-medium-r-normal--0-0-75-75-c-0-misc-fontspecific
-misc-nil-medium-r-normal--2-20-75-75-c-10-misc-fontspecific
-schumacher-clean-bold-r-normal--0-0-75-75-c-0-iso646.1991-irv
```

```
-schumacher-clean-bold-r-normal--10-100-75-75-c-60-iso646.1991-irv
-schumacher-clean-bold-r-normal--10-100-75-75-c-60-iso8859-1
-schumacher-clean-bold-r-normal--10-100-75-75-c-80-iso646.1991-irv
-schumacher-clean-bold-r-normal--10-100-75-75-c-80-iso8859-1
-schumacher-clean-bold-r-normal--12-120-75-75-c-60-iso646.1991-irv
-schumacher-clean-bold-r-normal--12-120-75-75-c-60-iso8859-1
-schumacher-clean-bold-r-normal--12-120-75-75-c-80-iso646.1991-irv
-schumacher-clean-bold-r-normal--12-120-75-75-c-80-iso8859-1
-schumacher-clean-bold-r-normal--13-130-75-75-c-80-iso646.1991-irv
-schumacher-clean-bold-r-normal--13-130-75-75-c-80-iso8859-1
-schumacher-clean-bold-r-normal--14-140-75-75-c-80-iso646.1991-irv
-schumacher-clean-bold-r-normal--14-140-75-75-c-80-iso8859-1
-schumacher-clean-bold-r-normal--15-150-75-75-c-90-iso646.1991-irv
-schumacher-clean-bold-r-normal--15-150-75-75-c-90-iso8859-1
-schumacher-clean-bold-r-normal--16-160-75-75-c-80-iso646.1991-irv
-schumacher-clean-bold-r-normal--16-160-75-75-c-80-iso8859-1
-schumacher-clean-bold-r-normal--8-80-75-75-c-80-iso646.1991-irv
-schumacher-clean-bold-r-normal--8-80-75-75-c-80-iso8859-1
-schumacher-clean-medium-i-normal--0-0-75-75-c-0-iso646.1991-irv
-schumacher-clean-medium-i-normal--12-120-75-75-c-60-iso646.1991-irv
-schumacher-clean-medium-i-normal--12-120-75-75-c-60-iso8859-1
-schumacher-clean-medium-i-normal--8-80-75-75-c-80-iso646.1991-irv
-schumacher-clean-medium-i-normal--8-80-75-75-c-80-iso8859-1
-schumacher-clean-medium-r-normal--0-0-75-75-c-0-iso646.1991-irv
-schumacher-clean-medium-r-normal--10-100-75-75-c-50-iso646.1991-irv
-schumacher-clean-medium-r-normal--10-100-75-75-c-50-iso8859-1
-schumacher-clean-medium-r-normal--10-100-75-75-c-60-iso646.1991-irv
-schumacher-clean-medium-r-normal--10-100-75-75-c-60-iso8859-1
-schumacher-clean-medium-r-normal--10-100-75-75-c-70-iso646.1991-irv
-schumacher-clean-medium-r-normal--10-100-75-75-c-70-iso8859-1
-schumacher-clean-medium-r-normal--10-100-75-75-c-80-iso646.1991-irv
-schumacher-clean-medium-r-normal--10-100-75-75-c-80-iso8859-1
-schumacher-clean-medium-r-normal--12-120-75-75-c-60-iso646.1991-irv
-schumacher-clean-medium-r-normal--12-120-75-75-c-60-iso8859-1
-schumacher-clean-medium-r-normal--12-120-75-75-c-70-iso646.1991-irv
-schumacher-clean-medium-r-normal--12-120-75-75-c-70-iso8859-1
-schumacher-clean-medium-r-normal--12-120-75-75-c-80-iso646.1991-irv
-schumacher-clean-medium-r-normal--12-120-75-75-c-80-iso8859-1
-schumacher-clean-medium-r-normal--13-130-75-75-c-60-iso646.1991-irv
-schumacher-clean-medium-r-normal--13-130-75-75-c-60-iso8859-1
-schumacher-clean-medium-r-normal--13-130-75-75-c-80-iso646.1991-irv
-schumacher-clean-medium-r-normal--13-130-75-75-c-80-iso8859-1
-schumacher-clean-medium-r-normal--14-140-75-75-c-70-iso646.1991-irv
-schumacher-clean-medium-r-normal--14-140-75-75-c-70-iso8859-1
```

```
-schumacher-clean-medium-r-normal--14-140-75-75-c-80-iso646.1991-irv
-schumacher-clean-medium-r-normal--14-140-75-75-c-80-iso8859-1
-schumacher-clean-medium-r-normal--15-150-75-75-c-90-iso646.1991-irv
-schumacher-clean-medium-r-normal--15-150-75-75-c-90-iso8859-1
-schumacher-clean-medium-r-normal--16-160-75-75-c-80-iso646.1991-irv
-schumacher-clean-medium-r-normal--16-160-75-75-c-80-iso8859-1
-schumacher-clean-medium-r-normal--6-60-75-75-c-40-iso646.1991-irv
-schumacher-clean-medium-r-normal--6-60-75-75-c-40-iso8859-1
-schumacher-clean-medium-r-normal--6-60-75-75-c-50-iso646.1991-irv
-schumacher-clean-medium-r-normal--6-60-75-75-c-50-iso8859-1
-schumacher-clean-medium-r-normal--6-60-75-75-c-60-iso646.1991-irv
-schumacher-clean-medium-r-normal--6-60-75-75-c-60-iso8859-1
-schumacher-clean-medium-r-normal--8-80-75-75-c-50-iso646.1991-irv
-schumacher-clean-medium-r-normal--8-80-75-75-c-50-iso8859-1
-schumacher-clean-medium-r-normal--8-80-75-75-c-60-iso646.1991-irv
-schumacher-clean-medium-r-normal--8-80-75-75-c-60-iso8859-1
-schumacher-clean-medium-r-normal--8-80-75-75-c-70-iso646.1991-irv
-schumacher-clean-medium-r-normal--8-80-75-75-c-70-iso8859-1
-schumacher-clean-medium-r-normal--8-80-75-75-c-80-iso646.1991-irv
-schumacher-clean-medium-r-normal--8-80-75-75-c-80-iso8859-1
-sony-fixed-medium-r-normal--0-0-100-100-c-0-iso8859-1
-sony-fixed-medium-r-normal--0-0-100-100-c-0-jisx0201.1976-0
-sony-fixed-medium-r-normal--16-120-100-100-c-80-iso8859-1
-sony-fixed-medium-r-normal--16-120-100-100-c-80-jisx0201.1976-0
-sony-fixed-medium-r-normal--16-150-75-75-c-80-iso8859-1
-sony-fixed-medium-r-normal--16-150-75-75-c-80-jisx0201.1976-0
-sony-fixed-medium-r-normal--24-170-100-100-c-120-iso8859-1
-sony-fixed-medium-r-normal--24-170-100-100-c-120-jisx0201.1976-0
-sony-fixed-medium-r-normal--24-230-75-75-c-120-iso8859-1
-sony-fixed-medium-r-normal--24-230-75-75-c-120-jisx0201.1976-0
-sun-open look cursor-----0-0-75-75-p-0-sunolcursor-1
-sun-open look cursor-----12-120-75-75-p-160-sunolcursor-1
-sun-open look glyph-----0-0-75-75-p-0-sunolglyph-1
-sun-open look glyph-----10-100-75-75-p-101-sunolglyph-1
-sun-open look glyph-----12-120-75-75-p-113-sunolglyph-1
-sun-open look glyph-----14-140-75-75-p-128-sunolglyph-1
-sun-open look glyph-----19-190-75-75-p-154-sunolglyph-1
10x20
12x24
12x24kana
12x24romankana
5x7
5x8
6x10
```

6x12

6x13

6x13bold

6x9

7x13

7x13bold

7x14

7x14bold

8x13

8x13bold

8x16

8x16kana

8x16romankana

9x15

9x15bold

a14

cursor

decw$cursor

decw$session

fixed

hanzigb16fs

hanzigb16st

hanzigb24st

heb6x13

heb8x13

k14

kana14

kanji16

kanji24

lucidasans-10

lucidasans-10

lucidasans-12

lucidasans-12

lucidasans-14

lucidasans-14

lucidasans-18

lucidasans-18

lucidasans-24

lucidasans-24

lucidasans-8

lucidasans-8

lucidasans-bold-10

lucidasans-bold-10

lucidasans-bold-12

lucidasans-bold-12
lucidasans-bold-14
lucidasans-bold-14
lucidasans-bold-18
lucidasans-bold-18
lucidasans-bold-24
lucidasans-bold-24
lucidasans-bold-8
lucidasans-bold-8
lucidasans-bolditalic-10
lucidasans-bolditalic-10
lucidasans-bolditalic-12
lucidasans-bolditalic-12
lucidasans-bolditalic-14
lucidasans-bolditalic-14
lucidasans-bolditalic-18
lucidasans-bolditalic-18
lucidasans-bolditalic-24
lucidasans-bolditalic-24
lucidasans-bolditalic-8
lucidasans-bolditalic-8
lucidasans-italic-10
lucidasans-italic-10
lucidasans-italic-12
lucidasans-italic-12
lucidasans-italic-14
lucidasans-italic-14
lucidasans-italic-18
lucidasans-italic-18
lucidasans-italic-24
lucidasans-italic-24
lucidasans-italic-8
lucidasans-italic-8
lucidasanstypewriter-10
lucidasanstypewriter-10
lucidasanstypewriter-12
lucidasanstypewriter-12
lucidasanstypewriter-14
lucidasanstypewriter-14
lucidasanstypewriter-18
lucidasanstypewriter-18
lucidasanstypewriter-24
lucidasanstypewriter-24
lucidasanstypewriter-8

lucidasanstypewriter-8
lucidasanstypewriter-bold-10
lucidasanstypewriter-bold-10
lucidasanstypewriter-bold-12
lucidasanstypewriter-bold-12
lucidasanstypewriter-bold-14
lucidasanstypewriter-bold-14
lucidasanstypewriter-bold-18
lucidasanstypewriter-bold-18
lucidasanstypewriter-bold-24
lucidasanstypewriter-bold-24
lucidasanstypewriter-bold-8
lucidasanstypewriter-bold-8
nil2
olcursor
olglyph-10
olglyph-12
olglyph-14
olglyph-19
r14
r16
r24
rk14
rk16
rk24
variable

APPENDIX

C

Linux around the World (Non-English Linux Distributions)

- Linux in Croatian

- Linux in French

- Linux in German

- Linux in Japanese

- Linux in Portuguese

- Linux in Russian

- Linux in Spanish

Linux in Croatian

MicroLinux

MicroLinux is a small Croatian-language distribution that is designed to sit on a DOS partition. This makes it convenient for users who can't repartition their Windows 95 systems and need to run both Windows (or DOS) and Linux.

```
HULK - Hrvatska udruga Linux korisnika
WWW: http://linux.hr/
```

Linux in French

Kheops Linux

Logiciels du Soleil from France produces Kheops Linux, a French version of the Red Hat distributions. Version 5.0 is currently available, and an upcoming French version of Red Hat 5.1 has been announced.

```
Logiciels du Soleil
1 rue Pasqualini
F-06800 Cagnes sur mer
France
E-mail: kheops@linux-kheops.com
WWW: http://www.linux-kheops.com/
```

MNIS Linux

MNIS produces a French distribution of Linux known as MNIS Linux. MNIS Linux is billed as a PC-based X Workstation and includes unique features such as the K Desktop Environment.

```
MNIS
28, rue Mahias
F-92100 Boulogne
France
E-mail: info@mnis.fr
WWW: http://www.mnis.fr/
```

Linux in German

Delix DLD Linux

Delix produces DLD Linux (which stands for Deutsche Linux Distribution) as well as selling other Linux products, including Red Hat Linux, Xi Graphics' Accelerated X servers, and the Common Desktop Environment (CDE). DLD includes a commercial X server, Red Hat's RPM package management system, the Adabas-D database, and more.

```
Delix Computer GmbH
E-mail: info@delix.de
WWW: http://delix.de/
```

Eagle Linux

Eagle Linux is a German Linux distribution for the Motorola 68000 series processors with specific installation support for Amiga computers. Support is provided for most popular Amiga models and most Amiga hardware and peripherals.

```
Media Computer Products GmbH
Altenbergstrasse 7
D-71549 Auenwald
Germany
WWW: http://www.eagle-cp.com/www/m68k.html
```

S.u.S.E. Linux

S.u.S.E. Linux is available in both English and German, but the Germany-based company makes the German-speaking market its primary focus. The German version of the distribution closely matches the English product, with similar extras like S.u.S.E.'s set of extra servers for XFree86 and a good set of demo commercial software for Linux.

```
S.u.S.E.
Gesellschaft für Software und Systementwicklung mbH
Gebhardtstraße 2
D-90762 Fürth
Germany
E-mail: info@suse.de
WWW: http://www.suse.de
```

Linux in Japanese

Debian JP Linux

The Debian JP Project is an attempt to provide a Japanese installer and Japanese packages for the standard Debian Linux distribution. The project has produced some beta code, and a final release should be available by the time you read this.

```
The Debian JP Project
WWW: http://www.debian.or.jp/index.html
```

Linux in Portuguese

Conectiva Linux

Conectiva Linux is a Portuguese version of Red Hat Linux produced by Conectiva Informática in Brazil. At the time of this writing, the current distribution of Conectiva Linux was based on Red Hat 5.

```
Conectiva Informática
Rua Prof. Rubens Elke Braga, 558
Parolin
Brazil
E-mail: info@conectiva.com.br
WWW: http://www.conectiva.com.br/
```

Linux in Russian

Open Kernel: Linux

Open Kernel: Linux from UrbanSoft is a Russian distribution based on Red Hat Linux that offers Russian console fonts, a Russian X Windows environment, and additional Russian packages that are not part of the standard Red Hat environment.

```
UrbanSoft
E-mail: info@usoft.spb.ru
WWW: http://www.usoft.spb.ru/
```

Linux in Spanish

Eurielec Linux

Eurielec Linux is yet another non-English Linux distribution based on Red Hat Linux, this time in Spanish. Eurielec Linux version 2.0 is based on the latest Red Hat Linux 5.1.

```
Eurielec - ETSI Telecomunicacinon-EnglisWWW:
http://www.etsit.upm.es/~eurielec/
```

Red Hat Linux's Default *sendmail.cf* File

```
#####################################################################
#####################################################################
#####
#####          SENDMAIL CONFIGURATION FILE
#####
##### built by root@porky.redhat.com on Thu Oct 30 01:33:15 EST 1997
##### in /usr/src/bs/BUILD/sendmail-8.8.7/cf/cf
##### using ../ as configuration include directory
```

```
#####
#####################################################################
#####################################################################

#####   @(#)cfhead.m4   8.9 (Berkeley) 1/18/97   #####
#####   @(#)cf.m4       8.24 (Berkeley) 8/16/95   #####




#####   @(#)redirect.m4   8.5 (Berkeley) 8/17/96   #####


#####   @(#)always_add_domain.m4   8.1 (Berkeley) 6/7/93   #####


#####   @(#)use_cw_file.m4   8.1 (Berkeley) 6/7/93   #####



#####   @(#)local_procmail.m4   8.6 (Berkeley) 10/20/96   #####




#####   @(#)check_mail.m4   3.3 (Claus Assmann) 1997-08-05   #####




#####   @(#)use_ip.m4       1.0 (Claus Assmann) 1996-11-23   #####


#####   @(#)use_names.m4    1.0 (Claus Assmann) 1996-11-23   #####


#####   @(#)use_relayto.m4  1.0 (Claus Assmann) 1996-11-23   #####
```

```
#####   @(#)check_rcpt4.m4   2.4 (Claus Assmann) 1997-08-28   #####



#####   @(#)check_relay.m4   3.0 (Claus Assmann) 1997-06-01   #####




#####   @(#)proto.m4  8.151 (Berkeley) 7/31/97   #####


# level 7 config file format
V7/Berkeley

##################
#   local info   #
##################

Cwlocalhost
# file containing names of hosts for which we receive email
Fw/etc/sendmail.cw

# my official domain name
# ... define this only if sendmail cannot automatically determine your domain
#Dj$w.Foo.COM


CP.

# "Smart" relay host (may be null)
DS

# place to which unknown users should be forwarded
#Kuser user -m -a<>
#DLname_of_luser_relay

# operators that cannot be in local usernames (i.e., network indicators)
CO @ % !

# a class with just dot (for identifying canonical names)
```

```
C..

# a class with just a left bracket (for identifying domain literals)
C[[

# Mailer table (overriding domains)
#Kmailertable dbm /etc/mailertable

# Domain table (adding domains)
#Kdomaintable dbm /etc/domaintable

# Generics table (mapping outgoing addresses)
#Kgenerics dbm /etc/genericstable

# Virtual user table (maps incoming users)
#Kvirtuser dbm /etc/virtusertable

# who I send unqualified names to (null means deliver locally)
DR

# who gets all local email traffic ($R has precedence for unqualified names)
DH

# dequoting map
Kdequote dequote

# class E: names that should be exposed as from this host, even if we masquerade
# class L: names that should be delivered locally, even if we have a relay
# class M: domains that should be converted to $M
#CL root
CE root

# who I masquerade as (null for no masquerading) (see also $=M)
DM

# my name for error messages
DnMAILER-DAEMON


CPREDIRECT

# file containing full e-mail addresses of spammers (for check_mail):
```

```
# spammer@address.domain "Error-Code Error-Text"
# or junk domains (for check_mail, check_relay):
# junk.domain   "Error-Code Error-Text"
# or IP addresses (for check_relay):
# D.X.Y.Z "Error-Code Error-Text"
# C.X.Y "Error-Code Error-Text"
# B.X "Error-Code Error-Text"
# A "Error-Code Error-Text"
Kjunk hash -a@JUNK /etc/mail/deny



# file containing IP numbers of machines which can use our relay
F{LocalIP} /etc/mail/ip_allow

# file containing names of machines which can use our relay
F{LocalNames} /etc/mail/name_allow

# file containing names we relay to
F{RelayTo} /etc/mail/relay_allow



# Configuration version number
DZ8.8.7


##############
#   Options   #
##############

# strip message body to 7 bits on input?
O SevenBitInput=False

# 8-bit data handling
O EightBitMode=pass8


# wait for alias file rebuild (default units: minutes)
O AliasWait=10
```

```
# location of alias file
O AliasFile=/etc/aliases

# minimum number of free blocks on filesystem
O MinFreeBlocks=100

# maximum message size
#O MaxMessageSize=1000000

# substitution for space (blank) characters
O BlankSub=.

# avoid connecting to "expensive" mailers on initial submission?
O HoldExpensive=False

# checkpoint queue runs after every N successful deliveries
#O CheckpointInterval=10

# default delivery mode
O DeliveryMode=background

# automatically rebuild the alias database?
#O AutoRebuildAliases

# error message header/file
#O ErrorHeader=/etc/sendmail.oE

# error mode
#O ErrorMode=print

# save Unix-style "From_" lines at top of header?
#O SaveFromLine

# temporary file mode
O TempFileMode=0600

# match recipients against GECOS field?
#O MatchGECOS

# maximum hop count
#O MaxHopCount=17
```

```
# location of help file
O HelpFile=/usr/lib/sendmail.hf

# ignore dots as terminators in incoming messages?
#O IgnoreDots

# name resolver options
#O ResolverOptions=+AAONLY

# deliver MIME-encapsulated error messages?
O SendMimeErrors=True

# Forward file search path
O ForwardPath=$z/.forward.$w:$z/.forward

# open connection cache size
O ConnectionCacheSize=2

# open connection cache timeout
O ConnectionCacheTimeout=5m

# persistent host status directory
#O HostStatusDirectory=.hoststat

# single thread deliveries (requires HostStatusDirectory)?
#O SingleThreadDelivery

# use Errors-To: header?
O UseErrorsTo=False

# log level
O LogLevel=9

# send to me too, even in an alias expansion?
#O MeToo

# verify RHS in newaliases?
O CheckAliases=False

# default messages to old style headers if no special punctuation?
O OldStyleHeaders=True
```

```
# SMTP daemon options
#O DaemonPortOptions=Port=esmtp

# privacy flags
O PrivacyOptions=authwarnings

# who (if anyone) should get extra copies of error messages
#O PostMasterCopy=Postmaster

# slope of queue-only function
#O QueueFactor=600000

# queue directory
O QueueDirectory=/var/spool/mqueue

# timeouts (many of these)
#O Timeout.initial=5m
#O Timeout.connect=5m
#O Timeout.iconnect=5m
#O Timeout.helo=5m
#O Timeout.mail=10m
#O Timeout.rcpt=1h
#O Timeout.datainit=5m
#O Timeout.datablock=1h
#O Timeout.datafinal=1h
#O Timeout.rset=5m
#O Timeout.quit=2m
#O Timeout.misc=2m
#O Timeout.command=1h
#O Timeout.ident=30s
#O Timeout.fileopen=60s
O Timeout.queuereturn=5d
#O Timeout.queuereturn.normal=5d
#O Timeout.queuereturn.urgent=2d
#O Timeout.queuereturn.non-urgent=7d
O Timeout.queuewarn=4h
#O Timeout.queuewarn.normal=4h
#O Timeout.queuewarn.urgent=1h
#O Timeout.queuewarn.non-urgent=12h
#O Timeout.hoststatus=30m

# should we not prune routes in route-addr syntax addresses?
#O DontPruneRoutes
```

```
# queue up everything before forking?
O SuperSafe=True

# status file
O StatusFile=/var/log/sendmail.st

# time zone handling:
#   if undefined, use system default
#   if defined but null, use TZ envariable passed in
#   if defined and non-null, use that info
#O TimeZoneSpec=

# default UID (can be username or userid:groupid)
O DefaultUser=8:12

# list of locations of user database file (null means no lookup)
#O UserDatabaseSpec=/etc/userdb

# fallback MX host
#O FallbackMXhost=fall.back.host.net

# if we are the best MX host for a site, try it directly instead of config err
#O TryNullMXList

# load average at which we just queue messages
#O QueueLA=8

# load average at which we refuse connections
#O RefuseLA=12

# maximum number of children we allow at one time
#O MaxDaemonChildren=12

# maximum number of new connections per second
#O ConnectionRateThrottle=3

# work recipient factor
#O RecipientFactor=30000

# deliver each queued job in a separate process?
#O ForkEachJob
```

```
# work class factor
#O ClassFactor=1800

# work time factor
#O RetryFactor=90000

# shall we sort the queue by hostname first?
#O QueueSortOrder=priority

# minimum time in queue before retry
#O MinQueueAge=30m

# default character set
#O DefaultCharSet=iso-8859-1

# service switch file (ignored on Solaris, Ultrix, OSF/1, others)
#O ServiceSwitchFile=/etc/service.switch

# hosts file (normally /etc/hosts)
#O HostsFile=/etc/hosts

# dialup line delay on connection failure
#O DialDelay=10s

# action to take if there are no recipients in the message
#O NoRecipientAction=add-to-undisclosed

# chrooted environment for writing to files
#O SafeFileEnvironment=/arch

# are colons OK in addresses?
#O ColonOkInAddr

# how many jobs can you process in the queue?
#O MaxQueueRunSize=10000

# shall I avoid expanding CNAMEs (violates protocols)?
#O DontExpandCnames

# SMTP initial login message (old $e macro)
O SmtpGreetingMessage=$j Sendmail $v/$Z; $b
```

```
# UNIX initial From header format (old $l macro)
O UnixFromLine=From $g    $d

# delimiter (operator) characters (old $o macro)
O OperatorChars=.:%@!^/[]+

# shall I avoid calling initgroups(3) because of high NIS costs?
#O DontInitGroups

# are group-writable :include: and .forward files (un)trustworthy?
#O UnsafeGroupWrites

# where do errors that occur when sending errors get sent?
#O DoubleBounceAddress

# what user id do we assume for the majority of the processing?
#O RunAsUser=sendmail


###########################
#   Message precedences   #
###########################

Pfirst-class=0
Pspecial-delivery=100
Plist=-30
Pbulk=-60
Pjunk=-100


####################
#  Trusted users   #
####################

# this is equivalent to setting class "t"
#Ft/etc/sendmail.ct
Troot
Tdaemon
Tuucp


#########################
#  Format of headers    #
#########################
```

```
H?P?Return-Path: <$g>
HReceived: $?sfrom $s $.$?_($?s$|from $.$_)
    $.by $j ($v/$Z)$?r with $r$. id $i$?u
    for $u; $|;
    $.$b
H?D?Resent-Date: $a
H?D?Date: $a
H?F?Resent-From: $?x$x <$g>$|$g$.
H?F?From: $?x$x <$g>$|$g$.
H?x?Full-Name: $x
# HPosted-Date: $a
# H?l?Received-Date: $b
H?M?Resent-Message-Id: <$t.$i@$j>
H?M?Message-Id: <$t.$i@$j>
#
######################################################################
######################################################################
#####
#####                       REWRITING RULES
#####
######################################################################
######################################################################


###########################################
###   Ruleset 3 - Name Canonicalization   ###
###########################################
S3

# handle null input (translate to <@> special case)
R$@                 $@ <@>

# strip group: syntax (not inside angle brackets!) and trailing semicolon
R$*                 $: $1 <@>              mark addresses
R$* < $* > $* <@>   $: $1 < $2 > $3        unmark <addr>
R@ $* <@>           $: @ $1                unmark @host:...
R$* :: $* <@>       $: $1 :: $2            unmark node::addr
R:include: $* <@>   $: :include: $1        unmark :include:...
R$* [ $* : $* ] <@> $: $1 [ $2 : $3 ]      unmark IPv6 addrs
R$* : $* [ $* ]     $: $1 : $2 [ $3 ] <@>  remark if leading colon
R$* : $* <@>        $: $2                  strip colon if marked
R$* <@>             $: $1                  unmark
R$* ;               $1                     strip trailing semi
```

```
R$* < $* ; >            $1 < $2 >              bogus bracketed semi

# null input now results from list:; syntax
R$@                     $@ :; <@>

# strip angle brackets - note RFC733 heuristic to get innermost item
R$*                     $: < $1 >              housekeeping <>
R$+ < $* >              < $2 >                 strip excess on left
R< $* > $+              < $1 >                 strip excess on right
R<>                     $@ < @ >               MAIL FROM:<> case
R< $+ >                 $: $1                  remove housekeeping <>

# make sure <@a,@b,@c:user@d> syntax is easy to parse - undone later
R@ $+ , $+              @ $1 : $2              change all "," to ":"

# localize and dispose of route-based addresses
R@ $+ : $+              $@ $>96 < @$1 > : $2   handle <route-addr>

# find focus for list syntax
R $+ : $* ; @ $+ $@ $>96 $1 : $2 ; < @ $3 >  list syntax
R $+ : $* ;             $@ $1 : $2;            list syntax

# find focus for @ syntax addresses
R$+ @ $+                $: $1 < @ $2 >         focus on domain
R$+ < $+ @ $+ >         $1 $2 < @ $3 >         move gaze right
R$+ < @ $+ >            $@ $>96 $1 < @ $2 >    already canonical

# do some sanity checking
R$* < @ $* : $* > $*    $1 < @ $2 $3 > $4      nix colons in addrs

# convert old-style addresses to a domain-based address
R$- ! $+                $@ $>96 $2 < @ $1 .UUCP >    resolve uucp names
R$+ . $- ! $+           $@ $>96 $3 < @ $1 . $2 >     domain uucps
R$+ ! $+                $@ $>96 $2 < @ $1 .UUCP >    uucp subdomains

# if we have % signs, take the rightmost one
R$* % $*                $1 @ $2                First make them all @s.
R$* @ $* @ $*           $1 % $2 @ $3           Undo all but the last.
R$* @ $*                $@ $>96 $1 < @ $2 >    Insert < > and finish

# else we must be a local name
R$*                     $@ $>96 $1
```

```
################################################
###   Ruleset 96 – bottom half of ruleset 3   ###
################################################

S96

# handle special cases for local names
R$* < @ localhost > $*    $: $1 < @ $j . > $2        no domain at all
R$* < @ localhost . $m > $* $: $1 < @ $j . > $2      local domain
R$* < @ localhost . UUCP > $*   $: $1 < @ $j . > $2  .UUCP domain
R$* < @ [ $+ ] > $* $: $1 < @@ [ $2 ] > $3           mark [a.b.c.d]
R$* < @@ $=w > $*          $: $1 < @ $j . > $3        self-literal
R$* < @@ $+ > $*           $@ $1 < @ $2 > $3          canon IP addr

# look up domains in the domain table
#R$* < @ $+ > $*         $: $1 < @ $(domaintable $2 $) > $3




# if really UUCP, handle it immediately

# try UUCP traffic as a local address
R$* < @ $+ . UUCP > $*        $: $1 < @ $[ $2 $] . UUCP . > $3
R$* < @ $+ . . UUCP . > $*    $@ $1 < @ $2 . > $3

# pass to name server to make hostname canonical
R$* < @ $* $~P > $*           $: $1 < @ $[ $2 $3 $] > $4

# local host aliases and pseudo-domains are always canonical
R$* < @ $=w > $*              $: $1 < @ $2 . > $3
R$* < @ $j > $*               $: $1 < @ $j . > $2
R$* < @ $=M > $*              $: $1 < @ $2 . > $3
R$* < @ $* $=P > $*           $: $1 < @ $2 $3 . > $4
R$* < @ $* . . > $*           $1 < @ $2 . > $3
```

```
#################################################
###   Ruleset 4 - Final Output Post-rewriting   ###
#################################################
S4

R$* <@>                    $@                      handle <> and list:;

# strip trailing dot off possibly canonical name
R$* < @ $+ . > $*       $1 < @ $2 > $3

# eliminate internal code - should never get this far!
R$* < @ *LOCAL* > $*    $1 < @ $j > $2

# externalize local domain info
R$* < $+ > $*           $1 $2 $3                 defocus
R@ $+ : @ $+ : $+       @ $1 , @ $2 : $3         <route-addr> canonical
R@ $*                   $@ @ $1                  ... and exit

# UUCP must always be presented in old form
R$+ @ $- . UUCP         $2!$1                    u@h.UUCP => h!u

# delete duplicate local names
R$+ % $=w @ $=w         $1 @ $2                  u%host@host => u@host




#############################################################
###    Ruleset 97 - recanonicalize and call ruleset zero    ###
###                 (used for recursive calls)              ###
#############################################################

S97
R$*                     $: $>3 $1
R$*                     $@ $>0 $1




#######################################
###    Ruleset 0 - Parse Address    ###
#######################################

S0

R$*               $: $>Parse0 $1                initial parsing
```

```
R$*                $: $>98 $1                 handle local hacks
R$*                $: $>Parse1 $1             final parsing

SParse0
R<@>               $#local $: <@>             special case error msgs
R$* : $* ; <@>     $#error $@ 5.1.3 $: "list:; syntax illegal for recipient addresses"
R<@ $+>            $#error $@ 5.1.1 $: "user address required"
R$*               $: <> $1
R<> $* < @ [ $+ ] > $*    $1 < @ [ $2 ] > $3
R<> $* <$* : $* > $*     $#error $@ 5.1.1 $: "colon illegal in host name part"
R<> $*                   $1
R$* < @ . $* > $*        $#error $@ 5.1.2 $: "invalid host name"
R$* < @ $* .. $* > $*    $#error $@ 5.1.2 $: "invalid host name"

# handle numeric address spec
R$* < @ [ $+ ] > $*      $: $>98 $1 < @ [ $2 ] > $3    numeric internet spec
R$* < @ [ $+ ] > $*      $#esmtp $@ [$2] $: $1 < @ [$2] > $3    still numeric: send

# now delete the local info - note $=0 to find characters that cause forwarding
R$* < @ > $*       $@ $>Parse0 $>3 $1         user@ => user
R< @ $=w . > : $*  $@ $>Parse0 $>3 $2         @here:... -> ...
R$- < @ $=w . >    $: $(dequote $1 $) < @ $2 . >    dequote "foo"@here
R< @ $+ >          $#error $@ 5.1.1 $: "user address required"
R$* $=0 $* < @ $=w . > $@ $>Parse0 $>3 $1 $2 $3    ...@here -> ...

SParse1
# handle virtual users
#R$+ < @ $=w . >    $: < $(virtuser $1 @ $2 $@ $1 $: @ $) > $1 < @ $2 . >
#R<@> $+ + $* < @ $* . >
               $: < $(virtuser $1 + * @ $3 $@ $1 $: @ $) > $1 + $2 < @ $3 . >
#R<@> $+ + $* < @ $* . >
               $: < $(virtuser $1 @ $3 $@ $1 $: @ $) > $1 + $2 < @ $3 . >
#R<@> $+ < @ $+ . >   $: < $(virtuser @ $2 $@ $1 $: @ $) > $1 < @ $2 . >
#R<@> $+            $: $1
#R< error : $- $+ > $*    $#error $@ $( dequote $1 $) $: $2
#R< $+ > $+ < @ $+ >    $: $>97 $1

# short circuit local delivery so forwarded email works
#R$+ . USENET < @ $=w . >    $#usenet $: $1    handle usenet specially
R$=L < @ $=w . > $#local $: @ $1             special local names
R$+ < @ $=w . > $#local $: $1                regular local name
```

```
# not local — try mailer table lookup
#R$* <@ $+ > $*      $: < $2 > $1 < @ $2 > $3        extract host name
#R< $+ . > $*        $: < $1 > $2                    strip trailing dot
#R< $+ > $*          $: < $(mailertable $1 $) > $2   lookup
#R< $~[ : $+ > $*    $>95 < $1 : $2 > $3             check — resolved?
#R< $+ > $*          $: $>90 <$1> $2                 try domain


# resolve remotely connected UUCP links (if any)

# resolve fake top level domains by forwarding to other hosts



# pass names that still have a host to a smarthost (if defined)
R$* < @ $* > $*      $: $>95 < $S > $1 < @ $2 > $3      glue on smarthost name

# deal with other remote names
R$* < @$* > $*       $#esmtp $@ $2 $: $1 < @ $2 > $3  user@host.domain

# if this is quoted, strip the quotes and try again
R$+                  $: $(dequote $1 $)              strip quotes
R$+ $=O $+           $@ $>97 $1 $2 $3                try again

# handle locally delivered names
R$=L                 $#local $: @ $1                 special local names
R$+                  $#local $: $1                   regular local names


#######################################################################
###    Ruleset 5 - special rewriting after aliases have been expanded    ###
#######################################################################

S5


# deal with plussed users so aliases work nicely
R$+ + *              $#local $@ $&h $: $1
R$+ + $*             $#local $@ + $2 $: $1 + *

# prepend an empty "forward host" on the front
R$+                  $: <> $1

# send unrecognized local users to a relay host
#R< > $+             $: < $L . > $( user $1 $)            look up user
```

```
#R< $* > $+ <> $*      $: < > $2 $3                    found; strip $L
#R< $* . > $+          $: < $1 > $2                    strip extra dot

# see if we have a relay or a hub
R< > $+                $: < $H > $1                       try hub
R< > $+                $: < $R > $1                       try relay
R< > $+                $: < > < $1 $(dequote "" $&h $) > nope, restore +detail
R< > < $+ + $* > $*    < > < $1 > + $2 $3                find the user part
R< > < $+ > + $* $#local $@ $2 $: @ $1                   strip the extra +
R< > < $+ >            $@ $1                              no +detail
R$+           $: $1 $(dequote "" $&h $)       add +detail back in
R< local : $* > $*     $: $>95 < local : $1 > $2   no host extension
R< error : $* > $*     $: $>95 < error : $1 > $2   no host extension
R< $- : $+ > $+        $: $>95 < $1 : $2 > $3 < @ $2 >
R< $+ > $+   $@ $>95 < $1 > $2 < @ $1 >


#################################################################
###   Ruleset 90 - try domain part of mailertable entry        ###
#################################################################

S90
#R$* <$- . $+ > $*     $: $1$2 < $(mailertable .$3 $@ $1$2 $@ $2 $) > $4
#R$* <$~[ : $+ > $*     $>95 < $2 : $3 > $4      check - resolved?
#R$* < . $+ > $*        $@ $>90 $1 . <$2> $3     no - strip & try again
#R$* < $* > $*          $: < $(mailertable . $@ $1$2 $) > $3     try "."
#R< $~[ : $+ > $*       $>95 < $1 : $2 > $3      "." found?
#R< $* > $*             $@ $2                    no mailertable match


#################################################################
###   Ruleset 95 - canonify mailer:[user@]host syntax to triple ###
#################################################################

S95
R< > $*                $@ $1                   strip off null relay
R< error : $- $+ > $*  $#error $@ $( dequote $1 $) $: $2
R< local : $* > $*     $>CanonLocal < $1 > $2
R< $- : $+ @ $+ > $*<$*>$*  $# $1 $@ $3 $: $2<@$3>   use literal user
R< $- : $+ > $*        $# $1 $@ $2 $: $3   try qualified mailer
R< $=w > $*            $@ $2                   delete local host
R< $+ > $*             $#relay $@ $1 $: $2      use unqualified mailer
```

```
######################################################################
###   Ruleset CanonLocal - canonify local: syntax              ###
######################################################################

SCanonLocal
# strip trailing dot from any host name that may appear
R< $* > $* < @ $* . >          $: < $1 > $2 < @ $3 >

# handle local: syntax - use old user, either with or without host
R< > $* < @ $* > $*            $#local $@ $1@$2 $: $1
R< > $+                        $#local $@ $1    $: $1

# handle local:user@host syntax - ignore host part
R< $+ @ $+ > $* < @ $* >       $: < $1 > $3 < @ $4 >

# handle local:user syntax
R< $+ > $* <@ $* > $*          $#local $@ $2@$3 $: $1
R< $+ > $*                     $#local $@ $2    $: $1


######################################################################
###   Ruleset 93 - convert header names to masqueraded form    ###
######################################################################

S93

# handle generics database
#R$+ < @ $=G . >          $: < $1@$2 > $1 < @ $2 . > @       mark
#R$+ < @ *LOCAL* >        $: < $1@$j > $1 < @ *LOCAL* > @    mark
#R< $+ > $+ < $* > @      $: < $(generics $1 $: $) > $2 < $3 >
#R< > $+ < @ $+ >         $: < $(generics $1 $: $) > $1 < @ $2 >
#R< $* @ $* > $* < $* >      $@ $>3 $1 @ $2       found qualified
#R< $+ > $* < $* >        $: $>3 $1 @ *LOCAL*     found unqualified
#R< > $*                  $: $1                   not found

# special case the users that should be exposed
R$=E < @ *LOCAL* >        $@ $1 < @ $j . >        leave exposed
R$=E < @ $=M . >          $@ $1 < @ $2 . >
R$=E < @ $=w . >          $@ $1 < @ $2 . >

# handle domain-specific masquerading
R$* < @ $=M . > $*        $: $1 < @ $2 . @ $M > $3  convert masqueraded doms
R$* < @ $=w . > $*        $: $1 < @ $2 . @ $M > $3
R$* < @ *LOCAL* > $*      $: $1 < @ $j . @ $M > $2
```

```
R$* < @ $+ @ > $*       $: $1 < @ $2 > $3        $M is null
R$* < @ $+ @ $+ > $*    $: $1 < @ $3 . > $4      $M is not null


######################################################################
###   Ruleset 94 - convert envelope names to masqueraded form    ###
######################################################################

S94
#R$+                    $@ $>93 $1
R$* < @ *LOCAL* > $*    $: $1 < @ $j . > $2


######################################################################
###   Ruleset 98 - local part of ruleset zero (can be null)      ###
######################################################################

S98

# addresses sent to foo@host.REDIRECT will give a 551 error code
R$* < @ $+ .REDIRECT. >         $: $1 < @ $2 . REDIRECT . > < ${opMode} >
R$* < @ $+ .REDIRECT. > <i>     $: $1 < @ $2 . REDIRECT. >
R$* < @ $+ .REDIRECT. > < $- > $# error $@ 5.1.1 $: "551 User has moved; please try "
➥ <$1@$2>



# check for junk domain/spammers
Sjunk
# lookup domain in database
R$*<@$+>          $:$1<@$(junk $2$)>
# exists? return
R$*<@$*@JUNK>     $@$1<@$2@JUNK>
# lookup address in database
R$*<@$+>          $:$1<@$(junk $1@$2 $:$2$)>
# exists? return
R$*<@$*@JUNK>     $@$1<@$2@JUNK>
# remove one subdomain, try again
R$*<@$-.$-.$+>    $: $>junk $1<@$3.$4>

Scheck_mail
# don't check these
R<$*@$=w>  $@ ok            shortcut
# idea from Steven Schultz
R<>        $: <$n @ $(dequote "" $&{client_name} $) >
```

```
# remove at least the dot...
R<$*@$*.>   <$1@$2>
R$*         $: $>3 $1              canonify
R$-         $@ ok
# no host without a . in the FQHN ?
R$*<@$->$* $#error $@ 5.1.8 $: 551 invalid host name $2, check your configuration.
# lookup IP address (reverse mapping available?)
#R$*<@[$-.$-.$-.$-]>$*   $: $1 < @ $[ [ $2.$3.$4.$5 ] $] > $6
# copy the result of the lookup
R$*         $:$1 $| $1
# now remove the dot
R$* $| $*<@$*.>$*        $: $1 $| $2<@$3>$4
# and check the database
R$* $| $*<@$*>$* $: $1 $| $>junk $2<@$3>
# match: return given error code (rhs of map)
R$* $| $*<@$*@JUNK>$*    $#error $@ 5.7.1 $: $3
# restore original value (after canonicalization by ruleset 3)
R$* $| $*         $: $1
# this is dangerous! no real name
# (see RFC 1123,sections 5.2.2 and 5.2.18)
#R$*<@$*$~P>$*    $#error $@ 4.1.8 $: 451 unresolvable host name $2$3, check your
➥ setup.



Scheck_rcpt
# first: get client address
R$+         $: $(dequote "" $&{client_addr} $) $| $1
R0 $| $*          $@ ok          client_addr is 0 for sendmail -bs
R$={LocalIP}$* $| $*     $@ ok    from here
# next: get client name
R$* $| $+     $: $(dequote "" $&{client_name} $) $| $2
R $| $*           $@ ok          no client name: directly invoked
#R$- $| $*         $@ ok          for those without full DNS...
R$*$=w $| $*      $@ ok          from here
R$*$={LocalNames} $| $*   $@ ok   from allowed system
# now check other side
R$* $| $*          $: $>3 $2
# remove local part
R$*<@$+.>$*          $: $>remove_local $1<@$2.>$3
# still something left?
R$*<@$+>$*          $#error $@ 5.7.1 $: 551 we do not relay
```

```
Sremove_local
# remove RelayTo part (maybe repeatedly)
R$*<@$*$={RelayTo}.>$*        $>3 $1 $4
R$*<@$=w.>$*                  $: $>remove_local $>3 $1 $3



SjunkIP
# lookup IP in database
# full IP address
R$-.$-.$-.$-    $: $(junk $1.$2.$3.$4 $)
# class C net
R$-.$-.$-.$-    $: $(junk $1.$2.$3 $: $1.$2.$3.$4 $)
# class B net
R$-.$-.$-.$-    $: $(junk $1.$2 $: $1.$2.$3.$4 $)
# class A net
R$-.$-.$-.$-    $: $(junk $1 $: $1.$2.$3.$4 $)

Scheck_relay
# check IP
R$+ $| $+       $: $1 $| $>junkIP $2
R$+ $| $*@JUNK  $#error $@ 5.7.1 $: $2
# check hostname
R$+ $| $+       $: $>junk <@$1>
R$*<@$*@JUNK>$* $#error $@ 5.7.1 $: $2
#
######################################################################
######################################################################
#####
#####                  MAILER DEFINITIONS
#####
######################################################################
######################################################################


###########################*****##############
###    PROCMAIL Mailer specification    ###
###########################*****################

##### @(#)procmail.m4   8.6 (Berkeley) 4/30/97  #####

Mprocmail,  P=/usr/bin/procmail, F=DFMSPhnu9, S=11/31, R=21/31, T=DNS/RFC822/X-Unix,
          A=procmail -Y -m $h $f $u
```

```
#####################################
###    SMTP Mailer specification    ###
#####################################

#####  @(#)smtp.m4    8.33 (Berkeley) 7/9/96  #####

Msmtp,          P=[IPC], F=mDFMuX, S=11/31, R=21, E=\r\n, L=990,
         T=DNS/RFC822/SMTP,
         A=IPC $h
Mesmtp,         P=[IPC], F=mDFMuXa, S=11/31, R=21, E=\r\n, L=990,
         T=DNS/RFC822/SMTP,
         A=IPC $h
Msmtp8,         P=[IPC], F=mDFMuX8, S=11/31, R=21, E=\r\n, L=990,
         T=DNS/RFC822/SMTP,
         A=IPC $h
Mrelay,         P=[IPC], F=mDFMuXa8, S=11/31, R=61, E=\r\n, L=2040,
         T=DNS/RFC822/SMTP,
         A=IPC $h


#
#   envelope sender rewriting
#
S11
R$+             $: $>51 $1              sender/recipient common
R$* :; <@>      $@                      list:; special case
R$*             $: $>61 $1              qualify unqual'ed names
R$+             $: $>94 $1              do masquerading


#
#   envelope recipient rewriting -
#   also header recipient if not masquerading recipients
#
S21
R$+             $: $>51 $1              sender/recipient common
R$+             $: $>61 $1              qualify unqual'ed names


#
#   header sender and masquerading header recipient rewriting
#
S31
```

```
R$+                 $: $>51 $1              sender/recipient common
R:; <@>             $@                      list:; special case

# do special header rewriting
R$* <@> $*          $@ $1 <@> $2            pass null host through
R< @ $* > $*            $@ < @ $1 > $2      pass route-addr through
R$*                 $: $>61 $1              qualify unqual'ed names
R$+                 $: $>93 $1              do masquerading


#
#   convert pseudo-domain addresses to real domain addresses
#
S51

# pass <route-addr>s through
R< @ $+ > $*            $@ < @ $1 > $2      resolve <route-addr>

# output fake domains as user%fake@relay

# do UUCP heuristics; note that these are shared with UUCP mailers
R$+ < @ $+ .UUCP. >     $: < $2 ! > $1              convert to UUCP form
R$+ < @ $* > $*         $@ $1 < @ $2 > $3           not UUCP form

# leave these in .UUCP form to avoid further tampering
R< $&h ! > $- ! $+      $@ $2 < @ $1 .UUCP. >
R< $&h ! > $-.$+ ! $+   $@ $3 < @ $1.$2 >
R< $&h ! > $+           $@ $1 < @ $&h .UUCP. >
R< $+ ! > $+            $: $1 ! $2 < @ $Y >     use UUCP_RELAY
R$+ < @ $+ : $+ >       $@ $1 < @ $3 >          strip mailer: part
R$+ < @ >               $: $1 < @ *LOCAL* >     if no UUCP_RELAY


#
#   common sender and masquerading recipient rewriting
#
S61

R$* < @ $* > $*         $@ $1 < @ $2 > $3       already fully qualified
R$+                     $@ $1 < @ *LOCAL* >     add local qualification
```

```
#
#  relay mailer header masquerading recipient rewriting
#
S71

R$+              $: $>61 $1
R$+              $: $>93 $1



#####################################################
###    Local and Program Mailer specification    ###
#####################################################

#####  @(#)local.m4    8.23 (Berkeley) 5/31/96  #####

Mlocal,          P=/usr/bin/procmail, F=lsDFMAw5:/|@qSPfhn9, S=10/30, R=20/40,
         T=DNS/RFC822/X-Unix,
         A=procmail -Y -a $h -d $u
Mprog,           P=/bin/sh, F=lsDFMoqeu9, S=10/30, R=20/40, D=$z:/,
         T=X-Unix,
         A=sh -c $u

#
#  Envelope sender rewriting
#
S10
R<@>         $n              errors to mailer-daemon
R$+          $: $>50 $1      add local domain if needed
R$*          $: $>94 $1      do masquerading

#
#  Envelope recipient rewriting
#
S20
R$+ < @ $* >     $: $1       strip host part

#
#  Header sender rewriting
#
S30
R<@>         $n              errors to mailer-daemon
R$+          $: $>50 $1      add local domain if needed
```

```
R$*               $: $>93 $1         do masquerading


#
#   Header recipient rewriting
#
S40
R$+               $: $>50 $1         add local domain if needed
#R$*              $: $>93 $1         do all-masquerading


#
#   Common code to add local domain name (only if always-add-domain)
#
S50
R$* < @ $* > $*   $@ $1 < @ $2 > $3             already fully qualified
R$+               $@ $1 < @ *LOCAL* >           add local qualification
```

Sources of Linux Information

The following list reflects different Internet resources where you can find more Linux-related information, download or purchase Linux distributions, and ask for help. By no means is this intended to reflect a complete list of Linux resources on the Internet; it is more a record of the sites I have found useful around the Internet in my years using Linux.

General Information

Linux Documentation Project	`http://sunsite.unc.edu/mdw/`
Linux Frequently Asked Questions with Answers	`http://www.cl.cam.ac.uk/users/iwj10/linux-faq/index.html`
Linux Hardware	`http://www.fokus.gmd.de/linux/linux-hardware.html`
linux-howto.com	`http://www.linux-howto.com/`
Linux Information Sheet	`ftp://rtfm.mit.edu/pub/usenet-by-hierarchy/comp/os/linux/answers/linux/info-sheet`
Linux Installation and Getting Started	`http://sunsite.unc.edu/mdw/LDP/gs/gs.html`
Linux International	`http://www.li.org/`
Linux Journal	`http://www.ssc.com/lj/index.html`
Linux Meta FAQ	`ftp://rtfm.mit.edu/pub/usenet-by-hierarchy/comp/os/linux/answers/linux/meta-faq`
Linux NOW!	`http://www.linuxnow.com/`
Linux Online	`http://www.linux.org/`
The Linux Resources	`http://www.linuxresources.com/`
The Linux Software Review	`http://karlsberg.usask.ca/~slg/lsr/lsr.html`
Linux System Administrators' Guide	`http://linuxwww.db.erau.edu/SAG/index.html`
Linux User Group Registry	`http://www.linux.org/users/index.html`
The Linux Web Ring	`http://nll.interl.net/lwr/`
Linux World	`http://www.sikesoft.com/`

The Network Administrators' Guide

`http://www.uni-tuebingen.de/zdv/projekte/`
`linux/books/nag/nag.html`

Woven Goods for Linux

`http://www.fokus.gmd.de/linux/`

Linux Distributions

Caldera OpenLinux

`http://www.caldera.com/`

Conectiva Linux (Portuguese)

`http://www.conectiva.com.br/`

Debian/GNU Linux

`http://www.debian.org/`

Delix Linux (German)

`http://delix.de/`

DLX Linux

`http://www.wu-wien.ac.at/usr/h93/h9301726/`
`dlx.html`

Eagle Linux (German, for Motorola 680x0 chips)

`http://www.eagle-cp.com/www/m68k.html`

Eurielex Linux (Spanish)

`http://www.etsit.upm.es/~eurielec/`
`redhat/index.html`

Hal 91

`http://home.sol.no/~okolaas/hal91.html`

Kheops Linux (French)

`http://www.linux-kheops.com/`

LinuxPPC (for PowerPC chips)

`http://www.linuxppc.org/`

Linux Pro Plus

`http://www.linuxmall.com/Allprod/lxcdr.html`

LinuxWare

`http://www.trans-am.com/linux.html`

MkLinux (for the Power Macintosh)

`http://www.mklinux.apple.com/`

MNIS Linux (French)

`http://www.mnis.fr/`

Red Hat Linux

`http://www.redhat.com/`

Slackware Linux

`http://www.slackware.org/`

Stampede Linux

`http://www.stampede.org/`

S.u.S.E. Linux (German and English)

`http://www.suse.com/`

TurboLinux

`http://www.turbolinux.com/`

Yggdrasil Linux

`http://www.yggdrasil.com/`

Mailing Lists and Newsgroups

alt.os.linux	news:alt.os.linux
comp.os.linux.admin	news:comp.os.linux.admin
comp.os.linux.advocacy	news:comp.os.linux.advocacy
comp.os.linux.announce	news:comp.os.linux.announce
comp.os.linux.answers	news:comp.os.linux.answers
comp.os.linux.development	news:comp.os.linux.development
comp.os.linux.development.apps	news:comp.os.linux.development.apps
comp.os.linux.development.system	news:comp.os.linux.development.system
comp.os.linux.hardware	news:comp.os.linux.hardware
comp.os.linux.help	news:comp.os.linux.help
comp.os.linux.misc	news:comp.os.linux.misc
comp.os.linux.networking	news:comp.os.linux.networking
comp.os.linux.setup	news:comp.os.linux.setup
comp.os.linux.x	news:comp.os.linux.x
Linux Mailing Lists	http://summer.snu.ac.kr/~djshin/linux/mail-list/index.shtml
LinuxWWW Mailing List Archives	http://linuxwww.db.erau.edu/mail_archives/

Non-Intel Platforms

ERAU SparcLinux Archive	http://linuxwww.db.erau.edu/sparclinux/
Linux Alpha FTP Archive	http://gatekeeper.dec.com/pub/DEC/Linux-Alpha/
Linux for BeBox	http://www.guru.dircon.co.uk/belinux/
Linux for Sparc Processors	http://www.geog.ubc.ca/s_linux.html
Linux/m68k for Macintosh	http://www.mac.linux-m68k.org/

The Linux/m68k Home Pages	http://www.clark.net/pub/lawrencc/linux/index.html
MkArchive	http://ftp.sunet.se/pub/os/Linux/mklinux/mkarchive/info/index.html
MkLinux Documentation Project	http://lands.dyn.ml.org/mklinux/
SGI-Linux	http://linus.linux.sgi.com/

Non-English Sites

EPC Home Page (Spanish)	http://www.arrakis.es/~epujol/linux/
Linux (Czech)	http://www.linux.cz/
Linux - Viel Unix für wenig Geld (German)	http://www.uni-tuebingen.de/zdv/projekte/linux/
Linux Indonesia (Indonesian)	http://www.linux.or.id/

Places to Buy Linux CD-ROMs

CD-ROM Shop	http://www.cdromshop.com/
CheapBytes	http://www.cheapbytes.com/
The Computer Underground	http://www.tcu-inc.com/
I-Link	http://i-linkcom.com/software.html
InfoMagic	http://www.infomagic.com/
Just Computers	http://www.justcomp.com/
Linux Central	http://linuxcentral.com/
Linux Mall	http://www.linuxmall.com/
Universal CD-ROM	http://www.bigmall.com/
Walnut Creek	http://www.cdrom.com/

Places to Download Linux and Linux Files

BLINUX's FTP Site	`ftp://leb.net/pub/blinux/`
Caldera's FTP Site	`ftp://ftp.caldera.com/pub/`
Debian's FTP Site	`ftp://ftp.debian.org/`
Georgia Tech's Linux Archive	`ftp://ftp.cc.gatech.edu/pub/linux/`
Linux Applications	`http://www.linuxapps.com/`
Linux Applications and Utilties for New Users	`http://www.ameritech.net/users/dbarber/index.html`
Linux Applications and Utilities Page	`http://www.hongik.com/linux//linapps.html`
Linux Kernel Archives	`ftp://ftp.kernel.org/`
Linux On-line's FTP Site	`ftp://ftp.linux.org/pub/`
Linux Software Map	`http://www.ssc.com/linux/resources/apps.html`
MIT's TSX-11 Linux Archive	`ftp://tsx.mit.edu/pub/linux/`
Red Hat's FTP Site	`ftp://ftp.redhat.com/pub/`
SunSite's Linux Archive	`ftp://sunsite.unc.edu/pub/Linux/`
Walnut Creek's FTP Site	`ftp://wcarchive.cdrom.com/pub/linux/`
Woven Goods for Linux's Software Page	`http://www.fokus.gmd.de/linux/linux-softw.html`

X-Windows

MetroLink	`http://www.metrolink.com/`
XFree86 Project	`http://www.xfree86.org/`
Xi Graphics	`http://www.xinside.com/`

The Linux Hardware Compatibility HOWTO

This appendix is the complete text of the Linux Hardware Compatibility HOWTO by Patrick Reijnen and is provided as a reference tool for installation of Linux. This document is based on the HTML version that is kept at `http://sunsite.unc.edu/mdw/HOWTO/Hardware-HOWTO.html`. The version used for this appendix is 98.2, dated 29 March 1998. Red Hat also keeps a version of the HOWTO specifically geared towards their distributions. The version for Red Hat 5.1 is at `http://www.redhat.com/support/docs/rhl/intel/rh51-hardware-intel.html`.

1. Introduction

1.1 Welcome

Welcome to the Linux Hardware Compatibility HOWTO. This document lists most of the hardware components (not computers with components built in) supported by Linux, so by reading through this document you can choose the components for your own Linux computer. As the list of components supported by Linux is growing rapidly, this document will never be complete. So, when components are not mentioned in this HOWTO, the only reason will be that I don't know they are supported. I simply have not found support for the component and/or nobody has told me about support.

Subsections titled "Others" list hardware with alpha or beta drivers in varying degrees of usability or other drivers that aren't included in standard kernels. Note that some drivers only exist in alpha kernels, so if you see something listed as supported but isn't in your version of the Linux kernel, upgrade.

The latest version of this document can be found on `http://users.bart.nl/~patrickr/hardware-howto/Hardware-HOWTO.html`, SunSite, and all the usual mirror sites. Translations of this and other Linux HOWTOs can be found at `http://sunsite.unc.edu/pub/Linux/docs/HOWTO/translations` and `ftp://sunsite.unc.edu/pub/Linux/docs/HOWTO/translations`.

If you know of any Linux hardware (in)compatibilities not listed here please let me know; just send mail.

Still need some help selecting components after reading this document? Check the "Build Your Own PC" site at `http://www.verinet.com/pc/`.

1.2 Copyright

Copyright 1997, 1998 Patrick Reijnen

This HOWTO is free documentation; you can redistribute it and/or modify it under the terms of the GNU General Public License as published by the Free Software Foundation; either version 2 of the license or (at your option) any later version.

This document is distributed in the hope that it will be useful, but without any warranty; without even the implied warranty of merchantability or fitness for a particular purpose. See the GNU General Public License for more details. You can obtain a copy of the GNU General Public License by writing to the Free Software Foundation, Inc., 675 Mass Ave., Cambridge, MA 02139, USA.

If you use this or any other Linux HOWTOs in a commercial distribution, it would be nice to send the authors a complimentary copy of your product.

1.3 System Architectures

This document only deals with Linux for Intel platforms. For other platforms, check the following:

- ARM Linux
  `http://www.arm.uk.linux.org/~rmk92/armlinux.html`

- Linux/68k

- Linux/8086
  `http://www.linux.org.uk/Linux8086.html`

- Linux/Alpha
  `http://www.azstarnet.com/~axplinux/`

- Linux/MIPS
  `http://www.fnet.fr/linux-mips/`

- Linux/PowerPC
  `http://www.linuxppc.org/`

- Linux for Acorn
  http://www.ph.kcl.ac.uk/~amb/linux.html
- Linux for PowerMac
  http://ftp.sunet.se/pub/os/Linux/mklinux/mkarchive/info/
  index.html

2. Computers/Motherboards/BIOS

ISA, VLB, EISA, and PCI buses are all supported.

PS/2 and Microchannel (MCA) is supported in the standard kernel 2.0.7. There is support for MCA in kernel 2.1.16 and newer, but this code is still a little buggy. For more information you can always look at the Micro Channel Linux Home Page (http://glycerine.itsmm.uni.edu/mca/)

2.1 Specific Systems

- IBM PS/2 MCA systems
  ftp://ftp.dcrl.nd.edu/pub/misc/linux/

Many new PCI boards are causing a couple of failure messages during boot time when "Probing PCI Hardware." The procedure presents the following message:

```
Warning : Unknown PCI device (8086:7100).  Please read
include/linux/pci.h
```

It tells you to read the pci.h file. From this file is the following quote:

```
    PROCEDURE TO REPORT NEW PCI DEVICES
We are trying to collect information on new PCI devices, using
the standard PCI identification procedure. If some warning is
displayed at boot time, please report
        - /proc/pci
        - your exact hardware description. Try to find out
          which device is unknown. It may be you mainboard chipset.
          PCI-CPU bridge or PCI-ISA bridge.
        - If you can't find the actual information in your hardware
          booklet, try to read the references of the chip on the board.
        - Send all that to linux-pcisupport@cao-vlsi.ibp.fr,
          and I'll add your device to the list as soon as possible
```

```
BEFORE you send a mail, please check the latest linux releases
to be sure it has not been recently added.

      Thanks
            Frederic Potter.
```

Normally, though, your motherboard and the unknown PCI devices will function correctly.

2.2 Unsupported

- Supermicro P5MMA with BIOS versions 1.36, 1.37 and 1.4. Linux will not boot on this motherboard. A new (beta) release of the BIOS that makes Linux boot is available at `ftp.supermicro.com/mma9051.zip`

- Supermicro P5MMA98. Linux will not boot on this motherboard. A new (beta) release of the BIOS that makes Linux boot is available at `ftp.supermicro.com/a98905.zip`

3. Laptops

For more information about Linux and laptops, the following site is a good starting point:

- Linux Laptop Homepage
  `http://www.cs.utexas.edu/users/kharker/linux-laptop/`

Other information related to laptops can be found at the following sites:

- Advanced Power Management
  `ftp://ftp.cs.unc.edu/pub/users/faith/linux/`

- Notebook battery status
  `ftp://sunsite.unc.edu/pub/Linux/system/power/`

- Non-blinking cursor
  `ftp://sunsite.unc.edu/pub/Linux/kernel/patches/console/`
  `noblink-1.7.tar.gz`

- Other general info
  `ftp://tsx-11.mit.edu/pub/linux/packages/laptops/`

3.1 Specific Laptops

- Compaq Concerto (pen driver)
  `http://www.cs.nmsu.edu/~pfeiffer/`

- Compaq Contura Aero
  `http://domen.uninett.no/~hta/linux/aero-faq.html`

- IBM ThinkPad
  `http://peipa.essex.ac.uk/tp-linux/tp-linux.html`

- NEC Versa M and P
  `http://www.santafe.edu/~nelson/versa-linux/`

- Tadpole P1000
  `http://www.tadpole.com/Support/linux.html`

- Tadpole P1000 (another one)

- TI TravelMate 4000M
  `ftp://ftp.biomath.jussieu.fr/pub/linux/TM4000M-mini-HOWTO`
  `.txt.Z`

- TI TravelMate 5100

- Toshiba Satellite Pro 400CDT
  `http://terra.mpikg-teltow.mpg.de/~burger/T400CDT-Linux.html`

3.2 PCMCIA

- PCMCIA
  `http://hyper.stanford.edu/HyperNews/get/pcmcia/home.html`

PCMCIA drivers currently support all common PCMCIA controllers, including Databook TCIC/2, Intel i82365SL, Cirrus PD67xx, and Vadem VG-468 chipsets. The Motorola 6AHC05GA controller used in some Hyundai laptops is not supported. See Appendix B for a list of supported PCMCIA cards.

4. CPU/FPU

Intel/AMD/Cyrix 386SX/DX/SL/DXL/SLC and 486SX/DX/SL/SX2/DX2/DX4 are supported. Intel Pentium, Pentium Pro, and Pentium II (basically it's a Pentium Pro with MMX) also work. AMD K5 and K6 work good, although older versions of K6 should be avoided as they are buggy. Setting "internal cache" disabled in BIOS setup can be a workaround.

Linux has built-in FPU emulation if you don't have a math coprocessor.

Experimental SMP (multiple CPU) support is included in kernel 1.3.31 and newer. Check the Linux/SMP Project page for details and updates.

- Linux/SMP Project
  http://www.linux.org.uk/SMP/title.html

A few very early AMD 486DXes may hang in some special situations. All current chips should be okay, and getting a chip swap for old CPUs should not be a problem.

The ULSI Math*Co series has a bug in the FSAVE and FRSTOR instructions that causes problems with all protected mode operating systems. Some older IIT and Cyrix chips may also have this problem.

There are problems with TLB flushing in UMC U5S chips in very old kernels (1.1.x).

- Enable cache on Cyrix processors
  ftp://sunsite.unc.edu/pub/Linux/kernel/patches/CxPatch030.tar.z

- Cyrix software cache control
  ftp://sunsite.unc.edu/pub/Linux/kernel/patches/linux.cxpatch

- Cyrix 5x86 CPU register settings
  ftp://sunsite.unc.edu/pub/Linux/kernel/patches/cx5x86mod_1.0c.tgz

5. Memory

All memory like DRAM, EDO, and SDRAM can be used with Linux. There is one thing you have to look at: normally the kernel is not supporting more than 64MB of memory. When you add more than 64MB of memory you have to add the following line to your LILO configuration file:

```
append="mem=<number of MB>M"
```

So, when you have 96MB of memory this should become

```
append="mem=96M"
```

Don't type a number higher than the number of MB you really have. This can present unpredictable crashes.

6. Video Cards

Linux will work with all video cards in text mode. VGA cards not listed below probably will still work with mono VGA and/or standard VGA drivers.

If you're looking into buying a cheap video card to run X, keep in mind that accelerated cards (ATI Mach, ET4000/W32p, S3) are MUCH faster than unaccelerated or partially accelerated (Cirrus, WD) cards.

"32 bpp" is actually 24-bit color aligned on 32-bit boundaries. It does NOT mean the cards are capable of 32-bit color; they still display 24-bit color (16,777,216 colors). 24-bit packed pixels modes are not supported in XFree86, so cards that can do 24-bit modes to get higher resolutions in other OSes are not able to do this in X using XFree86. These cards include Mach32, Cirrus 542x, S3 801/805/868/968, ET4000, and others.

6.1 Diamond Video Cards

Most currently available Diamond cards ARE supported by the current release of XFree86. Early Diamond cards may not be officially supported by XFree86, but there are ways of getting them to work. Diamond is now actively supporting the XFree86 Project.

6.2 SVGALIB (Graphics for Console)

- VGA
- EGA
- ARK Logic ARK1000PV/2000PV
- ATI VGA Wonder
- ATI Mach32
- Cirrus 542x, 543x
- OAK OTI-037/67/77/87
- S3 (limited support)
- Trident TVGA8900/9000
- Tseng ET3000/ET4000/W32

6.3 XFree86 3.3.1

Accelerated

- ARK Logic ARK1000PV/VL, ARK2000PV/MT
- ATI Mach8
- ATI Mach32 (16 bpp supported for cards with RAMDAC ATI68875, AT&T20C49x, BT481 and 2MB video ram)
- ATI Mach64 (16/32 bpp supported for cards with RAMDAC ATI68860, ATI68875, CH8398, STG1702, STG1703, AT&T20C408, 3D Rage II, internal, IBM RGB514)
- Chips & Technologies 64200, 64300, 65520, 65525, 65530, 65535, 65540, 65545, 65546, 65548, 65550, 65554
- Cirrus Logic 5420, 542x/5430 (16 bpp), 5434 (16/32 bpp), 5436, 544x, 546x, 5480, 62x5, 754x
- Gemini P1 (ET6000 chip)
- IBM 8514/A

- IBM XGA-I, XGA-II
- IIT AGX-010/014/015/016 (16 bpp)
- Matrox MGA2064W (Millennium)
- Matrox MGA1064SG (Mystique)
- Number Nine Imagine I128
- Oak OTI-087
- S3 732 (Trio32), 764 (Trio64), Trio64V+, 801, 805, 864, 866, 868, 86C325 (ViRGE), 86C375 (ViRGE/DX), 86C385 (ViRGE/GX), 86C988 (ViRGE/VX), 911, 924, 928, 964, 968
- See Appendix A for list of supported S3 cards
- SiS 86c201, 86c202, 86c205
- Trident 9440, 96xx, Cyber938x
- Tseng ET4000/W32/W32i/W32p, ET6000
- Weitek P9000 (16/32 bpp)
- Diamond Viper VLB/PCI
- Orchid P9000
- Western Digital WD90C24/24A/24A2/31/33
- Unaccelerated
- Alliance AP6422, AT24
- ATI VGA Wonder series
- Advance Logic AL2101/2228/2301/2302/2308/2401
- Cirrus Logic 6420/6440, 7555
- Compaq AVGA
- DEC 21030
- Genoa GVGA
- MCGA (320x200)
- MX MX68000/MX68010
- NCR 77C22, 77C22E, 77C22E+

- NVidia NV1

- Oak OTI-037C, OTI-067, OTI-077

- RealTek RTG3106

- SGS-Thomson STG2000

- Trident 8800CS, 8200LX, 8900x, 9000, 9000i, 9100B, 9200CXr, 9320LCD, 9400CXi, 9420, 9420DGi, 9430DGi

- Tseng ET3000, ET4000AX

- VGA (standard VGA, 4-bit, slow)

- Video 7/Headland Technologies HT216-32

- Western Digital/Paradise PVGA1, WD90C00/10/11/30

Monochrome

- Hercules mono

- Hyundai HGC-1280

- Sigma LaserView PLUS

- VGA mono

Others

- EGA (ancient, from c. 1992)
  `ftp://ftp.funet.fi/pub/Linux/BETA/Xega/`

6.4 S.u.S.E. X Server

S.u.S.E. is building a series of X servers based on the XFree86 code. These X servers support new video cards and are bug-fix releases for XFree86 X servers. S.u.S.E is building these X servers together with The XFree86 Project, Inc. These X servers will be in the next XFree86 version. These X servers can be found at `http://www.suse.de/index.html`. At this moment S.u.S.E. X servers are available for the following video cards:

- XSuSE ELSA Gloria X-Server

  - ELSA Gloria L, Gloria L/MX, Gloria S

- Video cards with the Alliance Semiconductor AT3D (also AT25) Chip

  - Hercules Stingray 128 3D

- XSuSE NVidia X-Server (PCI and AGP support, NV1 chipset and Riva128)

  - ASUS 3Dexplorer

  - Diamond Viper 330

  - ELSA VICTORY Erazor

  - STB Velocity 128

- XSuSE Matrox. Support for Mystique, Millennium, Millennium II, and Millennium II AGP

- XSuSE Trident. Support for the 9685 (including ClearTV) and the latest Cyber chipset

- XSuSE Tseng. W32, W32i ET6100, and ET6300 support

6.5 Commercial X Servers

Commercial X servers provide support for cards not supported by XFree86, and might give better performances for cards that are supported by XFree86. In general they support many more cards than XFree86, so I'll only list cards that aren't supported by XFree86 here. Contact the vendors directly or check the Commercial HOWTO for more info.

Xi Graphics, Inc.

Xi Graphics, Inc. (`http://www.xig.com/`) (formerly known as X Inside, Inc.) is selling three X server products (cards supported are sorted by manufacturer):

Accelerated-X Display Server

- 3Dlabs

  - 300SX

  - 500TX Glint

  - 500MX Glint

  - Permedia 4MB/8MB

  - Permedia II 4MB/8MB

- Actix
  - GE32plus 1MB/2MB
  - GE32ultra 2MB
  - GraphicsENGINE 64 1MB/2MB
  - ProSTAR 64 1MB/2MB
- Alliance
  - ProMotion-3210 1MB/2MB
  - ProMotion-6410 1MB/2MB
  - ProMotion-6422 1MB/2MB
- ARK Logic
  - ARK1000PV 1MB/2MB
  - ARK1000VL 1MB/2MB
  - ARK2000PV 1MB/2MB
- AST
  - Manhattan 5090P (GD5424) 512KB
- ATI
  - 3D Xpression 1MB/2MB
  - 3D Pro Turbo PC2TV 4MB/8MB
  - 3D Pro Turbo PC2TV 6144
  - 3D Xpression+ PC2TV 2MB/4MB
  - 3D Xpression+ 2MB/4MB
  - ALL-IN-WONDER 4MB/8MB
  - ALL-IN-WONDER PRO 4MB/8MB
  - Graphics Ultra (Mach8) 1MB
  - Graphics Pro Turbo (Mach64/VRAM) 2MB/4MB
  - Graphics Pro Turbo 1600 (Mach64/VRAM) 2MB/4MB

- Graphics Ultra Plus (Mach32) 2MB
- 8514/Ultra (Mach8) 1MB
- Graphics Ultra Pro (Mach32) 1MB/2MB
- Graphics Vantage (Mach8) 1MB
- VGA Wonder Plus 512KB
- VGA Wonder XL 1MB
- Video Xpression 1MB
- XPERT@Play 4MB/6MB/8MB
- XPERT@Work 4MB/6MB/8MB
- Video Xpression 2MB
- WinBoost (Mach64/DRAM) 2MB
- WinTurbo (Mach64/VRAM) 2MB
- Graphics Wonder (Mach32) 1MB
- Graphics Xpression 1MB/2MB
- Rage II (SGRAM) 2MB/4MB/8MB
- Rage II+ (SGRAM) 2MB/4MB/8MB
- Rage Pro 2MB/4MB/8MB
- Advance Logic
  - ALG2101 1MB
  - ALG2228 1MB/2MB
  - ALG2301 1MB/2MB
- Boca
  - Voyager 1MB/2MB
  - Vortek-VL 1MB/2MB
- Colorgraphic
  - Dual Lightning 2MB

- Pro Lightning Accelerator 2MB
- Quad Pro Lightning Accelerator 2MB
- Twin Turbo Accelerator 1MB/2MB
- Chips & Technology
  - 64300 1MB/2MB
  - 64310 1MB/2MB
  - 65510 512KB
  - 65520 1MB
  - 65530 1MB
  - 65535 1MB
  - 65540 1MB
  - 65545 1MB
  - 65550 2MB
  - 82C450 512KB
  - 82C451 256KB
  - 82C452 512KB
  - 82C453 1MB
  - 82C480 1MB/2MB
  - 82C481 1MB/2MB
- Cirrus Logic
  - GD5402 512KB
  - GD5420 1MB
  - GD5422 1MB
  - GD5424 1MB
  - GD5426 1MB/2MB
  - GD5428 1MB/2MB

- GD5429 1MB/2MB

- GD5430 1MB/2MB

- GD5434 1MB/2MB

- GD5436 1MB/2MB

- GD5440 1MB/2MB

- GD5446 1MB/2MB

- GD5462 2MB/4MB PCI and AGP

- GD5464 2MB/4MB PCI and AGP

- GD5465 2MB/4MB PCI and AGP

- GD54M30 1MB/2MB

- GD54M40 1MB/2MB

- Compaq

  - ProLiant Series 512KB

  - ProSignia Series 512KB

  - QVision 1024 1MB

  - QVision 1280 1MB/2MB

  - QVision 2000+ 2MB

  - QVision 2000 2MB

- DEC

  - DECpc XL 590 (GD5428) 512KB

- Dell

  - 466/M & 466/ME (S3 805) 1MB

  - OnBoard ET4000 1MB

  - DGX (JAWS) 2MB

  - OptiPlex XMT 590 (Vision864) 2MB

- Diamond
  - Fire GL 1000 Pro 4MB/8MB
  - Fire GL 1000 4MB/8MB
  - Stealth 3D 2000 2MB/4MB
  - Stealth 3D 3000XL 2MB/4MB
  - Stealth 64 Graphics 2001 1MB/2MB
  - Stealth 64 Graphics 2121XL 1MB/2MB
  - Stealth 64 Graphics 2201XL 2MB
  - SpeedStar 1MB
  - SpeedStar 64 Graphics 2000 1MB/2MB
  - SpeedStar 24 1MB
  - SpeedStar 24X 1MB
  - SpeedStar 64 1MB/2MB
  - SpeedStar Hicolor 1MB
  - SpeedStar PCI 1MB
  - SpeedStar Pro 1MB
  - SpeedStar Pro SE 1MB/2MB
  - Stealth 1MB
  - Stealth 24 1MB
  - Stealth 32 1MB/2MB
  - Stealth 64 VRAM 2MB/4MB
  - Stealth 64 DRAM 1MB/2MB
  - Stealth 64 Video VRAM (175MHz) 2MB/4MB
  - Stealth 64 Video DRAM 1MB/2MB
  - Stealth 64 Video VRAM (220MHz) 2MB/4MB
  - Stealth Hicolor 1MB

- Stealth Pro 1MB/2MB

- Stealth SE 1MB/2MB

- Stealth 64 Video 2001TV 2MB

- Stealth 64 Video 2121 1MB/2MB

- Stealth 64 Video 2121TV 1MB/2MB

- Stealth 64 Video 2201 2MB

- Stealth 64 Video 2201TV 2MB

- Stealth 64 Video 3200 2MB

- Stealth 64 Video 3240 2MB/4MB

- Stealth 64 Video 3400 4MB

- Viper 1MB/2MB

- Viper Pro 2MB

- Viper Pro Video 2MB/4MB

- Viper SE 2MB/4MB

- ELSA

  - VICTORY 3D 2MB/4MB

  - WINNER 1000 1MB/2MB

  - WINNER 1000AVI 1MB/2MB

  - WINNER 1000ISA 1MB/2MB

  - WINNER 1000PRO 1MB/2MB

  - WINNER 1000TRIO 1MB/2MB

  - WINNER 1000TRIO/V 1MB/2MB

  - WINNER 100VL 1MB

  - WINNER 2000 2MB/4MB

  - WINNER 2000AVI 2MB/4MB

  - WINNER 2000AVI/3D 2MB/4MB

- WINNER 2000PRO 2MB/4MB

- WINNER 2000PRO/X 2MB/4MB/8MB

- WINNER 3000-L 4MB

- WINNER 3000-M 2MB

- WINNER 3000-S 2MB

- WINNER 1024 1MB

- WINNER 1280, TLC34075 Palette 2MB

- WINNER 1280, TLC34076 Palette 2MB

- Gloria-XL

- Gloria-MX

- Gloria-L

- Synergy

- Everex

  - ViewPoint 64P 1MB/2MB

  - VGA Trio 64P 1MB/2MB

- Gateway

  - Mach64 Accelerator (Mach64/VRAM) 2MB

- Genoa

  - 5400 512KB

  - 8500/8500VL 1MB

  - Phantom 32i 8900 2MB

  - Phantom 64 2MB

- Hercules

  - Dynamite 1MB

  - Dynamite Pro 1MB/2MB

  - Dynamite Power 2MB

  - Dynamite 3D/GL

- Graphite 1MB
- Stingray 64 1MB/2MB
- Stingray Pro 1MB/2MB
- Stringray 1MB
- Terminator 3D 2MB/4MB
- Terminator 64/Video 2MB
- Graphite Terminator Pro 2MB/4MB
- HP
  - NetServer LF/LC/LE (TVGA9000i) 512KB
  - Vectra VL2 (GD5428) 1MB
  - Vectra XM2i (Vision864) 1MB/2MB
  - Vectra XU (Vision864) 1MB/2MB
- IBM
  - 8514/A 1MB
  - PC 300 Series (GD5430) 1MB
  - PC 300 Series (Vision864) 1MB/2MB
  - PC 700 Series (Vision864) 1MB/2MB
  - PS/ValuePoint Performance Series (Vision864) 1MB/2MB
  - VC550 1MB
  - VGA 256KB
  - XGA-NI 1MB
  - XGA 1MB
- IIT
  - AGX014 1MB
  - AGX015 1MB/2MB
- Integral
  - FlashPoint 1MB/2MB

- Leadtek
  - WinFast L2300 4MB/8MB
- Matrox
  - Comet 2MB
  - Marvel II 2MB
  - Impression (MGA-IMP/3/A/H, MGA-IMP/3/V/H, MGA-IMP/3/M/H) 3MB
  - Impression Lite (MGA-IMP+/LTE/P) 2MB
  - Impression Plus Lite (MGA-IMP+/LTE/V) 2MB
  - Millennium (MGA-MIL) 2MB/4MB/8MB
  - Millennium 220 (MGA-MIL) 2MB/4MB/8MB
  - Millennium PowerDoc (WRAM) 2MB/4MB/8MB
  - Millennium II (WRAM) 2MB/4MB/8MB PCI and AGP
  - Mystique (MGA-MYS) 2MB/4MB
  - Mystique 220
  - Matrox (con.t)
  - Impression Plus (MGA-IMP+/P, MGA-IMP+/A) 2MB/4MB
  - Impression Plus 220 (MGA-IMP+/P/H, MGA-IMP+/A/H) 2MB/4MB
  - Impression Pro (MGA-PRO/4.5/V) 4.5MB
  - Ultima Plus (MGA-PCI/2+, MGA-VLB/2+) 2MB/4MB
  - Ultima (MGA-ULT/2/A, MGA-PCI/2, MGA-VLB/2) 2MB
  - Ultima (MGA-ULT/2/A/H, MGA-ULT_2/M/H) 2MB
  - Ultima Plus 200 (MGA-PCI/4/200, MGA-VLB/4/200) 4MB
- MaxVision
  - VideoMax 2000 2MB/4MB
- Metheus
  - Premier 801 1MB

- Premier 928-1M 1MB

- Premier 928-2M 2MB

- Premier 928-4M 4MB

- Micronics

  - Mpower 4 Plus (Mach64) 1MB

- MIRO

  - miroCRYSTAL 10AD 1MB

  - miroCRYSTAL 12SD 1MB

  - miroCRYSTAL 12SD 2MB

  - miroCRYSTAL 20PV 2MB

  - miroCRYSTAL 20SD 2MB

  - miroCRYSTAL 20SV 2MB

  - miroCRYSTAL 22SD 2MB

  - miroCRYSTAL 40SV 4MB

  - miroCRYSTAL VR2000 2MB/4MB

  - miroMAGIC 40PV 4MB

  - miroMAGIC plus 2MB

  - miroVIDEO 12PD 1MB/2MB

  - miroVIDEO 20SD 2MB

  - miroVIDEO 20SV 2MB

  - miroVIDEO 20TD 2MB

  - miroVIDEO 22SD 2MB

  - miroVIDEO 40SV 4MB

- NEC

  - Versa P Series 1MB

- Nth Graphics

  - Engine/150 2MB

  - Engine/250 2MB

- Number Nine
  - GXE Level 10, AT&T 20C491 Palette 1MB
  - GXE Level 10, Bt485 or AT&T20C505 Palette 1MB
  - GXE Level 11 2MB
  - GXE Level 12 3MB
  - GXE Level 14 4MB
  - GXE Level 16 4MB
  - GXE64 1MB/2MB
  - GXE64pro 2MB/4MB
  - GXE64pro (-1600) 2MB/4MB
  - Imagine 128 2MB
  - Image 128 (-1280) 4MB
  - Image 128 Series 2 (DRAM) 2MB/4MB
  - Image 128 Pro (-1600) 4MB/8MB
  - Image 128 Series 2 (VRAM) 2MB/4MB/8MB
  - Image 128 Series III (Revolution 3D) (WRAM) 8MB/16MB PCI and AGP
  - Revolution 3D "Ticket to Ride" (WRAM) 8MB/16MB PCI and AGP
  - 9FX Motion331 1MB/2MB
  - 9FX Motion531 1MB/2MB
  - 9FX Motion771 2MB/4MB
  - 9FX Reality332 2MB
  - 9FX Reality772 2MB/4MB
  - 9FX Reality 334 PCI and AGP
  - 9FX Vision330 1MB/2MB
- Oak Technology
  - OTI-067 512KB

- OTI-077 1MB

- OTI-087 1MB

- OTI-107 1MB/2MB

- OTI-111 1MB/2MB

- Orchid

  - Fahrenheit 1280 Plus, ATT20C491 Palette 1MB

  - Fahrenheit 1280 1MB

  - Fahrenheit 1280 Plus, SC15025 Palette 1MB

  - Fahrenheit ProVideo 64 2MB/4MB

  - Fahrenheit Video 3D 2MB

  - Kelvin 64 1MB/2MB

  - Kelvin Video64 1MB/2MB

  - P9000 2MB

- Packard Bell

  - Series 5000 Motherboard 1MB

- Paradise

  - 8514/A 1MB

  - Accelerator 24 1MB

  - Accelerator Value card 1MB

  - Bahamas 64 1MB/2MB

  - Bali 32 1MB/2MB

  - VGA 1024 512KB

  - VGA Professional 512KB

- Pixelworks

  - WhirlWIN WL1280 (110MHz) 2MB

  - WhirlWIN WL1280 (135MHz) 2MB

- WhirlWIN WW1280 (110MHz) 2MB
- WhirlWIN WW1280 (135MHz) 2MB
- WhirlWIN WW1600 1MB
- Radius
- XGA-2 1MB
- Reveal
  - VC200 1MB
  - VC300 1MB
  - VC700 1MB
- S3
  - ViRGE 2MB/4MB
  - ViRGE/DX 2MB/4MB
  - ViRGE/GX 2MB/4MB
  - ViRGE/GX /2 2MB/4MB
  - ViRGE/VX 2MB/4MB
  - Trio32 1MB/2MB
  - Trio64 1MB/2MB
  - Trio64V+ 1MB/2MB
  - Trio64V2/DX 1MB/2MB
  - Trio64V2/GX 1MB/2MB
  - 801 1MB/2MB
  - 805 1MB/2MB
  - Vision864 1MB/2MB
  - Vision866 1MB/2MB
  - Vision868 1MB/2MB
  - 911 1MB

- 924 1MB

- 928 1MB

- 928 2MB/4MB

- Sierra

  - Falcon/64 1MB/2MB

- Sigma

  - Legend 1MB

- SPEA/V7

  - Mercury P64 2MB

  - Storm Pro 4MB

  - ShowTime Plus 2MB

  - STB

  - Evolution VGA 1MB

  - Horizon Plus 1MB

  - Horizon VGA 1MB

  - Horizon 64 1MB/2MB

  - Horizon 64 Video 1MB/2MB

  - Horizon Video 1MB

  - LightSpeed 2MB

  - LightSpeed 128 2MB

  - Nitro 3D 2MB/4MB

  - Nitro 64 1MB/2MB

  - Nitro 64 Video 1MB/2MB

  - PowerGraph VL-24 1MB

  - PowerGraph X-24 1MB

  - PowerGraph 64 3D 2MB

- PowerGraph 64 1MB/2MB
- PowerGraph 64 Video 1MB/2MB
- PowerGraph Pro 2MB
- Velocity 3D 4MB
- Velocity 64V 2MB/4MB
- Toshiba
  - T4900CT 1MB
- Trident
  - TGUI9400CXi 1MB/2MB
  - TGUI9420DGi 1MB/2MB
  - TGUI9440 1MB/2MB
  - TGUI9660 1MB/2MB
  - TGUI9680 1MB/2MB
  - TVGA8900B 1MB
  - TVGA8900C 1MB
  - TVGA8900CL 1MB
  - TVGA8900D 1MB
  - TVGA9000 512KB
  - TVGA9000i 512KB
  - TVGA9200CXr 1MB/2MB
- Tseng Labs
  - ET3000 512KB
  - ET4000 1MB
  - ET6000 2MB/4MB
  - VGA/16 (ISA) 1MB
  - VGA/16 (VLB) 1MB/2MB

- VGA/32 1MB/2MB
- ET4000/W32 1MB
- ET4000/W32i 1MB/2MB
- ET4000/W32p 1MB/2MB
- VLSI
  - VL82C975 (AT&T RAMDAC) 2MB
  - VL82C975 (BrookTree RAMDAC) 2MB
  - VL82C976 (Internal RAMDAC) 2MB
- Western Digital
  - WD90C00 512KB
  - WD90C11 512KB
  - WD90C24 1MB
  - WD90C26 512KB
  - WD90C30 1MB
  - WD90C31 1MB
  - WD90C33 1MB
  - WD9510-AT 1MB
- Weitek
  - P9100 2MB
  - P9000 2MB
  - W5186 1MB
  - W5286 1MB

Laptop Accelerated-X Display Server

- Broadax
  - NP8700 (Cyber 9385)

- Chips & Technology
  - 65510 512KB
  - 65520 1MB
  - 65530 1MB
  - 65535 1MB
  - 65540 1MB
  - 65545 1MB
  - 65554 2MB/4MB
  - 65555 2MB
- Cirrus Logic
  - GD7541 1MB/2MB
  - GD7543 1MB/2MB
  - GD7548 2MB
- Compaq
  - LTE 5400 (Cirrus Logic CL5478)
  - Presario 1090ES (NM 2093)
- Dell
  - Latitude XPi 896 (NeoMagic 2070)
  - Latitude XPi (NM 2070)
  - Latitude XPi CD 1MB (NM 2090)
  - Latitude LM (NM 2160)
  - Latitude CP (NM 2160)
  - Inspiron 3000 (NM 2160)
- Digital (DEC)
  - HiNote VP (NeoMagic 2090)

- Fujitsu
- Lifebook 435DX (NeoMagic 2093)
- Gateway 2000
  - Solo 2300 (NeoMagic 2160)
  - Solo 2300 SE (NM 2160)
  - Solo 9100 (C&T 65554)
  - Solo 9100XL (C&T 65555)
- Hewlett Packard
  - OmniBook 800 (NM 2093)
- Hitachi
  - Notebook E133T (NeoMagic 2070)
- IBM
  - VGA 256KB
  - ThinkPad 380D (NeoMagic 2090)*
  - ThinkPad 385ED (NeoMagic 2090)*
  - ThinkPad 560E (Cyber 9382)
  - ThinkPad 760XD (Cyber 9385)
  - ThinkPad 770 (Cyber 9397)
- Micron
  - TransPort XKE (NeoMagic 2160)
  - Millenia Transport (Cirrus Logic GD7548)
- NEC
  - Versa P Series 1MB
  - Versa 6230 2MB (NeoMagic 2160)
- NeoMagic
  - MagicGraph128/NM2070 896

- MagicGraph128/NM2070

- MagicGraph128V/NM2090

- MagicGraph128V+/NM2097

- MagicGraph128ZV/NM2093

- MagicGraph128XD/NM2160

- Sony

  - VAIO PCG-505 (NeoMagic 2097)

- Toshiba

  - T4900CT 1MB

  - Tecra 740CDT (C&T 65554)

- Trident

  - Cyber 9397

  - Cyber 9385

  - Cyber 9382

- Twinhead

  - Slimnote 9166TH (Cyber 9385)

* Numerous XiG customers have confirmed support.

Multi-Head Accelerated-X Display Server

Metro-X 2.3

Metro Link < mailto:sales@metrolink.com>

I don't have much more information about Metro-X as I can't seem to view the PostScript files they sent me. Mail them directly for more info.

The S3 ViRGE video card is said not to be supported by Metro-X.

7. Controllers (Hard Drive)

Linux will work with standard IDE, MFM, and RLL controllers. When using MFM/RLL controllers it is important to use ext2fs and the bad block checking options when formatting the disk.

Enhanced IDE (EIDE) interfaces are supported with up to two IDE interfaces and up to four hard drives and/or CD-ROM drives. Linux will detect these EIDE interfaces:

- CMD-640

- DTC 2278D

- FGI/Holtek HT-6560B

- RZ1000

- Triton I (82371FB) (with busmaster DMA)

- Triton II (82371SB) (with busmaster DMA)

ESDI controllers that emulate the ST-506 (MFM/RLL/IDE) interface will also work. The bad block checking comment also applies to these controllers.

Generic 8-bit XT controllers also work.

Starting with pre-patch-2.0.31-3 IDE/ATAPI is provided.

Other controllers supported:

- Tekram D690CD IDE PCI Cache Controller (with RAID level 1 mirroring and caching)

8. Controllers (SCSI)

It is important to pick a SCSI controller carefully. Many cheap ISA SCSI controllers are designed to drive CD-ROMs rather than anything else. Such low-end SCSI controllers are no better than IDE. See the SCSI HOWTO and look at performance figures before buying a SCSI card.

8.1 Supported

- AMI Fast Disk VLB/EISA (BusLogic compatible)

- Adaptec AVA-1502E (ISA/VLB) (AIC-6360). Use the AHA-152x driver.

- Adaptec AVA-1505/1515 (ISA) (Adaptec AHA-152x compatible)

- Adaptec AHA-1510/152x (ISA/VLB) (AIC-6260/6360)

- Adaptec AHA-154x (ISA) (all models)

- Adaptec AHA-174x (EISA) (in enhanced mode)

- Adaptec AHA-274x (EISA) (AIC-7771)

- Adaptec AHA-284x (VLB) (AIC-7770)

- Adaptec AHA-2920 (PCI). Use the Future Domain driver.

- Adaptec AHA-2940AU (PCI) (AIC-7861)

- Adaptec AHA-294x/U/W/UW/D/WD (AIC-7871, AIC-7844, AIC-7881, AIC-7884)

- Adaptec AHA-3940/U/W (PCI) (AIC-7872, AIC-7882) (since 1.3.6)

- Adaptec AHA-398x/U/W (PCI) (AIC-7873, AIC-7883)

- Adaptec PCI controllers with AIC-7850, AIC-7855, AIC-7860

- Adaptec on board controllers with AIC-777x (EISA), AIC-785x, AIC-787x (PCI), AIC-788x (PCI)

- Always IN2000

- BusLogic (ISA/EISA/VLB/PCI) (all models)

- DPT PM2001, PM2012A (EATA-PIO)

- DPT Smartcache/SmartRAID Plus,III,IV families (ISA/EISA/PCI).Take a look at http://www.uni-mainz.de/~neuffer/scsi/dpt/(EATA-DMA). Cards in these families are PM2011, PM2021, PM2041, PM3021, PM2012B, PM2022, PM2122, PM2322, PM2042, PM3122, PM3222, PM3332, PM2024, PM2124, PM2044, PM2144, PM3224, PM3334.

- DTC 329x (EISA) (Adaptec 154x compatible)

- Future Domain TMC-16x0, TMC-3260 (PCI)

- Future Domain TMC-8xx, TMC-950

- Future Domain chips TMC-1800, TMC-18C50, TMC-18C30, TMC-36C70

- ICP-Vortex PCI-SCSI Disk Array Controllers (many RAID levels supported). Patches for Linux 1.2.13 and 2.0.29 are available at `ftp://icp-vortex.com/download/linux/`. The controllers GDT6111RP, GDT6121RP, GDT6117RP, GDT6127RP, GDT6511RP, GDT6521RP, GDT6517RP, GDT6527RP, GDT6537RP, and GDT6557RP are supported. You can also use pre-patch-2.0.31-4 to pre-patch-2.0.31-9.

- ICP-Vortex EISA-SCSI Controllers (many RAID levels supported).Patches for Linux 1.2.13 and 2.0.29 are available at `ftp://icp-vortex.com/download/linux/`. The controllers GDT3000B, GDT3000A, GDT3010A, GDT3020A, and GDT3050A are supported. You can also use pre-patch-2.0.31-4 to pre-patch-2.0.31-9.

- Media Vision Pro Audio Spectrum 16 SCSI (ISA)

- NCR 5380 generic cards

- NCR 53C400 (Trantor T130B) (use generic NCR 5380 SCSI support)

- NCR 53C406a (Acculogic ISApport/Media Vision Premium 3D SCSI)

- NCR chips 53C7x0

- NCR chips 53C810, 53C815, 53C820, 53C825, 53C860, 53C875, 53C895

- Qlogic/Control Concepts SCSI/IDE (FAS408) (ISA/VLB)

- Quantum ISA-200S, ISA-250MG

- Seagate ST-01/ST-02 (ISA)

- Sound Blaster 16 SCSI-2 (Adaptec 152x compatible) (ISA)

- Tekram DC-390, DC-390W/U/F

- Trantor T128/T128F/T228 (ISA)

- UltraStor 14F (ISA), 24F (EISA), 34F (VLB)

- Western Digital WD7000 SCSI

8.2 Others

- AMD AM53C974, AM79C974 (PCI) (Compaq, HP, Zeos onboard SCSI)
  `ftp://sunsite.unc.edu/pub/Linux/kernel/patches/scsi/AM53C974-`
  `0.3.tgz`

- Adaptec ACB-40xx SCSI-MFM/RLL bridgeboard
  `ftp://sunsite.unc.edu/pub/Linux/kernel/patches/scsi/adaptec-`
  `40XX.tar.gz`

- Always Technologies AL-500
  `ftp://sunsite.unc.edu/pub/Linux/kernel/patches/scsi/al500-`
  `0.2.tar.gz`

- BusLogic (ISA/EISA/VLB/PCI) (new beta driver)
  `ftp://sunsite.unc.edu/pub/Linux/kernel/patches/scsi/BusLogic-`
  `1.3.0.tar.gz`

- Iomega PC2/2B
  `ftp://sunsite.unc.edu/pub/Linux/kernel/patches/scsi/iomega_`
  `pc2-1.1.x.tar.gz`

- Qlogic (ISP1020) (PCI)
  `ftp://sunsite.unc.edu/pub/Linux/kernel/patches/scsi/isp1020-`
  `0.5.gz`

- Ricoh GSI-8
  `ftp://tsx-11.mit.edu/pub/linux/ALPHA/scsi/gsi8.tar.gz`

8.3 Unsupported

- Parallel port SCSI adapters
- Non-Adaptec-compatible DTC boards (327x, 328x)

9. Controllers (I/O)

Any standard serial/parallel/joystick/combo cards. Linux supports 8250, 16450, 16550, and 16550A UARTs. Cards that support non-standard IRQs (IRQ > 9) can be used.

See National Semiconductor's "Application Note AN-493" by Martin S. Michael. Section 5.0 describes in detail the differences between the NS16550 and NS16550A. Briefly, the NS16550 had bugs in the FIFO circuits, but the NS16550A (and later) chips fixed those. However, there were very few NS16550s produced by National, long ago, so these should be very rare. And many of the "16550" parts in actual modern boards are from the many manufacturers of compatible parts, which may not use the National "A" suffix. Also, some multiport boards will use 16552 or 16554 or various other multiport or multifunction chips from National or other suppliers (generally in a dense package soldered to the board, not a 40-pin DIP). Mostly, don't worry about it unless you encounter a very old 40-pin DIP National "NS16550" (no A) chip loose or in an old board, in which case treat it as a 16450 (no FIFO) rather than a 16550A—Zhahai Stewart < `mailto:zstewart@hisys.com`> .

10. Controllers (Multiport)

10.1 Non-Intelligent Cards

Supported

- AST FourPort and clones (4-port)

- Accent Async-4 (4-port)

- Arnet Multiport-8 (8-port)

- Bell Technologies HUB6 (6-port)

- Boca BB-1004, 1008 (4/8-port) - no DTR, DSR, and CD

- Boca BB-2016 (16-port)

- Boca IO/AT66 (6-port)

- Boca IO 2by4 (4 serial/2 parallel, uses 5 IRQs)

- Computone ValuePort (4/6/8-port) (AST FourPort compatible)

- DigiBoard PC/X (4/8/16-port)

- Comtrol Hostess 550 (4/8-port)

- PC-COMM 4-port (4-port)

- SIIG I/O Expander 4S (4-port, uses 4 IRQs)

- STB 4-COM (4-port)

- Twincom ACI/550

- Usenet Serial Board II (4-port)

Non-intelligent cards usually come in two varieties, one using standard COM port addresses and 4 IRQs, and another that's AST FourPort-compatible and uses a selectable block of addresses and a single IRQ. (Addresses and IRQs are set using `setserial`.) If you're getting one of these cards, be sure to check which standard it conforms to. Prices are no indication.

10.2 Intelligent Cards

Supported

- Computone IntelliPort II (4/8/16-port)
  `ftp://ftp.computone.com/pub/bbs/beta/ip2linux-1.0.2.tar.gz`

- Cyclades Cyclom-8Y/16Y (8/16-port) (ISA/PCI)

- DigiBoard PC/Xe (ISA), PC/Xi (EISA) and PC/Xeve
  `ftp://ftp.digibd.com/drivers/linux/`

- Equinox SST Intelligent serial I/O cards
  `http://www.equinox.com/`

- Hayes ESP 1-, 2- and 8-port versions
  Included in kernel since 2.1.15. The driver for kernel versions 2.0.x can be found at `http://www.nyx.net/~arobinso`

- Stallion EasyIO (ISA)/EasyConnection 8/32 (ISA/MCA)

- Stallion EasyConnection 8/64/ONboard (ISA/EISA/MCA)/Brumby/Stallion (ISA)

Others

- Comtrol RocketPort (8/16/32-port)
  `ftp://sunsite.unc.edu/pub/Linux/kernel/patches/serial/comtrol-1.04.tar.gz`

- DigiBoard COM/Xi
  contact Simon Park (`mailto:si@wimpol.demon.co.uk`) or Mark Hatle
  (`mailto:si@wimpol.demon.co.uk`). NOTE: Both e-mail addresses seem
  not to exist any longer.

- Moxa C102, C104, C168, C218 (8-port), C320 (8/16/24/32 expandable) and
  C320T
  `ftp://ftp.moxa.com.tw/drivers/linux/`

- Specialix SIO/XIO (modular, 4 to 32 ports)
  `ftp://sunsite.unc.edu/pub/Linux/kernel/patches/serial/sidrv.taz`

11. Network Adapters

Ethernet adapters vary greatly in performance. In general, the newer the design
the better. Some very old cards like the 3Com 3C501 are only useful because they
can be found in junk heaps for $5 at times. Be careful with clones; not all are good
clones, and bad clones often cause erratic lockups under Linux. Read the Ethernet
HOWTO, `http://sunsite.unc.edu/LDP/HOWTO/`, for detailed descriptions of
various cards.

11.1 Supported

Ethernet

For Ethernet cards with the DECchip DC21x4x family the "Tulip" driver is available. More information on this driver can be found at `http://cesdis.gsfc.nasa`
`.gov/linux/drivers/tulip.html`.

- 3Com 3C501 - "avoid like the plague"

- 3Com 3C503, 3C505, 3C507, 3C509/3C509B (ISA)/3C579 (EISA)

- 3Com Etherlink III Vortex Ethercards (3C590, 3c592, 3C595, 3c597) (PCI), 3Com Etherlink XL Boomerang Ethercards (3c900, 3c905) (PCI), and 3Com Fast Etherlink Ethercard (3c515) (ISA)Newer versions of this driver are available at `http://cesdis.gsfc.nasa.gov/linux/drivers/vortex .html`Avoid the 3c900 card when possible as the driver is not functioning well for this card.

- AMD LANCE (79C960)/PCnet-ISA/PCI (AT1500, HP J2405A, NE1500/NE2100)

- AT&T GIS WaveLAN

- Allied Telesis AT1700

- Allied Telesis LA100PCI-T

- Ansel Communications AC3200 EISA

- Apricot Xen-II/82596

- Cabletron E21xx

- Cogent EM110

- Danpex EN-9400

- DEC DE425 (EISA)/DE434/DE435 (PCI)/DE450/DE500 (DE4x5 driver)

- DEC DE450/DE500-XA (Tulip driver)

- DEC DEPCA and EtherWORKS

- DEC EtherWORKS 3

- DEC QSilver's (Tulip driver)

- Fujitsu FMV-181/182/183/184

- HP PCLAN (27245 and 27xxx series)

- HP PCLAN PLUS (27247B and 27252A)

- HP 10/100VG PCLAN (J2577, J2573, 27248B, J2585) (ISA/EISA/PCI) More information at `http://cesdis1.gsfc.nasa.gov/linux/ drivers/100vg.html`

- ICL EtherTeam 16i/32 EISA

- Intel EtherExpress

- Intel EtherExpress Pro

- KTI ET16/P-D2, ET16/P-DC ISA (work jumperless and with hardware-configuration options)

- NE2000/NE1000 (be careful with clones)

- New Media Ethernet

- PureData PDUC8028, PDI8023

- SEEQ 8005

- SMC Ultra/EtherEZ (ISA)

- SMC 9000 series

- SMC PCI EtherPower 10/100 (Tulip driver)

- SMC EtherPower II (epic100.c driver)

- Schneider & Koch G16

- Western Digital WD80x3

- Zenith Z-Note/IBM ThinkPad 300 built-in adapter

- Znyx 312 Etherarray (Tulip driver)

ISDN

- Linux ISDN WWW page
  `http://www.ix.de/ix/linux/linux-isdn.html`

- 3Com Sonix Arpeggio
  `ftp://sunsite.unc.edu/pub/Linux/kernel/patches/network/sonix.tgz`

- AVM A1
  `ftp://ftp.franken.de/pub/isdn4linux/`

- Combinet EVERYWARE 1000 ISDN
  `ftp://sunsite.unc.edu/pub/Linux/kernel/patches/network/combinet1000isdn-1.02.tar.gz`

- Creatix PnP S0
  `ftp://ftp.franken.de/pub/isdn4linux/`

- ELSA Microlink PCC-16, PCF, PCF-Pro, PCC-8
  `ftp://ftp.franken.de/pub/isdn4linux/`

- ELSA QuickStep 1000
  `ftp://ftp.franken.de/pub/isdn4linux/`

- ICN ISDN cards
  `ftp://ftp.franken.de/pub/isdn4linux/`

- ITK ix1-micro rev.2
  `ftp://ftp.franken.de/pub/isdn4linux/`

- Octal PCBIT
  `ftp://ftp.franken.de/pub/isdn4linux/`

- Teles 8.0/16.0/16.3 and compatible ones
  `ftp://ftp.franken.de/pub/isdn4linux/`

- Teles S0
  `ftp://ftp.franken.de/pub/isdn4linux/`

ISDN cards that emulate standard modems or common Ethernet adapters don't need any special drivers to work.

Pocket and Portable Adapters

For more information on Linux and use of the parallel port, go to the Linux Parallel Port Home Page, `http://www.torque.net/linux-pp.html`

- Accton parallel port Ethernet adapter
  `http://paradigm.uor.edu/~harshman/linux/accton.html`

- AT-Lan-Tec/RealTek parallel port adapter

- D-Link DE600/DE620 parallel port adapter

Slotless

- SLIP/CSLIP/PPP (serial port)

- EQL (serial IP load balancing)

- PLIP (parallel port)—using "LapLink cable" or bi-directional cable

ARCnet

- Works with all ARCnet cards

Token Ring

- Any IBM Token Ring card not using DMA
- IBM Tropic chipset cards
- Madge Token Ring OCI 16/4 Mk2

FDDI

- DEC DEFEA (EISA)/DEFPA (PCI) (kernel 2.0.24 and later)

Amateur Radio (AX.25)

- Gracilis PackeTwin
- Ottawa PI/PI2
- Most generic 8530-based HDLC boards

PCMCIA Cards

- See Appendix B for complete list

11.2 Others

Ethernet

- Racal-Interlan NI5210 (i82586 Ethernet chip). Avoid this card. It is not functioning properly with the current driver.
- Racal-Interlan NI6510 (am7990 lance chip). Starting with kernel 1.3.66 more than 16MB RAM is supported.
- Racal-Interlan PCI card (AMD PC net chip 97c970)

ISDN

- SpellCaster's Datacomute/BRI, Telecomute/BRI (ISA)
  `ftp://ftp.franken.de/pub/isdn4linux/`

ATM

- Efficient Networks ENI155P-MF 155Mbps ATM adapter (PCI)
  `http://lrcwww.epfl.ch/linux-atm/`

Frame Relay

- Sangoma S502 56K Frame Relay card
  `ftp://ftp.sovereign.org/pub/wan/fr/`

Wireless

- Proxim RangeLan2 7100 (ISA)/630x (OEM mini-ISA)
  `http://www.komacke.com/distribution.html`

11.3 Unsupported

- Xircom adapters (PCMCIA and parallel port)

- IBM PCI Token Ring cards (all of them)

- Sysconnect/Schneider & Koch Token Ring cards (all of them)

12. Sound Cards

12.1 Supported

- 6850 UART MIDI

- Adlib (OPL2)

- Audio Excell DSP16

- Aztech Sound Galaxy NX Pro

- Crystal CS4232(PnP) based cards

- ECHO-PSS cards (Orchid SoundWave32, Cardinal DSP16)

- Ensoniq SoundScape

- Gravis Ultrasound

- Gravis Ultrasound 16-bit sampling daughterboard

- Gravis Ultrasound MAX

- Logitech SoundMan Games (SBPro, 44kHz stereo support)

- Logitech SoundMan Wave (Jazz16/OPL4)

- Logitech SoundMan 16 (PAS-16 compatible)

- MediaTriX AudioTriX Pro

- Media Vision Premium 3D (Jazz16)

- Media Vision Pro Sonic 16 (Jazz)

- Media Vision Pro Audio Spectrum 16

- Microsoft Sound System (AD1848)

- OAK OTI-601D cards (Mozart)

- OPTi 82C925 cards. Use the MSS driver and the isapnp tools

- OPTi 82C928/82C929 cards (MAD16/MAD16 Pro/ISP16/Mozart)

- OPTi 82C931 cards. See `http://oto.dyn.ml.org/~drees/opti931.html`

- Sound Blaster

- Sound Blaster Pro

- Sound Blaster 16

- Turtle Beach Wavefront cards (Maui, Tropez)

- Wave Blaster (and other daughterboards)

- Cards based on the ESS Technologies AudioDrive chips (688, 1688, 1868, etc.)

- AWE32/64 support is started in kernel series 2.1.x (check the Sound Blaster AWE mini-HOWTO by Marcus Brinkmann for installation details)

- MPU-401 MIDI

12.2 Others

- MPU-401 MIDI (intelligent mode)
  `ftp://sunsite.unc.edu/pub/Linux/kernel/sound/mpu401-0.2.tar.gz`

- PC speaker/Parallel port DAC
  `ftp://ftp.informatik.hu-berlin.de/pub/os/linux/hu-sound/`

- Turtle Beach MultiSound/Tahiti/Monterey
  `ftp://ftp.cs.colorado.edu/users/mccreary/archive/tbeach/`
  `multisound/`

12.3 Unsupported

The ASP chip on Sound Blaster 16 series is not supported. AWE32s onboard E-mu
MIDI synthesizer is not supported.

Nathan Laredo < `mailto:laredo@gnu.ai.mit.edu`> is willing to write
AWE32 drivers if you send him a complimentary card. He is also willing to write
drivers for almost any hardware if you send him free samples of your hardware.

Sound Blaster 16s with DSP 4.11 and 4.12 have a hardware bug that causes
hung/stuck notes when playing MIDI and digital audio at the same time. The
problem can happen with either Wave Blaster daughterboards or MIDI devices
attached to the MIDI port. There is no known fix.

13. Hard Drives

All hard drives should work if the controller is supported.

(From the SCSI HOWTO:) All direct-access SCSI devices with a block size of 256,
512, or 1024 bytes should work. Other block sizes will not work (note that this can
often be fixed by changing the block and/or sector sizes using the MODE SELECT
SCSI command).

Large IDE (EIDE) drives work fine with newer kernels. The boot partition must
lie in the first 1024 cylinders due to PC BIOS limitations.

Some Conner CFP1060S drives may have problems with Linux and `ext2fs`.
The symptoms are i-node errors during `e2fsck` and corrupt file systems. Conner

has released a firmware upgrade to fix this problem; contact Conner at 1-800-4CONNER (US) or +44-1294-315333 (Europe). Have the microcode version (found on the drive label, 9WA1.6x) handy when you call.

Certain Micropolis drives have problems with Adaptec and BusLogic cards. Contact the drive manufacturers for firmware upgrades if you suspect problems.

- Multiple device driver (RAID-0, RAID-1)
  `ftp://sweet-smoke.ufr-info-p7.ibp.fr/public/Linux/`

14. Tape Drives

14.1 Supported

- SCSI tape drives
  (From the SCSI HOWTO:) Drives using both fixed and variable length blocks smaller than the driver buffer length (set to 32K in the distribution sources) are supported. Virtually all drives should work. (Send mail if you know of any incompatible drives.)

- QIC-02 drives

- Iomega DITTO internal (ftape 3.04c and newer)

14.2 Others

- QIC-117, QIC-40/80, QIC-3010/3020 (QIC-WIDE) drives
  Most tape drives using the floppy controller should work. Various dedicated controllers (Colorado FC-10/FC-20, Mountain Mach-2, Iomega Tape Controller II) are also supported
  `ftp://sunsite.unc.edu/pub/Linux/kernel/tapes`

- ATAPI tape drives
  For these an alpha driver (`ide-tape.c`) is available in the kernel. ATAPI tape drives supported are:

  - Seagate TapeStor 8000

  - Conner CTMA 4000 IDE ATAPI Streaming tape drive

14.3 Unsupported

- Emerald and Tecmar QIC-02 tape controller cards—Chris Ulrich `<mailto:insom@math.ucr.edu>`

- Drives that connect to the parallel port (e.g., Colorado Trakker)

- Some high-speed tape controllers (Colorado TC-15)

- Irwin AX250L/Accutrak 250 (not QIC-80)

- IBM Internal Tape Backup Unit (not QIC-80)

- COREtape Light

15. CD-ROM Drives

For more information on CD-ROM drives, check the CD-ROM HOWTO at `http://sunsite.unc.edu/LDP/HOWTO/`.

15.1 Supported

Common CD-ROM Drives

- SCSI CD-ROM drives
  (From the CD-ROM HOWTO:) Any SCSI CD-ROM drive with a block size of 512 or 2048 bytes should work under Linux; this includes the vast majority of CD-ROM drives on the market.

- EIDE (ATAPI) CD-ROM drives (IDECD)
  Almost all double-, quad-, and six-speed drives are supported, including

  - Mitsumi FX400

  - Nec-260

  - Sony 55E

Proprietary CD-ROM Drives

- Aztech CDA268-01A, Orchid CDS-3110, Okano/Wearnes CDD-110, Conrad TXC, CyCDROM CR520ie/CR540ie/CR940ie (AZTCD)

- Creative Labs CD-200(F) (SBPCD)

- Funai E2550UA/MK4015 (SBPCD)

- GoldStar R420 (GSCD)

- IBM External ISA (SBPCD)

- Kotobuki (SBPCD)

- Lasermate CR328A (OPTCD)

- LMS Philips CM 206 (CM206)

- Longshine LCS-7260 (SBPCD)

- Matsushita/Panasonic CR-521/522/523/562/563 (SBPCD)

- MicroSolutions Backpack parallel port drive (BPCD)

- Mitsumi CR DC LU05S (MCD/MCDX)

- Mitsumi FX001D/F (MCD/MCDX)

- Optics Storage Dolphin 8000AT (OPTCD)

- Sanyo H94A (SJCD)

- Sony CDU31A/CDU33A (CDU31A)

- Sony CDU-510/CDU-515 (SOMYCD535)

- Sony CDU-535/CDU-531 (SONYCD535)

- Teac CD-55A SuperQuad (SBPCD)

15.2 Others

- LMS/Philips CM 205/225/202
  `ftp://sunsite.unc.edu/pub/Linux/kernel/patches/cdrom/lmscd0`
  `.4.tar.gz`

- NEC CDR-35D (old)
  `ftp://sunsite.unc.edu/pub/Linux/kernel/patches/cdrom/linux-`
  `neccdr35d.patch`

- Sony SCSI multisession CD-XA
  `ftp://tsx-11.mit.edu/pub/linux/patches/sony-multi-0.00.tar.gz`

- Parallel Port Driver
  `http://www.torque.net/linux-pp.html`

15.3 Notes

All CD-ROM drives should work similarly for reading data. There are various compatibility problems with audio CD–playing utilities, especially with newer low-end NEC drives. Some alpha drivers may not have audio support yet.

Early (single-speed) NEC CD-ROM drives may have trouble with currently available SCSI controllers.

PhotoCD (XA) is supported. The hpcdtoppm program by Hadmut Danisch converts PhotoCD files to the portable pixmap format. The program can be obtained from `ftp://ftp.gwdg.de/pub/linux/hpcdtoppm` or as part of the PBM utilities.

Also, reading video CD is supported in kernel series 2.1.3*x* and later. A patch is available for kernel 2.0.30.

Finally, most IDE CD-ROM changers are supported.

16. CD-Writers

Many CD-Writers are supported by Linux now. For an up-to-date list of CD-Writers supported, check the CD-Writing mini-HOWTO at `http://sunsite.unc.edu/LDP/HOWTO/mini/CD-Writing` or check `http://www.shop.de/cgi-bin/wini/lsc.pl`. Cdwrite (`ftp://sunsite.unc.edu/pub/Linux/utils/disk-management/`) and Cdrecord (`http://www.fokus.gmd.de/nthp/employees/schilling/cdrecord.html`) can be used for writing CDs. The X-CD-Roast package for Linux is a graphical front-end for using CD-writers. The package can be found at `ftp://sunsite.unc.edu/pub/Linux/utils/disk-management/xcdroast-0.96b.tar.gz`.

- Grundig CDR 100 IPW

- HP CD-Writer+ 7100

- HP SureStore 4020i

- HP SureStore 6020es/i
- JVC XR-W2010
- Mitsubishi CDRW-225
- Mitsumi CR-2600TE
- Olympus CDS 620E
- Philips CDD-522/2000/2600/3610
- Pinnacle Micro RCD-5020/5040
- Plextor CDR PX-24CS
- Ricoh MP 1420C
- Ricoh MP 6200S/6201S
- Sanyo CRD-R24S
- Smart and Friendly Internal 2006 Plus 2.05
- Sony CDU 920S/924/926S
- Taiyo Yuden EW-50
- TEAC CD-R50S
- WPI(Wearnes) CDR-632P
- WPI(Wearnes) CDRW-622
- Yamaha CDR-100
- Yamaha CDR-200/200t/200tx
- Yamaha CDR-400t/400tx

17. Removable Drives

All SCSI drives should work if the controller is supported, including optical (MO), WORM, floptical, Bernoulli, Zip, Jaz, SyQuest, PD, and others.

- Parallel port Zip drives
  `ftp://gear.torque.net/pub/`
- Parallel port Avatar Shark-250
  `http://www.torque.net/shark.html`

Removable drives work like hard disks and floppies: just `fdisk`/`mkfs` and mount the disks. Linux provides drive locking if your drives support it. `Mtools` can also be used if the disks are in MS-DOS format.

CD-R drives require special software to work. Read the CD-R Mini-HOWTO.

Linux supports both 512 and 1024 bytes/sector disks. Starting with kernel 2.1.32, Linux also supports 2048 bytes/sector. A patch to kernel 2.0.30 is available at `http://liniere.gen.u-tokyo.ac.jp/2048.html`.

The 2048 bytes/sector support is needed for

- Fujitsu magneto-optical disk drives M2513

Starting with pre-patch-2.0.31-3, IDE/ATAPI internal Zip drives, flopticals and PDs are supported.

- LS-120 floptical
- PD-CD

18. Mice

18.1 Supported

- Microsoft serial mouse
- Mouse Systems serial mouse
- Logitech Mouseman serial mouse
- Logitech serial mouse
- ATI XL Inport busmouse
- C&T 82C710 (QuickPort) (Toshiba, TI TravelMate)
- Microsoft busmouse
- Logitech busmouse
- PS/2 (auxiliary device) mouse

18.2 Others

- Sejin J-mouse
  `ftp://sunsite.unc.edu/pub/Linux/kernel/patches/console/jmouse`
  `.1.1.70-jmouse.tar.gz`

- MultiMouse. Use multiple mouse devices as single mouse
  `ftp://sunsite.unc.edu/pub/Linux/system/misc/MultiMouse-1.0.tgz`

- Microsoft Intellimouse

18.3 Notes

Touchpad devices like Alps Glidepoint also work, so long as they're compatible with another mouse protocol.

Newer Logitech mice (except the Mouseman) use the Microsoft protocol and all three buttons do work. Even though Microsoft's mice have only two buttons, the protocol allows three buttons.

The mouse port on the ATI Graphics Ultra and Ultra Pro use the Logitech bus-mouse protocol. (See the Busmouse HOWTO for details.)

19. Modems

All internal modems or external modems connected to the serial port should work. Alas, some manufacturers have created Windows 95–only modems. Check Appendix D for Linux-incompatible hardware.

A small number of modems come with DOS software that downloads the control program at runtime. These can normally be used by loading the program under DOS and doing a warm boot. Such modems are probably best avoided, as you won't be able to use them with non-PC hardware in the future.

All PCMCIA modems should work with the PCMCIA drivers.

Fax modems need appropriate fax software to operate. Also be sure that the fax part of the modem supports Class 2 or Class 2.0. It seems to be generally true for any fax software on Unix that support for Class 1.0 is not available.

- Digicom Connection 96+/14.4+ - DSP code downloading program
  `ftp://sunsite.unc.edu/pub/Linux/apps/serialcomm/smdl-`
  `linux.1.02.tar.gz`

- Motorola ModemSURFR internal 56K. Add a couple of lines to RC.SERIAL
  to account for IRQ and ports if they are non-standard.

- ZyXEL U-1496 series - ZyXEL 1.4, modem/fax/voice control program
  `http://www.pe1ch1.demon.nl/ZyXEL/ZyXEL-1.6.tar.gz`

- ZyXEL Elite 2864 series - modem/fax/voice control program
  `http://www.pe1ch1.demon.nl/ZyXEL/ZyXEL-1.6.tar.gz`

- ZyXEL Omni TA 128 - modem/fax/voice control program
  `http://www.pe1ch1.demon.nl/ZyXEL/ZyXEL-1.6.tar.gz`

20. Printers/Plotters

All printers and plotters connected to the parallel or serial port should work.
Alas, some manufacturers have created Windows 95–only printers. Check
Appendix D for Linux-incompatible hardware.

- HP LaserJet 4 series - free-lj4, printing modes control program
  `ftp://sunsite.unc.edu/pub/Linux/system/printing/free-lj4-`
  `1.1p1.tar.gz`

- BiTronics parallel port interface
  `ftp://sunsite.unc.edu/pub/Linux/kernel/patches/misc/bt-ALPHA-`
  `0.0.1.module.patch.gz`

20.1 Ghostscript

Many Linux programs output PostScript files. Non-PostScript printers can emulate PostScript Level 2 using Ghostscript.

- Ghostscript
  `ftp://ftp.cs.wisc.edu/pub/ghost/aladdin/`

Ghostscript Supported Printers

- Apple Imagewriter

- C. Itoh M8510

- Canon BubbleJet BJ10e (bj10e)

- Canon BubbleJet BJ200, BJC-210 (B/W only), BJC-240 (B/W only) (bj200)

- Canon BubbleJet BJC-600, BJC-610, BJC-4000, BJC-4100, BJC-450, MultiPASS C2500, BJC-240, BJC-70 (bjc600)

- Canon BubbleJet BJC-800 (bjc800)

- Canon LBP-8II, LIPS III

- DEC LA50/70/75/75plus

- DEC LN03, LJ250

- Epson 9-pin, 24-pin, LQ series, AP3250

- Epson Stylus Color/Color II/500/800 (stcolor)

- HP 2563B

- HP DesignJet 650C

- HP DeskJet, DeskJet Plus (deskjet)

- HP DeskJet 500, DeskJet Portable (djet500)

- HP DeskJet 400/500C/540C/690C/693C (cdj500)

- HP DeskJet 550C/560C/600/660C/682C/683C/693C/850/870Cse (cdj550)

- HP DeskJet 850/870Cse/870Cxi/680 (cdj850)

- HP DeskJet 500C/510/520/5540C/693C printing black only (cdjmono)

- HP DeskJet 600 (lj4dith)

- HP DeskJet 600/870Cse, LaserJet 5/5L (ljet4)

- HP DeskJet 500/500C/510/520/540/550C/560C/850C/855C `ftp:ftp.pdb.sni.de/pub/utilities/misc/hpdj-2.1.tar.gz`

- HP PaintJet XL300, DeskJet 600/1200C/1600C (pjxl300)

- HP LaserJet/Plus/II/III/4

- HP PaintJet/XL

- IBM Jetprinter color

- IBM Proprinter

- Imagen ImPress

- Mitsubishi CP50 color

- NEC P6/P6+/P60

- Oki OL410ex LED (ljet4)

- Okidata MicroLine 182

- Ricoh 4081/6000 (r4081)

- SPARCprinter

- StarJet 48 inkjet printer

- Tektronix 4693d color 2/4/8 bit

- Tektronix 4695/4696 inkjet plotter

- Xerox XES printers (2700, 3700, 4045, etc.)

Others

- Canon BJC600/800 color printers
  `ftp://petole.imag.fr/pub/postscript/ghostscript/bjc600/`

21. Scanners

For scanner support there is the package SANE (Scanner Access Now Easy). Information can be found at `http://www.mostang.com/sane/`. It can be downloaded from `ftp://ftp.mostang.com/pub/sane/`. This is a universal scanner interface. It comes complete with documentation and several front ends and back ends.

More information on handheld scanners can be found at `http://swt-www.informatik.uni-hamburg.de/~1willamo/scanner.html`.

21.1 Supported

- A4 Tech AC 4096/AS 8000P
  `ftp://ftp.informatik.huberlin.de/pub/local/linux/a4scan/a4scan.tgz`

- Adara Image Star I
  `http://fb4-1112.uni-muenster.de/ffwd/`
  `ftp://fb4-1112.uni-muenster.de/pub/ffwd/mtekscan-0.2.tar.gz`

- Conrad Personal Scanner 64, P105 handheld scanners
  `ftp://tsx-11.mit.edu/pub/linux/ALPHA/scanner/scan-driver-0.1.8.tar.gz`

- Epson GT6000
  `ftp://sunsite.unc.edu/pub/Linux/apps/graphics/capture/ppic0.5.tar.gz`

- Fujitsu SCSI-2 scanners
  contact Dr. G.W. Wettstein `<mailto:greg%wind.UUCP@plains.nodak.edu>`

- Genius ColorPage-SP2
  `http://fb4-1112.uni-muenster.de/ffwd/`
  `ftp://fb4-1112.uni-muenster.de/pub/ffwd/mtekscan-0.2.tar.gz`

- Genius GS-B105G handheld scanner
  `ftp://tsx-11.mit.edu/pub/linux/ALPHA/scanner/gs105-0.0.1.tar.gz`

- Genius GeniScan GS4500, GS4500A handheld scanners
  `ftp://tsx-11.mit.edu/pub/linux/ALPHA/scanner/gs4500-2.0.tar.gz`

- HighScreen Greyscan 256 handheld scanner
  `ftp://tsx-11.mit.edu/pub/linux/ALPHA/scanner/gs4500-2.0.tar.gz`

- HP ScanJet II series SCSI
  `ftp://sunsite.unc.edu/pub/Linux/apps/graphics/capture/hpscanpbm-0.3a.tar.gz`

- HP ScanJet IIc, IIcx, IIp, 3c, 4c, 4p, 5p, 5pse, plus
  `http://www.tummy.com/xvscan/`

- Logitech Scanman+, Scanman 32, Scanman 256 handheld scanners
  `ftp://tsx-11.mit.edu/pub/linux/ALPHA/scanner/logiscan-0.0.4.tar.gz`

- Microtek ScanMaker E3, E6, II, IIXE, III and 35t models
  `http://fb4-1112.uni-muenster.de/ffwd/`
  `ftp://fb4-1112.uni-muenster.de/pub/ffwd/mtekscan-0.2.tar.gz`

- Mustek M105 handheld scanner
  `ftp://tsx-11.mit.edu/pub/linux/ALPHA/scanner/scan-driver-0.1.8.tar.gz`

- Mustek HT800 Turbo, Matador 105, Matador 256 handheld scanners
  `ftp://tsx-11.mit.edu/pub/linux/ALPHA/scanner/scan-driver-0.1.8.tar.gz`

- Mustek Paragon 6000CX
  `ftp://sunsite.unc.edu/pub/Linux/apps/graphics/capture/muscan-2.0.6.taz`

- Nikon Coolscan SCSI 35mm film scanner
  `ftp://sunsite.unc.edu/pub/Linux/apps/graphics/capture/coolscan-0.2.tgz`

- Pearl 256 handheld scanner
  `ftp://tsx-11.mit.edu/pub/linux/ALPHA/scanner/scan-driver-0.1.8.tar.gz`

- UMAX SCSI scanners
  `ftp://tsx-11.mit.edu/pub/linux/ALPHA/scanner/umax-0.5.5.tar.gz`

The Mustek drivers work only with GI1904 interface cards. Eric Chang (`mailto:eric.chang@chrysalis.org`) has created a patch to use them with IF960 interface cards.

21.2 Others

- Genius GS-4000, ScanMate/32, ScanMate/GS handheld scanners
  `ftp://tsx-11.mit.edu/pub/linux/ALPHA/scanner/gs4500-2.0.tar.gz`

- Mustek HT105, M800 handheld scanners
  `ftp://tsx-11.mit.edu/pub/linux/ALPHA/scanner/scan-driver-0.1.8.tar.gz`

- Voelkner Personal Scanner 64 handheld scanner
  `ftp://tsx-11.mit.edu/pub/linux/ALPHA/scanner/scan-driver-0.1.8.tar.gz`

21.3 Unsupported

- Escom 256 (Primax Lector Premier 256) handheld scanner

- Genius ScanMate/256, EasyScan handheld scanners

- Mustek CG8000 handheld scanner

- Trust Ami Scan handheld scanner

22. Other Hardware

22.1 VESA Power Savings Protocol (DPMS) Monitors

Support for power savings is included in the Linux kernel. Just use `setterm` to enable support.

22.2 Touch Screens

The Metro-X X server is supporting the following touch screen:

- Carroll Touch serial touch screen.
  `http://www.carrolltouch.com/`

22.3 Terminals on Serial Port

Old terminals can easily be used under Linux by connecting them to the serial port of your system. At least the following terminals will be supported:

- VT52

- VT100

- VT220

- VT320

- VT420

22.4 Joysticks

Joystick support is in the latest XFree86 distributions (3.3.*x*) and in kernel versions 2.1.*xx*. For older kernels the links below are useful.

- Joystick driver
  ftp://sunsite.unc.edu/pub/Linux/kernel/patches/console/joystick-0.8.0.tgz

- Joystick driver (module)
  ftp://sunsite.unc.edu/pub/Linux/kernel/patches/console/joyfixed.tgz

22.5 Video Capture Boards/Frame Grabbers/ TV Tuners

A few programs are available that support TV tuners. These are:

- BTTV http://www.thp.uni-koeln.de/~rjkm/linux/bttv.html

- Xawtv

- Xtvscreen

- Data Translation DT2803

- Data Translation DT2851 Frame Grabber
  ftp://sunsite.unc.edu/pub/Linux/apps/video/dt2851-2.01.tar.gz

- Data Translation DT3155
  http://krusty.eecs.umich.edu/people/ncowan/linux/welcome.html

- Diamond DTV2000 (based on BT848)

- Dipix XPG1000/FPG/PPMAPA (based on TI C40 DSP). Most add-on cards are supported.
  http://www.thp.uni-koeln.de/~rjkm/linux/bttv.html

- Epix SVM

- Epix Silicon Video MUX series of video frame grabbing boards
  http://www.ssc.com/lj/issue13/npc13c.html

- FAST Screen Machine II
  `ftp://sunsite.unc.edu/pub/Linux/apps/video/ScreenMachineII`
  `.2.0.tgz`

- Hauppage Wincast TV PCI (based on BT848)
  `http://www.thp.uni-koeln.de/~rjkm/linux/bttv.html`

- Imaging Technology ITI/IC-PCI
  `ftp://ftp.gom-online.de/pub/IC-PCI/icpci-0.3.2.tar.gz`

- ImageNation Cortex I
  `ftp://sunsite.unc.edu/pub/Linux/apps/video/cortex.drv.1.1.tgz`

- ImageNation CX100
  `ftp://sunsite.unc.edu/pub/Linux/apps/video/cxdrv-0.86.tar.gz`

- ImageNation PX500 (being worked on). Ask for current status
  `mailto:rubini@linux.it`

- Imaging Technology Inc. IC-PCI frame grabber board
  `ftp://gandalf.expmech.ing.tu-bs.de/pub/driver/icpci-`
  `0.2.0.tar.gz`

- Matrox Meteor
  `ftp://sunsite.unc.edu/pub/Linux/apps/video/meteor-1.4a.tgz`

- Matrox PIP-1024
  `http://www.powerup.com.au/~sobeyp/pip_tar.gz`

- MaxiTV/PCI (based on ZR36120)
  `ftp://sunsite.unc.edu/pub/Linux/kernel/misc-cards/zr36120-`
  `971127.tgz`

- Miro PCTV (based on BT848)
  `http://www.thp.uni-koeln.de/~rjkm/linux/bttv.html`

- MuTech MV1000 PCI
  `ftp://sunsite.unc.edu/pub/Linux/apps/video/mv1000drv-0.33.tgz`

- MuTech MV200
  `http://www.powerup.com.au/~sobeyp/mu_tar.gz`

- Philips PCA10TV (not in production anymore)
  `ftp://ftp.il.ft.hse.nl/pub/tv1000/pctv1000.02.tgz`

- Pro Movie Studio
  `ftp://sunsite.unc.edu/pub/Linux/apps/video/PMS-grabber.3.0.tgz`

- Quanta WinVision B&W video capture card
  `ftp://sunsite.unc.edu/pub/Linux/apps/video/fgrabber-1.0.tgz`

- Quickcam
  `ftp://sunsite.unc.edu/pub/Linux/apps/video/qcam-0.7c-5.tar.gz`

- Sensus 700
  `http://www.robots.com/s700.htm`

- Smart Video Recorder III (based on BT848)
  `http://www.thp.uni-koeln.de/~rjkm/linux/bttv.html`

- STB TV PCI Television Tuner (based on BT848)
  `http://www.thp.uni-koeln.de/~rjkm/linux/bttv.html`

- Tekram C210 (based on ZR36120)
  `ftp://sunsite.unc.edu/pub/Linux/kernel/misc-cards/zr36120-971127.tgz`

- Video Blaster, Rombo Media Pro+
  `ftp://sunsite.unc.edu/pub/Linux/apps/video/vid_src-0.6.tgz`

- VT1500 TV cards
  `ftp://sunsite.unc.edu/pub/Linux/apps/video/vt1500-1.0.9.tar.gz`

22.6 Digital Camera

- HP Photo Smart Digital Camera
  `ftp://ftp.itojun.org/pub/digi-cam/`

22.7 UPS

Various other UPSes are supported; read the UPS HOWTO.

- APC SmartUPS
  `ftp://sunsite.unc.edu/pub/Linux/system/ups/apcd-0.5.tar.gz`

- APC-BackUPS 400/600, APC-SmartUPS SU700/1400RM
  `ftp://sunsite.unc.edu/pub/Linux/system/ups/apcupsd-2.2.tar.gz`

- UPSes with RS-232 monitoring port (genpower package)
  `ftp://sunsite.unc.edu/pub/Linux/system/ups/genpower-1.0.1.tgz`

- MGE UPSes
  `http://www.mgeups.com/download/softlib.htm` and `http://www`
  `.mgeups.com/download/software/linux/upsp.tgz`

- A daemon to shut down and up computers connected to UPSes. It is
  network-aware and allows server and client modes
  `ftp://sunsite.unc.edu/pub/Linux/system/ups/powerd-2.0.tar.gz`

22.8 Multifunction Boards

- Pro Audio Spectrum 16 SCSI/Sound interface card

22.9 Data Acquisition

The Linux Lab Project site collects drivers for hardware dealing with data acquisition; they also maintain some mailing lists dealing with the subject. I have no experience with data acquisition, so please check the site for more details.

- Linux Lab Project
  `http://www.llp.fu-berlin.de/`

- CED 1401

- DBCC CAMAC

- IEEE-488 (GPIB, HPIB) boards

- Keithley DAS-1200

- National Instruments AT-MIO-16F/Lab-PC+

- Analog Devices RTI-800/815 ADC/DAC board
  contact Paul Gortmaker <`mailto:gpg109@anu.edu.au`>

22.10 Watchdog Timer Interfaces

- ICS WDT500-P
  (`http://www.indcomp.src.com/products/data/html/wdt500-p.html`)

- ICS WDT501-P (with and without fan tachometer) (`http://www.indcomp`
  `.src.com/products/data/html/wdt500-p.html`)

22.11 Miscellaneous

- Mattel Powerglove

- AIMS Labs RadioTrack FM radio card
  `ftp://sunsite.unc.edu/pub/Linux/apps/sound/radio/radiotrack-1.1.tgz`

- Reveal FM Radio card
  `ftp://magoo.uwsuper.edu/docs/radio.html`

- Videotext cards
  `ftp://sunsite.unc.edu/pub/Linux/apps/video/videoteXt-0.6.tar.gz`

23. Related Sources of Information

- Cameron Spitzer's hardware FAQ archive
  `ftp://ftp.rahul.net/pub/cameron/PC-info/`

- Computer Hardware and Software Vendor Phone Numbers
  `http://mtmis1.mis.semi.harris.com/comp_ph1.html`

- Guide to Computer Vendors
  `http://guide.sbanetweb.com/`

- System Optimization Information
  `http://www.dfw.net/~sdw/`

24. Acknowledgments

Thanks to all the authors and contributors of other HOWTOs—many things here are shamelessly stolen from their works; to FRiC, Zane Healy, and Ed Carp, the original authors of this HOWTO; and to everyone else who sent in updates and feedback. Special thanks to Eric Boerner and lilo (the person, not the program) for the sanity checks. And thanks to Dan Quinlan for the original SGML conversion.

25. S3 Cards Supported by XFree86 3.3.1. (Appendix A.)

CHIPSETRAMDAC CLOCKCHIPBPPCARD 801/805AT&T 20C490 16 Actix GE 32/32+ 2MB Orchid Fahrenheit 1280(+) 801/805AT&T 20C490 ICD2061A 16 STB PowerGraph X.24 801/805 Del S3 805 Miro Crystal 8S Orchid Fahrenheit VA VL-41 805 S3 GENDAC 16 Miro 10SD VLB/PCI SPEA Mirage VLB 801/805SS2410 ICD2061A 8 Diamond Stealth 24 VLB/ISA 801/805AT&T 20C490 Ch8391 16 JAX 8231/8241, SPEA Mirage 801/805S3 GENDAC Miro Crystal 10SD 805i Actix GE 32i ELSA Winner 1000 ISA 928 AT&T 20C490 16 Actix Ultra 928 Sierra SC15025 ICD2061A 32 ELSA Winner 1000 ISA/VLB/EISA 928 Bt485 ICD2061A 32 STB Pegasus VL 928 Bt485 SC11412 16 SPEA(/V7) Mercury VLB 928 Bt485 ICD2061A 32 #9 GXE Level 10/11/12 928 Ti3020 ICD2061A 32 #9 GXE Level 14/16 928 928Movie Diamond Stealth Pro ELSA Winner 1000TwinBus ELSA Winner 1000VL ELSA Winner 2000 Miro Crystal 16S 864 ICD2061A Miro Crystal 20SD (BIOS 2.*xx*) 864 AT&T 20C498 ICS2494 32 Miro (Crystal) 20SD (BIOS 1.*xx*) 864 AT&T 20C498/ ICD2061A/ 32 ELSA Winner 1000 PRO VLB/PCI 864 STG1700 ICS9161 MIRO 20SD (BIOS 2.*x*) ELAS Winner 1000 PRO 864 STG1700 ICD2061A 32 Actix GE 64 VLB 864 AT&T 20C498/ ICS2595 16 SPEA(/V7) Mirage P64 DRAM (BIOS 3.*x*) AT&T 21C498 864 S3 86C716 SDAC 32 ELSA Winner 1000 PRO Miro 20SD (BIOS 3.*x*) SPEA Mirage P64 DRAM (BIOS 4.*x*) Diamond Stealth 64 DRAM Genoa Phantom 64i Miro Crystal 20SD VLB (BIOS 3.*xx*) 864 ICS5342 ICS5342 32 Diamond Stealth 64 DRAM (some) 864 SDAC Diamond Stealth 64 Graphics 2001 864 AT&T 20C498-13ICD2061A 32 #9 GXE64 PCI 864 ASUS Video Magic PCI V864 VidTech FastMax P20

CHIPSETRAMDAC CLOCKCHIPBPPCARD 964 ELSA Winner 2000 PRO-2,4 spider Tarantula 64 964 AT&T 20C505 ICD2061A 32 Miro Crystal 20SV PCI/40SV 964 Bt485 ICD2061A 32 Diamond Stealth 64 964 Bt9485 ICS9161A 32 SPEA Mercury 64 964 Ti3020 ICD2061A 8 ELSA Winner 2000 PRO PCI 964 Ti3025 Ti3025 32 #9 GXE64 Pro VLB/PCI Miro Crystal 40SV 964 IBM RGB 32 Hercules Graphite Terminator 64 868 S3 86C716 SDAC 32 ELSA Winner 1000AVI Miro Crystal 20SD PCI 868 AT&T 29C409 ELSA Winner 1000AVI 868 Diamond Stealth Video DRAM Diamond Stealth 64 Video 2120/2200 ELSA Winner 1000PRO/X #9 FX Motion 531 VideoLogic GrafixStar 500 968 Diamond Stealth 64 Video 3200 ELSA Gloria-4/8 ELSA Winner 2000AVI ELSA Winner 2000PRO/X-2/X-4/X-8 Genoa VideoBlitz III AV Hercules Graphite Terminator Pro 64 LeadTek WinFast S430 LeadTek WinFast S510 Miro Crystal 80SV Miro Crystal 20SV #9 FX Motion 771

VideoLogic GrafixStar 700 WinFast S430/S510 968 TVP3026 32 ELSA Winner 2000PRO/X Diamond Stealth 64 Video VRAM 968 IBM RGB 32 Genoa VideoBlitz III AVI Hercules Terminator Pro 64 STB Velocity 64 Video #9 FX Motion 771 Diamond Stealth 64 Video 3240/3400 968 TI RAMDAC Diamond Stealth 64 Video 3240/3400 732 (Trio32) 32 Diamond Stealth 64 DRAM SE (all Trio32 based cards) 764 (Trio64) 32 SPEA Mirage P64 (BIOS 5.x) Diamond Stealth 64 DRAM Diamond Stealth 64 Graphics 2xx0 #9 FX Vision 330 STB PowerGraph 64 (all Trio64 based cards)

CHIPSETRAMDAC CLOCKCHIPBPPCARD (Trio64V+) DSV3326 Diamond Stealth 64 Video 2001 DataExpert DSV3365 ExpertColor DSV3365 MAXColor S3 Trio64V+ ELSA Winner 1000TRIO/V Hercules Terminator 64/Video #9 FX Motion 331 STB Powergraph 64 Video VideoLogic GrafixStar 400 (Trio64V2) ELSA Winner 1000/T2D (ViRGE) Canopus Co. Power Window 3DV DSV3325 DataExpert DSV3325 Diamond Multimedia Stealth 3D 2000 Diamond Multimedia Stealth 3D 2000 PRO Diamond Stealth 3D 2000 Diamond Stealth 3D 2000 PRO Diamond Stealth 3D 3000 ELSA Victory 3D ELSA Victory 3DX ELSA Winner 3000-S Expertcolor DSV3325 Hercules Terminator 64/3D LeadTek WinFast 3D S600 MELCO WGP-VG4S #9 FX Motion 332 Orchid Tech. Fahrenheit Video 3D STB systems Powergraph 3D WinFast 3D S600 (ViRGE/DX) Hercules Terminator 3D/DX (ViRGE/GX) STB Nitro 3D (ViRGE/VX) ELSA Winner 2000AVI/3D ELSA Winner 3000 ELSA Winner 3000-L-42/-M-22 MELCO WGP-VX8 STB Systems Velocity 3D 911/924 Diamond Stealth VRAM 924 SC1148 DAC

NOTE: for the ViRGE/VX,DX,GX,GX2 chipsets you need XFree86 3.3.1. You should use the XF86_SVGA server.

26. Supported PCMCIA Cards (Appendix B.)

These cards are supported by David Hinds' PCMCIA package, and this list is taken from his Web page.

26.1 Ethernet Cards

- SMC, Megahertz, and Ositech cards use the smc91c92_cs driver
- 3Com and Farallon cards use the 3c589_cs driver
- Fujitsu, TDK, RATOC, CONTEC, Eagle and Nextcom cards use the fmvj18x_cs driver

All other cards use the pcnet_cs driver. Other NE2000-compatible cards that are not on the list are also likely to work with pcnet_cs.

- 3Com 3c589, 3c589B, 3c589C, 3c589D
- Accton EN2212, EN2216 EtherCard
- Allied Telesis CentreCOM CE6001, LA-PCM
- Asante FriendlyNet
- AST 1082 Ethernet
- CeLAN EPCMCIA
- CNet CN30BC, CN40BC Ethernet
- Compex/ReadyLINK Ethernet Combo
- Compex Linkport Ethernet
- Connectware LANdingGear Adapter
- CONTEC C-NET(PC)C
- Danpex EN-6200P2 Ethernet
- Datatrek NetCard
- Dayna Communications CommuniCard E
- Digital DEPCM-AA Ethernet
- Digital EtherWORKS Turbo Ethernet
- D-Link DE-650, DE-660
- Eagle NE200 Ethernet
- Edimax Technology Ethernet Combo
- EFA InfoExpress 205, 207 Combo
- Eiger Labs EPX-ET10T2 Combo
- ELECOM Laneed LD-CDWA, LD-CDX, LD-CDNIA, LD-CDY
- EP-210 Ethernet
- Epson Ethernet

- EtherPRIME Ethernet
- Explorer NE-10000 Ethernet
- EZLink 4109 Ethernet
- Farallon Etherwave
- Fiberline FL-4680
- Fujitsu FMV-J181, FMV-J182, FMV-J182A
- Fujitsu Towa LA501
- Gateway 2000 Ethernet
- Genius ME3000II Ethernet
- Grey Cell Ethernet
- GVC NIC-2000P Ethernet Combo
- Hitachi HT-4840-11 EtherCard
- Hypertec HyperEnet
- IBM CreditCard Ethernet Adapter
- IC-Card Ethernet
- Infotel IN650ct Ethernet
- I-O Data PCLA/T
- Katron PE-520 Ethernet
- Kingston KNE-PCM/M, KNE-PC2
- LANEED Ethernet
- LanPro EP4000A
- Lantech Ethernet
- Linksys EtherCard
- Logitech LPM-LN10T, LPM-LN10BA Ethernet
- Longshine Ethernet
- Macnica ME-1 Ethernet

- Maxtech PCN2000 Ethernet
- Megahertz XJ10BT, XJ10BC, CC10BT Ethernet
- Melco LPC-TJ, LPC-TS
- Micronet Etherfast Adapter
- NDC Instant-Link
- Network General "Sniffer"
- New Media EthernetLAN
- New Media LiveWire (NOT the LiveWire+)
- New Media BASICS Ethernet
- NextCom NC5310
- Novell/National NE4100 InfoMover
- Ositech Four of Diamonds
- Panasonic CF-VEL211P-B
- Planet SmartCom 2000, 3500
- PreMax PE-200 Ethernet
- Proteon Ethernet
- Ratoc REX-9822, REX-5588A/W
- Relia RE2408T Ethernet
- RPTI EP400, EP401 Ethernet
- SCM Ethernet
- SMC 8020BT EtherEZ (not the EliteCard)
- Socket Communications Socket EA LAN Adapter
- SuperSocket RE450T
- Surecom Ethernet
- SVEC PN605C
- TDK LAC-CD02x, LAK-CD021, LAK-CD022A, LAK-CD021AX Ethernet

- Thomas-Conrad Ethernet
- Trust Ethernet Combo
- Volktek NPL-402CT Ethernet
- Xircom CreditCard CE2

26.2 Fast Ethernet (10/100baseT) Adapters

- Linksys EtherFast 10/100
- Xircom CreditCard CE3

26.3 Token Ring Adapters

You should at least have kernel 1.3.72.

- IBM Token Ring Adapter
- 3Com 3c689 TokenLink III

26.4 Wireless Network Adapters

- AT&T GIS/NCR WaveLAN version 2.0
- DEC RoamAbout/DS
- Xircom CreditCard Netwave

26.5 ISDN

- ELSA PCMCIA

26.6 Modem and Serial Cards

Virtually all modem cards, simple serial port cards, and digital cellular modems should work. Also ISDN modems that emulate a standard UART are supported.

- Advantech COMpad-32/85 dual serial
- Quatech, IOTech dual RS-232 cards

- Quatech quad RS-232 card
- Socket Communications dual RS-232 card

26.7 Memory Cards

All SRAM cards should work. Unsupported flash cards can be read but not written.

- Epson 2MB SRAM
- IBM 8MB Flash
- Intel Series 2 and Series 2+ Flash
- Maxtor MobileMax 16MB Flash
- New Media SRAM
- TDK Flash Memory SFM20W/C 20MB

26.8 SCSI Adapters

Be careful. Many vendors, particularly CD-ROM vendors, seem to switch controller chips at will. Generally they will use a different product code, but not always: older (supported) New Media Bus Toaster cards are not easily distinguishable from the current (unsupported) Bus Toaster cards.

- Adaptec APA-1460, APA-1460A, APA-1450A SlimSCSI
- Digital SCSI II adapter
- Eiger Labs SCSI (Not the Eiger SS-1000)
- Future Domain SCSI2GO
- IBM SCSI
- Iomega ZIP Card
- IO-DATA PCSC-II, PCSC-II-L
- IO-DATA CDG-PX44/PCSC CD-ROM
- Logitech LPM-SCSI2
- Logitech LCD-601 CD-ROM

- MACNICA mPS110, mPS110-LP SCSI

- Melco IFC-SC2, IFC-DC

- NEC PC-9801N-J03R

- New Media Bus Toaster SCSI (older cards only)

- New Media Toast 'n Jam (SCSI only)

- Panasonic KXL-D740, KXL-DN740A, KXL-DN740A-NB 4X CD-ROM

- Pioneer PCP-PR1W CD-ROM

- Qlogic FastSCSI

- Raven CD-Note 4X

- RATOC REX-9530 SCSI-2

- Simple Technologies SCSI

- Sony CD-ROM Discman PRD-250

- Taxan ICD-400PN

- Toshiba NWB0107ABK, SCSC200B

26.9 ATA/IDE CD-ROM Adapters

You should at least have kernel 1.3.72.

- Argosy EIDE CD-ROM

- Caravelle CD-36N

- Creative Technology CD-ROM

- Digital Mobile Media CD-ROM

- EXP CD940 CD-ROM

- IO-DATA CDP-TX4/PCIDE, CDP-TX6/PCIDE, CDP-TX10/PCIDE, CDV-HDN6/PCIDE, MOP-230/PCIDE

- H45 Technologies Quick 2x CD-ROM

26.10 Multifunction Cards

You should at least have kernel 1.3.73.

- 3Com 3c562, 3c562B/C/D, 3c563B/C/D
- ActionTec Comnet EF336 modem 28.8 + Ethernet 10MB (only modem part works)
- IBM Home and Away Card
- Linksys LANmodem 28.8, 33.6
- Megahertz/U.S. Robotics EM1144, EM3288, EM3336
- Motorola Mariner
- Motorola Marquis
- Ositech Jack of Diamonds
- Xircom CreditCard CEM28, CEM33, CEM56

26.11 ATA/IDE Card Drives

These card drives are supported starting with kernel 1.3.72. Both Flash-ATA cards and rotating-media cards are supported.

26.12 Miscellaneous Cards

- Trimble Mobile GPS (uses serial/modem driver)

26.13 Cards with Separately Distributed Drivers

- IBM Smart Capture (Koji Okamura, mailto:oka@nanotsu.kobe-u.ac.jp)

26.14 Working on ...

People are working on the following cards:

- Nat'l Inst DAQCard (Eric Gonzalez, mailto:root@colomsat.net.co)

- Roland SCP-55 MIDI (Toshiaki Nakatsu, `mailto:ir9k-nkt@asahi.net.or.jp`)

- CyberRom CD-ROM (David Rowntree, `mailto:rowntree@dircon.co.uk`)

- IO DATA PCSC-II (Katayama Nobuhiro, `mailto:kata-n@po.iijnet.or.jp`)

- Macnica mPS-1x0 (Katayama Nobuhiro, `mailto:kata-n@po.iijnet.or.jp`)

- FORTEZZA encryption (Rex Riggins, `mailto:rriggins@radium.ncsc.mil`)

- Harris PRISM/AM79C930 (Mark Mathews, `mailto:mark@mail.absoval.com`)

- IBM Etherjet (Danilo Beuche, `mailto:danili@cs.tu-berlin.de`). The driver can be found at `http://www.first.gmd.de/~danilo/pc-driver`

- Teles

- Hayes ESP
  contact Dennis Boylan <`mailto:dennis@lan.com`>

- Hayes ESP
  contact Dennis Boylan <`mailto:dennis@lan.com`> PCMCIA

- Xircom CE3 (Werner Koch, `mailto:werner.koch@guug.de`)

26.15 Unsupported

- ActionTec Comnet EF336 modem 28.8 + Ethernet 10MB (Ethernet part not supported)

- Adaptec/Trantor APA-460 SlimSCSI

- CanonCompaq PCMCIA floppy drive

- New Media .WAVjammer and all other sound cards

- All 100baseT Ethernet adapters

- Panasonic KXL-D720, KXL-D745

- SMC 8016 EliteCard

- Telxon/Aironet wireless adapter

- Xircom CE II Ethernet/Modem

- Xircom CE-10BT Ethernet

27. Plug-and-Play Devices (Appendix C.)

For people having trouble getting Plug-and-Play devices to work, the ISA PnP utilities written by Peter Fox are available. Quote from the README:

> These programs allow ISA Plug-And-Play devices to be configured on a Linux machine.
>
> This program is suitable for all systems, whether or not they include a PnP BIOS.

Commands have been taken from the Plug and Play ISA specification Version 1.0a. (`ftp://ftp.redhat.com/pub/pnp/docs/`)

More information on ISA PnP utilities can be found on the Web site of Peter Fox: `http://www.roestock.demon.co.uk/isapnptools/`

Please let me know about hardware (not normally supported under Linux) which can be put to work with the aid of these utilities. A list of this hardware will be put in this appendix.

28. Linux-Incompatible Hardware (Appendix D.)

Some hardware manufacturers have created devices which are compatible with MS-DOS and Windows 95 only. They seem to emulate part of the normally available hardware in the devices by software packages sold together with the device. Specifications for these devices are not presented to the world so it is almost impossible to write drivers for these devices. A list of devices reported as being Linux-incompatible will be given.

Simply put, it is best to avoid hardware which states things like "Needs Windows" or "Windows only."

- Canon LBP-465 printer
- Hewlett Packard HP DeskJet 820xx printers
- Hewlett Packard HP DeskJet 720C, 722C printers

- Lexmark 1000 inkjet printer

- Sharp JX-9210 printer

- Boca Research 28.8 internal modem (model MV34AI)

- DSVD modem

- Multiwave Innovation CommWave V.34 modem (`http://www.multiwave.com/`)

- US Robotics WinModem series

- Zoltrix 33.6 Win HSP Voice/Speaker Phone modem

- Compaq 192 PCMCIA modem/serial card

- New Media Winsurfer PCMCIA modem/serial card

29. Glossary

AGP: Accelerated Graphics Port. A bus interconnect mechanism designed to improve performance of 3D graphics applications. AGP is a dedicated bus from the graphics subsystem to the core-logic chipset.
`http://www.euro.dell.com/intl/euro/r+d/r+dnews/vectors/vect_2-1/v2-1_agp.htm`

ATAPI: AT Attachment Packet Interface. A new protocol for controlling mass storage devices, similar to SCSI protocols. It builds on the ATA (AT Attachment) interface, the official ANSI Standard name for the IDE interface developed for hard disk drives. ATAPI is commonly used for hard disks, CD-ROM drives, tape drives, and other devices.

ATM: Asynchronous Transfer Mode

CDDA: Compact Disk Digital Audio. Capability of CD-ROM/Writer to read out audio tracks.

DMA: Direct Memory Access

EGA: Enhanced Graphics Adapter

EIDE: Enhanced IDE

EISA: Extended Industry System Architecture

FDDI: Fiber Distributed Data Interface. High-speed ring local area network.

IDE: Integrated Drive Electronics. Each drive has a built-in controller.

ISA: Industry System Architecture

ISDN: Integrated Services Digital Network

MCA: MicroChannel Architecture

MFM: Modified Frequency Modulation

MMX: Multimedia Extensions. Added to the newest generation of Intel Pentium processors. It offers better audio and video quality

PCI: Peripheral Component Interconnect. 32-bit bus designed by Intel.

RAID: Redundant Arrays of Inexpensive Disks. The basic idea of RAID is to combine multiple small, inexpensive disk drives into an array of disk drives which yields performance exceeding that of a single large expensive drive. There are five type of redundant array Architectures: RAID-1 through RAID-5. A non-redundant array of disk drives is referred to as RAID-0.
http://www.uni-mainz.de/~neuffer/scsi/what_is_raid.html

RLL: Run Length Limited

SCSI: Small Computer Systems Interface. A standard interface defined for all devices in a computer. It makes it possible to use a single adapter for all devices.
http://www.uni-mainz.de/~neuffer/scsi/what_is_scsi.html

SVGA: Super Video Graphics Adapter

UART: Universal Asynchronous Receiver Transmitter

VGA: Video Graphics Adapter

VLB: VESA Local Bus

WORM: Write Once Read Many

APPENDIX

G

Linux Command Reference

This reference provides a guide to using the common Linux commands and utilities found in the following directories in most Red Hat Linux installations:

/bin

/sbin

/usr/bin

/usr/sbin

The approach taken here is to provide a quick reference to the syntax and common options for many major Linux commands. More details about these commands and about commands not listed here are generally found in the man pages for the commands (accessed by typing **man <*command*>**).

In this reference, we present the overall syntax of commands using the style found in standard Linux man pages, and then provide a description of the command followed by a description of major flags and arguments.

In order to keep the reference to a reasonable size, most interactive programs, daemons, and Red Hat–specific commands have been excluded. Even so, there are almost 200 commands covered in this Appendix.

Commands appear in alphabetical order.

Commands Covered in This Reference

The following commands are covered in this reference:

arch	chgrp	depmod	fdisk
at	chkconfig	df	fgrep
atd	chmod	dir	file
atq	chown	dmesg	find
atrm	clear	dnsdomainname	finger
badblocks	compress	dnsquery	free
batch	cp	domainname	gpasswd
bc	crontab	du	grep
biff	cryptdir	e2fsck	groupadd
cal	date	echo	groupdel
cat	dc	egrep	groupmod
checkalias	decryptdir	false	groups

grpck	mail	pathchk	sync
gunzip	mailq	pidof	tail
gzexe	mailto	ping	tar
gzip	man	pppstats	timeconfig
halt	mattrib	ps	timed
head	mbadblocks	pwck	timedc
hostname	mcd	pwconv	top
id	mcopy	pwd	touch
ifconfig	mdel	pwunconv	traceroute
ifdown	mdeltree	quota	true
ifport	mdir	quotacheck	umount
ifup	messages	quotaoff	uname
insmod	mformat	quotaon	uncompress
kbd_mode	mkdir	rcp	unzip
kbdrate	mkdosfs	rdate	uptime
kill	mke2fs	rdist	useradd
killall	mkfs	repquota	userdel
ksyms	mkpasswd	rlogin	usermod
last	mkswap	rm	users
ldd	mlabel	rmdir	uudecode
less	mmd	rmmod	uuencode
lilo	mmove	route	vipw
listalias	modprobe	rsh	vmstat
ln	more	runlevel	w
loadkeys	mount	rup	wc
logger	mrd	rusers	whereis
login	mren	rwho	which
logname	mtype	rwhod	whoami
logrotate	mv	setclock	ypdomainname
lpd	netstat	setkeycodes	zcat
lpq	newgrp	showkey	zgrep
lpr	newusers	showmount	zip
lprm	nisdomainname	shutdown	zipgrep
ls	nslookup	sort	zipinfo
lsdev	passwd	statserial	zmore
lsmod	paste	su	znew

arch

Description	Displays the architecture of the machine on which Linux is running. For instance, `i586` represents a Pentium-based system, `i486` represents an 80486-based computer, and `axp` represents Linux running on an Alpha-based computer.
Syntax	`arch`
Important Flags and Options	None

at

Description	Schedules commands to be executed at a specific time. User is prompted for the commands, or the commands can be provided from a file. Each job is added to a schedule queue and is provided a job number.
Syntax	`at [-f filename] [-l] [-m] [-d job [job ...]] TIME`
Important Flags and Options	• `-d job`: Deletes a job specified by job number.
	• `-f filename`: Reads commands to be scheduled from the specified file rather than prompting for the commands.
	• `-l`: Displays commands in the schedule queue (the `TIME` argument is ignored).
	• `-m`: E-mails the user who scheduled the job once the job is finished, and includes any generated output in the body of the message.
Notes	Specifying times: Several options exist for specifying time, including these:
	• `HH:MM` specifies the hour and minutes, such as `11:15` or `22:30`. AM and PM suffixes are allowed, as in `11:15AM` or `11:30PM`.
	• `midnight` (`24:00` or `12:00PM`), `noon` (`12:00`), and `teatime` (`16:00`) are reserved words specifying the times indicated.
	• `MMDDYY`, `MM/DD/YY`, or `DD.MM.YY` can be used to indicate specific dates, as in `022598` or `25.02.98`.
	• `now` specifies the current time.
	• `tomorrow` specifies the next day.
	• Using a `+` can specify offsets in `minutes`, `hours`, `days`, or `weeks` from a specified time. For instance, to schedule a command for noon two days from the current day, you could use `noon + 2 days`.

atd

Description	Daemon that runs jobs scheduled for later execution by programs such as `at` and `batch`.
Syntax	`atd [-l load] [-b interval]`
Important Flags and Options	• `-b interval`: Indicates the minimum interval in seconds between the start of two batch jobs. By default, this is 60 seconds.
	• `-l load`: Specifies a load limit over which scheduled batch jobs will not be run. By default, this load is 0.8.

atq

Description	Displays jobs scheduled by **at** that are in the schedule queue. This is the same as **at -1**.
Syntax	**atq**
Important Flags and Options	None

atrm

Description	Removes specified jobs from the **at** schedule queue. This is the same as **at -d**.
Syntax	**atrm job [job ...]**
Important Flags and Options	None

badblocks

Description	Checks a device (usually a hard disk) for bad blocks.
Syntax	**badblocks [-o filename] [-w] device blocks-count**
Important Flags and Options	• **-o filename**: Specifies a file where results should be written instead of displaying them on the standard output.
	• **-w**: Uses a write test, instead of a read-only test, in which data is written to each block of the device and then reread from the block.
Notes	You should specify the device using the full Linux device path, such as **/dev/hda2** or **/dev/sdb3**. The number of blocks on the device is essential (this information can be determined using **fdisk**).
Warnings	Do not use the **-w** flag on devices that contain important data. Data stored on devices that are checked with the **-w** flag will get erased during the checking process.

batch

Description	Schedules commands to be executed at a specified time as long as system load levels permit. User is prompted for the commands, or the commands can be provided from a file. Each job is added to a schedule queue and is provided a job number.
Syntax	**batch [-f filename] [-m] TIME**
Important Flags and Options	• **-f filename**: Reads commands to be scheduled from the specified file rather than prompting for the commands.
	• **-m**: E-mails the user who scheduled the job once the job is finished and includes any generated output in the body of the message.
Notes	Specifying times: Several options exist for specifying time, including these:
	• **HH:MM** specifies the hour and minutes, such as **11:15** or **22:30**. **AM** and **PM** suffixes are allowed, as in **11:15AM** or **11:30PM**.
	• **midnight** (**24:00** or **12:00PM**), **noon** (**12:00**), and **teatime** (**16:00**) are reserved words specifying the times indicated.

- MMDDYY, MM/DD/YY, or DD.MM.YY can be used to indicate specific dates, as in 022598 or 25.02.98.
- now specifies the current time.
- tomorrow specifies the next day.
- Using a + can specify offsets in minutes, hours, days, or weeks from a specified time. For instance, to schedule a command for noon two days from the current day, you could use noon + 2 days.

bc

Description	An interactive, arbitrary-precision calculator. Processes all expressions in specified files as well as prompting user to provide expressions for evaluation.
Syntax	bc [file ...]
Important Flags and Options	None
Notes	The syntax of expressions used by bc is largely based on the C programming language. Refer to the bc man page for details.
	Expressions in files provided as arguments are processed before presenting a prompt to the user for entering additional expressions to be processed.

biff

Description	Notifies users when new mail arrives and indicates who sent the message.
Syntax	biff [ny]
Important Flags and Options	• n: Disables mail arrival notification when it is enabled.
	• y: Enables mail arrival notification when it is disabled.

cal

Description	Displays a calendar for a month or an entire year. If no month or year is specified, the current month's calendar is displayed.
Syntax	cal [-j] [-y] [month [year]]
Important Flags and Options	• -j: Specifies that Julian dates instead of Gregorian dates should be used.
	• -y: Displays a yearly calendar instead of a monthly calendar.
Notes	A single numeric argument specifies a year between the year 1 and the year 9999 (years must be complete—e.g., 1998, not 98). With two arguments, the first specifies the month numerically from 1 to 12 and the second the year from 1 to 9999.

cat

Description   Combines one or more files and displays them on the standard output. If no files are given, then the standard input is written to the standard output.

Syntax   `cat [-benstvAET] [–number] [–number-nonblank] [–squeeze-blank]`
➡ `[–show-nonprinting] [–show-ends] [–show-tabs] [–show-all]`
➡ `[file ...]`

Important Flags and Options
- `-A/–show-all`: Displays a $ at the end of each line, tab characters as ^I, and control characters preceded by a ^. This is the same as the combination of -v, -T, and -E.

- `-b/–number-nonblank`: Causes all non-blank lines to appear numbered. Numbering starts at 1.

- `-e`: Displays a $ at the end of each line and control characters preceded by a ^. This is the same as the combination of -v and -E.

- `-E/–show-ends`: Displays a $ at the end of each line.

- `-n/–number`: Causes all lines to appear numbered. Numbering starts at 1.

- `-s/–squeeze-blank`: Replaces sequences of multiple blank lines with single blank lines when displayed.

- `-t`: Displays tab characters as ^I and control characters preceded by a ^. This is the same as the combination of -v and -T.

- `-T/–show-tabs`: Displays tab characters as ^I.

- `-v/–show-nonprinting`: Displays control characters preceded by a ^.

checkalias

Description   Checks the user's file and then the system alias file in order to see if a specified alias is defined.

Syntax   `checkalias alias[, alias,...]`

Important Flags and Options   None

chgrp

Description   Changes the group ownership of one or more files or directories.

Syntax   `chgrp [-Rcfv] [–recursive] [–changes] [–silent] [–quiet] [–verbose]`
➡ `group file ...`

Important Flags and Options
- `-c/–changes`: Displays the names of only those files whose ownership is being changed.

- `-f/–silent/–quiet`: Suppresses display of error messages when a file's ownership cannot be changed.

- `-R/–recursive`: Recursively changes the ownership of all files in all subdirectories of any directory that has its ownership changed.

- `-v/–verbose`: Displays the results of all ownership changes.

Notes   The group can be specified either by name or by group ID.

chkconfig

Description	Manipulates or displays settings for system run levels.
Syntax	`chkconfig –list [name]`
	`chkconfig –add name`
	`chkconfig –del name`
	`chkconfig [–level levels] name <on|off|reset>`
	`chkconfig [–level levels] name`
Important Flags and Options	• `–add name`: Adds a new service for management by `chkconfig` and checks that the necessary start and kill entries exist. If entries are missing, they are created.
	• `–del name`: Deletes the named service from management; any links to it are also deleted.
	• `–level[levels`: Specifies numerically which run level a named service should belong to.
	• `–list name`: Lists all services that `chkconfig` knows about and any relevant information about them. If a named service is specified, only information about that service is displayed.
	• `off`: When specified after the service name, the service's status for the specified run level is changed to a stopped state. If no run level is specified, then this option affects run levels 3, 4, and 5.
	• `on`: When specified after the service name, the service's status for the specified run level is changed to a started state. If no run level is specified, then this option affects run levels 3, 4, and 5.
	• `reset`: When specified after the service name, the service's status for the specified run level is set to the default status indicated by the `init` script. If no run level is specified, then this option affects all run levels.

chmod

Description	Changes the access permissions of one or more files or directories.
Syntax	`chmod [-Rcfv] [–recursive] [–changes] [–silent] [–quiet] [–verbose]` ➥ `mode file ...`
Important Flags and Options	• `-c/–changes`: Displays the names of only those files whose permissions are being changed.
	• `-f/–silent/–quiet`: Suppresses display of error messages when a file's permissions cannot be changed.
	• `-R/–recursive`: Recursively changes the permissions of all files in all subdirectories of any directory that has its permissions changed.
	• `-v/–verbose`: Displays the results of all permission changes.
Notes	Modes can be specified in two ways: symbolically and numerically. When done symbolically, modes take the form `[ugoa][[+-=][rwxXstugo ...]`. The first element (`[ugoa]`) represents the users whose permissions are being affected (u=user who owns

the file or directory, **g**=all members of the group that owns the file or directory, **o**=any-one who is not the owner or in the owner group, **a**=all users). The + symbol means that the specified modes should be added to already specified permissions, the – symbol means the specified modes should be removed from existing permissions, and the = means that the specified modes should replace existing permissions. There are many different permissions that can be specified in the third element of the mode, including **r** for read permissions, **w** for write permissions, and **x** for execute permissions.

Full details of symbolic and numeric modes appear in the **chmod** man page.

chown

Description	Changes the user and/or group ownership of one or more files or directories.
Syntax	chown [-Rcfv] [–recursive] [–changes] [–silent] [–quiet] [–verbose] ➥ [user][:.][group] file ...
Important Flags and Options	• -c/–changes: Displays the names of only those files whose ownership is being changed.
	• -f/–silent/–quiet: Suppresses display of error messages when a file's ownership cannot be changed.
	• -R/–recursive: Recursively changes the ownership of all files in all subdirectories of any directory that has its ownership changed.
	• -v/–verbose: Displays the results of all ownership changes.
Notes	The user and group can be specified either by name or by IDs. User and group can be combined in several ways:
	• The user followed by a dot or colon followed by a group changes both the user and group ownerships to those specified.
	• The user followed by a dot or colon and no group changes the user ownership as specified and changes the group ownership to the specified user's login group.
	• If the colon or dot and group are specified without a user, then only group ownership is changed. This is the same as **chgrp**.
	• If the user is not followed by a dot or colon, then only the user ownership is changed.

clear

Description	Clears the terminal screen and resets the prompt and cursor location to the first line of the screen.·
Syntax	clear
Important Flags and Options	None

compress

Description	Compresses files or the standard input using Lempel-Ziv compression.

Syntax	`compress [-f] [-v] [-c] [-r] [file ...]`
Important Flags and Options	• `-c`: Returns compressed data on standard output rather than to a file as is the default when compressing a file.
	• `-f`: Forces compression of hard-linked files, which are ignored by default.
	• `-r`: Operates recursively. If a directory is specified as an argument, then compresses all files within that directory and in its subdirectories.
	• `-v`: Displays the percentage reduction in size for each file compressed.
Notes	When compressing files, **compress** replaces the original file with a file whose name has a **.Z** prefix but otherwise remains unchanged. This behavior is overridden by the `-c` flag. If no files are specified, the standard input is compressed and the results are returned through standard output.

cp

Description	Copies files and directories.

Syntax	`cp [-a] [-archive] [-b] [-backup] [-d] [-no-dereference] [-f]`
	➡ `[-force] [-i] [-interactive] [1] [-link] [-p] [-preserve] [-R]`
	➡ `[-recursive] [-s] [-symbolic-link] [-u] [-update] source`
	➡ `destination`
	
	`cp [options] source ... directory`

Important Flags and Options	• `-a/-archive`: Copies files and directories recursively, maintaining symbolic links as links and preserving ownership and permissions of the original files. This is the same as `-dpR`.
	• `-b/-backup`: Makes backup copies of files before the original files are overwritten.
	• `-d/-no-dereference`: Copies links as links rather than copying the files to which the links point.
	• `-f/-force`: Forces removal of existing destination files that need to be overwritten.
	• `-i/-interactive`: Prompts before overwriting existing destination files.
	• `-1/-link`: Makes hard links instead of copying files. This applies only to files, not to directories.
	• `-p/-preserve`: Preserves the ownership and permissions of the original files.
	• `-R/-recursive`: Recursively copies directories. That is, for every source directory specified, every file in the directory and all its subdirectories are copied while retaining the matching directory structure.
	• `-s/-symbolic-link`: Makes symbolic links instead of copying files. Source files must be specified with full paths.
	• `-u/-update`: Replaces only those destination files that have older modification times than the corresponding source files.
Warnings	Care needs to be taken with the `-f` flag when working as the root user. Making a mistake can cause important system files to be overwritten because the root user generally has write permission for all files and directories.

crontab

Description	Displays or alters a user's Cron table (`crontab`). The Cron table specifies scheduled actions that are executed by the Cron daemon.
Syntax	`crontab [-u user] file`
	`crontab [-u user] { -l|-r| -e }`
Important Flags and Options	• **-e**: Edits the `crontab` file of the user executing the command or the user specified by the **-u** flag. The editor invoked is specified by the **EDITOR** environment variable.
	• **-l**: Displays the contents of the `crontab` file of the user executing the command or the user specified by the **-u** flag.
	• **-r**: Deletes the `crontab` file of the user executing the command or the user specified by the **-u** flag.
	• **-u**: Specifies which user's `crontab` file to work with if it is not the same user as the one executing the command. This flag can only be used by the root user.
Notes	The format of entries in `crontab` files is discussed in Chapter 14, "General System Administration."

cryptdir

Description	Encrypts all files in a specified directory. If no directory is specified, then all files in the current directory are encrypted.
Syntax	`cryptdir [dir]`
Important Flags and Options	None
Notes	When encrypting files, you will be prompted twice for a password. This password is needed to unencrypt files. Encrypted files will have the `.crypt` extensions added to their names. Use `decryptdir` to decrypt the files.

date

Description	Displays or sets the current system date and time.
Syntax	`date [-u] [-universal] [MMDDhhmm[[CC]YY][.ss]]`
Important Flags and Options	• **-u/-universal**: Displays the time in Greenwich Mean Time (also known as Coordinated Universal Time).
Notes	If a date and time are provided as an argument, this is done entirely with numbers where the two-digit elements shown above represent the following values:

- **MM**: month
- **DD**: day of the month
- **hh**: hour
- **mm**: minute
- **CC**: century (first two digits of the year)
- **YY**: last two digits of the year
- **ss**: seconds

Keep in mind that only the root user can set the system clock.

dc

Description	An interactive, arbitrary-precision, reverse-polish notation calculator. Processes all expressions in specified files as well as prompting user to provide expressions for evaluation.
Syntax	`dc [file ...]`
Important Flags and Options	None
Notes	Detailed syntax of expressions used by **dc** is documented in the **dc** man page. Expressions in files provided as arguments are processed before presenting a prompt to the user for entering additional expressions to be processed.

decryptdir

Description	Decrypts all files in a specified directory. If no directory is specified, then all files in the current directory are encrypted. Files must have been encrypted with the **encryptdir** command.
Syntax	`cryptdir [dir]`
Important Flags and Options	None
Notes	You will be prompted for a password when decrypting files. You need to provide the same password used when encrypting the files, or the process will fail.

depmod

Description	Returns module dependencies on the standard output. These can be stored in a file and then used by **modprobe** for installing loadable modules.
Syntax	`depmod module1.o module2.o ...`
Important Flags and Options	None

df

Description	Displays free space on one or more mounted disks or partitions. If no files (or directories) are specified, then the free space on all mounted file systems is displayed. If filenames are specified, then the free space for the file system containing each file is displayed.
Syntax	`df [-T] [-t fstype] [-x fstype] [-all] [-inodes] [-type=fstype]` ➥`[-exclude-type=fstype] [-print-type] [filename ...]`
Important Flags and Options	• `-t/-type=fstype`: Displays information only for file systems of the specified type.
	• `-T/-print-type`: Displays the file system type for each file system reported.
	• `-x/-exclude-type=fstype`: Does not report information for file systems of the specified type.

dir

Description	Displays a listing of the files in a specified directory, in alphabetical order unless otherwise specified. By default, displays the contents of the current directory unless another directory is specified.
Syntax	`dir [-acCGlnrRStuU] [–all] [–no-group] [–numeric-uid-gid] [–reverse]` ➥ `[–recursive] [file ...]`
Important Flags and Options	• `-a/–all`: Shows all entries, including those whose names start with ".".

- `-c`: Sorts by the creation time of the file and, when displaying complete file information (with the -1 flag), displays the creation time.

- `-C`: Displays entries in columns.

- `-G/–no-group`: Prevents display of group information.

- `-l`: Displays files with long listing format.

- `-n/–numeric-uid-gid`: Lists user IDs and group IDs (UIDs and GIDs)– instead of names.

- `-r/–reverse`: Reverses order of entries when sorting.

- `-R/–recursive`: Recursively lists contents of subdirectories.

- `-S`: Sorts files by size.

- `-t`: Sorts by the modification time of the file and, when displaying complete file information (with the -1 flag), displays the modification time.

- `-u`: Sorts by the last access time of the file and, when displaying complete file information (with the -1 flag), displays the last access time.

- `-U`: Displays entries in their directory order rather than sorted.

dmesg

Description	Displays or manipulates the kernel ring buffer. This is where many bootup messages are kept.
Syntax	`dmesg [-c]`
Important Flags and Options	`-c`: Clears the ring buffer after displaying the contents.

dnsdomainname

Description	Displays the system's DNS domain name based on its fully qualified domain name.
Syntax	`domainname`
Important Flags and Options	None

dnsquery

Description	Queries DNS servers to look up information about a specified host.
Syntax	dnsquery [-n nameserver] [-t type] [-c class] [-r retry] [-p retry ➥ period] host
Important Flags and Options	• -c class: Specifies the class of records being searched for.
	• -n nameserver: Specifies the nameserver to use for the query. If not specified, then uses the default nameserver.
	• -p retryperiod: Specifies how long to wait before assuming the server is not responding.
	• -r retry: Specifies the number of times to retry the query if the server is not responding.
	• -t type: Specifies the type of query to make.
Notes	When specifying the type of query, possible types include:
	• A: Looks up the address only.
	• NS: Finds the nameserver for the host.
	• CNAME: Finds the canonical name for the host.
	• PTR: Finds the domain name pointer.
	• SOA: Finds the start of the authority record for the host.
	• MX: Finds the mail exchanges for the domain.
	• ANY: Finds anything and everything that can be found (this is the default behavior).
	When specifying classes of information, possible classes include:
	• IN: Internet (this is the default and you probably won't want to change it)
	• HS: Hesiod
	• CHAOS: Chaos
	• ANY: Any

domainname

Description	Displays or sets the system's NIS domain name. Without arguments or flags, the default behavior is to display the current NIS domain name.
Syntax	domainname [-F file] [–file file] [name]
Important Flags and Options	• -F/–file file: Indicates that the domain name should be set based on the contents of the specified file instead of expecting it as an argument on the command line.

du

Description	Displays a report of disk space usage for each specified file or directory as well as all subdirectories of specified directories. By default, displays information for all files and directories in the current directory.

Syntax	du [-abcksx] [-all] [-bytes] [-total] [-kilobytes] [-summarize] ➥ [-one-file-system] [file ...]
Important Flags and Options	• -a/-all: Displays usage information for files and directories.
	• -b/-bytes: Displays usage information in bytes.
	• -c/-total: Displays a total usage figure for all.
	• -k/-kilobytes: Displays usage information in kilobytes.
	• -s/-summarize: Displays a total for each argument and does not display individual information for each file or subdirectory inside a directory.
	• -x/-one-file-system: Skips directories that are not part of the current file system.

e2fsck

Description	Checks the state of a Linux second extended file system. This is the default file system used for Linux partitions.
Syntax	e2fsck [-cfnpy] [-B blocksize] device
Important Flags and Options	• -B blocksize: Specifies a specific block size to use in searching for the superblock. By default, the program will search at various different block sizes until it finds the superblock.
	• -c: Causes the **badblocks** program to be run and marks any bad blocks accordingly.
	• -f: Forces checking of file systems that outwardly seem clean.
	• -n: Opens the file system in a read-only state and answers "no" to all prompts to take action.
	• -p: Forces automatic repairing without prompts.
	• -y: Assumes an answer of "yes" to all questions.
Notes	The device to be checked should be specified using the complete Linux device path, such as **/dev/hda1** or **/dev/sdb3**. It is advisable that the file system not be mounted or, if you need to check the root file system or a file system that must be mounted, that this be done in single-user mode.

echo

Description	Displays a line of text, optionally without a trailing new line (a new line is included by default).
Syntax	echo [-ne] [string ...]
Important Flags and Options	• -e: Enables interpretation of backslashed special characters in the string.
	• -n: Disables output of a trailing new line.
Notes	Backslashed special characters include:
	• \b: backspace
	• \f: form feed

- \n: new line
- \r: carriage return
- \t: horizontal tab
- \\: backslash

egrep

Description
Searches files for lines matching a specified pattern and displays the lines. The pattern is interpreted as an extended regular expression.

Syntax
```
egrep [-bCciLlnvwx] [-number] [-e pattern] [-f file] [-byte-offset]
➥ [-context] [-count] [-regexp=pattern] [-file=file] [-ignore=case]
➥ [-files-without-match] [-files-with-match] [-line-number]
➥ [-revert-match] [-word-regexp] [-line-regexp] [pattern] file
➥ [file ...]
```

Important Flags and Options

- **-number**: Displays matching lines with the specified number of lines of leading and trailing context.

- **-b/-byte**-offset: Prints the byte offset of the match before each line.

- **-c/-count**: Instead of displaying matching lines, simply outputs a count of the total number of lines matching the expressions (when combined with -v, displays the total count of non-matching lines).

- **-C/-context**: Displays matching lines with two lines of leading and trailing context (this is the same as -2).

- **-e pattern/-regexp=pattern**: Uses the specified regular expression rather than one provided as an argument.

- **-f file/-file=file**: Uses the regular expression found in the specified file rather than one supplied as an argument.

- **-i/-ignore-case**: Ignores case in both the pattern and the files being searched.

- **-l/-files-with-matches**: Instead of displaying each matched line, simply displays the name of each file that contains at least one match for the regular expression.

- **-L/-files-without-match**: Instead of displaying each matched line, simply displays the name of each file that contains no matches for the regular expressions.

- **-n/-line-number**: Prefixes each output line with its line number in the file.

- **-v/-revert-match**: Displays non-matching lines instead of matching lines.

- **-w/-word-regexp**: Displays only those lines with matches for the regular expression that are complete words.

- **-x/-line-regexp**: Displays only those lines with matches for the regular expression that are complete lines.

Notes
The syntax of regular expressions used by **egrep** can be found in the **egrep** man page.

false

Description	Does nothing and returns a failure exit status.
Syntax	`false`
Important Flags and Options	None

fdisk

Description	Provides tools for manipulating partition tables. By default, `fdisk` starts ready to work with the current device unless a different device is specified as an argument.
Syntax	`fdisk [-l] [-s partition] [device]`
Important Flags and Options	• `-l`: Lists the partition tables for **/dev/hda**, **/dev/hdb**, and **/dev/sda** through **/dev/sdh** and then exits.
	• `-s partition`: Returns the size of the specified partition on the standard output and exits.

fgrep

Description	Searches files for lines matching a specified pattern and displays the lines. The pattern is interpreted as a list of fixed strings as opposed to regular expressions. Strings are separated by new lines and any of the strings can be matched.
Syntax	`fgrep [-bCciLlnvwx] [-number] [-e pattern] [-f file] [–byte-offset]` ➥ `[–context] [–count] [–regexp=pattern] [–file=file] [–ignore=case]` ➥ `[–files-without-match] [–files-with-match] [–line-number]` ➥ `[–revert-match] [–word-regexp] [–line-regexp] [pattern] file` ➥ `[file ...]`
Important Flags and Options	• `-number`: Displays matching lines with the specified number of lines of leading and trailing context.
	• `-b/–byte-offset`: Prints the byte offset of the match before each line.
	• `-c/–count`: Instead of displaying matching lines, simply outputs a count of the total number of lines matching the expressions (when combined with `-v`, displays the total count of non-matching lines).
	• `-C/–context`: Displays matching lines with two lines of leading and trailing context (this is the same as `-2`).
	• `-e pattern/–regexp=pattern`: Uses the specified pattern rather than one provided as an argument.
	• `-f file/–file=file`: Uses the pattern found in the specified file rather than one supplied as an argument.
	• `-i/–ignore-case`: Ignores case in both the pattern and the files being searched.
	• `-l/–files-with-matches`: Instead of displaying each matched line, simply displays the name of each file that contains at least one match for the pattern.

- `-L/-files-without-match`: Instead of displaying each matched line, simply displays the name of each file that contains no matches for the pattern.
- `-n/-line-number`: Prefixes each output line with its line number in the file.
- `-v/-revert-match`: Displays non-matching lines instead of matching lines.
- `-w/-word-regexp`: Displays only those lines with matches for the pattern that are complete words.
- `-x/-line-regexp`: Displays only those lines with matches for the pattern that are complete lines.

file

Description	Determines and displays the type of files.
Syntax	`file [-zL] [-f file] file ...`
Important Flags and Options	

- `-f file`: Reads the list of files to be checked from the specified file. These will be checked before checking files provided as arguments.
- `-L`: Causes symbolic links to be followed.
- `-z`: Attempts to look at the type of files inside compressed files.

find

Description	Looks for files below the specified paths that match all the criteria indicated by the options and takes any action indicated by the options. If no paths are specified, the search takes place below the current directory.
Syntax	`find [path ...] [options]`
Important Flags and Options	

- `-amin minutes`: Looks for files last accessed the specified number of minutes ago.
- `-anewer file`: Looks for files that were accessed more recently than the specified file was modified.
- `-atime days`: Looks for files last accessed the specified number of 24-hour periods ago.
- `-cmin minutes`: Looks for files whose status was last changed the specified number of minutes ago.
- `-cnewer file`: Looks for files whose status was last changed more recently than the specified file was modified.
- `-ctime days`: Looks for files whose status was changed the specified number of 24-hour periods ago.
- `-empty`: Looks for empty files or directories.
- `-exec command \;`: Executes the specified command. The string { } is replaced by the currently found file name and the command is repeated for each found filename.
- `-gid gid`: Looks for files with the specified numeric GID.
- `-group group`: Looks for files belonging to the named group.

- **-ilname pattern**: Looks for symbolic links whose names match the specified pattern in a case-insensitive manner.

- **-iname pattern**: Looks for files whose names match the specified pattern in a case-insensitive manner.

- **-ipath pattern**: Looks for files whose path matches the specified pattern in a case-insensitive manner.

- **-lname pattern**: Looks for symbolic links whose names match the specified pattern in a case-sensitive manner.

- **-maxdepth levels**: Descends at most the specified numbers of levels below the specified paths.

- **-mindepth levels**: Descends at least the specified number of levels below the specified paths before starting testing.

- **-mmin minutes**: Looks for files that were last modified the specified number of minutes ago.

- **-mount**: Does not descend any directories that are on other file systems than the current one.

- **-mtime days**: Looks for files that were last modified the specified number of 24-hour periods previously.

- **-name pattern**: Looks for files whose names match the specified pattern in a case-sensitive manner.

- **-newer file**: Looks for files modified more recently than the specified file.

- **-nogroup**: Looks for files whose numeric GID does not correspond to any existing group.

- **-nouser**: Looks for files whose numeric UID does not correspond to any existing user.

- **-ok command \;**: Executes the specified command for each file found after prompting the user. The string { } is replaced by the currently replaced filename.

- **-path**: Looks for files whose path matches the specified pattern in a case-sensitive manner.

- **-perm mode**: Looks for files whose permissions exactly match the specified mode. If **+mode** is used, then matches any of the specified permission bits; if **-mode** is used, then matches all of the specified permission bits.

- **-print**: Prints the full filename of all found files.

- **-regex pattern**: Looks for files whose names match the specified regular expression.

- **-size size[bckw]**: Looks for files of the specified size in the specified units. Units include **b** (512-byte blocks), **c** (bytes), **k** (kilobytes), and **w** (2-byte words).

- **-type type**: Looks for files that match the specified type. Types include **d** (directories), **f** (regular files), and **l** (symbolic links).

- **-uid uid**: Looks for files with the specified UID.

- **-user username**: Looks for files owned by the specified username or UID.

Notes

When providing numeric time information such as minutes and days, normally the match must be exact. Preceding the number with a + matches any value greater than the specified number and preceding a value with a – matches any value less than the number.

finger

Description	Looks up specified information about a user on the local system or remote systems. Users are specified on local systems by their username or their first or last name and on remote systems as **username@host**. With no users specified for the local system, all users logged in to the current system are listed. If a host with no username is provided in the form **@host**, then a list of all users logged into the remote system is displayed.
Syntax	`finger [user ...]`
Important Flags and Options	None

free

Description	Displays a report of free and used memory.
Syntax	`free [-b|-k|-m] [-s delay] [-t]`
Important Flags and Options	• `-b`: Displays the amount of memory in bytes.
	• `-k`: Displays the amount of memory in kilobytes (this is the default).
	• `-m`: Displays the amount of memory in megabytes.
	• `-s delay`: Displays continued reports separated by the specified delay in seconds.
	• `-t`: Displays an extra line containing totals.

gpasswd

Description	Administers the `/etc/group` file. Without flags, **gpasswd** allows changing of the specified group's password.
Syntax	`gpasswd group`
	`gpasswd -a user group`
	`gpasswd -d user group`
	`gpasswd -R group`
	`gpasswd -r group`
	`gpasswd [-M user,...] group`
Important Flags and Options	• `-a user`: Adds a user to the group.
	• `-d user`: Removes a user from the group.
	• `-M user,...`: Specifies one or more users who are members of the group.
	• `-r`: Removes the group password.
	• `-R`: Disables access to the group through the **newgrp** command.

grep

Description	Searches files for lines matching a specified pattern and displays the lines.
Syntax	`grep [-bCcEFGiLlnvwx] [-number] [-e pattern] [-f file] [-basic-` ➡ `regexp] [-extended-regexp] [-fixed-strings] [-byte-offset]` ➡ `[-context] [-count] [-regexp=pattern] [-file=file]` ➡ `[-ignore=case] [-files-without-match] [-files-with-match]` ➡ `[-line-number] [-revert-match] [-word-regexp] [-line-regexp]` ➡ `[pattern] file [file ...]`

Important Flags and Options

- `-number`: Displays matching lines with the specified number of lines of leading and trailing context.

- `-b/-byte`-offset: Prints the byte offset of the match before each line.

- `-c/-count`: Instead of displaying matching lines, simply outputs a count of the total number of lines matching the expressions (when combined with `-v`, displays the total count of non-matching lines).

- `-C/-context`: Displays matching lines with two lines of leading and trailing context (this is the same as `-2`).

- `-e pattern/-regexp=pattern`: Uses the specified pattern rather than one provided as an argument.

- `-E/-extended-regexp`: Treats the pattern as an extended regular expression (similar to `egrep`).

- `-f file/-file=file`: Uses the pattern found in the specified file rather than one supplied as an argument.

- `-F/-fixed-strings`: Treats the pattern as a list of new line separated strings, one of which must match. This is the same as `fgrep`.

- `-G/-basic-regexp`: Treats the pattern as a basic regular expression.

- `-i/-ignore-case`: Ignores case in both the pattern and the files being searched.

- `-l/-files-with-matches`: Instead of displaying each matched line, simply displays the name of each file that contains at least one match for the patterns.

- `-L/-files-without-match`: Instead of displaying each matched line, simply displays the name of each file that contains no matches for the patterns.

- `-n/-line-number`: Prefixes each output line with its line number in the file.

- `-v/-revert-match`: Displays non-matching lines instead of matching lines.

- `-w/-word-regexp`: Displays only those lines with matches for the patterns that are complete words.

- `-x/-line-regexp`: Displays only those lines with matches for the patterns that are complete lines.

Notes	The syntax of regular expressions used by `grep` can be found in the `grep` man page.

groupadd

Description	Creates a new group.
Syntax	`groupadd [-g gid [-o]] [-r] [-f] group`
Important Flags and Options	• `-f`: Prevents the program from exiting when trying to add a group that already exists. In this case, the group won't be altered.
	• `-g gid`: Uses the specified GID for the group instead of automatically assigning a value.
	• `-o`: Indicates that group IDs do not need to be unique.
	• `-r`: Adds a system account with a group ID lower than 499.

groupdel

Description	Deletes a group.
Syntax	`groupdel group`
Important Flags and Options	None

groupmod

Description	Modifies an existing group.
Syntax	`groupmod [-g gid [-o]] [-n groupname] group`
Important Flags and Options	• `-g gid`: Changes the group ID of the specified group to the new GID. This value must be unique unless `-o` is specified.
	• `-n groupname`: Changes the group name of the specified group to the new group name.
	• `-o`: Indicates that group IDs do not need to be unique.

groups

Description	Prints the groups that one or more users belongs to. If no user is specified, then displays the groups that the user running the command belongs to.
Syntax	`groups [username ...]`
Important Flags and Options	None

grpck

Description	Checks the integrity of a group file such as `/etc/group` or `/etc/gshadow`. If no files are specified, then the default files are checked.
Syntax	`grpck [-r] [group shadow]`
Important Flags and Options	• `-r`: Operates in read-only mode, not allowing any alterations to be made to the files.

gunzip

Description	Decompresses files compressed with the `gzip` command (as well as the `compress` ➡ command and the `zip` command).
Syntax	`gunzip [-cflrt] [-stdout] [-to-stdout] [-force] [-list] [-recursive]` ➡ `[-test] [name ...]`
Important Flags and Options	• `-c`/`-stdout`/`-to-stdout`: Writes output to standard output, keeping original file unchanged. By default, `gunzip` replaces the original compressed files with the uncompressed versions of the files.
	• `-f`/`-force`: Forces decompression even when a corresponding file already exists and will be overwritten by the decompressed file.
	• `-l`/`-list`: Lists files in the compressed file without decompressing.
	• `-r`/`-recursive`: Decompresses recursively, descending the directory structure and decompressing all files in subdirectories of directories named on the command line as arguments.
	• `-t`/`-test`: Tests the integrity of compressed files.

gzexe

Description	Creates an executable compressed file. If you compress a binary file or script with **gzexe**, then you can run it as if it were uncompressed. The file will simply uncompress into memory and execute, leaving the compressed version on your hard drive.
Syntax	`gzexe [-d] [name ...]`
Important Flags and Options	• `-d`: Uncompresses the specified file or files rather than compressing them.
Notes	When you compress a file named `filename`, the original, uncompressed file will be copied to `filename~` and the compressed file will retain the name `filename`. Once you have tested the compressed executable to see that it works, you can then delete the uncompressed copy.

gzip

Description	Compresses files using Lempel-Ziv encoding. The resulting file generally replaces the original, uncompressed file and will have a `.gz` extension.
Syntax	`gzip [-cdflrt] [-decompress] [-uncompress] [-stdout] [-to-stdout]` ➡ `[-force] [-list] [-recursive] [-test] [name ...]`
Important Flags and Options	• `-c`/`-stdout`/`-to-stdout`: Writes output to standard output, keeping original file unchanged. By default, `gzip` replaces the original, uncompressed files with the compressed versions of the files.
	• `-d`/`-decompress`/`-uncompress`: Decompresses the specified files, like `gunzip`, rather than compressing them.
	• `-f`/`-force`: Forces compression even when a corresponding file already exists and will be overwritten by the compressed file.
	• `-l`/`-list`: Lists files in a compressed file.

- -r/-recursive: Compresses recursively, descending the directory structure and compressing all files in subdirectories of directories named on the command line as arguments.
- -t/-test: Tests the integrity of compressed files.

halt

Description | Halts the system. If the system is not in run level 0 or 6, this is done by calling **shutdown**.

Syntax | halt [-n] [-w] [-d] [-f] [-i]

Important Flags and Options
- -d: Doesn't log the halt to /var/log/wtmp. By default, the halt is noted in this file.
- -f: Forces a halt or reboot without calling **shutdown**.
- -i: Shuts down network interfaces before halting.
- -n: Doesn't sync the file systems before halting.
- -w: Writes a record of a halt to /var/log/wtmp but doesn't actually halt the system.

Warnings | Care needs to be taken with this command. The -n flag, halting the system without syncing the disks, is of special concern because failing to sync the file systems before unmounting them can corrupt the data stored on them.

head

Description | Displays the first part of one or more files. By default, unless otherwise specified, the first 10 lines of each file are displayed. If no filenames are provided, then reads data from the standard input and displays the first section of the data, following the same rules as for files.

Syntax | head [-c number[bkm]] [-n number] [-qv] [-bytes number[bkm]] [-lines ➥ number] [-quiet] [-silent] [file ...]

Important Flags and Options
- -c/-bytes number: Displays the specified number of bytes from the start of each file. Optionally, the number can be followed by b for 512-byte blocks, k for kilobytes, and m for megabytes.
- -n/-lines number: Displays the specified number of lines from the start of each file.
- -q/-quiet/-silent: Prevents printing of filename headers when multiple files are being processed.

hostname

Description | Displays or sets the system's host name. If no flags or arguments are given, then the host name of the system is displayed.

Syntax | hostname [-a] [-alias] [-d] [-domain] [-f] [-fqdn] [-i] [-ip-address] ➥ [-long] [-s] [-short] [-y] [-yp] [-nis]

Important Flags and Options
- -a/-alias: Displays the alias name of the host if available.
- -d/-domain: Displays the DNS domain name of the host.

- **-f/-fqdn/-long**: Displays the fully qualified domain name of the host.
- **-i/-ip-address**: Displays the IP address of the host.
- **-s/-short**: Displays the host name without the domain name.
- **-y/-yp/-nis**: Displays the NIS domain name of the system.

id

Description	Displays real and effective user and group ID information for a specified user. If no user is specified, then prints the information for the user running **id**.
Syntax	**id [-gnruG] [-group] [-name] [-real] [-user] [-groups] [username]**
Important Flags and Options	

- **-g/-group**: Prints only the group ID.
- **-G/-groups**: Prints only the supplementary groups.
- **-n/-name**: Prints the user or group name instead of the ID number. Used in conjunction with **-u**, **-g**, or **-G**.
- **-r/-real**: Prints the real user or group ID instead of the effective ones. Used in conjunction with **-u**, **-g**, or **-G**.
- **-u/-user**: Prints only the user ID.

ifconfig

Description	Configures a network interface, or displays its status if no options are provided. If no arguments are provided, the current state of all interfaces is displayed.
Syntax	**ifconfig interface options address**
Important Flags and Options	

- **interface**: Specifies the name of the network interface (e.g., **eth0** or **eth1**).
- **up**: Activates the specified interface.
- **down**: Deactivates the specified interface.
- **netmask address**: Sets the network mask for the interface.
- **broadcast address**: Sets the broadcast address for the interface.
- **pointtopoint address**: Enables point-to-point mode for an interface, implying a direct link between two machines. Also sets the address for the other end of the link.
- **address**: Specifies the host name or IP address for the interface. This is required.

ifdown

Description	Disables a specified interface, such as **eth0** or **eth1**.
Syntax	**ifdown interface**
Important Flags and Options	None

ifport

Description	Sets the transceiver type for a specified network interface.
Syntax	`ifport interface type`
Important Flags and Options	• `type`: Specifies transceiver type. Possible types include: `auto` (automatic selection); `10baseT` (twisted-pair Ethernet); `10base2` (coaxial-cable Ethernet); `aui` (AUI interface Ethernet); `100baseT` (twisted-pair Fast Ethernet).

ifup

Description	Enables a specified interface, such as `eth0` or `eth1`.
Syntax	`ifup interface`
Important Flags and Options	None

insmod

Description	Installs a loadable module into the current kernel.
Syntax	`insmod [-fpsxX] [-o module_name] object_file [symbol=value ...]`
Important Flags and Options	• `-f`: Tries to load the module even if the version of the kernel and the expected kernel version do not match.
	• `-o module`: Explicitly names the module instead of basing the name on the object file for the module.
	• `-p`: Probes the module to make sure it is loaded.
	• `-s`: Logs activity to the system log daemon rather than standard output.
	• `-x`: Doesn't export the module's external symbols.
	• `-X`: Exports the module's external symbols (this is the default).

kbd_mode

Description	Displays or sets the keyboard mode.
Syntax	`kbd_mode [-a|-u|-k|-s]`
Important Flags and Options	• `-a`: Sets the keyboard to ASCII (XLATE) mode.
	• `-k`: Sets the keyboard to keycode (MEDIUMRAW) mode.
	• `-s`: Sets the keyboard to scanmode (RAW) mode.
	• `-u`: Sets the keyboard to UTF-8 (UNICODE) mode.

kbdrate

Description	Sets the repeat rate and delay time for the keyboard.
Syntax	`kbdrate [-r rate] [-d milliseconds]`
Important Flags and Options	• `-d milliseconds`: Sets the delay (before repeating) to the specified number of milliseconds.
	• `-r cps`: Sets the repeat rate to the specified number of characters per second. Not all values are possible. You should select from the following values: 2.0, 2.1, 2.3, 2.5, 2.7, 3.0, 3.3, 3.7, 4.0, 4.3, 4.6, 5.0, 5.5, 6.0, 6.7, 7.5, 8.0, 8.6, 9.2, 10.0, 10.9, 12.0, 13.3, 15.0, 16.0, 17.1, 18.5, 20.0, 21.8, 24.0, 26.7, 30.0.

kill

Description	Sends a kill signal to one or more running processes.
Syntax	`kill [-s signal|-p] pid ...`
	`kill -l`
Important Flags and Options	• `-l`: Displays a list of signal names.
	• `-p`: Prints the process ID of a specified process rather than sending it a signal.
	• `-s signal`: Sends the specified signal to the specified processes.
	• `pid`: Specifies either the ID of a process or its name. When specifying processes by name, all processes with the specified name will receive the signal.

killall

Description	Sends a signal to all processes sharing a common process name.
Syntax	`killall [-ei] [-signal] process ...`
	`killall -l`
Important Flags and Options	• `-e`: Forces the program to send the signal to only exact matches for process names longer than 15 characters.
	• `-i`: Asks for confirmation before sending the signal to each process.
	• `-l`: Displays a list of signal names.

ksyms

Description	Displays information about exported kernel symbols, including the address, name, and defining module.
Syntax	`ksyms [-a] [-m]`
Important Flags and Options	• `-a`: Displays all symbols, including those from the actual kernel.
	• `-m`: Displays module information, including the address and size of the module.

last

Description	Displays a history of user logins and logouts based on the contents of **/var/log/wtmp**. If a specific tty such as **tty0** or **tty1** is specified, then only logins to that tty are displayed.
Syntax	`last [-R] [-number] [-n number] [-adx] [name ...] [tty ...]`
Important Flags and Options	• `-a`: Forces the host name to be displayed in the last column.
	• `-d`: In the case of remote logins, displays all IP addresses as host names.
	• `-n number/-number`: Indicates how many lines of history to display.
	• `-R`: Suppresses the display of the host name in the report.
	• `-x`: Causes system shutdown and run level changes to be displayed along with logins and logouts.

ldd

Description	Displays shared library dependencies for one or more programs.
Syntax	`ldd [-dr] program ...`
Important Flags and Options	• `-d`: Reports missing functions after performing relocations.
	• `-r`: Reports missing data objects and functions after performing relocations.

less

Description	Displays a text file one screen at a time while allowing searching and backward scrolling.
Syntax	`less [-aeEGiINrsS] file ...`
Important Flags and Options	• `-a`: Causes searching to start after the last line on the screen. By default, searches include visible text.
	• `-e`: Causes `less` to exit the second time it encounters the end of a file. Otherwise, users must quit with the "`q`" command.
	• `-E`: Causes `less` to exit the first time it encounters the end of a file.
	• `-G`: Suppresses highlighting of strings found by a search.
	• `-i`: Causes searches to be case insensitive. This is ignored if the search pattern includes uppercase letters.
	• `-I`: Causes searches to be case insensitive even when the search pattern contains uppercase letters.
	• `-N`: Causes a line number to be displayed at the beginning of each line.
	• `-r`: Causes raw control characters to be displayed using caret notation (e.g., Ctrl+A is ^A).
	• `-s`: Squeezes consecutive blank lines into a single blank line.
	• `-S`: Chops lines wider than the screen rather than wrapping them to the next line.

lilo

Description	Installs the Linux boot loader.
Syntax	`lilo [C file] [-d deciseconds] [-q] [-D label] [-u device]`
Important Flags and Options	• `-C file`: Specifies a specific configuration file to use in loading the boot loader. The default configuration file is **/etc/lilo.conf**.
	• `-d deciseconds`: Indicates the number of deciseconds to wait at the Lilo prompt during booting before loading the default kernel.
	• `-D label`: Uses the kernel with the specified label as the default kernel rather than the first kernel in the configuration file.
	• `-q`: Displays the currently mapped files listing the kernels to be booted.
	• `-u device`: Uninstalls the boot loader for the specified device.

listalias

Description	Displays user and system aliases. If a regular expression is provided, then only aliases that match the expression are displayed.
Syntax	`listalias [-s|-u] [regular-expression]`
Important Flags and Options	• `-s`: Displays only system aliases.
	• `-u`: Displays only user aliases.

ln

Description	Makes links between files. When the last argument is a directory, then each of the other source files specified is linked into a file with the same name in the specified directory.
Syntax	`ln [-bis] [-backup] [-interactive] [-symbolic] source [dest]`
	`ln [-bis] [-backup] [-interactive] [-symbolic] source ... directory`
Important Flags and Options	• `-b/-backup`: Makes backups of files that are being removed.
	• `-i/-interactive`: Prompts when it is necessary to remove a destination file.
	• `-s/-symbolic`: Makes symbolic links instead of hard links.

loadkeys

Description	Loads compose key translation tables from one or more specified files. If no files are specified, the information is read from the standard input.
Syntax	`loadkeys [-c -clearcompose] [-d -default] [-m -mktable]` ↦ `[-s -clearstrings] [file ...]`
Important Flags and Options	• `-c/-clearcompose`: Clears the current accent table before loading new entries. If no entries are found, the table will be empty.

- -d/-default: Loads the default keymap.
- -m/-mktable: Prints a table on standard output of the current mappings.
- -s/-clearstring: Clears the kernel string table.

logger

Description

Places entries in the system log. If no messages are specified and no input file is provided, then the standard input is logged to the system log.

Syntax

logger [-is] [-f file] [-p priority] [-t tag] [message ...]

Important Flags and Options

- -f file: Logs the specified file to the system log.
- -i: Places the process ID of the process making the entry with each line in the log file.
- -p priority: Indicates the priority of the log entry.
- -s: Logs the message to standard error in addition to the system log.
- -t tag: Marks every line in the log entry with the specified tag.

login

Description

Log in to the system.

Syntax

login username

Important Flags and Options

None

logname

Description

Displays a user's username.

Syntax

logname

Important Flags and Options

None

logrotate

Description

Rotates log files, mailing the current file and then compressing it for archiving.

Syntax

logrotate [-s|-state file] configfile

Important Flags and Options

- -s/-state file: Uses the specified state file instead of the default /var/lib/logrotate.status.

lpd

Description	Runs the line printer spooler daemon to control printing to attached and remote printers. If a port number is specified, it overrides the default port to listen to for incoming requests.
Syntax	`lpr [-l] [port]`
Important Flags and Options	• `-l`: Logs valid network requests.

lpq

Description	Examines and displays the current status of a printer spool queue. If no printer is specified, then the default printer is queried. Normally, all jobs for the queried printer are displayed unless specific job numbers are given. If users are specified, only these users' print jobs will be displayed for the queried printer.
Syntax	`lpq [-l] [-Pprinter] [job ...] [user ...]`
Important Flags and Options	• `-l`: Prints all information about the files composing the job entry instead of just what will fit on one line. • `-Pprinter`: Queries the specified printer.

lpr

Description	Prints one or more files to the specified printer spool. If no files are indicated, then the standard input is sent to the printer spool. If no printer is specified, data will be sent to the default printer.
Syntax	`lpr [-Pprinter] [-#number] [-C class] [-J job] [-i [numcols]]` `➥ [-hlmrs] [file ...]`
Important Flags and Options	• `-#number`: Specifies the number of copies to print of each file. The default is one copy. • `-C class`: Prints the specified class name instead of the host name on the header page. • `-h`: Suppresses the printing of a header page. • `-i [numcols]`: Indicates that output should be indented by the number of blanks specified, or by 8 characters if no number is indicated. • `-J job`: Prints the specified job name instead of the filename on the header page. • `-l`: Allows control characters to be printed while suppressing page breaks. • `-m`: Sends an e-mail to the user when the print job is finished. • `-Pprinter`: Prints to the specified printer. • `-r`: Removes files after printing them. • `-s`: Creates a symbolic link to the file being printed rather than copying the file to the spool directory. This is useful when printing extremely large files.

lprm

Description	Deletes one or more jobs from a specified print queue. If no printer is specified, it attempts to remove the jobs from the default print queue. If a username is specified, all jobs owned by the user are removed, unless specific jobs are indicated.
Syntax	`lprm [-Pprinter] [job ...] [user ...]`
Important Flags and Options	• `-Pprinter`: Deletes jobs from the specified printer spool queue.

ls

Description	Displays a listing of files and directories. If no file or directory is specified, then the current directory's contents are displayed. By default, contents are sorted alphabetically.
Syntax	`ls [-acdlrRsStuX] [-all] [-time=ctime] [-time=status] [-directory]` ➡ `[-format=long] [-format=verbose] [-reverse] [-recursive] [-size]` ➡ `[-sort-size] [-sort=time] [-time=atime] [-time=access] [-time=use]` ➡ `[-sort=extension] [file|directory ...]`
Important Flags and Options	• `-a/-all`: Lists all files in the directory, including those that start with ".".
	• `-c/-time=ctime,-time=status`: Sorts entries by the change time of the files.
	• `-d/-directory`: Lists directory names only, without showing directory contents. By default, directory contents are listed.
	• `-l/-format=long/-format=verbose`: Lists files in long format, including file type, permissions, owner, and size.
	• `-r/-reverse`: Displays files in reverse order.
	• `-R/-recursive`: Lists the content of all subdirectories recursively.
	• `-s/-size`: Displays the size of files, in kilobytes.
	• `-S/-sort=size`: Sorts entries by file size starting with the largest file.
	• `-t/-sort=time`: Sorts entries by timestamp starting with the newest files.
	• `-u/-time=atime/-time=access/-time=use`: Sorts entries by the last access time.
	• `-X/-sort=extension`: Sorts files by file extension in alphabetical order.

lsdev

Description	Displays information about installed hardware.
Syntax	`lsdev`
Important Flags and Options	None

lsmod

Description	Displays a list of loaded modules.
Syntax	lsmod
Important Flags and Options	None

mail

Description	Sends and receives e-mails. The user will be prompted for the text of the message unless it is provided through the standard input. Also, other information such as the subject can be provided as a flag when sending messages, or the program can prompt for the information. If no options or arguments are specified, the current user's mailbox is opened for reading.
Syntax	mail [-s subject] [-c address,...] [-b address,...] address ... ➥ mail -f [mailbox] mail [-u user]
Important Flags and Options	• -b address,...: Indicates a list of addresses that should receive blind carbon copies of outgoing messages.
	• -c address,...: Indicates a list of addresses that should receive a carbon copy of outgoing messages.
	• -f [mailbox]: Reads mail from your inbox or the mailbox specified.
	• -s subject: Specifies the subject line of outgoing messages.
	• -u user: Opens the specified user's inbox for reading.
Notes	The mechanics of using mail to read messages is discussed in the mail man page.

mailq

Description	Displays the contents of the outgoing mail queue.
Syntax	mailq
Important Flags and Options	None

mailto

Description	Sends an e-mail to one or more recipients. If no recipients are indicated on the command line, the user will be prompted for the recipients. If no standard input is provided, then the user is prompted for the content of the message.
Syntax	mailto [-a character-set] [-c address,] [-s subject] [recipient ...]
Important Flags and Options	• -a character-set: Specifies an alternate character set, such as ISO-8859-8. The default is US-ASCII.
	• -c address,...: Specifies carbon-copy addresses
	• -s subject: Specifies the subject line of the message. If the subject is more than one word, enclose it in quotation marks.
Notes	To finish composing a message, use Ctrl+D or type a . alone on a blank line.

man

Description	Displays the manual page for a specified command.
Syntax	`Man command`
Important Flags and Options	• `command`: Specifies the command whose manual page is to be displayed.

mattrib

Description	Changes the attributes of a file on an MS-DOS file system such as a DOS floppy disk. This is similar to the DOS **ATTRIB** command.
Syntax	`mattrib [-a|+a] [-h|+h] [-r|+r] [-s|+s] msdosfile [msdosfile ...]`
Important Flags and Options	• `+a|-a`: Sets or unsets the archive bit.
	• `+h|-h`: Sets or unsets the hidden bit.
	• `+r|-r`: Sets or unsets the read-only bit.
	• `+s|-s`: Sets or unsets the system bit.
Notes	Use the + before an option to set a bit and the – to unset a bit.

mbadblocks

Description	Tests a DOS floppy disk for bad blocks. If any are found, they are marked in the disk's FAT.
Syntax	`mbadblocks drive:`
Important Flags and Options	None

mcd

Description	Changes the directory on an MS-DOS file system such as a floppy disk. If no argument is provided, then the current device and directory are displayed. Similar to the DOS **CD** command.
Syntax	`mcd [msdosdirectory]`
Important Flags and Options	None

mcopy

Description	Copies files in both directions between Unix and MS-DOS file systems such as floppy disks. Multiple files can be copied to a single directory when the directory is the last argument. Using a DOS drive designator such as `a:` implies a DOS file; otherwise a Unix file system is assumed. With only a single DOS file as an argument, this file will be copied to the current Unix directory. Similar to the DOS **COPY** command.

Syntax	`mcopy [-tnm] sourcefile targetfile`
	`mcopy [-tnm] sourcefile [sourcefiles ...] targetdirectory`
	`mcopy [-tnm] MSDOSsourcefile`
Important Flags and Options	• `-m`: Preserves file modification times when copying.
	• `-n`: Does not ask for confirmation when overwriting Unix files.
	• `-t`: Converts text files between Unix and DOS text files while copying.

mdel

Description	Deletes files on an MS-DOS floppy disk. Similar to the DOS **DEL** command.
Syntax	`mdel msdosfile [msdosfiles ...]`
Important Flags and Options	None

mdeltree

Description	Deletes one or more MS-DOS directories. Similar to the DOS **DELTREE** command.
Syntax	`mdeltree msdosdirectory [msdosdirectory ...]`
Important Flags and Options	None

mdir

Description	Displays the contents of a directory on an MS-DOS file system such as a floppy disk. If specific files are indicated, then only those files are listed. Similar to the DOS **DIR** command.
Syntax	`mdir [-w] msdosdirectory`
	`mdir [-a] [-f] [-w] msdosfile [msdosfile ...]`
Important Flags and Options	• `-a`: Lists hidden files as well as regular files.
	• `-f`: Displays files without listing total free space at the end of the listing.
	• `-w`: Displays files in wide output.

messages

Description	Displays a count of the number of messages in the user's inbox or, if named, in a specific mail folder.
Syntax	`messages [folder]`
Important Flags and Options	None

mformat

Description	Formats an MS-DOS floppy disk. Similar to the DOS **FORMAT** command.
Syntax	`mformat drive:`
Important Flags and Options	None

mkdir

Description	Creates one or more directories.
Syntax	`mkdir [-p] [-m mode] [–parents] [–mode=mode] [–help] [–version]` ➡ `directory ...`
Important Flags and Options	• `-m/–mode mode`: Sets the mode for the created directory using the same symbolic notation as the **chmod** command. If this is not specified, the default mode is assigned to the directory.
	• `-p/–parents`: Ensures that the parents of the specified directory exist and creates any missing parent directories needed.

mkdosfs

Description	Formats an MS-DOS file system on a specified device.
Syntax	`mkdosfs [-c] [-F fatsize] [-n name] device`
Important Flags and Options	• `-c`: Checks for bad blocks before formatting.
	• `-F fatsize`: Indicates the type of file allocation to create. This can be either **12** for a 12-bit FAT or **16** for a 16-bit FAT. The program will select the best option for you, usually **16**.
	• `-n name`: Sets the volume label to the specified name. The name can be up to 11 characters long. With no name, the volume label will not be set.

mke2fs

Description	Formats a Linux second extended file system.
Syntax	`mke2fs [-c] [-m percentage] [-L label] device`
Important Flags and Options	• `-c`: Checks for bad blocks before formatting.
	• `-L label`: Sets the volume label as specified.
	• `-m percentage`: Specifies the percentage of blocks to reserve for the superuser. This is set to 5 percent by default.

mkfs

Description	Creates a file system (similar to formatting a drive in DOS). Optionally, the number of blocks for the file system can be specified.
Syntax	`mkfs [-t fstype] [-c] [-l file] device [blocks]`
Important Flags and Options	• `-c`: Checks the device for bad blocks before formatting.
	• `-l file`: Reads the bad block list for the device from the specified file.
	• `-t fstype`: Specifies the type of file system that should be created. The default is minix if no other alternative can be found for the device in `/etc/fstab`.

mkpasswd

Description	Generates a random password and optionally assigns it to a user.
Syntax	`mkpasswd [-2] [-l number] [-d number] [-c number] [-C number]` ➥ `[-p file] [user]`
Important Flags and Options	• -2: Forces characters to alternate between the right and left hand when typing on a standard U.S. keyboard.
	• `-c number`: Specifies the minimum number of lowercase letters in the password.
	• `-C number`: Specifies the minimum number of uppercase letters in the password.
	• `-d number`: Specifies the minimum number of digits in the password.
	• `-l number`: Specifies the number of characters in the password.
	• `-p file`: Specifies the program to use to set the password. By default, this is `/etc/yppaswwd`or, if that is missing, `/bin/passwd`.
Notes	The use of the -2 flag makes it harder for the casual observer to see what is being typed by a user. But this can make it easier for a password-guessing program to guess the password.

mkswap

Description	Sets up a device as a swap area. The size of the file system can be specified in blocks if desired.
Syntax	`mkswap [-c] device [blocks]`
Important Flags and Options	• `-c`: Checks the device for bad blocks before creating the swap file system.
Notes	It is also possible to create swap files instead of swap partitions. Consult the `mkswap` man page for more information.

mlabel

Description	Labels an MS-DOS file system such as a floppy disk. If the label is not provided, the user is prompted for the label.
Syntax	`mlabel [-cs] drive:label`
Important Flags and Options	• `-c`: Clears the current label without any prompt to the user.
	• `-s`: Displays the current label.

mmd

Description	Makes one or more directories on an MS-DOS file system such as a floppy disk.
Syntax	`mmd msdosdirectory [msdosdirectory ...]`
Important Flags and Options	None

mmove

Description	Moves (also renames) MS-DOS files or directories. If the last argument is a directory, then all source files are moved into the target directory.
Syntax	`mmove sourcefile targetfile`
	`mmove sourcefile [sourcefile ...] targetdirectory`
Important Flags and Options	None

modprobe

Description	Loads one or more loadable modules, based on a pattern or a specified module object file.
Syntax	`modprobe module.o [symbol=value ...]`
	`modprobe -t tag pattern`
	`modprobe -a -t tag pattern`
	`modprobe -l [-t tag] pattern`
	`modprobe -r module`
	`modprobe -c`
Important Flags and Options	• `-a`: Loads all modules rather than the first module that loads successfully.
	• `-c`: Displays configuration information.
	• `-l`: Lists all modules of a specified type.
	• `-r module`: Unloads the specified module stack.
	• `-t tag`: Loads only modules marked with the specified tag.

more

Description   Displays one or more files screen-by-screen and allows for searching and jumping to an
                                     arbitrary location in the file.

Syntax   `more [-dlfs] [-number] [+number] [file ...]`

Important Flags and Options   • `-number`: Sets the number of lines per screen.

                                     • `+number`: Specifies the line to start on when displaying.

                                     • `-d`: Prompts the user at the end of each screen.

                                     • `-f`: Causes long lines not to be folded and to be counted as a single line.

                                     • `-l`: Prevents Ctrl+L from being treated as a form feed.

                                     • `-s`: Squeezes multiple blank lines into a single blank line.

Notes   For details of the commands that can be used when viewing files, consult the **more**
                                     man page.

mount

Description   Mounts a file system to a specified directory.

Syntax   `mount -a [-rw] [-t vfstype]`

                                     `mount [-rw] [-o options [,...]] device|dir`

                                     `mount [-rw] [-t vfstype] [-o options] device dir`

Important Flags and Options   • `-a`: Mounts all file systems in `/etc/fstab`. If a type is specified with `-t`, then only
                                       the file systems in `/etc/fstab` of the specified type will be loaded.

                                     • `-o`: See Note below.

                                     • `-r`: Mounts the file system in read-only mode. This is the same as `-o ro`.

                                     • `-t fstype`: Indicates the file system type.

                                     • `-w`: Mounts the file system in read-write mode. This is the same as `-o rw`.

Notes   Possible file system types for the `-t` flag include:

minix	nfs	coherent
ext	iso9660	
ext2	smbfs	
xiafs	ncpfs	
hpfs	affs	
msdos	ufs	
umsdos	romfs	
vfat	sysv	
proc	xenix	

For a list of options for the `-o` flag, consult the **mount** man page, which provides
detailed descriptions of the various options available.

mrd

Description	Removes one or more MS-DOS directories.
Syntax	`mrd msdosdirectory [msdosdirectory ...]`
Important Flags and Options	None

mren

Description	Renames an MS-DOS file. Similar to the DOS **REN** command, except that it can rename directories as well.
Syntax	`mren oldname newname`
Important Flags and Options	None

mtype

Description	Displays the contents of one or more MS-DOS files. Similar to the DOS **TYPE** command.
Syntax	`mtype [-ts] msdosfile [msdosfile ...]`
Important Flags and Options	• `-s`: Removes the high bit from data.
	• `-t`: Translates DOS text files to Unix text files before displaying them.

mv

Description	Renames and moves files. When a directory is the last argument, move all other specified files into that directory.
Syntax	`mv [-bfiu] [--backup] [--force] [--interactive] [--update]` ➥ `{source destination|source ... directory}`
Important Flags and Options	• `-b/--backup`: Makes a backup of files that are being moved.
	• `-f/--force`: Removes existing files that are about to be overwritten by the move without prompting.
	• `-i/--interactive`: Prompts before overwriting any existing files.
	• `-u/--update`: Does not overwrite an existing file if it has the same or newer modification time.

netstat

Description	Displays network status information, including connections, routing tables, and interface statistics. When no options are provided, a list of active sockets will be displayed.
Syntax	`netstat [-Mnrs] [-c] [-i interface] [--interface interface]` ➥ `[--masquerade] [--route] [--statistics]`

Important Flags and Options
- -c: Displays the select information every second until Ctrl+C interrupts it.
- -i [interface]/-interface [interface]: Displays information about a specified interface, or all interfaces if none is specified.
- -M/-masquerade: Displays a list of masqueraded sessions.
- -n: Shows numerical addresses instead of their host, port, or user names.
- -r/-route: Displays the kernel routing tables.
- -s/-statistics: Displays network statistics.

newgrp

Description
Logs the user into a new group, changing the user's group ID. If no group is specified, the group ID is changed to the user's login group ID.

Syntax
`newgrp [group]`

Important Flags and Options
None

newusers

Description
Reads a file containing a list of new users and creates the users. If no file is specified, the user information should be provided from standard input.

Syntax
`newusers [file]`

Important Flags and Options
None

Notes
The format of the file read by the **newusers** command is the same as the /etc/passwd file with the following exceptions:

- Passwords should not be encrypted. They will be encrypted when the user's account is created.
- If the group specified does not exist, the new group will be created.
- If the user's home directory doesn't exist, a new one will be created; if a directory with that name already exists, the ownership will be changed to that of the new user.
- Because this file will contain unencrypted passwords, it is essential that it be kept secure at all times.

nisdomainname

Description
Displays the current NIS domain name.

Syntax
`nisdomainname`

Important Flags and Options
None

nslookup

Description	Queries a DNS nameserver. Can be run in interactive mode. If no host name is provided, then the program enters interactive mode. By default, the DNS server specified in `/etc/resolv.conf` is used unless another is specified. If you want to specify a server but not look up a specified host, you must provide a - in place of the host.
Syntax	`nslookup [host|-[server]]`
Important Flags and Options	None
Notes	For instructions on the commands available in interactive mode, see the `nslookup` man page.

passwd

Description	Changes a user's password. When run by the root user, it can be used to change a specific user's password by providing the username as an argument.
Syntax	`passwd [username]`
Important Flags and Options	None

paste

Description	Merges corresponding lines from one or more files. Prints sequentially corresponding lines on the same line, separated by a tab with a new line ending the line. If no filenames are provided, input is taken from the standard input.
Syntax	`paste [-s] [-d delim-list] [—serial] [—delimiters list] [file ...]`
Important Flags and Options	• `-d/—delimiters list`: Specifies a delimiter to use instead of the default tab character. If more than one character is in the list, then the characters will be used consecutively, returning to the first character in the list after the final character has been used.
	• `-s/—serial`: Pastes the lines of one file followed by the lines from the next file, rather than one line from each file.

pathchk

Description	Checks the validity and portability of filenames. Specifically, checks that all directories in the path of the file have appropriate execute permission and that the length of each component of the path and filename is no larger than the maximum length for a filename component.
Syntax	`pathchk [-p] [—portability] file ...`
Important Flags and Options	• `-p/—portability`: Tests the length of each filename against POSIX.1 standards instead of the length limitations of the actual file system. Checks are also made for the portability of the characters used in the filename.

pidof

Description	Finds the process IDs of one or more named programs and displays the PIDs.
Syntax	`pidof [-s] [-x] [-o pid] [-o pid ...] program [program ...]`
Important Flags and Options	• `-o pid`: Omits the specified process ID from the list returned.
	• `-s`: Returns only a single PID.
	• `-x`: Returns the PIDs of shells running named scripts as well as named programs.

ping

Description	Sends echo request packets to a network host to see if it is accessible on the network.
Syntax	`ping [-R] [-c number] [-d] [-i seconds] host`
Important Flags and Options	• `-c number`: Stops sending packets after the specified number of packets have been sent.
	• `-d`: Outputs packets as fast as they come back or 100 times per second. The greater number will be generated. This option can only be used by the root user because it can generate extremely high volumes of network traffic. Care should be taken when using this option.
	• `-i seconds`: Specifies the number of seconds to wait between sending each packet. The default is one second. This option cannot be used along with the `-f` option.
	• `-R`: Records the route the packet takes and displays the route buffer of packets that have returned.

pppstats

Description	Displays statistics of PPP activities.
Syntax	`pppstats [-a] [-v] [-r] [-z] [-c <count>] [-w <secs>] [interface]`
Important Flags and Options	None

ps

Description	Displays status reports for currently running processes. Given a specific process ID as an argument, **ps** displays information about that particular process. Without options or arguments, **ps** displays the current user's processes.
Syntax	`ps [lumaxwrf] [txx] [pid ...]`
Important Flags and Options	• `a`: Shows processes owned by other users in addition to the current user's processes.
	• `f`: Displays processes in a tree showing which processes are children of which other processes.

- **1**: Displays information in long format.
- **m**: Displays memory information in the report.
- **r**: Displays only processes that are running.
- **txx**: Displays only those processes controlled by the tty specified by **xx**.
- **u**: Displays information in user format that includes the user name and start time of the format.
- **w**: Displays information in wide output mode, which prevents the truncation of commands to fit them on one line. For each **w** included as an option, an additional line is provided for displaying commands. Up to 100 **w** options may be used.
- **x**: Shows processes without a controlling terminal (this is useful for seeing daemons that were launched during the boot process and are still running.

pwck

Description	Checks the password file for errors and problems. The format of all entries is checked to be sure that valid information appears in each field. In addition, duplicate entries are found and the user is given the chance to delete poorly formatted or duplicate entries. If no password or shadow files are specified, the default **/etc/passwd** and **/etc/shadow** are used.
Syntax	`pwck [-r] [passwordfile shadowfile]`
Important Flags and Options	• **-r**: Executes in read-only mode so that no changes are made to the password file but the checks are done.

pwconv

Description	Copies entries from a password file to a shadow file, merging them with the existing shadow file. The new password file will be called **npasswd** and the new shadow file will be called **nshadow**.
Syntax	`pwconv`
Important Flags and Options	None

pwd

Description	Displays the name of the current directory.
Syntax	`pwd`
Important Flags and Options	None

pwunconv

Description | Restores a password from a shadow password file. The new password file will be called `npasswd`.

Syntax | `pwunconv`

Important Flags and Options | None

quota

Description | Displays a user's disk usage quota information. The root user can indicate specific users and groups and get reports about them. Non-root users can only view information about their own account and the groups to which they belong.

Syntax | `quota [-gu] [user|group]`

Important Flags and Options
- `-g`: Prints group quota for the groups that the user belongs to.
- `-u`: This is the default flag, causing the display of quota information for the user.

quotacheck

Description | Scans a file system for disk usage by a user or group and outputs the results to two quota files: `quota.user` and `quota.group`.

Syntax | `quotacheck [-g] [-u] [-a|filesystem]`

Important Flags and Options
- `-a`: Checks all file systems in the `/etc/fstab` file.
- `-g`: Checks for the files and directories used by a particular group ID.
- `-u`: Checks for the files and directory used by a particular user ID.

quotaoff

Description | Disables disk usage quotas for one or more file systems.

Syntax | `quotaoff [-g] [-u] [-a|filesystem ...]`

Important Flags and Options
- `-a`: Disables quotas for all file systems in `/etc/fstab`.
- `-g`: Disables group quotas for the specified file systems.
- `-u`: Disables user quotas for the specified file systems.

quotaon

Description | Enables disk usage quotas for one or more file systems.

Syntax | `quotaon [-g] [-u] [-a|filesystem ...]`

Important Flags and Options
- `-a`: Enables quotas for all file systems in `/etc/fstab`.
- `-g`: Enables group quotas for the specified file systems.
- `-u`: Enables user quotas for the specified file systems.

rcp

Description	Remote-copies one or more files between two systems. If the final argument is a directory, all other file arguments are copied to that directory.
Syntax	`rcp [-px] file ...`
Important Flags and Options	• `-p`: Preserves modification times and modes of the source file whenever possible.
	• `-x`: Turns on DES encryption for all copies.
Notes	Remote files and directories are specified with the form `remoteuser@remotehost:` ➥ `/path/to/file`.

rdate

Description	Retrieves the current time from one or more hosts on the network and displays the returned time.
Syntax	`rdate [-p] [-s] host ...`
Important Flags and Options	• `-p`: Displays the time returned from the remote system (this is the default behavior).
	• `-s`: Sets the local system's time based on the time retrieved from the network. This can only be used by the root user.

rdist

Description	Remotely distributes files in order to maintain identical copies on several hosts, preserving ownership, mode, and modification time wherever possible. If no destination directory is specified on the remote host, then the source files will be placed in the same location on the remote system.
Syntax	`rdist -c file|directory ... [login@]host[:directory]`
Important Flags and Options	• `-c`: Specifies a list of files to distribute to the remote system.
Notes	`Rdist` allows for controlling distribution from configuration files. This enables many more flags and options to be used. Consult the `rdist` man page for a complete description of this tool.

repquota

Description	Displays a summary of disk usage quotas for one or more file systems.
Syntax	`repquota [-gu] [-a|filesystem ...]`
Important Flags and Options	• `-a`: Displays reports for all file systems in `/etc/fstab`.
	• `-g`: Displays a report of group usage quotas for the specified file systems.
	• `-u`: Displays a report of user usage quotas for the specified file systems.

rlogin

Description	Logs in to a remote host.
Syntax	`rlogin [-Kx] [-l username] host`
Important Flags and Options	• `-K`: Turns off all Kerberos authentication.
	• `-l username`: Indicates that the connection should be logged in under the specified username rather than the user running `rlogin`.
	• `-x`: Turns on DES encryption for all data sent while logged in to the remote system.

rm

Description	Deletes one or more files or directories.
Syntax	`rm [-firR] [–force] [–interactive] [–recursive] file|directory ...`
Important Flags and Options	• `-f/–force`: Does not prompt the user for permission to delete files. This is dangerous if used as the root user.
	• `-i/–interactive`: Always prompts the user before deleting each file.
	• `-r/-R/–recursive`: Recursively removes the content of directories.

rmdir

Description	Deletes empty directories.
Syntax	`rmdir [-p] [–parents] directory ...`
Important Flags and Options	• `-p/–parents`: Removes the directory as well as all parents explicitly indicated on the command line as long as deleting the directory causes the parent to become empty.

rmmod

Description	Unloads one or more loaded modules.
Syntax	`rmmod [-as] module ...`
Important Flags and Options	• `-a`: Removes all unused modules.
	• `-s`: Sends all output to the system log instead of the display.

route

Description	Displays or alters the IP routing table. When no options are provided, the routing table is displayed.
Syntax	`route add [-net|-host] targetaddress [netmask Nm] [gw Gw] [[dev] If]`
	`route del [-net|-host] targetaddress [gw Gw] [netmask Nm] [[[dev] If]`

Important Flags and Options
- **add**: Indicates that a route is being added.
- **del**: Indicates that a route is being deleted.
- **[dev] If**: Forces the route to be connected to the specified interface.
- **gw Gw**: Specifies the gateway for the route.
- **-host**: Indicates the target is a host.
- **-net**: Indicates the target is a network.
- **netmask Nm**: Specifies the netmask for the route.

rsh

Description

Opens a shell on a remote system. If a command is provided, the command is executed on the remote host, the results are returned, and the connection is terminated.

Syntax

`rsh [-Kx] [-l username] host [command]`

Important Flags and Options
- **-K**: Disables Kerberos authentication.
- **-l username**: Attempts to connect to the remote host as a different user than the one running **rsh**.
- **-x**: Enables DES encryption for all data sent between the two hosts.

runlevel

Description

Displays the current and previous run level of the system.

Syntax

`runlevel`

Important Flags and Options

None

rup

Description

Displays the status of one or more remote systems. If no host is specified, then the status of all machines on the local network is displayed.

Syntax

`rup [-dhlt] [host ...]`

Important Flags and Options
- **-d**: Displays the local time on each host.
- **-h**: Sorts the entries by host name.
- **-l**: Sorts the entries by load average.
- **-t**: Sorts the entries by up time.

rusers

Description	Displays who is logged on to one or more machines on the local network. If no host is indicated, then all users logged in to all machines on the local network are displayed.
Syntax	`rusers [-1] [hostname ...]`
Important Flags and Options	• -1: Displays results in a long format, including user name, host name, tty being used by the user, and the time of login, among other information.

rwho

Description	Displays a list of users logged into all machines on the local network.
Syntax	**rwho**
Important Flags and Options	None

rwhod

Description	Answers incoming requests from the **rwho** client.
Syntax	**rwhod**
Important Flags and Options	None

setclock

Description	Sets the computer's hardware clock to the value of the current system clock.
Syntax	`setclock`
Important Flags and Options	None

setkeycodes

Description	Loads key mappings into the scancode-to-keycode mapping table. Arguments are provided in pairs with the first argument being the scancode for a key and the second being the keycode to be associated with it.
Syntax	`setkeycodes scancode keycode ...`
Important Flags and Options	None
Notes	To understand how to specify scancodes and keycodes, consult the **setkeycodes** man page.

showkey

Description	Displays scancodes and keycodes generated by the keyboard. The program remains active for 10 seconds after the last key is pressed.
Syntax	`showkey [-sk -scancodes -keycodes]`
Important Flags and Options	• `-k/-keycodes`: Displays keycodes.
	• `-s/-scancodes`: Displays scancodes.

showmount

Description	Shows the current state of mounts from an NFS server. If a host is specified, then only mounts from the particular host are displayed.
Syntax	`showmount [-ade] [-all] [-directories] [-exports] [host]`
Important Flags and Options	• `-a/-all`: Displays both the client's host name and the mounted directory using `host:directory` format.
	• `-d/-directories`: Displays only directories.
	• `-e/-exports`: Displays the server's list of exported directories.

shutdown

Description	Shuts down the system, stopping logins and possibly delaying before shutting down and issuing an optional warning message. When a time is specified, the shutdown will occur at the specified time; otherwise it occurs immediately.
Syntax	`shutdown [-rkhc] time [warning]`
Important Flags and Options	• `-c`: Cancels a running shutdown.
	• `-h`: Halts after shutting down.
	• `-k`: Sends the warning message but doesn't actually shut down the system.
	• `-r`: Reboots after shutting down.
Notes	The time can be specified as an absolute time in the form `HH:MM` or as a number of minutes to wait before shutting down in the form `+minutes`.

sort

Description	Sorts the lines contained in one or more text files and displays the results. If no files are indicated, data is taken from the standard input and sorted. The resulting sorted data is displayed to the standard output.
Syntax	`sort [-cu] [-t separator] [-o file] [-T tempdir] [-bdfMnr] [+POS1` ➡ `[-POS2]] [-k POS1[,POS2]] [file ...]`
Important Flags and Options	• `-b`: Ignores leading blanks in lines when trying to find sort keys.
	• `-c`: Checks whether the input data is sorted and prints an error message if it isn't. No sorting actually takes place.

- -d: Ignores all characters except letters, digits, and blanks in the sorting process.

- -f: Converts lowercase letters to uppercase letters during the sorting process.

- -k POS1[,POS2]: Specifies the field to use as the sorting key. The field will start at POS1 and run up until POS2 or the end of the line. Fields and character positions are specified starting at zero.

- -M: Sorts months. That is, any strings that starts with zero or more blanks followed by three letters are converted to uppercase and sorted as if they were abbreviated month names.

- -n: Compares strings numerically, which assumes that strings start with zero or more blanks followed by an optional sign and then a number.

- -o file: Outputs the results to the specified file instead of the standard output.

- +POS1 [-POS2]: Specifies the field to use as the sorting key. The field will start at POS1 and run up until POS2 or the end of the line. Fields and character positions are specified starting at zero.

- -r: Reverses the sort order.

- -t separator: Indicates that the specified separator should serve as the field separator for finding sort keys on each line.

- -u: When two lines compare as equal, only outputs the first.

statserial

Description	Shows the status of a serial port by displaying the signals on the pins of the port and the status of the handshaking line. If no device is specified, the default will be the value of the MODEM environment variable, or /dev/cua1 if the variable isn't set. The program will loop continuously, providing an updated status every second until Ctrl+C is pressed.
Syntax	statserial [-n|-d|-x] [device]
Important Flags and Options	

- -d: Displays the status of the port as a decimal number.

- -n: Disables looping and only displays a single status.

- -x: Displays the status of the port as a hexadecimal number.

su

Description	Runs a new shell under different user and group IDs. If no user is specified, the new shell will run as the root user.
Syntax	su [-flmp] [-c command] [-s shell] [-login] [-fast] [-preserve- ➥ environment] [-command=command] [-shell=shell] [-] [user]
Important Flags and Options	

- -c command/-command=command: Passes the specified command as a single command line to the shell instead of running the shell in an interactive mode.

- -f/-fast: Passes the -f option to the shell, which in the case of the C Shell and the Extended C Shell disables filename pattern expansion.

- **-/-l/-login**: Forces the new shell to be a login shell. This means new environment variables will be set, the path will change, and the current directory will switch to the user's home directory.
- **-m/-p/-preserve-environment**: Prevents the HOME, USER, LOGNAME, and SHELL environment variables from changing.
- **-s shell/-shell=shell**: Runs the specified shell instead of the default shell included in the password file.

sync

Description	Saves the disk cache to the physical disks. This forces any changed information to be saved to the disk.
Syntax	`sync`
Important Flags and Options	None

tail

Description	Displays the last part of one or more files. By default, unless otherwise specified, the last 10 lines of each file are displayed. If no filenames are provided, then reads data from the standard input and displays the last section of the data following the same rules as for files.
Syntax	`tail [-c number[bkm]] [-n number] [-q] [-bytes number[bkm]]` ➥ `[-lines number] [-quiet] [-silent] [file ...]`
Important Flags and Options	

- **-c/-bytes number**: Displays the specified number of bytes from the end of each file. Optionally, the number can be followed by **b** for 512-byte blocks, **k** for kilobytes, or **m** for megabytes.
- **-n/-lines number**: Displays the specified number of lines from the end of each file.
- **-q/-quiet/-silent**: Prevents printing of filename headers when multiple files are being processed.

tar

Description	Creates an archive file of one or more files or directories.
Syntax	`tar [-crtuxz] [-f tarfile] [-file tarfile] [-create] [-delete]` ➥ `[-preserve] [-append] [-same-owner] [-list] [-update] [-extract]` ➥ `[-get] [-gzip] [-gunzip] [file|directory ...]`
Important Flags and Options	

- **-c/-create**: Creates a new archive.
- **-delete**: Deletes files from an existing archive.
- **-f tarfile/-file tarfile**: Specifies the name of the archive file being created or read from.
- **-preserve**: Keeps permissions and order of files the same in the archive.

- -r/–append: Adds files to an existing archive.
- –same-owner: Signifies that extracted files keep their original owners.
- -t/–list: Displays a list of an archive's contents.
- -u/–update: Only adds files to an existing archive that are newer than the copy in the archive.
- -x/–extract/–get: Extracts files from an existing archive.
- -z/–gzip/–ungzip: Filters the archive through gzip when archiving and unarchiving.

timeconfig

Description	Configures time parameters. If a time zone is specified, then the system time zone is changed to the specified time zone. Otherwise, displays a list of available time zones.
Syntax	timeconfig [–utc] [timezone]
Important Flags and Options	• –utc: Assumes the system clock is running in Universal/Greenwich Mean Time.

timed

Description	Runs the time server daemon, which can synchronize the time with time on other machines on the local network.
Syntax	timed [-M] [-i network] [-n network]
Important Flags and Options	• -i network: Specifies which network the server belongs to, overriding any default choice made by timed.
• -M: Prepares to take on the job of the master time server if the master server crashes.
• -n network: Adds the specified network to the list of valid networks.

timedc

Description	Controls the timed daemon.
Syntax	timedc [clockdiff host ...|msite [host ...]|election host]
Important Flags and Options	• clockdiff host ...: Computes the difference between the system's clock and the time on the specified hosts.
• election host: Resets the election timer and ensures that a time master has been elected from among the slaves.
• msite [host ...]: Shows the master time server for the specified host or hosts. If no hosts are specified, shows the master for the current system.

top

Description	Displays a regularly updated report of processes running on the system.
Syntax	`top [d delay] [q] [c] [S] [s]`
Important Flags and Options	• c: Displays the complete command line of a process instead of just the command name.
	• `d delay`: Specifies the delay between updates, in seconds.
	• q: Causes updates to occur without any delays. If the root user runs **top** with this option, **top** will run with the highest possible priority.
	• s: Runs in a secure mode that prevents the use of dangerous interactive commands.
	• S: Statistics should be displayed in a cumulative manner. That is, CPU time should be reported for a process and its dead children as a total.
Notes	For a list of commands that can be used while **top** is running and for a description of the various fields in the reports, read the **top** man page.

touch

Description	Changes the timestamp of files without changing their contents. If a file doesn't exist, it will be created with a size of zero. By default, it uses the current time as the new timestamp.
Syntax	`touch [-acm] [-t MMDDhhmm[[CC]YY][.ss]] [-time=atime] [-time=access] [-time=use] [-time=mtime] [-time=modify] [-no-create] file ...`
Important Flags and Options	• `-a/-time=atime/-time=access/-time=use`: Changes only the access time.
	• `-c/-no-create`: Will not create files that don't exist.
	• `-m/-time=mtime/-time=modify`: Changes only the modification time.
	• `-t MMDDhhmm[[CC]YY][.ss]`: Sets the timestamp to the specified month, day, hour, and minutes plus, optionally, the specified century, year, or seconds. This overrides the default of using the current time.

traceroute

Description	Displays the route a packet travels to reach a remote host on the network.
Syntax	`traceroute [-ir] host`
Important Flags and Options	• `-i`: Specifies a network interface for outgoing packets. This is useful in systems with more than one network interface.
	• `-r`: Bypasses normal routing tables and attempts to send directly to an attached host.

true

Description	Does nothing and returns a successful exit status.
Syntax	`true`
Important Flags and Options	None

umount

Description	Unmounts a mounted file system. The file system is specified by either its device name, its directory name, or its network path.
Syntax	`umount -r device|directory|path ...`
Important Flags and Options	• `-r`: If unmounting fails, tries to remount the file system in read-only mode.

uname

Description	Displays selected system information. When no options are provided, the operating system name is displayed. When multiple pieces of information are requested, the display order is always: operating system, network host name, operating system release, operating system version, and machine type.
Syntax	`uname [-snrvma] [-sysname] [-nodename] [-release] [-machine] [-all]`
Important Flags and Options	• `-a`/`-all`: Displays all information.
	• `-m`/`-machine`: Displays the machine's type (that is, its hardware type).
	• `-n`/`-nodename`: Displays the machine's network host name.
	• `-r`/`-release`: Displays the operating system release.
	• `-s`/`-sysname`: Displays the operating system name. This is the default action when no options are specified.
	• `-v`: Displays the operating system's version.

uncompress

Description	Uncompresses files compressed with the `compress` program. If no files are specified, the standard input will be decompressed.
Syntax	`uncompress [-c] [file ...]`
Important Flags and Options	• `-c`: Sends the uncompressed data to the standard output instead of overwriting the old compressed file.

unzip

Description	Manipulates and extracts ZIP archives.
Syntax	`unzip [-cflptuz] [-d exdir] file[.zip]`
Important Flags and Options	• `-c`: Extracts files to the standard output, printing the name of each file as it is extracted.
	• `-d exdir`: Uncompresses the archive to the specified directory instead of the current directory.
	• `-f`: Extracts only those files that are newer than already-existing versions of the files.
	• `-l`: Displays the contents of the archive without extracting.
	• `-p`: Extracts files to the standard output without sending any other data such as filenames.
	• `-t`: Tests the integrity of files in the archive.
	• `-u`: Extracts files that are newer than already-existing versions of files as well as files that do not already exist in the extract directory.
	• `-z`: Displays the archive comment.
Notes	This is a powerful program that supports many modifiers. See the `unzip` man page for details.

uptime

Description	Displays the length of time the system has been running.
Syntax	`uptime`
Important Flags and Options	None

useradd

Description	Adds a user to the system. Alternately, the default values for new users can be changed. If no options are provided, the program will display the current default values for new users.
Syntax	`useradd [-d home_dir] [-e expire_date] [-f inactive_time]` ➥ `[-g initial_group] [-G group[,...]] [-s shell] [-u uid [-o]]` ➥ `username`
	`useradd -D [-g default_group] [-b default_home] [-f default_inactive]` ➥ `[-e default_expiration] [-s default_shell]`
Important Flags and Options	• `-b default_home`: Sets the default home directory prefix to the specified path. Only to be used when `-D` is used.
	• `-d home_dir`: Uses the specified home directory for the user instead of the default home directory.
	• `-D`: Indicates that default values for new users should be changed rather than that a new user should be created.

- -e expire_date: Specifies the expiry date for the account. The data is provided in MM/DD/YY format. When -D is used, -e will be used to set the default expiry for all new passwords as a number of days instead of in a date format.

- -f inactive_time: Indicates that once a password expires, the specified amount of time should elapse before permanently disabling the password. When -D is used, -f will be used to set the default amount of time before passwords will be disabled after expiring.

- -g initial_group: Specifies the default login group for the user. When used with -D, -g will specify the default group for all new users.

- -G group[,...]: Specifies other groups the user should belong to.

- -s shell: Specifies the default shell for the user. If not provided, the default shell for new users will be used. When used with -D, -s will specify the default shell for all new users.

- -u uid [-o]: Specifies a user ID for the user rather than automatically assigning one. The value must be unique unless the -o flag is used.

userdel

Description	Deletes a user's account.
Syntax	userdel [-r] user
Important Flags and Options	• -r: Deletes the user's home directory when deleting the account.
Notes	If you choose to delete the user's home directory, keep in mind that any other files the user owns that are outside their home directory are not deleted when their account is deleted. These have to be deleted manually. Such files might include the user's mail inbox, for example.

usermod

Description	Modifies the settings for an existing user's account.
Syntax	usermod [-d home_dir [-m]] [-e expire_date] [-f inactive_time] ➥ [-g initial_group] [-G group[,...]] [-l login_name] [-s shell] ➥ [-u uid [-o]] login
Important Flags and Options	• -d home_dir [-m]: Changes the user's home directory as specified and, if the -m option is used, moves the current home directory to the new location.

- -e expire_date: Sets a new expiry date for the account after which it will be disabled. The date should be in the form MM/DD/YY.

- -f inactive_days: Provides a new setting for the number of days after a password expires when it will be permanently disabled.

- -g initial_group: Defines a new login group for the user.

- -G group[,...]: Indicates which other groups a user should be a member of. If the user is currently a member of a group that is not on this list, they will be removed from the group.

- -l login_name: Changes the user's login name.
- -s shell: Changes the user's default shell as specified.
- -u uid: Changes the user's ID as specified.

users

Description	Displays the user names of current users on the system. This is normally found by looking at the contents of /etc/utmp. If a file is specified, the program will look in that file for the information.
Syntax	users [file]
Important Flags and Options	None

uudecode

Description	Decodes ASCII files created by **uudecode**, to recreate the original binary files. By default, the name of the decoded file will be the original name of the encoded file. If no files to decode are provided, then the standard input is decoded.
Syntax	uudecode [-o outputfile] [file ...]
Important Flags and Options	• -o outputfile: Specifies an alternate name for the resulting decoded file.

uuencode

Description	Encodes a binary file into a form that can be used where binary files cannot (such as with some mail software). If no file is provided, the standard input is encoded.
Syntax	uuencode [file]
Important Flags and Options	None

vipw

Description	Edits the system password file using the editor specified in the **EDITOR** environment variable.
Syntax	vipw
Important Flags and Options	None

vmstat

Description	Reports statistics about virtual memory.
Syntax	vmstat [delay [count]]

Important Flags and Options
- **count**: Indicates the number of times to repeat the report. If not specified, the report will repeat continuously until interrupted with Ctrl+C.
- **delay**: Indicates how often to repeat the report, in seconds. If not specified, then only one report is provided.

Notes
For details of the report generated by **vmstat**, read the **vmstat** man page.

w

Description
Displays a list of current users and the tasks they are running. If a user is specified, then only that user's tasks are displayed.

Syntax
`w [user]`

Important Flags and Options
None

wc

Description
Prints the number of bytes (characters), words, and lines in one or more documents. When multiple filenames are provided, each file will be counted and displayed separately and then a cumulative total will be displayed. If no files are specified, then the standard input is counted.

Syntax
`wc [-clw] [-bytes] [-chars] [-lines] [-words] [file ...]`

Important Flags and Options
- **-c/-bytes/-chars**: Displays only the number of bytes.
- **-l/-lines**: Displays only the number of lines.
- **-w/-words**: Displays only the number of words.

Notes
The results are displayed in this order: characters, words, lines. The values are separated by spaces.

whereis

Description
Attempts to locate the binary, source code, and man page files for one or more commands.

Syntax
`whereis [-bms] [-BMS directory ... -f] file ...`

Important Flags and Options
- **-b**: Searches only for binary files.
- **-B directory ... -f**: Searches only the specified directories for binary files. The **-f** flag is necessary to delineate the end of the directory list and the start of the file argument list.
- **-m**: Searches only for man pages.
- **-M directory -f**: Searches only the specified directories for man pages. The **-f** flag is necessary to delineate the end of the directory list and the start of the file argument list.
- **-s**: Searches only for source code.
- **-S directory ... -f**: Searches only the specified directories for source code. The **-f** flag is necessary to delineate the end of the directory list and the start of the file argument list.

Notes   The **whereis** command will search, at a minimum, the following directories for the
                     programs it is trying to locate:

                     /bin

                     /usr/bin

                     /etc

                     /usr/etc

                     /sbin

                     /usr/sbin

                     /usr/games

                     /usr/games/bin

                     /usr/emacs/etc

                     /usr/lib/emacs/19.22/etc

                     /usr/lib/emacs/19.23/etc

                     /usr/lib/emacs/19.24/etc

                     /usr/lib/emacs/19.25/etc

                     /usr/lib/emacs/19.26/etc

                     /usr/lib/emacs/19.27/etc

                     /usr/lib/emacs/19.28/etc

                     /usr/lib/emacs/19.29/etc

                     /usr/lib/emacs/19.30/etc

                     /usr/TeX/bin

                     /usr/tex/bin

                     /usr/interviews/bin/LINUX

                     /usr/bin/X11

                     /usr/X11/bin

                     /usr/X11R5/bin

                     /usr/X11R6/bin

                     /usr/X386/bin

                     /usr/local/bin

                     /usr/local/etc

                     /usr/local/sbin

                     /usr/local/games

                     /usr/local/games/bin

                     /usr/local/emacs/etc

                     /usr/local/TeX/bin

                     /usr/local/tex/bin

```
/usr/local/bin/X11
/usr/contrib
/usr/hosts
/usr/include
/usr/g++-include
```

which

Description	Displays the full pathname of one or more programs. Only programs that are on the path as specified by the **PATH** environment variable will be displayed.
Syntax	`which program ...`
Important Flags and Options	None

whoami

Description	Displays the current effective user ID.
Syntax	`whoami`
Important Flags and Options	None

ypdomainname

Description	Displays the system's NIS domain name.
Syntax	`ypdomainname`
Important Flags and Options	None

zcat

Description	Uncompresses one or more compressed files and displays the results to the standard output. If no files are specified, then the standard input is uncompressed and displayed.
Syntax	`zcat [-f] [file ...]`
Important Flags and Options	• **-f/-force**: Forces uncompression even when a corresponding file already exists and will be overwritten by the uncompressed file.

zgrep

Description	Searches one or more compressed files for a specified pattern.
Syntax	`zgrep [options] pattern file ...`
Important Flags and Options	None
Notes	For a list of possible entries and a discussion of pattern syntax, refer to the **grep** command.

zip

Description	Creates a ZIP archive from one or more files and directories.
Syntax	`zip [-efFgmrSu@] [zipfile [file1 file2 ...]]`
Important Flags and Options	• `-@`: Accepts the list of files to be archived from the standard input.
	• `-e`: Encrypts the archive after prompting for a password. The password will be necessary to extract files from the archive.
	• `-f`: Replaces entries in an existing archive only if the file is newer than the file currently in the archive.
	• `-F`: Tries to fix a damaged archive.
	• `-g`: Adds files to an existing archive.
	• `-m`: Moves files into the archive, deleting them from their original location once they are in the archive.
	• `-r`: Recursively works with directories, adding all files in subdirectories to the archive.
	• `-S`: Includes system and hidden files in the archive.
	• `-u`: Replaces entries in an existing archive if a file is newer than the file currently in the archive or if the file does not already exist in the archive.
Notes	The `zip` command offers many other options that have subtle, sometimes useful, impact on the behavior of the program. Consult the `zip` man page for more details.

zipgrep

Description	Searches for a pattern in one or more files in a ZIP archive using **egrep**. If no files in the archive are specified, then all files in the archive are searched.
Syntax	`zipgrep [egrepoptions] pattern zipfile file ...`
Important Flags and Options	None
Notes	For a complete discussion of **egrep**'s and `zipgrep`'s pattern syntax, refer to the **egrep** command.

zipinfo

Description	Displays details about ZIP archives, including encryption status, compression type, operating system used to create the archive, and more. By default, information about each file in the archive is also listed on separate lines. If no ZIP files are specified, the standard input will be processed.
Syntax	`zipinfo [-121M] zipfile[.zip] [file ...]`
Important Flags and Options	• `-1`: Lists only filenames, each on a separate line.
	• `-2`: Lists only filenames, including headers, trailers and comments.
	• `-l`: Lists information in long format (similar to `ls -l`).
	• `-M`: Displays information one page at a time in a fashion similar to `more`.

zmore

Description	Displays the contents of compressed text files, one screen at a time, allowing searching in much the same way as the `more` command. If no files are specified, the standard input will be used.
Syntax	`zmore [file ...]`
Important Flags and Options	None
Notes	See the `zmore` man page for a complete list of commands that can be used while viewing a file.

znew

Description	Converts files compressed with `compress` (`.Z` files) into the format used by `gzip` (`.gz` files). If no files are specified, then the standard input is processed.
Syntax	`znew [-ft9K] [file.Z ...]`
Important Flags and Options	• `-9`: Uses the best, but slowest, compression method.
	• `-f`: Forces compression even when a `.gz` file already exists.
	• `-K`: Keeps a `.Z` file if it will be smaller than the new `.gz` file.
	• `-t`: Tests the new `.gz` file before deleting the original `.Z` file.

A P P E N D I X

H

GNU General Public License

Version 2, June 1991

Copyright (C) 1989, 1991 Free Software Foundation, Inc.

675 Mass Ave, Cambridge, MA 02139, USA

Preamble

The licenses for most software are designed to take away your freedom to share and change it. By contrast, the GNU General Public License is intended to guarantee your freedom to share and change free software—to make sure the software is free for all its users. This General Public License applies to most of the Free Software Foundation's software and to any other program whose authors commit to using it. (Some other Free Software Foundation software is covered by the GNU Library General Public License instead.) You can apply it to your programs, too.

When we speak of free software, we are referring to freedom, not price. Our General Public Licenses are designed to make sure that you have the freedom to distribute copies of free software (and charge for this service if you wish), that you receive source code or can get it if you want it, that you can change the software or use pieces of it in new free programs; and that you know you can do these things.

To protect your rights, we need to make restrictions that forbid anyone to deny you these rights or to ask you to surrender the rights. These restrictions translate to certain responsibilities for you if you distribute copies of the software, or if you modify it.

For example, if you distribute copies of such a program, whether gratis or for a fee, you must give the recipients all the rights that you have. You must make sure that they, too, receive or can get the source code. And you must show them these terms so they know their rights.

We protect your rights with two steps: (1) copyright the software, and (2) offer you this license which gives you legal permission to copy, distribute and/or modify the software.

Also, for each author's protection and ours, we want to make certain that everyone understands that there is no warranty for this free software. If the software is modified by someone else and passed on, we want its recipients to know that what they have is not the original, so that any problems introduced by others will not reflect on the original authors' reputations.

Finally, any free program is threatened constantly by software patents. We wish to avoid the danger that redistributors of a free program will individually obtain patent licenses, in effect making the program proprietary. To prevent this, we have made it clear that any patent must be licensed for everyone's free use or not licensed at all.

The precise terms and conditions for copying, distribution and modification follow.

Terms and Conditions for Copying, Distribution and Modification

0. This License applies to any program or other work which contains a notice placed by the copyright holder saying it may be distributed under the terms of this General Public License. The "Program", below, refers to any such program or work, and a "work based on the Program" means either the Program or any derivative work under copyright law: that is to say, a work containing the Program or a portion of it, either verbatim or with modifications and/or translated into another language. (Hereinafter, translation is included without limitation in the term "modification".) Each licensee is addressed as "you".

    Activities other than copying, distribution and modification are not covered by this License; they are outside its scope. The act of running the Program is not restricted, and the output from the Program is covered only if its contents constitute a work based on the Program (independent of having been made by running the Program). Whether that is true depends on what the Program does.

1. You may copy and distribute verbatim copies of the Program's source code as you receive it, in any medium, provided that you conspicuously and appropriately publish on each copy an appropriate copyright notice and disclaimer of warranty; keep intact all the notices that refer to this License and to the absence of any warranty; and give any other recipients of the Program a copy of this License along with the Program.

    You may charge a fee for the physical act of transferring a copy, and you may at your option offer warranty protection in exchange for a fee.

2. You may modify your copy or copies of the Program or any portion of it, thus forming a work based on the Program, and copy and distribute such

modifications or work under the terms of Section 1 above, provided that you also meet all of these conditions:

a) You must cause the modified files to carry prominent notices stating that you changed the files and the date of any change.

b) You must cause any work that you distribute or publish, that in whole or in part contains or is derived from the Program or any part thereof, to be licensed as a whole at no charge to all third parties under the terms of this License.

c) If the modified program normally reads commands interactively when run, you must cause it, when started running for such interactive use in the most ordinary way, to print or display an announcement including an appropriate copyright notice and a notice that there is no warranty (or else, saying that you provide a warranty) and that users may redistribute the program under these conditions, and telling the user how to view a copy of this License. (Exception: if the Program itself is interactive but does not normally print such an announcement, your work based on the Program is not required to print an announcement.)

These requirements apply to the modified work as a whole. If identifiable sections of that work are not derived from the Program, and can be reasonably considered independent and separate works in themselves, then this License, and its terms, do not apply to those sections when you distribute them as separate works. But when you distribute the same sections as part of a whole which is a work based on the Program, the distribution of the whole must be on the terms of this License, whose permissions for other licensees extend to the entire whole, and thus to each and every part regardless of who wrote it.

Thus, it is not the intent of this section to claim rights or contest your rights to work written entirely by you; rather, the intent is to exercise the right to control the distribution of derivative or collective works based on the Program.

In addition, mere aggregation of another work not based on the Program with the Program (or with a work based on the Program) on a volume of a storage or distribution medium does not bring the other work under the scope of this License.

3. You may copy and distribute the Program (or a work based on it, under Section 2) in object code or executable form under the terms of Sections 1 and 2 above provided that you also do one of the following:

   a) Accompany it with the complete corresponding machine-readable source code, which must be distributed under the terms of Sections 1 and 2 above on a medium customarily used for software interchange; or,

   b) Accompany it with a written offer, valid for at least three years, to give any third party, for a charge no more than your cost of physically performing source distribution, a complete machine-readable copy of the corresponding source code, to be distributed under the terms of Sections 1 and 2 above on a medium customarily used for software interchange; or,

   c) Accompany it with the information you received as to the offer to distribute corresponding source code. (This alternative is allowed only for noncommercial distribution and only if you received the program in object code or executable form with such an offer, in accord with Subsection b above.)

   The source code for a work means the preferred form of the work for making modifications to it. For an executable work, complete source code means all the source code for all modules it contains, plus any associated interface definition files, plus the scripts used to control compilation and installation of the executable. However, as a special exception, the source code distributed need not include anything that is normally distributed (in either source or binary form) with the major components (compiler, kernel, and so on) of the operating system on which the executable runs, unless that component itself accompanies the executable.

   If distribution of executable or object code is made by offering access to copy from a designated place, then offering equivalent access to copy the source code from the same place counts as distribution of the source code, even though third parties are not compelled to copy the source along with the object code.

4. You may not copy, modify, sublicense, or distribute the Program except as expressly provided under this License. Any attempt otherwise to copy, modify, sublicense or distribute the Program is void, and will automatically terminate your rights under this License. However, parties who have

received copies, or rights, from you under this License will not have their licenses terminated so long as such parties remain in full compliance.

5. You are not required to accept this License, since you have not signed it. However, nothing else grants you permission to modify or distribute the Program or its derivative works. These actions are prohibited by law if you do not accept this License. Therefore, by modifying or distributing the Program (or any work based on the Program), you indicate your acceptance of this License to do so, and all its terms and conditions for copying, distributing or modifying the Program or works based on it.

6. Each time you redistribute the Program (or any work based on the Program), the recipient automatically receives a license from the original licensor to copy, distribute or modify the Program subject to these terms and conditions. You may not impose any further restrictions on the recipients' exercise of the rights granted herein. You are not responsible for enforcing compliance by third parties to this License.

7. If, as a consequence of a court judgment or allegation of patent infringement or for any other reason (not limited to patent issues), conditions are imposed on you (whether by court order, agreement or otherwise) that contradict the conditions of this License, they do not excuse you from the conditions of this License. If you cannot distribute so as to satisfy simultaneously your obligations under this License and any other pertinent obligations, then as a consequence you may not distribute the Program at all. For example, if a patent license would not permit royalty-free redistribution of the Program by all those who receive copies directly or indirectly through you, then the only way you could satisfy both it and this License would be to refrain entirely from distribution of the Program.

   If any portion of this section is held invalid or unenforceable under any particular circumstance, the balance of the section is intended to apply and the section as a whole is intended to apply in other circumstances.

   It is not the purpose of this section to induce you to infringe any patents or other property right claims or to contest validity of any such claims; this section has the sole purpose of protecting the integrity of the free software distribution system, which is implemented by public license practices. Many people have made generous contributions to the wide range of software distributed through that system in reliance on consistent application of that system; it is up to the author/donor to decide if he or she is willing to distribute software through any other system and a licensee cannot impose that choice.

This section is intended to make thoroughly clear what is believed to be a consequence of the rest of this License.

8. If the distribution and/or use of the Program is restricted in certain countries either by patents or by copyrighted interfaces, the original copyright holder who places the Program under this License may add an explicit geographical distribution limitation excluding those countries, so that distribution is permitted only in or among countries not thus excluded. In such case, this License incorporates the limitation as if written in the body of this License.

9. The Free Software Foundation may publish revised and/or new versions of the General Public License from time to time. Such new versions will be similar in spirit to the present version, but may differ in detail to address new problems or concerns.

Each version is given a distinguishing version number. If the Program specifies a version number of this License which applies to it and "any later version", you have the option of following the terms and conditions either of that version or of any later version published by the Free Software Foundation. If the Program does not specify a version number of this License, you may choose any version ever published by the Free Software Foundation.

10. If you wish to incorporate parts of the Program into other free programs whose distribution conditions are different, write to the author to ask for permission. For software which is copyrighted by the Free Software Foundation, write to the Free Software Foundation; we sometimes make exceptions for this. Our decision will be guided by the two goals of preserving the free status of all derivatives of our free software and of promoting the sharing and reuse of software generally.

No Warranty

11. BECAUSE THE PROGRAM IS LICENSED FREE OF CHARGE, THERE IS NO WARRANTY FOR THE PROGRAM, TO THE EXTENT PERMITTED BY APPLICABLE LAW. EXCEPT WHEN OTHERWISE STATED IN WRITING THE COPYRIGHT HOLDERS AND/OR OTHER PARTIES PROVIDE THE PROGRAM "AS IS" WITHOUT WARRANTY OF ANY KIND, EITHER

EXPRESSED OR IMPLIED, INCLUDING, BUT NOT LIMITED TO, THE
IMPLIED WARRANTIES OF MERCHANTABILITY AND FITNESS FOR A
PARTICULAR PURPOSE. THE ENTIRE RISK AS TO THE QUALITY AND
PERFORMANCE OF THE PROGRAM IS WITH YOU. SHOULD THE PRO-
GRAM PROVE DEFECTIVE, YOU ASSUME THE COST OF ALL NECES-
SARY SERVICING, REPAIR OR CORRECTION.

12. IN NO EVENT UNLESS REQUIRED BY APPLICABLE LAW OR AGREED
TO IN WRITING WILL ANY COPYRIGHT HOLDER, OR ANY OTHER
PARTY WHO MAY MODIFY AND/OR REDISTRIBUTE THE PROGRAM
AS PERMITTED ABOVE, BE LIABLE TO YOU FOR DAMAGES, INCLUD-
ING ANY GENERAL, SPECIAL, INCIDENTAL OR CONSEQUENTIAL
DAMAGES ARISING OUT OF THE USE OR INABILITY TO USE THE
PROGRAM (INCLUDING BUT NOT LIMITED TO LOSS OF DATA OR
DATA BEING RENDERED INACCURATE OR LOSSES SUSTAINED BY
YOU OR THIRD PARTIES OR A FAILURE OF THE PROGRAM TO OPER-
ATE WITH ANY OTHER PROGRAMS), EVEN IF SUCH HOLDER OR
OTHER PARTY HAS BEEN ADVISED OF THE POSSIBILITY OF SUCH
DAMAGES.

END OF TERMS AND CONDITIONS

Appendix: How to Apply These Terms to Your New Programs

If you develop a new program, and you want it to be of the greatest possible use
to the public, the best way to achieve this is to make it free software which everyone can redistribute and change under these terms.

To do so, attach the following notices to the program. It is safest to attach them to
the start of each source file to most effectively convey the exclusion of warranty;
and each file should have at least the "copyright" line and a pointer to where the
full notice is found.

```
<one line to give the program's name and a brief idea of what it does.>
Copyright (C) 19yy <name of author>
This program is free software; you can redistribute it and/or modify
it under the terms of the GNU General Public License as published by
```

```
the Free Software Foundation; either version 2 of the License, or
(at your option) any later version.
This program is distributed in the hope that it will be useful,
but WITHOUT ANY WARRANTY; without even the implied warranty of
MERCHANTABILITY or FITNESS FOR A PARTICULAR PURPOSE. See the
GNU General Public License for more details.
You should have received a copy of the GNU General Public License
along with this program; if not, write to the Free Software
Foundation, Inc., 675 Mass Ave, Cambridge, MA 02139, USA.
```

Also add information on how to contact you by electronic and paper mail.

If the program is interactive, make it output a short notice like this when it starts in an interactive mode:

```
Gnomovision version 69, Copyright (C) 19yy name of author
Gnomovision comes with ABSOLUTELY NO WARRANTY; for details type `show w'.
This is free software, and you are welcome to redistribute it
under certain conditions; type `show c' for details.
```

The hypothetical commands "show w" and "show c" should show the appropriate parts of the General Public License. Of course, the commands you use may be called something other than "show w" and "show c"; they could even be mouse-clicks or menu items—whatever suits your program.

You should also get your employer (if you work as a programmer) or your school, if any, to sign a "copyright disclaimer" for the program, if necessary. Here is a sample; alter the names:

```
Yoyodyne, Inc., hereby disclaims all copyright interest in the program
`Gnomovision' (which makes passes at compilers) written by James
Hacker.
<signature of Ty Coon>, 1 April 1989
Ty Coon, President of Vice
```

This General Public License does not permit incorporating your program into proprietary programs. If your program is a subroutine library, you may consider it more useful to permit linking proprietary applications with the library. If this is what you want to do, use the GNU Library General Public License instead of this License.

APPENDIX

I

Linux on Non-Intel Hardware

Linux is available for numerous hardware platforms other than the Intel x86 and Pentium microprocessors. This appendix serves as a quick overview of some of the major, interesting non-Intel versions of Linux that are available. For a comprehensive list of Linux ports that are available, consult Linux Online's list of hardware port projects at `http://www.linux.org/projects/ports.html`.

Linux for AP1000+

The AP1000+ is a multi-computer built by Fujitsu around the SPARC architecture. Multiple CPUs are connected by two networks. The system started with 16 CPUs and will be upgraded to 32 CPUs. The project for running Linux on this distributed multi-processing computer is being done at the Australian National University. Visit `http://cap.anu.edu.au/cap/projects/linux/` to learn more about the project.

Linux for the DEC Alpha Processor

DEC's Alpha CPU is widely hailed as an exemplary RISC CPU, offering one of the fastest processors on the market.

Linux for the Alpha CPU (`http://www.azstarnet.com/~axplinux/intro.html`) is perhaps among the most robust, stable, and highly tested versions of Linux for non-Intel hardware currently available. Everything from X Windows to networks to Web browsers works well, and emulation is even available to run many programs designed for the Intel x86 version of Linux.

Linux for Alpha runs on numerous DEC Alpha-based systems ranging from low-end Universal Desktop Boxes/Multias from Digital to high-end 500MHz systems.

Red Hat offers a version of Red Hat Linux 5.1 for the Alpha processor along with its Intel x86 and SPARC versions.

Embedded Linux

The ELKS (Embedded Linux Kernel Subset) project is aiming to create a version of Linux for embedded systems such as older 8086 and 80286 PCs, handheld computers, and embedded controller systems. The current version of Linux available from the project runs on PCs and requires about 512K of RAM for a full system.

The current version is far from complete, offering only the ability to boot, use virtual consoles, access floppy disks, and run a collection of small programs. This is a development system, but it highlights the flexibility that enables Linux to run under a variety of hardware constraints.

The ELKS project is online at `http://www.uk.linux.org/ELKS-Home/index.html`

Linux for Motorola 680x0 Processors

Linux/m68k is a port of Linux designed to run on Motorola 68020 through 68060 CPUs, such as those found in many Amiga, Atari, and Macintosh computers.

Robust, stable releases of Linux/m68k are currently available to run on Amiga and Atari systems, including the following systems:

- Amiga A2500
- Amiga A3000
- Amiga A3000T
- Amiga A4000/040
- Amiga A4000T/040
- Amiga A4000T/060
- Atari Falcon
- Atari Falcon with AfterBurner 040
- Atari TT
- Atari Medusa

In addition, development ports of Linux are under way to support other Motorola 680x0 systems, including:

- Macintosh systems (Classic, Mac II series, Mac LC, Performas, Centris, and Quadra systems, and many PowerBooks)

- HP 9000/300 workstations

- NeXT workstations

- Sun 3 workstations

More information is available at `http://www.linux-m68k.org/`.

Linux for MIPS Processors

Linux/MIPS is a port of Linux designed to run on most systems sporting MIPS processors, including:

- Acer PICA-61

- DECStation 5000/2x, 5000/100, and 3100

- MIPS Magnum 4000PC

- Olivetti M700-10

The current release is considered stable and includes networking and NFS support, with some shortcomings in support for on-board peripherals in some machines. While not yet available as a robust, complete distribution, it is possible to put together a complete distribution from the software on the project's Web site. Linux/MIPS is on the Web at `http://lena.fnet.fr/`.

Linux for the Power Macintosh

MkLinux is an attempt to run Linux on the Open Group Mach microkernel running natively on the Power Macintosh line of computers. Microkernel architecture is designed to ease porting of the OS, with the focus on porting the microkernel itself.

Apple Computer is fully supporting the MkLinux project, which has a Web site at `http://www.mklinux.apple.com/`. A complete distribution is currently available online or on CD-ROM.

Other projects aimed at porting Linux to the Power Macintosh include the PowerPC Linux distribution (which is discussed in the section on the PowerPC processor later in this appendix) and Powermac/Linux (`http://www.cs.wisc .edu/~tesch/linux_info/`). Both of these projects are versions of Linux that are native to the PowerPC processor (which is at the heart of Power Mac systems) instead of being layered on a microkernel. This design provides better performance but less portability to other hardware. The Powermac/Linux code, once a distinct project, has now been merged with the LinuxPPC source code developed by PowerPC Linux to produce one version of Linux for the PowerPC.

Linux for PowerPC Processors

Great strides have been made in supporting Linux on the PowerPC processor family. The LinuxPPC project (`http://www.linuxppc.org/`), which is managed and developed by PowerPC Linux, offers a stable and complete distribution that runs on a wide range of Power Macintosh computers, the BeBox from Be Computing, PowerPC-based RS/6000 systems from IBM, a wide range of systems from Power Computing, and workstations from Umax.

Supported applications and features include:

- PCI-bus systems
- SCSI and IDE hard disk drives
- Multimedia support
- Netscape Communicator
- X Windows and a wide range of window managers
- Java JDK 1.1.6

A project is also under way to develop an emulator of the Mac OS to run inside Linux on the PowerPC, just as Wine is an attempt to develop a Windows emulator for Linux for the Intel x86 CPU.

Linux for SGI Systems

SGI/Linux is a project of Silicon Graphics to port Linux to their hardware and then distribute it widely through Linux CD vendors. The project includes strong efforts to provide robust IRIX emulation in the distribution so that existing applications for SGI systems can be used under Linux, and consideration is being given to the ability to hot-swap between Linux and IRIX operating systems without completely rebooting the computer.

At the time of this writing, a pre-release distribution called Hard Hat 5.1 (a nearly-complete port of Red Hat Linux 5.1) is available. The major missing component is an X server, which is currently being developed.

SGI maintains a site for their Linux port at `http://www.linux.sgi.com/`.

Linux for SPARC Processors

S/Linux (`http://www.geog.ubc.ca/s_linux.html`) is the name of the project to port Linux to Sun's SPARC processors. Currently, the port is quite stable, and Red Hat now has a SPARC version of their distribution available (currently at release 5.1) along with Intel and Alpha versions of their distribution.

A separate Ultra/Linux project (Ultra Penguin) provides support for the newer UltraSPARC CPUs. Information is available at `http://ultra.linux.cz/`.

INDEX

Note to the Reader: Throughout this index **boldfaced** page numbers indicate primary discussions of a topic. *Italicized* page numbers indicate illustrations.

E

F

G

H

M

N

S

U

X

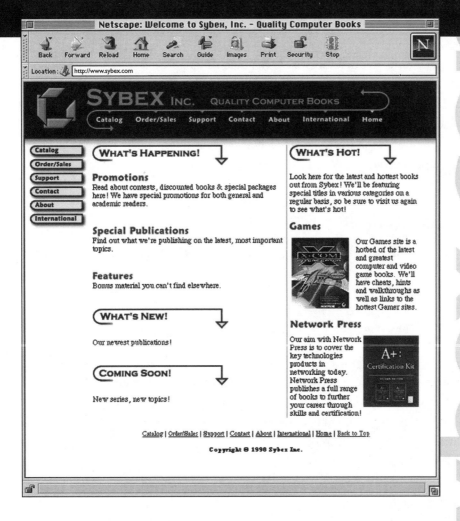

What's on This CD

The CD-ROM contains a complete copy of the freely redistributable version of Red Hat Linux 5.1, the latest version of this leading Linux distribution. The CD-ROM is based on the version distributed by Linux Central (http://www.linuxcentral.com). Red Hat 5.1 includes everything you need to set up a fully functional Linux workstation or server, including:

- X-Windows
- A selection of window managers
- Full networking support
- Internet client and server applications for e-mail, FTP, and the World Wide Web
- Multimedia support
- Much, much more…

System Requirements

To use Red Hat 5.1, you will need access to a personal computer with the following suggested minimum specifications:

- A 486 CPU or higher (in theory you can run Linux on a 386 system, but the performance will most likely be poor enough that it won't be worthwhile for most users)
- 16MB of RAM or more (you will notice a significant performance gain if Linux has 32MB or more of memory)
- A hard disk with at least 500MB of free disk space (if you can afford 1GB or more, this will greatly enhance your freedom to experiment with Linux and Linux applications)
- A CD-ROM drive (preferably an ATAPI/IDE CD-ROM or a SCSI CD-ROM drive)
- A backup of your current system in case you need to recover existing data or applications
- A video card and VGA or better monitor
- A keyboard and mouse

Software Support

Components of the supplemental Software and any offers associated with them may be supported by the specific Owner(s) of that material, but they are *not* supported by SYBEX. Information regarding any available support may be obtained from the Owner(s) using the information provided in the appropriate read.me files or listed elsewhere on the media.

Should the manufacturer(s) or other Owner(s) cease to offer support or decline to honor any offer, SYBEX bears no responsibility. This notice concerning support for the Software is provided for your information only. SYBEX is not the agent or principal of the Owner(s), and SYBEX is in no way responsible for providing any support for the Software, nor is it liable or responsible for any support provided, or not provided, by the Owner(s).

For additional support, please see Appendix E for a list of Linux-related resources that you can contact.